Dragonflies and Damselflies of the East

GW00673805

Dragonflies and Damselflies of the East

Dennis Paulson

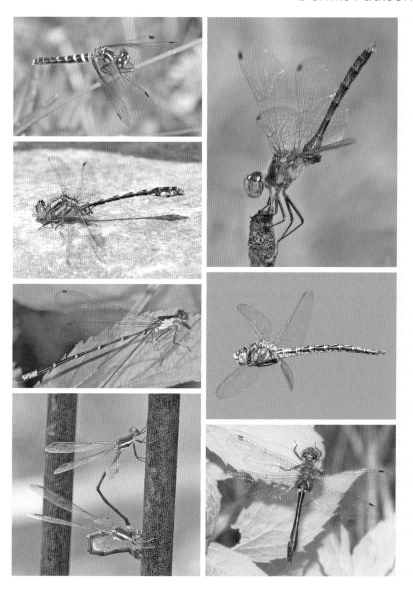

PRINCETON UNIVERSITY PRESS Princeton and Oxford

Published by Princeton University Press, 41 William Street, Princeton, New Jersey 08540
In the United Kingdom: Princeton University Press, 6 Oxford Street,
Woodstock, Oxfordshire OX20 1TW
press.princeton.edu

Jacket photograph: *Pantala flavescens* male © Greg Lasley

Library of Congress Cataloging-in-Publication Data

Paulson, Dennis R.
    Dragonflies and damselflies of the East / Dennis Paulson.
        p. cm.
    Includes bibliographical references and index.
    ISBN 978-0-691-12282-3 (hardback : alk. paper) — ISBN 978-0-691-12283-0 (pbk. : alk. paper)
    1. Dragonflies—East (U.S.)—Identification.   2. Dragonflies—Canada, Eastern—Identification.
    I. Title.
    QL520.2.A1P378 2011
    595.7'33—dc22

                                                                              2011002779

British Library Cataloging-in-Publication Data is available

This book has been composed in Myriad Pro
Printed on acid-free paper. ∞
Printed in China

10 9 8 7 6 5 4 3

Contents

Preface

The great recent interest in dragonflies has resulted in the publication of many good books dealing with them. There are now good technical manuals dealing with the entire North American fauna, and regional guides to damselflies, dragonflies, or both are appearing every year. Nevertheless, there are still no comprehensive field guides to all the Odonata of North America, and this book and a companion volume for western North America (*Dragonflies and Damselflies of the West*, Princeton, 2009) represent an attempt to fill that gap.

These books have two primary goals. The first is to make it possible to identify any of the 461 species of dragonflies and damselflies now known to occur in the United States and Canada. The second is to present material about their natural history that will prompt greater interest in their lifestyles. These insects are just as special as another group of well-loved insects, the butterflies, and there is no reason they cannot become as well known. We constantly alter the natural world, with both obvious and not-so-obvious effects, and we can hope that an increased knowledge of dragonflies will help us understand this world better, in particular the ecology and condition of our wetlands.

Global warming is bringing tropical species across our borders, and they are mixing with the ones already present. Natural wetlands are being filled and artificial ones created, and the forests that shelter many dragonflies are being cut down in some areas and regrown in others. Dragonflies are indicators of these changes if we understand them well enough. This is an exciting time in the study of the order Odonata, with so much amateur interest in the group and a concordant increase in our knowledge. Because of this, I hope these books will not only add to the enjoyment of all who choose to learn something about these fascinating animals but also add even more to what we already know about them.

I learned much about North American odonates when taken in the field or being accompanied by John Abbott, David Arbour, Richard Bailowitz, Jim Bangma, Allen Barlow, Giff Beaton, Bob Behrstock, Mike Blust, Sheryl Chacon, Duncan Cuyler, Jerrell Daigle, Doug Danforth, Marion Dobbs, Nick Donnelly, Bob DuBois, Sid Dunkle, Berlin Heck, Chris Hill, Bill Hull, Jim Johnson, Steve and Mary Jane Krotzer, Ed Lam, Greg Lasley, Charles Mills, Bryan Pfeiffer, Martin Reid, Martha Reinhardt, Larry Rosche, Jennifer Ryan, Judy Semroc, Gayle and Jeanell Strickland, Ken Tennessen, Mike Thomas, Sandy Upson, Michael Veit, Tom Young, and Bill Zimmerman. Messrs Beaton, Behrstock, Daigle, Danforth, Dobbs, Dunkle, Lasley, Reid, and Upson were especially appreciated repeated guides and companions. In addition, many of the other active field workers in North America have given me information about distribution, flight seasons, field identification, variation, habitat, and behavior of eastern Odonata. They include Maria Aliberti, Rob Alvo, John Belshe, Ethan Bright, Sharon Brown, Paul Brunelle, Burton Cebulski, Ken Childs, Glenn Corbiere, Dave Czaplak, John and Sue Gregoire, Greg Hanisek, George Harp, Kevin Hemeon, Tom Howard, Eric Isley, Ann Johnson, Colin Jones, Ellis Laudermilk, Jeremy Martin, David Moskowitz, Jeff Pippen, Herschel Raney, Mike Reese, Tom Schultz, Fred Sibley, Bill Smith, June Tveekrem, Tim Vogt, Erin White, and Hal White, and I hope I have not forgotten any of the others who belong on this list. Some of this information has come from the many online discussion groups that allow us all to communicate so freely about odonates.

I thank Nick Donnelly and John Abbott for making available the detailed information on distribution that greatly facilitated the construction of the range maps presented here. Giff Beaton and Allen Barlow read the entire manuscript and made many helpful suggestions. Mike May and Jessica Ware sent me unpublished phylogenetic studies that were very helpful. Christy Barton expertly rendered all of my hand-drawn range maps on the computer. I owe much to Linda Feltner for sharing her knowledge of Photoshop and graphic design with me. Natalia von Ellenrieder has my greatest appreciation for her precise anatomical drawings of species after species; without them, many more odonates would be unidentifiable! In addition, Rosser Garrison kindly let me use his drawings of dancers (*Argia*) that have graced the pages of other publications. Both of these friends have contributed greatly to the value of this book. I also thank Sid Dunkle for years of friendship and sharing both the problems and the joy of trying to come up with common names for all North American species. Working with the staff at Princeton University Press is always a pleasure, and I thank especially Robert Kirk, Dimitri Karetnikov, and Mark Bellis for their advice and cooperation. Elissa Schiff contributed expert copyediting. As always, Netta Smith deserves my undying gratitude for accompanying me in the field day after day, for sharing the fun and frustration of photographing dragonflies at all points of the compass, and for emotional and logistic support at all times.

I have learned much from additional field experience and the availability of many more photos while preparing this book. **Thus, there will be statements in this book that modify, perhaps even contradict, what was written in my earlier, western guide.**

Introduction

This book is a field guide to all the species of Odonata (dragonflies and damselflies) in the eastern United States and Canada, east of the western boundaries of Ontario, Minnesota, Iowa, Missouri, Arkansas, and Louisiana. I chose state and provincial boundaries rather than the exact middle of the continent because naturalists' interests and odonate record keeping are typically at this level. Because odonate diversity is higher in the East, the continent has been divided in this way to allocate similar numbers of species to the already published western guide and this eastern guide. The western book treated 348 species, and the present book contains 336 species. There is much overlap in species covered, as the total North American fauna at present is 462 species. Thus, about one-fourth of the species in each half of the continent do not occur in the other region and are covered in only one book. Species added to the fauna after each book was finished are briefly mentioned at the end.

Numerous species included in this book barely enter its geographic coverage from the west or south, but the great majority of the species covered are resident in the region. A few species recorded, mostly from southern Florida, may not have resident populations, or local resident populations may originate and then disappear. Because so few species are likely in these categories, all species have been treated equally.

I should make a few definitions clear at the outset. To geographers and biogeographers, North America includes Mexico, Central America, and the West Indies, but for convenience in this book I am restricting "North America" to Canada and the United States. A volume on all of North America would include hundreds more species, and we still do not know enough, nor have sufficient photographs, for a book on Mexican and Central American odonates. Numerous additional species that occur in northern Mexico or the West Indies might wander north in especially wet years or as a consequence of increasing global temperatures, some perhaps carried by prevailing winds or storms, and such additions to our fauna have been occurring at the rate of one or more species each year.

Although all Odonata are called dragonflies in other English-speaking countries, in North America many restrict the term "dragonfly" to the suborder Anisoptera and use "damselfly" for the suborder Zygoptera. I follow that practice in this book and use the term "odonate" when referring to both suborders. In the introductory sections, however, I may use "dragonfly" to refer to the entire order and "damselfly" when speaking only of that group. The word "ode" is used as a synonym by many odonate enthusiasts, with etymologically compromised modifications of it such as "odophile" (odonate lover).

Odonate species are grouped together by their fundamental similarities into ever-larger groups. Wing venation is an important character used to categorize families and genera, but it is de-emphasized here because it is not easily seen in the field. Nevertheless, there are good technical keys to odonates, and an understanding of their venation, as well as the details of the rest of their anatomy, is of value to the odonate enthusiast. Technical anatomical terms are kept at a minimum, but they are necessary from time to time, and they can be learned from the illustrations here.

Because we do not know the exact phylogeny (relationships and order of appearance over evolutionary time) of odonates, much less of most other groups of animals and plants, many authors have chosen to list species in alphabetical order by their scientific or common names rather than trying to associate them to show their relationships. This is commonplace in odonate books, but alphabetical order always places some closely related genera or species some distance apart in a list. Other books place species by their similarity in appearance (as in many flower books), which is helpful in a field guide but does not show relationships and often separates closely related species, so the reader is unaware of the relationship.

Thus, in these books, I have decided to attempt to place genera and species in a semblance of phylogenetic (taxonomic) order to emphasize their relationships. This is also appropriate because close relatives are often the species to be distinguished in a field guide. There

Sweetflag Spreadwing and Ruby Meadowhawk males—Walker Co., GA, August 2007, Marion M. Dobbs

is sufficient literature that in only relatively few cases have I had to use my own judgment. I hope the reader will become familiar with the order of the species, just as birders do in bird books (although it will probably be different in other books!).

Since the western guide was written, more information on phylogeny of the Libelluloidea (cruisers, emeralds, and skimmers) has become available that would shift the order of some of the genera in these books, but I am sticking with the order expressed in the western guide to avoid confusion. Similarly, it is now widely accepted that the spreadwings (Lestidae) are probably the most primitive damselflies.

See the Appendix for general references to odonates. An extensive list of references for the individual species was compiled but proved too voluminous to include in the published books. This Odonata Reference List can be downloaded at http://press.princeton.edu/titles/9538 .html.

Natural History of Odonates

Bird field guides normally do not discuss the general natural history of birds because that is so well known to naturalists in general and even to lay persons that it may not be necessary to know in order to identify the species. However, dragonflies are less well known, and they are such interesting animals that all who observe them in the field should know something about their lives. Of course, because they have a larval stage, much of what is important about them goes on out of sight of the usual observer.

Perching Dragonflies perch in many ways, as can by seen by looking at the photos in this book. Most of them, as typified by clubtails and skimmers, perch more or less horizontally, supported by their legs; the abdomen is often held above the substrate. These are *perchers*. Another whole group of dragonflies, typified by darners, hang from a perch, also supported by their legs clutched to the sides of the substrate. These are *fliers*. See below for how this correlates with feeding behavior. Percher dragonflies probably change their postures mostly for thermoregulation (temperature regulation). They can elevate or lower their abdomen with ease, and they can make it perpendicular to the sun's rays in the morning and evening to warm it maximally or point it directly at the sun at midday (*obelisking*) to minimize solar radiation falling on them. This is commonplace, especially in hot climates.

Wing positions are harder to understand, but among dragonflies they are varied only in the skimmer family. Some skimmers lift their wings when perched on a plant in an open, windy area, lifting them even more when the wind increases, and this is probably for aerodynamic reasons, to keep them stable on their perch. Certain genera of skimmers that routinely perch with wings up (pennants, for example) are those that most commonly perch in open, windy areas on thin, tenuous perches. On the other hand, many skimmers droop their wings in a forward position when they are relaxed, so perhaps that is the most "comfortable" position or takes the least energy to maintain. Dragonflies usually land on a perch with wings horizontal and then may droop them. If you approach such a dragonfly, it may raise its wings back up to horizontal, presumably the best position for a quick takeoff.

Calico Pennant male obelisking—St. Francois Co., MO, June 2009

Boreal Whitefaces basking—Nisku, AB, June 1975, Jim Erckmann

Damselflies hold their wings in one of two positions, the open wings of spreadwings (and several other tropical families) and the closed wings of all other damselflies. Open wings seem associated with large damselflies that forage by flycatching, and smaller flycatching damselflies such as dancers may hold their wings closed to avoid being conspicuous. A few pond damsels routinely hold their wings partially open.

Thermoregulation Temperature regulation is important to odonates, as they are *ectotherms*, their body temperature regulated by the ambient environmental temperature. (By contrast, we are *endotherms*, generating our own body temperature.) Perching dragonflies, as discussed above, can raise or lower their body temperature merely by the way they orient their body with regard to the sun's direction. Dragonflies are commonly seen perched on light substrates in early morning or late afternoon, or on cool middays, their body perpendicular to the sun's rays. When it is not sunny, they cannot do this, probably one of the reasons so many species remain dormant on cloudy days, even when temperatures are sufficient for their activity. Larger dragonflies, including all the fliers, can generate heat by the contraction of their big flight muscles, and they are considered active thermoregulators (the others are passive). The heat generated in the thorax can be transferred to the head and abdomen, and these dragonflies can be active at lower temperatures. They typically vibrate their wings while hanging up, and this makes them warm enough to become active.

Note that fliers such as darners and emeralds make up an impressive part of the odonate fauna at high latitudes. Note also that many of the species, both perchers and fliers, are darkly colored, absorbing rather than reflecting sunlight. On the contrary, many species of desert climates are pale-colored, better at reflecting sunlight. This may be effected by more extensive pruinosity. Some wide-ranging species vary from darker, or with a larger proportion of dark markings, in colder climates to lighter, or with a smaller proportion of dark markings, in hotter climates. This is especially apparent in patterned groups such as bluets, clubtails, and cruisers.

Roosting Odonates usually retire to dense vegetation for the night. Damselflies will fly into a clump of herbaceous vegetation and then crawl within it. They perch with abdomens parallel to plant stems and will move around the stem but not fly if disturbed at night (or at low temperatures). Spreadwings close their wings while roosting. Dragonflies are more likely to move up into shrubs and trees, even well up in the forest canopy, and hang on twigs and leaves on the edges of the vegetation, but some sleep in the weeds with the damsels. Little is known about this aspect of odonate biology. For the most part, odonates seem disoriented at night, but several species of skimmers, including Blue Dashers, have been reported feeding on moths at lights.

Flight One of the many special things about dragonflies is their superb flight ability. All four wings can be moved independently, as can often be seen in flight photos. The wings can not only be "beat" in the classical sense, moved up and down, but they can be rotated on their own axes somewhat like an airplane propeller. This allows great flexibility in just about every way a flying machine needs it. Dragonflies can fly forward at more than 100 body lengths/sec, backwards at more than 3 body lengths/sec, and hover, all while keeping their bodies horizontal. They can fly rapidly straight up and straight down, turn on a dime, or move forward or upward slowly, at almost stalling speed, to search for food items. Although at times they seem to move like a rocket, they probably do not exceed 30 miles/hr, the top speed of small birds.

Although masters of flight, odonates are still very much at the mercy of air currents. Strong winds carry the strongest of fliers, and damselflies especially may use the wind as a dispersal mechanism, flying up into the air column and drifting across the landscape. Sometimes on windy days large numbers of dragonflies appear where they were not present the day before, especially with winds from inland to coast, where the insects are able to resist being blown out over the water.

Migration We know something about the movements of adult odonates at their breeding sites from many mark-and-recapture studies, but much less about how far they disperse from their point of emergence and the likelihood of returning to that point. There is no doubt that some of these movements are substantial and that many individuals breed at locations well removed from their emergence site. Common Green Darners are well known as long-distance latitudinal migrants, much like birds, except there are two generations involved; the ones that fly north in the spring are the offspring of the ones that flew south in the fall, and vice versa! The same is probably true for Variegated Meadowhawks. Species of tropical origin such as both species of gliders and Red and Black Saddlebags move north from the tropics each summer and colonize high latitudes; perhaps their migration strategy is not that different from the others. Large numbers of a variety of darners and skimmers have been found in migratory flights of green darners in eastern North America, perhaps all migrating some distance. These flights have been along lakeshores and mountain ridges as well as the Atlantic coastline. Numerous species have been collected from offshore oil platforms in the Gulf of Mexico, damselflies such as Rambur's Forktail among them; these could be one-way dispersers or regular migrants. There is much yet to be learned about this.

Red Saddlebags female landing—Travis Co., TX, September 2005, Eric Isley

Slender Bluet male hovering—Aiken Co., SC, May 2008

Vision Dragonflies have the finest vision in the insect world. The compound eyes in the largest species have as many as 30,000 simple eyes (*ommatidia*) perceiving the world around them. Because the simple eyes are individual receptors, insect vision is somewhat of a mosaic, and dragonflies are very good at detecting movement. The tiniest movement in the distance stimulates one ommatidium after another. The eyes are so large, especially in darners, that they wrap around the head and afford almost 360° perception. Vision is relatively poor only directly behind and below a dragonfly, and dragonfly collectors learn that to their advantage. Damselflies, with their smaller eyes well separated, perhaps have enhanced depth perception for close-range distinction of aphids from the leaves on which they rest. Dragonflies have a wider range of color detection than mammals and, as can other insects, see into the ultraviolet (UV) range. Many species reflect UV, especially those that look bright blue or bright white to us, and they may look even brighter to other dragonflies.

Ringed Emerald eye—King Co., WA, September 1975, Truman Sherk

Feeding Odonates are all predators, in both adult and larval stages. Adults exhibit three different modes of foraging behavior that have equivalents in bird feeding behavior. Fliers fly around, either back and forth in a confined space or more extensively, and capture other flying insects by *hawking*. All other odonates are considered perchers. Among the perchers, *salliers* watch for flying prey from a perch and fly up to capture it, whereas *gleaners* alternate perching with slow searching flights through vegetation, where they dart toward stationary prey and pick it from the substrate. Gleaners may also flush an insect and chase it through the air. Typical hawkers include darners (called hawkers in the United Kingdom) and emeralds and certain groups of skimmers, for example gliders and saddlebags. Typical salliers include broad-winged damsels, spreadwings, dancers, clubtails, and most skimmers. Typical gleaners include pond damsels other than dancers.

Most dragonflies take small prey, much smaller than themselves. Tiny flies, leafhoppers, and beetles are common prey. Some species vary these with larger prey, for example other dragonflies and butterflies, and others seem to be specialists on large prey. Dragonhunters are well known to live up to their name, and some other clubtails also take large prey. Pondhawks commonly and darners more rarely prey on dragonflies up to their own size, and some pond damsels will take another damselfly of the same size, especially when the latter has just emerged and is quite vulnerable. Note that dragonflies that routinely take large prey are among the most effective biters when captured!

Predators and Predator Defense Many larger animals prey on odonates. Members of their own order are among the most important predators, as stated above. The other very important insect predators on odonates are robber flies on adults and ants on tenerals that have just emerged. Spiders are similarly important, both active predators and web-builders. Among vertebrates, birds are most important, taking a huge toll on tenerals in wetlands but also capturing many adults. Small falcons and large flycatchers are important predators, and some tropical bird groups (jacamars, bee-eaters) are even dragonfly specialists, their long, slender bills perfect for catching a dragonfly by the wings. Frogs and fish also take their toll at the water surface, as do lizards in the uplands. And below the water surface, fish, other odonates, water bugs and water beetles are among the most important predators on the larvae. Aquatic birds, including ducks and grebes, probably take a large number of them as well.

Dragonflies have their good vision and swift and agile flight to protect them from predators. Many are well camouflaged, especially when perching away from water. The mottled brown body coloration of some species, especially the females, enhances camouflage, as perhaps do the dark wingtips of many forest-dwelling skimmers, again especially the females.

Four-spotted Skimmer male with crane fly— Wood Co., WI, June 2007

Eastern Pondhawk male with female Variable Dancer—Lake Co., FL, April 2008

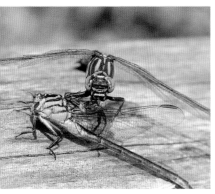

Blackwater Clubtail female with female Russet-tipped Clubtail—Telfair Co., GA, July 2003, Marion M. Dobbs

Powdered Dancer female with male Blue-tipped Dancer—Okaloosa Co., FL, July 2009

Rainbow Bluet female with leafhopper—Cook Co., IL, June 2008, Marla Garrison

Orb weaver with Spotted Spreadwings and teneral Autumn Meadowhawk— San Juan Co., WA, August 2007

Robber fly with female Aurora Damsel— White Co., GA, May 2006

Sundew with male Elfin Skimmer— Hillsborough Co., NH, June 2006

Tricolored Heron with male Red Saddlebags— Broward Co., FL, December 2008, Dan Logen

When not out in the open, damselflies usually perch along grass stems, grasping them tightly, and sidle around the stem to be on the far side from a potential predator. The well-separated eyes can look around a slender stem when the body is hidden. A few small dragonflies may effectively mimic wasps, gaining protection from predators that shy away from such well-protected insects.

Parasites Odonates have parasites just like all other animals, but a few types are evident to even the casual naturalist. The spheres that are commonly present on the lower side of the thorax or abdomen of odonates are water mites. The mite larvae find an odonate larva and climb aboard, remaining with it until it emerges, when they quickly transfer to the adult. They then gain both food and transport, perhaps to another wetland. While on the dragonfly, they suck body fluids and, if abundant enough, can reduce the host's survival. A much smaller num-

Skimming Bluet pair with water mites—Ocean Co., NJ, June 2008

ber of adult anisopterans are seen with tiny flies, usually on their wing bases, that are sucking blood from the wing veins. These are flies of the family Ceratopogonidae, the same family that features the pesky no-see-ums or sand flies. They are much more likely to be seen in the South, especially in subtropical areas.

Sexual Patrol Males of all odonates spend a lot of their time searching for females; natural selection demands it. Each species has a characteristic pattern of sexual patrol. Some species are territorial, each male staking out a territory and defending it. In the vast majority of species, this territory coincides with an optimal habitat for female egg laying, which of course coincides with optimal habitat for the larvae. Other species do not defend territories, for example, male darners that fly all around the shore of a lake or male damselflies that change perches frequently and do not remain in any particular place. Families with species that defend fixed territories include broad-winged damsels, clubtails, petaltails, and skimmers. Those in which males fly over long beats, not defending fixed territories but aggressive to any other males they encounter, include darners, spiketails, cruisers, emeralds, and some species among the clubtails and skimmers. Most damselfly males defend no more than the perch on which they rest at the moment.

Courtship and Mating Courtship behavior is fairly common in tropical damselflies, but few North American species practice it. It is best known in jewelwings of the genus *Calopteryx*. Among eastern dragonflies, male amberwings exhibit a form of courtship when they attempt to lead females to oviposition sites. In most North American odonates, the male just grabs the female, but she still chooses to mate with him or not. Although males will often attempt to mate with females of other species, most females are apparently able to detect by touch whether the male that grabs them is their own species.

Where odonates meet to mate has been called the *rendezvous*. In general, when a mature male odonate encounters a mature (or even immature) female of the same species at the rendezvous, he attempts to mate. In most species, the rendezvous is at the water, but many species, especially those that oviposit in tandem, also mate away from the water and then move to it to lay eggs. The male approaches the female from behind, grabs her with his legs, in some cases even biting her briefly, and immediately attempts to clasp her with his terminal appendages. A male dragonfly clasps the head of the female with two cerci on either side of her "neck" and the epiproct pressed tightly against the top of the head. In some dragonflies, the prothorax may also be involved in this *tandem linkage*. In jewelwings, spreadwings, and some pond damsels, the male's cerci are applied to the back of the prothorax and the two paraprocts to the top, holding it firmly. In other damselflies, the cerci contact the mesostigmal plates at the front

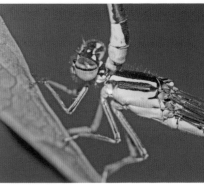

Tule Bluet tandem—Thurston Co., WA, July 2008, Dick Logan

Stream Bluet tandem—Worcester Co., MA, July 2008, Steven Price

of the synthorax, and the paraprocts the top and/or side of the prothorax. In damselflies that differ in their terminal appendages and mesostigmal plates, if the connection does not fit, the female is probably of a different species, and she is usually released. Less is known about how this works in dragonflies.

After the female is firmly clasped, a male damselfly will then take a few seconds to transfer sperm from the genital opening under his ninth segment to an organ of sperm storage, the *seminal vesicle*, under his second segment. He will then attempt to swing her abdomen forward to contact those genitalia with the tip of her abdomen. In dragonflies, males of most, possibly all, species transfer sperm to their second segment before hooking up with a female. When contact is made, the appropriate structures of the two sexes lock in place, and the penis transfers sperm through the female's genital pore into her vagina. Fertilization may take place immediately, or the sperm may pass into one or the other of two types of sperm-storage organs, the *bursa copulatrix* and the *spermatheca*. If sperm from another mating is already present, the male removes or flushes out much of it, thus making it highly likely that his sperm will fertilize her eggs.

At this time, the male supports them both on a perch in the majority of species (some copulate only in flight), and in dragonflies the female's legs grasp the male's abdomen. The copulatory, or *wheel*, position is unique to the Odonata, as is the distant separation of the male's genital opening and copulatory organs. That the position looks as much like a heart as a wheel has

Blue-striped Spreadwing sperm transfer—Hidalgo Co., TX, September 2008

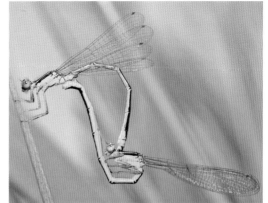

Rainbow Bluet copulation—
Cook Co., IL, June 2008,
Marla Garrison

Common Green Darner
copulation—Snohomish
Co., WA, June 2009,
Steven G. Mlodinow

Plains Clubtail
copulation—Travis
Co., TX, April 2010,
Eric Isley

been noted. Copulation lasts from a few seconds, for example in skimmers that mate in flight, to several hours in different odonate species.

Females of many species can retain live sperm throughout their lives, essentially fertilizing their own eggs as the eggs travel down the oviduct past the sperm-storage organs.

In a few studies in which most male dragonflies at a pond were removed, some remaining ones mated over 100 times! Males that have mated often have marks on their abdomen where the female legs have scratched them. This is especially obvious in species in which males develop pruinosity, as the pruinosity on the midabdomen is scratched off, and the signs are visible at some distance. Female dragonflies that have mated often have marks on their eyes where the male epiproct has scratched or even punctured the eyes.

Band-winged Meadowhawk in tandem with Eastern Amberwing—Penobscot Co., ME, August 2008, Vic Fazio

Male odonates attempt to mate with females not of their own species with a fairly high frequency. Apparently, recognition in some groups is not achieved until there is a tandem attempt, and the male and female structures that hook together during tandem do not quite fit. This happens commonly in damselflies and has been reported in most groups of odonates. Most of the time, no more than tandem is achieved, and that is often brief, but sometimes such mismated pairs actually achieve copulation. Hybrids have been reported in several odonate families.

Egg Laying and Hatching Eggs are laid into the water or bottom material (exophytic oviposition) or inserted into plants or other substrates (endophytic oviposition). Females that oviposit exophytically extrude eggs from the genital pore in their eighth segment, usually in flight. Quite a cluster of eggs may be formed before the female taps the water and releases them. The eggs typically sink into a bed of aquatic vegetation or onto the bottom. Some species, especially those of flowing waters, have eggs that adhere to the substrate in one way or another. Exophytic oviposition is very variable, some females tapping the water in the same spot for an oviposition bout and others flying rapidly over the water and dropping single eggs or egg clusters at intervals. In some species, eggs are dropped from above the water or even onto dry ground. Endophytic species have well-developed ovipositors and include all damselflies and petaltails and darners among the dragonflies. Large numbers of eggs can be laid by a single female, up to the low thousands.

Eggs may hatch after a few days, or embryonic development may take a month or more. In some species, the eggs overwinter and hatch the following spring. Each egg hatches into a very tiny *prolarva* that looks like a primitive insect form, quite different from the larva that will succeed it. When the eggs are laid above the water, the prolarva leaps and flips about until it gets to the water, at which time it will quickly molt into the second larval stadium (each stage is called a *stadium* or an *instar*). When the eggs are laid directly into the water, the prolarval stage may last only a few minutes.

Blue Dasher oviposition—Scott Co., IA, July 2009, Keith Wiggers

Variegated Meadowhawk tandem—Travis Co., TX, November 2005, Eric Isley

Banner Clubtail with egg mass—Jasper Co., TX, April 2010, Greg Lasley

Great Spreadwing tandem—St. Louis Co., MO, October 2008, Marion M. Dobbs

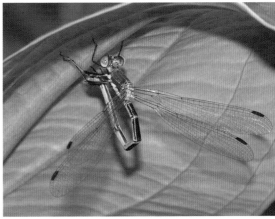

Amber-winged Spreadwing oviposition— Washington Co., MO, June 2009

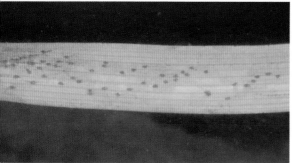

River Jewelwing eggs inserted in *Vallisneria*—Geauga Co., OH, June 2007, Judy M. Semroc

Lance-tipped Darner oviposition—Hampden Co., MA, September 2003, Glenn Corbiere

Larval Life History Although they have the standard head, thorax, and abdomen and six legs of all insects, odonate larvae (also called nymphs or naiads) look very different from the adults and lead a very different life. One thing they have in common is being predators, but the larvae capture their prey by shooting out their *labium*, a sort of lower lip (it has been called a "killer lip"), by hydrostatic pressure and grabbing with a pair of labial palps that open and shut on the prey. The labium then retracts and draws the prey into the mandibles. The larvae of damselflies, petaltails, clubtails, and darners have a flat labium with pointed palps that skewer the prey. The larvae of spiketails, cruisers, emeralds, and skimmers have a spoon-shaped labium with large palps that enclose the prey.

Dragonfly larvae respire through gills in their rectum, and the whole rear end of the abdomen is a respiratory chamber that draws water in and out and takes oxygen from it. Because of this ability, the rectum can also be used for jet propulsion under water. Finally, of course, it is the posterior end of the digestive tract, so in dragonflies the rectum is a multipurpose organ (calling it a *miraculous rectum* would not be extreme), one of their many unique attributes. Damselflies have three prominent caudal gills that function to extract oxygen from the water, and they can also use them to swim by waving them back and forth like a fish's tail. They are still able to respire after losing their gills, but not as well.

The larvae are very variable in what they do, more so than the adults. Some burrow just below the surface of sand and mud bottoms, grabbing midge larvae they encounter in their semifluid milieu; others squat in the bottom detritus with only their eyes and face exposed, striking out at fellow bottom dwellers; still others climb in the vegetation, stalking their prey as a cat stalks a mouse. Larvae of certain types live right out in the open in temporary ponds that lack larger predators, and some spreadwing larvae swim in stream pools like little fish. As you might guess, their shapes and colors vary in accord with their habits.

Collecting odonate larvae and keeping them in an aquarium is a wonderful way to learn about them. They are quite predatory and even cannibalistic, and to keep them from eating each other, put relatively few in each aquarium and give them lots of vegetation in which to hide. In a warm aquarium, they will grow quickly, even to metamorphosis. If you want to watch emergence, collect larvae in their last stadium and put them in an aquarium or large jar with a stick on which to emerge. Put a screen over it or they will be flying around your house.

Spreadwing larva—Taylor Co., GA, March 2005, Giff Beaton

Bluet larva—Taylor Co., GA, February 2006, Giff Beaton

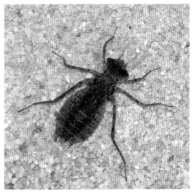

Comet Darner larva—Taylor Co., GA, March 2005, Giff Beaton

Baskettail larva—Taylor Co., GA, March 2005, Giff Beaton

Metamorphosis and Emergence The larvae undergo numerous molts, averaging around a dozen, as they grow and feed. In warm tropical pools, a larva may go through its entire development in as little as a month, but most temperate-zone species take at least several months. In colder waters, as in streams and mountain lakes and at higher latitudes, the larva may take several years to reach metamorphosis, growing through a few molts each summer. During the last few stadia, the adult wings begin forming inside wing pads extending back from the thorax

Dragonhunter emergence—Monroe Co., GA, May 2006, Giff Beaton

that become more prominent until they are bulging with the wings inside them. During this time, the larva is undergoing a metamorphosis to its adult state even as it remains active—one of the wonders of nature! It finally stops feeding and soon thereafter switches over to aerial respiration; it then leaves the water. Damselflies, clubtails, and some small skimmers often emerge just above the water, but other odonates typically move farther away from it, even climbing up into trees (long-distance travel is typical of cruisers).

The larva fixes itself to the substrate and then expands its thorax until a split appears in it. The thorax is first split by a little point on the front of the adult's thorax; look for this in the adults. It then emerges through the split and hangs backward from the larval skin. After its cuticle hardens for a while and its muscles become stronger, it reaches up and pulls itself out of the exuvia. The wings, folded like accordions, then begin to fill from the base with fluid transferred from the body and fairly soon reach full length. The fluid is then pumped back into the abdomen, and it expands. Finally, the wings open up, and very soon the *teneral* adult flies away. Clubtails and damselflies can manage the same process on horizontal substrates, coming out upright rather than hanging down. The cast skin left behind is called an *exuvia* (plural *exuviae*), and looking for exuviae is a good way to find out what species are breeding in an area, as the exuvia is just as good as the larva for identification. In many groups, it is easy to determine the species from the larva or exuvia, but in some, the species are similar enough that identification to genus is more practical.

To find adults emerging, exciting to watch although slow in tempo, you should know something about their emergence times. At temperate latitudes, most damselflies and clubtails emerge during the daytime, usually during the warmer periods at midday, whereas members of other families do so at night, the larger ones leaving the water a few hours after sunset so they are ready to fly as it gets light the next morning. As latitude increases, nighttime tem-

Florida Bluet male on Eastern Amberwing exuvia—Palm Beach Co., FL, November 2004, J. Lubchansky

Tawny Sanddragon female teneral + exuvia—Clay Co., FL, June 2004

Northern Bluet male and female emergence—Okanogan Co., WA, July 2009, Netta Smith

Northern Bluet mass emergence—Okanogan Co., WA, June 2008

peratures may be too cool for emergence, so darners, emeralds, and skimmers often emerge during the day in northern regions. A cold spell that ensues during emergence can delay or even stop the process. Conversely, with lower latitude, higher temperatures, and even more avian predators, even the clubtails emerge at night, although daytime emergence remains typical of damselflies. On a hot day, a damselfly can go from crawling out of the water to flying away in a half-hour or less, and they probably emerge in the daytime just because high temperature facilitates quick emergence. Where a species is abundant, emergence may be highly synchronized, producing real spectacles. This synchrony is usually a consequence of all the larvae overwintering in the last instar; thus, all are ready to emerge at about the same time when conditions permit.

Sexual Maturation After an odonate leaves the water as a teneral, its cuticle hardens, and the definitive color pattern is laid down, a combination of both pigments and structural changes. This color pattern can be held throughout life if it is the same as the mature color pattern, but the color itself may change over a course of days or weeks or even months as the individual becomes sexually mature and returns to the water, completing the cycle. These prereproductive adults are often called immatures (a name that should not be used for the larvae), and they may wander far and wide, even miles from the water. This is especially true of darners,

River Bluet immature male—Teton Co., WY, September 2007

Common Whitetail immature
male—Aiken Co., SC, May 2008

Common Whitetail mature male—
Washburn Co., WI, August 2008

which may fly up mountains much as butterflies do. Both immature and mature individuals of flier dragonflies may form feeding swarms, sometimes of mixed species. After the immature phase, most temperate-zone odonates live a surprisingly short time. Small damselflies live no more than a few weeks, larger dragonflies a month or two. Dying of old age is rarely observed in odonates, but at some lakes with an abundance of bluets, large numbers of dead ones have been observed floating on the surface toward the end of their flight season. Old individuals are often discolored, with tattered wings.

Odonate Anatomy

Understanding color-pattern descriptions of odonates is made easier by understanding their anatomy. All insects have three major body parts, the head, thorax, and abdomen. The *head* is involved in seeing and feeding (probably not much thinking), the *thorax* bears the wings and legs and thus is the locomotion center, and the *abdomen* bears the reproductive structures.

The head is made up of the huge eyes (smaller in damselflies) and what might be called the "face" (technically from top to bottom the *frons*, *clypeus*, and *labrum*). There is little else, al-

Purple Skimmer male—
Bay Co., FL, July 2009

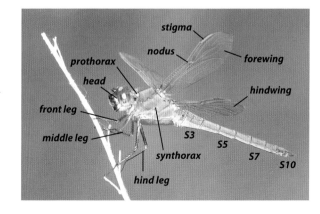

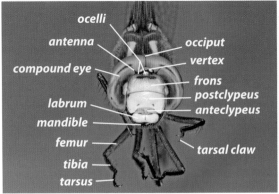
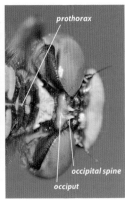

Lance-tipped Darner
male—Mahoning Co.,
OH, August 2006,
Judy M. Semroc

Appalachian Snaketail
female—Calhoun Co., AL,
April 2009, Giff Beaton

though sometimes field marks are located on the *vertex* (behind the frons) and the *occiput* (behind the eyes) or even the *labium* (the jointed lower lip). The coloration on the back of the head also varies and can be used as an identifying mark in some cases. Other anatomical features on the top of the head include the *ocelli* (singular *ocellus*), three tiny simple eyes arranged in a triangle that may serve to measure light intensity; and two small *antennae* that probably measure air speed but do not function as olfactory organs as in so many other insect groups. What looks like the "neck" of a dragonfly is actually its *prothorax*, on which are attached the first pair of legs. This tiny segment really does function somewhat as a neck, joining the head quite flexibly to the rest of the animal. The connection between head and prothorax is surprisingly narrow and seemingly flimsy, but it allows the head and body to be moved somewhat independently during flight. Look also at how odonates, at least the perching species, move their heads around while at rest. They are often looking for prey, but they can also spot predators, territorial rivals, and mates. Note also how the front legs are often tucked behind the head, perhaps not always necessary for perching.

Blue-fronted Dancer
female—Travis Co.,
TX, August 2003, Eric
Isley

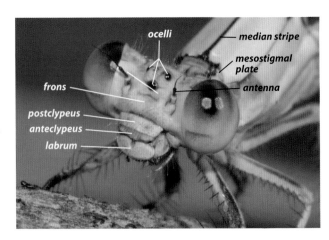

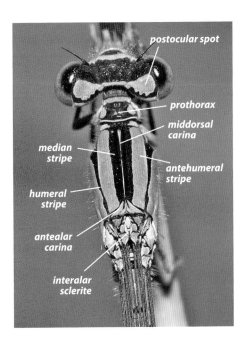

postocular spot

prothorax

middorsal carina

median stripe

antehumeral stripe

humeral stripe

antealar carina

interalar sclerite

Boreal Bluet male—
Millard Co., UT, July 2006,
Nicky Davis

The thorax, also called *pterothorax* or *synthorax*, houses the big important flight muscles. It is actually the fused *mesothorax* and *metathorax*, each with a pair of wings and a pair of legs. The part of the thorax in front of the forewing bases is anatomically the front. Thus, the thorax has a front, sides, and a bottom; the top would be the area containing and between the wings. This is harder to envision in damselflies, as their thorax is skewed so far backward to allow their wings to close over their abdomen that the front of the thorax looks like the top. I am going to remain consistent with anatomy and call the area in front of the wings the front of the thorax when describing color patterns of damselflies. The thorax is patterned in most species, and the patterns are consistent within and sometimes between families. In damselflies, the dark stripe on either side that extends from the base of the forewing to the second pair of legs is called the *humeral stripe*; a pale stripe at its anterior (inner, upper) edge is called the *antehumeral stripe*. These have been called "shoulder stripes" in some other books. Some damselflies have additional narrow dark stripes posterior to (outside, below) the humeral. In dragonflies, the stripes take different forms and can be much more complex.

The forewings and hindwings of damselflies are about the same (Zygoptera means *yoked wings*), whereas those of dragonflies are quite different, the hindwing being considerably broader and with different patterns of venation at the base (Anisoptera means *unlike wings*). All of our species have prominent markers on the wings, including the *triangle* (dragonflies) or *quadrangle* (damselflies), the *nodus*, and (in almost all species) the *pterostigma*. As do other authors, I use the shortened "stigma" for the pterostigma. Knowledge of venation will be of importance for species identification in some cases.

The 10-segmented abdomen carries the digestive tract and reproductive organs. It is probably longer than is necessary for that purpose just because it acts aerodynamically to put as much weight behind the wings as in front of them. Long abdomens tend to be slender, short abdomens wide. The secondary genitalia of males are carried under abdominal segments 2–3, usually very prominently. **Looking for that basal bulge in side view is the best way to quickly sex an odonate.** Females typically have wider abdomens, and these taper less to the rear than those of males, presumably because they carry a load of eggs. Abdomen shape is

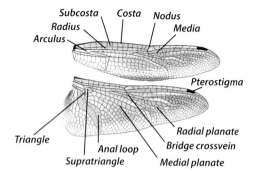

Wandering Glider wings (contrast increased digitally)

Subcosta Costa Nodus
Radius Media
Arculus

Pterostigma

Triangle

Anal loop

Supratriangle

Radial planate

Bridge crossvein

Medial planate

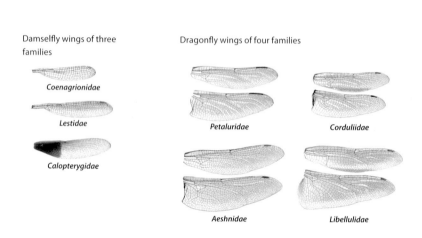

Damselfly wings of three families

Coenagrionidae

Lestidae

Calopterygidae

Dragonfly wings of four families

Petaluridae

Corduliidae

Aeshnidae

Libellulidae

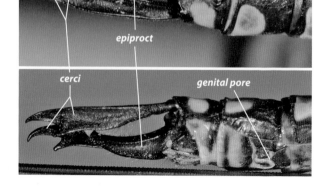

Blue-eyed Darner male appendages—Davis Co., UT, August 2006, Nicky Davis

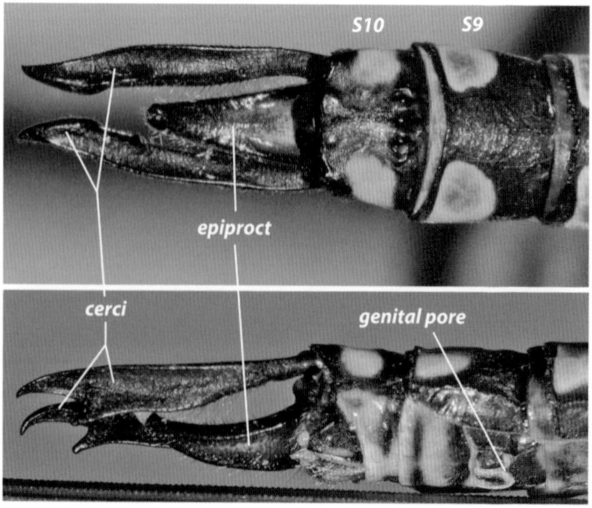

S10   S9

epiproct

cerci   genital pore

another important method of sex determination. The tenth segment (S10) carries the *cerci* of both sexes (upper appendages in males) and the *epiproct* (single lower appendage) in male dragonflies and *paraprocts* (paired lower appendages) in male damselflies. The female reproductive tract opens between S8 and S9 and may be protected by a *subgenital plate* (also called vulvar lamina, present in most dragonflies) or prolonged into a complex *ovipositor* (damselflies, petaltails, darners). Abdomens can be simply striped or spotted, with the spots arranged centrally or laterally, or more complexly patterned with linear and transverse markings.

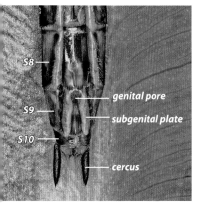

Common Baskettail female abdomen tip—Erie Co., PA, June 2006, Judy M. Semroc

American Rubyspot male abdomen tip—Utah Co., UT, June 2006, Nicky Davis

American Rubyspot female abdomen tip—Utah Co., UT, June 2006, Nicky Davis

Swift River Cruiser male and female—Rusk Co., WI, June 2007

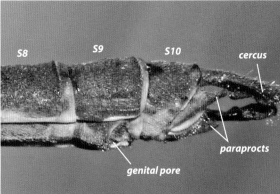

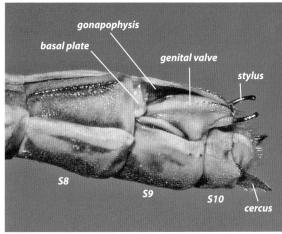

Odonate Colors

Dragonfly colors are produced in the same way as those of other organisms. Most of the blacks, browns, reds, and yellows are pigments of various types. Most of the blues are structural colors, produced by the microscopic structure of the surface of the cuticle reflecting blue light and letting the other wavelengths pass through. Greens are usually produced by adding yellow pigment to a blue-reflecting cuticle. Iridescent (metallic) colors are also structural. The translucent surface of the eyes makes their coloration particularly glowing. As the adult dragonfly develops within the larva, its pigment patterns are laid down, and they become more evident as it ages after emergence. Sexual maturation is often indicated by a dramatic change in color, often brought about by the deposition of pruinosity. Note that within a group (a genus or even a family) the great variety of colors and patterns are often part of a common theme, with the variation caused by the presence and relative size of dark markings and the pale colors between them.

Mature adults in a few groups can also change color, a phenomenon called reversible temperature-induced color change. This is known in some blue species that become gray at low temperatures (some dancers and mosaic darners). It is thought that this reduces their conspicuousness (of value when their temperature is lowered, as they are not so quick at escaping predation), but it also may enhance their ability to thermoregulate.

Odonate Names

A scientific name consists of a *genus* (plural *genera*) and a *species* name. The name is unique to the species and will allow reference to it in any language. Both words usually have Greek or Latin roots; Greek may actually be more common, so "Latin name" is a misnomer. Anyone with some knowledge of the classical languages or even of common words in biology will have an insight into the meanings of the names. For example, the Ringed Emerald is *Somatochlora albicincta. Somato* means "body" and *chlora* means "green" in Greek; *albi* means "white" and *cincta* means "ringed" in Latin. Thus, *Somatochlora albicincta* is a "white-ringed greenbody." Not all scientific names are so easily translated.

The scientific names and common names used herein are those in most recent use. With species being split (divided into more than one species) or lumped (combined with another species), changes in scientific names may still occur in the North American fauna. The Checklist Committee of the Dragonfly Society of the Americas has taken on the responsibility of keeping the North American checklist up to date by making taxonomic decisions and determining common names for North American species. These decisions are maintained and updated on a website at the Slater Museum of Natural History (http://www.pugetsound.edu/north-american-odonata). The checklist includes both the name of the person who described the species and the year of description.

Until relatively recently, most Odonata of the world lacked common names; odonatologists communicated entirely by scientific names. An attitude against using common names lasted through much of the twentieth century, but late in that century Sidney Dunkle and I, discussing the need to encourage wider studies of dragonflies by amateur naturalists, attempted to generate a set of common names for the North American fauna. That list was then published in *Argia*, the newsletter of the Dragonfly Society of the Americas, and was subject to criticism and suggestions by the membership. Changes were incorporated, and the list was officially endorsed by the society. That list is used herein, with a few recent changes to incorporate new species, newly recorded species, taxonomic changes, and correction of a few inappropriate names. Although stability is the ultimate goal, the naming of living organisms is always an ongoing process. The common names of species are considered "proper names" by many people using them, and thus their first letters are capitalized, that is, Filigree Skimmer rather than filigree skimmer. Group names are left uncapitalized, for example bluets or mosaic darners.

I strongly encourage all with a serious interest in dragonflies to consider learning both the common and scientific names. Almost all of the scientific literature on Odonata uses their scientific names, and most professional odonatologists communicate by the scientific names. This becomes essential as soon as one moves south of the U.S.-Mexican border and begins to encounter species not known from North America. Furthermore, knowing the genus to which a species belongs is immediately indicative of its relationships, whereas common names do not always provide that information. Genera of odonates are usually well defined, with a suite of characteristics (often morphological, ecological, and behavioral) that allow distinction from other genera. The genera of North American odonates have also been given common names, and those are written in lower case, as they are not to be considered proper names. At times in the text below, I use the real generic name rather than the generic common name, consciously promoting my philosophy. I also very often discuss the genus as a group to be compared with other such groups, as dragonfly genera are usually (but by no means always) discrete and recognizable. In fact, the generic name may be as easy to remember and quicker to say than the common name of the genus, e.g., *Orthemis* instead of tropical king skimmer or *Aeshna* instead of mosaic darner.

Finding Odonates

Because odonates are aquatic animals, the best place to find them, of course, is at the water. Wetlands of all types support populations, but some types are better than others. A warm, productive pond or lake with much aquatic vegetation should have a diverse array of species, and the species are often common and widespread ones that can be the first to be learned by a beginner. Many odonates are habitat specialists, and to find them you must locate their habitat. The best way to see a diversity of species is to explore a diversity of habitats, not just ponds and streams but as many different kinds of ponds and streams as there may be in the area. Large lakes and rivers have specialists not to be found on smaller wetlands. Tiny trickles and seeps may have still other specialists. Bogs and fens support different species, and some species even find habitats created by humans, such as reservoirs and farm ponds, to be optimal for their ecological needs. So-called "mitigation ponds" are being dug in many areas during construction projects, and, as they are usually fish-free and are often provided with instant aquatic vegetation, they can be especially good odonate habitats.

Because odonate presence varies in both space and time, you will also want to check each location at least several times over the flight season. Some species have surprisingly short periods of abundance, with most of the population emerging over a few days' time, present for less than a month, and then disappearing rapidly. Others have long flight seasons. In addition, there is year-to-year variation, with a species appearing at a wetland where it had not previously been present, perhaps remaining in abundance for a few years, then petering out over the next several years.

To be really devoted to finding odonates, you will have to get your feet wet. More species and more individuals will be seen by this method. Wet pants and muddy feet may be the costs for the benefits of great dragonfly experiences. The rewards for wet feet may be species that occur only at the outer edge of the belt of shore vegetation at ponds and lakes, species that occur on sand and gravel bars in rivers, and species that occur within flooded swamps. Some water bodies are thickly overgrown or with steep banks at shore, and getting out to the open water will avoid that. The best wading, of course, is in clear lakes or streams where you can see your feet! A boat of any sort may come in handy at such times, although odonates might be difficult to photograph or capture because they are disturbed by the boat approaching. Stop the boat in the midst of vegetation, and some will return.

Most species of odonates leave the waterside when immature, and they can then be found almost anywhere, in some cases even miles (or kilometers, if you are in Canada) from water. Look for them in sunny clearings or at the edges of roads and trails through forest and field. Walking along an open trail that parallels a stream, for example, may give you access to many species perching in the sun that are only at the stream at certain times of day. Some of the best looks at darners, river cruisers, and emeralds may come here, as you find them hanging up instead of incessantly cruising back and forth. If you see one of these long-bodied flier dragonflies cruising a beat, presumably feeding, watch it for a while and it may hang up, often when it captures something. You can then get a better look or approach for a photo opportunity. Some species aggregate to feed where their prey is concentrated, often in the lee of trees on windy days. You may be much more likely to find females, as well as immatures, away from water, but males are much more easily found at the water. Note also that females often outnumber males at the end of the flight season.

On a hot day, it can be too hot for odonates to remain in the sun for any length of time, and they will move into the shade during midday and early afternoon. At such times, it may be profitable to look for them in sheltered shaded areas, either at or away from the water. Species that normally perch out in the open may be hanging under branches to avoid the sun's direct rays. Similarly, if it is cooler, different opportunities present themselves. By visiting a dragonfly locality early in the morning, you may find some individuals sunning themselves, cool enough that they are easily approached even though perched in the open. As might be expected, the farther north you go, the lower the temperatures at which some dragonfly activity occurs, probably because northern species are specially adapted to function at lower temperatures.

Binoculars are of great value for getting closer looks at odonates, for example one perched over the water or up in a tree. Close-focus binoculars can be used to examine damselflies right at your feet, and in fact, my criterion for "close focus" is being able to focus on your own feet or closer. With such an optical aid, it might be possible in some cases to identify male damselflies from the structure of their appendages without capturing them.

When searching for odonates, it is best to alternate *near-looking* (even right at your feet if you are walking through vegetation) for damselflies and *far-looking* (up to 20–30 feet away) for the warier dragonflies. Some small damselflies are unlikely to flush from dense vegetation, and gently moving a net or even a stick through grasses, sedges, and other herbaceous vegetation can flush them out and bring them to your attention. Often I have caught small damselflies by sweeping an insect net through vegetation near water where I had no idea any were present. By this action, you can also examine more closely the damsels' predators (mostly spiders, the occasional robber fly or mantis) and prey!

Identifying Odonates

In times past, when faced with an unidentified dragonfly or damselfly, an odonate enthusiast had a simple, if not always easy, task: catch it and key it out. This normally necessitated preservation of the specimen, useful because it allowed the identification to be reconfirmed or possibly changed at any time. Nowadays, there is not only a much stronger desire but also a much greater possibility to identify the same individuals in the field, either with or without the aid of a net. If identification involves capture, the best tool to have, after the net, is a hand lens or other magnifier. Several types of good 10× hand lenses are sold in biological supply houses.

Short of capturing the specimen, the next best way to assure identification is to take what could be called "ID photographs," photos from sufficient angles to capture all important aspects of color pattern, details of wing venation, and even close-ups of appendages, hamules, and ovipositors. Photography has greatly assisted in the identification process, as photos can be taken and examined at leisure with identification guides in hand and, if sufficiently detailed, can serve as a voucher for the identification and for the record.

Because relatively few of the many people becoming interested in Odonata are collectors, more and more of the voucher "specimens" that support occurrence records of species are photos (see the website Odonata Central for a dramatic example of this). Photos are of course better than sight reports, which furnish no way of objectively assessing identifications and are dependent on the abilities of observers with all degrees of competence in making identifications. Nevertheless, photos may not always allow identification because (1) size cannot be judged; (2) color may be off because of the camera or the processing; (3) important identifying marks may not be visible; and (4) only examination in the hand distinguishes certain very similar species. Furthermore, those that are not permanently archived are not available for future study.

Short of that option, the observer's best chance for an identification is to observe all these features and either commit them to memory or take notes on them. Obviously if an identification guide is handy, this can be consulted on the spot. Look especially at overall coloration, including differences between thorax and abdomen; color of the eyes and face; and obvious patterning on the thorax and abdomen, which may be complex. Even the coloration of the stigmas, wing veins, legs, and/or appendages can be important to distinguish some species. Behavior can be an important adjunct, one of the first steps to decide whether you are looking at a darner or a clubtail, a pond damsel or a spreadwing.

When trying to identify odonates, remember that males of related species often differ from one another more than females do. So females can be difficult, even very difficult, to distinguish. Often a clue to identification of females comes from the presence of males of only one species of that group. If you see a mating pair, collect or photograph or watch it closely to learn more about what females look like. Bear in mind that males sometimes make mistakes, and mistakes are more likely to be seen in tandem pairs than in copulating pairs. As you become more familiar with the species, you will find these *heterospecific* pairs yourself. *Conspecific* pairs are the rule.

Beyond the simple instructions in what to look for, a few first principles should be understood. One of them is *variation*.

Just as in birds and butterflies, in fact all products of Mother Nature, dragonflies are variable. *Sexual* variation is the most obvious, as the majority of species are dimorphic in color, many of them strikingly so. All odonate species are sexually dimorphic in shape, so an important step in dragonfly identification is to be clear about the general ways in which the sexes differ and then apply these distinctions to the example under observation. You may immediately see that many of the individuals you initially thought were females were, in fact, immature males. **Being able to distinguish the sexes is a very important, often essential, step in identification.**

Adult odonates also vary in appearance with *age* just as much as birds and more than butterflies (which emerge from their pupae in fully adult colors). Most dragonflies change color as they move toward sexual maturation. The biggest problems in identification will be caused by the youngest individuals, which have not even reached their definitive "immature" coloration. Immatures are very common, so identification of mature, fully colored adults will have to be accompanied by the recognition that they may look distinctly different when younger. Often it is merely a case of a brightening and intensification of the color pattern, for example immature male bluets going from pale blue-gray to vivid blue or the yellow of an immature male meadowhawk maturing to bright red. Males often go through an immature stage in which they are patterned much like females but then change dramatically at maturity by adding a layer of *pruinosity* (a powdery bloom much like the one we see on plums) to part or all of their thorax and abdomen. Most pruinosity is whitish to pale blue. The aging process may lead to more changes, as when wings become darker and body colors duller. In some skimmers, old females may develop pruinosity and then look more like males. One thing to remember: **eye color will usually change during maturation**. Interestingly, color change continues to death; individuals may become discolored with advanced age, especially on the face and thorax. For example, most male Tule Bluets examined at the end of their flight season at one site had grayish-brown markings on the otherwise blue thorax.

Unlike many birds and butterflies, odonates do not vary *seasonally*, at least not in color. Blue Dashers and Hagen's Bluets in the East become smaller (because the larvae that emerge are smaller) over the course of the flight season, and such variation may be more common than we know. Changes with maturation and aging in whole populations will make for different-appearing individuals at the beginning and end of the flight season.

Only a few odonates are known to vary *geographically*, but some of that variation is sufficient that the species involved look rather different in different parts of North America. When obvious, this variation is discussed in the species account. There is also geographic variation that is not so obvious, and much of it has probably not been documented. Perhaps much of the geographic variation evident in odonates is correlated with climate; for example, populations in cooler areas may have more extensive black markings. This can be seen in northern populations of Boreal and Northern Bluets and seems fairly common in clubtails with wide latitudinal ranges. There is also some geographic variation in size, mentioned under certain species.

Finally, there is *individual* variation. This is evident in both size and coloration. All species vary in size, as will be evident in each species account. The variation is surprisingly great, much more so than in birds, and is caused by variation in size of the larvae at metamorphosis. Variation in coloration is a bit trickier. Some species seem invariable, presumably truest for species with a minimum of patterning. Any species that is patterned with stripes and spots and dashes and squiggles will vary in the extent of those markings. This is the case for wing as well as body markings. Usually the variation is finite, and differences among species can still be determined. Coloration itself also varies, usually just from a bit paler to a bit darker but sometimes more than that.

Polymorphism is a special kind of individual variation in which individuals appear in two or more discrete color patterns, with nothing in between. In North America, this is typical of females of many pond damsels and darners and a few spreadwings, with a brighter morph that looks something like the male of the species (usually with blue markings) and a duller morph quite differently colored from the male (often brownish or greenish). The male-like morph is usually called the *andromorph* (*andro* = male), the one that looks less like a male the *heteromorph* (*hetero* = different), and I use these terms throughout the book. No North American species has polymorphic males.

Odonates are variable. Color patterns, although often indicative, are not always definitive for identification. Most species are separable by their structure—male appendages or hamules, female mesostigmal plates or subgenital plates—and these structures will usually be definitive even when color patterns are not. Anyone who needs positive identification should strongly consider capturing the individuals in question.

Odonate Photography

Dragonflies and damselflies are wonderful photo subjects. So many of them are brightly colored and interestingly shaped that just sitting still they are photogenic. Many of them perch in the sunshine in conspicuous places, and walking around a wetland will provide photo op after photo op. Dragonfly photographers usually use lenses that are a combination of macro (for relatively close focusing) and telephoto (for magnification, especially of wary dragonflies). I use a 70- to 300-mm zoom lens that has macro capabilities at 300 mm, so I do not have to approach too closely and disturb my subject. I have also taken numerous photos with 400-mm telephoto lenses that focus down to 5 feet. If you are out photographing birds with such a lens, give dragonflies a try. In general, damselflies are easily approached, and they can be photographed with shorter lenses, but dragonflies can be quite wary. For whatever reason, some individuals will be much tamer than others, so just keep trying.

The best photos are taken with cameras on tripods, or at least with image-stabilized lenses, as you can make sure the dragonfly is in sharp focus and can shoot at a slow enough shutter speed to get a good depth of field on the subject and still gather in background light. Dragonflies may perch on flimsy stems, so they blow in the wind as flowers do, but if your subject is on a solid perch, you can often use a slow shutter speed. The alternative is to use a flash with a higher shutter speed. This works equally well in brightly or evenly lit situations, but the powerful flash on the subject means any distant background will be underexposed, even black. You can get around this when using flash by photographing dragonflies with backgrounds close enough to be well lit, but it is much better when they provide a smooth background (a dense bed of sedges all the same color, for example) than a cluttered one (a mass of twigs and leaves). However you do it, you will get better photos with the depth of field provided by a diaphragm opening of f/16 or f/18; f/22 or higher is even better. Otherwise, you are restricted to photos perpendicular to the subject and its wings—directly from the side for damselflies, directly from the top for dragonflies. Some photographers with an artistic bent may prefer subjects in partial focus.

There are really three components of successful dragonfly photography. The first two are science: familiarity with your camera equipment and its capabilities and knowledge of the subject matter. The third is art: taking photos that are beautiful and aesthetically pleasing. Perusal of the photos in this book will make it clear that the nature of the background is extremely important in photographing odonates. An uncluttered or out-of-focus background always shows the dragonfly or damselfly at its best, but the background can also furnish clues to habitat choice and behavior, so sometimes it will be an integral part of the photo. Few photos are as crisp and easy to interpret as those taken against a blue sky.

Digital photography is clearly becoming the medium for most of us. The biggest advantage of digital is that you can see your results immediately and know whether you have accomplished your photo goals then and there. One of the nicest advantages is being able to download your photos onto your computer and share them with friends and colleagues. Nowadays, a puzzling dragonfly photographed in the field might be identified by an expert at the other end of an e-mail message on the same day. Also, I find keeping track of digital images on the computer far easier than going through a huge slide collection (but many of us will have to do both).

Always, the hardest odonates to photograph are the "fliers," the ones that perch hanging up and often at some distance from the water. With persistence, by watching many of these dragonflies, you will eventually see one hang up at a place accessible to your stalking. Many of us photograph fliers by catching them and chilling them, but this is necessary only if you have a burning desire for a photo of that species, as posed individuals rarely perch in an entirely natural way. Many photos of fliers in this book are posed, and one of the real challenges will be to get photos of all of them naturally perched.

In fact, we need many more photos of dragonflies and damselflies in general. While searching for photos for this book, I discovered that a few species had not been photographed at all in a natural situation, and in others, no females are represented in photo collections. For variable species, there can never be too many photos. Time after time, I thought I knew the color pattern of a species, only to look at another photo and see unsuspected variation. My descriptions of the species became longer as I looked at more and more photos on the Internet or reexamined my own. A good collection of specimens can tell the story of variation, but only in pattern, not in color.

Much of the behavior of dragonflies, of course, involves flying, and they are much harder to photograph then. I hope that the present generation of camcorder-wielding birders will pay some attention to odonate behavior. Because they are small and quick, they are more difficult to follow with a lens, and thus, their behavior is more difficult to document than that of birds. But it is worth trying!

Odonate Collecting and Collections

Odonate collections form the raw material that has informed us about them over the last few centuries. This field guide could not have been written without a sizable collection for reference. We are still learning about the occurrence of most species, and voucher specimens are still essential to document distribution, even in this era of superb photographs and knowledgeable field observers. In addition, geographic variation cannot be understood without series of specimens from throughout the range of a species. Also, there are still some questions about species limits that can be settled only by researchers examining series of specimens. Independent of the scientific value of specimens is the heuristic value of handling them. Learning is most memorable by a hands-on approach, so I encourage everyone interested in dragonflies to acquire an insect net.

Although not everyone will wish to do so, the best way to learn to identify dragonflies is by catching them. Like butterflies, many species are easily identified in the field; but also like butterflies, some species may be identified only in the hand. The simplest way to learn their identity is to capture one, identify it in the hand, then either release it or collect and preserve it for a reference specimen. Take care not to catch tenerals (just emerged) unless you plan to keep them; they are very easily damaged if handled.

If you collect a dragonfly and plan to keep it, there are procedures that should be followed so the specimen is of greatest value to you and to a larger collection to which you may someday donate it. There is really no justification for killing a dragonfly except for education or research, but this can include your personal education or research. No North American odonate is rare enough that collecting a few specimens for these reasons in any way endangers its populations, but you should be aware that **collecting of any insects without a permit is prohibited in most parks and reserves**. In addition, certain species are officially protected because of their rarity in a particular region, and Hine's Emerald (*Somatochlora hineana*) is federally protected.

If you wish to make a collection, here is a summary of the steps to follow to collect a dragonfly for a specimen.

1. Catch it.	3. Acetone it.	5. Label it.
2. Envelope it.	4. Remove it.	6. Store it.

Catch it   Odonates are subject to predation, particularly by birds, and they are accordingly quite wary. They have quick responses and quick flight, so you must be even quicker. Even damselflies may move away rapidly, although they are sometimes easily approached.

If your intended "prey" is perched in the open, just sweep the net sideways, trying to center it. If it is in dense vegetation, the best strategy is to come down from above, as a sideways sweep may just flip the vegetation out of the net and the insect with it. Lift the end of the net, and your captive will often fly up into it. Grasp the net below it and turn the net over so you can reach in and grab it. They tend to fly up, and many a dragonfly has escaped instantly when the collector opens the bag to look inside!

For a dragonfly in flight, sweep sideways and quickly flip the net bag over, trapping it inside. It is always best to swing from behind and below, the area of an odonate's poorest vision. Both feeding individuals and those in sexual patrol flights may fly a regular beat, so you can anticipate their flight path. Do not be surprised if they fly out and around you on every pass. I have found that standing next to a shrub or tree apparently makes me less conspicuous.

You can usually grab any dragonfly with impunity, but the larger ones have big mandibles and can pinch. Only a few of the largest species can actually draw blood when they bite ("ouch" is only one of the four-letter words I have heard at that time), so if you are concerned, just watch what you are doing and grab them by the wings. Their wings are quite strong, without the shedding scales of butterflies. Again, tenerals are an exception to that statement.

Envelope it   Place it, always with wings folded back, in a glassine (stamp) envelope labeled with locality and date. To save time and for recordkeeping, I use a field number for each collection based on the year: 2011-1, 2011-2, etc. You can put more than one individual per envelope, but they may chew on each other, so put their heads at opposite ends. I write "T" on the envelope for pairs in tandem and "C" for pairs in copula, as it is important to keep track of pairs and keep them together in a collection. Make sure you have a pen with indelible ink.

Acetone it   After leaving your specimens in their envelopes for a while (for example, until you return home at night) so they can void their intestinal contents, kill them by immersing them briefly in acetone or injecting a drop of acetone into the thorax. Straighten the abdomen of each specimen, arranging the legs so they do not obscure the genitalia on the second abdominal segment of males. Line up each pair of wings so one lies under the other, and separate the forewings slightly from the hindwings to allow easier study of the wing venation. Put them back in their labeled envelopes and leave them submerged in acetone in a tightly closed plastic (e.g., Rubbermaid) container for 12–24 hr. Cut off a bit of both lower corners of the envelope so the acetone drains when you lift the envelope out.

Acetone extracts fat and water from specimens, and they dry much better and with better color preservation than when merely air-dried. However, you should **avoid breathing acetone fumes**. Work in a well-ventilated setting.

Specimens with extensive pruinosity may become discolored in acetone. In particular, male spreadwing damselflies and pruinose male skimmers such as Common Whitetail and Eastern Pondhawk change color rather drastically, so I now prefer not to place them in acetone unless the environment is so humid that they may not air-dry adequately.

Remove it Remove your specimens from the acetone and leave them in the open for a day so the acetone will evaporate. Preferably, have a well-ventilated spot away from people as it evaporates. Try to separate the envelopes for quickest evaporation. All dried dragonfly specimens are stiff and brittle, although those that have been acetoned are stronger and more resistant to breakage.

If you are unwilling or unable to use acetone, an alternative is to let the dragonfly die in the envelope; when it excretes feces from its abdomen, the abdomen dries better. Alternatively, you can kill odonates by freezing them. Make sure the abdomen is straightened rather than curved. Put the specimen in a dry and ant-proof place to dry thoroughly. A heat source such as a light bulb can promote rapid drying. Then continue as described below.

Label it All specimens should have the following information associated with them: locality, date, and collector (species name can be added later and changed if the specimen is re-identified). The label should be as exact as possible, as many odonates have very restricted habitat preferences and may only be at one spot in a larger landscape. Including latitude and longitude, easily acquired with today's GPS units, is a good idea, and elevation, especially in mountainous areas, is important. My wishful thinking has all odonate specimens on searchable databases some day, and the inclusion of all this information makes them easily mapped. Many collectors include habitat notes, at the very least something like "pond" or "slow, sandy stream" or "flying over clearing." This information associated with the time collected is of additional value. Pairs in tandem or in copula should always be so indicated.

Store it Store your specimens in a box protected from both humidity and possible pests such as carpet beetles, ants, or mice. For more useful and elegant storage, after they are dry switch them to Odonata specimen envelopes (available from the International Odonata Research Institute) with the collecting information printed or written on a 3 × 5 card; the specimen can then be examined without removal from the envelope.

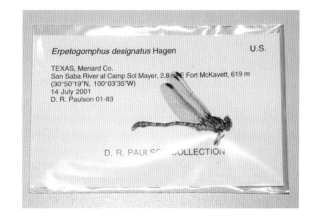

Dragonfly storage envelope

Dragonfly collection

You can devise your own storage system for your specimens. Many collectors keep them in boxes of appropriate sizes with a few mothballs in each box, stored on a shelf or in a cabinet or drawer. If you think your home is pest free, you can take your chances without mothballs, but you should check for bug damage frequently to confirm this.

Logically, the wings of pinned dragonfly specimens are usually spread, but for the most part they are not spread in enveloped specimens. You may wish to store a few specimens with wings spread for photography, drawing, and dorsal or ventral views of the specimens without having to remove them from the envelope. In addition, at least a few specimens of odonates with patterned wings should be stored with wings outspread.

To examine the wings of just one side, you can remove the specimen from the envelope and carefully (from front to back) slide a piece of white paper or card between the left and right wing pairs.

The larvae, of course, are collected in entirely different ways. The best way is with a strong dipnet or a metal net like a large tea strainer. Sweep it through aquatic vegetation or drag it over the bottom substrate, swish it around in the water to wash out the sediment, and then poke through it to see what is moving. Many larvae will remain immobile, so you will have to search for them. A good way to find stream larvae is to stir up the bottom sediment (rocks, sand, mud) while holding your net just downstream. Some larvae can be found by lifting rocks out of the water and scrutinizing them. This is most productive in tropical streams but would also be effective anywhere rock-dwelling species live.

Larvae to be retained for study should be preserved in 80% ethanol in vials that seal very well; evaporation is the bane of a preserved collection. Labels should be written with indelible ink on good archival paper; I have used parchment paper for years.

Finally, private collections are great for learning about and doing research on dragonflies, but they will be of maximal value if kept in excellent condition with accurate and complete data accompanying the specimens and ultimately donated to a permanent insect collection.

Odonate Threats and Conservation

Threats to odonate populations and species come in two forms, natural and human-caused (anthropogenic). Hurricanes, large forest fires, floods, and drought are all natural elements of our world, and they all surely have severe effects on local populations. They could likewise have severe effects on species with very limited ranges, for example, a single small island or restricted river drainage. However, at this time in the history of our planet, human activities are far more significant than those of Mother Nature.

Everywhere in the world, *habitat destruction* is the greatest threat to dragonflies and damselflies. Wetlands, essential habitats for the larvae and destinations for wandering adults, are being drained and filled at a dizzying rate. Thanks to concern about water birds, these activities have slowed in some regions, and mitigation efforts have provided new wetlands, some of them quite good for odonates. When riparian (waterside) vegetation is removed, odonate faunas shift away from habitat specialists toward the common and widespread species. Rivers themselves are not destroyed, but many factors are involved in their degradation as larval odonate habitats.

Chemical pollution is a problem in some areas, for example, rivers in the mining country of the Appalachians. At the most extreme, such rivers are lifeless, so odonates and all other creatures that might have lived there have disappeared. *Siltation* is another problem in rivers, silt brought in from altered and eroded landscapes burying larvae that need clean water from which to extract oxygen. Dams lead to siltation and, of course, entirely change the nature of rivers and streams, altering their odonate faunas as well. Furthermore, *boat traffic* on any water body produces waves that are likely to swamp and kill emerging dragonflies.

On rare occasions, elimination of a particular plant species may have a dramatic effect on odonates. Hyacinth Gliders, for example, seem closely tied to water hyacinths, and the concerted effort to rid southeastern waters of that pest plant has clearly reduced populations of the dragonfly. On the other hand, invasive aquatic plant species (another example is water chestnut) can severely alter aquatic ecosystems and have a negative impact on odonate populations.

Drought may turn out to be the most significant factor in reducing odonate populations in many parts of the world. Because of global climate change, many regions are experiencing unprecedented droughts, and that is the case all across North America. When shallow ponds have been dry for several years, their odonate fauna will have disappeared, and it remains to be seen how quickly such ponds will be recolonized. Even in the wet Southeast, rivers and underground aquifers can be sucked dry by human use, and human populations and water need are growing steadily.

With changing climate, not only has drought become more frequent but so have heavy rains, and streams are always at risk of being reamed out by *floods*. Severe floods can affect odonates by wiping out entire populations from rivers. Fast-moving water can scour a riverbed, removing silt and sand essential to larval habitat. Rising water can wipe out emerging individuals (as can the wake of a fast-moving boat), and a serious flood can decimate populations of adults confined to the riparian strip. It may take years for a scoured stream to regain its full diversity of aquatic creatures.

Wetlands are often altered by *artificial eutrophication*, the process during which the productivity of a wetland is enhanced beyond the normal range in nature. This condition, usually caused by runoff of fertilizers or other chemicals from the surrounding uplands, eventually results in a system that supports large numbers of just a few competitively successful species. Livestock can pollute water bodies when common, but they also contribute to habitat degradation by *grazing*. Cattle in particular are attracted to streams and ponds and quickly reduce shore vegetation to stubble. Even if larval habitats are relatively undisturbed, adults have no places to perch. This is especially serious in streams with a narrow band of riparian growth.

One factor we are still learning about is the effect of *fish* on dragonfly larvae. There is evidence that quite a few species of odonates survive best (or only) in the absence of fish. These species are adapted to live in fishless waters just as others are adapted to live with fish. But many water bodies, including previously fishless ones, have been stocked and restocked with fish, both native and nonnative, and this presumably has had profound effects on the odonates and other inhabitants of these wetlands. We will probably never know what these effects have been, as fish stocking has been going on for over a century and continues today. Furthermore, carp in particular muddy up water bodies because of their bottom foraging, and that in turn makes these water bodies poorer habitats for odonate larvae. Now still another series of introductions is taking place, as grass carp are introduced to clean up vegetation in some wetlands—vegetation that is surely important to some odonates. The effects of still other types of aliens are entirely unknown.

Odonates, although large and showy insects, are not noticed as much as birds and butterflies, not as charismatic as mammals, and not as edible as fish, so they have not received wide public attention. Nevertheless, their fate is coupled with that of wetlands, which are as much affected by human activities as any habitat on Earth. There is no reason why the Odonata could not become another of the "poster children" of wetland conservation, along with the waterfowl that have been the subjects of conservation concern for a long time. Dragonflies Unlimited has a nice ring to it!

One final point must be made: **dragonfly populations are not threatened by collecting.** Knowledge of insect population biology makes that clear. Our continued attempt to learn about them, however, is threatened by misguided attitudes that they should not be killed, not even for study. Under "collecting," I include any collecting the objective of which is education and/or research, including that done by school children and amateur naturalists just because of their desire to learn something about nature. Commercial collecting for profit, as has harmed some butterfly populations, has fortunately not been directed toward odonates, which are usually much less attractive than butterflies or beetles as dried specimens. But to support dragonfly conservation, we must support dragonfly research in all its forms, including the continued collection and preservation of specimens.

Odonate Research

What do we still need to learn about North American dragonflies? An answer of "everything" would not be too far off the mark. Adult behavior has been studied in detail for only a few species. Even those species have been studied only once or twice, and it is unlikely that a single study of a species describes it throughout its range. Reproductive behavior has been quantified for very few species. What are the differences among species in territory size, copulation time, number of eggs laid, number of oviposition sites, time of day of mating and oviposition, and other factors, and what is the significance of the differences?

It is easy to see dragonflies foraging, but foraging behavior has been even less quantified than reproductive behavior. Do different species have different dietary choices? How about feeding times, foraging heights, and foraging habitats? Are territorial breeders more likely to be territorial feeders? One of the easiest things to do with odonates is capture and mark them, and recognizing them as individuals leads to a higher level of understanding of their behavior.

We see odonates at the water and assume we know their habitat preferences, but does the abundance of adults correspond to the preferred habitat of the larvae? Although the larvae of almost all North American species have been discovered and described, we know very little about what they are doing beneath the water surface. Another interesting question to be answered is why so many similar species can be found together, for example, species of bluets and mosaic darners in some lakes and dancers in some streams.

Another fruitful avenue of research would be to document geographic variation in common species to try to gain a better understanding of gene flow and dispersal in different groups. There have been surprisingly few studies of geographic variation in common and widely distributed odonates.

Thermoregulation is quite important to odonates. Are there any damselflies that can regulate their body temperature in ways that have been shown for some dragonflies? Migration is another fascinating life strategy, so far studied only in Common Green Darners. What would a study of the highly migratory Variegated Meadowhawk reveal? How many odonate species migrate between the United States and Mexico?

Another area of odonate evolution that is poorly understood is their coloration. Why do so many species of skimmers have pale spots on segment 7? Why do clubtails often have yellow spots on the sides of their clubs? (In fact, why do clubtails have clubs?) Why is blue such a common color in males? What is the significance of the striping on the thorax in so many groups? Why are they not just solid-colored? This list of questions can be greatly extended.

There is no real line between amateur and professional odonatologists. It seems that very few people make a living carrying out Odonata research. Thus, the great majority of those studying and writing about odonates can be classified as nonprofessionals, and they are the ones who have contributed so much to our knowledge of dragonflies. I cannot emphasize enough how much these people (including the reader of these words) can continue to contribute, both by making observations and by sharing them with others. The proliferation of listserves on the internet has provided a medium by which much of this information is shared, but I will make a plea that you write up your observations for publication, whether in a scientific journal or a local newsletter, so they are preserved with more permanence than may be provided online.

Odonates in the East

In many groups of plants and animals, there is a biodiversity gradient, with higher diversity at lower latitudes. This gradient is absent or even reversed in Odonata east of the Mississippi, with New England states supporting large species lists and individual sites in the Northeast often with more species than their counterparts in the Southeast. For example, Sussex County, New Jersey, has perhaps the largest number of odonate species (145) known from any U.S. county. As the southern states become better studied, these differences may be less apparent, but note the substantial number of species restricted to the Northeast.

Because the geographic scope of this book is extensive, the regions covered by it vary substantially in numerous ways of significance to dragonflies: temperature, rainfall, seasonality, physiography, terrestrial vegetation cover, amount of human settlement, and regional knowledge of Odonata. Dragonflies are sun lovers, and temperature varies by latitude as well as by altitude. This latitudinal effect, interestingly, is not as strong in dragonflies as it is in many other groups of plants and animals. Apparently, dragonflies do relatively well in cooler climates as long as they have some warm summer days to sustain activity. Dragonflies need wetlands, so precipitation should be of importance to them. The East is uniformly wet and thus is full of freshwater wetlands to support odonates.

First records for odonate species are being noted for species after species, and most of them are records of southern species at the northern end of their ranges. This effect should be considered one of the more obvious bits of evidence for the effects of global warming on species and ecosystems.

Seasonality is still not as well documented for odonates as distribution. In the Southeast, many species of damselflies have known flight seasons throughout the summer. Nevertheless, in much of that region, damselfly populations plummet by midsummer, and few if any can be found of species that were abundant in April and May. In some species, numbers build up again in fall. This phenomenon may be a recent one, as I have been doing field work since 1960, and I do not recall such an obvious drop in damsel numbers in midsummer in Florida back in those days. It has been speculated that it could have something to do with the abundance of the very predatory Eastern Pondhawks in midsummer; more research is needed.

Explanation of Species Accounts

Size Measurements indicate the range in total length and hindwing length of each species in millimeters (**25.4 mm = 1 inch**), combining the sexes. They are taken mostly from the handbooks to North American Odonata, with modifications where records were lacking or inadequate. Ranges may not be so extreme at any time within a given population, as there is often seasonal and/or geographic variation, and it must be admitted that greater ranges may be a consequence of more specimens measured. Taking the midpoint between the extremes allows some comparison between species, but size can be used as a field mark only among species that differ substantially, say with no overlap between measurements. Bear in mind that females tend to be a bit bulkier than males and may have slightly longer hindwings, but males usually have a longer abdomen; thus, sexual dimorphism contributes to the range in measurements in each species.

Description A brief characterization of the species may be listed first, often referring only to the male, the sex that is usually more conspicuous to observers and the one that is more easily identified (sexism unintended). In some cases, this is followed by a description that applies to both sexes equally. Then males and females are described separately, often with additional information about sexually immature individuals. **Note that color patterns are usually described for viewing from above or one side; most odonates have pale undersides, not usually described.** The first abdominal segment (S1) is not usually described, as it is scarcely visible, but other abdominal segments are referred to by number. This seems more complicated than merely saying "tip of abdomen blue," but exactly which segments have the markings is very important in many cases of field identification. Complex patterns are shown in photos but are often not described except in comparisons for field identification. The photos are intended to convey the most information about appearance, so only brief descriptions of color patterns are included, with comments about variation and sexual differences. The photos augment the descriptions, but a good understanding of odonate structure helps to form a mental picture of each species. It must be emphasized that these descriptions refer to populations in the East; in a few species, those in the West or south of the U.S. border may look different.

Identification Comparison is the theme in this section. It is a good idea to read the generic accounts when trying to work out differences among species in a family. Species are compared only with those that overlap geographically *in the East*, so use of range maps is essential at all stages of identification. Unlike migratory birds, odonates are not expected outside their normal range, much less far from it. The tropical darners and skimmers that are likely exceptions to this are indicated. If you are concerned with a particular species, find out which other similar species occur in your area. The most similar species will often be distinguished first, followed by species that are less similar but could possibly cause identification problems. Species being compared are shown in boldface: **Seaside Dragonlet**. When comparison is with an entire group, it is shown in capitals: DRAGONLETS.

Having emphasized distribution, I must add that our level of knowledge is such that the range maps may not be the last word, so if you are outside the range of a species but not too far from it, do not dismiss it entirely, and comparisons are often made between two species not yet known to overlap. Two categories of distinguishing characteristics are used, although they are not always indicated as such. *Definitive* characters are those that are absolutely distinctive in distinguishing two species. *Indicative* characters are those that are often helpful in distinguishing two species but by themselves are not definitive. With the great amount of attention paid to odonates in recent years, especially by birders, who are likely to attempt to make an identification of every individual seen, we are realizing that there is more individual variation in these insects than we had thought. In some cases, characteristics that were once considered definitive field marks for species (for example, the amount of black on middle abdominal segments of bluets or the wing patterns of king skimmers) have been found to occur rarely in other species. Color characters especially may not always be trustworthy, and anyone who wishes to identify every individual may have to carry a net! Rare variants that have been documented in a species but are scarcely ever encountered are usually ignored in this book, and I am hoping this will cause a minimum of anxiety.

Natural History The accounts combine and summarize information from the published literature and my own observations, including the male at water, mating and oviposition, behavior away from water, and other information. Statements such as "oviposits in floating sedge stems" or "roosts at chest height" means that I have observed this or someone else has mentioned it for the species but does not necessarily mean it oviposits nowhere else or never roosts higher or lower. Also, such a statement for a species does not necessarily mean it is unique to that species within a genus or family, just that it has been noted. In many cases, statements are based on only a few observations, sometimes coming from scrutiny of my own and other photos; the internet is now a superb source of information of this sort. In some cases, a broad statement is made in the generic account that applies to all species in the genus, and this is not repeated in the species accounts. For this reason, it is also important to read the generic accounts. When there is detailed quantification, it usually comes from the literature and may be from just a single point in time and space. Because animals vary in behavior just as they do in color pattern, there is without doubt much variation beyond the parameters given (number of eggs laid, length of copulation, etc.). There are so many ways to describe the behavior of animals that I have tried to adopt some standards while trying to avoid having every account sound the same. Perching and flying heights are usually given in comparison with a person; heights of about 18 inches, 36 inches, 54 inches, and 72 inches are described as knee height, waist height, chest height, and head height (if over water, pretend to be walking on it). I encourage the reader to report all natural-history observations that vary substantially from what is written here or that are not described here, at the generic or specific level.

Habitat   A broad description of breeding habitat is given here. For most species, habitat choice was determined from my own observations, but I have used the literature for species less familiar to me. Bear in mind that odonates sometimes breed in atypical habitats and especially that nonbreeding immatures (and mature females) can be found well away from water and often in a great range of terrestrial habitats. The most common determinant of occurrence away from water is that, when immature, some species seem to prefer open and others wooded habitats. Much is yet to be learned about breeding habitats of some species, especially about the larval distribution that determines where we see breeding adults.

Flight Season   This information is available from a variety of well-documented sources, either published, on the Internet, or unpublished from those who keep such records. Because of space limitations, I include flight seasons only from these regions: Florida (FL), Georgia (GA), Iowa (IA), Kentucky (KY), Louisiana (LA), Maine (ME), New Jersey (NJ), Nova Scotia (NS), Ohio (OH), Ontario (ON), Quebec (QC), and Wisconsin (WI), with the assumption that this spread presents a good sample. When no information is available for a species in any of those regions, information is taken from the closest region adjacent to the area of this book. Also, seasons are not given for regions where the species is rare and obviously poorly known. Rather than list the extreme dates, I list the month in which they fall (but not months in which the earliest record is in the last two days or the latest record in the first two days), so these are rough approximations of the usual flight season. A species listed from June to October, for example, might actually be common from some time in June to some time in October, or it may not appear normally until July, or it may normally disappear in September. Note that these dates begin with emergence, and first appearance of mature individuals at the water will be some time later. **Regional references should be checked for details of flight seasons.**

Some species seem to occur throughout the year and are listed as such. Others are known to emerge as early as late January and may fly into early December; those are listed as January to December, and they may eventually be found to fly all year. For species that are common, we often have extreme records that are well beyond the normal times of occurrence. These provincial and state dates are guides to when you might expect to see the species, and it is unlikely you will see it in earlier or later months in that region.

Distribution   Comments about distribution that add to the information presented in the range maps are given here, including a rough idea of the distribution in western North America and the limits of distribution south of this region. In species confined to the East, there are often no further comments.

Comments Included here is information about taxonomy, subspecies, hybridization, name changes, possible additional species, and other matters not covered in the other sections.

Range maps These maps were drawn by hand, which may have resulted in slight inaccuracies of range boundaries. They are at a small enough scale that local publications should be consulted for fine details. They were constructed from our present knowledge (as of May 2010) of Odonata distribution in the East, primarily from the dot maps published by T. W. Donnelly. Many additional records have been established since those maps were published, with many of them published on Odonata Central, others in regional publications or on regional websites, and still others on various regional listserves (see Appendix for information), and all those I know about have been incorporated. Some regions are now better known than indicated in any of these sources, however, and additional unpublished records that have been submitted to me by regional experts have also been incorporated in the maps. The ranges are also continued into the immediate area to the west of the region covered by this book, in some cases slightly modified from those maps in the western guide because of new knowledge or a different interpretation of existing records. Odonate ranges are surprisingly irregular, and an attempt was made to closely define the known ranges. These range maps come with two assumptions. (1) The species is likely but not guaranteed to be found everywhere inside the shown range. In particular, it will be found mostly in its optimal habitats. (2) The species is unlikely to be found anywhere outside the shown range except in poorly known regions, although few regions of the East are still inadequately surveyed for Odonata.

Ranges can be defined fairly well in some states and provinces but not all of them, and the number of range borders that follow state lines are a clear indication of this. When records are well separated from one another, the gaps between them are shown, so the maps illustrate what we know of distribution at present, not what we assume is probably the case. The gaps are purposely emphasized to show regions where more fieldwork is indicated, and many of these gaps will doubtless be filled. Note, for example, how many species are known widely from Iowa but not in adjacent Minnesota. Nevertheless, some of the gaps are real, usually indicating a lack of appropriate habitat over substantial areas. The irregularity of the maps of some species is also a response to the mountainous terrain of the Allegheny-Appalachian chain: a lowland species may be present only in the lowlands, and a montane species only in the mountains where its occurrence is shown. Isolated records at a single locality that seem to be outside the periphery of the range of a species are indicated by dots, as are records of species that barely make it into the East. Some of the dots may represent vagrant occurrences, but this is not always known, and some definitely represent established populations. Bear in mind that the isolated records come from a great variety of sources, and it is possible that some of them are bogus (most likely from an incorrectly identified specimen in a published paper).

I have tried to make the maps detailed enough that people in each state and province will have a good idea of the known or expected distribution within that political entity. However, bear in mind that there may be few records from an area included in the range, range boundaries will certainly have to be modified, and field observers still have much to contribute to what we know about North American odonate distribution. In particular, the far north of Canada and parts of the eastern plains and Mississippi Valley remain especially poorly known. Look at maps such as those of Sweetflag Spreadwing and Horned Clubtail. Their complexity probably results from both habitat distribution and degree of knowledge, but there is nothing in nature that dictates a species distribution must be simple! **Finally, these maps represent records over a long time period; some species may now be absent from parts of their former range.**

Photos The photos included with each species account are intended to illustrate both what the species looks like and the specific field marks that are of value for identification. Much effort was expended to acquire photos different from those used in the previously published western guide, and I was able to find replacements for all but a few of the photos. Many photos were chosen to complement those that were available in the western guide, to make the two books together a more valuable unit. I attempted to find photos of both sexes of every species, but there seem to be no photos available at all for females of a small number of species. There is quite an admirable goal for this generation of odonate photographers! I have chosen to illustrate variation in species in which variation can cause confusion, for example, the different morphs and ages of female forktails. **Nevertheless, even with the number of photos available in these two books, they do not necessarily show all the variation in each species; please read the text.** The great majority of photos are natural, but a small number of individuals are posed; these are indicated. It is my hope that in the near future unposed photos of both sexes of all species will be available. Males are usually shown before females because they are the commonly seen sex, not because of sexist bias. Finally, to save space I have cut off some dragonfly wings and oriented many damselflies horizontally and some "fliers" vertically, no matter their original orientation. **All photos lacking a photographer's name are by the author.**

Drawings The line drawings, by Natalia von Ellenrieder and Rosser Garrison, were made from single specimens and thus do not necessarily look like the same structures in every individual of the species, but they are representative. They will be important in distinguishing among species of some genera when a specimen or live individual is in hand. They can also be used for confirmation of an identification.

Abbreviations and Conventions

TL   total length in millimeters
HW   hindwing length in millimeters
S1–10   abdominal segments 1–10
T1–5   thoracic stripes 1–5 (only in clubtails)

Damselflies   *Zygoptera*

Broad-winged Damsel Family   *Calopterygidae*

The large, showy damselflies of this family often display metallic bodies and/or colored wings. They are distinguished from other North American damselflies by broad wings with dense venation and no hint of the narrow petiole or "stalk" at the base that characterizes the other families. The nodus lies well out on the wing with numerous crossveins basal to it. Colored wings in this family are heavily involved in displays between males and of males to females. This is the only damselfly family in which individuals point their abdomen toward the sun (obelisking) at high temperatures. The closed wings are held either on one side of the abdomen or above it, which may relate to temperature regulation. Legs are rather long, and leg spines very long, appropriate to flycatching habits. This worldwide tropical family has only a few species in temperate North America and Eurasia. World 176, NA 8, East 7.

Jewelwings   *Calopteryx*

These are the most spectacular damselflies of temperate North America and Eurasia, all large with metallic green to blue-green bodies. Different species have wings that are clear, with black tips of different extent, or entirely black. Wing pattern is important for identification. Females are similar to males but usually duller and easily distinguished by white pterostigmas. That structure not as in other odonates, in this genus a group of white cells for sex recognition rather than functioning for flight. All live on clear streams and rivers. This is the group to watch if you wish to see odonate courtship behavior. Watch for wing clapping, wings suddenly opened and shut, which may be communication between individuals or for cooling. World 26, NA 5, East 5.

1 Superb Jewelwing   *Calopteryx amata*   TL 48–61, HW 33–42

Description Large metallic green damselfly, narrow wings with dusky wingtips. Male: Eyes medium brown. Entire body metallic green (can look blue), may have bronzy overtones on thorax. Face duller and may be glossed with red. Wings clear or faintly washed with yellowish tint, costal vein green; hindwing tip brown. *Female:* Colored like male but duller, fine pale lines on thorax, and yellow of underside extends onto lower sides. Abdomen more bronzy, tip with fine dorsal line and lower sides pale. Wings without dark tip; stigmas white, varying in size.

Identification Overlaps with **Appalachian Jewelwing** in mountains from West Virginia to North Carolina. Males easily distinguished by dark hindwing tip of **Superb**, although immature males barely shaded. Male **Appalachian** are generally more brilliant metallic green. Females very similar, but **Appalachian** always lacks white stigma (can be inconspicuous in **Superb**). **Superb** has green on sides of thorax continued to behind hindwing base, that area usually pale in **Appalachian**. Less similar to male **River** (much overlap in range) and **Sparkling Jewelwings** (very little overlap), both of which have both wingtips conspicuously dark. Female **River** also has dark wingtips, although not conspicuous in some because entire wings dusky. **Superb** further distinguished from **River** by narrower wings, pale ventral color extending slightly farther onto sides of thorax, and first antennal segment entirely pale. Female **Sparkling** in area of overlap have clear wingtips but are considerably smaller than **Superb** and entirely green on sides of thorax.

Natural History Both sexes perch up in shrubs over riffles; tend to stay in shrubby areas but may be in herbaceous plants along with River Jewelwings. Males highly territorial, aggres-

1.1
Superb Jewelwing
male—Essex Co., VT, June
2005, Bryan Pfeiffer/Wings
Photography

1.2
Superb Jewelwing
female—Coos Co., NH,
June 2006

sive displays by circling one another at high speed horizontally like other jewelwings, both in place and moving over water. Circle diameter quite variable (18 inches to at least 10 feet). Females often perch at breeding habitat.

Habitat Small, fairly swift rocky streams with abundant aquatic vegetation, usually in wooded landscape. At higher elevations in southern part of range.

Flight Season QC Jun–Jul, NS Jun–Aug, ME Jun–Aug, NJ May–Jul.

---

2 Appalachian Jewelwing *Calopteryx angustipennis* **TL 50–67, HW 33–40**

Description Large metallic green damselfly with narrow, unmarked wings. *Male:* Eyes brown. Body entirely metallic green, can look blue in some lights. Wing veins, especially anterior ones, metallic green, glowing in sun. *Female:* Colored like male but duller, thorax with fine pale lines and yellow underside; abdomen more bronzy, tip with fine dorsal line and pale lower sides. Both sexes lack stigmas.

2
Appalachian Jewelwing
male—Cumberland Co.,
TN, June 2006; female—
Rabun Co., GA, May 2008,
Giff Beaton

Identification Distinctly the longest-bodied jewelwing, making wings look relatively shorter than in other species. Also more of wing veins iridescent green than in other jewelwings. See **Superb Jewelwing**; both species with narrow wings, front and rear margins parallel in outer half of wing; no other species at all similar. Almost no overlap with **Sparkling** and **River Jewelwings**, and very different from **Ebony**.

Natural History Both sexes perch at waterside or on rocks in stream. Males circle one another very rapidly and very close together, both stationary and moving around; even three males may interact at once. Also fly rapidly over water, shockingly iridescent green toothpick in sun. Males seen to fall onto river surface and float downstream near female, presumably signaling current speed.

Habitat Rocky streams and rivers with moderate current, usually in woodland.

Flight Season KY May–Jul, GA May–Jun.

3 Sparkling Jewelwing   *Calopteryx dimidiata*   TL 37–50, HW 23–31

Description Slender metallic green damselfly with black wingtips. One of the smallest species in its family. *Male*: Eyes dark brown. Entire body metallic green, looks blue in some lights. Wings with terminal one-fifth black, slightly less in northern part of range. *Female*: Colored as male or somewhat more bronzy-green, usually with white stigma (smaller in northern part of range) and with black wingtips less crisply defined. Some have only hindwing tips black; others, mostly in northern part of range, have clear wings. Immature with reddish eyes, duller body color.

3
Sparkling Jewelwing
male—Richmond Co., GA,
May 2008; female—Lewis
Co., TN, June 2006

Identification Limited range overlap with somewhat similar **River Jewelwing**. Smaller than **River**, males with same amount of black on all wingtips (more on hindwing in **River**). Females rather like female **River** but tip of abdomen all dark (much of it conspicuously pale in **River**). In areas of overlap, white stigma of **Sparkling** usually much smaller than that of **River,** and wings tend to be clearer, less dusky. Even less overlap with larger **Appalachian** and **Superb Jewelwings**. Often occurs with **Ebony Jewelwing**, which is larger, with broad black wings. Some female **Sparkling** have darkish wings, never as dark as **Ebony** and distinctly narrower. In flight, looks like glowing green toothpick with flashing black wingtips dancing around, whereas black fluttering wings dominate appearance of **Ebony**.

Natural History Both sexes often together at breeding habitat, at least at some times of day. May remain active until almost dark. Males defend small territories with potential oviposition sites, flutter around and around each other in spiral flight over water and chase one another along up to 40 feet of stream; frequent contact at times. Spectacular to see, with brilliant green abdomen and flashing black wingtips. Also display to females that approach oviposition site in "floating cross display" by dropping to water and floating for short distance with wings partially spread and abdomen curled up. This repeated until female flips her wings, showing receptiveness, or leaves stream. Receptive female then courted with rapidly whirring wings, followed in some cases by copulation, which lasts about 2 min. Female oviposits by walking down leaf until submerged, often quite far, then laying several hundred eggs for about 15–20 min underwater. She then rises to surface, usually unreceptive to further male attention but remaining near water.

Habitat Sandy forest streams and rivers, usually acidic, with abundant aquatic vegetation and moderate to swift current. Less tied to woodland than Ebony and more often in open areas.

Flight Season NJ May–Sep, KY Jun–Aug, LA Mar–Sep, GA Apr–Oct, FL Feb–Nov.

Description Large green damselfly with black wingtips. *Male*: Eyes dark brown. Body glossy metallic green, looks blue in some lights. Wings with more than terminal third black, that on hindwing more extensive than on forewing, younger individuals with paler wingtips. More northerly populations often have more extensive black at wingtips. *Female*: Slightly duller or more bronzy; white stigma allows easy distinction from male. S8–10 with pale dorsal stripe and sides. Dark of wingtips can be more obscured; inner wing darker, so contrast less evident.

Identification Black wingtips makes it much like **Sparkling Jewelwing**, but hindwing markings more extensive than forewing in this species; also limited range overlap. See that species for differences in females. Some female **River Jewelwings** have wings dusky enough that wingtips do not contrast much, and a closer look is necessary to distinguish them from female **Ebony Jewelwing** where they occur together. Also, some female **Ebony** have darker wingtips. With experience, narrower wings of **River** readily noted. Black wingtips much less conspicuous in **Superb Jewelwing**.

Natural History Rarely seen very far from water. Both sexes at times common on streamside vegetation in optimal habitat. Males often seen in lengthy flights along shores of large rivers but typically perch over water and defend small territories, interacting constantly with somewhat irregular horizontal circling flights, some of them lengthy. Male stationary display to female spectacular, forewings fluttering and hindwings briefly halted so black tips prominent. Male flutters in front of female with abdomen tip raised, then lands and raises it further, exposing white under tip. Male also dives to water surface briefly with wings outspread. Male and female wing-clap to one another. Copulations last a few minutes, oviposition up to 24 min but usually much briefer (average 9 min). Females oviposit on floating, sometimes emergent, vegetation or back down stem and submerge for up to 50 min, usually with male in attendance at surface. Longevity of reproductive adults up to 28 days.

4.1
River Jewelwing
male—Penobscot Co.,
ME, June 2006;
female—Burnett Co., WI,
June 2007

4.2
River Jewelwing
male—Renfrew Co., ON,
July 2005; Bryan Pfeiffer/
Wings Photography

Habitat Clear streams of all sizes and rivers with slow to moderate current and beds of submergent aquatic vegetation. Typically more open and larger streams than those used by Ebony Jewelwing. However, the two often occur together, and River Jewelwings can be common on rather tiny wooded streams, as long as there is some sun penetration. Also seen at rocky shores of large lakes in some areas.

Flight Season ON May–Aug, QC May–Aug, NS Jun–Sep, IA Jun–Sep, WI May–Sep, ME Jun–Aug, OH Jun–Aug, NJ May–Jul.

Distribution Across continent through most of Saskatchewan and Alberta, widely in Pacific Northwest, and isolated range in western Nebraska and surrounding states.

5 Ebony Jewelwing *Calopteryx maculata* TL 39–57, HW 24–37

Description No other North American damselfly is metallic green with black wings. Large size alone distinctive. *Male*: Eyes dark brown. Brilliant metallic green (often looks blue) all over, with black wings. *Female*: Slightly duller, with conspicuous white stigma and wings somewhat paler at base than in male. Immatures distinguished by lighter brown eyes, also may have slightly paler wings.

Identification Females with somewhat paler wing bases could be mistaken for female **River Jewelwing**, but contrast between base and tip usually much greater in latter. Broader wings should also distinguish **Ebony**. Only other black-winged damselflies in range are some **Smoky Rubyspots**, with much narrower wings and black body.

Natural History Both sexes at and near water much of day, active until nearing sunset. Much wing clapping, opening wings slowly and closing them suddenly. Males may have "flights of attrition," bouncing around one another while staying close together but moving laterally, sometimes surprisingly long distances away from start. Flights persist for many minutes, presumably until one can not maintain interaction and flies away or lands. Males defend territories for up to 8 days around patches of submergent and floating vegetation in stream, bigger patches being more attractive. Females arrive at water well after males. Courtship display in front of female includes much wing fluttering and often showing white under abdomen tip, then landing on prominent white stigma of female and walking down wings to achieve tandem position. Copulation lasts a few minutes. Females return to male's territory, oviposit in rootlets and submergent vegetation of many types, even wet logs, at water surface; also may submerge entirely. Eggs laid at 7–10/min, may total 1800 in lifetime. Males guard females with which they have mated and often guard additional fe-

5
Ebony Jewelwing male,
female—Ashland Co., OH,
July 2007

males that oviposit in their territory, especially when females are at high density (likely because females are attracted to one another). Males that have lost territories may resort to "sneaking," attempting to mate with females on other males' territories. Night roosts may be communal, deep in tall grass. Often seen flying between night roosts in woodland and waterside, even across roads, where fluttery flight distinctive. Average longevity 2–3 weeks (including 11 days while immature), maximum 47 days. One avoided predation by Dragonhunter by dropping to water surface.

Habitat Slow-flowing woodland streams, usually associated with herbaceous vegetation. Tend to be more at rapids when that habitat is present. Occur on open banks when trees nearby (trees essential for roosting at night). May be abundant at small streams in woods where very few other species are present.

Flight Season ON May–Oct, QC May–Nov, NS May–Sep, IA May–Sep, WI May–Sep, ME Jun–Sep, OH May–Sep, NJ Apr–Oct, KY May–Oct, LA Mar–Oct, GA Mar–Oct, FL Feb–Dec.

Distribution West through most of Nebraska, Kansas, and Oklahoma.

Rubyspots *Hetaerina*

Wings narrower than in *Calopteryx* jewelwings, usually with small stigma in both sexes. Males unmistakable with red wing bases; wings vary from clear to black otherwise. Females appear much duller, may lack any hint of red in wings, but still large, usually metallic damselflies with heavily veined wings. Species of this genus among most obvious stream damselflies of New World tropics. World 37, NA 3, East 2.

Description Large metallic damselfly with conspicuous red wing bases. *Male*: Eyes dark reddish-brown, paler below and behind. Mostly metallic red head and thorax, shiny black abdomen. Bright red patches at wing base marked by white veins. Red varies in extent, at greatest almost to nodus. *Female*: Quite variable. Eyes brown over tan, paler than in male. Duller than male, dark colors of body vary from matte black to metallic green to metallic red (head and thorax only). Wings vary from almost uncolored to diffuse orange wash at base to dark orange filling same area as red in male. Pale stigma typically paler and more contrasty in female than in male.

Identification Larger than other closedwing damselflies except JEWELWINGS. Male could be confused only with **Smoky Rubyspot** (see that species) in East. Female distinguished from pond damsels by large size, densely veined wings, and metallic greenish to orange body with conspicuously striped thorax, usually (but not always) orange suffusion in wings. Stigmas whitish, relatively shorter than those of SPREADWINGS.

Natural History Both sexes rest on stems and leaves over water, sexes mixed more than in most damselflies. Commonly perches on small plants in midcurrent, also on rocks. May go into obelisk position in hot sun. Females probably territorial at water, as are males. Have been seen to concentrate in large numbers at dusk emergence of mayflies. Flight low and fast over water, quickly disappearing when disturbed. Resident males aggressive to intruders, performing horizontal circling flights until one leaves; display flights may last for minutes. Red wing spots in males increase in size to about 14 days. Larger spots in more successful territory holders but may reduce hunting success. No courtship, males merely seizing approaching females. Perched females reject inappropriate males by opening wings and

6
American Rubyspot male, female—Sevier Co., AR, August 2008, David Arbour

curving abdomen upward. Copulation brief, averaging 3 min in one study. Males mate infrequently, averaging less than once per day. Females oviposit on surface vegetation or by submerging entirely down to 3–5 inches, remain in a fairly small area, then emerge after up to an hour. Males remain on alert above their mate, apparently guarding against other males, but relatively seldom remate with her, although she may mate with a second male. Typically roost communally at night because of attraction to other roosting rubyspots; males often near their daytime territories. Some may remain on rocks over water for night roost. Maturation period about 6–10 days, average life expectancy about 10–15 days.

Habitat Clear, swift-running, sometimes rocky streams and rivers of all sizes with shore vegetation for perching and submergent vegetation for oviposition. In West, often on slower, even muddy streams. Common on open streams, also on wooded streams with plenty of sun.

Flight Season ON Jun–Oct, IA May–Oct, WI May–Oct, ME Aug–Sep, OH May–Oct, NJ May–Oct, KY May–Oct, LA Apr–Sep, GA Apr–Nov, FL Apr–Aug.

Distribution Widely in Southwest, extending north to Montana in plains and Oregon on Pacific coast, then south in uplands to Nicaragua.

7 Smoky Rubyspot *Hetaerina titia* TL 37–51, HW 25–30

Description Large black damselfly with variably colored wings.  *Male*: Eyes very dark brown, almost black. Body entirely black with slight greenish gloss, fine tan stripes on thorax. Usually with red patch in forewing obscured by dark patch in hindwing, most visible in flight. *Female*: Eyes brown over tan, many with conspicuous striped or spotted pattern. Thorax with metallic green markings on pale brown; abdomen mostly black. Wings vary from dusky to black, with no red and contrasty white stigmas. Only rubyspot with greatly varied wing coloration in both sexes, ranging from entirely black to mostly clear, with all in-between types. Extreme wingtips dark, more extensive in individuals with more black at base; tip and base coming together to produce entirely black wings. All extremes can be seen throughout season, but tendency for black-winged individuals in summer, clear-winged fall and spring.

Identification Individuals with mostly dark wings easily distinguished from other rubyspots and all other damselflies. Males with most lightly marked wings distinguishable from **American Rubyspot** by black body and dark wingtips, from other damselflies by large size, dense venation. Wings much narrower than in **Ebony Jewelwing**, another black-winged species. Females differ from female **American Rubyspot** in having less conspicuously striped thorax, markings green and brown, and almost always darker wings.

Natural History Tends to perch higher than American Rubyspot, usually on shaded pools rather than low on open riffles. May feed by flycatching out as much as 20–30 feet from branches well up in trees. Females not at water unless mating. Males flick open wings, showing red coloration, when another male flies over. Also circle one another in display flights 3–5 feet in diameter for at least brief periods (up to 30 sec) and move up and down stream while doing so. Tandem pairs often seen flying about, presumably looking for good oviposition site. Females oviposit underwater for long periods (up to 2 hr) with males perched above driving other males away from spot.

Habitat Slower streams in woodland, tends to be in more heavily shaded areas than American Rubyspot, also less likely to be at rocky riffles. Aquatic vegetation or rootlets from stream-bank trees essential for oviposition.

Flight Season ON Aug–Sep, IA Aug–Sep, OH Aug–Oct, KY Jun–Oct, LA Apr–Nov, GA May–Nov, FL all year.

Distribution Locally into western Oklahoma and Texas and southern New Mexico, south in lowlands to Costa Rica.

7.1
Smoky Rubyspot male—
Travis Co., TX, September
2007, Eric Isley; female—
Travis Co., TX, October 2006,
Eric Isley

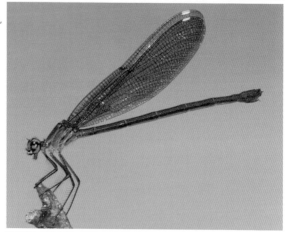

7.2
Smoky Rubyspot male—
Brantley Co., GA, October
2005, Giff Beaton

Spreadwing Family *Lestidae*

These are medium to large damselflies of worldwide distribution that usually hold their wings open, but several genera in the Old World keep them closed. All spreadwings close their wings at night, in bad weather, and when threatened by predators or males harassing females. Those in North America perch with long abdomen inclined downward, even vertically. Most are dark, with top of abdomen metallic and thorax metallic or with metallic stripes or spots, often also with pale stripes. Overall, they are not brightly colored, but males of our genera have blue eyes and face, and some Australian species are colored like bluets. Females of only a few species show blue colors. All have clear wings with stigma longer than in pond damsels, a definitive mark, and long legs with very long leg spines, as befits a predator on flying insects. Most are distinctly larger than pond damsels. World 152, NA 19, East 15.

Stream Spreadwings *Archilestes*

These are large damselflies with outspread wings, both species being larger than any pond spreadwing and much larger than any North American pond damsel. Unlike pond spreadwings, they show conspicuous pale stripes on sides of thorax. Males have blue eyes, females brown or blue (perhaps age variation). Mature males develop pruinosity on abdomen tip. They are found typically on streams but stray to ponds regularly, especially those associated with streams, and sometimes breed in them; they prefer fishless waters, where larvae swim in open like little minnows. Natural history is much like that of pond spreadwings. Males perch on branches and leaves over water, and pairs oviposit in woody stems, sometimes well above water. Other species occur from Mexico to Argentina. World 8, NA 2, East 1.

8 Great Spreadwing *Archilestes grandis* TL 50–62, HW 31–40

Description Very large spreadwing (largest North American damselfly) with yellow stripe on either side of thorax. Underside of thorax pale, becoming lightly pruinose. Abdomen dark brown to dark metallic green above. *Male*: Eyes and labrum blue. Thorax brown in front with full-length metallic green stripe on either side of midline, half-length stripe at rear edge of brown; sides yellow with another lighter brown stripe along lower sides, whole area developing pruinosity at maturity. Abdomen brown to black above with black apical rings on S3–7; S9–10 pruinose. *Female*: Eyes blue to brown, colored as male but distinguished by bulbous abdomen tip lacking pruinosity.

Identification Great Spreadwing looks twice size of POND SPREADWINGS, in steady flight over open water easily mistaken for dragonfly but wings and body much more slender.

Natural History Males perch over water, defend small territories. Females seized when they arrive. Pairs oviposit in tandem (or female released during oviposition) in leaf petioles or stems of herbaceous or woody plants, sometimes well above stream (perhaps highest known odonate oviposition at 44 feet above water). Oviposition lasts 15–180 min, with up to 230 eggs laid.

Habitat Slow streams, usually with wooded banks and may be in degraded situations in urban areas. Larvae may be seen swimming in open in pools, perhaps restricted to fishless waters.

Flight Season ON Aug–Oct, IA Aug–Oct, WI Jul–Sep, OH Jul–Oct, NJ Jul–Oct, KY Jun–Oct, GA Aug–Sep.

Distribution Across Southwest, north to northern California and Black Hills, then south in uplands to Venezuela. Range substantially expanded in East in historic times, perhaps because tolerance of poor-quality streams makes it a successful competitor.

8.1
Great Spreadwing male—
Travis Co., TX, July 2005,
Eric Isley

8.2
Great Spreadwing
female—St. Louis Co.,
MO, October 2008,
Marion M. Dobbs

Pond Spreadwings *Lestes*

Mature males have entirely bright blue eyes (more purplish with age, at least in some species), paler blue to whitish below, and pale blue labrum; male eye color not included in description unless different. Females usually have brown eyes and light brown to yellow labrum, but in at least some species females occur with blue eyes and labrum; not yet known whether this is function of age or perhaps genetic polymorphism, with brown and blue females as in some pond damsels. Tenerals are brown, then develop darker rings on middle abdominal segments, then become dark metallic above (green in most species), then acquire definitive coloration. Males become increasingly pruinose gray (or blue-gray) with age, pruinosity between wing bases and along sides of thorax, in some species the thorax becoming entirely pruinose gray. Mature males with part or all of S1 and S2 becoming pruinose, also S9 and usually S10 pruinose, sometimes extending onto S8. Pattern of pruinosity may be distinctive of species but also increases with age. Northern species and populations have more pruinosity on abdomen, typically S8–10 pruinose, whereas southern species and populations often have only S9 or S9–10 pruinose. Pattern on S2 distinctive for some species but also varies geographically. Females develop less pruinosity, typically with age on thorax and sometimes abdomen tip, most extreme about as pruinose as males of their species. Mature color pattern sufficiently variable that many will have to be captured to be sure of identification. Species distinction often must be based on appendage structure, less often color pattern of thorax; ovipositor size and shape important in females. Sex readily distinguished by shape, females with shorter, thicker abdomen with expanded tip.

Pond spreadwings are found on every continent (although barely into Australia), diverse in both temperate and tropical latitudes and often among the most common damselflies at marshy ponds and lakes. Arrival at water averages later in day than pond damsels. Individuals away from water often in woodland, where they forage in sunny spots and may take as much as several months to mature. Because of this, identifying immature individuals presents a challenge. Pond spreadwings tend to perch higher than pond damsels and forage by fly-catching. They also tend to stay in vegetation, but at times and places males may move out over open water in some numbers, flying low over surface like pond damsels but never hovering. Oviposition usually in tandem, females less often oviposit alone. Most lay eggs in vertical sedge or rush stems above water, female either staying at one level on the stem or moving up or down. World 84, NA 17, East 14.

9 Blue-striped Spreadwing *Lestes tenuatus* TL 39–44, HW 20–25

Description The blue-striped thorax identifies this tropical spread-wing. *Male:* Ground color of thorax bright blue, paler toward underside, with broad metallic bronze (may look green) median and humeral stripes; blue antehumeral stripe prominent. Abdomen metallic bronze to green above, S9 becomes whitish pruinose with  maturity. *Female:* Colored much like male but slightly duller and yellowish low on sides of thorax. Abdomen tip (S9–10) entirely dark, no pruinosity. Eyes dark blue and lighter blue above, yellow below.

Identification No other spreadwing occurs in restricted range in southern Florida. Might overlap with **Carolina** or **Swamp Spreadwings**, which show no blue on thorax; both have brown antehumeral stripes, males with S9–10 pruinose. **Southern Spreadwing** just to north lacks blue on sides of thorax and typically whitish pruinose there, may have narrow blue antehumeral stripe; female with no blue. Both sexes of **Blue-striped** only North Amer-

9.1
Blue-striped Spreadwing
male—Dade Co., FL, April 2005

9.2
Blue-striped Spreadwing female—
Hidalgo Co., TX, September 2008

ican spreadwings to show blue between wings, may become pruinose in male. **Antillean Spreadwing** of Florida Keys shows no blue on thorax in either sex. Female has swollen abdomen tip, top of S9 curved (straight in **Blue-striped**).

Natural History Males perch over water, usually in dense vegetation. Pairs oviposit in tandem. Perhaps spend dry season (winter) as adults, wet season (summer) as larvae.

Habitat Shallow cypress swamps and sinkholes in pineland.

Flight Season FL Aug–May.

Distribution Also south Texas south to Ecuador and Surinam and widely in Greater and Lesser Antilles.

---

10 Antillean Spreadwing *Lestes spumarius* TL 38–46, HW 20–25

Description A dull, slender tropical spreadwing of the Florida Keys. *Male:* Eyes mostly brown, with small blue area on top. Thorax whitish on sides, with prominent dark spot at ventrolateral angle. Median and humeral stripes wide, metallic green to bronze; fairly wide antehumeral stripes dull grayish. S9–10 become dull gray pruinose above. *Female:* Patterned like male but somewhat duller, eyes brown or blue. Thoracic stripes not contrasty, dark spot low on thorax conspicuous against white sides. Tip of abdomen mostly pale on sides, conspicuously swollen.

Identification No other spreadwing yet known from Florida Keys, no other similar damselfly there. See **Blue-striped Spreadwing**. Both cerci and paraprocts longer and more slender in this species than in **Blue-striped**.

Natural History Males perch low over water at tiny wooded sinkholes in pineland, often in dense growth where hard to see. Immatures among dense trees and shrubs nearby. Female oviposited solo in inch-wide buttonwood trunk three feet over water in shrub swamp. May be present as adults through winter dry season but only as larvae during rainy season.

10.1
Antillean Spreadwing
male—Monroe Co., FL, April
2005

10.2
Antillean Spreadwing
female—Monroe Co., FL,
April 2007, Steven Collins

10.3
Antillean Spreadwing
female—Monroe Co., FL,
December 2007

Habitat Shallow seasonal ponds in shrub-rich pineland in Florida Keys; greater variety of habitats, perhaps all seasonal wetlands, in West Indies.

Flight Season FL Jul–Apr.

Distribution Also in Bahamas and throughout Greater Antilles.

11 Rainpool Spreadwing   *Lestes forficula*   TL 35–44, HW 17–24

Description Distinctively marked tropical spreadwing, perhaps spreading in our region but not yet known from peninsular Florida. *Male*: Thorax with median stripe consisting of narrow metallic green stripe on either side of midline, then wide bright blue ante-humeral stripe (darkens with age), another narrow metallic green humeral stripe, and whitish below. Abdomen mostly dark, variably pruinose (always S9 but may extend to S8 and/or S10). *Female*: Poly-  morphic, eyes either brown, becoming dull bluish or greenish on top, or bright blue. Thorax pale olive with blue tinge or bright blue, both dark stripes very thin; lower sides and underside white, becoming faintly pruinose. From side, S8–10 prominently pale and becoming pruinose.

Identification Only spreadwing in range with narrow metallic stripes on either side of midline of thorax, visible at any age. Overlapping **Carolina**, **Slender**, and **Southern Spreadwings** have prominent dark median stripe, others (**Elegant**, **Swamp**) most of front of thorax dark metallic. Median ridge of thorax pale, unlike other species in range, and humeral stripe very narrow, not evident at a distance. Overall effect blue- and green-striped thorax in mature males.

Natural History Tropical-based species that spends dry season away from water, then returns to rain pools to breed in wet season. All-year flight season in Texas may indicate same life cycle with dormancy in winter, seems less likely in populations along Gulf Coast. Males and ovipositing pairs can be common in vegetation at shallow ponds, especially ephemeral ones. Pairs oviposit in upright plant stems at water level and up to a foot above it, sometimes female submerging her abdomen.

Habitat Shallow ponds and marshes with much emergent vegetation. Often common at seasonal pools but may occur in permanent waters, both swamps and marshes.

Flight Season LA Sep, AL Sep–Oct, FL Jul. All year in tropics.

Distribution May be more widespread along Gulf Coast. South in lowlands to Argentina, also in Greater and Lesser Antilles.

11.1
Rainpool Spreadwing
male—Hidalgo Co., TX,
September 2008

11.2
Rainpool Spreadwing
female—Hidalgo Co.,
TX, September 2008

12 Spotted Spreadwing *Lestes congener* TL 31–42, HW 18–23

Description Rather dull brown spreadwing with bicolored thorax showing prominent spots on underside. *Male:* Thorax brown, somewhat metallic in front, with very narrow tan antehumeral stripe and pruinose lower sides. Black humeral stripe wider above, usually widening abruptly in two steps to reach rear of hindwing base. Pair of black spots on each side of underside of thorax, just visible from side. Abdomen metallic dark brown above, S1–2 and S8–10 pruinose with maturity. *Female:* Eyes brown, paler below. Patterned as male but with pruinosity only on sides of thorax.

Identification In hand, and perhaps in side view when close, two dark spots on either side of thorax distinctive; other species may show one spot on each side, regularly in superficially similar **Northern, Southern,** and **Sweetflag** in same range. Very narrow antehumeral stripes, so front of thorax looks dark brown or even black and contrasts strongly with whitish sides in mature individuals of both sexes. Characteristic stepped line of demarcation between black front and pale rear of thorax distinctive but shared by quite different-looking **Swamp Spreadwing.** Pruinosity at abdomen tip not quite as pale and conspicuous in **Spotted** as in **Emerald, Lyre-tipped,** and **Northern** at same times and places. Rather differently colored **Amber-winged Spreadwing** has even larger dark markings under thorax.

Natural History Roosts mostly in woodland to 10 feet or more above ground, even well up in canopy of tall forests; in tall grass and shrubs in open country. Males can be abundant in tall emergent vegetation, pairs also reach high density. Many pairs mate away from water, then fly to oviposition site in tandem. Pairs oviposit from water surface to several feet above it, usually in slender stems and commonly over land at dried-up lake edges. Some variation in substrates used for egg deposition, but dead stems of bulrushes chosen in many areas. Pairs usually move downward on stem while ovipositing, single eggs deposited every few millimeters. Females often continue laying eggs after being released by male, especially in late afternoon.

12.1
Spotted Spreadwing male—
Harney Co., OR, July 2006,
Netta Smith

12.2
Spotted Spreadwing
female—Kittitas Co., WA,
September 2010, Netta Smith

Habitat Ponds and lakes of all sizes with at least some emergent vegetation.

Flight Season ON Jun–Oct, QC Jul–Oct, NS Jul–Oct, IA Jun–Oct, WI Jul–Oct, ME Jun–Nov, OH May–Nov, NJ Jul–Nov, KY May–Oct.

Distribution Widely in West from British Columbia and Northwest Territories south to California and New Mexico.

13 Carolina Spreadwing *Lestes vidua* TL 38–46, HW 21–25

Description Southeastern spreadwing with reddish thoracic stripes. *Male:* Eyes dark blue to violet above, bright blue below. Thorax with wide median and humeral stripes dark metallic green; fairly wide antehumeral stripes reddish-brown, narrowing abruptly at upper end. Lower sides of thorax yellowish, becoming faintly pruinose. Abdomen metallic green above, S1 and S9–10 becoming pruinose with maturity. *Female:* Eyes brown. Thoracic stripes as in  male. Abdomen typical of spreadwing, dark above, pale on sides and all of S10, S3–7 with prominent dark rings. At least some individuals develop blue on top of eyes and pruinosity on abdomen base and tip.

Identification **Southern Spreadwing** only really similar species in range, and the two often found together. **Carolina** differs from **Southern** by reddish-brown antehumeral stripe (typically gray, dull light brown, or blue in **Southern**) and dark blue to violet eyes in male (bright blue in **Southern** but also in some **Carolina**). Pruinosity in mature male equal on

13.1
Carolina Spreadwing
male—Palm Beach Co., FL,
February 2008, J.
Lubchansky

13.2
Carolina Spreadwing
female—Leon Co., FL,
April 2008

S9–10 in **Carolina**, less obvious on S10 in **Southern**. When not hidden by pruinosity, **Carolina** has additional short dark stripe just below hindwings that **Southern** lacks. **Carolina** also has a strong V-shaped dark marking just behind hind legs under thorax lacking in **Southern**. This mark may be obscured by pruinosity, and some **Southern** have it developed, but not the vivid mark present in **Carolina**. Male paraprocts also obviously longer in **Southern** (surpass distal tooth, almost reach inside curve of tip of cerci) than in **Carolina** (fall short of distal tooth). **Carolina** distinctly smaller than **Elegant** and **Swamp**, both of which more extensively metallic green; but note that **Swamp** can also have reddish-brown antehumeral stripe. Relatively shorter abdomen than **Slender**, which has no markings behind humeral stripe. Male **Slender** also has blue antehumeral stripes, lacks pruinosity on abdomen tip, and has white vein around wingtip.

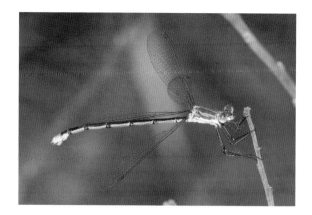

13.3
Carolina Spreadwing
immature female—Lake
Co., FL, April 2005

Natural History Males perch on sedge and grass stems at water, often just above surface. Pairs oviposit in same stems, may even descend underwater in tandem. May reach highest numbers in fall.

Habitat Shallow vegetated ponds of all sorts, in or out of woodland. Typical of fishless waters, perhaps confined to them.

Flight Season GA Feb–Nov, FL Feb–Dec.

14 Northern Spreadwing *Lestes disjunctus*   TL 33–42, HW 18–23

Description Common pond spreadwing all across northern North America. *Male:* Thorax in mature individuals varies from dark in front, pruinose on sides, with narrow blue antehumeral stripe and sometimes very narrow blue median stripe, to entirely pruinose (much less common). Abdomen metallic dark green above, S1–2 and S8–10 becoming completely pruinose with maturity. Pruinosity may vary with locality, age, or individual; not known. *Female:* Polymorphic, eyes brown or blue. Thorax with wide dark median stripe, wide dark humeral stripe widest at upper end, greenish or tan (blue in andromorph) antehumeral stripe narrowing at upper end, white lower  sides and underside. Abdomen entirely blackish above. Some females become almost as pruinose as males, in same areas of thorax and abdomen, perhaps limited to andromorphs.

Identification Looks superficially exactly like several other pond spreadwings, especially **Southern** and **Sweetflag** (see those species). Also much like **Lyre-tipped**, but both sexes differ in color of rear of head; differently shaped male paraprocts can be seen in hand and, with good view, in field. Females not distinguishable if rear of head not apparent. Remaining species in range all have differently colored thorax.

Natural History Mostly in herbaceous vegetation, may be some distance from water. Males frequent beds of dense emergent vegetation, perching from just above water to waist height, and can be very common there. Also present in more scattered vegetation and flying back and forth over open water. Sometimes breeds in shallow vegetated ponds that dry up each summer, more typical habitat of Emerald and Lyre-tipped Spreadwings. Females and tandem pairs arrive at water at midday, ovipositing pairs common through afternoon. Copulation lasts about 15 min. Pairs oviposit on live stems of bulrushes and sedges or dead stems of rushes and up to several feet above water, placing up to 6 eggs in one incision. Pairs also seen ovipositing entirely under water, coming up for air at intervals and then submerging again; unusual behavior in spreadwing. Sexual maturation in 16–18 days.

14.1
Northern Spreadwing
male—Kittitas Co., WA,
September 2007

14.2
Northern Spreadwing
female—Kittitas Co., WA,
September 2007

Habitat Well-vegetated ponds and lakes of all kinds; common in boggy situations.

Flight Season ON Jun–Sep, QC Jun–Sep, NS Jul–Oct, WI Jun–Sep, ME Jun–Oct, OH May–Aug.

Distribution Widely through West, from Alaska and Northwest Territories to northern California, Arizona, and New Mexico. Ranges of this and Southern Spreadwing incompletely known, extent of overlap may not be accurate.

Comments Formerly called Common Spreadwing, when combined with Southern.

15 Southern Spreadwing   *Lestes australis*   TL 36–46, HW 18–25

Description Common, brightly patterned eastern species. *Male*: Front of thorax metallic brown-black with light brown antehumeral stripe becoming blue with maturity. Light yellowish below, becoming whitish pruinose. Abdomen metallic green to bronze above. S1–2 and S8 pruinose low on sides, S9 entirely pruinose, S10 becoming lightly so in older individuals. *Female*: Eyes usually brown, may be blue-tinged with maturity. Colored much like male but not pruinose, antehumeral stripe usually pale tan.

Identification Distribution of this group of spreadwings not thoroughly worked out; **Southern** thought to coexist with **Northern** and **Sweetflag** in parts of

15.1
Southern Spreadwing
male—Okaloosa Co., FL,
July 2009

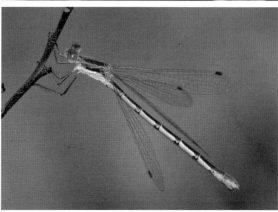

15.2
Southern Spreadwing
female—Early Co., GA,
April 2005, Giff Beaton

region. Probably not distinguishable except in hand from **Northern** by slightly larger size, males by blunt distal spine on inside of cerci (sharper in **Northern**, but difference not always obvious), slightly curved paraprocts (straight in **Northern**). Male **Southern** even more similar to **Sweetflag** but differs in slightly shorter hamules, narrower apical notch on S10, and slightly curved rather than straight paraprocts. In addition, male **Southern** never seem to develop completely pruinose thorax, as happens in some **Northern** and **Sweetflag**, and typically lack pruinosity on top of S8, but males in southern populations of **Sweetflag** may be indistinguishable from **Southern**. Pruinosity seems to increase with latitude, and northern populations of **Southern** might look more like the northern species! Female **Southern** easily distinguished from **Sweetflag** by much smaller ovipositor, but extremely similar to female **Northern** and probably not distinguishable in the field. In hand, ventral surface of ovipositor black in **Southern**, usually pale in **Northern** (sides black in both).

Natural History Foraging takes place in herbaceous vegetation away from water. Adults spend about 2 weeks away from water in sexual maturation, then another 10 days at water (maximum 50). Males occupy perches in grass and shrubs at water's edge for long periods, but little aggression is shown among individuals. May spend all day at water, visit only in morning, or show both morning and afternoon visits. Females come to water in afternoon, and mating peaks in later afternoon. Copulation takes 6–19 min, and pair spends an hour in tandem. Oviposition in standing reed stems above water. Both sexes average two matings during lifetime. Perhaps overwinters as adult in extreme south.

Habitat A wide variety of ponds and lakes with aquatic vegetation.

Flight Season IA May–Aug, OH Apr–Sep, NJ Apr–Sep, KY Apr–Oct, LA Mar–Dec, GA Mar–Nov, FL Mar–Jan.

Distribution West to western edge of plains states and eastern New Mexico. Ranges of this and Northern Spreadwing incompletely known, note range border running along state lines in some areas. Extent of overlap zone may be inaccurate, as some peripheral records for either species could be in error.

Comments Long considered a subspecies of *Lestes disjunctus*, under the name Common Spreadwing. With some structural differences and a somewhat different flight season, it probably deserves its rank as a full species, but genetic differences between the two are less than those between most species of spreadwings.

---

16 Sweetflag Spreadwing   *Lestes forcipatus*   TL 33–42, HW 20–26

Description Frustratingly similar to several others, best identified in field by looking for large ovipositor on females in pairs. *Male*: Thorax black in front with narrow blue-green antehumeral stripe, pale below, may be entirely gray pruinose in mature individuals. Abdomen metallic green-black above, at greatest extreme pruinose on S1, basal two-thirds of S2, and S8–10. Much variation, however; pruinosity in Georgia males restricted to S9–10. *Female*: Eyes blue as in  male. Thoracic pattern of broad dark median and humeral stripes and fairly broad pale antehumeral stripes as in similar spreadwings but rarely may become covered by pruinosity; also S8–10 become pruinose. Thus, female may end up colored like male, but shaped very differently.

Identification Color pattern virtually identical to **Northern Spreadwing**. In males at close range, look at S2 from above; entirely or mostly pruinose in **Northern**, apical third not so, looks shiny metallic, in **Sweetflag**. This character quite indicative but might not be definitive in populations that are less pruinose. May also work for females, in which S2 often becomes pruinose in mature **Northern**, apparently never in mature **Sweetflag**, thus should be good distinguishing mark in females with pruinose thorax. In hand, easiest structural difference to see in male is shape of notch at rear of S10, rounded and wider in **Sweetflag** and pointed and narrower in **Northern**. Also overlaps with **Southern**; see that species. **Sweetflag** has longer hamules than either **Northern** or **Southern**, 1.7 mm long or more in ventral view, with stalk longer than narrow pointed blade. You will have to compare species under magnification to see these microscopic differences. Females easily distinguished from **Northern** and all other North American spreadwings by ovipositor size, tip of ovipositor valves extending to or usually beyond tip of cerci unique in this species. Keep in mind that male pond spreadwings are well known to achieve tandem with wrong species!

Natural History Males and pairs can be common in appropriate habitat; mating and oviposition occur mostly in afternoon. Pairs usually oviposit in live stems of upright bulrushes, rushes, and cattails in fairly open stands up to several feet above shallow water or mud. Also in low sedges and buckbeans in floating mats and, of course, beds of sweet flag. Heavily pruinose females may perch in open at waterside like males.

Habitat Ponds and lakes with emergent vegetation, often associated with bogs or fens. Often in vernal pools, temporary ponds that dry during late summer.

Flight Season ON May–Oct, QC Jun–Sep, NS Jun–Sep, IA Jun–Jul, WI Jun–Sep, ME Jun–Oct, OH May–Sep, NJ May–Oct, KY Apr–Sep, GA Jun–Sep.

16.1
Sweetflag Spreadwing
male—Walker Co., GA,
August 2005, Giff Beaton

16.2
Sweetflag Spreadwing
female—Walker Co., GA,
August 2006, Giff Beaton

Distribution Poorly known in West but occurs sporadically from Northwest Territories south to Oregon and Colorado.

| 17 **Lyre–tipped Spreadwing** *Lestes unguiculatus* | TL 31–44, HW 17–24 |

Description Common northern spreadwing of temporary wetlands. *Male*: Thorax dark metallic brown in front, with narrow blue-green or tan median line and humeral stripes; sides pale blue to whitish with pruinosity. Abdomen metallic dark green or brown above; S1, sides of S2, sides and sometimes top of S8, and S9–10 pruinose with maturity. Some males at maturity, however, lack pruinosity; pairs of both types seen together. *Female*: Eyes brown or blue. Thorax me-  tallic brown in front with narrow median line and wider antehumeral stripe pale blue-green or yellow, sides pale blue-green or yellow. Abdomen entirely metallic brown to green above.

Identification Looks much like **Northern, Southern,** and **Sweetflag Spreadwings** in field, similarly variable. In hand, lyre-shaped paraprocts of male provide definitive identification; also visible at close range with careful look. Note that long, straight paraprocts of other species might be crossed at ends, superficially looking as if they diverged. In both sexes (important to identify females), **Lyre-tipped** has rear of head pale, others dark. Note that light pruinosity eventually covers rear of head in mature males of all four. Another distinction of males is that **Northern** and **Sweetflag** typically have upper surface of S2 mostly or entirely pruinose, whereas pruinosity appears only on sides of this segment in **Lyre-tipped** and **Southern**. Furthermore, male **Lyre-tipped** only species in this group in which pruinosity lacking from triangular area on top of S8. Ventral surface of ovipositor black in **Lyre-tipped**, as in **Southern** (but not **Northern**). **Lyre-tipped** usually has ends of stigmas conspicuously

17.1
Lyre-tipped Spreadwing
male—Harney Co., OR,
July 2006

17.2
Lyre-tipped Spreadwing
female—Houston Co.,
MN, July 2004, Greg Lasley

paler, not so in **Northern** (but **Southern** like **Lyre-tipped**). Female and immature male **Lyre-tipped** may have dark areas quite metallic green, need to be distinguished from **Emerald Spreadwing** by head color, male paraprocts, and smaller ovipositor.

Natural History Males spend much time at water resting on vertical stalks but do not defend perch sites, more commonly move from perch to perch. Approaching females taken in tandem immediately. Copulation lasts about 25 min but is often broken and resumed, accompanied by short flights in tandem. Pair then explores potential oviposition substrates for about a half-hour, then oviposits for over an hour, usually over relatively dry substrates rather than over water and typically backing down stem as eggs are laid. Pairs more and more common through afternoon. Female sometimes continues by herself. Living sedge, bulrush, bur-reed, and pitcher plant stems common substrates, and few hundred eggs laid at about 2/min, 1–2 per incision.

Habitat Shallow marshes and marshy edges of ponds and lakes, often in completely open areas and typically drying up in midsummer. These are exactly the habitats affected by drought, and this species declines wherever drought prevails. However, also quick to colonize newly flooded areas, including farm ponds, gravel pits, and other artificial wetlands, and presence varies greatly from year to year (for example, recorded widely in New Jersey in first half of twentieth century, not seen since). Usually most common spreadwing in prairie potholes. Immatures often abundant in grassy meadows.

Flight Season ON Jun–Oct, QC Jun–Sep, NS Jul–Aug, IA Jun–Oct, WI May–Sep, ME Jun–Sep, OH May–Oct, NJ Jun–Sep, KY May–Oct.

Distribution Widely in West from southern parts of Canadian provinces to northern California and eastern Colorado.

Description Long-bodied slender-looking spreadwing. Vein around extreme wingtips conspicuously pale. *Male*: Thorax black in front with rather wide blue antehumeral stripes, unmarked yellow on sides and underside. Abdomen typically lacking any pruinosity, but sometimes S9 pruinose, apparently more likely in northwestern part of range. Heavily pruinose between wing bases as all spreadwings. *Female*: Distinctly shorter than male, shaped more like other spreadwings. Eyes blue or blue over yellow. Pattern on thorax and abdomen as in male, no pruinosity.

Identification Males distinguished from other spreadwings by virtual lack of pruinosity on abdomen as well as looking longer than any other species of similar body bulk. Pale vein at extreme wingtips distinctive of both sexes. Not metallic like larger **Amber-winged**, **Elegant**, and **Swamp Spreadwings**, colored more like **Lyre-tipped**, **Northern**, and **Sweetflag** but reduced pruinosity distinctive. Absence of pruinosity always leaves conspicuous pale blue antehumeral stripes good for identification in both sexes. When others have those stripes blue, they are usually narrower. Abdomen length in female close enough to that of **Lyre-tipped**, **Northern**, and **Southern** that separating these four is difficult. **Lyre-tipped** usually has pale-tipped stigmas, but other three colored about the same. Pale wingtip vein always distinctive of **Slender** when visible, best viewed against dark background. S7 relatively longest in Slender, S9 obviously less than half length of S7 in **Slender**, not so extreme in others.

18.1
Slender Spreadwing male—Towns Co., GA, August 2008, Marion M. Dobbs

18.2
Slender Spreadwing female—Towns Co., GA, August 2008, Marion M. Dobbs

Natural History Males in shrubs and low tree branches in swampy woodland, also dense herbaceous vegetation at lake shores. Unlikely to be over open water. Emerge in great numbers from some wetlands and can be abundant in woodland during maturation. Maturation in color in about 2 weeks, reproductive activity at 3 weeks. Mating may take place away from water, and females oviposit solo, unusual in spreadwings, and about a foot above water. Eggs commonly laid in cattails, 1 egg per incision. After maturation may live for 6 weeks.

Habitat Lakes, ponds, and edges of slow streams with abundant emergent vegetation, usually associated with forest. Also found in vernal pools in and at edge of woodland.

Flight Season ON Jun–Oct, QC Jun–Sep, NS Jun–Sep, IA May–Oct, WI Jun–Sep, ME Jun–Oct, OH May–Oct, NJ May–Oct, KY May–Oct, GA Apr–Sep, FL Apr–May, Sep–Nov.

Distribution West to western Manitoba and eastern Colorado.

19 Emerald Spreadwing *Lestes dryas*	TL 32–40, HW 19–25

Description Rather stocky spreadwing with front of thorax emerald-green. *Male*: Thorax metallic green in front, pruinose white on sides, with narrow pale median and antehumeral lines; median line disappearing with maturity (also antehumerals in most individuals). Abdomen metallic green above, at maturity becoming pruinose on S1–2 and S9–10, often extending to S8. *Female*: Brown or blue eyes at maturity. Thorax metallic green in front with narrow pale median and antehumeral lines, yellow below. Abdomen entirely metallic green above, without pruinosity. Ovipositor relatively large, extending beyond tip of S10.

Identification Emerald green thorax and abdomen diagnostic along with stocky build (other green species such as **Elegant Spreadwing** are larger, longer), but bear in mind that in several species, even those in which adults lack green, dark part of abdomen may be green in immatures, and green highlight may show up on thorax. None is brilliant green like this species. Thorax and abdomen of **Emerald** sometimes look brownish, especially

19.1
Emerald Spreadwing male—
Chelan Co., WA, July 2008

19.2
Emerald Spreadwing female—
Chelan Co., WA, July 2008, Netta Smith

younger individuals, and oldest males can look quite black above. Note widened tips of paraprocts of male. Only **Sweetflag** has larger ovipositor.

Natural History Can be very common in shrublands and forest near breeding ponds. Breeding males and pairs tend to stay over dry rather than flooded parts of habitat. Pairs oviposit in live stems of sedges, grasses, and horsetails and hanging willow leaves, high above ground in the latter. One egg inserted in each incision.

Habitat Shallow ponds, marshes, and fens, often those that dry up in late summer; typically densely vegetated. Also found at edges of permanent wetlands but may not breed successfully where aquatic predators, either fish or dragonflies, are common.

Flight Season ON May–Sep, QC Jun–Sep, NS Jun–Sep, IA May–Jul, WI Jun–Sep, ME Jun–Sep, OH May–Aug, NJ Jun–Jul, KY Jun–Jul.

Distribution Widely in West from Alaska and Northwest Territories south to northern California and southern Rocky Mountains.

20 Swamp Spreadwing *Lestes vigilax* TL 42–55, HW 23–27

Description Large metallic green spreadwing. *Male*: Eyes dark blue-green with pale blue highlight over yellow green, looking somewhat bicolored. Thorax entirely metallic green to bronze in front or with narrow reddish-brown antehumeral stripes. Sides and underside pale yellow, becoming whitish pruinose, pruinosity obscuring border between dark and light parts of thorax, originally a wavy line. Abdomen metallic green to bronze above, becoming pruinose on S1 and S9–10 at maturity; sides of S2 and S8 also pruinose,

20.1
Swamp Spreadwing
male—Cumberland Co., ME,
July 2006

20.2
Swamp Spreadwing female—
Cumberland Co., ME, July 2006

20.3
Swamp Spreadwing
immature male—
Chesterfield Co., SC, May
2008

may extend to top of S8 in North. *Female*: Eyes brown over yellowish, blue in some (oldest?) individuals. Colored as male, but always with narrow pale reddish-brown antehumeral stripe. Abdomen duller than in male, with no pruinosity in most, but pruinose tip in a small percentage. Apparently females in some northern populations attain fully pruinose thorax if they live long enough!

Identification Longer-bodied than most other species in range, bulkier than **Slender Spreadwing** and metallic green rather than dark brown above. Cerci long, pair forming more acute angle where they meet than in other pond spreadwings. Long, very slender paraprocts also distinctive. Most like **Elegant Spreadwing**, which see.

Natural History Males usually perch in sheltered areas in shade, often in tangled vegetation, and are difficult to find. May also be in open, however. Tandem pairs oviposit in pickerel-weed stems and other plants at water surface, even well out from shore. Dull immatures found in dense herbaceous and shrubby vegetation near water, also well into forest away from water.

Habitat Wooded ponds and lakes with abundant emergent vegetation, often where shrubs grow in shallow water. Slow streams and bog-margined lakes included in this description.

Flight Season ON Jun–Sep, QC Jun–Aug, NS Jun–Sep, WI May–Oct, ME May–Oct, OH May–Sep, NJ May–Oct, KY May–Aug, LA Apr–Oct, GA Apr–Nov, FL Mar–Dec.

21 Elegant Spreadwing *Lestes inaequalis* TL 45–58, HW 25–31

Description Large metallic green spreadwing, distinctly larger in South. *Male*: Eyes dark blue-green with bright blue highlight over pale blue-green, strongly bicolored. Thorax metallic green to bronze in front, may show fine reddish-brown midline. Sides and underside pale yellow, rarely becoming whitish pruinose. Abdomen metallic green to bronze above, becoming pruinose on S9 and then S10 at maturity; sides of S1–2 also pruinose. *Female*: Eyes dark green over dull yellow to light green, strongly bicolored. Colored as male, but often with narrow pale reddish-brown antehu-

21.1
Elegant Spreadwing male—
Gloucester Co., NJ, June 2008

21.2
Elegant Spreadwing female—
Worcester Co., MA, June 2006, Tom
Murray

meral line. Minimal or no pruinosity on most, but underside of thorax and abdomen tip may become pruinose in oldest individuals.

Identification Impressively large size and mostly metallic upperside at maturity distinctive. Eyes more strikingly bicolored (actually tricolored) than in any other species but **Swamp Spreadwing**. Both sexes distinguished from that quite similar species by pale rear of head and pale tibiae (dark in mature **Swamp** but pale in immatures). Pruinosity in male **Elegant** usually not obscuring sharp border between front and sides of thorax, as it does in **Swamp**. At close range, look for distinctive long paraprocts in male, extending beyond tips of cerci. Female distinguished from **Swamp** by metallic green on top of S10 (pale or pruinose in **Swamp**), also slightly larger ovipositor valves, extending beyond lower edge of S10 and dark below (valves in **Swamp** entirely pale). Tiny basal plate of ovipositor pointed in **Swamp**, squared off in **Elegant**. Typically, pale antehumeral stripe in female narrower in **Elegant** than in **Swamp**, abdominal pattern brighter green. **Amber-winged Spreadwing** also with green and yellow thorax, not as elongate and with dark markings under thorax. Much longer-bodied than **Emerald Spreadwing** with similar green thorax.

Natural History Males perch low in shrubs and other emergent vegetation and fly over open water, where they can be quite conspicuous. Also often land under leaves and stems, less apparent at those times. Often in shade and more active later in day. Usually not very common. Reported to oviposit on upper surface of water-lily leaves, presumably also in other substrates. Also feed among herbaceous vegetation in weedy clearings.

Habitat Lakes, ponds, and slow streams with abundant vegetation, for example water lilies and sedges, in or out of woodland. Most likely pond spreadwing on slow forest streams.

Flight Season ON May–Aug, QC Jun–Aug, IA Jun–Jul, WI Jun–Aug, ME Jun–Aug, OH May–Sep, NJ May–Aug, KY May–Aug, LA Apr–Aug, GA Apr–Sep, FL Apr–Aug.

Description Large green and yellow spreadwing with amber-tinted wings and distinctive markings on sides of thorax. *Male*: Eyes bright sky-blue, paler below. Thorax metallic greenish in front without pale stripes (may become frosted with pruinosity); lower sides and underside yellow with irregular dark stripes, becoming whitish pruinose. Abdomen metallic dark green, S1 and S9–10 (more rarely S8) pruinose above. *Female*: Eyes blue above, yellow below. Thorax and abdomen as in male, only pruinosity develops on underside of thorax.

Identification No other spreadwing has amber wings (not always obvious), and no other spreadwing has dark stripes across bright yellow sides of thorax. Bulkiest of pond spread-wings, although **Elegant** and **Swamp** are as long. Superficially most like those two species because of large size, green thorax, and sparse pruinosity but differs in wing color and very short paraprocts. Most like **Swamp**, mature male differs in pruinosity usually on S9–10 rather than S8–10, although probably total overlap. Best mark short paraprocts when they can be seen, as well as wing coloration. Differs further from **Elegant** in having entirely dark tibiae and frosty, even bluish-looking, thorax. Bicolored blue and yellow eyes of female also distinctive, although shared with female **Swamp Spreadwing**.

Natural History Males and copulating and tandem pairs perch on or near tips of sedge and grass stems at about knee height close to water, sometimes in shrubs. More active fliers along lake shores and out over open water than other spreadwings, impressively large and fast, perhaps while searching for females. Appears more likely to take larger prey such as other damselflies, including teneral spreadwings. Mating in afternoon. Females oviposit in tandem or solo from just above water to several feet up on sedge, cattail, rush, and bur-reed stems, also commonly under water-plantain and on top of water-lily leaves. Eggs laid in clusters, averaging 6–7 per cluster.

Habitat Variety of permanent lakes and ponds with at least some emergent vegetation. Has been found in everything from bog lakes to pasture ponds, but usually considered charac-teristic of fishless wetlands.

Flight Season ON May–Aug, QC May–Aug, NS Jun–Aug, IA Jun–Aug, WI Jun–Aug, ME Jun–Aug, OH May–Sep, NJ Jun–Aug, KY May–Sep.

22.1
Amber-winged Spreadwing
male—Phelps Co., MO,
June 2009

22.2
Amber-winged Spreadwing
female—Clermont Co., OH, May
2008, William Hull

Pond Spreadwings - male appendages

Blue-striped
Spreadwing

Antillean
Spreadwing

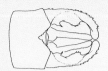

Rainpool
Spreadwing

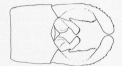

Spotted
Spreadwing

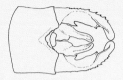

Carolina
Spreadwing

Northern
Spreadwing

Southern
Spreadwing

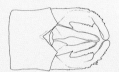

Sweetflag
Spreadwing

Lyre-tipped
Spreadwing

Slender
Spreadwing

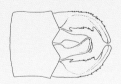

Emerald
Spreadwing

Swamp
Spreadwing

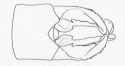

Elegant
Spreadwing

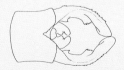

Amber-winged
Spreadwing

Pond Spreadwings - female abdomen tip

Blue-striped Spreadwing

Antillean Spreadwing

Rainpool Spreadwing

Spotted Spreadwing

Carolina Spreadwing

Northern Spreadwing

Southern Spreadwing

Sweetflag Spreadwing

Lyre-tipped Spreadwing

Slender Spreadwing

Emerald Spreadwing

Swamp Spreadwing

Elegant Spreadwing

Amber-winged Spreadwing

Pond Damsel Family   *Coenagrionidae*

This largest family of damselflies is the second-largest family of odonates. Almost anywhere in the world, they are usually the most common damselflies in open ponds and marshes. There are also many species on streams, but other families often dominate on tropical streams, and most damselflies have narrow wings; thus, a commonly used name "narrow-winged damsels" is not very informative. They are generally small species, a few as large as spreadwings. The wings are held closed in all but a few species in which they are held half-open, less open than in spreadwings. The color pattern has similar elements in almost all genera. The eyes in most are black or dark brown above, brightly colored below, and it is that color that is used in their description. The "face" is often paler than the top of the head, and most species have postocular spots, pale spots contrasting with the dark head just in from the back of each eye; they may be connected by a pale line of the same color or not. The thorax typically has a dark median stripe, a pale antehumeral stripe, and a dark humeral stripe, the sides and underside pale. Sometimes the pale stripe is interrupted. In males, the abdomen is all dark, mostly pale, or some intermediate combination of dark and pale, often with a contrastingly colored tip. Females usually have slightly thicker abdomens than males (they carry all those eggs), and an ovipositor is present but not usually as prominent as in spreadwings. Females typically but not always share the male's head and thorax pattern but usually have the abdomen darker above, with less pattern. Females in some genera are polymorphic, one morph colored more like the male, the other duller. World 1140, NA 105, East 65.

Eurasian Bluets   *Coenagrion*

This diverse group of temperate Eurasian species with a few North American representatives look essentially like typical blue American bluets, *Enallagma*, but may or may not be closely related to them. No field characters differentiate males definitively, so they will have to be distinguished individually from various American bluets as well as each other. From above, black on female abdomen covers entire upper surface of each segment except for narrow basal ring, whereas black on middle segments of many American bluets bulges at posterior end and tapers at anterior end somewhat like a torpedo. Black markings fall well short of front of segment in *Enallagma*, leaving a conspicuous ring. Also, most *Enallagma* usually have at least one distinct dark stripe visible around the middle of each eye (less obvious in males), but *Coenagrion* lack these stripes and typically have a larger and more contrasty dark area forming a "cap" on the eye. In hand, male *Coenagrion* have forked paraprocts in side view, shared by a few *Enallagma*, and females lack vulvar spine, present in *Enallagma*. In habits they resemble *Enallagma* but tend to be more common in dense herbaceous vegetation, and they are all northerly distributed. World 41, NA 3, East 3.

23 Prairie Bluet   *Coenagrion angulatum*   TL 27–33, HW 16–22

Description Northern plains bluet with mostly black abdomen.
Male: Eyes black over pale greenish. Thorax with wide black median and moderate humeral stripe, blue antehumeral about as wide as humeral; also fine but conspicuous black line low on sides of thorax. S1–2 blue, S2 with black subapical bar; S3–6 black with basal blue rings, widest on S3 and becoming narrower to rear; S7 almost entirely black; S8–9 blue, S10 blue on sides. *Female*: Poly-

morphic, pale areas greenish or blue. Thorax striped as in male. Abdomen entirely black above, conspicuously pale on sides, with narrow pale rings at end of each segment, slightly wider and distinctly blue on S7–9; S8 with pair of dorsal blue spots at base.

Identification Few other male bluets in its range with blue S1–2 and S8–9 but mostly black middle abdominal segments. Barely overlaps with **Skimming Bluet**, which is smaller and

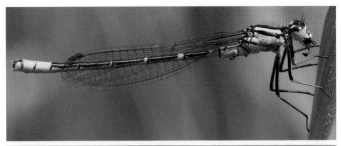

23
Prairie Bluet male—Oak Lake, MB, June 2010, Deanna Dodgson;
female—Hillside Beach, MB, June 2009, Deanna Dodgson

has top of S2 and virtually all of S3–8 black. FORKTAILS in its range have green-striped thorax. **Stream Bluet**, in different habitat and more slender, differs in same way in color pattern as **Skimming**. Of closely related species, female much like **Taiga Bluet** but pale spots at base of S8 usually distinctive. However, some **Prairie** lack those spots, distinguished by rear border of prothorax three-lobed (not so in **Taiga**) with scarcely evident pale rim (prominent pale border in **Taiga**). Much less pale color on abdomen than vividly ringed **Subarctic Bluet**. Females of co-occurring species of AMERICAN BLUETS (*Enallagma*) such as **Alkali**, **Boreal**, **Familiar**, **Northern**, **River**, and **Tule** also have broader rings of pale color on middle segments and characteristic torpedo shape of black on each segment rather than straight edge of Eurasian bluet. However, two *Enallagma*, **Hagen's** and **Marsh Bluets**, rather similar because abdominal markings less obviously different. Nevertheless, both have bulges that hint at torpedo pattern; they also lack basal spots on S8 and have smaller postocular spots than **Prairie Bluet**. Check for dark horizontal stripes around eyes to be sure if you have *Enallagma* (striped) or *Coenagrion* (not).

Natural History Extremely abundant at some prairie wetlands. Males common in dense grass rather than over open water. Sexual maturation takes about a week. Copulation for 20 min or more. Oviposition typically in tandem on submergent vegetation at surface. In emergent vegetation, pair backs down under water and may remain for up to 30 min, then floats to surface and flies away, still in tandem. Females lay 150–200 eggs in each of several clutches.

Habitat Prairie lakes, ponds, sloughs, and slow streams, usually with much marsh vegetation, some of them sufficiently shallow to go dry at times.

Flight Season ON Jun, IA Jun; probably May–Jul.

Distribution Across Canadian prairies and boreal forest to northern British Columbia, scattered records north and west to Alaska.

Description Far northern bluet with divided antehumeral stripes. *Male*: Eyes black over blue. Moderate median and humeral stripes, blue antehumeral slightly wider than humeral and divided near upper end, looking something like exclamation mark (although *interrogatum* means to question!). That stripe rarely only constricted, not broken, even more rarely undivided. Conspicuous black stripe on sides of thorax expanded at upper and lower ends. Abdomen

blue with prominent black U on S2 with arms wider than base, S3 with black apical ring, then each subsequent segment with more and more black, so S4 appears half black, S5 three-quarters black, S6 seven-eighths black and S7 with very narrow blue basal ring; S7 also has blue tip, S8–9 blue, and S10 black above. *Female*: Polymorphic, either blue like male or green. Eyes brown over pale green. Thoracic stripes as in male. Abdomen mostly black above, but S1 pale, S2 extensively pale on sides, forming black torpedo but with exaggerated base; conspicuously pale basal ring on S3–8, also larger area on S8–9, and S10 pale.

Identification Divided antehumeral stripe distinctive (although may occur in **Skimming** and **Taiga Bluets**), as is conspicuous black stripe low on sides of thorax with bulges in it like string of pearls. Blue on end of S7 distinguishes **Subarctic** from other two Eurasian bluets in rare individuals with unbroken antehumeral stripe. Extensive blue on abdomen base and tip not like any other eastern bluet except **Azure**, which has more at ends and less in middle, also distinctly more slender; distinguished because of thoracic pattern in any case. Female distinguished from other bluets by divided antehumeral stripe and much pale color at abdomen tip. No other female bluet in range has most of S9–10 blue as well as tip of S8.

Natural History Males and pairs in tandem in dense vegetation, not usually over open water; copulating pairs often perch in shrubs up to head height. Pairs or lone females oviposit in floating sedge and grass leaves and stems and upright grass stems.

Habitat Boreal fens and bogs, usually associated with sphagnum and other aquatic mosses but often in shrubs.

Flight Season ON Jun–Jul, QC May–Sep, WI Jun–Aug, ME Jun–Jul.

Distribution Widely in western Canada to eastern Alaska.

24
Subarctic Bluet
male—Heckman
Pass, BC, July 2006,
Netta Smith;
female—Whiteshell
Provincial Park, MB,
June 2008, Larry de
March

Description Widespread and common northern bluet of sedge marshes with much black on abdomen and U-shaped mark on S2; lower sides of thorax sometimes greenish. *Male:* Eyes black over blue-green. Thorax with wide median and moderate humeral stripe, relatively narrow antehumeral stripe sometimes broken into exclamation point, more often in some populations than others. Fine black line just behind humeral stripe from wing base halfway down thorax. Black U on S2 with base wider than arms; S3–5 about half blue, half black; S6–7 almost all black; S8–10 blue, with black on top of S10 and often paired apical markings on S9. *Female:* Poly-

morphic, either light pinkish-brown or bright greenish to blue-green. Entire top of abdomen black from S2 to S10, with fine pale basal rings on each segment; narrow apical rings on S7–9 blue in both morphs. Some individuals have base of S8 pale, however. Immature males can have fully blue markings on abdomen but tan thorax.

Identification Males with more black on abdomen than other small bluets that occur with them, in characteristic pattern of U-shaped mark on S2, then two short and one long black section before blue tip. Black mark on S2 different proportions than similar U-shaped mark on **Subarctic Bluet**, which also always has interrupted antehumeral stripe. Northern populations of **Boreal** and **Northern Bluets**, with much more black than elsewhere, may have U-shaped mark on S2, but larger than **Taiga** and without additional black stripes behind humeral stripe. **River Bluet** also show U-shaped mark but larger, with long cerci. No other bluet has paired black apical markings on S9 or fine but conspicuous black line just behind humeral stripe. No other male bluet shows green on thorax as this species often does. Females of other Eurasian bluets usually have extensive pale areas on S8 or S8–9, as do those of some AMERICAN BLUETS. But see **Prairie** for additional characters, and note unstriped eyes and lack of pale basal markings on middle abdominal segments as characters for Eurasian bluets. American bluets of ponds and lakes with no pale color on S8–9 usually have middle abdominal segments extensively marked with pale areas and never have apical blue rings on S7–8. Some small Atlantic-coast bluets (**Little**, **New England**, **Pine Barrens**)

25
Taiga Bluet
male—Chelan
Co., WA, June
2004;
female—
Kittitas Co., WA,
June 2007,
Netta Smith

very similar but lack pale rear border of prothorax and fine black line behind humeral stripe characteristic of **Taiga**; also have vulvar spines.

Natural History Males abundant in appropriate habitat, females and pairs generally harder to find than those of American bluets. Males and tandem pairs stay within dense grasses and sedges, rarely if ever over open water and fly less strongly than American bluets. Also on open sphagnum mats. Males cruise through vegetation rapidly in search of females. Pairs oviposit on both floating and emergent plant stems, abdomen tip usually just below surface.

Habitat Sedge marshes and fens and well-vegetated pond and lake edges, also in sedge beds at large lakes. Often in stands of water horsetail. Common in habitats of both other North American representatives of group. In shadier, cooler habitats in southern parts of range.

Flight Season ON May–Aug, QC May–Sep, NS Jun–Jul, WI Jun–Aug, ME Jun–Jul, OH Jun–Jul.

Distribution Across western Canada to eastern Alaska, south in mountains to northern California and central Rockies.

American Bluets *Enallagma*

Large genus of small to medium-sized damselflies, primarily in temperate North America but a few in Eurasia. Typical species are mostly blue, the amount of black variable with species. Relatively recent evolutionary radiation has produced a confusing assemblage of similar bluets in the East, best distinguished structurally. Another group has the abdomen mostly black, the tip variably blue, also exhibiting much variation. Also another group of yellow to red species and small group of mostly violet species. Postocular spots vary from small and isolated ("spots") to large and connected or almost connected by an occipital bar ("dumbbell") to narrow and connected ("line"). Eyes in females usually with more distinct horizontal stripe around middle. Pond species typically have much blue on the abdomen, whereas stream species more likely to have a black abdomen with a blue tip. Thorax typically patterned with black stripes, wide median and narrow humeral; pale antehumeral stripe usually wider than humeral. Males rarely and females more often show pale line on median carina dividing median stripe, but this line characteristic of some species. Blue bluets show "torpedo" pattern from above on most abdominal segments: pointed at anterior end, then parallel-sided and often constricted just before bulging at posterior end. Many species have polymorphic females, either brown (sometimes green) or blue. Eurasian bluets (*Coenagrion*) are very similar to the mostly blue American bluets, but males have paraprocts that are slightly forked in side view, and females lack a vulvar spine, characters visible only in hand. Otherwise, they are best distinguished by characteristics of the included species.

Stream bluets typically perch facing the shore at the tip of a branch or leaf projecting from shore; they also commonly hover for long periods over water, both of these behaviors distinguishing them from dancers that share this habitat. Both copulating and tandem pairs are frequently seen. In tandem oviposition, males grasp substrate or, if no substrate is available, they lean forward whirring wings, not resting still in vertical position as typical of dancers. Blue bluets are distinguished from mostly blue dancers usually by having black on top of the eyes (a black "cap" usually absent in dancers), black on top of S2 (on sides in dancers) and S10 (no black in dancers), and almost all lacking black stripes low on S8–9 (most dancers have them). Female bluets easily distinguished from female dancers if eyes can be seen; those of most bluets with at least one horizontal stripe, not so in dancers. Many bluets can be distinguished from one another in the field by relative proportions of blue and black on various abdominal segments, but some of mostly blue species have to be captured to be distinguished by appendages. Some females are distinguished only by close examination of mesostigmal plates. Interestingly, relatively rarely are two mostly blue bluets found to be common at the same place and time. Habitat differences, even if not well understood by us, separate them. World 46, NA 37, East 33.

Description Large bluet of running water with long appendages. Postocular spots usually without occipital bar. *Male:* Eyes black over blue. Thorax with wide median and narrow to wide humeral stripes, in some populations narrowed toward upper end and then widened into spot. Black subapical spot on S2, in some connected to lateral markings as U-shaped mark. Black ring extending forward as point on S3 and beyond, black more extensive but point shorter on each succeeding segment until black filling most of S7 and cut straight across; S8–9 blue, S10 black. Upper part of cerci conspicuously long and straight. *Female:* Polymorphic, brown or blue. Eyes brown over tan. Thorax as male. Abdomen black above on all segments, on S3–7 pointed forward into pale basal ring; black on S9–10 not fully covering segment.

Identification Male resembles many other bluets, especially **Alkali** and **Tule Bluets** because of much black on middle segments; former more likely to occur with it. Looks a bit larger than **Tule**. Postocular spots usually bridged by line in **Tule**, not so in **Alkali** and **River**. Long cerci of male, with ventral process, distinctive from all other bluets. Narrow humeral stripe distinctive where found; female may be distinguishable from similar **Familiar** and **Tule Bluets** by this mark, otherwise only in hand. **Alkali Bluet** has similar humeral stripe but usually entirely pale S8. Usually only bluet common on open rivers.

Natural History Both sexes in open herbaceous vegetation, often perch on ground like dancer. Males perch on stems at outer edge of vegetation beds. Pairs or single females oviposit on emergent and floating vegetation; females may go entirely under water, down to several inches deep, for as long as a half-hour.

Habitat Streams and small rivers, mostly in open country but often with riparian borders; also flowing irrigation canals.

Flight Season ON Jun–Sep, IA Jun–Sep, WI Jun–Aug.

Distribution Widely in West from southern Alberta and Oregon south locally to northern California and New Mexico.

26
River Bluet male—Teton Co., WY, September 2007; immature female—Uinta Co., WY, July 2008, Greg Lasley; blue female—Teton Co., WY, September 2007

Description Common bright blue bluet of Southeastern ponds. Postocular spots form transverse line. *Male*: Eyes blue with slight amount of black above. Thorax with usual bluet stripes, humeral slightly narrower than antehumeral. Black markings include large round apical spot on S2, larger narrow rings on S3–6, S6 often prolonged forward into long point; S7 black above with narrow blue basal ring; S8–9 blue, S10 black above. Midabdomen black rings usually narrow but sometimes more extensive, extending forward as much as midsegment. *Female*: Polymorphic, brown or pale bluish. Eyes brown over pale greenish or tan. Thorax as male. Abdomen with all segments continuously black above, only slight indication of torpedo-shaped markings.

Identification Numerous other all-blue bluets in range. Should be distinguishable from **Big Bluet** by size alone, but smaller individuals of **Big** complicate this. **Big** usually has median stripe on thorax divided by fine blue carina, a generally dependable field mark. Otherwise, capture and scrutiny of appendages are necessary. **Familiar** more easily distinguished from **Atlantic** by good look at large cerci of former; also, postocular spots often larger in **Familiar** and without occipital bar, but overlap. Males of slightly smaller Atlantic-coast species (**Little, New England, Pine Barrens, Sandhill**) differ by usually lacking occipital bar; also, **New England** and **Sandhill** have obvious black spots on S8, **Pine Barrens** usually does, and **Little** has purplish thorax. Male **Boreal, Hagen's, Marsh,** and **Northern Bluets** also very similar, tend to have larger postocular spots, much wider than occipital bar if that is present. Capture and study of appendages may be necessary. Females of all of these species even more similar, not so different in postocular spots, so in-hand perusal of mesostigmal plates even more essential for positive identification. Female **Atlantic** distinguished from **Familiar** by narrower postocular spots, often no wider than occipital bar, and from **Big** by smaller size and lack of fine pale line down front of thorax. Cerci of female **Atlantic** about half length of S10, slightly more than half in **Familiar**. **Pine Barrens** female has obvious pale color on S8, all others look about the same.

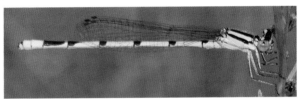

27
Atlantic Bluet
male—Charlton Co.,
GA, July 2007; brown
female—Glynn Co.,
GA, November 2005,
Giff Beaton; blue
female—Early Co.,
GA, September 2005,
Giff Beaton

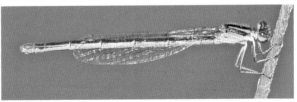

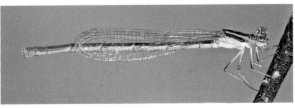

Natural History Males range all over typical well-vegetated ponds, usually perching on stems above water. Pairs oviposit in tandem on horizontal stems or female solo on vertical stems, moving underwater headfirst and briefly while male waits above.

Habitat Shallow grassy ponds, less often lake borders, in open or open woodland; typical of fishless waters. Often in acid, sphagnum-bordered ponds in North.

Flight Season NJ May–Oct, GA Mar–Nov, FL all year.

28 Familiar Bluet *Enallagma civile*   TL 28–39, HW 16–21

Description Abundant and widespread bright blue bluet, typical of early-succession habitats. Postocular spots not connected in most populations, can be very small or even absent in North. *Male*: Eyes blue with small black cap. Thoracic stripes typical bluet, widest black median, somewhat narrower blue antehumeral, and quite narrow black humeral. Abdomen blue with black apical markings on S2–7, beginning as spot on S2, pointed and somewhat wider spots on S3–5, covering two-thirds of S6 and almost all of S7; S8–9 blue, S10 black above. *Female*: Polymorphic, brown or blue. Eyes tan to greenish tan with brown cap. Thorax as in male. Abdomen  black above, covering all segments, but typical bluet torpedo pattern evident.

Identification Largely blue middle segments should distinguish male from other bluets with more black. Readily distinguished from very similar **Boreal**, **Northern**, and **Vernal Bluets** by distinctively shaped cerci clearly longer than paraprocts (reverse in other three) and black marking on S2 a spot touching rear of segment (bar separated from rear in others where they overlap with **Familiar**). In areas where most overlap takes place, **Familiar** usually has distinctly smaller postocular spots. Also, other three species tend to be early season, reaching high populations and then disappearing, whereas **Familiar** remains common through summer. **Familiar** slightly larger than **Hagen's** and **Marsh** that overlap with it widely but colored very similarly. **Familiar** often has relatively wider antehumeral and narrower humeral stripes than the two smaller species, thus showing more blue in front

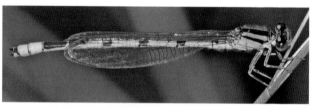

28
Familiar Bluet
male—Catron Co.,
NM, July 2007;
brown
female—
Maricopa Co., AZ,
January 2010,
Pierre Deviche;
blue female—
White Co., GA,
June 2003, Giff
Beaton

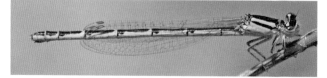

view of thorax, but they overlap. Blue on sides of S10 comes up a bit higher in **Familiar** (to level of top of cerci) than in **Boreal**, **Hagen's**, **Marsh**, **Northern**, and **Vernal** (only to bottom of cerci), just visible from above in this species and could be useful character. **Atlantic** and **Big** similar in extent of S10 blue but have narrower postocular spots and barely perceptible cerci. Furthermore, **Big** usually larger, with divided median stripe on thorax and more black on middle segments. Male **Familiar** occasionally are rather strongly purplish-tinged, and this variation may occur in other blue bluets as well (normal in **Little Bluet**); not well documented. Males of other small Atlantic-coast bluets (**New England, Pine Barrens, Sandhill**) always or usually have black markings on S8. Female much like those of other blue bluets with black on entire abdomen, will have to be identified in hand. Catch mating pairs (especially in wheel, unlikely to be heterospecific) to learn female characteristics.

Natural History Extremely abundant at many sites but surprisingly local. Males spend much of day at water but do not visit each day while reproductively mature. Males arrive at water in late morning and remain at peak numbers until midafternoon. Mating peaks by midday. Copulation lasts about 20 min. Tandem pairs oviposit in soft plant tissues of all kinds at and below surface, up to a few inches above water in shrub stems. Pair engages in exploratory flights in which female tests substrate and often lays some eggs, pair then moving again. These flights are surprisingly lengthy, averaging 34 min and moving substantial distances. Then at some appropriate site, female backs underwater to continue ovipositing, and male releases her before his head gets wet. Female may also back down stem, then lay eggs as she ascends. Underwater oviposition bouts last about 10–30 min, female then popping to surface. Male typically waits for her there and grabs her again, pair moving to new site. Females often reject attempts at second tandems, whether by first mate or another male. No underwater oviposition at some sites, probably because of lack of appropriate plants. Entire course of oviposition may last 2 hr. Both sexes average just over one mating in lifetime. Unlike many other bluets, more of a summer than a spring species, and common well into fall.

Habitat Lakes, ponds, open marshes, and slow streams, even margins of rivers, as long as some emergent vegetation is present. Broad habitat tolerance, including preference for newly created wetlands, may explain widespread abundance. In at least some areas, seems characteristic of newly created wetlands, disappearing as succession (or competition?) changes conditions. Also found in brackish waters near coast, along with Big Bluets.

Flight Season ON May–Oct, NS Jun–Oct, IA May–Oct, WI May–Oct, ME Jun–Oct, OH May–Nov, NJ May–Oct, KY Apr–Oct, LA Mar–Nov, GA Mar–Dec, FL all year.

Distribution Not as ubiquitous as one might think because of wide range; very local in some areas. Widely in West north to southern Oregon and southern Saskatchewan, south through Mexico and Central America at increasingly higher elevations to Venezuela.

29 Tule Bluet *Enallagma carunculatum* TL 26–37, HW 14–22

Description Common bluet of northern marshes with much black on abdomen. Postocular spots usually form narrow dumbbell. *Male*: Eyes blue with black cap. Median stripe broad, humeral stripe narrow, antehumeral wider than humeral. Abdomen with large black apical spot on S2; apical black mark on S3–6 somewhat pointed forward and occupying more than half of segment, longest on S6; most of S7 black; S8–9 blue, S10 black above. Rare vari-ants have most segments almost entirely black, thus abdomen looking black with blue tip. *Female*: Polymorphic brown or blue; blue may be absent from middle segments, may be golden-yellow instead. Eyes tan with brown cap. Thorax as in male. Abdomen black above, black expanded apically and narrowed basally, extending forward in point on S3–8, with narrow but varying pale ring at base of each. From above, black on each segment shaped like fat candle in small candle-holder (another way of saying torpedo-shaped).

Identification Male easily distinguished from most coexisting bluets (**Boreal, Familiar, Ha-**

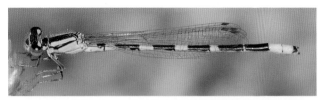

29
Tule Bluet male,
brown
female—Grant
Co., WA, August
2007; blue
female—Grant
Co., WA, August
2005

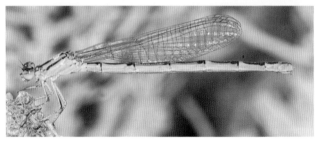

gen's, **Marsh**, **Northern**, **Vernal**) by much black on all middle abdominal segments, exceeding blue on all segments. **Alkali** and **River** quite similar but usually more blue than black on S3–4, also **River** usually lacks occipital bar between postocular spots and has distinctly longer cerci. Female looks like other bluets with black covering most of abdomen, could be distinguished only by looking at mesostigmal plates in hand.

Natural History Typical bluet in habits, with males and tandem pairs perching all over shore and emergent vegetation and flying well out over open water, even of very large lakes. Very common in optimal habitats. On average, copulation lasts 21 min, exploration for oviposition sites 11 min, surface oviposition 58 min, and underwater oviposition 20 min. Pairs and solo females oviposit in standing bulrushes and presumably other plants. Mayflies and small flies common prey.

Habitat Marshy and open lakes, ponds, and slow streams and rivers, occurring commonly at larger and more eutrophic lakes than some of its relatives. Often common at lakes and ponds with tall cattail growth where other bluets are lacking. Also found at marl and saline lakes, but not as characteristic of extreme environments as Alkali Bluet.

Flight Season ON May–Oct, QC Jun–Sep, NS Jul–Sep, IA May–Sep, WI Jun–Oct, OH Jun–Sep, NJ May–Sep, KY Jun–Jul.

Distribution Widespread and abundant throughout West, north to southern Canada and south to northern Baja California.

Description Small bluet of lakes and ponds with brown eyes and mostly black abdomen. Postocular spots small, isolated. *Male:* Eyes brown over tan to greenish, small streak of blue across front. Thorax with broad median and humeral stripes, antehumeral no wider than humeral and may be constricted or even interrupted in some individuals (more likely in

Southeast). Abdomen mostly black with blue at base forming wavy line down S2 (because black both on top and sides of segment) onto base of S3; in some, line interrupted by black on top and sides in contact; otherwise S8–9 blue but with black low on sides. Faintly indicated basal rings on S3–7 either blue or whitish. *Female*: Eyes brown over tan. Thorax as male. Abdomen entirely black above, black extending well down sides of segments. S8 above with paired blue squarish marks or entirely blue. Females during copulation and oviposition may replace blue markings with dull gray-brown.

Identification Several aspects of male coloration unusual among blue bluets. Blue streak on eyes otherwise brown above is unique, as other blue bluets have mostly blue eyes. Entirely black S10 is shared with **Turquoise** but no other blue bluet. Perhaps most like **Turquoise** but smaller, less elongate, and typically on ponds rather than streams. **Turquoise** has blue eyes, joined postocular spots, no black on sides of S2. Male **Slender Bluet** differs in same ways as **Turquoise** but also has narrow humeral stripes and more blue on abdomen base, and thorax looking overall bluer. Perhaps most like **Lilypad Forktail** in habitat and habits, as well as black body with blue thorax and abdomen tip, but **Lilypad** has mostly blue eyes, a black ring around blue abdomen base, and more blue on abdomen tip (a bit on both S7 and S10). Female **Skimming Bluet** differs from other similar-looking damselflies in its range with black abdomens in having pale markings only on top of S8. Closest might be young andromorph **Rambur's Forktail**, still with blue thorax, but in that species entire S8 is blue, not just top. Barely overlapping in range, female **Purple Bluet** also similar, rarely as bright

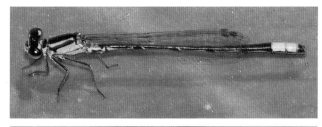

30
Skimming Bluet male—Ocean Co., NJ, June 2008; male—Richmond Co., GA, May 2006; female— Worcester Co., MA, June 2006

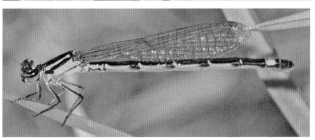

blue as **Skimming** and with antehumeral stripes broader than humeral (the reverse in **Skimming**).

Natural History Males perch on lilypads, algal mats, and emergent grasses and sedges and fly quickly from one perch to another, low over water as name indicates. Often hover over open water, unlike Lilypad Forktail. Pairs and solo females oviposit in floating debris and vegetation after lengthy copulation in shrubs away from water.

Habitat Lakes, ponds, and slow streams with clear water, usually with abundant beds of water lilies or other floating vegetation.

Flight Season ON May–Sep, QC Jun–Sep, IA May–Sep, WI May–Sep, ME Jun–Sep, OH May–Oct, NJ May–Oct, KY May–Sep, LA Mar–Aug, GA Mar–Nov, FL Feb–Oct.

Distribution West in plains to eastern Colorado.

Description Slender bluet of ponds with more blue on abdomen tip than in other species. Postocular spots very large, joining blue color on back of head. *Male*: Eyes blue, black cap reduced. Black and blue, thorax with moderate median stripe and narrow humeral stripe. Abdomen mostly black above with blue on sides of base and extensive at tip: S1 blue, S2 blue with black apical spot, S3 blue at base and on sides, S4–6 with narrow basal ring, S7–10 blue with black basal spot on S7, S10 with much black above. *Female*: Eyes black over brown; postocular spots yellowish to greenish. Body black and blue, no heteromorph. Thorax blue with wide median and relatively narrow humeral stripes, antehumeral stripe slightly wider than humeral. Abdomen mostly black above, conspicuously blue on sides of S1–3, entire base of S7 (with narrow black line down middle), and pair of basal spots on S8.

Identification Male distinguished by mostly black abdomen with long blue tip, including distal part of S7, and extensive blue at base as well. Other slender bluets with mostly black abdomen (**Pale, Skimming, Stream, Turquoise**) have less blue on base and only S8–9 at most blue at tip. **Attenuated Bluet**, with some blue on S7, has less blue at base and is distinctly longer. Female **Azure's** pattern of big blue spot on base of S7 unique in its range. Also note combination of greenish postocular spots with blue thorax.

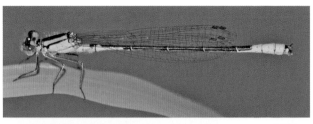

31
Azure Bluet
male—
Washington Co.,
MO, June 2009;
female—Walker
Co., GA, August
2005, Giff Beaton

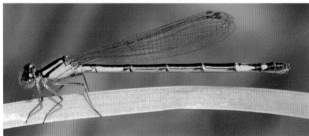

Natural History Males perch on edge vegetation and fly low over water. Copulation lasts 10–20 min. Pairs oviposit on surface vegetation. Some females climb down stem headfirst, released by male immediately. Submerged solo oviposition, sometimes rather deep, lasts 5–25 min. Blue colors in female turn gray during oviposition. Males remain nearby and seize females when they emerge, but females refuse to copulate again.

Habitat Ponds and lakes of all sizes with much emergent vegetation; may be especially common at small boggy ponds. Usually restricted to fishless waters, where it can be the only common bluet, and quick to colonize newly formed wetlands.

Flight Season ON Jun–Sep, QC Jul–Aug, NS Jun–Sep, IA May–Sep, WI May–Sep, ME Jun–Oct, OH May–Oct, NJ May–Oct, KY Apr–Oct, GA Apr–Sep.

Distribution Also slightly farther west in Oklahoma and Texas.

32 Big Bluet   *Enallagma durum*   TL 34–44, HW 17–25

Description Largest blue bluet in region, most common on large lakes and in coastal region. Postocular spots form very narrow transverse line. *Male*: Eyes blue with small black cap. Thorax typical of blue bluets but dorsal carina usually blue, bisecting wide black median stripe. Abdomen blue, with black markings a large apical spot on S2, apical spots (almost rings) on S3–6 narrowly pointed toward front, top of S7 except narrow basal ring, and top of S10. *Female*: Polymorphic, brown or blue. Eyes tan, darker above. Thorax as male, also with pale line dividing median stripe. Abdomen entirely black above with usual torpedo pattern on S3–7.

Identification Typical individuals larger than other bluets, distinctive because dark markings of middle abdominal segments more drawn out in long point toward front than in **Atlantic** and **Familiar**, only other largish mostly blue bluets in range and habitat (very little overlap with **Boreal**, **Northern**, and **Vernal** farther inland). Small percentage of individuals smaller and some with less black on abdomen, so capture and scrutiny of appendages in side view may be necessary for certainty. **Familiar** easily distinguished by long cerci equaling S10 in length (barely visible in **Big**). Female resembles females of numerous other bluets, perhaps separable by size and pale median carina of thorax. Otherwise, mesostigmal plates must be examined in hand. In **Big**, gap between plates narrower than plates; in **Atlantic** and **Familiar**, about the same width.

32
Big Bluet male,
female—Wakulla
Co., FL, July 2009

Natural History Males perch on grass and sedge in beds of same. Females oviposit under water, head down, while male guards above. Regularly takes other damselflies as prey.

Habitat Large sandy lakes and lower reaches of rivers, even extending into brackish estuaries. Occurs all across Florida Peninsula. Only common bluet at some large water bodies near coast.

Flight Season ME Jul–Aug, NJ May–Nov, LA Apr–Oct, FL Feb–Dec.

Distribution South on Gulf Coast of Mexico to Tamaulipas.

---

33 Alkali Bluet *Enallagma clausum*　　　　　　　　　　　　　　TL 28–37, HW 16–23

Description Large bluet characteristic of alkaline lakes but occurring in other habitats. Postocular spots large, forming dumbbell. *Male*: Eyes blue with black cap. Wide median and antehumeral, narrow humeral stripes. Abdomen with much black: subapical spot on S2 almost touching end of segment, apical markings reaching half length of segment on S3–5, more than half on S6 and four-fifths of S7, typically increasing regularly to rear; S8–9 blue, S10 black on top. *Female*: Polymorphic, orange-brown (may have greenish thorax) or blue. Eyes tan or pale greenish with brown cap. Median thoracic stripe usually split lengthwise by pale carina. Abdomen typical of blue bluets, S2 with anchor-shaped marking usually extending entire length of segment; torpedo markings of equal length on S3–7, with pale basal rings prominent, and S8 entirely pale (rarely with black middorsal line); black on S9–10 slightly reduced in comparison with other species.

Identification Male marked most like **River Bluet** in having S3–5 almost equally blue and black; **Boreal, Familiar, Northern,** and **Vernal** have less black, **Tule** more black. At close range in side view, male **Alkali** distinguished from **Familiar** and **River** by short cerci, from Boreal group (**Boreal, Northern,** and **Vernal**) by shorter, more curved paraprocts. Female

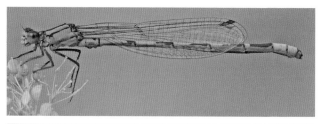

33
Alkali Bluet
male—Grant Co.,
WA, September
2008, Steven G.
Mlodinow; brown
female, blue
female—Grant
Co., WA, August
2008

has more pale color on abdomen than all others of this group, S8 entirely pale, and much pale color at base of all middle segments. Females of Boreal group usually with some black on S8, other female bluets with S8 entirely black above. Very narrow humeral stripe, often widened into dot near upper end as in some dancers, distinctive except from **River Bluet**, female of which usually has mostly dark S8. Of species in its range, only **River** female usually has median thoracic carina pale. In female **Alkali**, lower end of middorsal carina on thorax constricted and slightly elevated, unique among this group.

Natural History Males perch on lakeside rocks and grasses or fly over water; perching on bare ground more likely than in other bluets. Perhaps in absence of competition, reaches tremendous densities in preferred lakes, at least in West; sufficiently abundant in some areas to produce bluish cast to lake surface, even hundreds of tandem pairs visible at once. Females and pairs oviposit directly on floating alga mats and alga-covered rocks in lakes with no emergent vegetation, both at water surface and well beneath it, at least to a foot deep.

Habitat In West, occupies alkaline lakes and ponds, some of them too alkaline for any other odonates. Also may be at edge of large, slow-flowing rivers. Emergent vegetation present or not. Farther east, occurs in large lakes of more normal chemistry.

Flight Season ON Jun–Jul, IA Jun–Aug, WI Jul–Aug.

Distribution Widely through arid parts of West, from southern Canadian provinces south to southern Nevada and southern New Mexico.

34 Northern Bluet *Enallagma annexum* TL 29–40, HW 17–24

Description Typical mostly blue bluet that can be very abundant at northern latitudes. Postocular spots large, forming dumbbell. *Male*: Eyes black over blue. Thorax with wide median stripe and narrow humeral stripe. Black subapical, often crescent-shaped, bar on S2, black rings on S3–5, widest on S5; most of S6–7 black; S8–9 blue, S10 black above. *Female*: Polymorphic, either brown or blue. Eyes dark brown over light brown. Thorax as male. Abdomen mostly black above; pale basal rings on S3–8, brown or blue often more extensive on S8, at most may fill segment; S9–10 black.

Identification Not distinguishable from **Vernal Bluet** except with difficulty in hand (see that species); **Vernal** often in habitats with

34.1
Northern Bluet male—Okanogan Co., WA, June 2008, Netta Smith; blue female— King Co., WA, September 2008

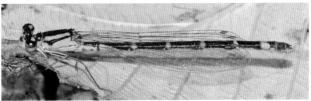

34.2
Northern Bluet pair with brown female—Okanogan Co., WA, July 2009

fish, **Northern** not so. Impossible to distinguish from **Boreal Bluet** except in hand (also possible with sharp close-range photos of appendages). With hand lens look at cerci from above; **Northern** has projection like little lip toward rear, **Boreal** has similar projection on inside of each cercus. Also looks much like **Familiar Bluet**, but that species has cerci longer than paraprocts, reverse of that in **Northern**, and black marking on S2 usually larger, touching rear of segment (separated from it in **Boreal** and **Northern** where they overlap in range with **Familiar**). Also very similar to **Alkali Bluet**, but most individuals have less black on S5. **Hagen's** and **Marsh Bluets** colored very similarly but smaller with, on average, smaller postocular spots, most noticeable when comparison possible and especially evident in females. In most (or all?) areas of overlap, bar on S2 in **Northern** distinguishes it from both smaller species, which have larger spot on that segment. Female much like female **Alkali** and **Boreal Bluets**, will have to be distinguished in hand by examination of mesostigmal plates. With hand lens, note that rear edge of mesostigmal plate well-defined in **Northern**, blends with rest of thorax in **Boreal**. Plates in **Alkali** more like **Northern**, but median carina strongly constricted near front end and pair of pits on top of prothorax. **Pine Barrens Bluet** also with pale base of S8, distinctly smaller. Females of other similar bluets lack pale color on top of S8.

Natural History Typical of bluets, males at water in large numbers, perched in all vegetation types, although more commonly at edges rather than inside dense stands, and flying over open water, forming blue haze over water where abundant. Mating usually takes place in sunny clearings near water, tandem pairs then flying to water. Copulation lasts 10–27 min. Pairs oviposit flat on floating vegetation, not up on emergents, and vascular plants preferred over algae. Much exploratory oviposition by pair, followed by period of actual egg laying in tandem. Pair eventually separates, and female moves below surface headfirst. Male remains guarding for some time but often gives up. Submerged oviposition up to 90 min.

Habitat Marshy and open lakes and ponds. Typically in fish-free water bodies in East, common in bog lakes.

Flight Season ON May–Sep, QC Jun–Aug, NS May–Oct, IA Jun–Aug, WI May–Aug, ME May–Aug, OH May–Jul, NJ May–Jul.

Distribution Throughout West, from far North to northern Baja California and southern New Mexico.

Comments Known in previous North American literature as *Enallagma cyathigerum*. That name is now considered to be restricted to the Eurasian species that looks much like *annexum* but is genetically distinct from it. Has hybridized with Vernal Bluet.

Bluets - male appendages 1

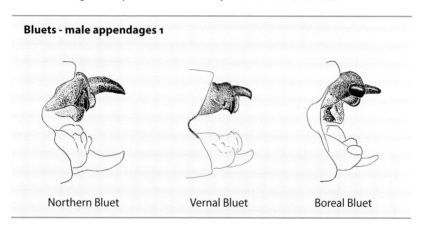

Northern Bluet   Vernal Bluet   Boreal Bluet

---

35 Vernal Bluet *Enallagma vernale* TL 30–34, HW 18–20

Description Locally distributed bluet almost identical to Northern. *Male*: Eyes black over blue. Thorax with wide median stripe and narrow humeral stripe. Black subapical, often crescent–shaped, bar on S2, black rings on S3–5, widest on S5; most of S6–7 black; S8–9 blue, S10 black above. *Female*: Polymorphic, either brown or blue. Eyes dark brown over light brown. Thorax as male. Abdomen mostly black above; pale basal rings on S3–8, brown or blue often more extensive on S8, at most may fill segment; S9–10 black.

Identification Cannot be distinguished from **Boreal** or **Northern Bluets** in field, not even with binoculars. Also very similar in color pattern to **Familiar**, **Marsh**, and **Hagen's Bluets**. In hand, virtually identical to **Northern**, differs in very fine details of male appendages. Each cercus has a knob at its distal end, and basal to that knob, male **Vernal** has a small black tooth bordering a tiny depression. These characters lacking in **Northern**, but either variation or hybridization produces intermediate individuals. Females not distinguishable, although some have S8 entirely black, very rare condition in **Boreal** and **Northern**. Many populations, however, contain only one of these species, and once sampled these can be given a name. See under Habitat.

35
Vernal Bluet
male—Coos Co.,
NH, June 2006;
blue female—
Windsor Co., VT,
Jun 2004, Michael
H. Blust

Natural History Behavior essentially like that of closely related Boreal and Northern Bluets.
Habitat Typically in lakes and slow streams, including boggy ones, often with fish. In the
range of Vernal, Boreal and Northern Bluets usually in boggy lakes and ponds without fish.
Flight Season ON May–Jul, QC May–Sep, NS May–Aug, WI May–Jun, ME May–Jun.
Distribution Also one record farther north in Ontario, near Hudson Bay (not mapped).
Comments Has hybridized with Northern Bluet.

36 Boreal Bluet *Enallagma boreale*　　　　　　　TL 28–36, HW 17–22

Description Typical mostly blue bluet, abundant at northern latitudes. Postocular spots large, forming dumbbell. *Male*: Eyes blue
with black cap. Thorax with wide median stripe and narrow humeral stripe. Abdomen with black subapical umbrella-shaped bar
on S2 (extends to end of segment in some), black rings on S3–5,
widest on S5; most of S6–7 black; S8–9 blue, S10 black above. *Female*: Polymorphic, either brown or blue. Eyes dark brown over
light brown. Thorax marked as in male. Abdomen mostly black
above; pale basal rings on S3–8, brown or blue usually more extensive on S8, at most may fill segment; S9–10 black.

Identification Indistinguishable from **Northern** and **Vernal Bluets** except by structural differences apparent with magnification (differences listed under **Northern**). **Boreal** and
Northern, occurring widely across North America, comprise a pair of species that in the
field will have to be lumped (they have been called "borthern" or "nobo" bluets). To survey
them where they are common, I usually catch 10 males and check their appendages. Also
very much like **Familiar Bluet**, with which it overlaps over a relatively small region; **Familiar** has cerci longer than paraprocts (reverse of that in **Boreal**), larger postocular spots, and
black marking on S2 larger, touching rear of segment. **Hagen's** and **Marsh Bluets**, more
likely to occur with **Boreal**, are slightly smaller, usually have slightly smaller postocular
spots, and also differ by larger size of black spot on S2. Male appendages also allow easy
distinction. **Boreal** also much like **Alkali Bluet**, but males have slightly less black on middle
abdominal segments. Occurs with **Tule Bluet** in some areas, males easily distinguished by
extent of black on middle segments and different appendages. Females differ from most
female bluets by having extensive pale color on S8; other species so colored (see **Alkali**
and **Northern**) will have to be distinguished in hand by examining mesostigmal plates.

36
Boreal Bluet
male   Coos Co.,
NH, June 2006;
brown female—
Apache Co., AZ,
July 2007; blue
female—Kittitas
Co., WA, August
2006

Natural History Males fly over open water and perch on emergent vegetation; can be at high densities. Pairs form at or away from water, sometimes abundant along open corridors in woodland. On average, copulation lasts 23 min, exploration for oviposition sites 11 min, surface oviposition 67 min, and underwater oviposition 23 min. Pairs oviposit in tandem. Mayflies and small flies common prey. Mean life expectancy of reproductive adults 4 days, maximum 17 days.

Habitat Ponds and lake margins with much emergent vegetation, including cold bog ponds and muskeg. Apparently restricted to fishless ponds in East, unlike situation in West.

Flight Season ON May–Sep, QC May–Aug, NS May–Sep, IA Jun–Jul, WI May–Aug, ME May–Aug, OH May–Jun, NJ May–Jul.

Distribution Throughout West, from far North south through much of California and Rocky Mountain uplands to Durango in Mexico.

---

37 New England Bluet *Enallagma laterale*   TL 25–28, HW 15–16

Description Small northeastern bluet with black marking on S8. Postocular spots relatively narrow, not connected to narrow occipital bar between them. *Male:* Eyes blue with black cap. Typical bluet thoracic stripes. Abdomen with black markings large apical spot on S2; elongate spots, pointed at front, on S3–5 becoming wider to rear; three-fourths of S6 and all of S7; and top of S10. Pair of elongate, irregular lateral black markings on S8. Rare dark individuals

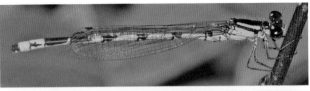

37
New England
Bluet male—
Merrimack Co.,
NH, June 2006;
female—Morris
Co., NJ, May 2005,
Allen Barlow

have more black on middle segments, black markings on S8 connected in U shape. *Female*: Pale green, bluish when immature. Eyes brown over tan. Thorax as in male. Abdomen almost entirely black above, markings narrowing slightly toward front of each segment.

Identification Males look almost identical to **Pine Barrens Bluet**, but black mark on S8 averages larger and always present, more likely to be conspicuous from a little distance. Typically **New England** has antehumeral stripe as wide as or wider than humeral, **Pine Barrens** has it narrower. Middle abdominal markings usually pointed in **New England**, usually notched in **Pine Barrens**; compare on S4–5. However, both species vary, and identification should always be checked in hand where they overlap. The terminal notch in side view of the cerci of **New England** is easily seen under low magnification. Bear in mind that dark mark on S8 occurs rarely in other bluets, including **Marsh** and **Hagen's**. The latter two species and **Atlantic** and **Familiar Bluets** have less black on middle abdominal segments than **New England** and usually wider antehumeral stripes, even up to 2× width of humeral. Male **Little Bluet** lacks black mark on S8 and is more purplish-blue. Female indistinguishable from **Hagen's**, **Little**, and **Marsh** except for mesostigmal plates; much like **Pine Barrens** but never with pale base of S8.

Natural History Many localities support only a single species of these small Atlantic-coast bluets, but they can be very common. Also easy to miss among large numbers of Hagen's Bluets that live in same habitats. Females seen ovipositing in sphagnum.

Habitat Clear, open sandy lakes with beds of shore and floating vegetation, often spring-fed and sphagnum bog-margined.

Flight Season ME Jun–Jul, NJ May–Jun.

38 Pine Barrens Bluet *Enallagma recurvatum* TL 26–29, HW 14–17

Description Small northeastern bluet often with black marking on S8. Postocular spots relatively narrow, usually no occipital bar between them. *Male*: Eyes bluish or greenish with black cap. Typical bluet thoracic stripes, but antehumeral stripe always narrower than humeral and sometimes constricted toward upper end. Abdomen with black markings including large apical spot on S2; rings, square-ended or notched at front, on S3–5 becoming wider to rear;  three-fourths of S6, four-fifths of S7, all of S8, and top of S10. Often pair of narrow irregular lateral black markings on S8. *Female*: Polymorphic, brown or blue, even pale greenish. Eyes brown over tan. Thorax as in male. Abdomen almost entirely black above, except S8 extensively pale at base, black marking pointed in front.

Identification Male most like **New England Bluet,** but dark mark on S8 usually less obvious, and antehumeral stripe as wide as humeral. Usually more black than blue on middle abdo-

38
Pine Barrens Bluet
male, female—
Ocean Co., NJ,
June 2008

men (**New England** almost always less black than blue on S4, **Pine Barrens** about half; **New England** half or less black on S5, **Pine Barrens** more than half). Middle abdominal markings may furnish field mark, usually pointed in front in **New England** and square or notched in **Pine Barrens**. But confirm in hand if there is any doubt. Note that dark mark on S8 occasionally occurs in **Hagen's** and **Marsh Bluets**, which also have less black on middle abdominal segments, as do **Atlantic** and **Familiar Bluets**. Female distinguished from all similar species by pale base of S8 (note that some of the larger mostly blue bluets are similarly marked).

Natural History Males common in dense shore vegetation, even over land near water; may shun open water at some locales. Abundant and only bluet at some lakes, shares others with Scarlet and Skimming Bluets.

Habitat Lakes and ponds, including bog ponds, with much shore vegetation.

Flight Season NJ May–Jun.

39 Little Bluet *Enallagma minusculum* TL 24–28, HW 14–16

Description Small northeastern bluet with purplish tinge. Postocular spots relatively narrow, usually no occipital bar between them. *Male*: Eyes greenish with dusky area above. Typical bluet thoracic stripes; top of thorax often more purplish-blue. Abdomen with black markings including large apical spot on S2 occupying half of segment and with prominent anterior corners, rings on S3–6 occupying half of S3 and becoming wider to rear, almost all of S7, and  almost all of S10. *Female*: Polymorphic, brown or blue. Eyes brown over tan or pale greenish. Thorax stripes as in male. Abdomen almost entirely black above, markings narrowing slightly toward front of each segment.

Identification Overlapping with several small (smaller than **Boreal** and **Familiar** types) bluets, male of this one distinguished from all by more purplish color, especially on thorax. Lacks black markings on S8 characteristic of **New England** and, to lesser degree, **Pine Barrens**. Individuals with less purplish cast easily mistaken for **Hagen's** or **Marsh**, which usually have less black on middle segments and large postocular spots connected by occipital bar. Also, black spot on S2 straight across in front and usually extended laterally in **Little**, rounded in other two. Female not distinguishable from most of these except by mesostigmal plates; **Pine Barrens** differs by having pale base of S8.

Natural History Males can be common in vegetation at lake edge. Oviposition in tandem in emergent and floating plants in shallow water.

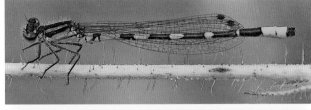

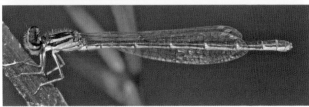

39
Little Bluet
male—Kings Co.,
NB, July 2006,
Denis Doucet;
female—
Barnstable Co.,
MA, July 2004,
Glenn Corbiere

Habitat Sandy lakes with wooded or shrubby shores, usually with beds of sedges, grasses, and/or water lilies.
Flight Season NS Jul–Aug, ME Jun–Aug.

40 Sandhill Bluet *Enallagma davisi* TL 28–32, HW 15–18

Description Small southeastern bluet with black marking on S8. Postocular spots relatively narrow, usually lacking occipital bar between them. *Male*: Eyes blue with black cap. Typical bluet thoracic stripes. Abdomen with black markings including large apical spot on S2, narrow rings on S3–4, then wider rings occupying almost half of S5, four-fifths of S6 and all of S7, and top of S10. Pair of elongate, irregular lateral black markings on S8. *Female*: Polymorphic, brown or blue. Eyes brown over tan. Thorax stripes as in male. Abdomen almost entirely black above, except S8 slightly to extensively pale at base, black marking pointed in front.

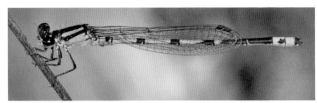

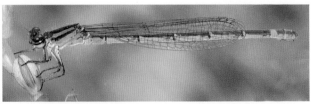

40
Sandhill Bluet
male—Richmond
Co., GA, May 2006;
brown
female—
Chesterfield Co.,
SC, May 2008;
blue female—
Richmond Co., GA,
May 2006

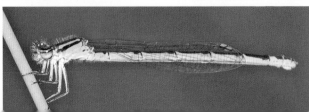

Identification No overlap with other small Atlantic coast bluets with black markings on male S8 (fortunately!). Most similar regional species **Atlantic** and **Familiar Bluets**, which are slightly larger and paler and lack those markings. Note occurrence of **Little Bluet**, also without black on S8, in nearby coastal lakes in North Carolina (no overlap in range known). Female **Sandhill** distinguished from **Little** as well as somewhat larger **Atlantic** and **Familiar Bluets** by pale base of S8.

Natural History Males perch on emergent grass and sedges at and near shore, flying over water relatively little. Both sexes feed in herbaceous vegetation away from water.

Habitat Sand-bottomed lakes with shore vegetation and open water.

Flight Season GA Mar–May, FL Jan–Apr.

41 Marsh Bluet *Enallagma ebrium* TL 28–34, HW 16–21

Description Small very common bluet of northern regions. Postocular spots large, forming dumbbell; rarely separated spots. *Male*: Eyes blue with black cap. Typical bluet thoracic stripes. Abdomen with black markings including large apical spot on S2, rings on S3–5 becoming slightly wider to rear, top of most of S6 and all of S7, and top of S10. Rarely with more black on middle abdominal segments. *Female*: Polymorphic, brown or blue. Eyes brown over tan or pale greenish. Thorax as in male. Abdomen entirely black above, with torpedo markings.

Identification Most like **Hagen's Bluet** in both sexes, not distinguishable except in hand, although difference in male cerci may be visible with close-focus binoculars. Male colored also like **Familiar**, **Boreal**, **Northern**, and **Vernal Bluets** with which it may occur, distinguishable by smaller size and, from last three species in much of area of overlap, by spot on S2 usually touching rear of segment. Capture and scrutiny of

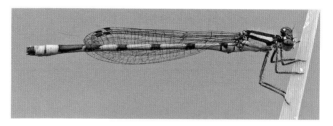

41.1
Marsh Bluet male—
Penobscot Co., ME,
June 2009, Bryan
Pfeiffer/Wings
Photography

41.2
Marsh Bluet blue female—
Pend Oreille Co., WA, August
2008, Jim Johnson

broader median and humeral stripes and narrower antehumeral stripes. Both also usually on still waters. Females of other stream bluets (**Blackwater, Stream, Turquoise**) have blue at abdomen tip.

Natural History Males perch at water level or up to a foot or more above it, often on flat leaves and usually rather inconspicuous because of dark coloration. Pairs may oviposit in floating detritus or plant rootlets just below surface. Like other stream bluets, density usually lower than those of ponds.

Habitat Small to medium streams with slow to swift current.

Flight Season GA Mar–Nov, FL all year.

Distribution Also in Cuba.

Comments Formerly combined with Antillean Bluet *Enallagma coecum* of the West Indies other than Cuba but now considered distinct species.

---

44 Stream Bluet *Enallagma exsulans*   **TL 31–37, HW 17–21**

Description Slender bluet of streams with mostly black abdomen and distinctly greenish tinge on head and thorax. Postocular spots form narrow dumbbell. *Male:* Eyes turquoise with black cap. Thorax greenish-blue with usual bluet stripes, humeral distinctly wider than antehumeral. S2–7 black above, S8 with black extending backwards in point almost full length of segment. Sides of S2–3 conspicuously blue or tinged with greenish; blue basal rings on S4–7; sides of S8 and S10 and all of S9 blue. *Female:* Polymorphic, either green or blue on thorax. Eyes greenish with black cap. Thorax as in male  but often pale middorsal carina; humeral stripe often divided lengthwise by brown stripe, losing distinctness of stripe in extreme cases. Abdomen black above, conspicuously greenish or blue on sides, S9–10 blue with pair of black basal spots or more extensive black basal triangle on S9. Rare darker individuals have almost all of top of S9 black, palest individuals with S8 blue at tip, S9–10 entirely blue.

Identification Other male bluets with abdomen mostly black above include **Azure, Skimming, Slender**, and **Turquoise**, last one most likely in habitat of **Stream**. **Turquoise** most similar but with more blue at abdomen tip and never greenish on head and thorax. **Slender** with narrow humeral stripes, also S8–9 entirely blue as in **Turquoise**. **Azure** with much more blue on thorax and abdomen base and **Skimming** smaller, again with S8–9 entirely blue. Female's greenish head, thorax, and abdomen base together with blue abdomen tip distinguish her from most other damselflies. However, see **Blackwater, Rainbow,** and **Turquoise Bluets**, with very similar females.

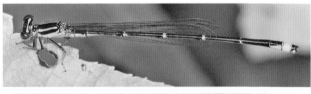

44
Stream Bluet
male—Talbot Co.,
GA, May 2006;
green female—
Holmes Co., OH,
July 2007

Natural History Males hover a foot over water of pools for long periods, then perch on stems of herbaceous plants growing in or extending over water. Pairs often common. Mating takes place at water or in nearby woodland. Copulation lengthy for bluet, lasting 55–119 min, then pair remains in tandem for some time after that before oviposition begins. Egg laying may begin before or after pair separates, and males may accompany females for part or all of oviposition, which can be completely underwater for 15–31 min. Water-willow is common substrate. Pairs and single females also oviposit at surface on beds of submergent vegetation.

Habitat Medium streams to large rivers with slow to moderate current, often with much water-willow. Also vegetated lake shores in northern part of range. Persists in degraded streams.

Flight Season ON Jun–Sep, QC Jun–Aug, NS Jun–Sep, IA May–Sep, WI Jun–Sep, ME Jun–Sep, OH May–Oct, NJ May–Sep, KY May–Sep, LA Apr–Sep, GA Apr–Sep.

Distribution West in southern plains states, south in eastern Mexico to Hidalgo.

45 Blackwater Bluet *Enallagma weewa* TL 30–39, HW 16–23

Description Very dark and slender bluet of southeastern streams. *Male*: Eyes medium brown over pale brown, head all dark. Thorax metallic black above, gray on sides. Abdomen black, gray on sides of S1–2; S9 blue. *Female*: Eyes as in male, horizontal striping evident; postocular spots very narrow. Polymorphic, thorax pale blue or brown, wide brown median and humeral stripes dark brown split by pale brown. Abdomen black above, paler on sides; S9–10 blue except black dorsal triangle on S9.

Identification Male unmistakable by very slender appearance, all dark coloration and blue S9. At a glance, might be mistaken for **Blue-tipped Dancer** of same streams, but behavior very different, and thoracic stripes should always be visible on dancer. Female quite similar to other two stream bluets in range, **Stream** and **Turquoise**, although a bit more slender. **Turquoise** female typically has more blue at abdomen tip, including on S8, and wider antehumeral stripes. **Stream** female often but not always green on thorax; black marking on S9 usually with two points, not one as in **Blackwater**.

Natural History Males perch on grass stems and other vegetation overhanging dark water; can be quite inconspicuous, sometimes only abdomen tip apparent. Also spend much time hovering for lengthy periods over water, a foot or so above surface, sometimes with abdomen bent downward near end. Females and immatures in nearby thickets. Pairs oviposit in

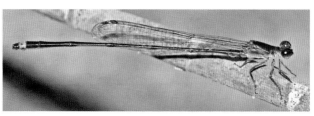

45
Blackwater Bluet
male—
Chesterfield Co.,
SC, May 2008, Jim
Johnson;
female—
Richmond Co., GA,
May 2006

tandem on floating vegetation at surface, or female may submerge alone. Female with abdomen tip bent down in pairs flying over stream. Seen to capture emerging gnats over stream in late afternoon.

Habitat Wooded streams with moderate current, usually with sand bottoms but dark, tannin-rich water. Sometimes at larger rivers and where streams flow through swamps.

Flight Season NJ Jun–Sep, LA Apr–Sep, GA May–Nov, FL Feb–Nov.

---

46 **Attenuated Bluet** *Enallagma daeckii*   TL 35–47, HW 19–25

Description Very long, slender bluet with scarcely any black on head, thorax, and abdomen tip. Postocular spots large, head almost entirely pale. *Male*: Eyes blue over green. Thorax with median and humeral stripes very narrow, at quick glance appearing all blue. Abdomen black above, blue on sides of S2 and base of S3, distal third of S7 and all of S8–10 blue. *Female*: Eyes tan, darker above, with two distinct brown lines encircling upper half. Thorax greenish, tinged with blue (blue in younger individuals). Abdomen black above, scarcely any basal rings evident; S9–10 blue.

Identification Size and slenderness set it off immediately. **Pale Bluet** most similar, distinctly smaller and with less or no blue on top of S7. **Slender Bluet** also smaller and only S8–9 black above. Female very much like female **Pale**, other than size best field mark may be conspicuous horizontal dark rings around eyes in this species. Also like female **Slender**, but latter with S8 largely blue. Might be mistaken for rather slender female **Furtive Forktail** of same habitat, latter slightly smaller and with front of thorax and tip of abdomen black.

Natural History Males perch in and fly through shrubby thickets and tall grasses, higher than most other damselflies and moving leisurely along with much hovering. Long abdomen in damselflies apparently facilitates hovering. Pairs in tandem move through grass and shrubs at same levels, impressively long as a pair, then drop to lower vegetation to oviposit. Pair backs down herbaceous stem, then male releases female and she may go well below surface.

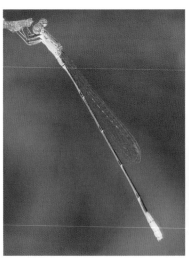

46
Attenuated Bluet male—Telfair Co., GA, May 2006;
female—Telfair Co., GA, April 2005, Giff Beaton

Habitat Shrubby borders of wooded sand-bottomed lakes and swamps. Always associated with woodland.

Flight Season NJ Jun–Aug, KY May–Jun, LA Apr–Jun, GA Apr–Jun, FL Apr–Sep.

47 Rainbow Bluet *Enallagma antennatum* TL 27–33, HW 15–21

Description Stream-dwelling bluet unmistakable because of orange face, greenish thorax, and blue abdomen. Postocular spots form narrow interrupted line. *Male*: Eyes orange in front, green behind, yellow below. Face orange, postocular spots blue. Thorax bluish-green, median and humeral stripes wide, antehumeral stripe quite narrow and yellowish or chartreuse; median stripe may be divided by pale line. Legs mostly yellowish. Abdomen black above, blue on sides of S1–3, light green on sides of S4–7, narrow blue basal rings on S3–7; black stripe on top of S8 narrows to rear, shows bright blue sides, S9 all blue, S10 black above. *Female*: Eyes brown above, yellow below. Thorax, legs, and sides of abdomen yellowish to yellow-green. Middorsal carina pale, humeral stripe usually with fine pale line dividing upper part. Abdomen black above with terminal blue rings on S7–8, much of S9–10 bluish and greenish.

Identification No other damselfly colored like male. Even with rear view, yellowish legs give it away. Could easily be mistaken for FORKTAIL because of greenish thorax and mostly black abdomen, but orange face and legs peg it as this species. Female much like female **Stream** and **Turquoise Bluets** but yellower, especially on face. Amount of blue at abdomen tip somewhat variable in these three species, but usually **Rainbow** has top of S9 mostly black, **Stream** and **Turquoise** mostly blue; pale line down center of S9 characteristic of **Rainbow** when present. Humeral stripe usually solid black in **Rainbow** except for fine pale line dividing upper half; **Stream** and **Turquoise** usually with humeral stripe divided by wide pale line or entirely brown. **Rainbow** has pale tubercle at mediodorsal corner of mesostigmal plates, not present in **Stream**. **Turquoise** usually has same tubercle dark, but some individuals have both carina and tubercle pale.

Natural History Males perch on stems at outer edge of vegetation at edges of pools. Pairs oviposit in grass at water surface; female reported to descend below surface.

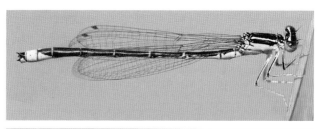

47
Rainbow Bluet
male—Rutland
Co., VT, June 2005,
Bryan Pfeiffer/
Wings
Photography;
female—Lanark
Co., ON, June
2008, Steven
Collins

Habitat Slow streams and rivers lined with beds of emergent vegetation, typically in open country. Also at ponds along stream courses.

Flight Season ON May–Aug, QC Jun–Aug, IA Jun–Sep, WI May–Aug, OH May–Sep, KY Jun–Aug.

Distribution West across plains, from southern Saskatchewan south to northern Texas.

---

48 Turquoise Bluet   *Enallagma divagans*   TL 27–36, HW 17–22

Description Slender bluet of streams with prominent blue abdomen tip. Postocular spots form narrow dumbbell. *Male*: Eyes blue with small black cap and horizontal dark stripe. Thorax typical bluet but with antehumeral and humeral stripes about same width. Abdomen black with blue on S1, sides of S2, and sides of base of S3; S8–9 entirely blue, S10 black (some individuals show blue low on sides). Some West Virginia males have much black on top of S8. *Female*: Eyes brown above, tan below. Thorax blue like male or blue mixed with dull greenish; humeral stripe all black or largely obscured by brown (most common). Some individuals with pale middorsal carina. Abdomen black above, blue along sides, variable blue at tip. S8 all black or with extensive blue tip; S9 all blue or with pair of basal black triangles; S10 all blue.

Identification Male most like **Stream Bluet** and often found in same habitat but lacks blue rings, and S8–9 all blue, whereas **Stream** has narrow but conspicuous blue rings on middle segments and black covering most or all of top of S8 (occasional **Turquoise** may show some black). Blue more often visible on sides of S10 in **Stream** than in **Turquoise**. **Turquoise** quite blue, but head and thorax of **Stream** either blue or light green. Also much like **Slender Bluet**, which differs in having more extensive blue coloration: larger postocular spots, narrower black humeral stripe, more blue at abdomen base. Female much like female **Stream Bluet**, but brown on humeral stripe when present covers most of stripe rather than dividing it lengthwise as in **Stream**. **Turquoise** commonly has tip of S8 blue, all black in **Stream** (but also some **Turquoise**). **Turquoise** female blue, never green as are many female **Stream Bluets**, and eyes usually brown (**Stream** with green to turquoise eyes). Postocular spots narrower in **Stream**, no more than 2× as wide as occipital bar, usually >2× as wide in **Turquoise**; difference not dramatic. Immature and many mature females probably distinguishable only by mesostigmal plates, those in **Stream** parallel-sided and with pit immediately behind them, **Turquoise** slightly more triangular, with no pit.

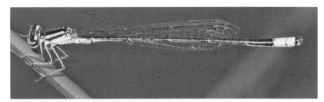

48
Turquoise Bluet
male—Taylor Co.,
GA, May 2006;
female—Santa
Rosa Co., FL, April
2008

Also like **Rainbow Bluet** but always more blue at abdomen tip. Immature females of orange bluet group (**Florida, Golden, Orange, Vesper**), with light blue thorax and blue abdomen tip, look much like female **Turquoise**, but all have less blue at abdomen tip, much black on top of S9.

Natural History Males perch low at stream margins or hover over water a few inches up for long times. Tandem pairs may be common in woody vegetation near water, then move to water to oviposit in submergent vegetation at surface. Female may back down stems by herself for up to 30 min, with male waiting above.

Habitat Small woodland streams with moderate current and swampy areas with slight current. Also wooded shores of large lakes and reservoirs, even ponds, in upland areas.

Flight Season ME Jun–Sep, OH May–Jul, NJ May–Aug, KY May–Jul, LA Mar–Jun, GA Mar–Jul, FL Mar–May.

49 Pale Bluet *Enallagma pallidum* — TL 30–36, HW 16–20

Description Slender southeastern bluet with much light blue on thorax and abdomen tip. *Male*: Eyes entirely blue, head blue with only narrow black stripe between eyes. Thorax light blue with quite narrow black median and humeral stripes. Abdomen black above, blue on S1, sides of S2, and all of S8–10. *Female*: Eyes light blue over tan; head mostly blue with fine black markings. Thorax light blue with narrow median and humeral stripes mostly tan with blackish edges. Abdomen black above, pale on sides. S8 blue with black basal triangle, S9–10 entirely blue.

Identification Extensive blue on tip distinguishes it from most other bluets with mostly black abdomens. **Attenuated Bluet** longer, as its name implies, and blue extends forward to tip of S7; also has even less conspicuous black markings on thorax. See that species for additional differences. **Slender, Stream,** and **Turquoise** all with black at extreme tip of abdomen. **Slender** most like **Pale** because of so much blue on head and thorax, so always check for wider median stripe and black on abdomen tip of **Slender**. Females of these two extremely similar, **Slender** often but not always with more conspicuous median stripe and black marking on S8 narrow, often pointed (broad rectangle in **Pale**).

Natural History Males and tandem pairs fly among and perch on shrubs. Tandem oviposition in stems at or just below water level.

Habitat Shrubby, swampy areas at the edge of ponds and lakes, sometimes slow streams.

Flight Season GA Apr–Jun, FL Apr–Aug.

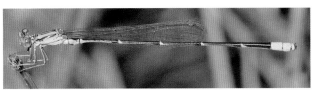

49
Pale Bluet
male—Tattnall
Co., GA, May 2006,
Marion M. Dobbs;
female—Tattnall
Co., GA, May 2005,
Giff Beaton

Description Slender bluet (of course!) of pond habitats with rather fine thoracic stripes. Postocular spots large, head largely pale with black lines dividing pale areas. More blue on prothorax than related species. *Male:* Eyes blue over blue-green, no black cap. Thorax with relatively limited black markings, median stripe only moderate width and, in southern populations, may be split lengthwise by pale stripe and so reduced as to be almost lacking; humeral stripe quite narrow. Abdomen black above, prominently blue on sides of S2–3 with full-length black mark on S2 somewhat buoy-shaped (becoming wider toward rear then suddenly contracted); narrow basal blue rings on S3–7, S8–9 blue, and S10 black above, blue below. *Female:* Eyes greenish or bluish over tan, rather finely striped. Thorax blue like male but dark stripes may be even more reduced, greenish-brown rather than black. Abdomen pale bluish on sides, black above; black marking on S2 as in male and blue basal rings and typical torpedos on S3–7; S8–10 all blue except black basal spot on S8 of variable size, pointed behind. Some females strongly greenish on thorax and all but tip of abdomen (polymorphic?).

Identification Limited black on thorax of male distinctive, somewhat like **Attenuated Bluet,** but that species in swamps and longer and more slender with more blue on abdomen tip, including part of S7. Similar **Pale Bluet** also in swamps, also entirely blue S10. **Turquoise Bluet** has darker head and eyes, wider humeral stripe, and no blue on S10. **Azure Bluet** has more black on head and much more blue at both base and tip of abdomen. Female also like **Azure,** but both sexes of **Slender** easily distinguished by narrow humeral stripe. Female **Pale Bluet** very similar; see that species.

Natural History Males perch in shore vegetation or fly and hover well out over water. Tandem pairs also hover for lengthy periods over water. Copulation lengthy and may be broken and resumed. Female oviposits in tandem with male supported in air or solo, at surface or submerged.

Habitat Lakes and ponds, open or with abundant vegetation.

Flight Season ON Jun–Aug, IA Jun–Aug, WI Jun–Jul, OH May–Oct, NJ May–Sep, KY Jun–Aug, LA Apr–May, GA May–Jul.

Comments Two subspecies listed in literature: *E. t. traviatum* east of Allegheny-Appalachian chain, then east of Mississippi River in South; *E. t. westfalli* west of that area. Males of western populations have distinctly thicker cerci, one of relatively few documented instances of geographic variation in appendage shape.

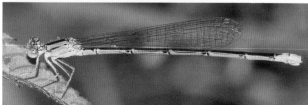

50
Slender Bluet
male—Richmond
Co., GA, May 2006;
female—Floyd
Co., GA, May 2006

Description Tiny bluet with doubled thoracic stripes. Postocular spots form narrow interrupted line, dashes at ends may be small, isolated. *Male:* Eyes blue. Both median and humeral stripes divided longitudinally into pair of narrow stripes. Abdomen with S1–2 with black stripe above, expanded subapically on S2; S3 with narrow black line ending in apical ring; S4–6 with apical ring sharply pointed at front; S7 mostly black above but also pointed in front; S8–9 entirely blue, S10 black above. *Female*: Eyes tan. Thorax tan with stripes  as in male. Black along top of all abdominal segments except S9–10 (sometimes tip of S8), which are blue. Sides of middle segments also blue, brighter toward rear.

Identification Besides very small size for bluet, doubled median and humeral stripes in both sexes unique among group, thorax looking finely instead of coarsely striped. Narrow black line on largely blue S3 also unique. Female distinctive among typical bluets in gradually becoming bluer toward rear, with tan head, thorax, and abdomen base but increasing blue on sides and then tip of abdomen. No DANCER colored exactly like this either. Male **Double-striped** a bit darker blue than **Familiar Bluet**, with which it often occurs.

Natural History Males and tandem pairs can be very common, almost swarming among beds of vegetation and flying well out over open water. Both spend much time hovering over open water, characteristic of species. Females oviposit in tandem or solo after being released by male, on floating sedges or submergent vegetation they can reach from surface. Females also descend underwater, breaking tandem before male is submerged and sometimes male hovering above.

Habitat Ponds, lake margins, and slow streams with much emergent vegetation.

Flight Season ON May–Sep, IA May–Sep, WI Jun–Aug, OH May–Oct, NJ May–Oct, KY May–Oct, LA Mar–Oct, GA Apr–Oct, FL May–Sep.

Distribution West in plains to eastern Colorado, farther south over to southeastern California, and south in Mexico to Baja California, Chihuahua, and Tamaulipas. Has increased dramatically in East in recent decades, pushing northward and eastward from original southwestern range.

51
Double-striped
Bluet male—
Floyd Co., GA, May
2006; female—
Yazoo Co., MS,
May 2005, Giff
Beaton

Description Bright orange-red and black southeastern pond damsel. Postocular spots narrow, forming continuous slightly curved stripe. *Male*: Eyes red. Thorax red, paler low on sides, with somewhat metallic-black median and humeral stripes and narrow stripe low on sides; antehumeral about same width as or slightly narrower than black stripes. Abdomen black to tip except S1–2 red  with large black apical spot on S2, also basal fifth of S3 and again

52
Cherry Bluet male—Lake
Co., FL, April 2008; female,
immature male—Leon
Co., FL, April 2005

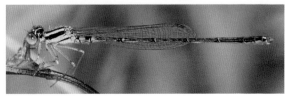

low on sides of S9–10; finally, very narrow basal ring (a bit paler orange) on S4–6. *Female*:
Eyes brown over lighter brown with horizontal stripes. Thorax pale orange with black
stripes like male, including lower side stripe. Abdomen shiny black above to tip, dull pale
orange on sides. Immatures greenish to yellowish to orange, like Burgundy but unlike Florida and Orange Bluets, in which they are blue.

Identification Nothing else much like it in range, which does not overlap with that of very
similar **Scarlet Bluet**. Most similar is **Burgundy Bluet**, which is a bit smaller and darker,
showing less red. The dark stripes look blue or purple in **Burgundy**, usually black (but
rarely purplish) in **Cherry**. Best mark is red on abdomen base in **Cherry**, not evident in **Burgundy**. Females very similar, but **Burgundy** a bit darker orange, with relatively narrower
antehumeral stripe and more conspicuous dark lateral stripe on thorax. Distinguished from
orange female **Florida** and **Orange Bluets** by lack of orange on top of abdomen tip.

Natural History Males commonly perch on lilypads as well as grasses and sedges. Usually in
more open situations than Burgundy Bluet. Become common at water late in day, like related species; may be absent in morning. Females in tandem pairs oviposit in grass stems or
on underside of lilypads.

Habitat Natural sand-bottomed ponds and lakes with abundant vegetation but plenty of
open water.

Flight Season LA Mar–Sep, GA Mar–Nov, FL Feb–Dec.

---

53 Scarlet Bluet *Enallagma pictum*   TL 30–34, HW 15–18

Description Bright red and black pond damsel of narrow Atlantic
coast belt. Postocular spots narrow, forming continuous slightly
curved stripe. *Male*: Eyes red. Thorax red, with black median and
humeral stripes and narrow stripe low on sides; antehumeral about
same width as or slightly narrower than black stripes. Abdomen
black to tip except S1 and sides of S2 and basal half of S3 red, sides
of S8–10 orange. *Female*: Eyes brown over lighter brown with hori-

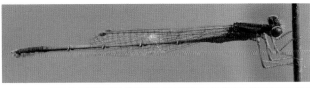
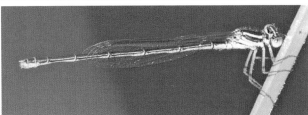

53
Scarlet Bluet
male—Burlington
Co., NJ, July 2009,
Allen Barlow;
female—Atlantic
Co., NJ, June 2008

zontal stripes. Thorax pale orange with black stripes like male, lower side stripe conspicuous. Abdomen black above to tip, dull pale orange on sides, extending slightly higher on S9–10.

Identification No other red and black damselfly like this one in its range; very different from **Eastern Red Damsel**. Female almost identical to female **Orange Bluet**, but abdomen black above to tip, lacking orange tip of **Orange**. Antehumeral stripe narrower than humeral in **Scarlet**, broader in **Orange**. Note bright orange female **Lilypad Forktail** superficially similar and in same habitat but with orange abdomen tip.

Natural History Active throughout day but males hang in shade of leaning sedge stems during hot midday. Most perch on sedge stems but also on lilypads. Tandem pairs in afternoon.

Habitat Sand-bottomed lakes and ponds with clear open water, often surrounded by narrow belt of emergent sedges and grasses and with much floating vegetation. Pine Barrens of New Jersey stronghold of largest populations.

Flight Season ME Jul–Aug, NJ May–Sep.

54 Burgundy Bluet *Enallagma dubium* TL 25–30, HW 12–17

Description Black and red bluet with purple thoracic stripes. Post-ocular spots form narrow, slightly curved, transverse line. *Male*: Eyes red, purplish above. Thorax red with purple-black stripes, both median and humeral wide; narrow dark stripe on sides of thorax as well. Abdomen black with red-purple gloss at base and tip, orange to red-orange low on sides of S1–3 and S7–10. *Female*: Eyes orange above, yellowish below. Thorax marked as male but pale  color orange instead of red. Abdomen entirely black above, dull pale orange on sides. Immature with pale colors pale greenish.

Identification Only really similar species in Southeast is **Cherry Bluet**; see that species. Not known to overlap with **Scarlet Bluet** farther north. Female rather like female **Orange Bluet** but smaller, with much wider humeral stripe with metallic overtones and no orange at abdomen tip. **Citrine**, **Furtive**, and **Rambur's Forktails** with bright orange thorax show no thoracic stripes.

Natural History Males perch in dense grass or on floating leaves (often water lilies) or fly for extended periods over open water; very difficult to see over dark water. Pairs copulate in shrubs, then oviposit in tandem on water lilies (often on underside through hole in leaf) and other floating vegetation. One oviposition bout may take up to 30 min.

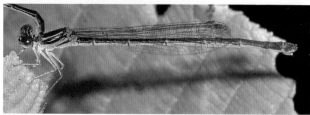

54
Burgundy Bluet
male—
Chesterfield Co.,
SC, May 2008, Jim
Johnson;
female—
Chesterfield Co.,
SC, May 2008

Habitat Sandy ponds with abundant shore vegetation, usually dense grass, and/or beds of floating vegetation, especially water lilies. In open or surrounded by swamp or forest. Also at slow streams edged by herbaceous vegetation.
Flight Season LA Apr–Sep, GA Mar–Sep, FL Mar–Sep.

55 Orange Bluet *Enallagma signatum* TL 28–37, HW 15–21

Description Slender orange bluet with orange abdomen tip. Postocular spots form transverse line. *Male:* Eyes orange. Thorax orange with moderately wide black median and humeral stripes, pale antehumeral about as wide as humeral. Abdomen mostly black with orange sides of S1–2, very narrow basal rings on S3–7, low on sides of S8, all of S9, and sides of S10. *Female:* Polymorphic, may be orange, duller than male; blue (perhaps only younger individuals); or greenish. Eyes brown over greenish or tan. Thoracic stripes as in male, humeral a bit narrower. Abdomen black above, most of S9 and all of S10 pale. Immature of both sexes with pale colors pale blue, gradually turns orange.

Identification Both sexes look just like closely related **Florida Bluet**. Male differs only in shape of cerci, slightly longer than S10 in **Orange** and shorter in **Florida**. Male somewhat like male **Vesper Bluet** but orange instead of yellow and blue. Obviously orange in contrast with the distinctly red **Cherry** and **Scarlet Bluets**. Female **Vesper Bluet** has much narrower humeral stripe (see that species for more information). Female **Burgundy, Cherry,** and **Scarlet Bluets** have much wider humeral stripe and no pale color on tip of abdomen. See **Florida Bluet** for difficult distinction from that species. Blue female also like female **Turquoise Bluet** but less pale color at abdomen tip and no brown in humeral stripe. When faced with puzzling individual, recall that immature **Orange Bluet** of both sexes can be fairly bright blue, and immature female can have brown humeral stripe and look very much like female **Stream Bluet**. Antehumeral stripe usually wider than median stripe in **Orange**, narrower in bona fide blue species.

Natural History Away from water, may be up in trees. Males and pairs in tandem usually at outer edge of grass and sedge beds, fly well out over open water when disturbed. Also common where water lilies cover surface. Although at times seen earlier, most common at water later in day, with late afternoon peak and activity at least until dark, averaging not quite as late as Vesper Bluet. Good example of a species for which midday surveys may be

55
Orange Bluet
male—Cameron
Co., TX, October
2004, Greg Lasley;
female—Warren
Co., GA, April
2005, Giff Beaton;
immature
male—McCurtain
Co., OK,
September 2008,
David Arbour

inadequate, although mating has been observed as early as midday. Often become more common at water when clouds obscure sun. Pairs oviposit in water lilies and floating grass and on algal mats; female or even pair may submerge completely for 10–20 min. May take 12 days to mature, reproductive life as long as 3 weeks.

Habitat Lakes, ponds, and slow streams, quite broad habitat choice. Tolerates polluted situations.

Flight Season ON Jun–Oct, QC Jun–Aug, NS Jul–Aug, IA May–Oct, WI May–Aug, ME Jun–Sep, OH May–Oct, NJ May–Oct, KY Apr–Sep, LA Feb–Nov, GA Mar–Nov, FL all year.

Distribution West across plains to eastern Colorado and south in Mexico to Tamaulipas.

56 Florida Bluet *Enallagma pollutum*   TL 28–37, HW 14–19

Description Slender orange bluet with orange abdomen tip, almost restricted to Florida. Postocular spots form transverse line. *Male*: Eyes orange. Thorax orange with moderately wide black median and humeral stripes, pale antehumeral about as wide as humeral. Abdomen mostly black with orange sides of S1–2, very narrow basal rings on S3–7, low on sides of S8, all of S9, and sides of S10. *Female*: Polymorphic, may be orange, duller than male, or blue (perhaps only younger individuals). Eyes brown over greenish or tan. Thoracic stripes as in male, humeral a bit narrower. Abdomen black above, most of S9 and all of S10 pale. Immature of both sexes with pale colors pale blue, gradually turns orange.

Identification Only other very similar species **Orange Bluet**, found through range of **Florida**, although absent from extreme southern Florida. Only **Florida Bluet** found south of Tamiami Trail. Male **Orange** has longer cerci, clearly longer than S10; about length of S10 or slightly shorter in **Florida**, without long tip. Male **Orange** typically has tiny orange spot in

Pond Damsel Family   **117**

56
Florida Bluet male—
Broward Co., FL,
February 2009, J.
Lubchansky; female—
Collier Co., FL,
December 2007;
immature male—Palm
Beach Co., FL, February
2009, J. Lubchansky

center of prothorax, lacking in **Florida**. Females even more similar, but **Orange** typically has less black on S9, triangle rather than rectangle. Overlap makes this less than definitive. Both have pair of pits on middle lobe of prothorax. In **Florida**, they are about at midlength, with most of adjacent pale spot in front of pit. In **Orange**, they are farther forward, with most of pale spot behind pit. **Orange** seems more likely to have green female than **Florida**, but this needs further checking. Don't be fooled by blue immatures of either species. See **Orange Bluet** for differences from other similar species.

Natural History Males and pairs in tandem fly over open water and perch in grasses and sedges and flat on lilypads. More common at water later in day and under clouds, pairs active until virtually dark. Oviposition in tandem or alone, on plant stems or floating algal mats and starting at water surface. Female may submerge tip of abdomen and head and thorax, leaving wings exposed (as a conduit to the air?), or go entirely below surface down to about 2 inches, remaining for 3 min or more. Deposits few eggs (32 in one instance) in stem, then moves to nearby stems and repeats one after another, all with male attached.

Habitat Open ponds, lakes, and slow streams and canals, occurring almost anywhere a bluet might be found in peninsular Florida.

Flight Season FL all year.

Description Slender bluet with yellow thorax and restricted blue abdomen tip, active in evening. Postocular spots narrow dumbbell or transverse line. *Male:* Eyes yellow, more orange above. Thorax yellow with narrow dark brown median stripe, sometimes with pale carina, and quite narrow brown humeral stripe. Abdomen black above, sides of S2–3 bright yellow and narrow pale yellowish basal ring on S3–7; S9 all blue, S10 black above, blue below. *Female:* Eyes orange-brown over yellow. Surprisingly variable and probably

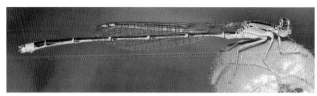

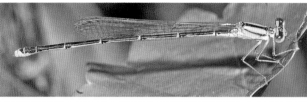

57
Vesper Bluet
male—Richmond
Co., GA, May 2006;
female—Lake Co.,
FL, April 2008;
immature
female—
Richmond Co., GA,
May 2006

polymorphic, thorax usually greenish to pale turquoise but can be yellow to orange; perhaps geographic variation also involved. Abdomen black above except sides of S9 and all of S10 either blue as in male or more rarely yellow-orange; this variation may not be in all populations. Immature of both sexes with pale colors light blue.

Identification Combination of yellow-orange thorax and blue abdomen tip makes male and blue-tipped female unique in region except for very similar **Golden Bluet** often found in same habitat. **Golden** distinguished by broad black thoracic stripes in both sexes. Orange-tipped female like **Florida** and **Orange Bluets**, as are immatures of both sexes, but **Vesper** has narrower humeral stripe. At close range, it can be seen that **Vesper's** antehumeral stripe pale to lower end, where it ends at mesostigmal plate, whereas that of **Orange** narrowly but clearly bordered by black at lower end (also the case in **Florida** and **Golden**). Both species have pair of pits on top of prothorax where male paraprocts contact female; those in **Vesper** right in middle, those in **Orange** a bit closer to front (**Florida** and **Golden** like **Vesper**). Immature females also look much like female **Turquoise Bluet**, although they only rarely occur together; **Vesper's** narrow humeral stripe, never interrupted by brown, again furnishes distinction. **Turquoise** also has more blue on tip, involving S8 as well as S9–10.

Natural History Spends most of day in vegetation, even up in trees, not far from water. Activity of males at water starts in midafternoon and can peak after sunset, later than most other damselflies are flying. Males perch on low vegetation at water, much attracted to lilypads; also commonly fly out over open water. Pairing and oviposition peak still later, and tandem pairs and single females may continue to oviposit when completely dark. Females may mate while still in immature color.

Habitat Typically lakes with much emergent vegetation, usually where woodland available at or near shore.

Flight Season ON Jun–Sep, QC Jun–Aug, NS Jun–Aug, IA Jun–Oct, WI May–Sep, ME Jun–Sep, OH May–Sep, NJ May–Sep, KY May–Jul, LA Apr–Aug, GA Mar–Nov, FL Feb–Nov.

Distribution Sparsely in southern plains, west to eastern Colorado.

58 Golden Bluet *Enallagma sulcatum* TL 28–36, HW 14–18

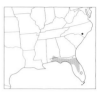

Description Distinctive Florida bluet with orange thorax, blue-tipped abdomen. Postocular spots form narrow, slightly curved line. *Male*: Eyes orange, blackish on extreme top. Thorax orange with broad median and humeral stripes, narrow lower side stripe; antehumeral narrower than humeral. Abdomen black above; sides of S1–2 orange, S9 and sides of S10 blue. *Female*: Colored much like male, but eyes brown above, dull orange below. Abdomen black, orange on sides of S1–2, S10 entirely blue. Immatures with postocular spots and thorax blue to greenish instead of orange.

Identification Only damselfly similar to mature individuals of either sex is **Vesper Bluet**, identically colored but with narrower black thoracic stripes (some northern **Vesper**, outside range of **Golden**, have wider median stripes). Both are common at some Florida lakes. Blue immature males distinguished from **Florida** and **Orange Bluets** by shape of cerci, shorter and square-ended. Blue immature females (or orange-tipped mature females if they exist) should be distinguishable from immature **Florida** and **Orange** by all black S9. Also female **Golden** has pit behind each mesostigmal plate, lacking in other species.

Natural History Males and pairs perch in grass beds and fly out over water, well into evening like related species; also on lilypads. Can be very abundant. More active during day than Vesper Bluets, mating seen at least as early as midday.

Habitat Sand-bottomed lakes with beds of shore vegetation, both grasses and water lilies, and open water.

Flight Season FL Feb–Nov.

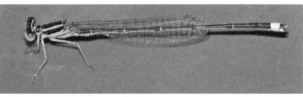

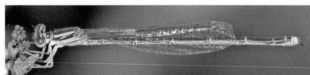

58
Golden Bluet
male, female—
Lake Co., FL, April
2008

Bluets - male appendages 2

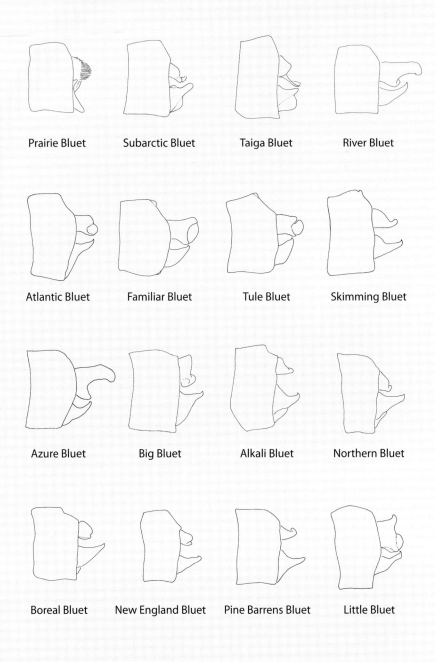

Prairie Bluet

Subarctic Bluet

Taiga Bluet

River Bluet

Atlantic Bluet

Familiar Bluet

Tule Bluet

Skimming Bluet

Azure Bluet

Big Bluet

Alkali Bluet

Northern Bluet

Boreal Bluet

New England Bluet

Pine Barrens Bluet

Little Bluet

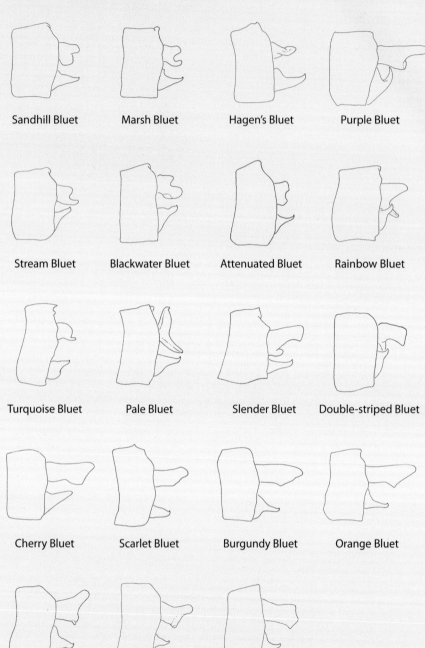

Sandhill Bluet Marsh Bluet Hagen's Bluet Purple Bluet

Stream Bluet Blackwater Bluet Attenuated Bluet Rainbow Bluet

Turquoise Bluet Pale Bluet Slender Bluet Double-striped Bluet

Cherry Bluet Scarlet Bluet Burgundy Bluet Orange Bluet

Florida Bluet Vesper Bluet Golden Bluet

Bluets and Yellowface - female mesostigmal plates

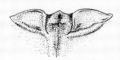

Prairie Bluet

Subarctic Bluet

Taiga Bluet

River Bluet

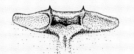

Atlantic Bluet

Familiar Bluet

Tule Bluet

Skimming Bluet

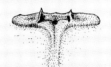

Azure Bluet

Big Bluet

Alkali Bluet

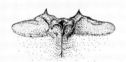

Northern Bluet

Vernal Bluet

Boreal Bluet

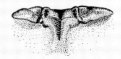

New England Bluet

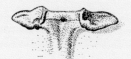

Pine Barrens Bluet

Little Bluet

Sandhill Bluet

Marsh Bluet

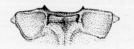

Hagen's Bluet

Purple Bluet

Stream Bluet

Blackwater Bluet

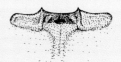

Attenuated Bluet

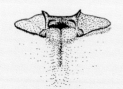

Rainbow Bluet

Turquoise Bluet

Pale Bluet

Bluets and Yellowface - female mesostigmal plates, *(continued)*

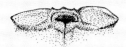

Slender Bluet

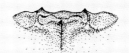

Double-striped Bluet

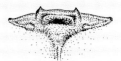

Cherry Bluet

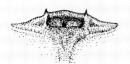

Scarlet Bluet

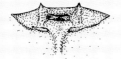

Burgundy Bluet.tif

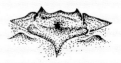

Orange Bluet

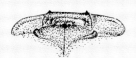

Florida Bluet

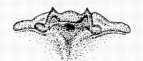

Vesper Bluet

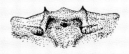

Golden Bluet

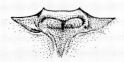

Caribbean Yellowface

This genus has two very similar species, the other one in western Mexico. They are much like *Enallagma* bluets and presumably are related to them, but the yellow face of males easily distinguishes them. The very long cerci are longer than in most bluets and conspicuous at close range. World 2, NA 1, East 1.

59 Caribbean Yellowface *Neoerythromma cultellatum* TL 27–31, HW 13–16

Description Mostly black-bodied bluet-like pond damsel with bright yellow face. Postocular spots large, not quite connected by narrow bar that itself can be divided in middle. *Male*: Eyes yellow in front, black above, greenish below. Black humeral stripe broad, antehumeral stripe about as broad, usually yellow-green but may be blue; sides of thorax blue. Most individuals have prominent narrow black side stripe and short stripe ending in spot between it and humeral stripe. Abdomen black, with blue S1–2, basal rings on S3–6, posterior sides of S7, and S8–9. Black V-shaped mark covers much of top of S2, and S10—unlike many bluets—entirely black. *Female*: Face dull greenish. Eyes brown over greenish-tan. Thorax as male but antehumeral stripe blue or pale colors of thorax pale green (perhaps polymorphic). Abdomen black above, extensive blue to blue-green on sides of S1–2, less extensive on S3–7, and extending over base as narrow ring; S8 blue with large black subapical spot or black with blue basal ring, S9 blue with black basal spot or black with blue only low on sides, S10 entirely blue.

Identification No other eastern damselfly blue and black with bright yellow face. Very long cerci of male also distinctive. Females much like some species of BLUETS but show more obvious black stripe on sides of thorax, together with small spot there, also mixture of blue and black on S8–9 different from any other. No trace of dark horizontal line around eye typical of BLUETS. Fortunately overlaps in range with no blue BLUETS, which are almost absent from tropical lowlands. Female **Purple Bluet** might be seen with it, but that has pale color only on top of S8, **Yellowface** on last three segments. Blue immature female **Florida Bluet** has blue only on top of S10. Most commonly co-occurring damselfly usually **Rambur's Forktail**.

Natural History Often rests flat on lilypads but also perches on emergent grasses and sedges at outer edge of vegetation. Associated with open water rather than dense vegetation. Commonly flies out over open water, much like many bluets, and stays just above surface. Pairs and single females oviposit on floating or emergent vegetation (often stone-

59
Caribbean
Yellowface
male—Laguna
Tortuguero,
Puerto Rico,
March 2009, Netta
Smith; female—
Limón Province,
Costa Rica, March
2006, William A.
Haber

wort where it occurs) at water surface, often laying eggs in semicircle under floating leaves. Male elevated during egg laying.

Habitat Large open ponds or canals, usually with narrow band of grasses or sedges at shore, much less commonly ponds fairly densely vegetated with floating vegetation. Often near coast, may breed in slightly brackish water.

Flight Season FL Feb–Dec.

Distribution Also in Greater Antilles and from south Texas south in lowlands to Venezuela.

Forktails   *Ischnura*

Forktails are very small to small damselflies of worldwide distribution, including many oceanic islands. Often in dense vegetation, a few species also fly over open water. "Forktail" refers to a forked projection at end of S10 in males of most species. Eyes in mature individuals appear to have a dark cap, with horizontal stripes often but not always evident below it and usually lacking in fully mature individuals. Males typically have blue-tipped black abdomen, an easy distinction from the bluets and dancers that have mostly blue abdomens, but some species of both of those groups have patterns somewhat like forktails. Dark abdominal markings usually parallel-sided, covering top of abdomen, unlike many bluets in which black markings on middle abdominal segments narrow and pointed in front. The combination of green thorax and blue-tipped abdomen is mostly typical of forktails. Females of many species are polymorphic, heteromorphs orange at first and then becoming dark or pruinose and andromorphs brightly colored like male; heteromorphs always more common. Forktails tend to stay near water even when immature, unlike most other damselflies. Copulating pairs are frequently seen in some species, infrequently in others; the sightings presumably are correlated with length of copulation, which varies greatly in forktails. Oviposition is usually into plant tissues at and just below water surface, and not in tandem in any eastern forktails, unlike most other pond damsels. This is probably because the sexes are at water together, and females have effective ways of discouraging male attention, so male contact guarding is unnecessary. Males of four species—Citrine, Fragile, Furtive, and Lilypad—are very distinctive among forktails and among all coexisting damselflies. However, some females are very similar and might be identifiable only in the hand. World 69, NA 14, East 6.

60 Lilypad Forktail   *Ischnura kellicotti*   TL 24–31, HW 12–18

Description Medium-sized brightly colored forktail inextricably linked to water lilies. *Male*: Eyes dark blue with large black cap. Postocular spots large, blue. Thorax blue with wide median and humeral stripes. Abdomen black, bright blue on S1, much of S2, tip of S7, and much of S8–10. *Female*: Eyes green with black cap; postocular spots blue. Thorax and abdomen base as male, abdomen tip with less blue (top of S8–10). Increasingly pruinose with age, pattern more difficult to make out, but blue thorax and abdomen tip still evident. Immature female patterned as mature female but all  pale areas bright orange; intermediates rarely seen. Change from orange to blue with age quite unusual among odonates. Also noteworthy is wing-color change in both sexes, from bright amber in just-emerged individuals to clear as in most damselflies, with blue upper surface of forewing stigmas in male.

Identification Very distinctive species, most likely to be mistaken for co-occurring **Skimming Bluet**. **Lilypad** differs from **Skimming** by bright blue eyes (mostly brown in **Skimming**), larger postocular spots, and blue on top of S10. Note that blue on S2 crosses rear part of segment in **Lilypad**, only front part in **Skimming**. Orange or heavily pruinose females might be mistaken for immature or mature female **Eastern Forktail**, respectively, but orange abdomen tip or blue thorax rather than white or gray makes for easy distinc-

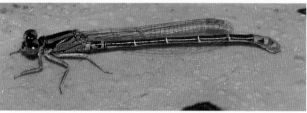
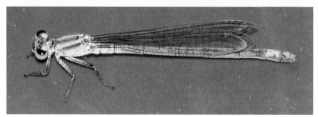

60
Lilypad Forktail
male, orange
female—Evans
Co., GA, May 2006;
blue female—
Atlantic Co., NJ,
June 2008

tion. Then there is typical **Lilypad Forktail** behavior; **Eastern** rarely rests on lilypads (but may do so). Note possibility of confusing orange females with male **Cherry** or **Scarlet Bluets**, which have much less orange on abdomen tip.

Natural History Both sexes common in breeding habitat; almost invariably perch flat on lilypads, with abdomen curled down near end to touch leaf (for support? predator detection?). Flight rapid and low between perches, streaking rather than fluttering; perhaps better flight for coping with wind or avoiding predation. Both orange and blue females mate, but mating seldom seen, so perhaps female mates only once. Copulation lasts about 20 min. Larvae live under water-lily leaves. Few odonates so closely tied to a single type of plant.

Habitat Ponds and lakes with extensive beds of water lilies of any species, including water shield.

Flight Season ON Jul–Sep, ME Jun–Aug, OH Jun–Jul, NJ May–Sep, LA Mar–Sep, GA Mar–Nov, FL Feb–Dec.

---

61 Furtive Forktail *Ischnura prognata*   TL 30–37, HW 14–20

Description Long, slender forktail of southern swamps. *Male*: Eyes green, tiny postocular spots blue, thorax green with black stripes, abdomen black above, yellowish on sides; S9 blue. *Female*: Immature with eyes dull orange; face, postocular spots, thorax except thin black midline, and S1–3 bright orange; rest of abdomen black above. With maturity, eyes green, head and front of thorax dull metallic brownish, sides of thorax pale, whitish to greenish or bluish. Often a small dark triangle on sides of thorax at wing base just behind dark median stripe. Abdomen black above with varying amounts of gray pruinosity.

61
Furtive Forktail
male—Floyd Co.,
GA, May 2006;
immature
female—Glynn
Co., GA, April
2008, Giff Beaton;
female—
Chattooga Co.,
GA, May 2005,
Marion M. Dobbs

Identification Only forktail so long and slender. If size and shape not sufficient, presence of blue only on S9 is a good mark for males (**Rambur's** has blue on S8 also). Mature females distinguished from other dark species with at least some abdominal pruinosity (**Citrine**, **Eastern**, **Fragile**) by often pale bluish or greenish sides (others are usually gray to white), stigmas graded from dark proximally to light distally (others all dark). Dull-colored mature female **Rambur's** also looks like **Furtive** but less elongate, rarely if ever overlap in habitat. **Rambur's** typically has pale postocular spots; **Furtive** lacks them. Immature females colored much like immature female **Citrine** but much larger; also **Citrine** shows much more orange on abdomen, S1–5 and S9–10. Immature female **Rambur's** has less orange, usually only on S1–2 (S1–3 in **Furtive**). Long, slender **Attenuated** and **Pale Bluets** of same habitat show much more blue in both sexes. In far southern Florida, see **Lucifer Swampdamsel**.

Natural History Both sexes, mature and immature, usually present together in preferred habitat; apparently do not wander away from water; and never move into open habitats. Move slowly through dense beds of vegetation in flight, even up into lower tree branches; long abdomen probably adaptation to hovering. Females oviposit alone.

Habitat Swamps and swampy borders of slow streams, always under canopy. Usually associated with dense growth of herbaceous plants such as tall grasses, water smartweed, and lizard's tail.

Flight Season OH Apr–May, LA Feb–Sep, GA Feb–Dec, FL all year.

---

62 Rambur's Forktail *Ischnura ramburii*   TL 27–36, HW 15–19

Description Large, brightly marked southern and coastal forktail. *Male*: Eyes green with black cap, tiny postocular spots blue. Thorax green with wide median and humeral stripes; antehumeral stripe narrow, rarely broken. Abdomen shiny black above, golden on sides; S8 blue, S9–10 black above, blue on sides. Populations at far western edge of U.S. range and farther south in tropics with all of S9 blue also. *Female*: Polymorphic. Heteromorph with postocular spots, thorax, and S1–2 bright orange with black midline, abdomen

62.1
Rambur's Forktail
male—Suwanee
Co., FL, April 2008;
andromorph
female—Monroe
Co., FL, December
2007

62.2
Rambur's Forktail
immature
heteromorph
female—Clay Co.,
FL, June 2004;
heteromorph
female—Dade
Co., FL, January
2006, Giff Beaton

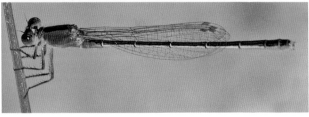

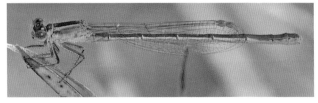

otherwise entirely black above, pale greenish on sides of S3–7 and orange on sides of S8–10. Thorax becoming duller and eventually orangey-brown to greenish-brown with maturity, with faint paler antehumeral stripe; sides of abdomen pale tan throughout. At least some females with conspicuous blue-green postocular spots, may be lost with further maturation. Andromorph colored just like male, also varying geographically, with blue thorax when immature.

Identification Males and andromorph females easily distinguished from all other damselflies in range by large size (for a forktail) and blue S8 and sides of S9. Other forktails in range with green, striped thorax and blue abdomen tip are smaller and have S8–9 blue, S8 with black stripe on side (**Eastern**), or longer and more slender with S9 blue (**Furtive**). **Lilypad Forktail** and several bluets superficially similar, but all with blue thorax. Immature andromorph female **Rambur's** also with blue thorax, but no others with abdomen tip similarly colored. See also female **Furtive Forktail**.

Natural History Both sexes at or near water most of time. Where common, large sleeping aggregations have been found at waterside. Males and sometimes mating pairs can be very common in preferred habitats, often more out in open than other forktails, at edge of vegetation beds. Both female morphs commonly seen in pairs, orange immatures less commonly. Copulation very lengthy, averaging 200 min and up to almost 7 hr, majority occurring in afternoon. Females of copulating pairs typically grab substrate, unlike most pond damsels but apparently characteristic of at least some forktails. Abdomen has to be very flexible to do this. Oviposition solo, mostly in late afternoon, in floating leaves, stems, and debris, sometimes with tip of abdomen submerged. May spend minutes perched in one spot moving only tip of abdomen to deposit eggs. Regular predator, females especially, on other small damselflies (including their own species); mostly tenerals but some older.

Habitat Occurs in great variety of habitats in lowland range—lakes, ponds, marshes, ditches, even brackish waters, as long as some shore vegetation such as grasses and sedges present. Especially common near coast and but not known to breed in full salt water.

Flight Season ME Jul–Sep, NJ May–Oct, KY Jun–Jul, LA all year, GA Feb–Dec, FL all year.

Distribution Across Southwest to southeastern California and south to Venezuela and throughout West Indies.

Description Typical small forktail with black-striped green thorax and blue abdomen tip. *Male:* Eyes and face bright green, postocular spots bluish. Thorax bright green, with black median and humeral stripes. Rarely antehumeral stripe constricted as in Fragile Forktail. Abdomen black except S1 and sides of S2 green, S8–9 blue, each with short but thick black stripe low on sides. Achieves mature color in 1 day. *Female:* Polymorphic. Heteromorph when young with orange postocular spots, thorax, and abdomen base. Thorax with wide black median and narrow black humeral stripes. Abdomen orange on S1–2 and much of S3, remainder shiny black above.

63.1
Eastern Forktail
male, immature
heteromorph
female—Jackson
Co., WI, June 2007;
female—Wayne
Co., OH, July 2007

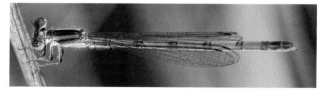

63.2
Eastern Forktail andromorph female—Coos Co., NH, June 2006; male with interrupted antehumeral stripe—Waushara Co., WI, June 2007, Ken Tennessen

Mature females become entirely gray pruinose with black median and humeral stripes still visible, face and eyes green. Females take almost a week to achieve mature color. Immature andromorph very rarely seen, colored as male but thorax bluer and more black on base of S8. Indistinguishable from heteromorph when mature.

Identification Nothing in range exactly like this very common species, with green, black-striped thorax and blue S8–9. Orange immature females distinguished from similar forktails by black humeral stripe, from orange bluets by entirely black abdomen tip. Mature females of **Citrine** and **Fragile Forktails** similar, see those species. Mature female with obscure pruinosity and thus conspicuous thoracic stripes could be mistaken for BLUET, easily distinguished by black "cap" on eyes.

Natural History One of most abundant damselflies in many parts of its range. Males perch in dense vegetation at waterside or cruise through it looking for prey and females. Females also present at water and in nearby herbaceous vegetation. Both orange and pruinose females mate. Copulation lasts about 40 min. Most females mate only once, then use male's sperm to fertilize all eggs they lay. Females repel other damselflies, including males of their own and other species, by fluttering wings and curving abdomen downward. Oviposition solo on floating or emergent stems of grasses, sedges, and other marsh plants; commonly on dead leaves. Females much more likely than males to eat other damselflies, teneral and mature.

Habitat Ponds, lakes, marshes, and slow streams, even edges of large rivers, as long as beds of vegetation in quiet water are present. Very wide habitat choice, but not in bogs or fens. Not always obvious in dense grass and sedges but usually quite visible at edges, where they can be very common.

Flight Season ON May–Oct, QC May–Sep, NS May–Sep, IA May–Oct, WI May–Oct, ME May–Nov, OH Apr–Nov, NJ Apr–Nov, KY Apr–Sep, GA May–Sep.

Distribution Distinctly less common in southern coastal lowlands than in interior. In fact, occurrence in coastal South Carolina is in question. Also west to western edge of plains.

---

64 Fragile Forktail *Ischnura posita* **TL 22–31, HW 10–16**

Description Tiny dark forktail with bright exclamation points on thorax. In some areas, early spring individuals largest. *Male:* Eyes green, face yellow-green. Mostly shiny black, thorax with interrupted (rarely complete) antehumeral stripe and sides light green, becoming slightly pruinose with age. Abdomen black, sides of S1–2 light green. Very rarely with bit of blue on top of S9 and/or S10 (Mexican subspecies with more). All pale markings yellow-green or even yellow in western part of range. *Female*: Immature as male but postocular spots and thoracic color pale to bright blue. As in male, very rarely bit of blue on abdomen tip or pale thoracic stripe complete. Pattern becomes obscure with age, may be almost covered by gray pruinosity on thorax and abdomen, but thoracic pattern usually remains at least faintly visible.

Identification In flight, especially in sun, males look like tiny spot of golden-green moving through vegetation, because bright thoracic pattern only feature visible. All black abdomen and interrupted antehumeral stripe distinctive. Often found with equally small **Citrine Forktail**, mature female similar but a bit more robust and with pruinosity usually obscuring black median thoracic stripe that is visible in **Citrine**. Mature female might be mistaken for same of **Eastern Forktail**, but a bit smaller and interrupted humeral stripe usually visible even through pruinosity. **Fragile** females more likely to have fine dark lateral thoracic stripe than **Eastern**, and line of demarcation between dark dorsal and pale ventral color on S8 often more irregular in **Eastern**. Note **Fragile** females lack vulvar spine on S8 present in **Eastern**.

Natural History Usually remains within dense vegetation, both herbaceous and shrubby, but also in open on beds of floating plants such as water lilies, pondweeds, and mare's tail. Seems likely to come out from vegetation during cooler, cloudy weather, perhaps because predation from larger odonates unlikely then. Males perch from water surface up to waist high. Females oviposit solo on duckweed and other floating vegetation and emergent stems, even a few inches above water level. Night roost sites average higher than daytime perches and abdomen more elevated, perhaps to catch morning sun. As other forktails, females persistent predators on other damselflies.

Habitat Ponds, lake shores, swamps, ditches, and slow streams with abundant herbaceous vegetation, including spring-fed. Often in dense grass or sedge beds as other forktails but also common in other herbaceous plant beds in shady wooded situations. High tolerance for pollution.

Flight Season ON May–Sep, QC Jun–Sep, NS May–Aug, IA May–Oct, WI May–Sep, ME May–Oct, OH Apr–Oct, NJ Apr–Oct, KY Apr–Oct, LA all year, GA all year, FL all year.

Distribution Also one record from eastern Newfoundland (not mapped). West to western Oklahoma and Texas and south through eastern Mexico to Guatemala.

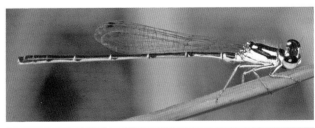

64
Fragile Forktail
male—Floyd Co.,
GA, May 2006;
female—
Chesterfield Co.,
SC, May 2008

Description Tiny mostly yellow damselfly, unique in male forewing stigmas not at wing edge. *Male*: Eyes yellow in front, green behind, with large black cap. Thorax striped green and black, with narrow antehumeral and wide humeral stripe. Abdomen yellow, green at extreme base; S1–2 black above, S3–6 with black basal spearpoint and apical ring, may be joined on S6; S7–10 all yellow or, at lower latitudes, S7 mostly black. Forewing stigmas orange, removed from wing margin behind thickened white vein; hindwing stigmas normal, black. *Female*: Eyes dull greenish with brown cap, prominently banded with black. Thorax black in front, gray on upper sides, white on lower sides. Abdomen black above, eventually becoming pruinose gray, often faintly banded with darker gray. Immature with face, postocular spots, pale areas on thorax and abdomen orange (extending to S5 or further). During maturation, S6–8 and parts of S5 and S9 become black above, then entire abdomen. Thorax gradually becomes greenish, abdomen increasingly pruinose at maturity.

Identification Yellow males unmistakable. Orange immature females differ from immature **Eastern Forktail** by lacking conspicuous dark humeral stripe, from **Furtive** and **Rambur's** by smaller size, more orange at abdomen base (only S1–2 in **Rambur's**, S3–4 in **Furtive**) and broader median stripe than in **Furtive**. Mature females in wetter areas more likely to be dull blackish, in drier regions can be quite pale gray pruinose. In either case, very similar to mature females of other pruinose species, **Eastern** and **Fragile Forktails**, but distinguished by shiny black median stripe on front of thorax (pruinosity obscures stripe in other species) with no trace of distinct humeral stripe (sometimes obvious in other species). Although considerably smaller, at one stage of development female **Citrine** with dull orangish-olive thorax could look much like mature heteromorph **Rambur's**. **Rambur's** never becomes pruinose on abdomen and often has bright blue postocular spots.

Natural History Both sexes can be found at very high densities in appropriate habitat, sometimes both matures and immatures rising in clouds when disturbed from dense veg-

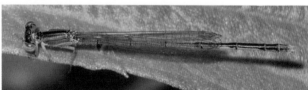

65
Citrine Forktail
male—Decatur
Co., GA, July 2007;
immature
female—Floyd
Co., GA, May 2006;
female—Orange
Co., FL, April 2008

etation at shallow grassy or sedgy ponds. Mating seldom seen, probably because most females mate only once, then use sperm of that male to fertilize all eggs they lay. Copulation throughout day, with both immature and mature females, may last until after dark. Oviposition much less often seen than in other forktails; solo females insert eggs methodically into upright and floating stems and leaves, including grasses, water lilies, and sphagnum.

Habitat Ponds and lake margins densely vegetated with grasses and/or sedges, also temporary ponds with similar vegetation, at least in southern part of range. Common in sphagnum bogs in some areas. Good disperser, taken by winds far above ground, so may turn up in inappropriate habitats.

Flight Season ON Jul–Sep, NS Aug, IA Jun–Sep, ME Aug, OH May–Nov, NJ Apr–Oct, KY May–Oct, LA Feb–Nov, GA Feb–Jan, FL all year.

Comments Population in Azores parthenogenetic, lacking males. Females lay eggs that give rise to females. No other odonate known to practice this method of reproduction.

Distribution Through Southwest west to southern California and south in lowlands to Venezuela; isolated populations on Galapagos (only damselfly there) and Azores. At times numbers appear north of usual range, perhaps colonies that wax and wane with climatic conditions.

Red Damsels *Amphiagrion*

This distinctive genus, with one variable or two closely related species, is confined to North America; its nearest relatives are not obvious. Males are bright red, often with much black, females duller. Thorax bulky and quite hairy, with a hairy tubercle (bump) beneath it exaggerated in western populations. World 2, NA 2, East 1.

66 Eastern Red Damsel *Amphiagrion saucium*   TL 22–27, HW 14–17

Description Small, slender red or orange damselfly of dense vegetation. *Male*: Eyes reddish-brown, paler below, with horizontal stripes; head black, with no postocular spots. Thorax black in front, reddish on sides, line of demarcation between two irregular; entirely black in northwestern part of region. Abdomen bright red, variably marked at tip with black. Amount of black varies from almost none to paired black blotches on S7–10, sometimes S6. Mark-ings take up increasing part of segment toward rear. Legs red in much of range, black in northwestern part. *Female*: Eyes light brown, faintly striped; head lightly marked with black. Thorax dull orange. Abdomen red-orange, variation in black markings at abdomen tip much as in male.

Identification No other small red damselfly normally occurs with it. No other female damselflies in range plain unmarked reddish to reddish-brown, including abdomen. Might barely overlap with **Duckweed Firetail** on Atlantic coast. Males of latter species have much red on head, narrower black on front of thorax, and no black on abdomen. Female **Firetail** dull brown, darker on top of thorax and abdomen. **Firetail** typically in swamps with duckweed, **Red Damsel** in bogs or sedge marshes. Note some heteromorph female FORKTAILS with much orange on thorax and abdomen, but not red like male **Red Damsel** and with more black on abdomen than female **Red Damsel**.

Natural History Both sexes common in dense vegetation near and at breeding habitat. Perch on sedge or grass stems, not flat leaves. Oviposition in tandem on floating vegetation and debris.

Habitat Sedge-filled marshes, seeps from streams, acid bogs.

Flight Season ON May–Aug, QC Jun–Aug, NS May–Aug, IA May–Aug, WI May–Aug, ME May–Jul, OH May–Aug, NJ May–Aug, KY May–Sep, GA Apr–Jun.

66.1
Eastern Red Damsel male, female—Floyd Co., GA, May 2006

66.2
Eastern Red Damsel "western" male—Houston Co., MN, July 2004, Greg Lasley

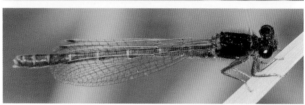

Comments In western part of region, from Minnesota and Wisconsin south to Missouri and Illinois, individuals are a bit more robust, with higher bump under thorax, and typically much darker, with entirely black thorax and legs. The abdomen is shorter as well as thicker, the wings usually reaching the end of S7 (usually no further than middle of S6 farther east). These have been considered intermediates between this species and Western Red Damsel, *Amphiagrion abbreviatum*, and if that is indeed the case, the two should be considered one species. At present, all populations in the range of this book are listed as *saucium*, but it is possible the western populations, even as far east as Wisconsin and the Upper Peninsula of Michigan, should be considered *abbreviatum*. More study is needed, especially in the Great Lakes region.

Aurora Damsel *Chromagrion*

This monotypic genus is confined to eastern North America. Half-open wings, thoracic color pattern, and long appendages are unique among North American pond damsels. Anterior side of quadrangle in wings is exceptionally long. Thought to be most closely related to *Pyrrhosoma*, red damselflies with three species in Eurasia. World 1, NA 1, East 1.

67 Aurora Damsel *Chromagrion conditum* TL 31–39, HW 20–26

Description Like large bluet with partially open wings, easily recognized by lack of humeral stripes and yellow on sides. Black front of thorax with wavy edges and no postocular spots. *Male*: Eyes blue, with or without one or two fine black stripes around them. Face blue, most of head black with no postocular spots. Middorsal black stripe on thorax with wavy edges; sides of thorax blue with yellow spot low on each side. Abdomen black with S1, sides of S2, basal  rings on S3–7, and S8–9 bright blue. *Female*: Polymorphic, similar to male or with entirely yellow thorax sides. Eyes blue or brown above, gray below, with two black stripes around upper half.

67
Aurora Damsel
male—Jackson
Co., WI, June 2007;
immature
female—Floyd
Co., GA, May 2005;
blue female—
Penobscot Co.,
ME, June 2006

Identification Some stream-dwelling AMERICAN BLUETS somewhat similarly colored, but all have stripes on thorax, median stripe straight-edged, and no trace of yellow. Long appendages differentiate male from other blue pond damsels, also lack of postocular spots. Half-open wings and long appendages may cause confusion with POND SPREADWINGS, but different thoracic pattern and blue color instead of pruinosity make distinction easy. Also note short stigmas in comparison with spreadwings.

Natural History Often perches with wings half-open, good field mark at a distance. Males perch on vegetation in open but spend much time in slow flight over water, presumably looking for stationary females. Copulation for 24–54 min, tandem exploration 12–52 min, oviposition 24–51 min. Pairs oviposit at water surface, male supported upright by female and may be carried at least partially underwater by her. Males and pairs most common at water at midday. Flight season relatively early.

Habitat Vegetated edges of clear ponds such as beaver ponds, sphagnum bogs, and slow streams, very often spring fed. Also in wooded swamps with cold water flowing through. Usually in low numbers, even in optimal habitat, and not often found far from water.

Flight Season ON May–Aug, QC May–Aug, NS May–Aug, WI May–Jul, ME May–Jul, OH May–Jul, NY May–Aug, NJ May–Jul, KY May–Aug, GA Apr–Jun.

These neotropical damselflies are predominantly red, but there are also a few blue species in South America. Unlike most other North American pond damsels, they lack postocular spots. They are commonly associated with floating vegetation, from tiny duckweeds to water lettuce. Two regional species are distinguished only in hand but may not occur together. World 58, NA 3, East 2.

68 Desert Firetail *Telebasis salva*   TL 24–29, HW 12–16

Description Small red pond damsel of southwestern wetlands, barely enters East. *Male* Eyes red above, yellowish below. Head black with no postocular spots, face red. Thorax red to red-orange on sides, paler below; wide black median stripe with irregular outer edge and reddish carina; prominent black streak on sides corresponding to humeral stripe, and small black markings closer to wing bases. Abdomen entirely red. *Female* Eyes light orange-brown. Thoracic markings as in male. Abdomen brown, with faintly indicated paler narrow basal rings and darker apical rings on S3–8. Abdomen can be rather bright, even reddish like male.

Identification Not known to overlap with any other red damselfly in East. See **Duckweed Firetail. Eastern Red Damsel** more robust, with relatively shorter abdomen, darker head and thorax, and much black at end of abdomen. Females more similar, but female **Firetail** always has narrow black line down front of thorax, female **Red Damsel** more black.

Natural History Males become common at water in late morning and early afternoon, followed by buildup in numbers of tandem pairs, but disappear from water later in day. Copulation lasts an hour or more, oviposition a half hour or more. Pairs oviposit flat on floating vegetation or in grass and other upright emergents; females submerge no more than abdomen. When away from water, may roost up to head height in woody vegetation, and probably mate away from water, then fly to it in tandem. Reproductive life up to 22 days.

Habitat Ponds and slow streams, typically in open country but may be bordered by trees and shrubs as long as sun penetrates. Usually associated with floating vegetation such as

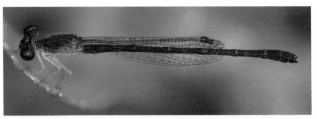

68
Desert Firetail
male—Hidalgo
Co., TX, October
2005, J.
Lubchansky;
female—Hidalgo
Co., TX,
September 2008

duckweed or beds of algae, often called "pond scum." Also inhabit grass and sedge beds where floating vegetation lacking.

Flight Season Probably all summer.

Distribution Across southernmost states to central California, then south to Venezuela.

Description Small red pond damsel of duckweed carpets in wooded southeastern wetlands. *Male*: Eyes red above, yellowish below. Head black with no postocular spots, face red. Thorax reddish on sides, paler below; wide black median stripe with irregular outer edge and reddish carina; prominent black streak on sides corresponding to humeral stripe, and small black markings closer to wing bases. Abdomen entirely red. *Female*: Eyes brown to reddish brown above, tan below. Head brown with black markings. Thoracic markings as in male but light brown on sides, paling to whitish below. Abdomen brown, upper surface darker and may be almost blackish, with narrow pale basal rings on S3–8.

Identification Ranges of two firetail species approach in southwestern Arkansas but so far not found together. Cerci in this species obviously more than half length of paraprocts, about half in **Desert**. Hind lobe of prothorax with two small processes pointing up in **Desert**, no such processes in **Duckweed**. Female abdomen tends to be less marked, more reddish brown in **Desert**, darker and more patterned in **Duckweed**, with little hint of reddish. Habitat choice sufficiently different that they may never be found together, but if so, they would have to be distinguished in hand. See **Eastern Red Damsel**, possible overlap. Dull female could be mistaken for BLUET or FORKTAIL, but look for distinctive thoracic pattern. **Citrine**, **Furtive**, and **Fragile Forktails** share habitat.

Natural History Males fly low over and rest on carpet of duckweed on water surface. Pairs oviposit in tandem on same carpet. Also found in dense grass, sedges, and ferns.

Habitat Swamps, usually under canopy and typically with an abundance of duckweed or water lettuce, less commonly in water lilies or grass beds.

Flight Season KY Jun–Jul, GA May–Sep, FL Jan–Nov.

69
Duckweed Firetail
male—
Hempstead Co.,
AR, August 2008,
David Arbour;
female—
Issaquena Co., MS,
May 2005, Giff
Beaton

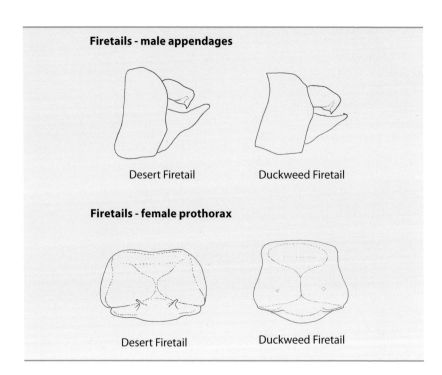

Firetails - male appendages

Desert Firetail   Duckweed Firetail

Firetails - female prothorax

Desert Firetail   Duckweed Firetail

Swampdamsels *Leptobasis*

Small neotropical group of slender, swamp-dwelling damselflies, three of which have recently been discovered in tropical parts of North America (Red-tipped Swampdamsel, *L. vacillans*, was found in south Texas after the western predecessor to this guide was published). Most have dramatic color change with age, although not closely related to other genera such as *Hesperagrion* that do the same. Females of most species have exceptionally long ovipositors. At least some species spend the long tropical dry season as immature-colored adults, and this may be universal in the group. World 8, NA 3, East 1.

70 Lucifer Swampdamsel *Leptobasis lucifer*   TL 31–33, HW 14–17

Description Slender, distinctively colored south Florida swamp damselfly. *Male*: Eyes green with black cap; face green. Thorax green with black median and humeral stripes. S1–2 also greenish; S3–6 black above, yellowish below; S7–10 red-orange, S7 with blackish wash above. *Female*: Eyes duller, entirely off-yellow. Thorax pale green with brown median and humeral stripes. S1 green, S2–7 black or brown above, dull orange below. S8–10 dull greenish to orangish, with some pruinosity at maturity. Immature female with thorax and abdomen base pale blue instead of green, S8–10 dull orange. Immature male not seen but may have blue-striped thorax.

Identification Nothing else in range looks like mature male of this species. Female distinguished from all co-occurring damselflies, including rather similar-sized mature female **Furtive Forktail**, by lightly indicated humeral stripe as well as relatively large ovipositor. Immature might be mistaken for dull **Everglades Sprite** but larger and with no trace of contrasty dark area below pale antehumeral stripe.

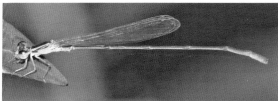

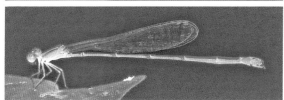

70
Lucifer Swampdamsel
male, female—Collier Co.,
FL, December 2007, Netta
Smith

Natural History Both sexes found in or at edge of dense swamp forest, usually flying slowly through and around shrubs throughout warm part of day, presumably looking for prey on leaves. Upon prey capture, damselfly perches for a few moments to devour it. Much more likely to be seen where sun penetrates canopy. Females oviposit in aquatic vegetation at the surface.

Habitat Dense to open cypress swamps with abundant shrubs, flooded seasonally.

Flight Season FL Dec–Mar.

Distribution Also known from southern Mexico to Costa Rica; not known from West Indies, but Cuba could be source of Florida population.

Comments Formerly called Lucifer Damsel, *Chrysobasis lucifer.*

Sprites *Nehalennia*

These are very small damselflies of North and South America, with another species widely distributed in Eurasia. Top of head, front of thorax, and abdomen are metallic green in four temperate species, black in two tropical ones. Tropical species have postocular spots and pale antehumeral stripes; temperate species lack antehumeral stripes when mature (some females have very narrow stripes) and lack postocular spots (narrow occipital bar present). All have blue on sides of thorax and tip of abdomen. Typically they inhabit dense sedge and grass beds and are less conspicuous than other damselflies, but they may be very common. Poking around in vegetation with a net or branch may be necessary to find them. Long tibial spines and wings held above abdomen when perched may indicate they are flycatchers. Wing position is also an identification clue, shared only with dancers in North America. In temperate species, pairs oviposit with male held up like little blue-tipped stick. World 6, NA 5, East 5.

71 Tropical Sprite *Nehalennia minuta*   TL 25–30, HW 12–15

Description Small, slender damselfly of Lower Florida Keys woodland, much blue when mature. *Male:* Eyes entirely blue. Blue postocular spots narrow, connected. Thorax black medially, mostly blue on sides. Abdomen black above, blue to pale brown on sides, with narrow blue basal rings on S3–7. S8–10 blue with black apical  spot on S8. Immatures with pale areas light brown. *Female:* Eyes mostly brown, small blue cap. Colored much as male but somewhat duller.

Identification Everglades Sprite only very similar species in its range. Male **Tropical** has S8–10 almost entirely blue (pale in immature), mostly black above in **Everglades**. Male eye color also good distinction, all blue in **Tropical** and dark-capped in **Everglades**. Male **Ever-**

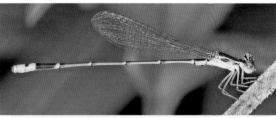

71
Tropical Sprite
male, female—
Trinidad, July
2004, John C.
Abbott/Abbott
Nature
Photography;
immature
male—Monroe
Co., FL, February
2002, R. A.
Behrstock/
Naturewide
Images

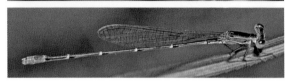

glades has flange projecting upward at rear of prothorax; **Tropical** lacks it. Mature individuals of both sexes with wide dark stripe on side in **Tropical**, mostly lacking in **Everglades** (immatures look similar). Females extremely similar, especially immatures; again, **Tropical** has less black on abdomen tip. **Everglades** female has hind margin of prothorax trilobed, deeply notched; cut straight across in **Tropical**, with no middle lobe. Only other small dark damselflies in Florida Keys would be females of **Citrine** and **Rambur's Forktails**, either with much orange on thorax and abdomen base or abdomen all dark above.

Natural History Adults stay within herbaceous vegetation at and near their breeding sites. Immatures more often seen (although they can be very obscure), usually within woodland. Pairs oviposit in tandem in grass throughout the day.

Habitat In Florida, tiny sinkholes, usually surrounded by shrubs, in pineland. In tropics, more varied but usually with much marsh vegetation.

Flight Season FL Oct–Feb; all year in tropics.

Distribution Also from northern Mexico south to Brazil and throughout Greater Antilles.

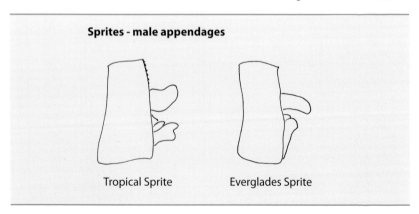

Sprites - male appendages

Tropical Sprite   Everglades Sprite

Description Tiny dark damselfly of Peninsular Florida and Gulf Coast, shows much blue when mature. *Male*: Eyes blue, blackish above and paling to whitish below. Narrow pale postocular spots joined by bar. Very narrow pale blue antehumeral stripe at outer edge of front of thorax, with black humeral stripe varying in thickness. Sides of thorax blue, brownish in younger individuals. Abdomen black, sides of S1–2, S8–9, and all of S10 blue; also narrow blue basal rings on S3–9, scarcely visible from above. *Female*: Perhaps polymorphic. Some colored exactly like male, others with sides of thorax brown. Immature patterned as mature but all pale areas tan rather than blue; sides of thorax with brown stripe. Males of population in Florida Panhandle with more blue on abdomen tip; black dorsal marking may be virtually lacking from S9.

Identification Tropical Sprite only species in its range much like it, and that species so far known only from Lower Keys, where **Everglades** rare. See that species. **Southern Sprite,**

72.1
Everglades Sprite male— Bay Co., FL, July 2009, Marion M. Dobbs; female—Bay Co., FL, July 2009

72.2
Everglades Sprite pair— Bay Co., FL, July 2009, Marion M. Dobbs

similarly small and slender, is metallic green above with a bit more blue visible on abdomen tip. Mature **Fragile Forktails** show no trace of blue and have divided antehumeral stripes closer to middle of thorax. Immature **Fragile** can have bluish thorax but still show green eyes and typical striping. No females of similarly small dark damselflies have S10 blue.

Natural History Adults apparently spend much time away from water and are often seen in immature coloration, perhaps a lengthy maturation period waiting for rains. Immatures usually within woodland and can be very difficult to see; may perch well up in trees. At other times, numerous individuals, including bright adults and pairs, found resting on leaves and twigs at ground level in woodland near water. Often wave abdomen up and down after landing. Found frequently at lights at night. Mating seen only during rainy season (summer to fall). Pairs oviposit in tandem on floating leaves with male erect.

Habitat Grass and sedge marshes; may retire to woodland, even middle of dense forest, when not breeding. Breed in tiny sinkholes in pineland adjacent to Everglades as well as in open Everglades (where locally abundant).

Flight Season FL all year.

Distribution Found on upper Texas coast in 1918, not since.

---

73 Southern Sprite *Nehalennia integricollis*   TL 20–25, HW 11–14

Description Tiny metallic green and blue southeastern damselfly. *Male*: Eyes blue with dark brown to black cap; fine blue occipital bar extending one-third width of head without eyes, paired posterior thickenings somewhere along its length. Thorax metallic green in front, blue on sides. Abdomen metallic green above, blue on sides of S1–2, sides of S8, and all of S9–10 except for paired black streaks on top of S9. *Female*: Eyes blue with brown cap, usually bit duller than male. Color as in male, but thorax yellow below (may be tinged with blue) and blue on abdomen confined to S10 and spot

at tip of S9, sometimes sides of S9 as well. Immature duller, with narrow postocular spots joined by fine line and very fine pale antehumeral stripe. Tenerals are whitish (perhaps all sprites are so colored), look different from most other damselflies.

Identification Male **Sedge Sprite** very similar to male **Southern** but slightly more blue at abdomen tip, including tip of S8; note limited overlap in these two species. Andromorph female **Sedge** with much more blue at abdomen tip than female **Southern**, but heteromorph looks identical. Must be distinguished by prothorax shape, pair of deep notches at

73
Southern Sprite
male—Jasper Co.,
TX, May 2005;
female—
Chesterfield Co.,
SC, May 2008

rear in **Sedge** and no notches in **Southern**. **Sphagnum Sprite** has more blue than **Southern** in both sexes; see also that species. Immature **Southern** might be confused with BLUET or FORKTAIL, but pattern of pale color on abdomen tip as well as very small size should be distinctive.

Natural History Can be very common in dense vegetation, so close search is always advised when looking for sprites. Often detected only by sweeping net through grass beds. Pairs remain in tandem for oviposition in floating vegetation and grass and sedge stems at water level. While laying eggs, female holds abdomen between wings.

Habitat Ponds and lakes with dense vegetation, usually sedges or grasses, at shore or throughout.

Flight Season NJ Jun–Aug, LA Apr–Sep, GA Apr–Sep, FL Mar–Nov.

74 Sedge Sprite *Nehalennia irene* TL 24–29, HW 13–17

Description Small metallic green and blue northern damselfly. *Male*: Eyes blue with black cap; head metallic green with very fine blue occipital bar one-third width of head without eyes. Thorax metallic green in front, blue on sides. Abdomen metallic green above, S8–10 blue with bilobed black marking on base of S8 and pair of black spots on top of S9; also sides of S1–2. *Female*: Polymorphic in overall range; heteromorphs, with yellow thorax and blue only at tip of S10, overwhelmingly predominant in most of East. Andromorph with blue thorax and a bit less blue at abdomen tip than male, usually little or no blue on S8; occurs widely but much more common at west end of region.

Identification See **Southern** and **Sphagnum Sprites**, both of which may occur with it.

Natural History Abundant at many localities. Mostly associated with dense beds of sedge and often much more common than first apparent, as many individuals deep in vegetation, both short and tall. Sometimes seen in more open vegetation, however, and can be common on open sphagnum mats. Pairs oviposit in upright or floating stems, mosses, and detritus just below water surface.

Habitat Wide variety of habitats, from sedgy lake and pond shores to sedge meadows, bogs, and fens.

74
Sedge Sprite—
male Grafton Co.,
NH, June 2006;
heteromorph
female—Coos
Co., NH, June
2006; andromorph
female—Wood
Co., WI, June 2007

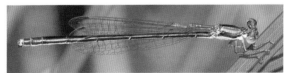

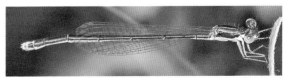

Flight Season ON May–Sep, QC May–Aug, NS May–Sep, IA Jun–Aug, WI May–Sep, ME Jun–Sep, OH May–Aug, NJ May–Aug.

Distribution Across northern North America to Alaska, south in mountains to northern California and southern Wyoming.

75 Sphagnum Sprite *Nehalennia gracilis* TL 25–30, HW 13–17

Description Slender green damselfly with extensive blue abdomen tip. *Male*: Eyes blue; fine occipital bar extends half width of head without eyes. Thorax metallic green in front, blue on sides. Abdomen metallic green above, blue on sides of S1–2 and blue S8–10. Rarely may show very fine blue antehumeral stripe. *Female*: Like male but eyes sometimes duller, more greenish. Thorax blue or yellow below. More likely to have fine blue antehumeral stripe. Blue on abdomen tip variable but always less than male. At most extensive, S8 with bilobed black marking extending almost to end of  segment and S9 with two separated black markings continuing same pattern. At least extensive, S8 black and S9 blue with bilobed black marking; S10 always blue. This may represent polymorphism, as in Sedge Sprite.

Identification Important to correctly sex sprites, as male of one species can be colored like female of another. Both sexes of **Sphagnum** have more blue on abdomen tip than same sex of **Sedge** or **Southern Sprite**, either of which can occur with it. Latter two species never have all three last segments blue, as in male **Sphagnum**. Female **Southern** have blue only on tip of S9 and S10; same is true for most female **Sedge** in East, but those with most blue overlap with **Sphagnum** (and male **Sedge** looks much like female **Sphagnum** with least blue). Female **Sphagnum** more likely to retain very narrow antehumeral stripe into maturity, **Sedge** not. Occipital bar, if it can be seen, great field mark; see descriptions for each species. Female **Sedge** has trilobed rear edge of prothorax, **Southern** no projections,

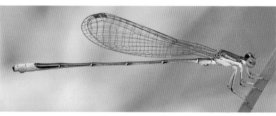

75
Sphagnum Sprite
male—Hancock
Co., ME, July 2009,
Bryan Pfeiffer/
Wings
Photography;
heteromorph
female—Wayne
Co., OH, July 2007;
andromorph
female—Wood
Co., WI, June 2007

Sphagnum slightly notched in center plus erect point at lower end of thoracic carina lacking in other two.

Natural History May be very common in chosen habitat but not especially obvious when within dense vegetation. Often only blue thorax or abdomen tip reveals presence. Usually seen perched on sedge or grass stems. Mating more common in afternoon; oviposition in tandem.

Habitat As name implies, very often associated with sphagnum bogs but also in tall grass and other dense vegetation at lake and pond edges where no sphagnum present.

Flight Season ON Jun–Aug, QC Jun–Sep, NS Jun–Aug, WI Jun–Jul, ME May–Sep, OH May–Jul, NJ May–Aug, FL Apr–May.

Distribution Very spotty within southern and western part of range.

Sprites - female prothorax

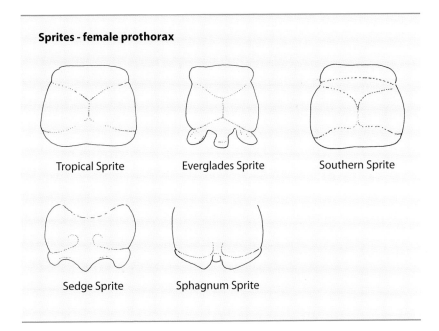

Tropical Sprite Everglades Sprite Southern Sprite

Sedge Sprite Sphagnum Sprite

Dancers *Argia*

The flight style of dancers gives them their name, a bouncy or jerky movement through the air quite different from the smooth forward motion of bluets, forktails, and other pond damsels and more like jewelwing flight. They are much more likely to land flat on rocks, logs, or soil than other types of pond damsels, and they stay in the open, not moving slowly through vegetation as do many other pond damsels. Males show varying proportions of blue and black, not so different from bluets in coloration but quite different in behavior. Most species are blue, but coloration is just as varied as in other large genera, many species lavender or violet, some dark purple or almost entirely black, and even a red species. A few add brilliant red eyes and copper thorax to the basic dancer color pattern. Unlike other pond damsels, a few even have dark wings. They usually perch with wings raised above the abdomen (all other North American pond damsels except sprites hold them alongside the abdomen) and sally forth after flying insects (others glean from vegetation). The wings have a slightly shorter petiole (they become broader closer to the base), probably an adaptation for quick and strong flight to catch flying insects, and the long tibial spines that characterize the genus are surely effective in that activity. Many, perhaps all, species open and then close the wings in what has been called "wing clapping."

Blue dancers are usually distinguished from bluets by humeral stripe either notched at end, clearly forked into two branches, or distinctly narrowed in middle and expanded to a spot at the upper end (bluets never forked, same width throughout or smoothly narrowed to upper end). Seepage Dancer an exception, looks much like bluet but holds wings above abdomen. Dancers with blue-tipped abdomen have blue S10, whereas bluets with blue tips have S10 black on top (except long, slender Attenuated Bluet and Pale Bluet, both with mostly black abdomen). Also, black markings are usually on sides of S2 in dancers, on top in bluets. In female dancers, dark markings on abdomen are paired dorsolateral spots or stripes; in other pond damsels, dark markings are central, either covering entire top of segment or, in most bluets, torpedo-shaped. Finally, female dancers lack vulvar spine present on American bluets.

Although most species perch on rocks or ground in open areas, some prefer vegetation. At water, they typically perch along overhanging stem or leaf facing stream rather than hanging at tip facing shore, as do bluets; this is an excellent clue. Copulating pairs are infrequently seen (copulation must be brief), but tandem pairs are commonly seen moving about habitat and ovipositing. Typically females insert eggs in plant tissues at and just below water surface, males either grasping plant stem or, more commonly, held vertically in air (not all pond damsels do this). Pairs aggregate at good oviposition sites, perhaps attracted because pair already present indicates no predators. Exposed rootlets of streamside trees in swift currents are preferred by many species for egg laying. Some, especially females, will have to be captured for identification. This largest genus of Odonata in the New World is well represented in North America, although most species are southwestern. World 113, NA 32, East 12.

76 Seepage Dancer   *Argia bipunctulata*   TL 23–30, HW 13–18

Description Small bluet-like dancer of vegetation beds. Head dark above, no postocular spots, but pale occipital bar present. *Male*: Eyes blue. Entirely blue except for these black markings: wide median and humeral stripes on thorax; black blotch at end of S2; rings at end of S3–5; mostly black S6, blue on dorsal base; and all of S7. *Female*: Eyes tan with dark brown cap. Thorax patterned as male but light areas light tan. Abdomen mostly pale brown on S1–3, S4–5 mostly black above and at end and pale on sides, S6–7 and S9–10 black, S8 entirely pale tan above. Apparently no blue females.

Identification No really similar dancer in East. **Springwater** is larger with much less heavily striped thorax and black lateral markings on midabdomen. Could overlap with **Aztec**, also small but with much less black on thorax. Distinguished from all BLUETS that might be similar by wings held above abdomen and very wide humeral stripe, much wider than blue antehumeral, so thorax looks mostly black in front. Also lacks prominent postocular spots of most bluets (has tiny blue dots nearer center of head). Blue bluets such as **Atlantic, Double-striped**, and **Familiar** also have black on top of S10, lacking in blue dancers. Also distinctive of both sexes of **Seepage** is pale line bordering top of each eye. No other female dancer has mostly dark abdomen, black at tip but with pale S8. Female BLUETS with S8 pale have sides of S9–10 pale, not black.

Natural History Populations are scattered because of special habitat needs and not very dense where they occur. Their lifestyle, rather sedentary perching in low and often dense vegetation, is different from that of most other dancers in their range.

Habitat Seepage or bog waters with abundant sedges, also weedy flowing ditches.

Flight Season OH Jun–Sep, NJ May–Sep, KY Jun–Jul, LA May–Aug, GA May–Sep, FL Mar–Aug.

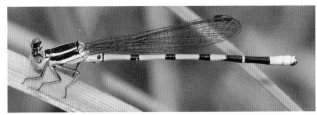

76
Seepage Dancer
male—Aiken Co.,
SC, May 2008;
female—
Champaign Co.,
OH, August 2007,
William Hull

Description Widespread eastern dancer with unpatterned thorax. Front and top of head blue, black at rear with small separated post-ocular spots. *Male*: Eyes blue in front, brown behind, look all blue in face view. Thorax blue in front, pale whitish-tan on sides, with conspicuous black polygon above each middle leg. Abdomen mostly black above, pale tan on sides; S8–10 blue, with black low on sides, rarely extending up onto top of S8. Males often have gray-violet thorax, much duller than usual, this color more likely at low temperatures or in tandem. *Female*: Polymorphic. Eyes brown, darker  above; lack of blue in eyes in andromorph good distinction from male. Black blotch at base of middle leg smaller or even lacking. Andromorph with all blue thorax as in male, blue extending back along sides of basal abdominal segments; heteromorph entirely brown. Abdomen black above, dorsolateral markings often split by fine pale line but continuous from S2 to S9. Ovipositing blue females also become duller, blue-gray. Some females are green, and color change with age documented in individual females.

Identification No other species colored just like male, with almost entirely blue thorax and blue abdomen tip. Unique even with gray thorax, in either case isolated black lower end of humeral stripe conspicuous. Females much like female **Powdered Dancer**, with unmarked thorax, and can be difficult. **Blue-fronted** has more vividly striped abdomen tip, with conspicuous ventrolateral stripe on S9 that is mostly lacking in **Powdered**; thus, **Powdered** shows large pale area on sides of abdomen tip. **Blue-fronted** also more likely to have partially developed black humeral stripe. Typical dancer wing position and behavior distinguish from female BLUETS with minimal thoracic striping.

Natural History Commonly perches on ground but also low in vegetation. At one pond, males arrived early and became spaced at 6-foot intervals, typically at water for about 3 hr but not retaining territories from day to day. Often aggressive toward other males, rarely to pairs. Females arrive about 2 hr after males, maximum mating just past midday. Copulation lasts 10–27 min, tandem exploration 10–50 min, and tandem oviposition 53–115 min. About

77.1
Blue-fronted
Dancer
male—Telfair Co.,
GA, July 2007; dull
male—Wayne Co.,
OH, July 2007

77.2
Blue-fronted
Dancer brown
female—Holmes
Co., OH, July 2007;
blue female—
Ashland Co., OH,
July 2007

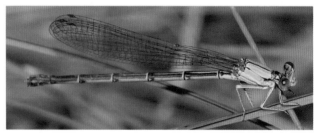

half of females continue ovipositing alone for 20 min after release by males. Horizontal floating substrates typically used for egg laying, with pairs concentrating in small areas. Both sexes reproductively active for about 1 week, averaging about one and one-half matings; maximum age about 1 month after maturity.

Habitat Very wide habitat choice includes rivers and streams, less often ponds and lakes, especially larger ones. More typical of larger, muddier rivers than smaller streams.

Flight Season ON Jun–Sep, IA May–Sep, WI Jun–Aug, OH May–Sep, NJ Jun–Sep, KY May–Oct, LA Apr–Nov, GA Apr–Oct, FL Apr–Aug.

Distribution West to western edge of plains, north to northern Colorado, also in southeastern Arizona and south in lowlands of eastern Mexico to Nuevo León.

78 Powdered Dancer *Argia moesta*   TL 37–42, HW 22–29

Description Large dull brown to black dancer with areas of whitish pruinosity ("powder"). Head almost entirely pale in pale western populations, pale postocular line in dark eastern populations. *Male*: Eyes brown, in some populations darker on top, or pale gray-brown. Heavily marked immatures with wide median stripe and wide humeral stripes, some populations with humeral stripe forked or entirely divided with outer fork wider. Wide and complete black stripes on abdomen make it mostly black above with contrasty white rings at base of S3–7 (at most extreme these may show tinge of blue); S9–10 pale except for dorsolateral stripes. Pruinosity varies with population: in most of region may be only on front of head, front of thorax, and S9–10 at most; in drier regions covering head, all of thorax, and S8–10. Thoracic pattern at least faintly visible no matter how pruinose. *Female*: Polymorphic, either entirely light brown or largely blue on head and thorax; usually brown more common than blue. Blue individuals may be green when younger, and their thorax typically turns gray when mating (face remains blue). Thoracic pattern also very variable, in many females obviously striped, with wide median stripe and narrow, either unforked or widely forked humeral stripe; never broad humeral stripe as in males. Striped females seem most common in Southeast. Other females relatively lightly marked with only fine median and humeral stripes, thorax essentially unmarked. Abdomen with wide complete dorsolateral stripes on S2–9 enclosing brown middorsal stripe; obvious ventrolateral stripe on S8, but S9–10 pale from side. Dorsolateral stripes may almost fuse, so abdomen looks entirely dark above.

Identification Typical heavily pruinose mature male like nothing else, as pruinosity rare in male pond damsels. Note that some, especially western, individuals look so blue that confusion with **Blue-fronted Dancer** is possible; such individuals also have abdomen dusted with pruinosity. Male POND SPREADWINGS have pruinose thorax and abdomen tip but are

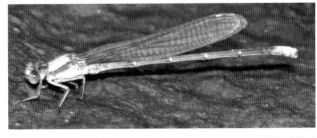

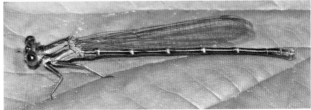

78.1
Powdered Dancer
male—Phelps Co.,
MO., June 2009;
immature
male—Burnett
Co., WI, June 2007

78.2
Powdered Dancer
brown
female—Jasper
Co., GA, July 2007;
striped blue
female—Ashland
Co., OH, July 2007

78.3
Powdered Dancer
pairs—Ashland
Co., OH, July 2007

otherwise very different from **Powdered Dancer**. Immature males quite variable but could be distinguished by outer fork of humeral stripe much wider than inner and entirely black abdomen with S9–10 pale, with or without stripes. Female distinguished from female **Blue-fronted Dancer** by almost entirely lacking ventrolateral stripe on S9, so abdomen tip looks pale from side rather than striped. In hand, helpful mark is relatively long stigma, often with crossvein contacting it in middle; in all other eastern dancers, crossveins at ends of stigmas. Immature and female **Powdered** with well-defined thoracic stripes actually rather similar to immature and female **Dusky Dancer**, but pale line within divided humeral stripe of **Dusky** wavy, that of **Powdered** straight. Some BLUETS look somewhat similar; always note wing position and flight style.

Natural History Males typically perch on rocks at shore or out in water, also on streamside vegetation. May hover over water for lengthy periods, much more likely to do so than other dancers; typically face upstream but perhaps merely into wind. Also more likely than other dancers to perch with wings alongside abdomen. Males can be abundant in late morning, tandem pairs not until midafternoon, but copulating pairs much less often seen. Copulation lasts 14–31 min, tandem exploration 3–49 min, oviposition 37–67 min. Females oviposit at surface or submerged, either solo or in tandem (even with submerged male), to several feet below surface; may stay under for 30 min. Pairs often aggregate in large numbers, even landing on each other while female probing with abdomen. Eggs laid in almost any substrate in live or dead plant tissue, including algal films on rocks. Sexual maturation takes about 2 weeks, average adult longevity 3 weeks, maximum 4 weeks. Perhaps pruinosity confers resistance to high temperatures, as this may be the only odonate active at streams on sunny days exceeding 37°C. Females commonly eat damselflies (including their own species), especially tenerals.

Habitat Streams and rivers, from muddy to sandy but often rocky, with wooded or open banks; also on irrigation canals. Typical of largest rivers inhabited by dancers but may also be on quite small streams. Also on large lakes in northern parts of range. One of the most successful dancers, common farther north than most others.

Flight Season ON Jun–Oct, QC May–Sep, NS Jun–Sep, IA May–Sep, WI May–Sep, ME May–Sep, OH May–Oct, NJ Jun–Sep, KY May–Oct, LA Apr–Oct, GA Apr–Nov, FL Mar–Nov.

Distribution Across Southwest to southeastern California and south in Mexico to Jalisco and Tabasco.

79 Blue-ringed Dancer *Argia sedula* TL 30–34, HW 18–21

Description Common small, mostly black dancer with bright blue rings and blue abdomen tip. Sexual dimorphism more extreme than in most dancers. *Male*: Eyes blue. Postocular spots small, separated. Median and humeral stripes very wide, so thorax mostly black in front with narrow blue antehumeral stripe (which can be incomplete). S2 with black side stripes widely fused above, S3–7 black with conspicuous blue basal rings of variable width, sometimes virtually absent; S8–10 blue with black lower side stripes. Black on middle segments slightly constricted toward rear, so small

79
Blue-ringed Dancer
male—Telfair Co., GA, July
2007; female—Ashland
Co., OH, July 2007;
dark-winged female
Suwanee Co., FL, April
2008

amount of tan or blue may show from sides. Males in tandem often have postocular spots and front of thorax dull blue-gray, much duller than usual, and this color also characteristic of individuals at low temperatures. *Female*: Eyes brown; head entirely pale above. Body color light brown. Thoracic markings dull and obscure; wide brown median stripe usually faintly evident with median carina a black hairline, and wide brown forked humeral stripe may also be visible. Mature females show touch of pale blue-green on tiny plates at wing bases. Abdominal markings brown, consisting of apical spot on S2–4 becoming more obscure on rearward segments, dorsolateral spots or stripes on S3–5 or S3–6 similarly disappearing into dull brown patternless S7–10, becoming paler toward end. Pale bluish-green basal rings and sides evident on S3–6 in some, perhaps sign of maturity. Wings distinctly amber-tinted.

Identification Conspicuous rings distinguish male from dark, blue-tipped male BLUETS of same streams. Male most like **Paiute Dancer**, may barely overlap in East. **Blue-ringed** has thorax mostly black in front, with relatively narrow antehumeral stripes, whereas **Paiute** shows more blue, with those stripes wide. **Paiute** has narrower pale rings on abdomen but two per segment in middle. Female **Blue-ringed** less patterned than most other brown female damselflies, in some almost patternless and only black markings on upright mesostigmal plates and hairline median carina of thorax. Also more likely to have wings brownish. **Paiute** somewhat similar but has prominent black markings on all segments back to S9. Recall that most teneral damselflies look dull brownish and almost patternless.

Natural History Males perch on herbaceous vegetation at streamside, much more likely on vegetation than rocks. Females often common in open areas near water, perched in low vegetation and on ground. Pairs oviposit in live herbaceous stems or floating dead vegetation at water surface. Reproductive life averages 4–5 days, maximum 2 weeks.

Habitat Small to large streams and rivers, often most common where much herbaceous vegetation along shore but also found in open, rocky stretches. Wide habitat tolerance probably contributes to general abundance and wide range.

Flight Season ON Jun–Sep, OH Jun–Sep, NJ Jun–Aug, KY Jun–Sep, LA Apr–Oct, GA Apr–Nov, FL all year.

Distribution Across Southwest to northern Colorado and southern Nevada and California, then south in Mexico to Baja California, Querétaro, and Veracruz.

80 Paiute Dancer · *Argia alberta* · TL 27–32, HW 16–20

Description Small blue and black dancer of sedgy habitats. Head with much black above, postocular spots quite narrow. *Male*: Black of top of head extends out as short stripe onto each eye, as if eye has black pupil. Thorax blue with black median and fairly wide forked humeral stripes. Fork varies from rarely absent to one-third of stripe length. S1–2 blue, S2 with narrow black dorsolateral stripes ending in bulge and turning inward to point, like neck, head, and bill of bird. Middle segments of abdomen with black dorsolateral stripes almost filling space available (rarely leaving fine middorsal line), so looks dark with narrow blue rings and light brown to blue on sides. At darkest, entire middle of abdomen black; at lightest, stripes may end so second blue ring visible at two-thirds length of middle segments. S7 entirely black above, S8–10 blue with black low on sides (little on S8, extensive on S10). *Female*: Polymorphic, entirely brown or thorax light blue, abdomen light brown to blue. Eyes tan with limited dark brown cap. Color pattern as in male but humeral stripe often narrower, abdomen with narrow to broad incomplete dark pointed dorsolateral stripes and dorsal blotches at ends of segments; stripes complete and vivid on S7–9.

Identification Male **Paiute** more purplish-blue than other dancers with which it might occur. Although not known to overlap in East, most like **Blue-ringed Dancer**, complicated because latter with much more pale color on abdomen in western part of range, thus looks

80
Paiute Dancer
male, female—
Harney Co., OR,
July 2006

much like **Paiute** in side view. **Paiute** usually has wider antehumeral stripes (thorax looks as much blue as black in front) and narrower, forked humeral stripes, but overlap. **Blue-ringed** usually with wider basal rings that make its name appropriate, those rings convex behind (when prominent in **Paiute**, usually concave behind). Heteromorph female **Paiute** not too dissimilar from **Blue-ringed**, but paired abdominal markings usually prominent, not so in **Blue-ringed**. Tip of abdomen entirely pale in female **Blue-ringed**, with black markings in **Paiute**. Female **Paiute** also somewhat like female **Variable**, but dark markings on middle abdominal segments broken into spots rather than continuous stripes. Female **Springwater** also similar to **Paiute** but has much narrower humeral stripes and no markings on S8.

Natural History Males can be common in and at edge of dense marsh vegetation, especially tall bulrushes, also out in low sedges, especially when at water. Pairs become more common in midafternoon.

Habitat Shallow sedge marshes, often associated with springs, hot springs in the northern part of the range. Also small sandy streams that flow out of such springs, with slight current and abundant sedges.

Flight Season IA Jun–Aug.

Distribution Across interior West to western Montana and eastern California, south in Mexico to Chihuahua.

---

81 Variable Dancer *Argia fumipennis* TL 29–34, HW 18–23

Description Small dancer with striking geographic variation; see below. Western/northern subspecies *A. f. violacea* described. *Male*: Eyes brown above, violet below. General coloration violet. Thorax with narrow median stripe and narrow humeral stripe with long and divergent fork; lower sides white. Black markings on abdomen include narrow dorsolateral line ending in triangle on S2, complete or almost-complete rings on S3–6, almost all of S7, and conspicuous lower edges of S8–10. S8 violet-blue, S9 blue, S10 blue tinged slightly with violet, unique color pattern among North American

damselflies. *Female*: Eyes brown. Coloration brown or reddish-brown with thoracic markings as male (rarely bluish tinge on thorax). Abdomen with dorsolateral black stripes con-

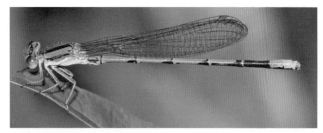

81.1
Variable Dancer
(*violacea*)
male—Lewis Co.,
TN, June 2006;
female—Floyd
Co., GA, May 2006

81.2
Variable Dancer
(*fumipennis*)
male—Liberty
Co., FL, April 2008;
female—Leon
Co., FL, April 2005

tinuous on all middle segments, extending back to S8 and faintly on S9; most of last three segments pale but also indistinct black ventrolateral stripe on S8. No blue female. *A. f. fumipennis* of Southeast colored like *violacea*, but wings dark brown. *A. f. atra* of Florida with similarly dark wings but S3–7 entirely black where other subspecies violet. Abdomen darker in females of both dark-winged subspecies than in *violacea*.

Identification Only other violet dancer occurring with **Variable** is **Kiowa**, which has S8–10 entirely blue, with no purple tinge on S8. Female has narrow forked or unforked humeral stripe and dark abdominal stripes extending length of S8 and onto S9, much as female **Paiute**. Midabdominal markings in **Paiute** spots, in **Variable** continuous stripes. Similarly, female **Aztec** has elongate spots on midabdomen rather than stripes.

81.3
Variable Dancer
(*atra*) male—
Suwanee Co., FL,
April 2008;
female—Lake Co.,
FL, April 2008

Natural History Common over riffles and in vegetation along pools. Males rest on rocks, ground, or vegetation at water. Often slowly open and close wings, especially dark-winged populations. Copulation in Florida lasted about 24 min on average, exploration 34 min, oviposition 58 min. Pairs oviposit on live and dead plant stems and detritus at surface, occasionally submerging.

Habitat Wide habitat choice, from small streams and ditches with much vegetation to open sandy lake shores. Often in stands of sedges and grasses. More often at ponds than other dancers.

Flight Season ON May–Sep, QC Jun–Sep, NS Jun–Sep, IA May–Sep, WI Jun–Sep, ME Jun–Oct, OH May–Sep, NJ May–Oct, KY May–Sep, LA Mar–Oct, GA Mar–Nov, FL all year.

Distribution West to western edge of plains from Montana to New Mexico, also southern Arizona and south in uplands of Mexico to Durango and Hidalgo.

Comments This species is the only North American odonate that has been given subspecies common names. Populations over much of region are of subspecies *Argia fumipennis violacea*, often called Violet Dancer. Dark-winged *A. f. fumipennis* of southeastern Coastal Plain, north to North Carolina and west to Mississippi, has been called Smoky-winged Dancer, and black-bodied *A. f. atra* of Florida Peninsula is Black Dancer. Use of species common name for all subspecies is encouraged, however. Intermediates between subspecies are common in all areas where they meet.

82 Aztec Dancer *Argia nahuana*   TL 28–35, HW 18–23

Description Small sky-blue dancer of southwestern weedy streams. *Male:* Bright blue all over, thorax with narrow black median and humeral (usually forked) stripes. S2 with pair of subapical black spots, S3–6 with black ring at rear, S7 mostly black, S8–10 blue with black stripe low on sides. Rare lightly marked individuals have median stripe narrower, humeral stripe unforked, and/or S7 all blue. *Female:* Polymorphic, brown or blue (andromorph rare). Eyes brown in brown female, blue in blue female. Color pattern as male but black dorsolateral stripes ending in points along each abdominal segment, continuous on S7, usually incomplete on S8–9, lacking on S10.

82
Aztec Dancer
male, female—
Chihuahua,
Mexico,
September 2005

Identification Only two other dancers in its range are mostly blue. Male differs from **Spring-water** in slightly smaller size, often forked humeral stripe, and lack of anterior black markings on middle abdominal segments. Differs from **Seepage** in much less black on head and thorax; ranges not known to overlap. Female much like female **Springwater**, but S8 striped (unmarked in **Springwater**). Heteromorph female quite similar to female **Variable**; capture will be necessary to distinguish them. Inner edge of mesostigmal plates in Variable separated by greater than width of each plate in **Variable**, less than that width in **Aztec**. Andromorph female **Aztec** quite different from females of these other species; also has blue eyes, unusual in female dancers.

Natural History Typically perches in vegetation at riffles. Pairs oviposit in herbaceous vegetation, including grass leaves, at water level.

Habitat Small streams with open banks but abundant emergent vegetation, both sedges and watercress. Usually at riffles rather than pools.

Flight Season NE Jun–Aug.

Distribution West to Pacific coast, north to southern Oregon and northern Nevada, south in Mexico to Jalisco.

83 Kiowa Dancer *Argia immunda*   TL 33–38, HW 19–25

Description Robust dull purple dancer, heavily marked with black. *Male*: Eyes violet, paler beneath. Head, thorax, and much of abdomen violet. Thorax with wide median stripe, moderately wide forked humeral stripe. Black abdominal markings include large polygon on S2, wide black rings and large black basal spots on S3–6, black spots larger toward rear, often fused with ring on S6 and rarely reach ring on S3–5; S7 almost entirely black; S8–10 blue with  continuous black stripe low along sides. *Female*: Polymorphic. Eyes brown. All brown or head, thorax, and S8–10 blue. Patterned as male, but dorsolateral abdominal spots usually longer, in some forming stripes. S8–10 usually plain but may have indistinct ventrolateral stripe, especially on S8.

Identification Male distinctive by dull violet coloration with large basal spots on middle segments, making abdomen look heavily spotted. **Variable Dancer**, another violet species with basal markings on middle segments, has markings much smaller, so middle segments

83
Kiowa Dancer
male—Travis Co.,
TX, July 2006, Eric
Isley; blue
female—Hidalgo
Co., TX, May 2005

largely unspotted. Exceptionally dark individuals, with only pale rings on middle segments, recall **Blue-ringed Dancer** but of course are violet. Heavily marked middle segments of female contrast with unmarked S8–10. **Springwater** also similar but has narrow, unforked humeral stripe.

Natural History Males and pairs common in vegetation in riffles, where they oviposit in green stems. Females often on ground away from water.

Habitat Small to medium rocky streams in open; may have shrubby or riparian borders.

Flight Season Not recorded in East, presumably midsummer.

Distribution Across Southwest to Arizona, also Black Hills of South Dakota, then south to Belize.

84 Springwater Dancer *Argia plana*   TL 33–40, HW 22–25

Description Common blue dancer of the Southwest. *Male*: Mostly blue, with blue eyes. Thorax with moderate median stripe and narrow unforked humeral stripe (rarely forked) widening at lower end. Black on abdomen: S2 with narrow (sometimes interrupted) stripe ending in triangle on each side; rings on S3–6, becoming wider on posterior segments; long pointed spot on S4–6, (rarely S3–6) joined to ring on S6; S7 mostly black with slight extension backward from  pale basal ring (rarely with more blue); S8–10 entirely blue. Immature males may be mixed blue and pale violet. *Female*: Polymorphic, either brown or blue, with eyes usually brown. Blue females can be that color all over or just on thorax and/or abdomen tip. Thoracic markings as in male. Pointed narrow dorsolateral stripes on S2–7, fused with apical ring on S7; S8–10 entirely pale or rarely with small pair of elongate basal spots on S9.

Identification No other bright blue male dancers in range in this region except **Aztec** and **Seepage**, both of which have no spots on sides of middle abdominal segments. In addi-

84
Springwater
Dancer
male—
Montgomery Co.,
AR, May 2006;
brown
female—Brewster
Co., TX, November
2007, Netta Smith;
blue female—
Dallas Co., TX,
June 2008, David
Arbour

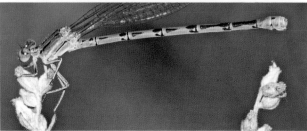

tion, **Seepage** has bold black thoracic stripes. Distinguished from bright blue BLUETS by behavior, thoracic pattern, and blue S10. **Variable** violet instead of blue, with forked humeral stripe. Female **Springwater** differs from **Kiowa** and **Variable Dancers** by narrow, usually unforked humeral stripe; from **Aztec** by unmarked S8–9 (or S9 with basal spots; both segments striped in **Aztec**).

Natural History Males typically perch on vegetation at shore or in water. Males live more than 11 days, females more than 8 days after maturation, and both sexes mate one or two times during their lives. Males not territorial but may be spaced about 3 feet apart along streams because of aggressive behavior toward intruders. Copulation takes 19–40 min, tandem exploration 16–35 min, and oviposition 38–56 min. Pairs oviposit at surface in aquatic vegetation or floating detritus, also in damp clay adjacent to spring; separate quickly after oviposition.

Habitat Small to medium shallow streams, rocky and sandy, in or out of woodland; may be on quite small spring runs and hillside trickles, often at tiny seeps with no other species of dancers. Considered indicative of springs in some parts of range.

Flight Season IA Jun–Sep, WI Jun–Sep.

Distribution Across Southwest to western South Dakota and Arizona, south in uplands to Guatemala.

Comments Populations from west Texas west are violet rather than blue.

Description Violet dancer barely entering region. *Male:* Eyes violet,
darker above. Basic body color violet, thorax with fine black median and humeral lines and whitish sides; black smudge on side of
S2, black rings on S3–6, wider on S5 and much wider on S6; S7
mostly black and S8–10 blue, with very little black low on sides. *Female:* Eyes brown. Polymorphic, either rich tan all over or thorax
and abdomen base pale blue-green. Thorax marked as male, abdo-
men either entirely pale with black blotches at ends of S3–6 or, in addition, narrow black
dorsolateral stripes from S3 to S7; S8–10 always entirely pale.

85
Emma's Dancer
pair—Grant Co.,
OR, August 2004

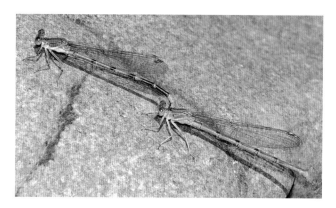

Identification No other violet/purple damselfly in its range except **Variable Dancer**. Male
differs from that species by larger size and very narrow median stripe. Fine median stripe
and lightly marked abdomen, with unmarked S8–9, unique combination for female.
Natural History Males common at breeding habitat farther west. Females in nearby uplands, and pairs come to water in afternoon, sometimes in clusters at appropriate oviposition sites. These include floating vegetation of all sorts, rootlets of streamside trees, and
emergent shore vegetation. Tandem pairs also common away from water, perhaps form
there, and spend hours paired. More likely to perch on rocks and ground than vegetation.
Habitat Moderate to large streams and rivers, typically rocky but also with sand or mud substrates and with open banks or shrubby or riparian borders. Typical of larger rivers but occurs also on small, swift, rocky streams; in West also at large lakes with open, rocky shores in
both forested and desert regions.
Flight Season IA Jun, NE Jun–Sep.
Distribution Also from western Nebraska west to southwestern British Columbia, south to
central California and southern Colorado.

Description Dark but vividly marked dancer of eastern forests. Postocular spots small and separated to nonexistent, may be dashed
line in younger individuals. *Male:* Eyes dark brown over tan, with
tinge of blue. Thorax dark violet in front, whitish on sides, with
rather narrow median stripe but quite broad humeral stripes. Abdomen entirely black with very narrow pale rings on S5–7, S9–10
blue. Males in tandem often have front of thorax dull red-violet,
duller than usual, and this color also characteristic of individuals at

86
Blue-tipped
Dancer
male—Ashland
Co., OH, July 2007;
brown
female—Monroe
Co., GA, May 2006;
blue female—
Decatur Co., GA,
July 2007

low temperatures. *Female*: Polymorphic, entirely brown or head, thorax and abdomen base bright blue. Eyes dark brown over tan or greenish gray. Thorax with narrow median stripe and fairly broad forked humeral stripe, outer fork widest. Abdomen mostly black above, S10 and sometimes tip of S9 pale.

Identification Only dancer with its combination of violet, black, and white thorax and blue only at extreme abdomen tip. Thorax color distinguishes from blue-tipped stream-dwelling BLUETS such as **Stream** and **Turquoise**. Males also colored somewhat like **Blackwater Bluet**, a much more slender species. Distinguished from all BLUETS by entirely blue S10. Other female dancers in range and habitat with mostly dark abdomen are **Blue-fronted**, **Dusky**, and **Powdered Dancers**. Differs from all by its combination of prominently striped thorax and mostly black abdomen tip. Female **Dusky** has fully forked humeral stripe and striped abdomen tip. Females with bright blue, vividly striped thorax could also be mistaken for stream BLUETS, distinguished by lack of blue abdomen tip.

Natural History Males perch on streamside vegetation and rocks, often in shade. Also commonly hover over water, more than other dancers except Powdered. Females typically on ground in sunny patches in woodland, but both sexes prefer vegetation to rocks. Pairs oviposit on floating leaves, twigs, and rootlets, even on wet wood above water, sometimes in large aggregations.

Habitat Small wooded sandy streams with slow to moderate current and with or without riffles, less often larger rivers. More tied to forest streams than other dancers in its range but also found in degraded and urban streams.

Flight Season ON Jun–Sep, IA May–Sep, WI Jun–Jul, OH May–Sep, NJ Jun–Sep, KY May–Oct, LA Mar–Sep, GA Mar–Oct, FL Mar–Oct.

Distribution West to western Kansas.

87 Dusky Dancer *Argia translata* TL 32–38, HW 19–23

Description Slender dark dancer with limited blue. Postocular spots small, separated; younger individuals with line between them. *Male*: Eyes bright blue-violet. Thorax when immature shows moderate median stripe and fairly broad but almost completely split humeral stripes. Humeral stripe area, then entire thorax, becomes entirely dark gray to blackish with pruinosity during maturation. Abdomen black with narrow bluish basal rings on S3–6 or S3–7, most also with blue rings on S8–9, blue extending backward on sides of segments to produce somewhat blue-tipped abdomen. Considerable variation in this, from no blue to almost all of S9–10 blue above. Males in tandem undergo dramatic transformation, brightly marked thorax with pale tan to whitish sides and antehumeral stripes contrasting with black humeral stripes; single males sometimes seen like this, presumably after mating. *Female*: Polymorphic, light areas usually brown or with blue on head and dorsal stripe on abdomen. Thorax as immature male with deeply divided humeral stripe, outer fork wider. Black dorsolateral stripe on S2–10, fused with black apical ring top on S3–6; S7 mostly black. Contrasty ventrolateral stripe on S8–9 and base of S10, so abdomen tip vividly striped in side view.

Identification No other dancer, or pond damsel for that matter, has abdomen almost entirely dark in male. Limited blue on abdomen tip not shared by any other species. Female most likely mistaken for female **Powdered** with striped thorax, but latter lacks lower dark stripe at abdomen tip and has different configuration of humeral stripes.

Natural History Males perch on rocks or vegetation adjacent to water. Pairs oviposit in herbaceous vegetation and rootlets at riffles. In woodland away from water, perches in trees.

Habitat Small to medium slow-flowing sandy or rocky streams or larger rivers, in quite open areas or with wooded banks.

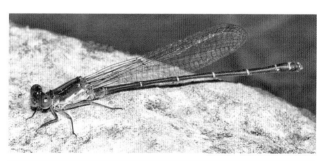

87.1
Dusky Dancer male—Ashland Co., OH, July 2007; female—Hidalgo Co., TX, September 2008

87.2
Dusky Dancer
pair—Tamaulipas,
Mexico,
November 2006,
Marion M. Dobbs

Flight Season ON Jun–Sep, ME Jul–Oct, OH Jun–Sep, NJ Jun–Sep, KY Jun–Oct, GA Jun–Oct.
Distribution Across Southwest to southern Arizona and south in lowlands to Argentina.
Most widespread species of dancer, but absent from most of southeastern Coastal Plain
even though common in lowland tropics.

Dragonflies   *Anisoptera*

Petaltail Family   *Petaluridae*

These dragonflies are often considered the most primitive living odonates. They are characterized by large size, very long stigmas, somewhat clubtail-like small eyes (but brown, not green or blue), camouflage colors, and semiterrestrial larvae that live in mud or burrows and forage at night on terrestrial insects and spiders. Broad, petal-like cerci of males of the Australian species have given the family its scientific and common names. Females have ovipositors like those of darners but unlike other North American dragonflies. Different authors have placed them at the base of dragonfly evolution or in a somewhat more advanced but still early group. Formerly among the dominant odonates and with much greater distribution, there remain relict species in moist climates of Australia, New Zealand, Chile, Japan, and northwestern and eastern North America. World 11, NA 2, East 1.

Gray Petaltail   *Tachopteryx*

This big dull-colored petaltail is a widespread inhabitant of southeastern forests. Sufficiently distinct in both adult and larval anatomy to warrant a genus of its own, it is a typical petaltail in behavior. World 1, NA 1, East 1.

88 Gray Petaltail   *Tachopteryx thoreyi*   TL 71–80, HW 48–53

Description Large brownish-gray and black dragonfly with separated eyes. *Male*: Eyes brown with gray highlights, becoming grayer with maturity; face gray-brown. Thorax slightly purplish gray with wide black humeral stripe and single black side stripe. Abdomen same color gray, strongly banded with black at rear of S3–7, rest black. *Female*: Similarly colored, readily distinguished by ovipositor and slightly thicker abdomen.

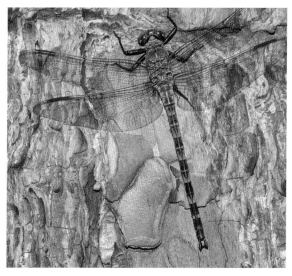

88.1
Gray Petaltail male—
Jasper Co., TX, May 2005

Identification Nothing else like it. Other large dragonflies in range more brightly marked with yellow, usually with eyes blue or green and mostly with eyes larger and touching. Perching behavior alone is good field mark, although some DARNERS also land on tree trunks. All are colored differently, most much smaller.

Natural History Surprisingly common near good habitat. Flight fast and direct. Rests on flat surfaces at any angle—rocks, fallen logs, tree trunks, stone walls—flat against substrate, where sometimes very well camouflaged. Could this be the normal perching mode in the early evolution of dragonflies? Commonly perches vertically on tree trunks from waist height up to 15 feet, also on large stones and rock walls closer to ground. Very likely to land on light-colored net or clothing, a dragonfly you can actually attract by standing in or walking slowly through its habitat! Also quite easily approached, surprisingly tame for large dragonfly. Feeds by sallying out from perch after flying insects, including quite large ones such as butterflies and other dragonflies. Also lazy figure-eight foraging flights to catch small insects in clearings. Sexual maturation in 2–3 weeks, adult life span to 7 weeks. Males not territorial but spend much time at limited breeding sites, also encountered in forest clearings and edge, sometimes at some distance from seeps. Males typically search for females by flying up and down tree trunks. Copulation well up in trees. Females oviposit into wet soil or tiny puddles. Larvae in wet mud, usually under leaves.

Habitat Shallow, mucky seeps in forested areas, flat or on hillside and associated with either streams or ponds; also sedge-covered open fens in Ozarks. Ranges from breeding habitat into open woodland, pine flatwoods.

Flight Season OH May–Aug, NJ Jun–Aug, KY May–Aug, LA Apr–Jul, GA Apr–Jul, FL Mar–Jun.

88.2
Gray Petaltail female—
Liberty Co., FL, April 2008

Darners are large dragonflies with large eyes and long abdomens that fly continuously or hover intermittently, then hang vertically when they perch. Some individuals may land horizontally on logs, rocks, or the ground to warm themselves in the sun at lower temperatures. The abdomen, especially of the male, is swollen at the base and often constricted at S3. Male cerci in most are long and fairly simple and make the abdomen seem longer. Female cerci also typically are long and often distinctive, but in many species are broken off during oviposition, so the female abdomen looks thicker and shorter than that of the male. Females have well-developed ovipositors, unlike most dragonflies. The thorax in most shows two side stripes, and the abdomen usually has a complex pattern of pale spots. They are the only fliers that have blue coloration on their bodies. Other flier dragonflies are spiketails, river cruisers, and emeralds. Spiketails have much smaller eyes, not quite or barely touching in middle, and black or dark brown bodies with two yellow stripes on either side of thorax (many darners share this, but their base color is brown rather than black). River cruisers have large eyes but only a single stripe on each side of the thorax and large central spots or rings on the abdomen, darners paired spots (some are ringed). Most emeralds have brilliant green eyes and brown or metallic black and green bodies, sometimes with green highlights. Female darners have well-developed ovipositors, whereas spiketails have a pointed, projecting subgenital plate, and river cruisers and emeralds lack any special modifications for egg laying. Wing venation also distinguishes families. Wings tend to become suffused with yellowish to brown in older darners. World 443, NA 42, East 30.

Pygmy Darners   *Gomphaeschna*

These are the smallest and most primitive North American darners, with more open wing venation than other species. The thorax is heavily patterned with pale markings. They are the only darners with a forked male epiproct. Female cerci are very short and narrow. Not common, they are found in swamps and bogs, flying early in the season. They often perch on tree trunks, where they are well camouflaged. World 2, NA 2, East 2.

89 Harlequin Darner   *Gomphaeschna furcillata*   TL 53–60, HW 29–36

Description Small, complexly patterned woodland darner. *Male*: Eyes green, face white with black across top of frons. Thorax brown with numerous greenish or pale bluish stripes and small pale orange markings that make the sides mostly pale with a jagged brown pattern. Abdomen black, with pale green (sometimes pale orange) apical dorsolateral forward-pointing triangles on S3–9, also tiny paired triangles at midsegment S3–7 and some individuals have basal orange triangles on S3–6. Also large irregular ventrolateral markings, blue on S3 and orange on S4–8, produce complexly  patterned abdomen as well. Cerci narrow, well separated at base and arched outward and then approaching again at tips. *Female*: Colored more or less as male but eyes gray-brown with greenish tinge, stripes on thorax and triangles on abdomen more whitish than green. Cerci very short. Forewings may develop wash of color beyond nodus.

Identification Distinguished by very small size for a darner, dull coloration. T-spot on frons with extensive black at base, almost no crossbar; no other darner except **Taper-tailed** similar (see that species). No other darner of any size has such an irregular thoracic pattern or combination of pale green and golden spots on abdomen. **Mottled Darner** also with irregularly patterned thorax but distinctly larger, abdomen dark with blue spots, no overlap in flight seasons. **Springtime Darner**, another small spring-flying darner, has blue-spotted

89.1
Harlequin Darner male—Early
Co., GA, March 2007, Giff Beaton

89.2
Harlequin Darner female—Westchester
Co., NY, June 2009, Clarence Holmes

abdomen and regular thoracic stripes and normal T-spot. Breeding habitat different, but both may be seen cruising over clearings in feeding flight. All other darners in range distinctly larger with different color patterns.

Natural History Both sexes perch on tree trunks and commonly land on clothing of one stalking them! Males fly back and forth over breeding habitat or hover quite low, often changing direction, then move and hover again. Females oviposit in rotten wood at water level or a bit above. Cruises over clearings in rapid flight from low to well up in trees when foraging; active until late in day.

Habitat Shallow pools and ditches in swampy areas or sphagnum bog ponds. Adults often seen at seasonal or spring-fed pools in swamps, perhaps may be successful there.

Flight Season ON May–Aug, QC Jun–Jul, NS May–Jul, WI Jun–Jul, ME May–Jul, OH May–Jun, NJ Apr–Jun, KY May–Jun, LA Feb–Apr, GA Mar–May, FL Jan–Apr.

---

90 Taper-tailed Darner · *Gomphaeschna antilope* · TL 52–60, HW 30–36

Description Small woodland darner with complex but rather dull pattern. *Male:* Eyes greenish over brown; face brown with white markings across middle and along edges. Thorax brown with pale bluish stripes and black irregular markings scattered across its surface; black more concentrated on lower sides, with yellowish crescent-shaped spot above hind legs. Abdomen mostly looks mottled, but distinct series of pale greenish-tan paired apical triangles on S2–9, becoming smaller to rear. *Female:* Colored much like male, but eyes brown and with more pale and less dark color on abdomen, pale triangles more obscure. Forewings may develop spot of color at nodus.

Identification Most similar species closely related **Harlequin Darner**, which is a bit more brightly marked in any view. In males, pale blue-gray triangles on abdomen disappear toward rear in **Taper-tailed**, still contrast in **Harlequin**. **Harlequin** usually has pale orange basal triangles on abdomen lacking in **Taper-tailed**. Male cerci wide at base in **Harlequin**,

90

Taper-tailed Darner male—Liberty Co., FL, April 2008, posed; female—Georgetown Co., SC, May 2008, Bruce Grimes

then converge toward tip, in side view slightly curved downward; same close together and parallel in **Taper-tailed**, in side view straight. Wings of **Taper-tailed** slightly broader than those of **Harlequin**, but **Harlequin** has two or more bridge crossveins, only one in **Taper-tailed**. Females can look almost identical, but if they can be seen, placement of amber wing markings diagnostic. Also, female **Taper-tailed** abdomen usually has lateral orange markings as well as dorsal; **Harlequin** usually only dorsal. Definitive identification by counting bridge crossveins. See **Harlequin Darner** for differences from other kinds of darners.

Natural History Rapid foraging flights from near ground to treetops prolonged over sunny clearings in pinewoods. Low fliers usually restricted in extent and allow close scrutiny and capture. Males usually seen, so could these be sexual patrol flights? Male and female were collected at a termite swarm. Both sexes land on tree trunks or hang under branches. May mate away from water. Oviposition in wet wood above water.

Habitat Swamps and bogs in Coastal Plain.

Flight Season NJ May–Jul, LA Apr–May, GA Mar–Apr, FL Jan–Jun.

Spotted Darners *Boyeria*

This small genus of brown darners occurs in temperate North America and Eurasia. North American species are brown with pair of pale spots on either side of the thorax; Eurasian species with striped thorax are more like other darners. All have in common crossveins in basal space in wings, perhaps relating them to some tropical genera with the same character. As in tropical forest darners, the large eyes and broad wings allow slow flight in dark habitats. Most fly low over woodland streams, often late in the day. World 7, NA 2, East 2.

91 Fawn Darner *Boyeria vinosa* TL 60–71, HW 39–46

Description Rather plain brown stream darner with bold pale spots on thorax. *Male*: Eyes dark brown with blue to greenish wash above, paler brown below. Thorax brown with two small but bold pale yellow to white spots on either side, made more conspicuous by darker areas around them. Some individuals with hint of greenish frontal stripes. Abdomen brown with tiny and rather faint yellowish markings scattered along it. Wings dark brown at extreme bases, become suffused with brown in older individuals. *Female*: As male but eyes without blue, abdomen conspicuously thicker. Cerci slender, pointed, longer than S10 in East, shorter in western part of range.

Identification For only very similar species see **Ocellated Darner**. Easily distinguished from the similarly brownish, forest-inhabiting **Twilight Darner** of southeastern Coastal Plain if bright pale thoracic spots or brown wing spots visible. **Shadow** and **Springtime Darners**, overlapping widely in range and habitat with **Fawn**, have vivid pale thoracic stripes and larger spots on abdomen. **Swamp Darner** larger, with green-striped thorax. From above, dark brown basal wing spots quite conspicuous against lighter brown body of **Fawn**, often sufficient for identification.

Natural History Both sexes cruise around clearings or over water to feed and hang vertically from almost any sort of shaded perch low in woodland, on cliffs, or under bridges. Males patrol streams low over water and usually near shore, typically in late or very late afternoon

91
Fawn Darner male—Ottawa, ON, July 2007, Chang-Won Seo, posed; female—Ottawa, ON, August 2007, Chang-Won Seo, posed

but also at other times of day, including dawn. May fly when too dark to see them clearly, intermingled with bats. Beats very greatly in length. Presumably looking for females, males often spend much time moving slowly along the bank, poking in and out of root tangles and downed branches, circling projecting sticks, and not hovering as other darners do. Also forage while doing this, sometimes capturing damselflies as large as rubyspots that they flush. Flight very low and somewhat fluttery, almost butterfly-like, distinguishing it from other stream-patrolling darners. Mating occurs at any time, even at dusk; copulation at rest in shrubs or trees. Females oviposit in wet wood at and just below water level, often flying around potential site for minutes at a time without actually laying eggs. Well known for landing on legs of people wading in streams and attempting oviposition with predictable consequences, one source of myth that dragonflies sting. An individual staying in one place rather than passing through is more likely a female.

Habitat Streams with some current, from very small streams deep within woodland to moderate-sized rivers in semiopen country. Varied bottom types and with or without rocks. Sometimes along lake shores.

Flight Season ON Jun–Oct, QC Jun–Aug, NS May–Oct, IA Jul–Oct, WI Jun–Oct, ME May–Nov, OH Jun–Oct, NJ May–Oct, KY Jun–Oct, LA May–Nov, GA Jun–Nov, FL May–Dec.

Distribution Also in northern Nebraska.

92 Ocellated Darner *Boyeria grafiana* TL 63–65, HW 40–43

Description Brown northern stream darner with bold yellow spots on side of thorax. *Male:* Eyes dark brown with greenish wash above, paler brown below. Thorax brown with two small but bold pale yellow spots on either side, made more conspicuous by darker areas around them. Some individuals with narrow greenish frontal stripes. Abdomen brown with small yellow spots low on sides of S2 and S4–8; more diffuse yellow marking on S3. Also fine yellow

92
Ocellated Darner
male—Gatineau
Park, QC, August
2008, Chang-Won
Seo, posed;
female—
Northumberland
Co., NB, August
2007, Denis
Doucet

Darner Family **171**

markings across both base and middle of most abdominal segments. Wings with no more than hint of dark brown at extreme base. *Female:* As male but dorsal abdominal markings may be more obvious, abdomen thicker. Cerci shorter than S10.

Identification Very similar to **Fawn Darner** and may not be distinguishable in flight but usually looks overall grayer, and anterior thoracic stripes usually more prominent. At rest, look for generally darker, grayer brown coloration; larger yellow spots on abdomen (always conspicuous, can be obscure in **Fawn**); and less brown at wing bases. Eyes of male **Ocellated** a bit brighter green than male **Fawn**. Both have yellow spots under abdomen, larger in **Ocellated**. Difference in yellow spot on S2 at close range, as male auricles yellow above and below (only above in **Fawn**). **Ocellated** of both sexes more likely than **Fawn** to show fine yellow dorsal markings. No other darners like this pair of species; female **Shadow Darner** flies low over streams, can be very dull, but has yellow thoracic stripes.

Natural History Usually roosts in forest shade for much of day, then begins flight low over river in late afternoon (or all day when cooler). Flight more rapid than similar-looking Fawn Darner, not as meticulous in inspecting every nook and cranny.

Habitat Usually in swift, rocky, forested rivers of uplands, rather different habitat than Fawn Darner but sometimes occurring together.

Flight Season ON Jun–Oct, QC Jun–Sep, NS Jun–Oct, ME Jun–Sep, OH Aug–Sep, NJ Jul–Oct, KY Jul–Oct.

Swamp Darner *Epiaeschna*

This very large darner is superficially like the pilot darners but with different wing venation and a prominent spine in the male projecting upward from the end of S10. Related to Cyrano Darner and some Old World genera also with no hint of constriction ("waist") near the abdomen base. World 1, NA 1, East 1.

93 Swamp Darner *Epiaeschna heros*   TL 82–91, HW 52–59

Description Large dark darner with brown, green-striped thorax and green-ringed abdomen. *Male:* Eyes blue, face brown. Thorax brown with green stripes. Abdomen dark brown to black with pale green rings, two to three per segment. *Female:* Colored as male but eyes with more brown, less blue, at maturity. Also distinguished by thicker abdomen and lack of epiproct; cerci about size of male's.

Identification Most similar is **Regal Darner**, less robust but just as long. **Regal** differs in having overall paler look, thorax and abdomen base with more green than brown on both sides and front and more brightly marked abdomen, with green line down center of basal segments as well as green rings (only ringed with green in **Swamp**). Male **Regals** also have green eyes (blue in **Swamp** and mature female **Regal**) and green face (brown in **Swamp**). Stem of T-spot on frons in **Swamp** very broad, as broad as pale green spots on either side (narrower in **Regal**, bordered by green extending down side of face). Female cerci shorter and persistent in **Swamp**, longer and lost at maturity in **Regal**. Flight style different (see **Regal**). Small **Swamp Darner** might be mistaken for superficially similar **Cyrano Darner**, as they fly in similar ways over swampy pools. Both have blue eyes and green-striped brown thorax, but **Cyrano** has much more extensive green all over slightly thicker abdomen, as well as projecting frons.

Natural History Adults fly back and forth through swamps or forest, sometimes in large numbers, also forage over open areas in woodland habitats. Flight from near ground to well up in trees. Males flying at chest height over ponds and stream pools may be searching for females. Sexes often meet away from water for mating, then female oviposits in wood-

93.1
Swamp Darner male—
McCurtain Co., OK, June 2009,
David Arbour

93.2
Swamp Darner female—
McCurtain Co., OK, July
2009, David Arbour

land pools or extensive swamps, usually in wet dead wood just above water level but also in mud or up on standing trunks. Some swarms on Atlantic coast in fall thought to be migrants.

Habitat Swamps and slow streams for breeding, more confined to woodland than Regal Darner. Larvae may develop in very shallow pools, perhaps even seasonal ones.

Flight Season ON May–Sep, QC Jul–Aug, IA Apr–May, WI May–Sep, ME Jun–Sep, OH Apr–Aug, NJ Apr–Oct, KY Apr–Sep, LA Feb–Oct, GA Mar–Nov, FL Feb–Oct.

Distribution Also slightly farther west from Kansas to Texas.

Cyrano Darner *Nasiaeschna*

This is another relatively primitive genus confined to eastern North America, probably most closely related to the Swamp Darner and several Old World genera. It is characterized by a rather stocky body, with no waist, and projecting frons. World 1, NA 1, East 1.

Description Stocky, mostly greenish darner of eastern swamps. *Male*: Eyes blue, face green to blue-green above, chartreuse to dull yellow on front. Thorax brown with green stripes: short and L-shaped on front, first side stripe jagged and interrupted, second straight and complete. Abdomen with complex striped pattern, mostly green in middle above brown dorsolateral and green ventrolateral zones; tapers toward tip. *Female*: Colored as male, abdomen thicker with very short cerci.

Identification Looks thick-bodied in comparison with other darners, with no hint of waist (this is true of most female darners, however). In hand, large, angled frons distinctive, also visible at close range in flight. Jagged thoracic stripes and abdomen with as much green as brown distinguish it from **Regal** and **Swamp Darners** that fly in similar places. Combination of blue eyes and all green body markings distinguish from all MOSAIC DARNERS.

Natural History Males fly regular, often fairly short (but as long as 40 feet), beats at waist to head height over open water. Abdomen usually held slightly curved in flight, wings above horizontal and fluttered continuously. Both sexes fly low and slow and pluck prey from herbaceous vegetation, unusual feeding method for flier dragonfly. Prey items, often large and regularly other odonates up to moderate-sized clubtails, are immediately taken to a perch in vegetation and eaten. Taking large prey more typical of this species than most other darners, perhaps associated with use of gleaning as foraging method. Also cruise back and forth over clearings in forest at about head height but rarely seen to perch, and then often well up in tree. May forage until dusk. Females oviposit in sodden logs or stumps at water's edge or up to 10 in above it, remaining for lengthy periods in one spot.

94.1
Cyrano Darner female—Denton Co., TX, June 2009, Troy Hibbits; male—Price Co., WI, June 2007, posed

94.2
Cyrano Darner
male—McCurtain
Co., OK, June
2008, Berlin Heck

Habitat Wooded wetlands of all kinds; swamps, lake edges, and slow streams. Border of at least shrubs if not trees seems necessary. Floating and emergent vegetation present or not. Widespread but usually not common.

Flight Season ON Jun–Jul, IA Jun–Jul, WI Jun–Jul, ME Jun–Jul, OH Jun–Aug, NJ May–Jul, KY May–Aug, LA Mar–Oct, GA Mar–Aug, FL all year.

Distribution Also slightly farther west from Kansas to Texas. Scarce and local in upland portions of range.

Springtime Darner   *Basiaeschna*

Superficially this is like larger mosaic darners but is a member of a more ancestral group, with more primitive wing venation. The eyes are smaller than those of mosaic darners, the line where they meet no more than twice the length of the occiput (three times or more in mosaic and neotropical darners). It also inhabits woodland streams and flies in spring, unlike most mosaic darners. World 1, NA 1, East 1.

95 Springtime Darner   *Basiaeschna janata*   TL 53–64, HW 32–40

Description Small early-season stream darner patterned much like mosaic darners but smaller than any of those that occur with it and with small brown spot at base of each wing. *Male:* Eyes brown with blue tinge, face dull yellow-brown. Lateral thoracic stripes bright yellow to whitish, bit of blue at upper ends; frontal stripes narrow and dull greenish, scarcely visible. Abdomen spotted with blue. Appendages simple, quite narrow in top view. *Female:* Eyes brown, face brownish. Polymorphic, abdominal spots green or blue. Cerci very narrow, slightly shorter than S9–10. Wings become brown in old females.

Identification Color contrast between yellow-white thoracic stripes and blue abdominal spots more striking than in most other darners; dull eye color in mature male also distinctive. Flight season of **Springtime** separates it in time from most MOSAIC DARNERS; small size and basal wing spots also distinctive. In Canadian part of **Springtime's** range, might be found in same area as **Zigzag Darner**, but latter inhabits different habitats and has different flight season, and **Zigzag**, true to its name, has zigzag thoracic stripes. Also marked only with blue, whereas **Springtime** has yellow to whitish thoracic stripes. **Cyrano Darner** could be on same stream, more likely later in summer; distinguished by larger size, higher

95
Springtime Darner female—McCurtain Co., OK, April 2010, Berlin Heck;
male—Price Co., WI, June 2007

and slower flight, curved abdomen, and green markings. In forest shade, blue color of fly-ing individuals may not be obvious, so could be mistaken for unrelated species, for exam-ple, **Stream Cruiser** or cruising CLUBTAIL. With familiarity, behavioral differences allow distinction even when color patterns cannot be seen.

Natural History Males fly long beats rapidly up and down streams, at knee height or lower and usually near shore when on larger rivers. Often capture damselflies while cruising. Ac-tive at water from dawn until dark, one of the common dusk-flying species. Both sexes hang up in trees, sometimes in weeds, and often seen in low feeding flights in clearings at forest edge, within few hundred yards of breeding sites. Females oviposit in upright herba-ceous plants and floating leaves (for example, bur-reed and spatterdock) out in current, often with abdomen submerged.

Habitat Woodland streams and rivers with some current; also at beaver ponds along stream course and, sometimes, rock-bordered lakes.

Flight Season ON May–Jul, QC May–Aug, NS May–Aug, WI May–Aug, ME May–Aug, OH May–Jul, NJ Apr–Jul, KY Mar–Jun, LA Mar–Apr, GA Mar–May, FL Mar–Apr.

Distribution Also slightly farther west in Oklahoma and Texas, one record in Saskatchewan.

Two-spined Darners *Gynacantha*

This is the largest genus of darners and is well represented in both New and Old World trop-ics. Most are shades of brown, but many have bright green or blue markings on thorax and abdomen base. Some have basal wing markings, and wings of mature adults can be quite brown. Females have prominent two-spined structure projecting downward from S10, prob-ably involved with steadying abdomen for egg laying. All but a few species are dusk fliers, and their biology is poorly known. Large eyes and broad wings fit them for their daytime flight in forests and dusk flight in clearings. The two North American species are rather similar, but the group includes very small to very large species. World 85, NA 2, East 1.

Description Plain brown dusk-flying forest darner. *Male*: Eyes brown, may become dull greenish when fully mature; mature individuals have tiny but notable crosswise streak of green near front edge of each eye. Entirely light brown from face to abdomen tip. Small black spots on thorax and faint indications of patterning on abdomen. Mature individuals at brightest with front of thorax greenish, light green sclerites between wings, and fine light green  abdominal rings and lines. Abdomen very slightly constricted at S3. *Female*: Colored exactly as male, with thicker abdomen. Cerci long, narrow, and pointed, break off to half length in mature females. With age, wings of both sexes become increasingly suffused with brown.

Identification Not similar to any other regional species except **Fawn Darner**, which has vivid yellow spots on sides of thorax and never any green markings. Differs from **Phantom** and **Pale-green Darners** of similar habits in larger size, mostly brown thorax. Note **Mocha**

96.1
Twilight Darner male—Dade Co., FL., December 2007, Netta Smith

96.2
Twilight Darner female— Puntarenas Province, Costa Rica, February 2009, R. A. Behrstock/ Naturewide Images

Emerald, an all-brown emerald that is smaller and darker and with very different terminal appendages. Unlike most darners, this one does not fly beats over water.

Natural History Both sexes patrol for small insects in dusk feeding flights, sometimes in large numbers and usually at woodland edge. May establish "beats" along edges a few feet wide and 40–50 feet long. Rarely fly above head height. Commonly enters buildings after dusk flight and may be found next morning. Dusk flights occur even in suburban areas with few trees. Unidirectional dusk flights of thousands of individuals seen in late fall in southern Florida. Daytime roosts within forest also usually below head height, difficult to see because abdomen often backed by vertical stem and wings invisible in shade. Mating in forest away from water, apparently at any time of day. Female searches out shallow pools in or at edge of woodland and oviposits in rotten wood or mud. May lay eggs in depressions before they fill with rain, and late-emerging adults may live for months to breed in next rainy season.

Habitat Wooded swamps and low-lying woodland, even in shaded garden pools; no minimal size for larval habitat.

Flight Season GA Sep–Dec, FL all year.

Distribution From northern Mexico south in lowlands to Brazil and throughout West Indies. Vagrant recorded in Oklahoma.

Three-spined Darners *Triacanthagyna*

Closely related to two-spined darners, with very large eyes and broad wings, these display three prominent spines under S10 of females rather than two. Most species are smaller than two-spined darners, very slender, and all have green and brown thorax and dark abdomen with fine green markings. Forest-based and crepuscular, they make up a prominent component of dragonfly dusk flight throughout the New World tropics. World 9, NA 3, East 2.

97 Pale-green Darner *Triacanthagyna septima* TL 59–66, HW 34–43

Identification Small light green and brown pale-legged darner of south Florida. Abdomen not constricted at S2–3. *Male*: Eyes blue-green, face olive. Thorax light green with faintly indicated brownish wash on front. Abdomen mostly brown, sides of S1–2 greenish  also light green dorsal stripe on S2 and fine transverse markings on middle segments becoming narrow and more obscure toward rear. *Female*: Colored about as male; eyes greenish to brown, perhaps never with blue. Cerci long, narrow, and pointed, broken off in mature individuals. Close look at appendages necessary to determine sex, as females with appendages look much like males. Unlike most tropical dusk-flying darners, wings not darker with age.

Similar Species Distinguished from **Phantom Darner** of similar size, shape, and habits by entirely green rather than striped thorax and pale rather than dark legs; also note lack of "wasp waist." Much rarer than **Phantom**. Conspicuously smaller than **Twilight Darner**, with thorax green rather than brown or greenish-tinged. Both have pale legs. Closest to **Blue-faced Darner** in size and even in color pattern, but that species darker overall with dark legs and usually blue face. Mature **Blue-faced** much more brightly colored than **Pale-green**, also has fine green median line down length of abdomen not present in **Pale-green**.

Natural History Both sexes hang up during day in woodland, usually dense, and forage at forest edge from ground level to well up in trees at dusk; may be second flight at dawn when warm enough. Breeding poorly known, but females probably oviposit in fallen logs and branches in depressions on dry forest floor that fill with water at beginning of rainy season.

97.1
Pale-green Darner
male—Hidalgo Co., TX,
September 2008

97.2
Pale-green Darner
female—Madre de Dios
Department, Peru, July
2002, Netta Smith

Habitat Should be in dense woodland that floods seasonally. Breeds in forested swamps in tropics, so much potential breeding habitat in south Florida.

Flight Season FL Nov; all year in tropics.

Distribution Known in East from single record in Big Cypress Swamp, Collier County, Florida; perhaps only a vagrant. Also from south Texas south to Bolivia and Brazil and throughout West Indies.

---

98 Phantom Darner *Triacanthagyna trifida*   **TL 62–75, HW 40–47**

Description Green-striped dusk-flying darner of southeastern coastal plain. Abdomen constricted at S2–3. *Male:* Eyes blue, face dull greenish with black T-spot on frons. Thorax mostly green, with broad brown median stripe and three narrow brown stripes on each side. Abdomen brown to black, with S1–2 and base of S3 mostly green (complex pattern on top of S2) and fine transverse green markings, two per segment, on S2–9. Sclerites between wings mostly blue with maturity. *Female:* As male but eyes greenish when mature. Male may stay in immature coloration (green eyes, green between wings) for weeks or even months before finally acquiring mature coloration late in season. Wings of both sexes become increasingly suffused brown with age.

Identification Most similar in general appearance to **Blue-faced Darner**, a species that flies during the day. **Blue-faced** has a blue face and almost entirely green thorax, plus median green line on abdomen. Very young **Blue-faced**, however, have a green face and traces of brown stripes on the thorax; look at eyes (dull bluish) and characteristic dorsal line on abdomen. Also, "wasp waist" characteristic of **Phantom**. Of the dusk fliers, **Pale-green**

98.1
Phantom Darner
male—Collier Co.,
FL, December 2007,
posed

98.2
Phantom Darner
male, immature
female—Collier Co.,
FL, December 2007,
Netta Smith; male
posed

Darner also has all green thorax and pale legs, **Twilight Darner** larger, mostly brown without stripes on thorax.

Natural History Hangs up during day in deep shade, typically from small branches of shrubs. Appears at dusk flying over open areas near woodland, from just above ground up to tree canopies, sometimes in virtual swarms. Flight typically more erratic and often higher than that of larger Twilight Darner. Flies until too dark for observer to see clearly. Seen going round and round in swarms of gnats. May come into buildings and be found there following morning, and sometimes a shorter dawn flight. Infrequently seen foraging during broad daylight, even at midday, seemingly more prone to do this than are other dusk-fliers. Breeding behavior unknown; males have been seen patrolling over muddy forest depressions.

Habitat Dense interior of forests and swamps for roosting, seasonal flooding for breeding.

Flight Season GA Sep–Dec, FL Jul–Feb.

Distribution Scarce in northern part of range. Also throughout West Indies.

Pilot Darners *Coryphaeschna*

These are rather large neotropical darners, the mature males with conspicuously green thorax and black abdomen (some tropical species are entirely red). Males have simple appendages. Females typically have very long cerci that are easily broken off; their presence is a sign of immaturity. Adults are usually associated with forest but may breed in open marshes. They forage well above ground (thus "pilot darners"), even among treetops, sometimes in large aggregations and often with other species. World 8, NA 3, East 3.

99 Blue-faced Darner *Coryphaeschna adnexa* TL 66–69, HW 42–45

Description Medium-sized darner of Florida with blue face, green thorax, slender brown abdomen. *Male*: Eyes green with bright blue margins or mostly blue, face and rear of head blue. Thorax green with fine brown suture lines. Abdomen with fine green line down center and two narrow green rings around each segment (one on  S9, none on S10). Teneral with wide brown stripes on thorax, quickly obscured. *Female*: Colored as male but face green with blue tinge, abdomen often somewhat richer brown. Green crossbands on abdomen more likely to bend at ends and partially outline segments, also green spots low on sides of more basal segments. Might also be distinguished by intact cerci distinctly longer than those of male; cerci lost in older females.

Identification Few darners in this region with entirely green thorax, brown abdomen. Most similar is **Mangrove Darner**, larger and with no hint of blue on eyes or face, also brown dash on either side of front of thorax. **Regal Darner**, similar in shape and habits but much larger, has brown stripes on thorax. Note that thorax in teneral **Blue-faced** striped just like **Regal**, distinguish by size and brown abdomen of **Blue-faced**. Rare **Pale-green Darner** is paler, with pale legs and greenish face. GREEN DARNERS all much bulkier, relatively shorter abdomens.

Natural History Males patrol back and forth low over floating vegetation. Females oviposit in floating vegetation, for example water lettuce, just above water. Both sexes in feeding flight, sometimes numerous individuals, from near ground to treetops. Flies within tiny woodland clearings as well as out in open, then hangs up under branch at about head height.

Habitat Ponds, usually covered with floating vegetation such as water lettuce, water hyacinth, or duckweeds. Usually associated with forest.

Flight Season FL all year.

Distribution From south Texas south in lowlands to Argentina, also Greater Antilles.

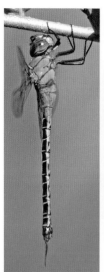

99.1
Blue-faced Darner female—Hillsborough Co., FL,
October 2003, Giff Beaton; male—Collier Co., FL,
December 2007, posed

99.2
Blue-faced Darner immature
male—Palm Beach Co., FL,
May 2008, J. Lubchansky

---

100 Mangrove Darner   *Coryphaeschna viriditas*   **TL 76–85, HW 50–59**

Description Large green and black darner of south Florida, mostly
coastal. *Male*: Eyes and face green, narrow T-spot on frons. Thorax
and abdomen base (S1–3) green with sparse brown markings, including fine lines on sides of thorax and short dashes on front. Abdomen black with pattern of fine green rings and median stripe
ending on S7. Each segment is actually outlined in green (slightly interrupted at outside
edge), with a green cross in the middle. *Female*: Colored as male, but eyes become blue at
maturity. With age, wings suffused with saffron color in both sexes.

Identification Superficially like **Regal Darner** but slightly smaller, this species easily distinguished by all green thorax. **Blue-faced Darner**, a smaller species, has a plain green thorax,
but mature males and females have blue eyes and face. However, immature **Blue-faced**
have green eyes and face and may look much like **Mangrove**. Look for fine dark dash on
either side of front of thorax on **Mangrove**, lacking in **Blue-faced** (immature **Blue-faced**
may show trace of it). Also, much stronger green line along outside edge of abdominal segments in **Mangrove**, outlining segment in lateral view, than in **Blue-faced**; this difference
more evident in males. **Blue-faced** so far not found in Florida Keys, stronghold of **Mangrove Darner**. GREEN DARNERS have very different abdominal patterns than pilot
darners.

Natural History Most often encountered while in foraging flight, from low to well above
ground in clearings among trees. Lengthy watching may be rewarded with a better look
when one hangs up in tree, as low as head height. Like Regal Darner, pairs may encounter
each other away from water, then copulate in tree; after mating, female heads for wetland
to oviposit. Also seen flying over water bodies such as canals in mangroves at midday, but
these may have been feeding individuals, as those collected were immature.

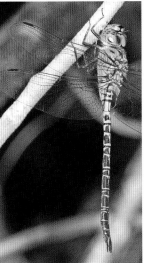

100
Mangrove
Darner male,
female—Dade
Co., FL,
December 2007

Habitat Often associated with coastal mangroves and perhaps breeds in them, especially in areas flooded with fresh water (not known to breed in sea water). May be in mangroves in Florida Keys because they furnish dense forest adjacent to uncommon freshwater wetlands. Also in forest away from coast. Known to breed in open freshwater marshes in tropics.

Flight Season FL Dec–Aug.

Distribution Also from northern Mexico south to Bolivia and Paraguay and throughout Greater Antilles.

---

101 Regal Darner   *Coryphaeschna ingens*   TL 86–90, HW 54–59

Description Large darner with green- and brown-striped thorax, green-ringed black abdomen. *Male*: Eyes green, face green with brown crossline. Thorax green with wide brown stripes. Abdomen black with narrow green dorsal line and fine narrow green rings around it, two to three each on middle segments. *Female*: Colored as male but with blue eyes when mature, green when immature. This may be primary way sexes distinguished away from water.

Very long, slender cerci in immature female shed with maturity. Wings in immature female orange at base, clear beyond, this reversed in maturity, when much of wings become brownish-orange.

Identification See **Swamp Darner**, closest in size and color to this species and overlapping with it extensively. **Regal** with more green, less brown on thorax. Flight styles somewhat different, **Swamp** zipping through air like fighter plane, **Regal** with more buoyant flight like glider. Birders should think of difference between merlin and kestrel, although this is surely indicative and not definitive. When wings suffused with orange, tends to be more toward tip and rear edge in **Regal**, more in center and front edge in **Swamp**. Intact female cerci longer in **Regal** than in **Swamp**. See **Mangrove Darner** also.

Natural History Unusual among dragonflies in males not patrolling at wetlands, but pairs meet and mate away from water. Apparently both "immature" and mature females mate. Both sexes in feeding swarms from near ground to high in air at any time, including dawn,

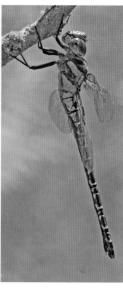

101.1
Regal Darner
male—Palm
Beach Co., FL,
September
2008,
J. Lubchansky;
female—
Travis Co., TX,
April 2008, Eric
Isley

101.2
Regal Darner
immature
female—Indian
River Co., FL,
March 2009,
Bob Martinka

but especially late afternoon to dusk; in open or among trees, sometimes in large numbers. May be mixed with other large species such as Common Green Darners or Prince Baskettails. Tends to feed on quite small prey, including swarming mosquitoes and mayflies. Females oviposit in emergent or floating vegetation at lake or pond shores, even in fairly dense marshes. Spend much time dropping into vegetation and rising again, as if testing for appropriate and/or safe site, meanwhile with abdomen curled downward, perhaps to discourage male attention. Both sexes hang up in shrubs and trees.

Habitat Breeds in open ponds and lakes in wooded areas, roosts in woodland. Also commonly hunts over open areas.

Flight Season LA Apr–Oct, GA Apr–Sep, FL Jan–Oct.

Distribution Also Bahamas and Cuba.

These bright and contrastingly patterned dragonflies fly over lakes and marshes throughout temperate regions of the northern hemisphere, where they dominate dragonfly faunas. Often seen away from water, sometimes at great distances, they commonly form mixed-species feeding swarms, probably aggregating only because their flying prey is aggregated. Both sexes move from water body to water body, not at all tied to one place (probably true of most if not all mosaic darners). Typical coloration includes a frontal stripe on each side of front of thorax, a pair of slanted stripes on either side of thorax, often green shading down into blue, and a series of paired blue spots down the entire length of the abdomen. Females in most species are polymorphic, with male-colored andromorph and usually more common heteromorph with yellow stripes and spots; green is also an alternate color to blue in some. Check out enough mating pairs and you will usually see both morphs. Males either fly regular beats along the shoreline or hover here and there in a smaller territory, but some of them circumnavigate a pond or lake and then move on to another one, all to search for females ovipositing in shore vegetation. Females disturbed during oviposition usually fly rapidly up into trees. Also may be quickly grabbed, even by males of other species, which usually results in awkward flight and then release. Males can be identified by combination of thoracic stripe shape, abdominal pattern, and appendage type. With enough practice, some species can be picked out as they fly by, but please believe that this is tricky! Because you do not see these dragonflies perch very often, capturing them and identifying them in the hand is the best way to find out what species are present.

Neotropical darners (*Rhionaeschna*), very similar to but recently separated from mosaic darners, are distinguished by pale lateral borders to T-spot on frons and tubercle under S1 in both sexes. Some marks to look for to distinguish mosaic and neotropical darners that fly together include (1) shape of male appendages, whether simple, paddle, or forked; (2) eye color bright blue, darker turquoise, or clearly greenish; (3) face unmarked or with obvious dark stripe on frontoclypeal suture; (4) lateral thoracic stripes wide or narrow, straight or notched, extended posteriorly or not at upper ends; (5) presence or absence of markings between lateral thoracic stripes; (6) S10 black or with prominent blue or white spots; (7) pale spots under most abdominal segments or not; and (8) much hovering or continuous flight along shore. Females are much more difficult to distinguish but share the facial, thoracic, and abdominal patterning (but not necessarily coloration) of males and may have distinctive ovipositors or cerci. Note that stigma in males is dark above, in females pale. Identification problems are greater in the North, where more species occur together. Bear in mind that several other genera of this family can be mistaken for mosaic darners, especially Springtime Darner. World 41, NA 15, East 12.

Description Slender, dark northern darner, with limited blue. Lateral thoracic stripes straight (may be slight extension at wing base) and narrow, all blue or blue above, greenish below (no yellow). Frontal stripes very narrow, greenish. *Male*: Eyes turquoise. Cerci with prominent ventral tubercle in side view at about one-fourth length. *Female*: Polymorphic, common andromorph colored exactly as male; heteromorph, with yellow-green spots on abdomen, much less common. Cerci large and conspicuous, obviously longer than S9–10 and acutely pointed. Abdomen slender and wasp-waisted as in male.

Identification For both sexes, dark color, with narrow, straight thoracic stripes, limited blue on abdomen and none on S10, distinctive, Superficially most similar **Shadow Darner** has

102.1
Black-tipped
Darner
female—
Frederick Co.,
MD, August
2007, Steven
Collins, posed;
male—Price Co.,
WI, August
2008, posed

102.2
Black-tipped Darner
female—Skamania Co.,
WA, September 2007, Jim
Johnson, posed

paddle appendages, pale spots under abdomen. Female **Black-tipped** identified by looking amazingly like male, same narrow-waisted shape and bright color; large cerci simulate male appendages.

Natural History Males fly along lake shores or over marshes, often above vegetation at head height or above. May patrol and defend entire small pond, usually for short periods and then move to another nearby wetland. But also hover at length over small coves, chasing all intruders. Known to displace and even prey on male Canada and Green-striped Darners when patrolling. Both sexes more common at water later in day. Females behave exactly like males, presumably mimicking them to avoid harassment when ovipositing, but often fly lower, below tops of sedges. If a seeming male darner, flying among other males in the same manner, suddenly lands and begins ovipositing, it is probably this species. Abdomen of female more slender than in other darners, enhancing similarity to male. Oviposits both well above water level and at water level, on emergent or floating plants, even mud; abdomen may be submerged to wings. Rushes, cattails, irises, bur-reeds, and other plants used; living soft rush especially preferred. Sometimes in single-species or mixed feeding swarms, often forming in the afternoon.

Habitat Clear lakes and ponds, often with associated bog vegetation, in forested regions. Bur-reed usually common.

Flight Season ON Jun–Sep, QC Jul–Oct, NS Jun–Oct, WI Jun–Oct, ME Jun–Oct, OH Jul–Oct, NJ Jul–Oct.

Distribution Local west to British Columbia and Washington.

103 Sedge Darner *Aeshna juncea*   TL 61–69, HW 40–46

Description Common northern darner of sedgy lakes. Lateral thoracic stripes wide and straight, may be slight posterior extension; long streak parallel to and between them and often short streak in front of anterior one. Frontal stripes well developed and conspicuous. Fine black line across face. Whitish spots beneath middle abdominal segments (not in all individuals). *Male*: Eyes greener than in most other common species. Lateral thoracic stripes blue above and yellow-green below. Very wide in some individuals, with in-between streak especially prominent. Blue abdominal spots relatively small but well developed on S10. *Female*: Polymorphic, heteromorph with green-tinged eyes and yellow-green markings, andromorph with blue-tinged eyes and blue markings. Cerci rather small for mosaic darner, not as long as S9–10.

Identification Combination of simple appendages and broad, straight thoracic stripes good for this species. Pale streak between stripes more prominent than in other species. Stripes much broader than in **Variable Darner**, lacking prominent indentations and extensions of **Canada**, **Green-striped**, **Lake**, and **Subarctic Darners**. Most similar to **Subarctic** and often occurs with it. Identification can be tricky and may have to be resolved by scrutinizing hamules of individuals in hand, but careful look at thoracic-stripe shape will usually do it. Female also with well-developed and fairly long pale stripe between especially broad and

103
Sedge Darner male—
Baker Co., OR, August
2005, posed;
female—Baker Co., OR,
August 2004, posed

straight lateral thoracic stripes. Closest in pattern because of broad, straight lateral stripes would be **Black-tipped Darner**, which has no in-between stripe. Also, female **Sedge** one of few species with obvious pale spots under abdomen (usually); thoracic pattern distinct from that of **Canada, Green-striped, Shadow**, and **Subarctic**, the other species. See **Subarctic** for differences from female **Sedge**.

Natural History Most abundant darner in many northern wetlands. Males fly widely about a foot over extensive sedge beds or with much lengthy hovering, also along vegetated lake shores at knee height and below. Patrol flights over sedges 30 feet long or shorter. Females oviposit at water level or just below in emergent grasses and sedges or matted roots, also into moss. Female either moves short distance when disturbed or leaves water like a shot. Many oviposit when males not present. Adult life to 70 days (prereproductive period to 35 days).

Habitat Extensive sedge marshes and mossy fens, also lakes, ponds, and ditches with emergent vegetation.

Flight Season ON Jul–Aug, QC Jun–Sep, NS Jun–Sep.

Distribution Widely in far Northwest through Alaska, south in mountains to Oregon and New Mexico; also across northern Eurasia.

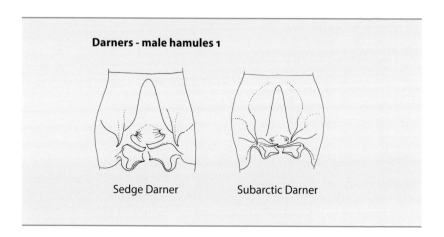

Darners - male hamules 1

Sedge Darner   Subarctic Darner

104 Subarctic Darner *Aeshna subarctica* TL 63–68, HW 40–46

Description Northern darner of bogs and fens. Black line across yellow face. Lateral thoracic stripes notched and extended, less so than some other species. Short, thin streak between stripes and often narrow partial streak just in front of anterior one. Frontal stripes relatively thin, reduced. Pale spots beneath middle abdominal segments. *Male*: Eyes green, similar to Sedge Darner in being less bluish than other mosaic darners. Thoracic stripes bluish above  and yellow-green below. *Female*: Polymorphic, female abdomen with blue or yellow or greenish yellow spots. Cerci longer than S9–10.

Identification Often flying with very similar **Sedge Darner**, from which it is distinguished by narrower thoracic stripes with slight notch in front and extension to rear. Minor but distinctive difference in black stripe across face, widening at ends in **Subarctic** but not in **Sedge**. Male hamules quite different, only evident in hand with magnification. Females distinguished from **Sedge** by longer cerci (distinctly longer than S9–10, about 6–7 mm in length, no longer or shorter than those segments in **Sedge**, about 4–5 mm), shorter ovipositor (just

104

Subarctic Darner male—Whitehorse, YT, August 2009, Syd Cannings, posed; green female, blue female—Wasco Co., OR, September 2007, Jim Johnson, posed

reaches end of S9, surpasses it in **Sedge**). Both sexes distinguished from **Canada** and **Green-striped Darners** by black line across face, less distinct notch on first lateral thoracic stripe. Breeding habitat important clue for **Subarctic**.

Natural History Males fly back and forth at waist height over floating beds of sphagnum and other mosses in lakes or muskeg pools, hover in one spot, then move to another. Patrol flights not usually along shorelines. Some males remain in restricted areas for minutes at a time, others wander farther. Females oviposit in mosses and sedges at water surface, usually at the edge of open water. Both sexes cruise in darner assemblages in woodland clearings. Adult life to 70 days (prereproductive period to 35 days). Appears later in season than most other darners, at least in some areas.

Habitat Typically fens and bogs with abundant growth of sphagnum and other mosses.

Flight Season ON Jul–Sep, QC Jul–Sep, NS Aug–Oct, WI Jul–Sep, ME Aug–Sep, NJ Aug–Sep.

Distribution Widely in far North, west to Alaska and south in mountains to Oregon and Montana; also across northern Eurasia.

<hr>

105 Green-striped Darner *Aeshna verticalis*   **TL 62–72, HW 41–47**

Description Common northeastern darner with green thoracic stripes. Lateral thoracic stripes notched and extended, mostly green but some blue above, especially posterior stripe; frontal stripes broad, green. *Male*: Eyes greenish. *Female*: Polymorphic, most heteromorphs with green or yellow-green spots, rarely blue. Cerci relatively large, distinctly longer than S9–10, widest near middle; often broken off at maturity.

Identification Much like **Canada Darner** but lateral thoracic stripes mostly green (mostly blue in **Canada**, rarely mostly blue in **Green-striped**), slightly less notched than in **Canada** (thus much less notched than **Lake**), and extension along wing base ("flag") often but not

105
Green-striped
Darner male,
female—
Westmorland Co.,
NB, August 2007,
Denis Doucet,
posed

always becomes wider at end (stays narrow in **Canada**). In addition, stripes usually brighter and more contrasting. Female differs in same ways. Variation sufficient that some individuals may not be identifiable from color pattern. Differs from other species in same way as **Canada**, including spots under abdomen. Fine teeth on upper surface near tip of cerci in male **Canada** can be seen under magnification; lacking in **Green-striped**. Hamules also different, those of **Green-striped** shorter and strongly curved inward at front, those of **Canada** longer and pointing forward. Difference in female genital valves apparent in hand: grooves on ventral surface extend about to tip in **Canada**, end well before tip in **Green-striped**.

Natural History Both sexes often perch on tree trunks. Males patrol as in other mosaic darners, fairly high and often along border between open water and vegetation. May also be over dense stands of grasses and sedges or sphagnum beds. Females oviposit in bur-reed stems and pondweed, usually just above waterline. Feeds in clearings away from water, may join feeding swarms.

Habitat Forest ponds and lakes with much aquatic vegetation.

Flight Season ON Jun–Oct, QC Jun–Oct, NS Jul–Oct, WI Jun–Sep, ME Jul–Oct, OH Aug–Oct, NJ Jul–Sep.

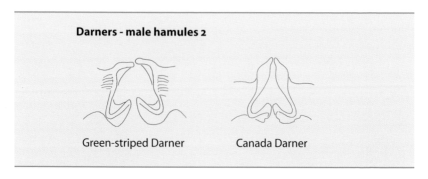

Darners - male hamules 2

Green-striped Darner   Canada Darner

Description Common darner of northern lakes. Lateral thoracic stripes notched and extended, yellow spot between them; frontal stripes well developed. Pale blue or gray spots under most abdominal segments. *Male*: Lateral thoracic stripes blue, may shade to green below; frontal thoracic stripes well developed, greenish; abdominal spots moderate sized and blue. *Female*: Polymorphic, heteromorph with yellow-tinged brown eyes and yellow-green markings, andromorph with blue-tinged brown eyes and blue markings. May lack frontal stripes.

Identification Very similar to **Green-striped Darner**, distinguished by mostly blue lateral thoracic stripes and minor differences in stripe shape (see that species). Either species may occasionally show stripe color of the other. Also rather similar to **Lake Darner**, but both sexes distinguished by being smaller, with no black stripe on face, and pale spots under abdomen. Posterior lateral thoracic stripe slightly indented or incurved in front in **Canada**, distinctly notched in **Lake**. Male flight style different, with much hovering in **Canada** and steady flight in **Lake**. Female distinguished from darners other than **Green-striped** by combination of unmarked face, notched/extended thoracic stripes, and pale spots under abdomen. Others with ventral abdominal spots include **Sedge**, **Shadow**, and **Subarctic Darners**, first two with straight stripes and last with notched stripe but no extension. Female **Lance-tipped** also rather like **Canada** and **Green-striped**, but distinctly larger cerci and second lateral thoracic stripe wider at upper end, extending downward along rear edge of thorax.

Natural History Males fly slowly along shore at about waist height, usually back and forth in defined territory of no more than 30–65 feet, and very often hover over and cruise through

106.1
Canada Darner green female, male—Wasco Co., OR, August 2008, posed

106.2
Canada Darner blue female—Bayfield Co., WI, August 2008, Ryan Brady

Darner Family **191**

tall beds of grasses and sedges for lengthy periods, at intervals dropping to surface for quick or extended female search. Copulation usually in shrubs near water. Females oviposit in plant stems, moss, algae, and mud at water level, usually in marshy area rather than at shore. Away from water, perches on tree trunks or hangs from branches. Common in early evening darner feeding swarms in clearings near woodland. Blue, green, and yellow markings of males may be subdued gray when active at relatively low temperatures, brighten as air warms.

Habitat Lakes and ponds in forest zone with abundant emergent vegetation; often associated with bogs and beaver ponds.

Flight Season ON Jun–Oct, QC Jun–Oct, NS Jun–Oct, IA Sep–Oct, WI May–Oct, ME Jun–Oct, OH Aug–Oct, NJ Jun–Oct.

Distribution Locally across far North to Yukon, south in mountains to California and Montana; isolated population in northwestern Nebraska.

107 Lake Darner *Aeshna eremita* TL 66–79, HW 41–52

Description Larger than other mosaic darners, largest darner in much of its range. Lateral thoracic stripes notched and extended, pale spot or streak between them. Much blue on abdomen, none beneath it. *Male*: Eyes turquoise above, black line across face. Lateral thoracic stripes blue or blue shading to green below; spot or streak between them blue or green; frontal stripes greenish. *Female*: Polymorphic, with either blue, as in male, or green stripes and spots.

Identification Larger than other mosaic darners, also recognized by continual cruising flight along lake shores. **Canada** and **Green-striped Darners** most similar species in most of range because of simple appendages and thoracic pattern. **Lake** larger than either, with black line across face, no pale spots under abdomen, and notched posterior lateral thoracic stripe. Female identified by size, thoracic pattern, black face line, and relatively large cerci.

Natural History Males fly rapidly over open water or along lake shores at about knee height, often with long abdomen drooping at tip. Usually stay out of vegetation and no hovering, unlike most other mosaic darners. Sometimes move into beds of dense vegetation to search for females, however. Males remain at water late in afternoon and may continue flying until dark (under midnight sun in far north!). Perching sites for both sexes typically bare

107
Lake Darner
male—
Whatcom Co.,
WA, September
2008, posed;
green
female—San
Juan Co., WA,
August 2007,
Netta Smith,
posed; blue
female—
Ottawa, ON,
September
2006,
Chang-Won Seo

twigs, tree trunks, or ground. Females oviposit on floating logs, in stems of emergent herbaceous plants, and in tangles of rootlets on vertical banks at or just below water surface. May come to water in large numbers during moderate rain.

Habitat Typically wooded lakes and large ponds, sometimes slow streams.

Flight Season ON Jun–Oct, QC Jun–Oct, NS Jun–Oct, WI Jun–Oct, ME May–Oct.

Distribution Across far north to Alaska, south to Washington and in mountains to Utah and Colorado.

---

108 Variable Darner *Aeshna interrupta*   TL 61–72, HW 41–46

Description Lateral thoracic stripes narrow and straight or narrow and slightly irregular (in unforested western part of region), or divided into upper and lower spot (in forested eastern part of region); frontal stripes poorly developed or absent. Fine black line across face. *Male:* Eyes rather dark blue, face pale greenish. Thoracic stripes mostly blue, may be yellow below; upper spots may be blue, lower ones yellow-green. Large amount of blue on abdomen, S3 usually looks all blue on sides, with only narrow black dorsal line. Isolated whitish to pale blue spots on S10 (spotted individuals may lack pale markings on that segment). *Female:* Polymorphic, andromorph with blue-tinged eyes and blue body markings, heteromorph with brown eyes and yellow body markings.

Identification Both sexes distinguished from all other mosaic and neotropical darners by lateral stripes being narrow or reduced to spots. Often hard to see thoracic markings on males in flight, even with good look in passing, whereas stripes usually obvious on other species. Whitish spots on S10 visible on perched individual good mark to distinguish males,

108.1
Variable Darner spotted pair—
Washington Co., VT, August 2006,
Bryan Pfeiffer/Wings Photography

108.2
Variable Darner striped male, Pyper Lake, BC, July
2006, posed; striped blue female—Grant Co., OR,
July 2008, Greg Lasley

as those spots on other species blue. However, those few without spots on S10 could be mistaken for **Black-tipped** or **Shadow Darners**, both of which have smaller blue abdominal spots. Female much like female **Shadow** but lacks pale spots below. Female **Variable** also rather like female **Blue-eyed**, which has bump under S1.

Natural History Males fly rapidly or slowly along shorelines or stop to hover and inspect vegetation beds, looking for laying females. Often at edge between open water and cattails, also over dense sedge beds. Tends to fly back and forth over apparently defined territory. Both sexes feeding and at water until dark. Where common, copulating pairs regularly seen in flight, also tandem pairs; some of the latter could be mismatched (males are indiscriminate). Females oviposit on floating sedge and grass stems, upright herb and shrub stems, and wet logs. Regularly in mixed feeding swarms of several species of mosaic darners. Often perch on tree trunks, also on ground at higher latitudes. Commonly encountered far from water in mountain clearings, probably "hilltops" like butterflies. Most abundant darner by far on Canadian prairies and locally common over much of range.

Habitat Lakes and ponds of all sorts, even small ones, usually with dense shore vegetation but at least some open water. From lowlands to well up in mountains.

Flight Season ON Jun–Sep, QC Jun–Oct, NS Jun–Oct, IA Jul–Sep, WI Jun–Oct, ME Jun–Oct, NJ Aug–Sep.

Distribution Across northern North America to Alaska, south to mountains of California, northern Arizona, and New Mexico.

Comments Several named subspecies differ in shape of thoracic stripes or structure of male cerci. *A. i. interrupta* occurs in eastern forest zone. In that subspecies, lateral thoracic stripes broken into two pairs of above-and-below spots (thus *interrupta*). *A. i. lineata*, which has narrow, linear thoracic stripes, is subspecies of prairies west of that zone; both types in Wisconsin.

Description Mosaic darner with irregular thoracic pattern, markings pale blue to whitish. *Male*: Eyes dull bluish, face pale blue. Anterior thoracic stripes short and jagged, and whitish spot low on either side of front. Anterior lateral stripe deeply incised and hooked forward at top, posterior stripe very broad, and two whitish spots fill up most of space between them. Abdomen with S1 mostly blue in lateral view and usual complement of paired blue spots, including  large ones on S10. Underside of middle abdominal segments also with white to pale blue spots. *Female*: Eyes brown over yellow, face yellow. Thorax patterned identically but with yellow or blue-gray markings (polymorphism?). Abdomen brown with yellow markings like those of male.

Identification Among mosaic darners, no other colored like this on thorax, which looks mostly pale blue (yellow in female) because so heavily marked. Extension of lower end of anterior lateral stripe across humeral suture onto front of thorax diagnostic among large mosaic darners (also present in otherwise quite different **Azure** and **Zigzag**). Abdomen looks much like those of other species, except side view of S1 shows it to be almost entirely pale; mostly brown (pale posterior half at most) in other mosaic darners. Considerably smaller **Harlequin** and **Taper-tailed Darners** have complexly marked thorax but very differently colored abdomen; also don't overlap in flight season.

Natural History Forages in clearings and open woodland, may be higher and faster than related species. Often perches on tree trunks. Males fly along close to shore vegetation or bog mat, examining nooks and crannies at water level as most mosaic darners do and hovering often. Patrol shorelines at any time of day, perhaps more common late in afternoon. One female oviposited in mud on drying lake bed among stranded lilypads. Visiting females depart quickly when disturbed.

109

Mottled Darner male—Vilas Co., WI, August 2008, posed; female—MA, 1994, Blair Nikula

Habitat Lakes and ponds, often bog-fringed and with abundant water lilies and arrowhead.

Flight Season ON Jun–Oct, QC Jul–Aug, NS Jul–Sep, WI Jun–Sep, ME Jul–Oct, OH Aug–Sep, NJ Jul–Oct.

110 Zigzag Darner *Aeshna sitchensis* TL 57–60, HW 37–40

Description Small darner with lateral thoracic stripes narrow and so strongly notched and extended that they form zigzag shape. Stripes often broken and may have spot or streak in between. Frontal stripes reduced or lacking. *Male*: Eyes brown mixed with blue around edges. All pale markings light blue, no green or yellow. *Female*: Polymorphic, heteromorph with eyes brown with blue highlights, thoracic stripes yellow, abdominal spots yellow to white. Andromorph with eyes and pale markings blue.

Identification Small size and very blue abdomen of males obvious. From above, blue spots on midabdomen much like those of other darners, but spots get conspicuously larger toward rear until they cover more than half of segment, unlike all others but similar **Azure**. Only these two northern darners are so small and blue. Compared with **Azure Darner**, abdomen has alternating brown and blue along sides and more brown than blue from above. Pattern on top of frons also diagnostic, black transverse stripe in front of eyes bulging forward at either end like crescent in **Zigzag**, not so in **Azure**. Also check length of eye seam (see under **Azure**). Female abdomen more dark than pale from above.

Natural History Both sexes perch on ground, gravel roads, logs, tree trunks, and other usually light-colored substrates, males more commonly out in breeding habitat. Rather tame, and often land on light-colored clothing or net. Males perch on patches of light-colored moss raised above surrounding marsh, alternating low flights (knee height) over open meadows with more perching than other mosaic darners. Difference perhaps more apparent than real because they are easy to see when perched and other species are hidden in trees and shrubs. Pairs easier to find than in other mosaic darners, probably for same reason; tend to perch in low shrubs rather than on ground but also fly into woodland as do

110
Zigzag Darner
male—
Heckman Pass,
BC, July 2006,
Netta Smith;
inset
male—
Heckman Pass,
BC, July 2006;
blue
female—
Whiteshell
Provincial Park,
MB, July 2007,
Larry de March

other species. Males at times fly above tall sedges much like Sedge Darner but usually at small, shallow pools. Females oviposit at water level in dense grass or sedges or at edge of open water, often in moss beds, into algal mats, or on mud. Retire to open woodland and clearings when away from breeding habitat, but feed both at and away from bogs, males while in sexual patrol

Habitat Fens and cold-water pools with low sedges and mosses, often bordered by shrubby or wooded uplands and usually shallow with little open water. May dry up in midsummer.

Flight Season ON Jun–Sep, QC Jun–Sep, NS Jun–Sep, WI Aug–Sep, ME Jun–Aug.

Distribution Across far North to Alaska, south in mountains to Oregon and Utah.

---

111 Azure Darner *Aeshna septentrionalis*   TL 54–63, HW 35–40

Description Small darner with lateral thoracic stripes narrow and so strongly notched and extended that they form zigzag shape. Stripes often broken. Frontal stripes reduced or lacking. *Male*: Eyes blue. All pale markings light blue, no green or yellow. *Female*: Polymorphic, blue just as male or with yellow markings, pale markings of abdomen less extensive than in male.

Identification Should only be confused with similar-sized and also northerly occurring **Zigzag Darner**. Both sexes of **Azure** differ by having more pale color on abdomen, blue or yellow spots sufficiently close that from side abdomen looks just about all blue or yellow, from above more pale than dark. Pale spots distinct and separate in **Zigzag**. However, both are variable, and color patterns on some individuals may be less than diagnostic. Markings on top of frons distinctive, in this species black bar in front of eyes narrow at ends, not bulging forward as in **Zigzag**. Perhaps best close-range characteristic is eye seam, line where eyes meet: short in **Azure**, no longer than length of occiput, distinctly longer than occiput in **Zigzag**.

Natural History Both sexes perch commonly on ground, rocks, tree trunks, and moss, usually light-colored. Boulders more commonly used than by Zigzag Darners. Males fly low

111.1
Azure Darner male—
Heckman Pass, BC, July
2006

111.2
Azure Darner
female—Haines
Junction, YT, June 2003,
Jim Bangma, posed;
inset male—Old Crow,
YT, Rob Cannings

over marshy areas or floating moss mats much like male Zigzags. Females oviposit in mosses and soupy mud ("muskeg slime") at edge of pools. The northernmost dragonfly.

Habitat Fens and shallow ponds, similar to Zigzag Darner habitat, but sphagnum and other mosses characteristically present.

Flight Season ON Jun–Jul, QC Jul–Sep.

Distribution Across far North to Alaska, south in mountains to British Columbia; isolated population in southern Alberta.

112 Lance-tipped Darner *Aeshna constricta* TL 65–73, HW 42–45

Description Brightly marked darner with lateral thoracic stripes notched and extended; frontal stripes well developed. *Male:* Thoracic stripes blue to green or chartreuse, extensive blue on abdomen. Paddle appendages. *Female:* Abdomen shape about as male's. Polymorphic, with duller yellow-marked heteromorph and brighter blue-marked andromorph, andromorph very bright and male-like. Heteromorphs may have largely yellowish wings. Cerci

112.1
Lance-tipped Darner
male—Kent Co., NB,
September 2006, Denis
Doucet

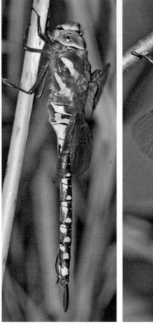

112.2
Lance-tipped Darner
green female—Dutchess
Co., NY, August 2008,
Jeffrey S. Pippen; blue
female—Bayfield Co., WI,
August 2008, Ryan Brady

large and lance-shaped (thus common name), persistent and conspicuous. Cerci only as long as S9–10 because S9 very large, almost twice as long as S10, distinctly larger than same segment in females of other species. Also, pale spots on S9 large and square, distinctly larger than those on S8 and extending lower on sides.

Identification Lateral thoracic stripe shape, with anterior stripe notched in front and drawn out to rear at top distinguishes from **Shadow Darner**, only other paddletail with which it occurs. Only other female mosaic darner with similarly large cerci is very differently colored **Black-tipped**, with smaller and smaller-spotted S9. Female marked something like female **Canada** and **Green-striped** but with larger cerci, slightly different thoracic pattern. Second lateral stripe usually wide at upper end, extends slightly downward along rear edge of thorax in **Lance-tipped**; stripe remains narrow at upper end in others. Large pale spot on S9 another mark for female **Lance-tipped**.

Natural History Males fly beats along shores or through semiopen cattails. Females brightly colored as males and fly over water like them, perhaps mimicking them to avoid harassment by other species. Oviposit on upright stems and leaves of cattails, sweetflag, and other robust plants up to waist height above moist or dry ground; also commonly at surface, including on peat soil. Egg laying slow and methodical, may lay only few eggs in given stem. To avoid male harassment may fly with abdomen bent down sharply. Often in mixed feeding swarms. Typically hang in low shrubs or herbaceous vegetation.

Habitat Shallow marshy ponds and similar edges of larger lakes, commonly in open country. Breeding occurs in ponds that dry up every year, unusual for darners, and may be restricted to fishless waters.

Flight Season ON Jul–Oct, QC Jul–Oct, NS Jun–Sep, IA Jul–Oct, WI Jul–Oct, ME Jul–Oct, OH Jun–Oct, NJ Jul–Nov, KY Aug–Oct.

Distribution Across northern plains to southern British Columbia, Washington, and northern Nevada, scattered records south to Oregon and New Mexico.

113 **Shadow Darner** *Aeshna umbrosa*	TL 64–73, HW 41–47

Description Dark darner with narrow, straight lateral thoracic stripes, some with posterior "flags" at upper end; frontal stripes usually narrow but present. Abdominal spots quite small; also pale spots under abdomen. *Male*: Eyes turquoise. Lateral thoracic stripes blue-green above, yellow-green below. Abdominal spots quite small, blue in western part of region but may also have green spots toward end of abdomen; may be all green in eastern part of region. Occasional individuals have pair of tiny pale spots on S10. Paddle appendages. *Female*: Polymorphic, heteromorph with brown eyes and yellow to greenish markings, andromorph with blue-tinged eyes, greenish to yellow thoracic stripes, and blue abdominal spots. Cerci rounded at tip, longer than S9–10, usually broken off at maturity.

Identification Abdominal spots small enough that they may be scarcely visible as one flies by. Male distinguished from **Lance-tipped Darner**, with which it may occur, by smaller ab-

113.1
Shadow Darner
male—Bayfield Co., WI,
September 2008, Ryan
Brady

113.2
Shadow Darner
pair—Bayfield Co.,
WI, September
2008, Ryan Brady

dominal spots, black S10, and pale spots under abdomen. Blue anteroventral spot on S7 distinctly larger than posterodorsal spot, unlike most other mosaic darners; easily seen in side view of perched individuals. Also from **Lance-tipped** by narrower thoracic stripes. Female as other darners with fairly narrow, straight thoracic stripes (especially **Black-tipped**) but with conspicuous pale spots under abdomen. Dorsal abdominal spots generally small, makes abdomen of female also look darker than in most other species. Lack of apparent cerci may be indicative mark, as much more frequently broken off in **Shadow** than others. Rear of head pale in **Shadow**, dark in most other species; must look carefully for this even in hand.

Natural History Males fly beats up and down streams and along lake shores, with much hovering while facing shore, even as long as 30 sec in one spot. Often fly low, closer to water than other species, but much variation; finding a female is the point of the exercise. May patrol and defend entire small pond, usually for period of less than 1 hr, and typically move from one patrol area to another, often at different water bodies. Both sexes much more common at water later in day, and morning surveys may not reveal their presence. Females oviposit on logs and twigs in water or on moist tree trunks or earth banks, sometimes well above water and even in rather dry situations. Less likely to use living plants than most other darners. Perhaps because of woody oviposition substrates, females much more likely than other mosaic darners to break off cerci as they mature. Feeding flights in clearings and at woodland edges, from ground level to tree canopy. As name implies, often pursues all activities in shade. Regularly flies until too dark to see it clearly, much like tropical dusk-flying darners. Usually one of last species of autumn, flying along with Autumn Meadowhawk.

Habitat Lakes, ponds, even small ones, marshes, and slow streams. More common on streams than other mosaic darners. Colonizes small suburban ponds readily. Mostly in uplands in South.

Flight Season ON Jun–Oct, QC Jun–Oct, NS Jun–Oct, IA Jul–Oct, WI Jun–Oct, ME Jun–Nov, OH Jul–Nov, NJ Jun–Nov, KY Jun–Oct, GA Aug–Dec.

Distribution Across much of North America to the Pacific coast, north to Northwest Territories and south to northern California and New Mexico.

Comments Two subspecies often recognized, *A. u. umbrosa* throughout East. Extremes quite different, far western populations (*A. u. occidentalis*) with considerably larger blue spots on abdomen.

Darners - male appendages

Canada Darner   Shadow Darner   Blue-eyed Darner

Neotropical Darners   *Rhionaeschna*

Resembling mosaic darners, both sexes are distinguished in hand or at close range from the side by a low but fairly evident bump (tubercle) under the first abdominal segment. In addition, the black T-spot on the frons is bordered by a conspicuously paler area on either side in neotropical darners, not so in mosaic darners. In male neotropical, the blue marking on the rear of S2 is flat in front, not connected to a middorsal blue line (connected in mosaic). Females of both genera are patterned the same. Forked appendages in males of our two species are distinct from those of mosaic darners; also, eyes are brighter blue. Besides shape, sexes distinguished from above by dark stigmas in male, pale in female. As in mosaic darners, females of most species are polymorphic, with heteromorph more common. Males tend to fly continuously rather than hovering. The group is characteristic of South and Central America, with a few species extending north all the way to Canada. World 41, NA 5, East 2.

114 Blue-eyed Darner *Rhionaeschna multicolor* TL 65–69, HW 42–45

Description Blue-eyed darner of western edge of region. *Male*: Eyes and face bright sky-blue. Thoracic stripes straight and narrow, pale blue; frontal stripes vary from narrow to absent. Cerci forked at tip. *Female*: Polymorphic, heteromorph with brown eyes and yellow body markings. Andromorph with blue-tinged eyes and face, yellow to blue-green stripes on thorax, and blue spots on abdomen.

Identification Bright sky-blue eyes and forked cerci of male allow easy distinction from all other darners except **Spatterdock**. Not known to overlap, but see that species. Female distinguished in hand from all MOSAIC DARNERS by tubercle under S1, in field with more difficulty. Those in its range with straight and relatively narrow thoracic stripes for which it could be mistaken include at least **Shadow** and **Variable Darners**. Differs from **Shadow** in larger blue spots on abdomen, none beneath it, but too similar to **Variable** where they overlap to be identifiable unless tubercle or pale areas next to T-spot seen.

Natural History Males fly over open water and along shores, usually continuously but occasionally hovering briefly, typically at waist height. Usually less likely to hover than mosaic darners but may have well-defined beats along short length of shoreline. Often alternate open-water flight with slow and low patrol through dense tall emergent vegetation. Copulating pairs perch from near ground up into trees, often flying for some time back and forth over water before finding good perch. Females oviposit in dense emergent vegetation and on floating plant stems and leaves and woody branches in open water, laying eggs above or below waterline. Both sexes wander far from water when not breeding, liable to be seen anywhere away from water, including cruising over city yards and parking lots. May occur in mixed feeding swarms. On very hot days, roost well within cover of riparian trees, sometimes in groups, and may fly until dusk.

114
Blue-eyed
Darner
male—Whatcom
Co., WA,
September 2008;
female—Benton
Co., WA, August
2008, Greg
Lasley

Darner Family **201**

Habitat All kinds of lakes, ponds, slow streams, and canals, especially common in highly productive, open marshy lakes and in open rather than wooded areas.

Flight Season IA Jun–Sep, WI Jul–Aug.

Distribution Martha's Vineyard record from 1943. Also throughout West, north to southern British Columbia and Montana and south in uplands of Mexico to Michoacan.

<table>
<tr><td>**115 Spatterdock Darner** *Rhionaeschna mutata*</td><td>**TL 74–76, HW 44–51**</td></tr>
</table>

Description Early summer darner with bright blue eyes associated with water lilies. *Male*: Eyes and face bright sky-blue, all body markings blue. Lateral thoracic stripes straight, slightly indented, and expanded at upper ends. Frontal thoracic stripes vary from absent to moderately developed. Abdominal markings as other mosaic and neotropical darners, may or may not have small pale spots on S10. Cerci forked at tip. *Female*: Polymorphic, heteromorph with  brown eyes and yellow body markings. Andromorph with blue-tinged eyes and face, yellow to blue-green stripes on thorax, and blue spots on abdomen.

Identification Brightly colored at close range but looks rather dark and dull at a distance. No other darner like this one except **Blue-eyed**. At present, not known to overlap, but they come close, and **Blue-eyed** such a successful species that it may move farther east. Only obvious difference in color pattern is that both sexes of **Spatterdock** have broader, more irregular lateral thoracic stripes. Abdomen distinctly longer in **Spatterdock**, about 4.5× length of thorax (only 4× in **Blue-eyed**); difference in shape evident in photos. Male cerci very similar, but fork at end shallower in **Spatterdock**. In comparing females in hand, tubercle under S1 slightly smaller and cerci slightly longer in **Spatterdock** than in **Blue-eyed**. Female **Spatterdock** distinguished from female MOSAIC DARNERS most readily in hand by tubercle under S1; most similar to striped type of **Variable**. In dorsal view, pale spot on either side of T-spot also distinctive. Flies earlier in season than most of them, usually only darner of that type present at water in June.

Natural History Males cruise slowly back and forth a few feet above water, usually over center of ponds rather than along edges. Females oviposit in spatterdock and other plants. Both sexes hang up on shrubs in nearby woodland.

115
Spatterdock
Darner
male—Sussex
Co., NJ, June
2004, Sheryl
Chacon;
female—Centre
Co., PA, June
2005, Michael H.
Blust

Habitat Usually at fishless ponds, may or may not be covered with water lilies (including spatterdock).

Flight Season ON May–Jun, IA May–Jun, WI Jun–Jul, OH May–Sep, NJ May–Jul, KY May–Jun.

Green Darners *Anax*

These large, robust darners are among the largest of dragonflies in most regions. North American species have bright green thorax, but some Old World species are quite different, for example, black and yellow ringed or entirely red. The thorax is bulky, the abdomen swollen at base and a bit thicker and relatively shorter than in many other large dragonflies (but excessively long in Giant Darner, the largest dragonfly in North America). Male hindwings without the sharp angle on inner corner that is characteristic of other darners; also lacking are projecting auricles on S2. Adults fly swiftly and directly along shorelines or over open water, less likely to hover than most other darners. World 29, NA 5, East 3.

116 Amazon Darner *Anax amazili* TL 70–75, HW 49–52

Description Robust darner with green thorax and white-spotted abdomen. *Male*: Eyes brownish gray to blue-gray, face green. "Bull's-eye" on top of frons with blue border interrupted at front. Thorax bright green. Abdomen with S1–2 bright green; sides of S1 white, forming what looks like ring from side, small blue median  spots on S2. Rest of abdomen black to dark brown with whitish irregular spots on sides of S3–9. With age, abdomen darkens, and spots eventually become obscure, white ring becomes green. *Female*: Colored exactly as male.

Identification Most like **Common Green Darner**, but white-spotted or entirely dark abdomen distinctive, as is white or pale green basal ring conspicuous from sides. **Blue-faced** and **Mangrove Darners**, also with green thorax, are much more slender as well as having fine green lines on dark abdomen.

Natural History Both sexes, or perhaps only females, spend dry season as adults, then females oviposit by themselves in herbaceous vegetation both above and below water level or in completely dry basins. Breed in temporary wetlands just as rains come, larvae developing quickly as top predators in fishless ecosystems. Males less often seen than females,

116
Amazon Darner
male—Hidalgo
Co., TX, October
2008, Jan
Dauphin;
female—
Hidalgo Co., TX,
October 2008,
Greg Lasley

rarely at water; probably mate away from water, unlike other green darners. Often seen in feeding flights that may be low and fast during day and at dusk; occasionally comes to lights during dusk flight. Other individuals encountered roosting at head height in woodland.

Habitat Open ponds and marshes; temporary waters preferred in tropics.

Flight Season FL Jun–Oct.

Distribution Not certainly established as a breeding species in eastern United States but perhaps does so, from number of recent records in Florida. Alternatively, perhaps regular summer movement of individuals north from tropics, with small enough numbers that males and females unlikely to find one another. Regular in south Texas, ranges south in lowlands to Argentina; also Galapagos and West Indies.

Description Large darner with green thorax, red abdomen. Legs especially long. *Male*: Eyes green to blue-green. Thorax and S1–2 green, S3–10 intensely red-orange, only faintly patterned. *Female*: Colored as male but abdomen duller, more reddish brown, more obviously patterned with paler spots, and slightly thicker and shorter. Immatures of both sexes have more prominent spots, which vary from whitish to quite blue. One of few darners lacking any marking on top of frons.

Identification Basically unmistakable. However, confusion possible, especially between female **Comet** and immature and female **Common Green Darner**, which may have reddish-purple abdomen. **Common Green** at all ages has dark stripe along top of abdomen and "bull's-eye" on top of frons.

Natural History Males fly along or off shore, tend to stay a bit higher and farther out from shore than Common Green Darners. Cruise long distances in larger bodies of water but easily watched at length in small ones. Single male may cruise around entire shore of midsized pond. Flight at waist to chest height. Females oviposit in vegetation, including floating and

117
Comet Darner male—Charlton Co., GA, September 2009, Giff Beaton;
female—Hart Co., KY, June 2006, posed

standing grass stems; eggs usually laid just below surface. May come to water in some numbers on cloudy mornings when males not present. Egg-laying females usually remain at one spot only briefly, perhaps 10–20 sec, then move to another nearby spot. Much less often seen away from water than Common Green Darner.

Habitat Shallow lakes and ponds, typically with extensive beds of grasses and lacking fish. Comet Darner larvae probably top predators in these wetlands.

Flight Season ON Jun–Jul, ME Jun–Jul, OH Jun–Jul, NJ May–Sep, KY Mar–Jun, LA Apr–Oct, GA Mar–Oct, FL Feb–Nov.

Distribution Ranges slightly farther west in Oklahoma and Texas.

---

118 Common Green Darner *Anax junius* TL 68–78, HW 46–53

Description One of most common and characteristic North American dragonflies. Thorax green, abdomen with black dorsal stripe that becomes wider toward tip. *Male:* Eyes dull greenish, paler below. Face greenish, frons blue above with "bull's-eye" pattern. Thorax bright to dull grass-green. Abdomen with S1 green, S2–6 bright blue, S7–8 duller, S9–10 often bluish-green, S9–10 mostly dark. *Female:* Polymorphic, most females with S1–2 green, S3–10 brown above and gray-green on sides. Minority colored much as male, at brightest with S2–10 black above and pale blue on sides. Immature

118.1
Common Green Darner
male—Hidalgo Co., TX,
November 2005

118.2
Common Green Darner
female—Greenlee Co.,
AZ, July 2007

of both sexes with S3–10 reddish violet. Wings uncolored or orange-tinted in immatures, with age become increasingly suffused with amber, especially in females.

Similar species One of two widespread eastern darners with bright green thorax. **Comet Darner** with entirely bright red or reddish-brown abdomen, but reddish-purple immature **Common Green** may be mistaken for female **Comet**; look for pattern on top of frons. Abdominal pattern also different, **Common Green** with black stripe down middle, not so in **Comet**. **Amazon Darner** rather similar but has pale ring at abdomen base, spotted abdomen, blue border of bull's-eye on frons interrupted at front. Among unrelated dragonflies, **Great Pondhawk** most similar; also large and green but has green-and-black banded abdomen, perches rather than hangs. PILOT DARNERS, often flying in same areas in far South, look more slender than green darners.

Natural History Feeding over open areas, sometimes in small swarms and at any time of day, perhaps most often at dawn and dusk. Prey mostly small insects but all the way up to mosaic darners and distasteful butterflies. May hover facing into light breeze. Perching tends to be lower than in other darners and in open areas, often in herbaceous vegetation (most darners perch higher in shrubs or trees). Males fly rapidly over open water or along shorelines, mostly from knee to waist height. Copulating pairs fly away from water. Tandem pairs fly low over water and land in open to oviposit (thus males do not fly into vegetation as some other darners do when looking for females). Oviposits in both upright and floating stems and leaves, dead or alive, also woody branches, usually 1–2 min at each stop. Only North American darner that normally oviposits in tandem, but some females manage by themselves. Single males pay much attention to pairs, trying to land on them; male of pair flutters, and female curls abdomen down and closes wings to deter this. Tandem pairs sometimes seen in flight far from water, regularly in southbound migration. Large proportion of populations in most areas migratory. One of the earliest species to appear in the North, well before many resident species have emerged. Great numbers in southern Florida in spring at times, perhaps individuals eventually moving north, as mating not seen at that season; one such concentration was thought to consist of recently emerged individuals. Mature adults move north in spring throughout East, appearing before any are found emerging (exceptions known). These individuals breed, their larvae develop during summer, and their offspring emerge in late summer, then fly south in immature colors. Huge southbound flights have been noted along Atlantic and Gulf coasts and in Great Lakes. Apparently collect at coastlines but also seen along mountain ridges in Pennsylvania and Arkansas; some cross Gulf of Mexico. Most or all of these individuals may mature and breed along the way, as tandem pairs are seen in southbound flights and much breeding is observed from at least New Jersey southward in fall. The same individuals or others presumably continue to move south and ultimately may breed somewhere in eastern Mexico, Florida, and the West Indies, their larvae developing during winter and their offspring moving north in spring. Probably all regions also have "resident" populations more like other dragonflies, emerging in spring from larvae that overwintered locally and breeding near emergence sites.

Habitat Lakes and all but smallest ponds, also slow streams. Because of migratory nature, liable to be seen anywhere at or away from water.

Flight Season ON Mar–Dec, QC May–Sep, NS Jun–Oct, IA Apr–Oct, WI Apr–Oct, ME May–Nov, OH Apr–Oct, NJ Mar–Dec, KY Mar–Dec, LA all year, GA all year, FL all year.

Distribution Extent of both summer range and winter range of migratory populations poorly known; research needed both in middle latitudes and in tropics. Throughout western United States north to southern Canadian provinces, south regularly through much of Mexico (rarely farther south) and West Indies. Vagrant to Bermuda, United Kingdom, France, Alaska, and northeastern Asia.

Alert and fast-flying, many of them rare, local, and with brief flight seasons, clubtails are considered the most exciting group by many dragonfly enthusiasts. Despite their great diversity and local abundance, their behavior is very poorly known. They are cryptically colored and spend much time at rest and thus are not as obvious as the aerial darners and brightly colored skimmers. Although taking flying prey from a perch as most skimmers do, and similarly with worldwide distribution, clubtails are different from skimmers in many ways. Appropriately named, males of most species have a slender abdomen with the terminal segments expanded into a distinct club. This is rare in other families, but note cruisers and clubskimmers. Clubs are smaller in females, and even males of a few species lack this attribute, but all the family should be recognizable by the relatively small, widely separated eyes. Eye color is blue, green, or an intermediate turquoise in all but a few species and can be an important field mark. A typical clubtail has a pale thorax with dark stripes, or what looks like a dark thorax with pale stripes if the dark color is more extensive. The stripes do not correspond exactly with stripes in other families, so for ease of reference, *the dark stripes visible from the side are indicated by T plus numbers from front to back.* Stripe T1, on the front of the thorax, is often called the *antehumeral* stripe, T2 the *humeral*, T3 the *interpleural*, and T4 the *metapleural* stripe. A small proportion of species have a fifth stripe, T5, at the rear edge of the thorax. The abdomen is typically dark with pale rings and/or streaks or spots along the top and spots or rings in side view; thus, complexly patterned.

Spiketails are the only other dragonflies with small, blue to green eyes, and the eyes just about touch in that family. In addition, all are black or brown and yellow and perch with abdomen declined, even vertically. Most clubtails perch on the ground or on twigs with abdomen inclined upward, curled down a bit at the end, although larger clubtails often perch with drooped abdomen, and many species perch flat on leaves. Obelisking is common in species that perch in the open, often resulting in the abdomen held straight up. Other than the skimmers, this is the only dragonfly family in which this position is adopted. Many species fly with abdomen slightly curved, as when they perch. Oviposition as in skimmers, by striking the water surface and releasing eggs, but females of at least some species build up substantial egg masses at the end of the abdomen while at rest and perch in a characteristic way, with abdomen curved upward, the eggs supported by sharply bent-down segment 10. After a few moments of producing the egg mass, the female then drops them quickly in the water and goes back to a perch to repeat the process.

There is little sexual dimorphism in coloration, but females often have more pale, less dark color on the abdomen. Color change with maturation is commonplace, younger individuals

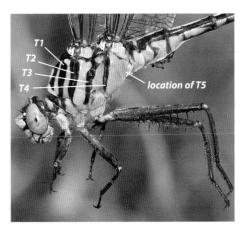

Thoracic stripes in Southeastern
Spinyleg male—Early Co., GA, July 2007

with yellow markings that turn to dull gray-green in older ones. The pale ground color is thus rarely important as a field mark except to distinguish some species by their bright green thorax, but specifics of pattern are very important. Geographic variation is evident in some species, individuals in drier and hotter parts of the species' range paler, with paler markings more extensive than the same species in wetter regions. Finally, clubtails are often much more common than they seem, as may be indicated by the abundance of their exuviae on a river bank or lake shore. Many species emerge during the day, and as their emergence is relatively rapid in the hot sun, they are good subjects for watching this process from beginning to end. World 961, NA 101, East 80.

Sanddragons *Progomphus*

Sanddragons are medium-sized, mostly tropical clubtails with irregularly patterned thorax and slightly developed club in males. With few exceptions, they are the only clubtails with any color in the wings, a spot of brown at base of all wings. Males characteristically have flat, pale cerci that show up prominently at the abdomen tip. They are usually seen along sandy shores, as their larvae are highly modified as sand burrowers. World 69, NA 4, East 3.

119 **Common Sanddragon** *Progomphus obscurus*   TL 47–53, HW 28–33

Description Rich brown and yellow clubtail of sandy habitats. *Male:* Eyes blue-gray, becoming olive-green; eyes of mature males can become golden above, perhaps only eastern clubtail so colored. Face dull yellowish with two faint brown stripes crossing it. Thorax yellow with brown stripes, T1–2 thick and partially to entirely fused; T3–4 connected at lower ends. Abdomen dark brown to black with yellow rear-pointing triangles (much like burning candles) on S2–6; S7–10 entirely dark or with pair of small dorsolateral squares at base and pale line at outer edge of S8. Cerci cream-colored. Dark brown markings at base of all wings. *Female:* Colored as male, eyes blue-gray.

119.1
Common Sanddragon male—
Decatur Co., GA, July 2007

119.2
Common Sanddragon female—
Caldwell Co., TX,
May 2005

Identification Pale appendages on all-dark abdomen tip distinctive of both sexes of this heavily marked species, richer yellow and brown than other clubtails of its habitat. Basal wing markings also distinctive in comparison with most species. Barely overlaps with **Tawny Sanddragon**, distinguished by black- or dark-brown-tipped abdomen with or without very limited pale markings. Thoracic markings distinctive if visible, T3–4 fused only at lower ends, pale stripe obvious between them (most of that area dark in **Tawny**). In area of overlap, **Tawny** usually at lakes, **Common** at streams. Also overlaps with **Belle's Sanddragon**, which can be distinguished by larger size; longer, more pointed cerci; and more obvious yellow markings on sides of terminal segments. In area of overlap, **Belle's** usually at sandy lakes or trickles, **Common** at larger streams.

Natural History Males perch on sand beaches of pools, right at edge facing water, or fly low over water in what can be lengthy patrol flights, including hovering over riffles. Also land on rocks on rocky/sandy rivers. Not aggressive in territory defense. Prefer open rather than shrubby banks. Abdomen elevated when perched, on ground or on twigs, and obelisks dramatically at midday. Pairs copulate for up to 15 min on ground or in shrubs near water. Female oviposits on erratic path, taps water once on yard-long approach run; also may drop eggs from above surface. Males have been seen guarding ovipositing females, unusual among clubtails.

Habitat Sandy woodland streams; sandy lakes in northern part of range. Sometimes on rocky rivers, presumably where sand available among rocks.

Flight Season ON Jun–Jul, IA Jun–Sep, WI Jun–Sep, ME Jun–Aug, OH May–Aug, NJ Jun–Sep, KY Jun–Aug, LA Apr–Aug, GA May–Sep, FL Apr–Aug.

Distribution West to eastern Colorado and New Mexico.

---

120 Tawny Sanddragon *Progomphus alachuensis* TL 52–57, HW 30–35

Description Rich brown sanddragon of Florida sand lakes. *Male:* Eyes gray, with slight greenish or bluish tinge; face tan, with faint darker transverse markings. Thorax yellow with brown stripes; T1–2 fused, T3–4 largely fused with two pale spots remaining at middle

120.1
Tawny Sanddragon male—
Charlton Co., GA, July 2007

120.2
Tawny Sanddragon female—
Clay Co., FL, July 2007, Giff Beaton

and below. Abdomen black with long yellow dorsal triangles, yellow more extensive on S7; S8–10 brown, S8 yellow at base. Cerci long, cream-colored. Wings with brown markings at extreme base. *Female*: Like male but more extensively marked with yellow on abdomen. where pale markings tend toward yellow-orange.

Identification Only sanddragon in peninsular Florida, overlaps with **Common** at north end of range but in different habitat. Differs from that species by abdomen tip brown, yellow-marked (especially on S8), instead of almost entirely black. Some populations of **Common** have brown-tipped abdomen, but always very reduced yellow markings. **Belle's** that occurs at lakes west of range of **Tawny** also has black-tipped abdomen. Other clubtails in range of this one have neither brown spots at wing bases nor white cerci; most have dark markings, black rather than brown.

Natural History Males perch on sandy shores or more commonly in low vegetation near shore, facing water. Much chasing between this species and Two-striped Forceptails common in same habitat. Females usually away from water, rarely seen except for breeding. Oviposit while in rapid, erratic flight with occasional dips to water surface; may also drop eggs from a foot above water while in slow, almost hovering, flight.

Habitat Sand-bottomed lakes, usually with clear water and often with bed of emergent vegetation near shore. Water lilies may also be common. Occurs at some sandy streams in southern Florida, well south of range of Common Sanddragon.

Flight Season GA Jun–Oct, FL Apr–Aug.

---

121 Belle's Sanddragon   *Progomphus bellei*   TL 54–60, HW 33–37

Description Vividly marked, black-clubbed sanddragon of southeastern sand lakes and streams. *Male*: Eyes gray with greenish tinge; face yellow with obscure brown markings. Thorax with broad brown stripes (looks dark brown with yellow stripes); T1–2 broad, fused; T3–4 connected by crosspieces, broad at lower end and narrow at upper end, leaving three pale spots between them, one at upper end. T3–4 may be fused completely in North Carolina  populations. Abdomen black with long yellow dorsal markings on S3–7, narrowed in middle and pointed at end. S8 with pair of dorsolateral yellow squares at base, S8–9 with irregular yellow markings on sides. Cerci long, cream-colored. Wings with brown markings at extreme base. *Female*: Colored as male but more yellow on sides of terminal segments.

Identification Prominent flat pale cerci and brown markings at wing bases mark this as a sanddragon. Very similar to **Common Sanddragon** but distinctly larger, with conspicuous

121.1
Belle's Sanddragon
male—Bladen Co.,
NC, June 2008, Ricky
Davis

121.2
Belle's Sanddragon
female—Liberty Co.,
FL, June 2009, Troy
Hibbitts

pale markings on sides of abdomen tip. **Common** rarely has small markings in this area, but they can be very similar to those of **Belle's**, although always less extensive. Thoracic markings distinctly different in the two, **Belle's** showing much less yellow. Male cerci longer, more acutely pointed; difference easily seen with binoculars.

Natural History Males perch on sandy shores of lakes or tiny streams, also on twigs and cypress knees, at intervals flying out on patrol flights about a foot above the water. Females nearby in herbaceous vegetation.

Habitat Open sand-bottomed lakes in forested landscape, also where small forest streams on sandy soil emerge into sunny openings.

Flight Season FL May–Aug.

Distribution Apparent gap in distribution may be real, as appropriate habitat seems to be lacking in between.

Greater Forceptails *Aphylla*

A widespread neotropical group, these large, short-legged clubtails have a long, slender abdomen with not much of a club, but a prominent leaflike projection on either side of S8 enhances the clubtail look. The brown male cerci are large and forceps-like, the epiproct almost lacking, but the lower edge of S10 is pointed on either side, visible in side view; female cerci are yellow to orange. The thorax is dark with vivid pale stripes, the abdomen largely reddish from the side and with only a weakly ringed look. Related to lesser forceptails (*Phyllocycla*) and leaftails (*Phyllogomphoides*) of Texas and southward and often occurring with them but more likely to occur on open lakes and ponds than other large clubtails. World 24, NA 3, East 2.

122 Broad-striped Forceptail *Aphylla angustifolia* TL 62–68, HW 36–42

Description Large Texas clubtail with broad pale stripes on thorax and slender, patterned abdomen. *Male*: Eyes blue-green, face with narrow brown bars crossing it. Thorax looks brown with yellow stripes, as all five dark stripes quite wide, T1–2 partially fused. Basal segments of abdomen brown with yellow on sides and base, forming ringed pattern on S2–4 or 5. End segments more uniformly colored, reddish; become darker brown with age. Narrow orange  flange on S8–9. *Female*: Colored much as male, but abdomen more uniform orange with yellow markings, apparently not becoming as dark with age; flange on S8–9 virtually nonexistent.

Identification Easily distinguished from **Two-striped Forceptail** by many more stripes on thorax. Not much like any other large clubtail in range except **Russet-tipped Clubtail**.

122.1
Broad-striped Forceptail male—
Travis Co., TX, August 2009, Eric Isley

122.2
Broad-striped Forceptail female—
Travis Co., TX, September 2009, Eric Isley

Thoracic stripes wider in **Two-striped**, so thorax looks darker, and male appendages very different. Club in **Russet-tipped** also paler, brighter reddish.

Natural History Males perch on twigs and leaves over water, from near ground to waist height or above, rarely on ground. Occasionally fly along shore to new perch, even when not disturbed, but have definite preferred perches. Both sexes feed in open areas nearby.

Habitat Lakes and ponds, pools on rivers and streams.

Flight Season LA Jun–Aug.

Distribution Ranges south to Guatemala and Belize.

Comments From its range in Texas, it is very likely that the Narrow-striped Forceptail, *Aphylla protracta*, occurs in at least southwestern Louisiana. It differs from the Broad-striped by having distinctly narrower pale thoracic stripes, is usually more reddish looking overall, and has a narrower club.

123 Two-striped Forceptail   *Aphylla williamsoni*   TL 71–76, HW 37–43

Description Large southeastern clubtail with vivid pale thoracic stripes. *Male:* Eyes blue, face with dark brown crossbars. Thorax dark brown with three widely spaced yellow stripes on each side, second and fourth light stripes of other forceptails lacking. Abdomen dark brown with yellow markings on sides of basal segments, terminal segments mostly orange. Flanges on S8 bright yellow, contrasting with red-orange sides of segment. *Female:* Colored as male but more likely to show narrow and incomplete pale thoracic stripe between prominent ones.

Identification Unmistakably a forceptail from its overall look, distinguished from **Broad-striped Forceptail** and other clubtails that occur with it by having only two wide pale stripes visible on each side of thorax and only a single stripe visible on either side of front. Otherwise, looks much like **Broad-striped**, large and dark and with strong reddish cast to posterior abdomen. Bright yellow flanges contrasting with darker sides of S8 in male distinctive. Female abdomen darker, with smaller pale markings than in **Broad-striped**, going along with overall darker-looking thorax.

Natural History Males perch on twigs and tall reeds at shore, often at waist height or above, and fly out at other large dragonflies, persistently at their own species. Most perching well above ground, but at least females seen on ground. Both sexes quite wary when perched,

123.1
Two-striped Forceptail
male—Howard Co., AR,
August 2009, Charles Mills

123.2
Two-striped Forceptail
female—Bay Co., FL, July
2009

may ascend into treetops when disturbed. Patrol flights may cover 60 feet or more. Abdomen slightly curved in flight, sometimes hovers. May remain active at water until dark, unlike most other clubtails. Oviposition may be limited to late in day and is varied, from hovering to rapid flight and from tapping water to dropping eggs from above.

Habitat Slow streams and rivers, canals, and a great variety of sand-bottomed lakes and ponds, among the most ecologically broad-based of American clubtails.

Flight Season LA Apr–Nov, GA Jul–Oct, FL Apr–Nov.

Pond Clubtails *Arigomphus*

This small group is primarily distributed in central and eastern North America. Males have rather narrow clubs, females clubless abdomens. Most species are relatively plain and pale, gray or dull greenish combined with black or dark brown, but a few are brighter, chartreuse and reddish-brown. The front of the thorax is mostly pale, the median stripes paired, relatively narrow, and well separated, even obscure in some species; few other eastern clubtails are marked this sparsely. The sides of the thorax are only lightly marked behind T1 and T2. S10 and appendages are often pale. Other distinctions are structural, including long subgenital plates that project downward in females of some species. They are more likely to be at lakes and ponds than species of related genera. World 7, NA 7, East 7.

Description Slender northern clubtail with lightly striped thorax, both sexes with "horns." *Male:* Eyes blue, face unmarked. Thorax with T1 incomplete at upper end, well-developed T2, very narrow lower end of T3, and barely indicated T4. Legs black, inside of front femora pale. Abdomen black with pale grayish to yellow dorsal stripe, becoming spearpoints to rear and ending at base of S8; also pale spot on top of S10. S8–9 with rusty edges, contrasting with  yellow everywhere else. No club, but slight flange on S8. Cerci and epiproct very wide, like branched horns. *Female:* Color pattern as male; pale color on sides of abdomen comes up higher. Hind femora mostly pale. Occiput large, bilobed, with pair of slightly curved black horns at base.

124.1
Horned Clubtail male—
Ottawa, ON, May 2004,
Chang-Won Seo

124.2
Horned Clubtail female—
Burnett Co., WI, June 2007

Identification Male distinguished from most co-occurring clubtails by absence of club and minimal striping on sides of thorax, but two other pond clubtails rather similar. **Horned** distinguished from **Lilypad** and **Unicorn** by very wide branched cerci, less pale color on S10, and yellow instead of rust on sides of narrow club. Females more similar, **Horned** usually with less yellow on top of S10 and typically an obvious yellow triangle on top of S8 (little or no marking on that segment in **Lilypad** and **Unicorn**). At close range note prominent bilobed occiput and black horns of female **Horned**. **Jade Clubtail** has even sparser markings on thorax, mostly pale abdomen, and green eyes. COMMON CLUBTAILS with minimal clubs all have more heavily marked thorax.

Natural History Males perch on bare ground or rocks or flat on leaves at waterside or fly back and forth along shore or over water. Females often perch on leaves higher in woodland, where males go when disturbed.

Habitat Lakes, ponds, and slow streams, may be quite muddy.

Flight Season ON May–Aug, QC Jun–Jul, IA May–Jul, WI Jun–Aug.

Distribution Also in Black Hills of South Dakota and adjacent states.

---

125 Lilypad Clubtail *Arigomphus furcifer*   TL 46–54, HW 27–31

Description Slender northeastern pond clubtail with dramatically forked male cerci. *Male:* Eyes blue to turquoise, face unmarked. Front of thorax with narrow stripes, incomplete below. T1 fairly broad and complete, T2 narrower and approaches T1 at upper end. T3–4 very narrow, T3 only half height. Legs black, inside of front femora pale. Abdomen black with pale green spearpoints back to S7, S8–9 black, S10 with yellow dorsal stripe; cerci yellow. Sides of

125.1
Lilypad Clubtail
male—Wood Co., WI,
June 2007

125.2
Lilypad Clubtail
female—Ottawa, ON,
June 2007, Chang-Won
Seo

Clubtail Family   **215**

S8–10 reddish (may be dark in southern populations). Narrow flange on S8 only, producing slight club. *Female:* Color pattern as male, yellow on top and sides of abdomen more extensive; may have short pale triangle on top of S8.

Identification Often occurs with **Unicorn Clubtail**, differs in S10 not fully pale, T1–2 touching at upper ends, slightly more heavily striped on sides of thorax, reddish (in most populations) color more prominent at tip of abdomen. Less similar to **Horned Clubtail**, which has S10 mostly black with huge, forked cerci in male; pale markings on sides of abdomen tip yellow rather than reddish in both sexes. In front view, T1 in **Horned** separated from T2 but incomplete at upper end. COMMON CLUBTAILS with narrow abdomens that might occur with **Lilypad** all have much more broadly striped thorax.

Natural History Both sexes forage in sunny clearings near breeding habitats. As name implies, males commonly perch on lilypads and other vegetation, but also on sandy shores and rocks. Females tap water to oviposit.

Habitat Lakes, ponds (including bog ponds), and slow streams, usually with much aquatic vegetation.

Flight Season ON May–Aug, QC Jun–Jul, WI May–Jul, ME Jun–Aug, OH May–Jul, NJ May–Aug.

---

126 Unicorn Clubtail *Arigomphus villosipes*　　　　　TL 50–58, HW 29–36

Description Slender northeastern pond clubtail with S10 all pale. *Male:* Eyes turquoise to blue, face unmarked. Front of thorax with narrow stripes, incomplete below. T1 and T2 relatively narrow, well separated. T3 scarcely evident at lower end, T4 narrow but complete. Legs black, inside of front femora pale. Abdomen black with yellow spearpoints back to S7; S8–9 black, S10 entirely pale, including cerci. Sides of S8–9 obscurely marked with dull reddish. S8 with narrow flange, very slightly clubbed. *Female:* Color pattern as male, much yellow on lower sides of abdomen. Both sexes have hornlike projection from occiput that gives species its name.

Identification Most similar to **Lilypad Clubtail** and often occurs with it. Distinguished by entirely pale S10, male with less complex cerci. See **Lilypad** for other differences. **Horned Clubtail** very similar, usually less yellow on S10 but can have as much as **Unicorn**. Conspicuously pale S10 also distinguishes **Unicorn** from other co-occurring clubtails.

126.1
Unicorn Clubtail male—
Hart Co., KY, June 2006

126.2
Unicorn Clubtail
female—Hamilton Co.,
OH, July 2008, William Hull

Natural History Males perch on sandy and muddy shores facing water, also on logs, docks, lilypads, algal mats, and up in vegetation. Dramatic obelisking at hot midday. Also fly back and forth over water. Can be very common, one male every 10 feet of shore.

Habitat Typically mud-bottomed lakes and ponds, including beaver ponds, with or without much vegetation. May occur in rather degraded urban situations, along with Common Whitetails.

Flight Season ON May–Aug, ME Jun–Jul, OH Apr–Aug, NJ May–Aug, KY May–Jul.

---

127 Jade Clubtail *Arigomphus submedianus* TL 51–55, HW 34–36

Description Eastern prairie clubtail with green eyes and ruddy abdomen tip. *Male*: Eyes grass-green, face pale greenish-tan. Thorax pale greenish, T1 wide and distinct, T2 narrower, others indistinct or lacking. Legs tan, ends of femora and inside of tibiae black. Abdomen dull greenish-gray to yellowish with dark brown dorsolateral apical triangular markings on S2–6, narrow dark rings between them; S7–9 rich brown, S10 paler orangey, appendages yellow. *Female*: Colored as male, eyes a bit duller.

Identification Eyes greener than in other pond clubtails, although not much more so than in **Bayou Clubtail**; differently colored abdomen tip easily distinguishes these two. Most like **Stillwater Clubtail** except for eye color but appearing a bit paler overall. Also T1 distinctly wider than T2, reduced marking on sides of thorax. Of these pale prairie-pond clubtails, S9 obviously longer than S8 in female only in **Jade**. Other superficially similar clubtails in range include **Flag-tailed Spinyleg**, with wider T2, middle abdominal segments white but with dark markings extensive, almost continuous, and much longer hind legs.

Natural History Perches on or near ground, males at water's edge. Forages in open and semi-open areas near woods.

Habitat Large mud-bottomed lakes, sloughs, and canals, also some slow-flowing rivers.

Flight Season WI Jun–Jul, KY May–Jul, LA May–Jul.

Distribution Ranges slightly farther west in Nebraska, Oklahoma, and Texas.

127.1
Jade Clubtail male—
Howard Co., AR, June
2008, Charles Mills

127.2
Jade Clubtail female—
Bowie Co., TX, June 2008,
Mike Dillon

128 Stillwater Clubtail *Arigomphus lentulus* TL 48–58, HW 29–36

Description Eastern prairie clubtail with blue eyes and ruddy abdomen tip. *Male*: Eyes blue to turquoise, face pale greenish. Thorax pale greenish with T1 and T2 prominent, sometimes partially fused; T3 and T4 faintly indicated. Femora chartreuse, tipped black; tibiae black and white striped. Abdomen yellowish-green at base, duller yellow-gray on S3–6, S2–6 with apical dorsolateral blackish blotches forming somewhat ringed pattern. S7–10 rusty, in some individuals  darker above and some yellowish on sides; S8 often darker than S9. Appendages pale yellow. *Female*: Colored as male but dark markings on abdomen less extensive.

Identification Most similar to other pond clubtails with which it occurs. Both sexes differ from quite similar **Jade Clubtail** by more heavily striped thorax; latter also has quite green eyes. Differs from **Bayou Clubtail** by more reddish abdomen tip (dark brown in **Bayou**) and wider T1–2. In female **Jade**, S9 slightly longer than S8, about same length in **Bayou** and **Stillwater**. In female **Stillwater**, dark markings on sides of abdomen usually form continu-

128.1
Stillwater Clubtail
male—Howard
Co., AR, May 2008,
Charles Mills

128.2
Stillwater Clubtail
female—McCurtain Co.,
OK, June 2008, David
Arbour

ous dark stripe; markings on other two species interrupted. Both sexes colored somewhat like **Russet-tipped Clubtail** but that species has sides of thorax prominently striped.

Natural History Males rest on shore or grass stems or twigs facing water. Both sexes forage low in sunny clearings.

Habitat Open muddy ponds and other still waters.

Flight Season KY May–Jun.

Distribution South through eastern Texas.

---

129 Bayou Clubtail *Arigomphus maxwelli*   **TL 50–54, HW 29–32**

Description Rather pale midsouth clubtail with blackish abdomen tip. *Male*: Eyes green to turquoise, face pale yellow to whitish. Thorax gray-green with narrow but well-defined T1–4, T3 and T4 sometimes incomplete. Legs black, hind femora with pale base; tibiae black inside, pale outside. Abdomen dull pale yellow with dark brown markings covering much of sides of S2 and forming irregular apical rings on S3–6; S7–9 very dark brown, S10 light brown, appendages yellowish. Club distinct but not very wide. *Female*: Colored as male but paler, dark markings on abdomen smaller, tip lighter brown. Femora with more pale color.

Identification Much like **Stillwater Clubtail** but with darker abdomen tip in both sexes, greener eyes. Typically S7 entirely dark in **Bayou**, patterned in **Stillwater**. Thoracic stripes T1 and T2 narrow and well separated in **Bayou**; T1 wider and closer to T2, sometimes partially fused, in **Stillwater**. Femora in **Bayou** with less light color than in **Stillwater**, may look all dark in males. More prominent thoracic stripes and darker abdomen tip easily distinguish from somewhat similarly colored **Jade Clubtail**. Slightly more contrast between greener thorax and yellower abdomen than in other pond clubtails. Female somewhat like **Russet-tipped Clubtail** but less heavily marked thorax and more heavily marked abdomen.

129.1
Bayou Clubtail
male—Hempstead
Co., AR, June 2008,
Charles Mills

129.2
Bayou Clubtail
female—Harris Co.,
TX, April 2007,
Martin Reid

Natural History Males perch on ground or rocks at edge of water bodies, move into woodland when not at water.

Habitat Shallow ponds such as borrow pits and slow-flowing ditches in open or woodland edge, more likely at streams than other pond clubtails.

Flight Season LA May–Jun.

130 Gray-green Clubtail   *Arigomphus pallidus*   TL 60–62, HW 37–38

Description Grayish southeastern clubtail with green eyes and brown-spotted abdomen; perhaps the dullest North American clubtail. *Male:* Eyes bright green, face unmarked. Thorax gray, often green-tinged; virtually unmarked in some, very fine brown T2 and less evident T4 only markings visible at a distance. Some individuals, however, have all four stripes fairly well developed. Legs brown, tibiae tan outside.  Abdomen pale grayish-tan with faint brown dorsolateral stripes on S1–3, dark terminal spots on S4–6, S7 becoming darker to rear and S8–9 or 10 entirely brown; S10 sometimes and appendages always pale. S7–8 with prominent flanges, abdomen slightly clubbed. *Female:* Color pattern as male, including bright eyes, but with no club. Thoracic and abdominal stripes tend to be a bit broader and more evident. Legs tan, brown-striped.

130.1
Gray-green Clubtail
male—Wayne Co., GA,
May 2006

130.2
Gray-green Clubtail
female—Early Co., GA,
July 2007

Identification Usually looks gray at a distance. Bright green eyes stand out against dull, pale body coloring in this species; frontal stripes on thorax barely visible in most. Nothing else like it in southern part of region, but overlaps with somewhat similar **Bayou**, **Jade**, and **Stillwater** in western Kentucky. More heavily striped individuals in that area could be distinguished from all others by combination of green eyes, gray thorax, paler abdomen tip with usually patterned S7.

Natural History Males typically perch on ground near water and on low-growing aquatic vegetation such as water lilies but also in low vegetation away from water, no more than a foot above ground. Females perch low or higher up in shrubs in woodland. Females oviposit by tapping methodically and somewhat irregularly in shallow water at the base of cypress trees or near shore.

Habitat Slow streams, ponds, and lakes with much vegetation or more open. Often at borrow pits, also cypress swamps. Only clubtail besides Two-striped Forceptail to penetrate to southern tip of Florida.

Flight Season KY May–Jun, GA Apr–Jul, FL Mar–Oct.

Pond Clubtails - male appendages

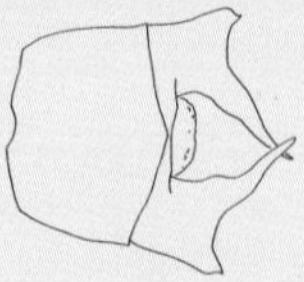

Horned Clubtail

Horned Clubtail

Lilypad Clubtail

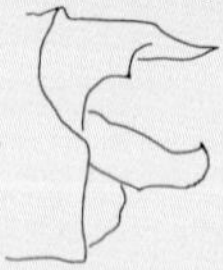

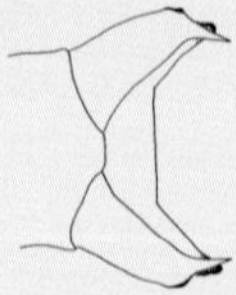

Lilypad Clubtail

Unicorn Clubtail

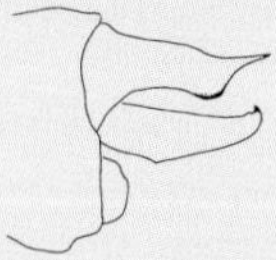

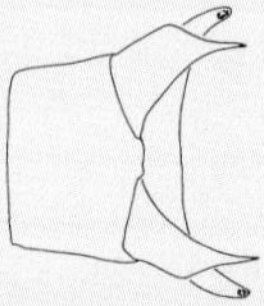

Unicorn Clubtail

Jade Clubtail

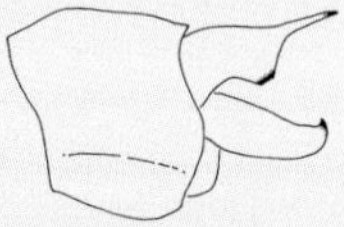

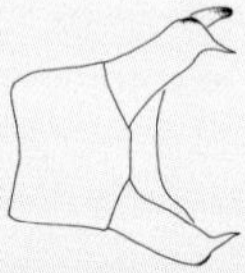

Jade Clubtail

Stillwater Clubtail

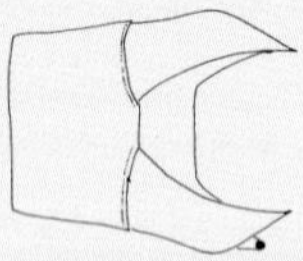

Stillwater Clubtail

Bayou Clubtail

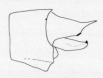

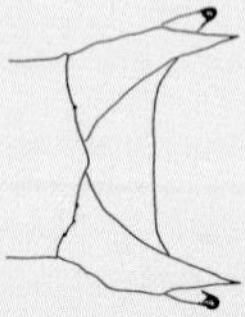

Bayou Clubtail

Gray-green Clubtail

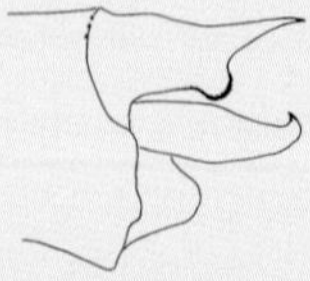

Gray-green Clubtail

Distributed widely in temperate North America and Eurasia, this constitutes the largest genus of odonates in North America. Many species are locally distributed and often quite uncommon, notwithstanding the name of group, but many are common or even abundant in the right habitat during the peak of an often brief flight season. In some species, much of spring emergence at one place happens on very few days. Most species are on streams and rivers but with quite varied substrates, a few on sandy lakes and ponds. Some members of this genus are known for the striking "roller-coaster flights" they perform, as if rapidly drawing a series of shallow U figures in the air. I have seen this in common clubtails and hanging clubtails, and it may be more widespread in the family. Species vary greatly in size (some half the bulk of others) and pattern, although not so much in color. Most change color as they mature, with pale areas of thorax bright yellow or yellow-green when young and gray in old age, less contrasty with dark areas. Yellow color on abdomen remains through maturity, however. Dark colors range from brown to black, even in the same species, perhaps also a function of age (black = young, brown = old). Because of this, descriptions of color patterns may use "dark" and "pale" instead of trying to pin down the variable colors. All species striped on abdomen base, so differences in markings described mostly for S3–10.

This genus has been divided into subgenera, although authors differ in which ones they recognize. The species below are grouped in subgenera to facilitate discussion. Subgenera I recognize in the East include *Gomphus*, *Hylogomphus*, *Gomphurus*, and *Stenogomphurus*. Some odonatologists use another subgenus, *Phanogomphus*, as a substitute for *Gomphus* (in that case, the species of *Hylogomphus* are then considered the true members of subgenus *Gomphus*). *Gomphurus* are typically large species with well-developed clubs and long legs. *Stenogomphurus* have been included with *Gomphurus* but are really rather distinct. *Hylogomphus* are the smallest members of the genus, with prominent clubs like miniature *Gomphurus*. *Gomphus* species are more varied in size and shape, most without well-developed clubs and with legs shorter than those of *Gomphurus*. Other characters are in wing venation, structure of penis and hamules, and larval morphology. Features of genitalia are sometimes visible at close range or in photos at just the right angle but are more readily seen in the hand. Species of one group can look much like species of another. Finally, not until a molecular phylogeny of the genus is attempted will we have a better insight into the relationships within this large group. World 51, NA 38, East 35.

Subgenus Gomphus

This may be a catch-all subgenus, as the species vary from moderately clubbed to scarcely clubbed, from very brightly marked to very dull. They are united by features of venation, genitalic structure, and larval morphology but may yet prove to be not so closely related, especially North American versus Eurasian. Some members of this group are the only common clubtails that are restricted to lakes and ponds. None is as big and showy as a *Gomphurus*, although Pronghorn Clubtail could easily be mistaken for one. Mating pairs fly away from water, sometimes not far, for extended copulation at rest. Several species of the group—Ashy, Cypress, Dusky, Lancet, Pronghorn, and Rapids—have been seen in the peculiar roller-coaster flight, a series of shallow concave parabolas that may go on for several seconds, usually over land. Perhaps all species do it. Could this be an adaptation for predator evasion, or is it a display flight of some sort? Most species are early-spring fliers, among the earliest of odonates to emerge in their area. The group occurs all across North America (17 species) and Eurasia (13 species).

Description Most abundant small clubtail in East, thorax more dark than pale. Quite variable in intensity of coloration, darkest individuals in New England. *Male:* Eyes blue, face unmarked. Thorax with T1–2 wide, almost touching; T3–4 also wide, minimal pale stripe between them; narrow T5 also present. Legs brown to black, outer surface of tibiae pale. Abdomen brown to black with dorsal pale spearpoints on S3–8, each mark with point almost reaching end of segment at palest extreme, not much more than half length in darker individuals. S9 with wide yellow stripe above, S10 with bit of yellow in palest individuals; yellow restricted and dull in darkest northeastern ones, can be almost lacking above. Sides of S8–9 with wide, irregular yellow margins. Common name from downward-projecting blade on cerci. *Female:* Colored much as male, slightly less yellow at end of abdomen. Femora paler than those of male.

Identification Differs from other species with dark, somewhat obscure thoracic pattern (**Ashy** and **Dusky Clubtails**) in smaller size, usually obvious although narrow pale stripe between T1 and T2 (usually scarcely or not at all evident in **Ashy** and **Dusky**), often more

131.1
Lancet Clubtail pale male—Jackson Co., WI, June 2007

131.2
Lancet Clubtail female— Franklin Co., MA, June 2006

131.3
Lancet Clubtail dark
male—Carroll Co., NH,
June 2006

yellow on top of S9, and straight rear edge of occiput (convex in **Ashy** and male **Dusky**, wavy edged in female **Dusky**) all noteworthy. Size alone distinguishes them (but not in photos!). Very slightly more clubbed than those two species, with better-developed flanges projecting from S8–9. In hand, lancet-shaped cercus distinctive. Female subgenital plate with long, pointed lobes in **Dusky**, short, pointed lobes in **Lancet**, barely evident in **Ashy**. Small southern species that might occur with it (**Cypress, Diminutive, Sandhill**) have dark stripes on light thorax. See also **Oklahoma Clubtail**.

Natural History Males perch on ground or rock adjacent to water, facing it, with no over-water patrols. Both sexes perch on sandy roads and other open substrates near breeding habitats, even in tiny clearings in woods; also up on leaves, but seldom far from ground; commonly on lilypads. Females oviposit by flying rapidly over water, tapping every few feet, often perching between bouts to build up ball of eggs (or just hovering briefly, perhaps to bring more eggs into position).

Habitat Wide, including slow streams, ponds, sandy lakes, and even bogs. Appears to be more restricted to ponds in northern part of range.

Flight Season ON May–Aug, QC May–Aug, NS May–Sep, WI May–Aug, ME May–Aug, OH May–Jul, NJ Apr–Aug, KY Apr–Jul, GA Mar–Jul, FL Apr–May.

132 Oklahoma Clubtail   *Gomphus oklahomensis*   TL 46–49, HW 26–30

Description Small, slender clubtail of southwestern part of region. *Male*: Eyes blue, face pale. Thorax with T1–2 separated by very narrow pale line, T3–4 wide with diffuse pale area between them. Legs brown, outer surface of tibiae pale. Abdomen with fairly wide dorsal stripe broken into spearpoints on S3–8, shortest on 8; S9 with pale dorsal stripe, S10 with small pale spot. Sides of S8-9 broadly pale-margined. *Female*: Colored as male, more yellow visible on sides of abdomen. Pale stripe on S8 narrow to absent, on S9–10 usually conspicuous.

Identification Smaller than similarly colored **Ashy Clubtail**, its most likely associate, and distinguished by separated T3 and T4 (fused in **Ashy**). Also quite similar to **Pronghorn Clubtail**, a slightly larger species with substantially wider club in male and more contrast pattern and more yellow at end of abdomen in female. Also a bit smaller than **Sulphur-tipped**, usually with less yellow on abdomen tip, but overlap, and these individuals very difficult. More pale area between T3–4, S9 a bit narrower and longer, and femora paler, often striped with dark, in **Sulphur-tipped**. Some may have to be taken in hand, when size difference is evident and differences in appendages and subgenital plates can be checked. Perhaps no overlap in range with very similar **Lancet Clubtail**; male of that species differs in structure by "lancet" rather than subterminal tooth visible in lateral view of cerci, no ex-

132.1
Oklahoma Clubtail
male—Hempstead
Co., AR, April 2009,
Charles Mills

132.2
Oklahoma Clubtail
female—Jasper Co.,
TX, May 1998, R. A.
Behrstock/Naturewide
Images

ternal tooth in dorsal view. Both sexes differ by middorsal thoracic stripe parallel-sided (slightly wider below in **Lancet**). Barely overlaps with **Rapids Clubtail**, differs from that species by much yellow on top of club and yellow-striped tibiae.

Natural History Both sexes perch on sandy ground or low in vegetation.

Habitat Sandy ponds and lakes with mud bottoms and slow streams, in or out of woodland.

Flight Season LA Mar–May.

---

133 Rapids Clubtail *Gomphus quadricolor*   TL 42–45, HW 25–27

Description Small, dark clubtail of northeastern rivers. *Male*: Eyes blue to turquoise, face unmarked. Thorax with T1–2 broad, in contact at both ends. T3–4 narrow, gray or whitish area between them. Legs black. Abdomen black with restricted dorsal and lateral spots at base of S3–7; extensive yellow on sides of S8–9, rest of tip black. Legs black. *Female*: Colored like male but yellow dorsal markings extend much of segment from S3–7, middle segments usually but not always with yellow streaks behind lateral spots.

133.2
Rapids Clubtail female—Jackson
Co., WI, June 2007

Identification Mostly black abdomen with conspicuous yellow sides of S8–9 distinguishes this species from all in subgenus *Gomphus* except following species. Slightly larger **Beaverpond** and **Harpoon** quite similar; very close look or capture may be required to distinguish them. In both sexes of **Rapids**, black on top of S8 just reaches edge of segment at rear; edge of segment yellow throughout in **Beaverpond** (variation between both conditions in **Harpoon**). Anterior hamule shaped like bird claw, somewhat like **Harpoon** and very different from **Beaverpond**. Posterior lobe, behind hamules, is black and square-shaped in **Rapids**, black and higher than wide in **Harpoon**, intermediate in shape in **Beaverpond** but light-colored and excessively hairy. Female **Rapids** has darker abdomen, usually only pale basal spots on sides of middle segments; other species have pale stripes as well. The two *Stenogomphurus* species (**Cherokee** and **Sable**) also look something like **Rapids** but are slightly smaller with no yellow on S9 in mature males; females and immatures have that yellow, however, but all can be distinguished by narrower, scarcely visible, T3–4. Narrower club distinguishes male **Rapids** from all similarly colored *Gomphurus* and *Hylogomphus*; female *Gomphurus* are larger, female *Hylogomphus* a bit stockier. Also, S9 longer than S8 in **Rapids**, shorter in others.

Natural History Males perch on rocks in river or at shore, also low vegetation. At both riffles and pools. Pairs found as far as several hundred yards from their breeding habitat.

Habitat Rocky and gravelly, mud-bottomed rivers with moderate to fast current, generally on the large side.

Flight Season ON Jun–Jul, WI May–Aug, OH May–Jul, NJ May–Jun, KY May–Jun.

Description Rather sharply marked clubtail of northern ponds. *Male*: Eyes blue, face unmarked. Thorax with T1–2 broad, fused along entire length or partially separated by very fine line. T3 very narrow, T4 broader, both complete and well separated. Legs black, inside of front femora pale. Abdomen with yellow dorsal stripe from long, narrow triangles, becoming shorter and shorter and represented by tiny streak on S8. Yellow basal lateral spots conspicuous, often additional midlength spot on any of S4–7. Entire margins of S8–9 yellow, border between black and yellow on S8 variable but somewhat distinctive; also yellow on lower edge of S10. *Female*: Colored like male; more extensive yellow markings on sides of abdomen.

Identification Often recognizable because pale stripes on front of thorax quite wide below, forming broader-based triangles in front view than in similar species, including **Harpoon** and **Rapids**. In **Beaverpond**, these pale stripes rounded above, in **Harpoon** they hook outward, and in both **Beaverpond** and **Rapids** there may be an isolated adjacent dot. **Harpoon Clubtail** very similar to **Beaverpond**; see that species for discussion of that and other similar species.

134.1
Beaverpond Clubtail
male—Westmorland Co.,
NB, June 1998, Denis
Doucet

134.2
Beaverpond Clubtail
female—Piscataquis Co.,
ME, June 2006, Netta
Smith

Natural History Males perch on ground and rocks at breeding habitat or take short flights along shore or over water. Females can be common along sunny roads in and near breeding habitats when few males are seen in same areas.

Habitat As name implies, usually on coldwater ponds rather than streams, but beaver ponds are associated with streams, so some individuals will be at running water.

Flight Season ON May–Jul, QC May–Jul, NS May–Aug, ME May–Jul, NJ May–Jun.

135 Harpoon Clubtail *Gomphus descriptus* TL 48–52, HW 29–32

Description Brightly marked clubtail of northern streams. *Male*: Eyes blue or turquoise, face unmarked. Thorax with T1–2 broad, fused along entire length or partially separated by very fine line. T3 very narrow, T4 broader, both complete and well separated. Legs black. Abdomen with yellow dorsal stripe from long, narrow triangles, becoming shorter and shorter and represented by tiny streak on S8. Tiny yellow basal lateral spots on S4–7, may be lacking; S7 usually with tiny terminal spot. Entire margins of S8–9 yellow, that on S8 with irregular upper margin, low in middle and extending up from both ends. *Female*: Colored like male but additional yellow streaks along sides of abdomen.

Identification Extremely like **Beaverpond Clubtail** in thoracic stripes and abdominal pattern; often identified just by habitat, but this can be flawed. Perhaps best quick mark furnished by pale stripes on front of thorax. In **Harpoon**, pale stripe broader above, wraps

135.1
Harpoon Clubtail male—Merrimack Co., NH, June 2006

135.2
Harpoon Clubtail female—Coos Co., NH, July 2003, Tom Murray

around T1 to form little hook. In **Beaverpond**, stripe narrow and more or less pointed above (so more triangular), no hook (may be tiny pale dot separated from it). On average, **Harpoon** has less yellow on sides of abdomen, one small spot or no yellow on each middle segment, whereas **Beaverpond** has one larger spot and often a second spot behind that. **Harpoon** may have spot at end of S7, **Beaverpond** at midlength; these spots distinctive when present. **Harpoon** usually has less yellow on sides of S8 and pattern different, but possibly overlap. In **Beaverpond**, single lobe projects slightly down from black into yellow on side of segment; in **Harpoon**, often two lobes projecting farther into yellow. **Beaverpond** often has dorsal spot at base of S8, **Harpoon** never; thus only presence of spot significant. Hamules quite different looking but may have to have dragonfly in hand to see them clearly. Anterior hamule almost as long as posterior and sickle-shaped in **Harpoon**, much shorter than posterior and blunt in **Beaverpond**. Also, posterior lobe behind hamules as high as posterior hamules in **Harpoon**, distinctly lower in **Beaverpond**. Females differ in color pattern in same minor ways that males do, and female **Harpoon** has pale stripe on rear of femur lacking in **Beaverpond**. Subgenital plate less than half length of S8 in **Harpoon**, more than half length in **Beaverpond**. **Rapids** another rather similar species of subgenus *Gomphus* with narrow black abdomen and big lateral spots on S8–9. That species has shorter dorsal abdominal markings in males, reduced lateral abdominal markings in females, and narrower, less fused T1–2, T1 barely reaching brown line at upper end of thorax in both sexes. Females of some *Hylogomphus* species superficially similar but smaller, with stockier abdomens; most have narrower thoracic stripes. Female *Stenogomphurus* (**Cherokee**, **Sable**) a bit larger than *Hylogomphus* but also differ from **Harpoon** in same way in thoracic patterns. Also have black markings on face lacking in **Harpoon**.

Natural History Males perch on rocks and up on tree leaves on and along river, then fly out in patrol flight. Mature females rarely seen. Ovipositing females perch briefly with upcurved abdomen while producing egg mass. Both sexes forage in nearby clearings.

Habitat Clear, small to medium-sized sandy streams and rivers with good current.

Flight Season ON May–Jul, QC May–Aug, NS Jun–Jul, ME Jun–Jul, NJ May–Jul.

---

136 Ashy Clubtail *Gomphus lividus* TL 48–56, HW 29–34

Description Slender and rather dull brown and whitish stream clubtail, one of most common and widespread species. *Male*: Eyes blue, face entirely pale or with faint crosslines. Thorax with T1–2 wide, fused; T3–4 wide, fused; and T5 well developed; really a dark thorax with pale stripes. Legs brown, outer surface of tibiae pale tan. Abdomen dark brown to black with yellowish spearpoints covering much of middle segments, reduced to less than half length by S8. Some individuals with top of S9 yellow as well. Poorly defined yellowish markings along sides of S8–9. *Female*: Colored as male, but spearpoints extending entire length of segments, more than half on S8; S9–10 mostly pale.

Identification One of group of common clubtails with rather dull coloration, very wide dark thoracic stripes, and scarcely any indication of club. Extremely similar **Dusky Clubtail** averages a bit darker, with different appendages, but these two are among the most difficult pairs of species to distinguish in the field, even though territorial males tend to be in different habitats. **Dusky** with prominent lateral tooth on cerci viewed from above, **Ashy** angled but without tooth. Also, epiproct relatively wider in **Dusky**. In side view, **Dusky** also has prominent downward-projecting tooth on each cercus, **Ashy** lacks it. Females easily distinguished by subgenital plate, scarcely evident in **Ashy** and with two pointed lobes that extend almost one-third length under S8 in **Dusky**. Perhaps distinguishable by eye color in some cases, **Ashy** tending toward blue-purple and **Dusky** tending toward blue-green. **Ashy** distinguished from **Lancet Clubtail** by obviously larger size, different appendages. **Lancet** with downward-projecting blade on cercus in lateral view, **Ashy** without. Subgeni-

136.1
Ashy Clubtail
male—Floyd Co.,
GA, May 2006

136.2
Ashy Clubtail
female—Murray
Co., GA, May 2006

tal plate in female **Lancet** with two obvious pointed lobes. See **Lancet** for additional differences. **Harpoon Clubtail** of same habitat generally brighter, more contrastily marked with narrower dark stripes on light thorax.

Natural History Away from water usually low on rocks, sand, or shrubs. Males perch on sand, rocks, or logs at shore; patrol until late afternoon, even in shade. Oviposits by tapping water near bank at intervals of a few inches.

Habitat Slow-flowing wooded streams and rivers, also edges of large wave-beaten lakes.

Flight Season ON May–Aug, QC Jun–Jul, WI May–Aug, OH May–Jul, NJ May–Jul, KY Apr–Aug, LA Mar–Jun, GA Mar–Jun, FL Mar–May.

| **137 Dusky Clubtail** *Gomphus spicatus* | **TL 46–50, HW 26–30** |

Description Slender clubtail, dull in maturity, usually at lakes. *Male*: Eyes blue, face pale. Thorax with T1–2 wide, fused; T3–4 wide, mostly fused. Legs dark brown, outer surface of tibiae tan. Abdomen with narrow pale spearpoints shortening to rear, half length on S7, very short on S8; S9–10 dark. Margins of narrow S9 faintly yellow. *Female*: Colored as male but dorsal spearpoints slightly more conspicuous, as is yellow margin on S9; also pale dorsal stripe on S10.

137.1
Dusky Clubtail
male—Price Co., WI,
June 2007

137.2
Dusky Clubtail
female—Carroll Co.,
NH, June 2006

Identification **Ashy Clubtail** similar enough to cause constant identification challenge. Easily differentiated by different appendages in hand, difference hard to see in field. **Dusky** has prominent tooth on outer surfaces of cerci, also prominent tooth beneath, visible from side; **Ashy** has neither. Hamules also quite different: anterior as long as posterior in **Ashy**, much shorter in **Dusky**. **Lancet Clubtail** similarly colored but much smaller; see that species. No other dull clubtail with slender abdomen in its range. Females differ by subgenital plates; see illustrations and description under **Lancet**.

Natural History Males perch on ground and low vegetation, including water lilies, at edge of water, immatures and females in woodland clearings nearby. Usually perch on or near ground, often on sandy roads and other wide-open areas.

Habitat Clear-water lakes with open sandy shores or dense grass beds along shore; also large ponds, including bog ponds. Sometimes slow streams flowing into lakes.

Flight Season ON May–Aug, QC May–Aug, NS May–Aug, ME May–Aug, OH May–Jul, NJ May–Jun.

Description Small, rather dull southeastern clubtail of sandy streams. Smaller at southern end of range. *Male*: Eyes blue, face unmarked. Occiput concave in center, projects as slight lobe at either end. Thorax with T1–2 fairly wide, barely separated, T1 not reaching top of segment; T3–4 of moderate width, separated by less than their own width. Legs light brown, outer surface of tibiae paler. Abdominal pattern somewhat obscure with brown lateral stripe fading out on terminal segments, yellow dorsal stripe continuous to S8 or S9. Sides of S7–9 yellowish, mottled with brown. Individuals in western part of range more contrastingly colored, with blacker abdomen. S10 mostly dark in darker individuals, mostly pale in paler ones. Club moderately developed. *Female*: Colored like male, eyes a bit duller and abdominal pattern even more obscure. Occiput as male.

Identification Differs primarily in structure from slightly smaller but very similar **Sandhill Clubtail** but rarely if ever found together. In dorsal view, cerci of **Sandhill** with external tooth lacking in **Cypress**. Anterior hamules of **Cypress** straight, nestled into posterior hamule; anterior hamules of **Sandhill** more slender and curved forward, clearly separated from posterior hamule. Lobed occiput margin of both sexes of **Cypress** distinctive in hand and may be visible at close range. In females, S9 a bit narrower and S10 a bit longer in **Sandhill**

138.1
Cypress Clubtail
male—Columbia
Co., FL, April 2005

138.2
Cypress Clubtail
female—Polk Co.,
FL, April 2005

than in **Cypress**, making the abdomen tip look slightly more pointed. Overlaps slightly with **Lancet Clubtail**, which has broader thoracic stripes, T3–4 fused and T1–2 almost fused. **Diminutive** has more slender abdomen, scarcely clubbed, and S9 distinctly longer than S8. Pattern somewhat brighter also. **Hodges's** and barely overlapping **Westfall's** shaped like **Diminutive**, much more vividly patterned black and yellow than **Cypress**.

Natural History Males perch at edge of water, facing it; also out on lilypads or on twigs but always low. Often return to exact spot from which flushed. Patrol flights over water with raised abdomen. Copulation fairly lengthy, often on ground, and may be well away from water. Females either dash around and tap water erratically or hover in one spot 6 inches or so above the water, descend and tap, then rise and do it again. Oviposit in floating detritus as well as open water.

Habitat Lowland rivers and streams, often bordered by cypresses; also found at lakes, typically more heavily vegetated and muddier than the open sandy lakes preferred by Sandhill Clubtail.

Flight Season GA Mar–Jun, FL Feb–May.

---

139 Sandhill Clubtail *Gomphus cavillaris*   TL 37–45, HW 20–25

Description Small far-southeastern clubtail of sandy lakes, with two distinctive subspecies. Description refers to *G. c. cavillaris. Male*: Eyes blue, face with faint brown crossline. Thorax with T1–4 all of moderate width, well separated. Legs brown. Abdomen brown on sides, complete yellowish dorsal stripe through S8 or S9, bordered by lighter brown dorsolateral stripes and extensive yellow sides on S7–9; S10 mostly darker brown. Club moderately developed. *Female*: Colored like male but duller, abdominal pattern rather obscure and varying from medium brown to light tan, more pale color on sides. *G. c. brimleyi* much more contrastingly colored, with dark brown thoracic stripes; legs black and yellow striped; abdomen dark brown to black, with narrow yellow dorsal stripe extending to S8; sides of S7–9 yellow but with some darker markings; S10 all dark. Female with much yellow on sides of abdomen.

Identification Three other small clubtails in this subgenus likely to occur with **Sandhill**, although no two species regularly occur at the same lake. **Cypress** so similarly colored to **Sandhill** that structural characters necessary to separate them (see **Cypress Clubtail**). **Hodges's** somewhat similar but has narrower and darker abdomen with very little indica-

139.1
Sandhill Clubtail (*cavillaris*) male—Clay Co., FL, April 2005

139.2
Sandhill Clubtail (*cavillaris*) female—Lake Co., FL, April 2008

139.3
Sandhill Clubtail
(*brimleyi*) male—
Leon Co., FL, April
2005

139.4
Sandhill Clubtail
(*brimleyi*) female—
Leon Co., FL, April
2008

tion of club and less yellow on sides of it, S8 almost all black above. **Lancet** has broader thoracic stripes, T3–4 fused. No habitat overlap and perhaps no range overlap with **Diminutive** or **Westfall's**, which are more vividly black and yellow even than *brimleyi* subspecies of **Sandhill** and have S9 longer than S8. **Clearlake Clubtail** at same lakes with **Sandhill** but larger with distinctive very long S9.

Natural History Males perch at shore or on sand near vegetation edge away from shore. At some locations, chose leaves and twigs on sand over sand itself, but always very low. Also at times actively fly and hover over water, well into afternoon, with abdomen elevated; patrol flights last up to 30 sec. Copulating pairs rest on ground and in low vegetation away from water. May take large prey (grass mantis as long as dragonfly).

Habitat Sand-bottomed clear lakes, where they can be abundant.

Flight Season GA Mar–Apr, FL Jan–May.

Comments The two subspecies are quite distinct in color pattern. *G. c. cavillaris* inhabits the Florida Peninsula and *G. c. brimleyi* the Florida Panhandle and far southern Alabama, with an isolated population at large lakes in Bladen County, North Carolina.

Description Small restricted-range southeastern clubtail of boggy ponds and lakes. *Male:* Eyes blue, face with faint crossline. Thorax with T1–2 broad but distinct, T1 pointed above. T3–4 broad, narrow area between them gray. Legs dark brown, outer surface of tibiae yellow. Abdomen mostly black, well-developed yellow dorsal stripe extends back to S8, where only half length. Small anterior yellow spots on sides of S3–7, more yellow on S7. Extensive yellow on sides of S8–9, S8 penetrated from above by black, bilobed marking. Club scarcely evident. *Female:* Colored like male, more yellow or whitish all along sides of abdomen.

Identification Very slender black and yellow abdomen, with scarcely a hint of a club, distinctive, as is S9 longer than S8. **Cypress** and **Sandhill** barely overlap, if at all; both have distinct club in male and more pale color on abdomen. Same with **Lancet**, which overlaps somewhat more; it has fused T3–4. All three have shorter S9. **Clearlake Clubtail** distinctly larger with even longer S9 and narrower thoracic stripes.

Natural History Males perch on sand at edge of vegetation back from shore, can be very common. Both sexes perch in herbaceous vegetation in sunny clearings near breeding habitat, even during good weather more of them away from than at water.

Habitat Ponds, lakes, and slow streams, typically acid and bog-margined, with sphagnum and pitcher plants.

Flight Season GA Apr–May.

140.1
Diminutive Clubtail
male—Richmond
Co., GA, May 2006

140.2
Diminutive Clubtail
female—Richmond
Co., GA, May 2006

Description Small clubtail of woodland streams on Florida Panhandle. *Male:* Eyes blue to turquoise, face with faint crossline. Thorax with T1–2 broad but distinct, T1 pointed above. T3–4 of moderate width and distinct. Legs blackish, outer surface of tibiae yellow. Abdomen mostly black, well-developed yellow dorsal markings on S3–8, variable in extent on middle segments but decrease in length toward rear. Small anterior yellow spots on sides of S3–7, more yellow on S7. Extensive yellow on sides of S8–9, S8 penetrated from above by black, bilobed marking. Club scarcely evident. *Female:* Colored like male but complete whitish or yellow stripe all along sides of abdomen.

Identification Slender black and yellow abdomen distinctive. Much like **Diminutive,** but no overlap in range; this species paler between T3 and T4. May not occur with **Hodges's**; latter has shorter S9 and lacks bilobed marking on sides of S8. **Cypress** and **Lancet** both with browner abdomen, wider club, shorter S9.

Natural History Both sexes and pairs rest on ground near breeding habitat. Males may patrol briefly over water.

Habitat Small boggy ponds and streams through woodland.

Flight Season FL Mar–Apr.

Comments Very closely related to Diminutive Clubtail but distinctive enough for species status.

141.1
Westfall's Clubtail
male—Santa Rosa Co., FL,
April 2008

141.2
Westfall's Clubtail female—
Santa Rosa Co., FL, April 2004,
Giff Beaton

Clubtail Family **237**

Description Small Gulf-coast clubtail of slow-flowing rivers. *Male*: Eyes blue, face unmarked. Thorax with T1–2 moderate width, T1 interrupted above. T3–4 moderate width, well separated. Legs brown, inner surface of femora and outer surface of tibiae yellow. Abdomen black with narrow yellow dorsal stripe filling most of middle segments to S7, very short on S8. Yellow basal spot on sides of S3–6, much more yellow on S7 and fully yellow sides of S8–9, with slight amount of black mottling. *Female*: Colored like male but yellow markings almost continuous on sides of abdomen.

Identification Narrow, mostly black abdomen and boldly striped thorax with well-separated stripes distinctive, also restricted range. Occurs with **Westfall's**, which has S9 longer than S8, entirely dark femora, and bilobed black marking on sides of S8 (**Hodges's** occasionally has hint of same marking). **Cypress** and **Sandhill** have wider clubs and less vividly black and yellow abdomen, with more yellow on top of club. **Lancet** has broader, joined thoracic stripes. **Clearlake** larger, with wider club and very long S9.

Natural History Males perch on sand and low vegetation at breeding habitat. Both sexes and pairs also in nearby clearings.

Habitat Clean, sandy rivers and streams with slow current through woodland.

Flight Season LA Mar–Apr, FL Mar–May.

142.1
Hodges's Clubtail
male—Santa Rosa Co., FL,
April 2008

142.2
Hodges's Clubtail
female—Santa Rosa Co.,
FL, April 2008

Description Brightly marked southeastern lake clubtail with long abdomen tip. *Male*: Eyes turquoise, face with narrow but distinct black crossline. Thorax with T1–2 fairly narrow, well separated; T3–4 even narrower and farther apart. Legs black, tan on inner surface of femora. Abdomen black with very limited yellow (small basal dorsal and lateral spots on S3–7) except prominent yellow edges on S7–9 (wide on S8–9); S10 also yellow on sides. *Female*: Colored like male but with sides of abdomen mostly yellow.

Identification Quite distinctive species because of very long S9. Might occur with smaller **Diminutive** or **Westfall's Clubtails**, both of which have S9 elongate, but not so long as **Clearlake**. Relatively narrow and widely separated thoracic stripes also different from similar species that might occur with it. **Cypress** and **Sandhill** (this species in same habitat) both with normally shaped abdomens and wider stripes on thorax.

Natural History Males fly back and forth over water and perch on open patches of shoreline, stumps, logs, tree trunks, and lily pads. May perch crosswise on tree trunks, unusual for any dragonfly. Make long flights out over water, sometimes not returning to same spot. Female oviposits by hovering for many seconds, perhaps to build up egg ball, then fast low flight and sporadic water-tapping.

Habitat Clear sandy lakes with some silt deposit and wooded or open shores; often but not always water lilies. Some are cypress-bordered.

Flight Season LA Apr, GA Apr, FL Mar–Apr.

143.1
Clearlake Clubtail male—
Leon Co., FL, April 2005

143.2
Clearlake Clubtail
female—Telfair Co., GA,
April 2010, Marion M.
Dobbs

144 Sulphur-tipped Clubtail *Gomphus militaris* TL 47–53, HW 28–33

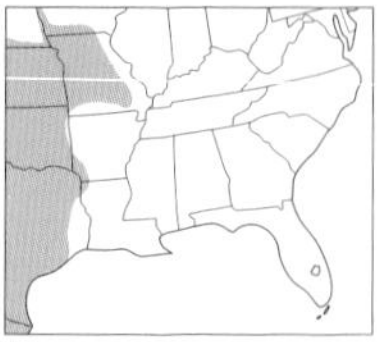

Description Small southwestern clubtail with moderate club and more yellow than similar species. *Male*: Eyes blue, face unmarked. Thorax with T1–2 just separated, T3–4 moderate width with well-defined pale area between them. Abdomen with usual spear-points, shortening on S7 and half segment length on S8. S9 with broad pale stripe, S10 with narrow stripe. In arid western part of range, dark markings on club much reduced, so most of S8 and all of S9 yellow. *Female*: Colored as male, more yellow on sides of abdomen, with pale areas exceeding dark lateral stripe. S9 with yellow dorsal and lateral stripes almost touching, S10 with much yellow.

Identification Pale color more extensive, especially at abdomen tip, than in most other clubtails occurring with it. Club narrower and with more yellow than in somewhat larger **Cocoa** and **Plains** and similar-sized **Pronghorn Clubtail**. Can look fairly much like **Pronghorn**, as color patterns just about overlap. Look for pale streak on outside of femur in **Sulphur-tipped**. **Sulphur-tipped** also with much more yellow than in narrow-abdomened **Oklahoma Clubtail** found at same ponds. Could be confused with equally bright yellow **Flag-tailed Spinyleg**, but that species larger, with narrower thoracic stripes, prominent yellow-orange club and longer legs.

Natural History Males perch on sandy shores and in low vegetation at water and fly out and back at intervals; females on similar perches away from water.

Habitat Small to medium slow-flowing rivers and large open ponds and lakes.

Flight Season IA Jun–Jul.

Distribution West to eastern Colorado and New Mexico and south in Mexico to Nuevo León.

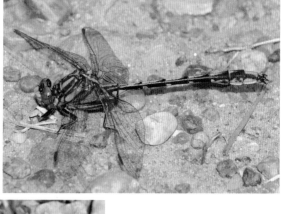

144.1
Sulphur-tipped Clubtail male—Bastrop Co., TX, May 2005

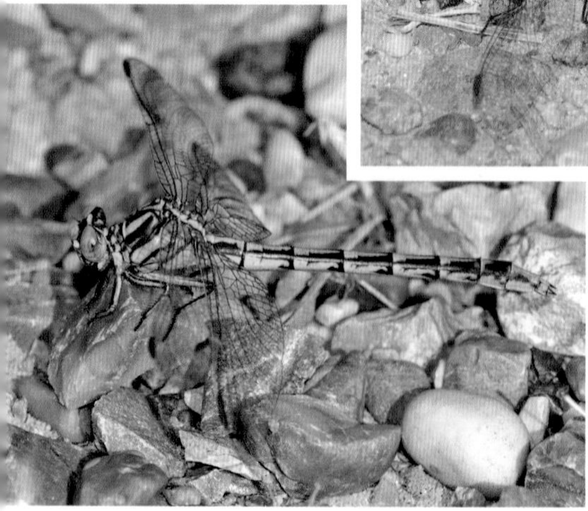

144.2
Sulphur-tipped Clubtail female—Howard Co., AR, June 2009, Charles Mills

Description Small midwestern clubtail with moderate, brightly spotted club. *Male*: Eyes blue, face unmarked. Thorax with T1–2 wide, narrowly separated; T3–4 wide, partially fused; T4 may be interrupted above. Legs black, outer surface of tibiae pale. Abdomen black with wide pale dorsal stripe on S1–7, pointed on each segment and almost reaching tip; shorter triangle on S8, less than half segment; S9 with wide yellow, S10 with yellow spot. Margins of S8–9 entirely yellow. *Female*: Colored about like male but more yellow visible on sides of abdomen, most of S10 yellow above. Femora with yellow stripe. Tiny horn between each lateral ocellus and eye.

Identification Easily mistaken for very similar **Plains Clubtail**; see that species for details of distinction. More brightly marked, with wider club, than other small clubtails of subgenus *Gomphus* in its range, much darker overall than somewhat similarly shaped **Sulphur-tipped**. Also smaller and shorter-legged, with smaller club, than larger *Gomphurus* such as

145.1
Pronghorn Clubtail male—
Winneshiek Co., IA, July
2004, Greg Lasley

145.2
Pronghorn Clubtail female—
Pope Co., AR, June 2008,
Herschel Raney

Cobra, Cocoa, Midland, and **Ozark Clubtails** with which it occurs. These four all have more dark than light on sides of S8, and all but **Cocoa** have entirely dark tibiae.

Natural History Both sexes perch typically in open on ground or rocks or in weeds or low shrubs. Assume obelisk posture at midday. May fly up and down pools and riffles on occasion but do not hover at length over riffles as some larger clubtails do and may also search for mates away from water. Females oviposit close to bank by tapping water at irregular intervals a few feet apart, depositing 30–50 eggs with each tap.

Habitat Slow-flowing sandy or muddy streams with or without rocks and in or out of woodland, also medium to large lakes in North.

Flight Season ON May–Aug, IA May–Aug, WI Jun–Aug, OH May–Aug, KY May–Jun.

Distribution West locally across northern states to British Columbia and Washington, also northeast Colorado and north and central Texas.

---

146 Tennessee Clubtail *Gomphus sandrius* TL 48–52, HW 29–32

Description Medium-sized clubtail of very restricted range with moderate yellow-spotted club. *Male*: Eyes turquoise, face unmarked. Thorax with T1–2 fairly broad but separate, T1 not quite reaching top of segment. T3 narrow, incomplete above; T4 slightly wider and complete. Legs dark brown to black, outer surface of tibiae yellow. Abdomen with extensive yellow, including dorsal triangles that extend almost full length of middle segments but only half length on S7–8; S9 with broad yellow dorsal stripe, S10 with yellow spot. Sides of S3–7 with basal yellow spot, also isolated yellow spots on posterior segments. Sides of S8–9 extensively yellow, with characteristic dark pattern at rear of S8 that encloses isolated yellow

146.1
Tennessee Clubtail
male—Maury Co., TN,
June 2006

146.2
Tennessee Clubtail
female—Rutherford
Co., TN, June 2010,
Greg Lasley

spot. *Female*: Colored like male but more extensive yellow on sides of abdomen and S10 entirely yellow above. Femora also with much yellow.

Identification Co-occurring **Handsome Clubtail** a bit larger, T3–4 narrower, less yellow on club, and tibiae entirely black. Much like closely related **Pronghorn Clubtail,** although no known overlap. **Pronghorn** has broader thoracic stripes, S3–4 often fused; both sexes with less yellow on hind femur than **Tennessee**. Male cerci quite different, those of **Pronghorn** with much more prominent exterior tooth.

Natural History Males perch on bedrock at shore of stream facing water, may also patrol over pools. One female oviposited in fast low flight over pool below riffle, striking water at intervals of 6 feet or more.

Habitat Shallow streams with moderate current flowing over bedrock.

Flight Season Entire range Jun.

Subgenus Hylogomphus

This subgenus features brightly patterned species with prominent clubs, all of them smaller than similarly shaped *Gomphurus* and usually with larger clubs than any of subgenus *Gomphus*. This is a difficult group, and in-hand identification is recommended until you learn which species live where. The six species are restricted to eastern North America.

147 Green-faced Clubtail *Gomphus viridifrons* TL 45–46, HW 27–28

Description Small green-faced clubtail with mostly black club prominent but not as wide as widest *Hylogomphus*. *Male*: Eyes green, face with one dark crossbar. Thorax with T1 and T2 well developed, in contact at upper end. T3 and T4 narrow, T3 incomplete above, T4 sometimes barely visible. Ground color of thorax gray in mature individuals, contrasting with yellow abdominal markings.  Legs black. Abdomen black with restricted pale markings including fine narrow dorsal triangles and small basal lateral spots on S3–7; usually larger lateral spot on S8 may extend half length of segment; may be tiny spot on S9. *Female*: Colored much like male, but lateral abdominal markings larger, much yellow on sides of S7–9, that on S9 visible from above. Big, backward-pointing black spines on vertex, usually visible against yellow of occiput.

Identification This and **Mustached Clubtail** a bit larger than other co-occurring *Hylogomphus* (**Piedmont**, **Spine-crowned**), with less yellow on the slightly narrower male club.

147.1
Green-faced Clubtail
male—Scott Co., TN,
June 2006

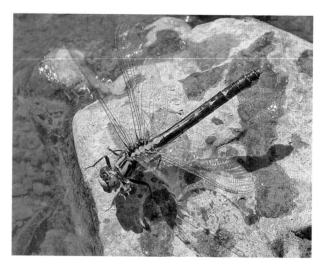

147.2
Green-faced
Clubtail female—
Ashtabula Co., OH,
June 2004, John
Pogacnik

Much like **Mustached** but less black on face, T4 often obscure or absent (well defined in **Mustached**). Female *Hylogomphus* will always be difficult and should be identified by capture and examination of subgenital plate (extends almost full length of S8 in this species). Also, female **Green-faced** has spines on vertex much more prominent than in poorly named **Spine-crowned**. Could be mistaken for dark stream species in other subgenera, for example **Cherokee**, **Harpoon**, and **Sable Clubtails**, differs by wider club in male. Male hamules black, project farther (just about height of abdomen) in this species than in most others found with it.

Natural History Males perch on rocks out in the current and seem very wary. May be only *Hylogomphus* more likely to be found in this habitat than on leaves overhanging smaller streams. Also hover over pool just above riffle, facing wind and being slowly carried backward, then dart forward and hover in same place again.

Habitat Good-sized rocky rivers with moderate to swift current, sand and silt on bottom.

Flight Season ON May–Jun, WI May–Aug, OH May–Jul, KY May–Jun, GA May–Jun.

148 Mustached Clubtail *Gomphus adelphus* TL 39–45, HW 24–28

Description Common small river clubtail with moderate mostly black club, black-marked face. *Male:* Eyes green or turquoise; face with conspicuous black crossbands. Thorax with T1–2 well developed, in contact at upper end. T3 narrow and incomplete above, T4 slightly wider and quite distinct. Legs black. Abdomen black with restricted pale markings including short narrow to somewhat broader dorsal triangles on S3–7; S8–9 with faintly indicated yellowish area along outer edges. *Female:* Colored as male except more yellow on abdomen; dorsal markings longer and conspicuous yellow spots on sides of S3–9. Prominent spines on either side of vertex, just above eyes.

Identification Very much like **Green-faced Clubtail** but with pattern of dark stripes across face (**Green-faced** has only one) and usually better-defined lateral thoracic stripes. Typically less yellow on club in **Mustached** (often with none), but the two overlap. Other *Hylogomphus* have much more yellow on sides of somewhat wider clubs. Females differ only in head and thorax patterns.

Natural History Males perch on rocks in or at edge of river or on broad leaves of overhanging trees and shrubs up to head height. Also hover over water at heads of riffles with abdo-

148.1
Mustached Clubtail
male—Burnett Co., WI,
June 2007; inset male—
Algonquin Provincial Park,
ON, June 2008, Steven
Collins

148.2
Mustached Clubtail
female—Penobscot Co.,
ME, June 2006,
Netta Smith

men raised and hind tibiae extended. Tend to leave water during hot midday period. Both sexes often common in sunny clearings nearby, often well up on leaves. Females perch on rocks with abdomen curved up to produce egg masses between oviposition bouts.

Habitat Streams and rivers with slow to fairly swift current, sand or mud bottom, often with rocky riffles. Also at some lakes with exposed shores.

Flight Season ON May–Aug, QC May–Jul, NS Jun–Aug, WI May–Aug, ME May–Aug, NJ May–Jun.

Description Small brightly marked stream clubtail with prominent club. *Male*: Eyes blue-gray to greenish gray; face unmarked. Thorax with T1–2 well developed, may be fused. T3–4 thin, T3 usually incomplete above. Legs black. Abdomen with pattern of short dorsal triangles and tiny lateral spots on S3–7 (additional yellow on sides of S7), large yellow spots on sides of S8–9 (reaching end of S9 but not S8). *Female*: Colored as male. T1 and T2 usually not fused. Pair of spines on vertex barely visible.

Identification Differs from **Green-faced** and **Mustached Clubtails** in smaller size, no dark markings on face, much more yellow on club in males. Very little overlap with **Green-faced** but females much alike in color pattern. Must be distinguished by head spines or subgenital plate, much shorter in this species. Much like **Piedmont** and overlaps with it in southern

149.1
Spine-crowned Clubtail male—
Worcester Co., MA, June 2006,
Tom Murray, posed; inset
female—Allegheny Co., MD, June
2008, Steven Collins

149.2
Spine-crowned Clubtail
female—Sussex Co., NJ,
June 2008

uplands. May not be distinguishable in field from **Spine-crowned**, but latter has larger subapical tooth on cerci and conspicuously smaller anterior hamules. Females easily distinguished in hand by length of subgenital plate (more than half length of S8 in **Piedmont**, less than half in **Spine-crowned**).

Natural History Males patrol back and forth about a foot above the water, occasionally hovering, and perch on shore or rocks or up in vegetation.

Habitat Large to medium-sized shallow rivers with moderate current, mud substrate, and at least scattered rocky riffles.

Flight Season ME May–Jul, NJ May–Jul.

---

150 Piedmont Clubtail *Gomphus parvidens*　　　　　　TL 39–46, HW 25–31

Description Small clubtail with prominent yellow-sided club. Distinctly larger in Alabama than farther east. *Male*: Eyes blue to turquoise; face with faint dusky crosslines. Thorax with T1–2 broad, separate or just barely touching; T3 faint, incomplete above; T4 narrow but complete. All stripes broader and more distinct in Alabama. Legs black. S4–7 with short dorsal triangles and tiny lateral spots at base. S8–9 with big yellow lateral spots, barely reaching

150.1
Piedmont Clubtail
male—Chesterfield Co.,
SC, May 2008

150.2
Piedmont Clubtail
female—Richmond Co.,
GA, May 2006

end of S8. *Female*: Color pattern as in male. Pointed conical turbercle between each lateral ocellus and adjacent eye margin.

Identification Barely overlaps with all other *Hylogomphus* species, probably rarely occurs with any of them. Much yellow on club distinguishes males from male **Green-faced** and **Mustached**, also lacks black facial markings of **Mustached**. Scarcely marked sides of thorax differentiate both sexes from **Banner** and **Twin-striped**. Looks just like **Spine-crowned**, would have to be distinguished in hand. **Spine-crowned** has larger ventral tooth on cerci of male. Occiput of male **Spine-crowned** projects beyond rear margin of eyes and with slightly curved border in **Spine-crowned**, falls short of eye margin and with straight border in **Piedmont**.

Natural History Males perch on leaves over water, fly out on presumed patrol flight at intervals. Foraging immature and mature individuals can be common in woodland clearings near river.

Habitat Small, slow-flowing sandy streams in woodland.

Flight Season GA Apr–Jun.

---

151 Twin-striped Clubtail *Gomphus geminatus* TL 39–47, HW 24–29v

Description Only small clubtail with wide, yellow-sided club in limited range. *Male*: Eyes dark blue or turquoise, paler below; face with faint dusky crosslines. Thorax with T1–2 broad, touching or not, may leave isolated yellow dot at top; T3–4 narrower but prominent and clearly separated. Legs black. Abdomen with pointed basal spots on top and sides of S4–7, on S7 extending all along edge of segment. S8–9 extensively yellow on sides. *Female*: Colored as  male, yellow on abdomen a bit more extensive and femora paler at base. No spines on vertex.

Identification Combination of conspicuous and distinct T3–4 and much yellow on sides of S7 distinguishes both sexes of this species from other *Hylogomphus* (may coexist only with **Banner Clubtail**, with dusky area between T3 and T4 and bulky, widely divergent cerci in male). No other very small clubtail in range has prominent club in male.

151.1
Twin-striped Clubtail
male—Santa Rosa Co., FL,
April 2008

151.2
Twin-striped Clubtail
pair—Walton Co., FL,
April 2008

Natural History Males perch on or hang from leaves over and near streams, knee to head
height. Pairs in woodland, may be at some distance from breeding habitat. Female builds
up ball of eggs while perched with abdomen elevated (probably many clubtails do this).
Habitat Small sandy streams with little to moderate current in woodland.
Flight Season FL Mar–Jun.

---

152 Banner Clubtail   *Gomphus apomyius*   TL 35–37, HW 23–25

Description Quite small clubtail with wide black, yellow-sided club.
Male: Eyes blue to turquoise, face unmarked. Thorax with T1–2 well
developed, almost touching, T3–4 also well developed with pale
area between them rather narrow and obscured. Legs black. Abdomen black with pale dorsal stripe on S1–2, narrow basal triangles
on S3–7; large basal spot on sides of S3, tiny spots on S4–6, basal
spot and margin on S7, and entire sides of widely clubbed S8–9
yellow. *Female*: Color pattern about as male, eyes somewhat
bluer; minimal or no club. Short, conical tubercle on either side of
vertex.

Identification Differs from all *Hylogomphus* that might occur with it (all but **Mustached**) in
broad T3–4 not clearly separated. Very wide extent of black cerci also distinctive for male,
although similar in **Piedmont**. Female, with scarcely any club, distinctive in small size and
bright markings, including bold dorsal and lateral yellow spots on middle abdominal segments. These markings are distinctive against clubtails other than *Hylogomphus*, for example, PYGMY CLUBTAILS that have dorsal stripe and lateral spots and LEAST CLUBTAILS that
have rings.

Natural History Males perch on leaves at chest height over stream, rarely on rocks, or hover
over riffles with abdomen raised and club prominent. Active in morning until temperature
rises, then back into shady woodland. Females on leaves in woods nearby. Quite
uncommon.

Habitat Small, clean woodland streams with acid water and sand bottom and accumulations
of organic detritus.

Flight Season NJ Apr–Jul, LA Mar–Apr, GA Mar–May.

Clubtail Family   **249**

152.1
Banner Clubtail
male—Cumberland
Co., NJ, June 1999,
Steve Walter

152.2
Banner Clubtail
male—Jasper Co., TX,
April 2010,
Greg Lasley

152.3
Banner Clubtail
female—Jasper Co.,
TX, April 2010,
Greg Lasley

The 13 species of this subgenus, restricted to North America, are among the favorites of drag-onfly aficionados. They are relatively large and strikingly marked, with a conspicuous to very conspicuous club in males (somewhat smaller in females) and long hind legs. They seem to have a predilection for butterflies, and even dragonflies, and perhaps the long legs aid in the capture of large prey. Species of other subgenera tend to have narrower clubs, although there are well-clubbed species in other subgenera that make identification more difficult. Thus, when considering a *Gomphurus* in the East, one must also think about species in subgenera *Gomphus* (Pronghorn Clubtail much like Plains) and *Hylogomphus* (like miniature *Gomphurus*) as well as species in the hanging clubtail genus *Stylurus* (some shaped about like *Gomphurus*). Finally, there are numerous species in this subgenus that look very similar to one another, and these similar species may be flying on the same river.

153 Midland Clubtail *Gomphus fraternus* TL 48–55, HW 28–33

Description Small black northern *Gomphurus* with moderate club. *Male*: Eyes greenish, face unmarked. Thorax dull yellow with dark frontal stripe straight-edged; T1–2 wide, partially fused; T3 as a half-line and T4 as a line. Legs black. Abdomen yellow at base with brown dorsolateral stripes on S2; yellow spearpoints on S3–8, shorter on S7 and only small triangle on S8; S8–9 with large yellow spots on sides covering half of S8 and all of S9. *Female*: Colored as male. Rear border of occiput with tiny central tooth. Yellow stripe on hind femur.

153.1
Midland Clubtail
male—Jackson Co.,
WI, June 2007

153.2
Midland Clubtail
female—Price Co.,
WI, June 2007

Identification Complete overlap with **Handsome Clubtail**, patterned identically but usually shows tiny yellow triangle at base of S9 lacking in **Midland**. For differences in hand, see **Handsome**. **Plains Clubtail** usually has more yellow on top of S8–10 and two well-defined stripes on sides of thorax with whitish area between them; also yellow stripes on tibiae. **Cobra Clubtail** has even wider club with less yellow on sides (none on S7, small spot on S8) and better-defined lines on sides of thorax as well as dark markings on face. Barely overlaps with **Blackwater** and **Gulf Coast**, both of which have wider clubs; **Blackwater** lacks yellow triangle on S8 and has less yellow on sides of club, **Gulf Coast** with strongly developed stripes on sides of thorax. **Splendid Clubtail** perceptibly larger, with fine lines across face and shorter yellow markings on top of abdomen (no spot on S8). **Skillet Clubtail** with distinctly wider club, fainter dark lines on sides of thorax. **Midland** barely overlaps with **Cocoa**, latter much more brownish and with complete T3. Also similar to **Septima's**, with slight range overlap, but **Septima's** with narrower club and usually no yellow spot on S8. Smaller **Pronghorn** and **Tennessee Clubtails** have more yellow on top of abdomen tip, with S9 all yellow above, and stronger stripes on sides of thorax.

Natural History Both sexes perch on roads and sandy banks. Males also fly rapidly over riffles, hovering from time to time. Often feeds on other dragonflies, including the very predatory Eastern Pondhawk. Females oviposit in rapids and breaking waves, in rapid straight flight.

Habitat Clean streams with moderate current and rock and mud substrates, also large, wave-washed lakes in northern part of range.

Flight Season ON May–Aug, QC Jun–Jul, IA May–Aug, WI May–Aug, OH Apr–Aug, KY May–Jul.

Distribution Extends farther west in Manitoba.

Description Brightly marked *Gomphurus* of restricted interior range. *Male*: Eyes blue to turquoise; face unmarked. Thorax with T1–2 broad, often joined and almost fused. T3–4 narrow, T3 interrupted in middle. Legs black. Abdomen with well-developed pale dorsal stripe, markings shortening to triangles on S6–9, decreasing in size until very small on S9. Large yellow lateral spots on S8–9, extending less than half segment length on S8. *Female*: Colored as male, yellow spots on sides of S8 and top of S8–9 averaging a bit smaller. Tiny horn between each lateral ocellus and adjacent inner eye margin.

Identification Almost identical to **Midland Clubtail** but dorsal spot on S9 present, lacking in **Midland**. Male cerci of **Handsome** with slight tooth on outer edges, no such tooth in

154.1
Handsome Clubtail
male—Metcalfe
Co., KY, June 2006

154.2
Handsome Clubtail
female—Metcalfe
Co., KY, June 2006

Midland. Female **Midland** has tiny tooth on occiput lacking in **Handsome**; **Handsome** has tiny horn at inner eye margins lacking in **Midland**. Leg color might be of use in females, in which hind femora in **Midland** have conspicuous pale stripe, usually lacking in **Handsome**. Some similar species (**Cobra, Gulf Coast, Skillet, Splendid**) lack yellow dorsal markings on S8–9; others (**Plains, Pronghorn, Tennessee**) have much more yellow there.

Natural History Males perch flat on small pale rocks in river in areas with much sun, also fly up and down riffles. Both sexes forage in weedy meadows separated from rivers by tree groves, perching low in vegetation.

Habitat Fair-sized rocky rivers in wooded areas.

Flight Season OH May–Jul, KY May–Jul.

---

155 Septima's Clubtail *Gomphus septima* TL 53–62, HW 32–36

Description Dark brown *Gomphurus* with reduced markings on sides of thorax and relatively narrow, dark club. *Male*: Eyes turquoise, face unmarked. Thorax with T1–2 broad, much fused; T3 very fine, only lower third visible; T4 narrow but complete. Legs brown, tibiae darker. Abdomen with pale line on S3–7 extending entire length of segment, falling slightly short on S7; S8–9 with no dorsal markings but with conspicuous pale lateral spots, half  length on S8, full length on S9. May be tiny dorsal spot at base of S8, perhaps more characteristic of Delaware River population. Small pale basal spots on sides of S4–6, longer on S7. *Female*: Colored as male, dorsal abdominal stripes slightly more extensive and more yellow on sides of abdomen. Pointed tubercle between each lateral ocellus and eye.

Identification Of *Gomphurus* species, differs from **Blackwater, Cobra**, and **Gulf Coast** in unmarked face, narrower club, virtually plain sides of thorax. Plain thorax as well as darker club also distinguishes it from **Cocoa**. Very little overlap if any with quite similar **Midland** (slightly smaller) and **Splendid** (slightly larger), which are usually blacker, **Midland** with more evident dorsal spot on S8 (often lacking in **Septima's**). On average, T1 and T2 fused at upper ends in **Septima's**, barely touching in **Midland**, and separate in **Splendid**.

Natural History Males on rocks and logs at breeding habitat, both sexes feeding in nearby clearings, where they rest on ground and flat on leaves. Males appeared to be on territory on floating walkway over lake near slow, sandy stream that may have been breeding habitat. One copulating pair flew into treetops, others in grass. Often leave water during heat of midday. Mating observed as late as 7 p.m., oviposition even later. One female extruded eggs while perched on rock, then flew over water in wide loops, tapping thrice at 4-m intervals, and then flew up into treetops.

155.1
Septima's Clubtail male—Chesterfield Co., SC, May 2008

155.2
Septima's Clubtail female—Chesterfield Co., SC, May 2008

Habitat Moderate to large wooded rivers with some current, usually rocky but with fine sand and silt for larval habitat.

Flight Season NJ May–Jun.

Comments *G. s. delawarensis*, described from the Delaware River, differs slightly in structure from *G. s. septima* from Alabama to the Carolinas, and the dark markings are a bit darker.

156 Ozark Clubtail *Gomphus ozarkensis* TL 50–53, HW 29–32

Description Dark brown *Gomphurus* with moderate club and limited distribution. *Male*: Eyes turquoise, face yellow. Thorax with T1–2 wide and fused, T3–4 wide and almost fused. Legs black. Abdomen with narrow yellow dorsal stripe, half-length on S7 and quarter-length on S8. Club moderate with yellow lateral spots small and basal on S8, entire length of segment on S9. *Female*: Colored as male but slightly more yellow on sides of abdomen, including S8; dorsal stripe on S7 may be full length and S10 with some yellow above.

Identification The few common clubtails in its range include one species with similarly fused thoracic stripes. **Pronghorn Clubtail** superficially similar but smaller and with more yellow on abdomen, including bright yellow sides of S8–9 and top of S9. Also similar are two slightly larger species with lateral thoracic stripes better separated. **Cocoa Clubtail** has less yellow on S8 and often lighter brown abdomen tip, and **Cobra Clubtail** more vividly black and yellow and with black lines across face. **Cobra** also lacks small yellow dorsal spot on S8 present in **Ozark**. **Splendid** has only fine lines on sides of thorax and is much larger; **Gulf Coast** also much larger. **Plains** and **Sulphur-tipped Clubtails** with much more yellow on club as well as separated thoracic stripes.

Natural History Males perch on rocks or gravel at shore or in river much of day but also fly out over river and hover close to water facing prevailing wind. Usually near riffle. Females

156.1
Ozark Clubtail male—
Phelps Co., MO,
June 2009

156.2
Ozark Clubtail
female—Clark Co., AR,
May 2006

also perch near river, sometimes as easy to find as males, also on ground and low vegetation in clearings away from water.

Habitat Medium to large rivers with alternating pools and riffles, gravel and silt to sandy bottoms, mostly in forested areas.

Flight Season Entire range Apr–Jul.

157 Cocoa Clubtail *Gomphus hybridus* TL 50–52, HW 27–29

Description Brown southeastern *Gomphurus* with moderate club. *Male*: Eyes blue-gray, face dull yellow. Thorax yellow with wide and almost fused T1–2, well-developed T3–4 with space between them somewhat grayish. Legs brown, tibiae with outer surface of tibiae paler. Abdomen yellow at base with blackish dorsolateral stripes on S1–2, S3–6 black with continuous yellow dorsal spearpoints; S7–10 distinctly more brownish with yellow spearpoint on S7, small basal spot on S8, yellowish mottling on sides of S8 and much yellow on sides of S9. *Female*: Colored as male, slightly more yellow on sides of abdomen. Very tiny spine between lateral ocelli and inner eye margins.

Identification Differs from all other co-occurring moderately clubbed clubtails by browner coloration, especially on club; dark markings usually brown rather than black or blackish-brown (but some individuals are darker). Besides that, differs further from **Plains, Pronghorn, Sulphur-tipped,** and **Tennessee** by much less yellow on top and sides of club; from **Blackwater, Gulf Coast,** and **Splendid** by distinctly smaller size; from **Cobra** and **Skillet** (scarcely overlap) by much narrower club; from **Handsome, Midland,** and **Septima's** by

157.1
Cocoa Clubtail
male—Greene Co.,
GA, May 2006

157.2
Cocoa Clubtail
female—Chester
Co., SC, May 2008

heavier thoracic striping, with T1–2 often fused and T3–4 complete and fairly thick. Barely overlaps with rather similar **Ozark**, but latter also with more yellow on sides of club.

Natural History Both sexes perch on ground or in vegetation (generally low) at and near water. Males usually on sandy and gravelly beaches.

Habitat Clear sand- and silt-bottomed rivers, often with rocks.

Flight Season GA Mar–May, FL Mar–Apr.

---

158 Plains Clubtail *Gomphus externus* TL 52–59, HW 30–33

Description Widely distributed *Gomphurus* with moderate club. *Male*: Eyes turquoise, face yellowish. Thorax yellowish-green with T1–2 wide and almost fused, T3–4 wide and close together. Legs black, tibiae yellow on outer surface. Abdomen yellow at base with wide brown dorsolateral stripes on S2, S3–7 black to brown with narrow yellow spearpoints above, widening to rectangle that covers S9; S8–9 also with entirely yellow edges; S10 mostly brown with yellow dorsal spot. Some individuals with dark markings more restricted, thoracic stripes

158.1
Plains Clubtail
male—Little River
Co., AR, April 2006,
Charles Mills

158.2
Plains Clubtail
female—Hamilton
Co., OH, June 2008,
William Hull

narrower and more yellow on abdomen tip. Narrower thoracic stripes in northwestern part of range. *Female*: Colored as male. Tiny pale horn between each lateral ocellus and inner eye margin.

Identification Most similar to member of another subgenus, **Pronghorn Clubtail**, and much overlap in range. In fact, very slightly smaller **Pronghorn** essentially identical in color pattern. Best mark may be edge of S8, usually entirely yellow in **Pronghorn** but with some dark markings in **Plains**. Also, look at hind legs, length of which distinguishes subgenera. When back along body, they extend to or beyond middle of S2 in **Plains**, not to middle in **Pronghorn**. Easily distinguished in hand by male appendages (epiproct wider than narrow cerci in **Plains**, same width as "horned" cerci in **Pronghorn**) and female subgenital plate (each half long and pointed in **Plains**, short and wide in **Pronghorn**). Also, slender arms of epiproct of **Plains** rather dramatically curved upward in side view, whereas thicker epiproct of **Pronghorn** less curved; may be visible in close view. **Sulphur-tipped Clubtail** smaller, with greater extent of yellow on abdomen tip and much yellow on femora (black in **Plains**). In color pattern distinct from other *Gomphurus* with which it might occur because of extensive yellow on top of S8–9 (very little or none in any of the others) and rather wide T3 and T4 (similar in **Ozark),** these stripes well separated in **Cobra** and **Cocoa,** narrower in **Gulf Coast** (larger) and **Handsome**, quite fine and T3 incomplete in **Midland**, **Splendid** (larger), and **Skillet**. Club much narrower than in **Cobra** or **Skillet**.

Natural History Males perch on ground near water with abdomen elevated and occasionally fly long beats over river. Usually perch flat on leaves when away from water. Copulating pairs in low vegetation near water. Females oviposit by straight flight over river, tapping water at intervals. One female produced 5100 eggs when abdomen dipped in glass of water.

Habitat Sandy or muddy streams and rivers with moderate current, open grassy or wooded banks.

Flight Season IA May–Sep, WI Jun–Jul, OH Jun–Aug, KY Jun–Jul.

Distribution Across plains to eastern Montana, south to New Mexico and west Texas; also southern Idaho and northern Utah.

---

159 Cobra Clubtail *Gomphus vastus* TL 47–57, HW 28–34

Description Dark *Gomphurus* with wide club like cobra's hood. Size distinctly larger in southern part of range. *Male*: Eyes green, face yellow with black horizontal markings. Thorax with T1 very wide but interrupted above, T2 narrower; T3–4 narrow but prominent, well separated; T3 rarely incomplete above. Legs black. Abdomen with narrow dorsal stripe on S3–7 extending only half length on most segments, thus quite interrupted; looks like series of pointed dashes. Lateral yellow spots on club small and basal on S8, large and full length on S9. *Female*: Colored as male but more yellow on sides of abdomen, dorsal abdominal stripes more complete. Tiny pointed tubercle between lateral ocellus and eye margin.

Identification With large range, overlaps with every other eastern *Gomphurus*. Males with very wide club and minimal yellow stripe on abdomen, thus very dark looking. **Blackwater** and **Gulf Coast Clubtails** quite similar, usually more continuous dorsal abdominal stripe, **Gulf Coast** with dorsal spot on S8. **Blackwater** with least amount of yellow on sides of club, reaching less than halfway on S9 (more than halfway on other two). **Gulf Coast** also with finer black lines on face. Structural differences apparent in females in hand. Branches of subgenital plate sharply pointed in **Blackwater** and **Cobra**, blunt in **Gulf Coast**. Edges of S9 approximately straight in **Blackwater**, gently convex in **Cobra**, and both S8 and S9 look shorter in latter. **Gulf Coast** somewhat in between. **Splendid Clubtail** also similar to **Cobra** but less heavily marked face, fine lines on sides of thorax, and larger yellow spot on sides of S7 (although that spot varies from fairly large to virtually absent in **Cobra**). **Ozark Clubtail** somewhat similar but with wider thoracic stripes (T3–4 fused) and tiny spot of yellow on top of S8. **Plains Clubtail** slightly smaller and browner overall, with T3–4 broader and club with more yellow on sides, S9 all yellow above. **Pronghorn Clubtail** distinctly smaller and with much yellow on top of club. **Cocoa** with narrower brown club, and all

159.1
Cobra Clubtail
male—Monroe Co.,
GA, June 2008,
Giff Beaton

258 Dragonflies

159.2
Cobra Clubtail
male—Monroe Co.,
GA, June 2008, Giff
Beaton

159.3
Cobra Clubtail
female—Hamilton
Co., OH, June
2008, William Hull

other *Gomphurus* (**Handsome**, **Midland**, **Septima's**, **Skillet**) with finer lines on sides of thorax.

Natural History Males perch on shore, or on rocks in rocky rivers, with abdomen elevated, then fly beats up and down. Usually fly a few feet above water, slow when facing wind and may hover in slight breeze. Both sexes typically perch on leaves with abdomen inclined downward. Males at one river active until dark, constantly wing-whirring. Copulating pairs perch in tall weeds, shrubs, and trees at head height and above. Females oviposit by flying rapidly, sometimes far from shore, and tapping water at intervals to release eggs.

Habitat Rivers and streams with slow to moderate current and sandy or silty bottoms, with or without rocks. Also large, rock-bordered lakes in north.

Flight Season ON Jun–Jul, QC Jun–Jul, IA May–Jul, WI May–Aug, OH May–Aug, KY May–Aug.

Distribution Slightly farther west in central Texas.

160 Gulf Coast Clubtail *Gomphus modestus* TL 55–63, HW 34–37

Description Large black southern *Gomphurus* with prominent club. *Male*: Eyes green; face yellow, crossed by two fine black lines. Thorax prominently striped; T1–2 wide, almost touching, T3–4 narrower but still well-developed. Legs black. Abdomen with narrow yellow dorsal stripe becoming less complete to rear, widening on S7, small basal spot or not on S8; well-developed club, with large yellow lateral spots on S8–9 not reaching end of segments. *Female*: Colored as male, bit more yellow on top and sides of abdomen.

160.1
Gulf Coast Clubtail
male—Perry Co., MS,
June 2009, Troy
Hibbitts

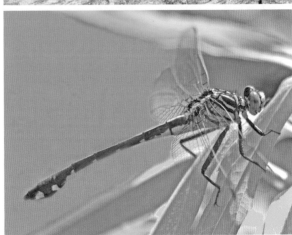

160.2
Gulf Coast Clubtail
female—San Jacinto
Co., TX, May 2007,
Martin Reid

Identification Most other *Gomphurus* in its range at least a bit smaller. **Blackwater** most similar, with less yellow on sides of S8–9 and heavier facial markings. S8 usually with dorsal yellow spot in **Gulf Coast** males, producing three-spotted effect in dorsal view of that segment; spot usually lacking in **Blackwater** and **Cobra**. **Cobra** also very similar, almost same size in South and colored just abut identically. Male secondary genitalia distinctly larger in **Cobra**, hamule and posterior lobe project as high as pale color on side of S2; obviously less than that in **Gulf Coast**. Female **Gulf Coast** very similar to **Cobra**; perhaps best field mark size of yellow lateral spot on S8, slightly larger in **Gulf Coast** (usually more than half the length of S9, less than half in **Cobra**). In hand, upper black line across face no wider than ocelli in **Gulf Coast**, distinctly wider in **Cobra**. Also, subgenital plate narrower and with more pointed tips in **Cobra**; comparison probably necessary. **Ozark** with fused T1–2, T3–4; other barely overlapping *Gomphurus* (**Midland**, **Septima's**, **Splendid**) with finer lateral thoracic markings. Superficially similar to **Black-shouldered Spinyleg** but differs in quite different thoracic pattern, also much more yellow on top of club in **Spinyleg**.
Natural History Males perch along streams on bank or leaves. Quite uncommon.
Habitat Large, slow-flowing rivers over rock and sand substrates.
Flight Season LA May, FL Jun.

Description Large, impressive *Gomphurus* of southeastern lowland rivers. *Male*: Eyes green, face with broad dark crossbands producing quite dark effect. T1–2 broad, well separated; T3–4 narrow but conspicuous. Legs black. Abdomen with dorsal markings on S3–6 narrow, strongly attenuated and not exceeding two-thirds of segment; that on S7 broader, half length. Small basal spots on sides of S3–6, much more extensive on S7, extending almost half length.

Small lateral spots on S8–9, less than half length. Club very wide, S8 with wide black flange. *Female*: Colored as male, club narrower.

Identification Size and wider club differentiate it from most similar species, especially distinctly smaller **Cocoa**, **Midland** (perhaps no overlap), and **Septima's**. Rather like both **Gulf Coast** and **Splendid Clubtails**, differs by no dorsal spot on S8, less yellow on sides of S8–9, and heavier facial markings. Little overlap in range with either one. **Cobra Clubtail** has

161.1
Blackwater Clubtail
male—Long Co., GA,
May 2006

161.2
Blackwater Clubtail
female—Wayne Co., GA,
May 2006

even more yellow on sides of S9, extending length of segment. **Black-shouldered Spinyleg** of same habitat has different thoracic pattern.

Natural History Males perch on shore, branches or leaves at water's edge, also on sides of cypress trees in water. Commonly capture other odonates, including jewelwings and smaller clubtails. Female oviposits by flying low over water and hitting surface at intervals. Seen at one river remaining active until dark, constantly wing-whirring.

Habitat Slow sand-bottomed streams and rivers running through woodland. Some lakes on the Florida Peninsula also support populations.

Flight Season GA Mar–Aug, FL Mar–Aug.

---

162 Splendid Clubtail *Gomphus lineatifrons*   TL 67–69, HW 38–45

Description Large, dark *Gomphurus* of upland rivers. *Male*: Eyes turquoise to green, face with fine black crosslines. Thorax with T1–2 broad, usually not touching. T3–4 narrow, T3 usually interrupted but rarely complete. Legs black. Abdomen with yellow dorsal stripes becoming shorter toward rear, about half length on S7. Sides of S8–9 with big yellow blotches, half length on S8 and from three-fourths to almost full length on S9. Club relatively narrow for

162.1
Splendid
Clubtail
male—Rusk Co.,
WI, June 2007

162.2
Splendid
Clubtail
female—Lewis
Co., TN, June
2006

Gomphurus. Female: Eyes may be greener than those of males. Coloration similar but yellow abdominal stripes slightly longer, more yellow low on sides of middle segments.

Identification Large size and lack of yellow dorsal markings on S8–9 distinguish it from most other *Gomphurus* in range. See **Blackwater** and **Gulf Coast**, both of which it overlaps slightly, and **Cobra**, with much overlap. Middorsal thoracic stripe an excellent field mark, narrow and parallel-sided in **Splendid**, distinctly widening below in **Blackwater**, **Cobra**, and **Gulf Coast** (but also parallel-sided in all smaller *Gomphus* and mid-sized moderate-clubbed *Gomphus* such as **Pronghorn** and **Tennessee Clubtails**; the latter have much more yellow on club). Thoracic pattern of **Splendid** quite different from that of **Black-shouldered Spinyleg**.

Natural History Males perch on dark rocks associated with riffles or fly back and forth or hover over riffle with abdomen up at 20°. Both sexes in sunny clearings nearby.

Habitat Good-sized rivers with much mud, usually with rocks and cobbles.

Flight Season WI May–Jul, OH May–Jul, KY May–Jul, GA May–Jun.

163 Skillet Clubtail *Gomphus ventricosus* TL 48–53, HW 24–33

Description Small northeastern *Gomphurus* with hugely widened club. *Male:* Eyes green to turquoise, face unmarked. Thorax with T1–2 broad, joined above. T3–4 very narrow, usually interrupted so sides of thorax almost plain. Legs black. Abdomen with yellow dorsal stripe extending full length of middle segments, tiny basal triangle extended as very narrow line most of length of S7. Very wide club with big yellow spots on sides extending full length of seg-

163.1
Skillet Clubtail male—
Hampshire Co., MA,
June 2006

163.2
Skillet Clubtail female—
Hampshire Co., MA, June 2008,
Glenn Corbiere

ments but with wide black flange bordering pale spot on S8. *Female*: Colored as male but yellow abdominal stripe a bit wider; club distinctly smaller but impressive for female. Hind femur with pale stripe at base. Tiny to rather well-developed horn between lateral ocellus and eye.

Identification Startlingly wide club with yellow-spotted, black-edged S7 distinctive of both sexes. Other wide-clubbed *Gomphurus* lack black margin to yellow markings on S7. Very lightly marked sides of thorax and wide T1–2 simulate **Black-shouldered Spinyleg**, which is larger with much smaller club.

Natural History Considered rare in most areas, it may just be an infrequent visitor to its breeding habitat. Males fairly common, females occasionally seen, at rivers in Wisconsin. Feeds in weedy fields up to a few hundred yards from breeding habitat.

Habitat Midsized to large pristine rocky rivers with fine sediment for larval habitat, usually slow to moderate current.

Flight Season WI May–Aug, OH May–Aug, KY May–Jun.

Subgenus Stenogomphurus

This subgenus includes two southeastern United States species often placed in *Gomphurus*. Their slender, dark abdomens with minimal clubs and relatively short legs, as well as differently structured hamules and minor larval differences, argue against that placement. Nor do they fit within any of the other subgenera. Pale color in mature males gray-green, in females and immatures bright yellow. The wingtips are slightly dusky, unique among North American clubtails.

164 Cherokee Clubtail *Gomphus consanguis*   TL 48–50, HW 32–37

Description Small southeastern mountain clubtail with lightly marked dark abdomen and narrow club. *Male*: Eyes turquoise; face pale, unmarked. T1–2 broad and full length; T3–4 narrow and full length. Legs black. Abdomen black with limited yellow; fine streaks on S2–3, narrow basal triangles on S4–7. Sides of S8–9 with large yellow patches when immature, lost or almost lost at maturity but narrow yellow flanges retained on S7–8. *Female*: Colored like male,  but yellow on abdomen a bit more extensive, including streaks and spots on sides of middle segments and same patches on sides of S8–9 visible in young males. Wingtips slightly dusky in females and young males (only visible with pale background).

Identification Smallish size and minimal yellow on abdomen good marks for this species,

164.1
Cherokee Clubtail male—
Chattooga Co., GA, June
2006, Giff Beaton

164.2
Cherokee Clubtail
female—Chattooga
Co., GA, May 2003,
Giff Beaton

but several somewhat similar ones. See **Sable Clubtail** for differences. Of slender-bodied members of subgenus *Gomphus* in range, **Harpoon Clubtail** most like **Cherokee,** but male slightly less clubbed and less yellow on sides of club. **Harpoon** has much more prominent appendages, looking bulky in both side and top view. T1 and T2 usually fused above in **Harpoon**, separate in **Cherokee**. **Rapids** may not overlap with **Cherokee,** differs by broader lateral thoracic stripes. Some *Hylogomphus* (**Green-faced, Piedmont**) look similar but are smaller, males with much wider clubs.

Natural History Males perch on leaves low over stream, fly out over it in short, slow patrol flights.

Habitat Small forest streams with silt bottom, often spring-fed.

Flight Season GA May–Jun.

165 Sable Clubtail *Gomphus rogersi* TL 47–50, HW 31–

Description Small southeastern highland clubtail with dark abdomen and narrow club. *Male:* Eyes green to turquoise; face pale, variably marked with black crosslines. T1–2 broad and complete, touching at ends and often with stripe between them restricted and topped with spot; T3–4 fine, T3 incomplete. Legs black. Abdomen black, with tiny pale triangles at base of S3–6. Scarcely evident club, S7–9 with fine yellow flange. *Female:* Colored like male but a bit  more yellow on abdomen, including fine dorsal lines on segments and prominent patches on edges of S8–9. Wingtips slightly dusky in both sexes.

Identification Distinguished from quite similar **Cherokee Clubtail** (only rarely found on same stream) by T3 being incomplete or lacking. Overall darker, more likely to have black markings on face, also black front of occiput (pale in **Cherokee**). Fine pale line well separated from wider spot between T1 and T2 (usually slightly wider line merely expanded at top in **Cherokee**) and pale abdominal markings at absolute minimum in males, never more than edge of S8–9 (female abdomens much more similar). See **Cherokee** for species similar to both that species and this one. Slender, dark abdomen produces superficial similarity to LEAST CLUBTAILS and PYGMY CLUBTAILS. Distinguished from those distinctly smaller species by mostly pale sides of thorax, lack of pale lateral spots or rings on abdomen, and different appendages.

Natural History Males perch on sunlit vegetation overhanging stream or on flat rocks in shade at head of riffle, fly up into trees when disturbed. Males have been seen apparently guarding ovipositing females, very unusual for clubtail.

165.1
Sable Clubtail
male—Sussex
Co., NJ, June
2007, Tom
Murray, posed

165.2
Sable Clubtail
female—Pickett Co.,
TN, June 2006,
Giff Beaton

Habitat Small, clear forest streams up to 15 feet in width, alternating short pools with rocky riffles. Usually sand or gravel bottom. Often occur just below impoundments.
Flight Season NJ May–Jun, KY May–Jul.

Common Clubtails - male appendages

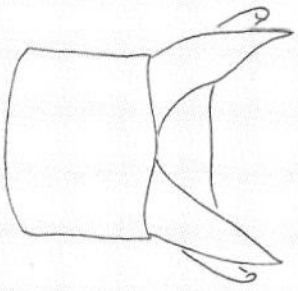

Lancet Clubtail

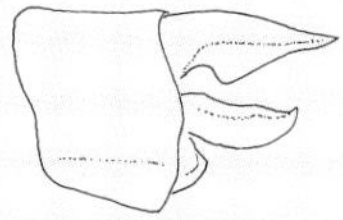

Lancet Clubtail

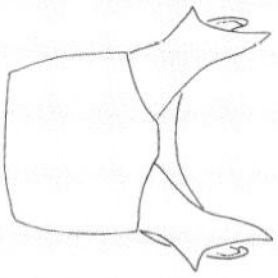

Oklahoma Clubtail

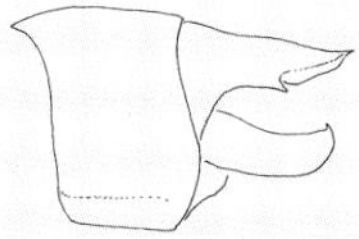

Oklahoma Clubtail

Rapids Clubtail

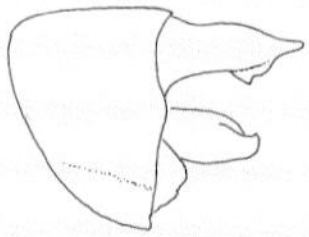

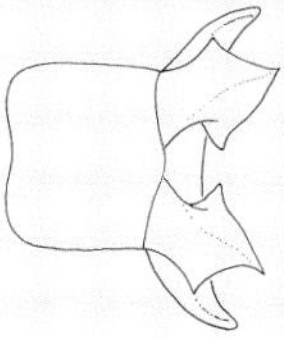

Rapids Clubtail

Beaverpond Clubtail

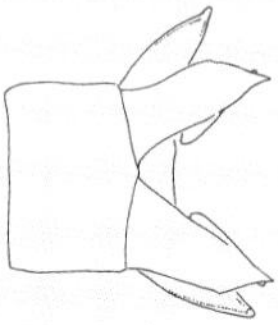

Beaverpond Clubtail

Harpoon Clubtail

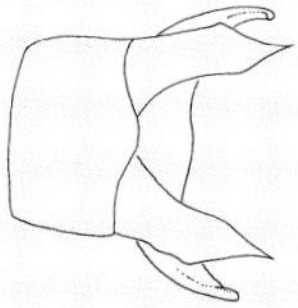

Harpoon Clubtail

Ashy Clubtail

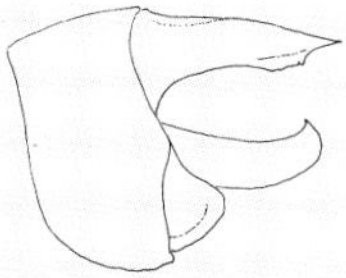

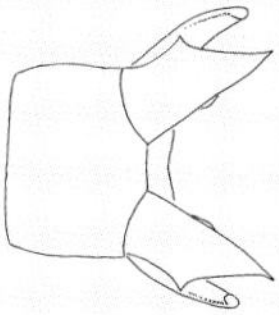

Ashy Clubtail

Dusky Clubtail

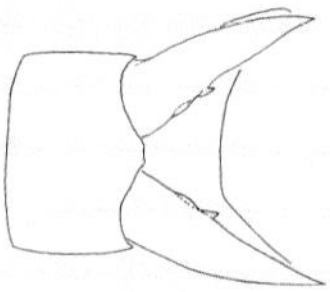

Dusky Clubtail

Cypress Clubtail

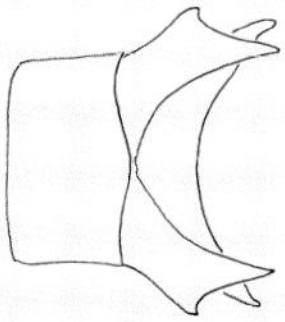

Cypress Clubtail

Sandhill Clubtail

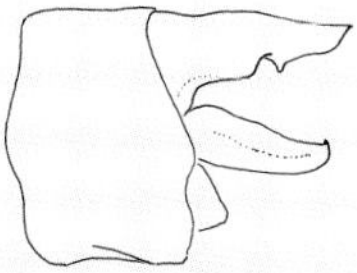

Sandhill Clubtail

Diminutive Clubtail

Diminutive Clubtail

Westfall's Clubtail

Westfall's Clubtail

Hodges's Clubtail

Hodges's Clubtail

Clearlake Clubtail

Clearlake Clubtail

Sulphur-tipped Clubtail

Sulphur-tipped Clubtail

Pronghorn Clubtail

Pronghorn Clubtail

Tennessee Clubtail

Tennessee Clubtail

Green-faced Clubtail

Green-faced Clubtail

Mustached Clubtail

Mustached Clubtail

Common Clubtails - male appendages *(continued)*

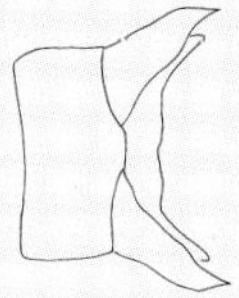

Spine-crowned Clubtail

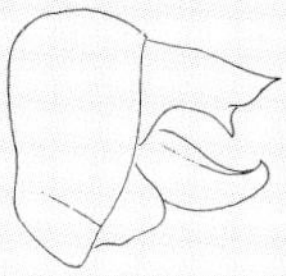

Spine-crowned Clubtail

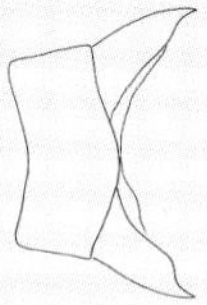

Piedmont Clubtail

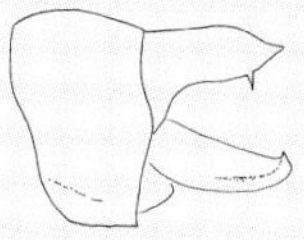

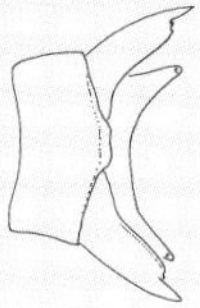

Piedmont Clubtail

Twin-striped Clubtail

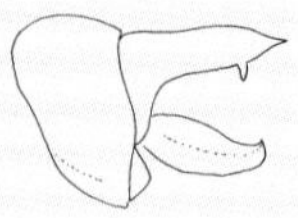

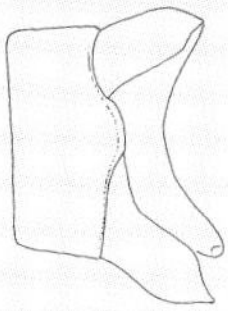

Twin-striped Clubtail

Banner Clubtail

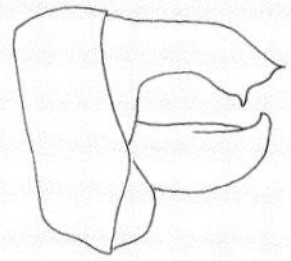

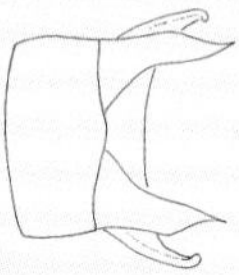

Banner Clubtail

Midland Clubtail

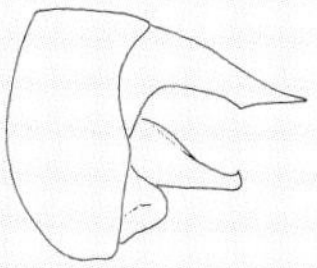

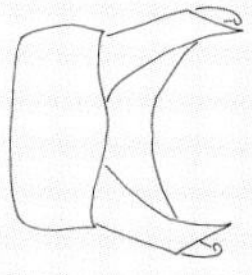

Midland Clubtail

Handsome Clubtail

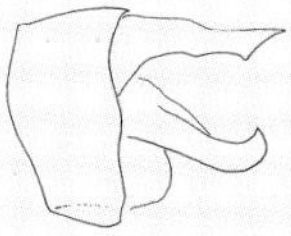

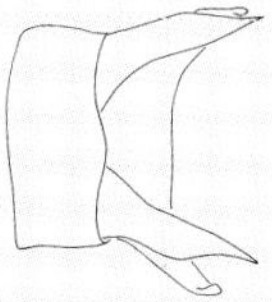

Handsome Clubtail

Septima's Clubtail

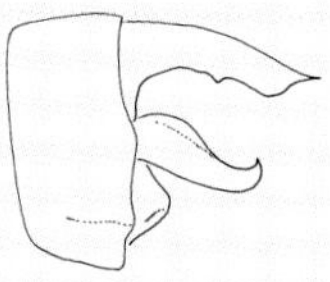

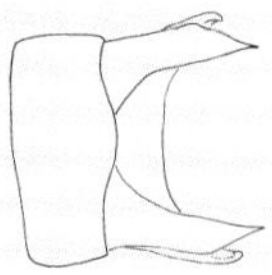

Septima's Clubtail

Ozark Clubtail

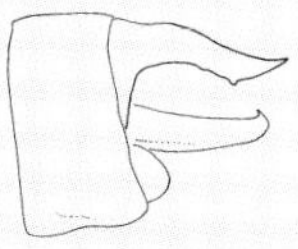

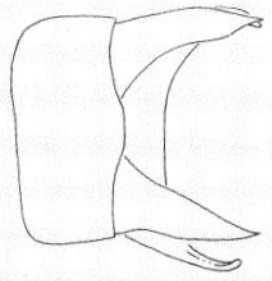

Ozark Clubtail

Cocoa Clubtail

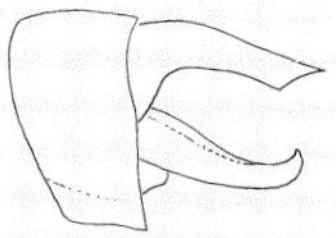

Cocoa Clubtail

Plains Clubtail

Plains Clubtail

Cobra Clubtail

Cobra Clubtail

Gulf Coast Clubtail

Gulf Coast Clubtail

Blackwater Clubtail

Blackwater Clubtail

Splendid Clubtail

Splendid Clubtail

Skillet Clubtail

Skillet Clubtail

Cherokee Clubtail

Cherokee Clubtail

Sable Clubtail

Sable Clubtail

Common Clubtails - female subgenital plate

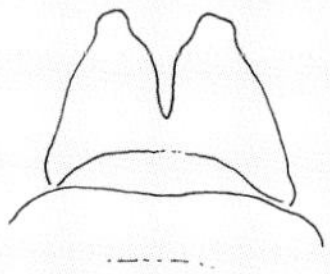

Lancet Clubtail

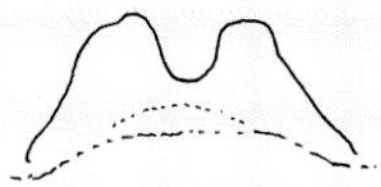

Oklahoma Clubtail

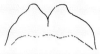

Rapids Clubtail

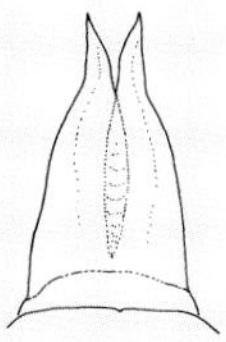

Beaverpond Clubtail

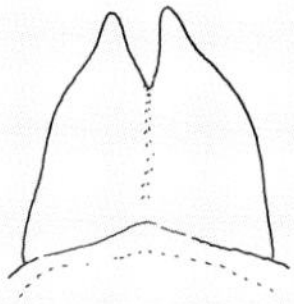

Harpoon Clubtail

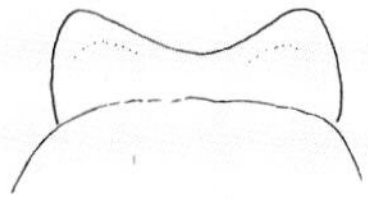

Ashy Clubtail

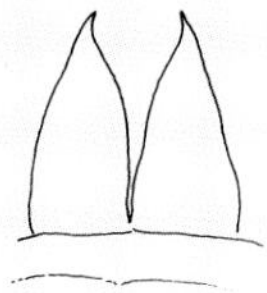

Dusky Clubtail

Cypress Clubtail

Sandhill Clubtail

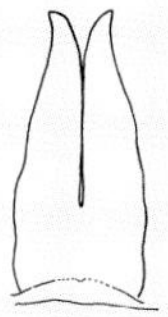

Diminutive Clubtail

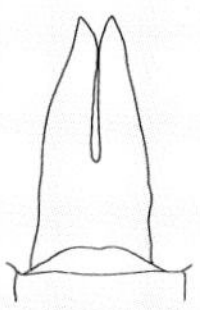

Westfall's Clubtail

Hodges's Clubtail

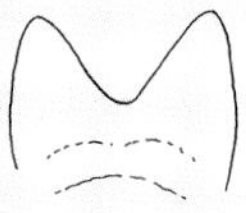

Clearlake Clubtail

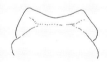

Sulphur-tipped Clubtail

Pronghorn Clubtail

Tennessee Clubtail

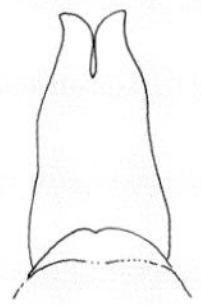

Green-faced Clubtail

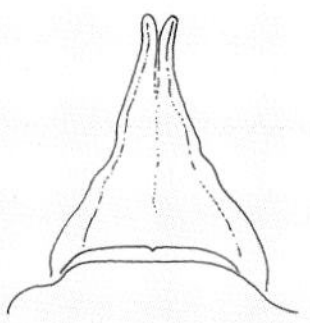

Mustached Clubtail

Common Clubtails - female subgenital plate (continued)

Spine-crowned Clubtail

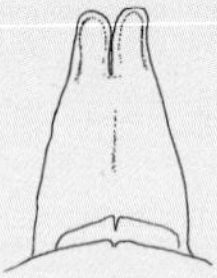

Piedmont Clubtail

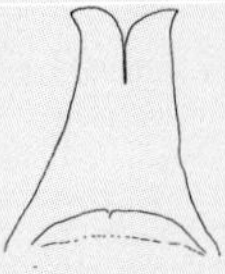

Twin-striped Clubtail

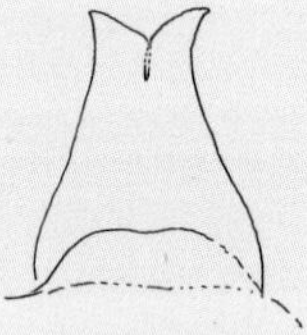

Banner Clubtail

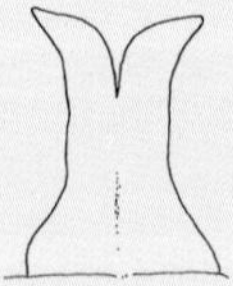

Midland Clubtail

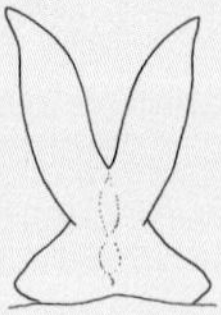

Handsome Clubtail

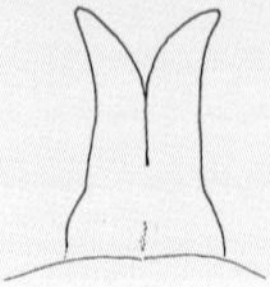

Septima's Clubtail

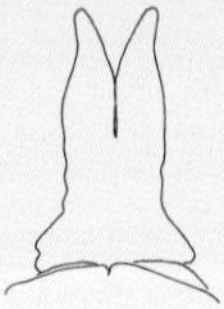

Ozark Clubtail

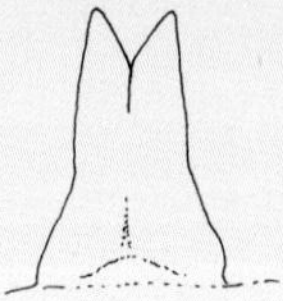

Cocoa Clubtail

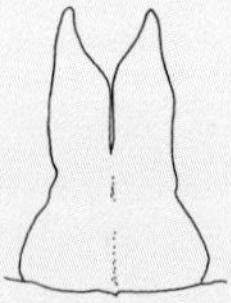

Plains Clubtail

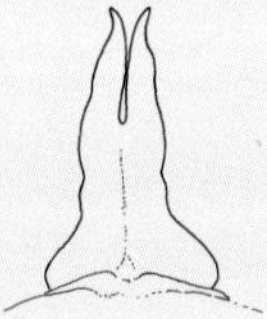

Cobra Clubtail

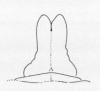

Gulf Coast Clubtail

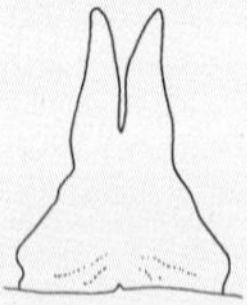

Blackwater Clubtail

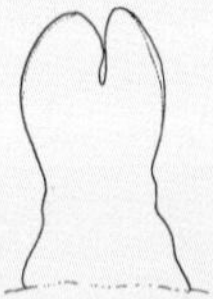

Splendid Clubtail

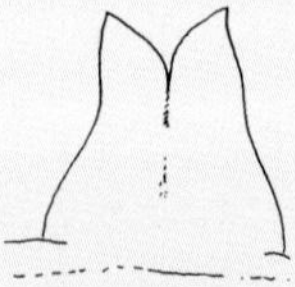

Skillet Clubtail

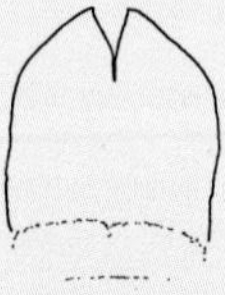

Cherokee Clubtail

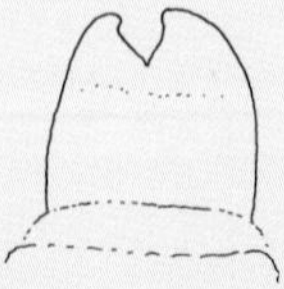

Sable Clubtail

As the name implies, members of this genus typically perch with abdomen hanging down, even to the vertical. This is in part because they have a long abdomen and often perch on leaves, which bend downward under their weight. But this position distinguishes them from most other eastern clubtails (forceptails often perch similarly). Perhaps correlated with this, their hind legs are rather short. Do not be confused by tenerals of other species that may hang down for a while immediately after emergence. Some hanging clubtails also perch flat on ground or rocks, even with abdomen elevated slightly, but not on twigs with abdomen elevated as typical of many other clubtails. Otherwise, they look much like common clubtails. Most of them spend much time in flight over water, leading to speculation whether species of this genus may feed in flight rather than from a perch like most other clubtails. The thoracic pattern is distinctive of certain species, yellow stripes on front of thorax not connected to yellow above or below. World 30, NA 11, East 10.

166 Riverine Clubtail *Stylurus amnicola* TL 47–49, HW 29–33

Description Boldly marked clubtail with distinctive thoracic stripes and moderate club. Perceptibly larger in southern part of range. *Male:* Eyes dark turquoise, face pale with dark irregular markings. Thorax with complex pattern on front, like flower in vase with leaf on either side; T1–2 very wide, only faint line between them, T3–4 narrow and well separated. Legs black, base of hind femora and inside of front femora pale. Abdomen with usual dorsal spearpoints on S2–7, short yellow triangle on S8; small yellow spot on sides of S7, large spots almost filling sides of S8–9. *Female:* Colored

as male but complete dorsal stripe on S1–7, yellow basal triangle on S8–9. Interrupted yellow stripe and spots on sides of middle segments, more prominent spots on S8–9. Middle femora also pale-based.

Identification Pattern on front of thorax diagnostic. Also very wide T1–2 and much less prominent side stripes. Superficially like **Black-shouldered Spinyleg** because of that, and front of thorax even somewhat similar, but smaller and shorter-legged, wider club with more yellow on sides and less on top. Of other hanging clubtails, most like **Elusive Clubtail**, but different thoracic patterns distinguish them. Not especially like any COMMON CLUBTAIL because of thorax, but note other black and yellow species, **Cobra Clubtail** with

166.1
Riverine Clubtail
male—Juneau Co.,
WI, August 2008, Ken
Tennessen

166.2
Riverine Clubtail
female—
Hampshire Co.,
MA, July 2008,
Glenn Corbiere

distinctly wider club and **Pronghorn Clubtail** with more yellow on abdomen tip. Smaller than **Arrow Clubtail**, wider club with more prominent yellow.

Natural History Rarely seen except during emergence. Adults hang out in treetops except for brief visits to breeding habitat, when males tend to stay over midriver for brief periods. However, sometimes cruise up and down along slow-flowing pool for some time. Most likely to find immature individuals near river after emergence.

Habitat Medium to large slow-flowing to rapid rivers with varied bottom types, in or out of woodland.

Flight Season ON Jul–Aug, QC Jun–Jul, IA Jun–Sep, WI Jun–Aug, OH Jun–Sep.

Distribution Also slightly farther west in Nebraska. Records very sparse in parts of range.

---

167 Laura's Clubtail *Stylurus laurae*   TL 60–64, HW 36–42

Description Large clubtail with strongly striped thorax and club with yellow sides. *Male:* Eyes green, face pale with two dark crossbars. Yellow stripes on front of thorax not connected below to yellow collar. Thorax with T1 wide, narrowly separated from T2; T3–4 narrow but distinct, usually gray rather than yellow between them. Legs dark brown, femora partially pale. Abdomen mostly black, becoming brown on terminal segments. Pale dorsal stripe complete on S1–5, then shorter on S6–7. Sides of S3–6 with tiny pale basal spots, S7 with narrow pale edge, S8–9 entirely yellow on sides with slightly darker edges. *Female:* Colored as male, more yellow on sides of middle segments of abdomen.

Identification Greener eyes, darker abdomen tip, narrower pale stripe between T1 and T2, and usually gray area between T3 and T4 distinguishes **Laura's** from **Russet-tipped Clubtail**; front of thorax also different. See also **Townes's** and **Yellow-sided Clubtails**. Somewhat similar to *Gomphurus* COMMON CLUBTAILS, but completely dark top and broadly yellow sides of club distinctive, as is thoracic pattern. Also, flight season generally later than *Gomphurus*.

Natural History Males perch on overhanging leaves and branches from near the water to above head height, less often on rocks and logs (but more often than other hanging clubtails). Fly out over riffles briefly and then back to perch. Present at midday but may stay ac-

167.1
Laura's Clubtail male—
Aiken Co., SC,
August 2005, Lois Stacey

167.2
Laura's Clubtail female—
Liberty Co., FL, June 2005,
Giff Beaton

tive at water into early evening. Oviposits by tapping water at short intervals, not as wild a flight as many other clubtails. Feeds from trees at forest edge.

Habitat Clear shallow forest streams with rocky riffles, sand or mud bottoms.

Flight Season ON Jul–Aug, OH Jun–Sep, KY Aug–Sep, LA Apr–Jul, GA Jun–Oct, FL May–Aug.

---

168 Shining Clubtail *Stylurus ivae*   TL 58–61, HW 35–41

Description A slender but wide-clubbed, rather yellow southeastern clubtail of late autumn. *Male*: Eyes green above, yellow below; face unmarked. Thorax with very broad T1, fused with half-height, much narrower T2 in unusual pattern, leaving yellow spot at top of broad brown stripe. T3–4 very fine, T3 widely interrupted in most individuals. Thorax looks entirely yellow on sides from distance. Femora mostly yellow, tibiae dark brown. Middle segments of ab-

domen obscurely marked with irregular brown stripes on sides of S3–6, yellow rings at anterior end of segments. S7–10 mostly yellow on sides, orange to orange-brown above, with well-developed club. *Female*: Colored as male, some individuals with abdominal markings darker and extending to S9; no club.

Identification No other species in range with wide yellow-orange club of male. **Russet-tipped Clubtail** with darker, more reddish club. Both sexes also distinctive in virtually unmarked sides of thorax behind very broad brown area. **Yellow-sided Clubtail** with similar thorax has much darker abdomen. Much more yellow on abdomen than **Black-shouldered Spinyleg** with vaguely similar thoracic pattern. Flies in late fall when large proportion of clubtail species already finished flight seasons.

Natural History Both sexes feed in clearings. Males perch on leaves over stream, fly out in lengthy slow patrols with periods of hovering.

Habitat Small sand-bottomed streams in woodland.

Flight Season GA Sep–Oct, FL Sep–Nov.

168.1
Shining Clubtail
male—Gadsden Co.,
FL, October 2005,
Giff Beaton

168.2
Shining Clubtail
female—Geneva
Co., AL, October
2008, Steve Krotzer

Description Finely striped black and yellow clubtail of limited southeastern range. *Male*: Eyes green, face with fine brown cross-lines. Thorax with T1 broad, well separated from T2, which divided by fine pale line; T3–4 narrow but distinct, T4 usually finer than T3. Femora tan, striped with brown; tibiae brown. Abdomen mostly black with fine yellow dorsal line down each segment, becoming shorter to rear and split into basal oval and terminal fine line, basal  markings extending to S8. Sides of S7–9 with irregular yellow blotches, bordered outside by black. *Female*: Colored as male, but eyes a bit paler below, thoracic stripes may be finer, and more yellow on top and sides of abdomen; no club.

Identification Almost all black abdomen, with dull yellow low on sides, and evenly striped thorax, with longitudinally split T2, distinctive. **Yellow-sided** most similar but much more contrast between wide T1–2 and narrow T3–4. Also usually in smaller streams. **Russet-**

169.1
Townes's Clubtail male—
Mobile Co., AL, July 2008,
Steve Krotzer

169.2
Townes's Clubtail
female—Mobile Co., AL,
June 2000, Steve Krotzer

tipped and **Shining** have yellowish to reddish clubs, but **Laura's** can look very similar to **Townes's**. It is larger, with a more reddish tinge to club and a different thoracic pattern in lateral view. **Townes's** may barely overlap with **Riverine**, with distinctive thoracic pattern, and **Arrow**, larger with narrower club and much more heavily striped thorax.

Natural History Both sexes perch on tree leaves with abdomen hanging down, sometimes well above ground; males usually right over water, females near or away from it.

Habitat Fair-sized, slow-flowing, sand-bottomed rivers with silt in quiet areas.

Flight Season FL Jun–Sep.

---

170 Yellow-sided Clubtail   *Stylurus potulentus*   TL 48–52, HW 30–34

Description Small clubtail of central Gulf Coast with bright yellow sides to thorax and mostly black abdomen. *Male:* Eyes blue, face brown above. Thorax with T1 very broad, fused with narrower T2 and with tiny pale dot at upper end. T3–4 very fine, scarcely visible so sides of thorax look all yellow. Legs black, femora with some yel-

170.1
Yellow-sided Clubtail
male—Calhoun Co.,
FL, July 2000,
Steve Krotzer

170.2
Yellow-sided Clubtail
female—Calhoun Co.,
FL, July 2009

low at base; hind femora mostly yellow. Abdomen mostly black, very fine broken yellow dorsal line back to base of S7. Irregular yellow blotches on sides of S7–9, usually bordered laterally by brown or black. Club moderately developed. *Female*: Colored as male, dorsal abdominal stripe complete and yellow on sides of abdomen tip duller, obscure; club scarcely evident.

Identification Somewhat like **Townes's Clubtail**, found in same area, but differs in brighter yellow sides of thorax, with less distinct striping. Identical to **Townes's** in dorsal view except **Townes's** shows an additional pale stripe on front of thorax; also, **Yellow-sided** eyes bluer (green in **Townes's**). **Laura's** also similar but distinctly larger with reddish tinge to club, eyes green, and thoracic striping more like **Townes's**.

Natural History Both sexes commonly perch low in shrubs and herbs at woodland edge near breeding habitat. Present in morning and afternoon, not at hot midday.

Habitat Slow-flowing woodland streams with sand and mud bottoms.

Flight Season FL May–Aug.

Description Distinctive vividly ringed northeastern clubtail, male with impressive club. *Male:* Eyes green, dark X-shaped mark with pale center across face. Light markings very pale yellow to white rather than yellow to gray of other common and hanging clubtails. Thorax with T1–2 fused, forming broad dark area, or incompletely fused, separated by fine pale line and dot. T3–4 as broad as pale area between them, in some individuals partially connected along

length of stripes. Legs black. Abdomen black, S3–7 with whitish ring at anterior end forming ringed pattern. Short pale dorsal triangles on S7–8, irregular pale spots on sides of S7–9. Club well developed, broader than other *Stylurus*, S8–9 with wide flanges and much wider than S10. *Female*: Patterned much like male, but narrow pale dorsal line on abdomen as well as rings; pale color brighter yellow than in male. T3–4 more extensively fused, small pale spots on sides of abdominal segments, and more likely to be fine pale dorsal line through S7.

Identification Quite different from any other clubtails in range; co-occurring **Arrow Clubtail** superficially similar but with spotted, not ringed, abdomen and with much narrower club in male. Might be mistaken for SPIKETAIL at first glance, especially when hanging

171.1
Zebra Clubtail
male—Vilas Co., WI,
September 2006,
Ken Tennessen

171.2
Zebra Clubtail
female—Douglas
Co., WI, August
2006, Gervase
Thompson

down. **Tiger Spiketail**, with ringed abdomen, most similar, especially to female **Zebra** with much narrower club than male. But SPIKETAILS have very different thoracic pattern, dark with light stripes, and lack pale lateral markings on abdomen tip of clubtail. Also fliers rather than perchers, and male **Tiger Spiketail** flies in very different habitat from **Zebra Clubtail**.

Natural History Males fly up and down rivers not far above surface, hovering from time to time; beats may be 50–100 feet long. Usually at riffles rather than pools, and active through much of day. More likely to perch on rocks in river than other hanging clubtails and usually perch not far from horizontal; also less likely to make extended flights over water. Very territorial, males chasing one another and river cruisers. Females rarely seen, probably up in trees, and observed copulation high in trees. Ovipositing females visit water briefly and seem stealthy. Make brief oviposition run over shallow riffle, tap water a few times, and land in tree, probably to build up egg mass before doing it again.

Habitat Clean rivers and streams with sand or sand and cobble bottoms and moderate current in wooded landscape; usually much gravel and at least scattered rocks.

Flight Season ON Jun–Sep, QC Jun–Sep, NS Aug–Oct, WI Jun–Sep, ME Jul–Sep, KY Aug–Sep.

---

172 Elusive Clubtail *Stylurus notatus* TL 52–64, HW 30–35

Description Large, dark clubtail with moderate club, adults not often seen. *Male*: Eyes blue, face pale but with brown bar across upper part. Yellow stripes on front of thorax not in contact with yellow at either end. Thorax with T1–2 wide, joined at top; T3–4 narrow but distinct. Legs black. Abdomen black, pale stripe on S1–2; small pale triangles on S3–8, shorter than typical clubtail spearpoints (perhaps longer in some individuals). Sides of S3–6 with tiny  pale basal spots, S7–9 with large pale spot at base reaching half length or more. *Female*: Colored as male, more yellow on sides of middle segments of abdomen. Hind femora pale at base.

Identification Lack of any reddish color distinguishes **Elusive** from **Russet-tipped Clubtail**, thoracic pattern from similarly colored and often co-occurring **Riverine Clubtail**. Superficially much like **Arrow Clubtail**, which has broader lateral thoracic stripes and more elongate S9. Abdomen more slender than in **Cobra**, **Midland**, **Plains**, and **Pronghorn Clubtails**, color pattern brighter than in **Ashy** and **Dusky Clubtails**.

172.1
Elusive Clubtail male—Ottawa, ON,
September 2009, Christine Hanrahan

172.2
Elusive Clubtail female—Hamilton Co.,
OH, September 2007, William Hull

Natural History Justifies its name, as rarely seen except during emergence. Adults fly into forest canopy to feed and come back to breeding habitat briefly to breed. Even when at water, usually far out from shore and difficult to capture, photograph, or observe!

Habitat Large, slow-flowing rivers, less often large lakes.

Flight Season ON Jun–Oct, QC Jun–Sep, IA Jun–Sep, WI Jun–Oct, OH May–Sep, KY Jul–Oct.

Distribution Records very sparse in parts of range, especially Canada west of Quebec. In Michigan apparently only near the Great Lakes. Isolated records in Northwest Territories, Saskatchewan, western Manitoba, and western Nebraska.

173 Russet-tipped Clubtail *Stylurus plagiatus*   TL 57–66, HW 30–40

Description Wide-ranging clubtail of southern regions with well-defined reddish club. *Male*: Eyes turquoise to blue, face unmarked but slightly clouded with age. Thorax with T1–4 all present, well separated. Femora medium brown, darker toward end; tibiae blackish. Abdomen blackish with pale spearpoints on S3–6, small pale triangle on S7; most of S7–10 reddish orange, yellower on sides, with narrow blackish margins on club. *Female*: Colored as male, abdomen less conspicuously marked and appearing mostly brownish with orangey tip. Little indication of club.

Identification Russet-tipped abdomen distinctive from most clubtails. Somewhat like **Sulphur-tipped Clubtail**, overlapping in southwest part of region. **Sulphur-tipped** smaller, with much more contrast abdominal markings, including dark stripes down abdomen onto club; **Russet-tipped** has duller abdomen, obscurely patterned club. Females especially like female **Broad-striped Forceptail**, but side stripes of thorax always narrower in **Russet-tipped**, abdomen much more clubbed in male. See also **Laura's** and **Shining Clubtails**.

Natural History Probably mostly in trees when not at water. Males often seen hanging vertically in trees or less often in more horizontal position, especially when on leaves. Active

Clubtail Family **281**

173.1
Russet-tipped Clubtail
male—Floyd Co., GA,
September 2007, Marion
M. Dobbs; inset male—
Hamilton Co., OH,
September 2007, William
Hull

173.2
Russet-tipped Clubtail
female—Juneau Co.,
WI, August 2008, Ken
Tennessen

throughout day. Sexual patrol in back-and-forth flight over breeding habitats, usually over riffles and often hovering. Females rarely seen, mating pairs usually in trees well above head height. Females oviposit in rapid flight, tapping open water at long intervals. Very successful species, exceeding all other members of genus in range and flight season.

Habitat Slow-flowing rivers and streams down to fairly narrow ones, in or out of woodland. Common at some lakes in peninsular Florida.

Flight Season IA Jul–Oct, WI Jun–Oct, OH May–Sep, NJ Jul–Oct, KY Jul–Sep, LA Jun–Oct, GA Jun–Nov, FL Apr–Nov.

Distribution Extends slightly farther west in Kansas to Texas and south in eastern Mexico to Nuevo León, also separate populations in western Texas to southeastern California.

Description Long, slender, vividly patterned river clubtail. *Male*: Eyes green, face pale but washed with brown, especially on upper part. Thorax with T1–2 broad, spot and narrow pale line between them like upside-down exclamation point. T3–4 fairly broad, separated by pale stripe about same width or narrower. Legs black. Abdomen mostly black, S3–8 with pale dorsal markings a basal triangle and, in some individuals, an additional line beyond it (not on S8). Pale markings on sides tiny basal spots on S3–7 and large, irregular spots on sides of S7–9, those on S8–9 mostly bordered on edge with black. Club rather narrow. Hamules very large, anterior ones sickle-shaped and prominent in side view. *Female*: Colored as male, but much more prominent yellow spots on sides of abdomen, spots not as prominent on last segments. No club, but S9 with narrow yellow flange. Femora mostly brown. Pair of curved spines just behind each lateral ocellus, another pair between each ocellus and inner eye margin.

Identification The long abdomen with especially long S9 and narrow club in male gives this species a distinctive shape, and its color pattern is different from other species that might

174.1
Arrow Clubtail
male—Waupaca Co.,
WI, September 2008,
Ken Tennessen

174.2
Arrow Clubtail
female—Waupaca Co.,
WI, September 2008,
Ken Tennessen

fly with it. Most like barely overlapping **Townes's Clubtail** but larger and with different thoracic pattern, also S9 shorter than wide rather than the reverse as in **Arrow**. See also **Elusive Clubtail**.

Natural History Immatures spend lengthy period away from water, usually in woodland. Males have long patrol flights over breeding habitat, not far above water surface and along shore or farther out over open water, often in shade. Intersperse hovering, a bouncy flight that seems to come from alternating fluttering and gliding, with extremely rapid, low, straight flight "like an arrow." Becomes more common at water later in afternoon.

Habitat Good-sized rivers in forested landscapes with some current, producing long riffles.

Flight Season ON Jul–Sep, QC Jun–Aug, WI Jun–Aug, ME Jul–Sep, OH Aug–Oct, NJ Jul–Oct, KY Jul–Oct.

---

175 Brimstone Clubtail   *Stylurus intricatus* TL 41–45, HW 26–32

Description Small, mostly yellow clubtail of the Missouri River valley. *Male:* Eyes blue, face pale. Thorax with T1–4 narrow, all well separated; T3–4 even narrower than T1–2. Legs yellow and black striped. Abdomen mostly yellow, black hourglass markings on sides of S3–6, scarcely any other dark markings. *Female:* Colored as male, a bit more black on S2 and S7.

Identification No other clubtail in range of this small yellow species very similar. Barely overlapping **Sulphur-tipped Clubtail** probably most like it but has more heavily striped thorax and prominent brown stripes along club. Yellow immature and female MEADOWHAWKS have eyes neither separated nor blue.

Natural History Males fly rapidly back and forth low over water in short beats, hovering at intervals, or perch in streamside shrubs hanging at 45° angle or on logs; relatively rarely on ground. Females more often in shrubs near water, not perching as high as some other hanging clubtails. Copulation at rest in shrubs for an hour or more. Females oviposit by tapping at intervals while in rapid flight.

175.1
Brimstone Clubtail
male—Imperial Co., CA,
July 2006, Paul G.
Johnson

175.2
Brimstone Clubtail
female—Imperial Co., CA,
June 2009, Gary Suttle

Habitat Typically slow-flowing, warm muddy rivers in open country but with associated riparian shrubs and/or trees; sometimes in irrigation canals.
Flight Season IA Jul–Sep.
Distribution A western species, ranging farther west in Nebraska and Kansas as well as scattered among river basins in southern Saskatchewan and Alberta, Wyoming and Utah, northern Nevada to southwestern Arizona, and New Mexico and western Texas.

Hanging Clubtails - male appendages

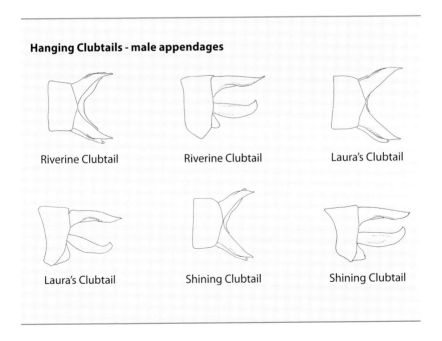

Riverine Clubtail   Riverine Clubtail   Laura's Clubtail

Laura's Clubtail   Shining Clubtail   Shining Clubtail

Hanging Clubtails - male appendages (continued)

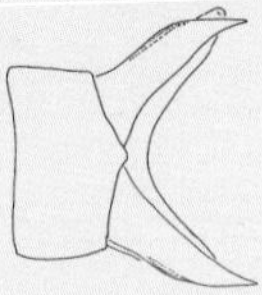

Townes's Clubtail

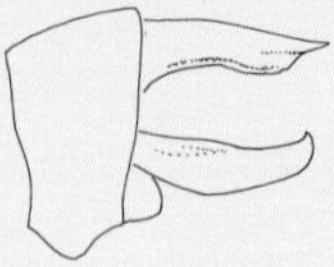

Townes's Clubtail

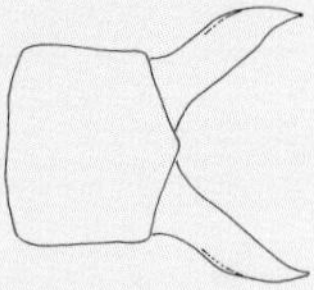

Yellow-sided Clubtail

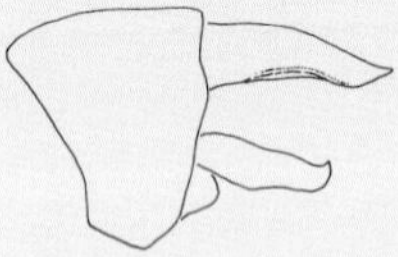

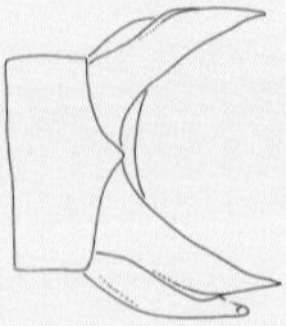

Yellow-sided Clubtail

Zebra Clubtail

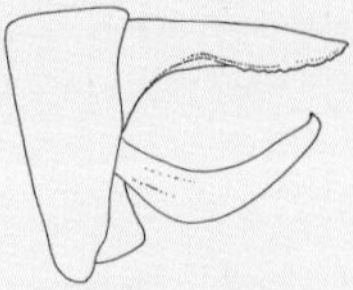

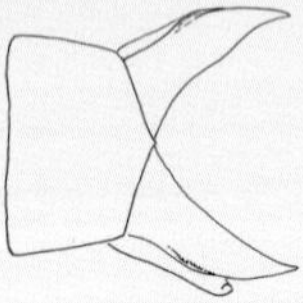

Zebra Clubtail

Elusive Clubtail

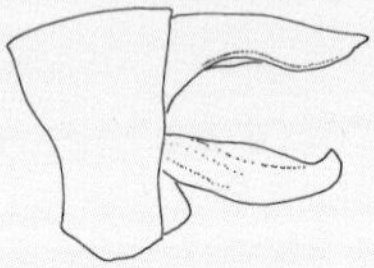

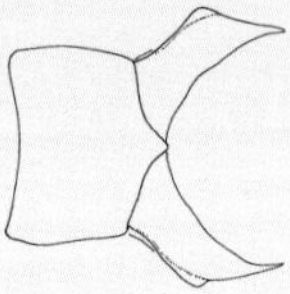

Elusive Clubtail

Russet-tipped Clubtail

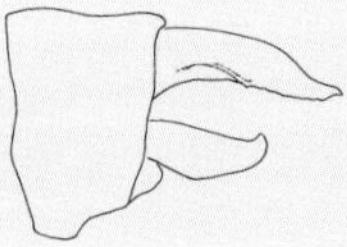

Russet-tipped Clubtail

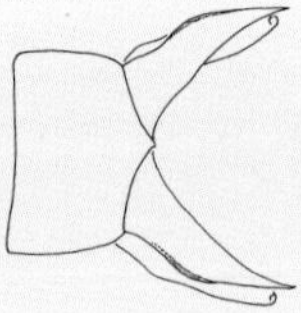

Arrow Clubtail

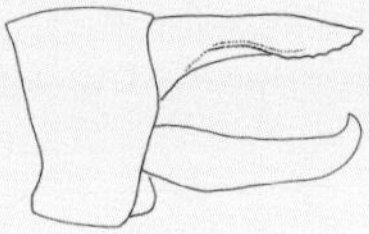

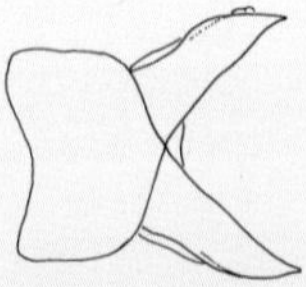

Arrow Clubtail

Brimstone Clubtail

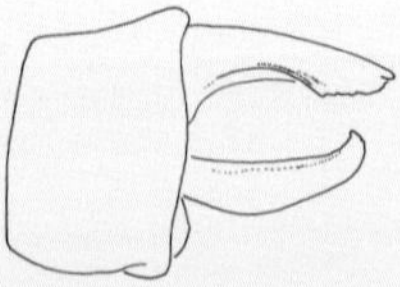

Brimstone Clubtail

Hanging Clubtails - female subgenital plate

Riverine Clubtail

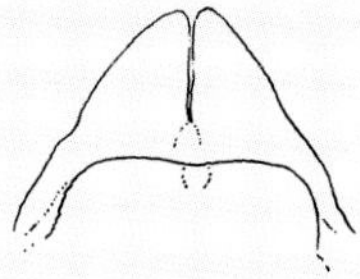

Laura's Clubtail

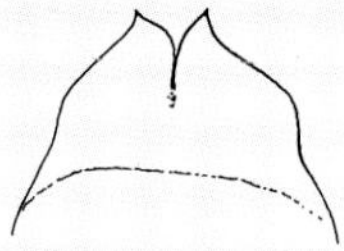

Shining Clubtail

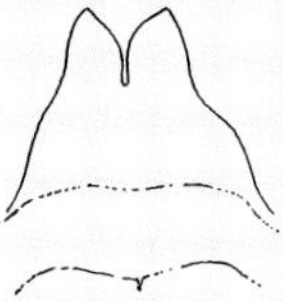

Townes's Clubtail

Yellow-sided Clubtail

Zebra Clubtail

Elusive Clubtail

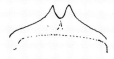

Russet-tipped Clubtail

Arrow Clubtail

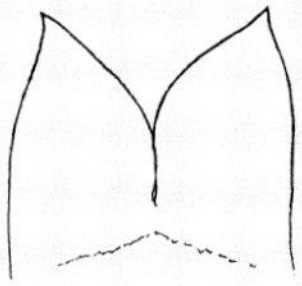

Brimstone Clubtail

Found only in central and eastern North America, spinylegs stand out by very long hind legs with prominent large spines on femur, presumably adaptations for capturing large prey. Otherwise they resemble some *Gomphus* species, especially subgenus *Gomphurus*, which also have long hind legs, but larger than all but a few of them and with club not as wide in males. World 3, NA 3, East 3.

176 Black-shouldered Spinyleg *Dromogomphus spinosus* TL 53–68, HW 32–40

Description Large, long-legged rather dark clubtail with moderate club and characteristic wide dark stripes on otherwise pale thorax. *Male:* Eyes green, face yellow. Thorax yellow to gray with frontal stripe split into widely separated narrow lines joined at top and bottom to produce characteristic pattern. T1–2 very wide and fused or almost fused to make very broad dark brown stripe on either side of front; sides entirely yellow except for dark half-line for T3 and complete line for T4. Abdomen mostly black with yellow to gray line down middle of all segments, wider on basal segments  and interrupted and expanded into triangles on S8–9 and spot covering much of S10. Yellow markings low on sides of most segments, forming obvious spots on sides of S7–9. Quite a bit of individual variation, some with virtually no yellow on club. *Female:* Colored as male, abdomen slightly thicker so club not as pronounced.

Identification This distinctive species most likely mistaken for COMMON CLUBTAILS of subgenus *Gomphurus*, with their large size, long legs, and striking color patterns, but club not as prominent. Fortunately, **Black-shouldered Spinyleg** only clubtail with its broad thoracic stripes. Very different-looking than closely related **Flag-tailed** and **Southeastern Spinylegs**, and not much else even vaguely similar. Rather prominent dorsal abdominal

176.1
Black-shouldered
Spinyleg male—
Telfair Co., GA, July
2007

176.2
Black-shouldered
Spinyleg female—
Calhoun Co., FL,
July 2009

stripe may distinguish it from similar species with less pale color. Note: colored somewhat like much larger and similarly long-legged **Dragonhunter**, but latter has broad, fused T3–4 and even less club.

Natural History Males perch on leaves up to waist height or above or on ground or rocks near water, facing stream. Also on rocks in water, either pools or riffles. May obelisk in mid-day sun. Come in slowly to land, legs extended suddenly just before landing. Alternate perching and flying up and down or hovering over stream at knee to waist height, abdomen tilted upward. Females and immatures in woodland nearby, usually perched up in vegetation and often in shade. Pairs fly into trees for lengthy copulation. Females oviposit in rapid flight, skimming water and tapping it every few feet.

Habitat Rocky and muddy streams and rivers from small to large, more often in woodland. Also in rocky lakes in northern part of range.

Flight Season ON May–Sep, QC Jun–Aug, NS Jun–Sep, WI Jun–Aug, ME Jun–Sep, OH May–Sep, NJ Jun–Sep, KY May–Oct, LA May–Sep, GA May–Sep, FL Apr–Nov.

Distribution Slightly farther west in Oklahoma and Texas and isolated record in southern South Dakota.

---

177 Flag-tailed Spinyleg   *Dromogomphus spoliatus*   TL 56–65, HW 32–36

Description Large, long-legged brightly marked clubtail with largely yellow-orange abdomen tip. *Male:* Eyes light blue or turquoise, face yellowish-tan. Thorax dull yellow with rather narrow T1–4, T3 often broken. Abdomen with S1–2 mostly yellowish, dark brown dorsolateral blotches on S2; S3–6 white with blackish dorsolateral markings, smaller anterior one connected or not to larger posterior one; from side, may present appearance of two black-and-white rings alternating on each segment; S7–10 yellow to orange, S7–9 often with brown markings above. *Female:* Colored as male, abdomen less clubbed.

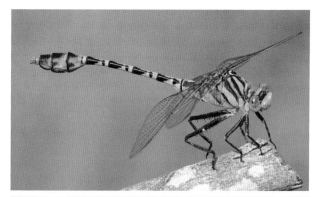

177.1
Flag-tailed Spinyleg male—Travis Co., TX, June 2009, Eric Isley

177.2
Flag-tailed Spinyleg male—Travis Co., TX, August 2009, Eric Isley

Identification Common name comes from club being laterally compressed, very conspicuous like flag from side but not very wide in top view. A few other clubtails in range share general appearance of ringed midabdomen with orange S7–10. **Jade** and **Stillwater Clubtails** both a bit smaller, with pale yellow or cream-colored abdomen and only one large dark marking on each middle segment. **Flag-tailed Spinyleg** has white midabdomen with two apparent markings per segment. **Cobra, Plains,** and **Sulphur-tipped Clubtails** have dark markings continuous along sides of abdomen and darker, more conspicuous markings on yellow club. GREATER FORCEPTAILS, often in same habitats, have much less well-developed club; also not as black-and-white looking as this species. **Black-shouldered Spinyleg** very differently colored, with smaller club.

Natural History Males perch on elevated perches at waterside, also low on rocks, or fly out over water with much hovering. Abdomen up to vertical obelisk on sunny midday, but also hanging down in some individuals perched in shrubs.

Habitat Slow-flowing rivers and large, sometimes muddy, ponds.

Flight Season ON Jul–Aug, IA Jun–Sep, OH Jun–Sep, KY Jun–Sep, LA Jun–Aug, GA May–Sep.

Distribution Extends farther west in Oklahoma and Texas, also record from southeastern New Mexico and south in Mexico to Tamaulipas.

178 Southeastern Spinyleg   *Dromogomphus armatus*   TL 64–74, HW 36–41

Description Southeastern clubtail with long, spiny hind legs and orange-tipped abdomen. *Male:* Eyes green; face pale with narrow, faint dark crosslines. Thorax yellowish with dark brown stripes. T1–4 all well defined and separate. Legs black. Abdomen mostly yellowish, prominent black dorsolateral stripes from S1 to S6; Tip (S7–10) somewhat orange-tinged. Dorsolateral stripe brown and may be rather obscure, leaving mostly orangish tip. Club of moderate size, somewhat flattened from side to side. *Female:* Colored as male but scarcely any club; S7–10 can be quite orange.

Identification Most like **Flag-tailed Spinyleg**, but that species has pale rings interrupting striped pattern of abdomen and slightly more "flag"-shaped club. Also, **Southeastern** has complete dark stripes on top of S7, **Flag-tailed** incomplete. Eyes green in **Southeastern**, blue in **Flag-tailed**. Almost no overlap in range. Quite distinct from **Black-shouldered Spinyleg**. Only other clubtails in range with mostly orange to yellow abdomen tip are **Rus-**

178.1
Southeastern Spinyleg
male—Santa Rosa Co.,
FL, May 2008,
Kelly Jones

178.2
Southeastern Spinyleg
female—Stewart Co.,
GA, July 2005, Giff
Beaton

set-tipped and **Shining Clubtails** and **Two-striped Forceptail**. All three have much shorter, pale-based hind legs and more obscurely marked abdomens. **Shining** furthermore virtually lacks lateral thoracic stripes, and **Two-striped** has dark thorax with two pale side stripes.

Natural History Perches on ground or up in vegetation, at water or in sunny clearings. Commonly seen away from breeding habitat, often resting on sandy roads with abdomen elevated. Female seen to tap water few times for less than 1 min, then land in tree, then back to water few minutes later; presumably building up egg ball as many (all?) clubtails do. Butterflies common prey.

Habitat Small streams, even trickles and seeps, through sandy woodland, both pine and hardwoods. Much smaller streams than those inhabited by other two spinylegs.

Flight Season GA Jun–Aug, FL Jun–Nov.

Dragonhunter *Hagenius*

This genus includes the largest of North American clubtails, with long hind legs, poorly developed club, and wide, flat larva that resembles a wood chip. It is closely related to the equally large and fierce *Sieboldius* of Asia. World 1, NA 1, East 1.

179 Dragonhunter *Hagenius brevistylus*   TL 73–90, HW 47–58

Description Long-legged, black and yellow monster dragonfly with small head that often flies with abdomen tip curled down. Size increases to south. *Male*: Eyes green, face yellow with fine black line across it. Thorax yellow with broad T1 and T2 fused (leaving tiny spot) or almost fused, broad T3 and T4 almost fused; yellow stripe between pairs narrower than dark area. Abdomen black with yellow on sides of basal segments and narrow yellow spearpoints, shortening to rear and becoming triangles by S7–8; yellow basal spots on sides of middle segments expanding into larger spots on  sides of S8–9. Slight club widest on S9, unlike most other clubtails. *Female*: Colored as male but much more yellow visible on sides of abdomen, yellow on top and sides of S8 in contact. Little indication of club.

Identification No other clubtail as large as this one, might be more likely mistaken for SPIKETAIL or RIVER CRUISER as it flies by, but notice different pattern of yellow on black on both

179.1
Dragonhunter
male—Washington
Co., VT, July 2005,
Bryan Pfeiffer/Wings
Photography

179.2
Dragonhunter
female—Lincoln Co.,
TN, June 2006

thorax and abdomen. Perched individual not like anything else, although note somewhat similar appearance but smaller size, wider club, and different thoracic pattern of **Black-shouldered Spinyleg**. Narrow club distinguishes **Dragonhunter** from the largest *Gomphurus* clubtails such as **Blackwater**, **Gulf Coast**, and **Splendid**.

Natural History Both sexes perch on tree and shrub branches over water, often hanging down a bit and seeming awkward, too large for perch. Perch held distinctively in crook of long, spiny hind legs, but awkwardness confirmed when one crashes into tangle of twigs, flutters, and then flies out again! Also perches flat on ground or rocks near water. Males fly leisurely up and down streams or along shorelines, looking for prey and/or females, with abdomen a bit elevated, tip curled down. Wild chases even up into treetops when one encounters another. Females flying in same manner look exactly like males; quite unusual for female clubtail to spend nonbreeding time at water, perhaps not subject to male harassment. Preys on other odonates and butterflies and presumably other large insects. Ebony Jewelwings are common prey, and Dragonhunters may be most common at streams where jewelwings are abundant. Other clubtails also common prey, including largest species occurring with it such as Blackwater Clubtail. Typically oviposits facing vertical stream banks, hovering and dropping forward to the water to tap once, then rising (and backing up!) to drop and tap again, changing position every tap or every few taps. This may be continued for several minutes. Also by long flights over open water and reported to drop eggs from above water. Immatures of both sexes in shrubby areas near water, usually quite wary. Adults at water usually approachable.

Habitat Wide variety of streams and rivers, less commonly lakes. As other top predators (cougars, wolves, great horned owls), seem to be able to utilize all habitats. This may be because larva not a burrower (rests among detritus), thus not tied to any particular substrate.

Flight Season ON Jun–Sep, QC Jun–Aug, NS Jun–Oct, WI Jun–Aug, ME Jun–Sep, OH Jun–Sep, NJ Jun–Sep, KY May–Sep, LA May–Aug, GA May–Sep, FL Apr–Nov.

Distribution Slightly farther west in central Texas. Extensive range also typical of large predators.

Ringtails *Erpetogomphus*

With diversity centered in Mexico, these are neotropical relatives of temperate snaketails, although none of them have horned females. Male ringtails are moderately clubbed, females not; legs are short. Ground color of thorax green in most species. From side, middle of abdomen black with conspicuous pale rings visible on each segment, often yellow as they extend across top; S7 with wide white band; and club reddish, orange, or yellow and black. Snaketails instead show yellow spots on each segment, no white rings on the side, and club not differently colored. Males typically perch on the ground or on rocks or twigs over water; females perch similarly but visit water only for breeding. World 22, NA 6, East 1.

180 Eastern Ringtail *Erpetogomphus designatus*   TL 49–55, HW 30–35

Description Ringtail with dark stripe on front of thorax incomplete below, small patches of color at wing bases. *Male*: Eyes light blue, face pale greenish with two faintly indicated light brown stripes across front. Thorax dull light green with narrow but well-developed stripes T1–4; T1 incomplete at both ends. Abdomen with S1–6 mostly black with pale yellow to off-white basal ring and yellow dorsal stripe on each segment; S7 similar but with more orange, S8–10 entirely orange or S8–9 with much brown or black above. *Female*: Colored as male but yellow more extensive on top of abdomen, black markings more reduced. All wings with well-defined brown spots at base.

180.1
Eastern Ringtail male—Caldwell Co., TX, July 2004

180.2
Eastern Ringtail female—Caldwell Co., TX, June 2008, Giff Beaton

Identification No other ringtails in its range in East. Occurs with a number of SNAKETAILS, all of which have green thorax, but none of them has a black and white ringed abdomen with reddish tip like this species.

Natural History Both sexes on ground or on twigs up to head height, can be some distance from water. Males fly up and down riffles on beats 10–20 feet long, hover for short periods facing wind, then move again. Also perch on rocks and in low vegetation. Abdomen usually elevated slightly, up to vertical at midday. Females oviposit in pools, fairly erratic with one tap on each yard-long run.

Habitat Sandy and gravelly streams and rivers, even large ones.

Flight Season KY Jun–Sep, GA May–Oct, FL Jun–Aug.

Distribution West to western Kansas and eastern New Mexico, south in uplands of Mexico to Durango and Nuevo León. Isolated records in Montana, South Dakota, and western New Mexico.

Snaketails *Ophiogomphus*

These beautiful green clubtails are much sought by dragonfly enthusiasts, as they usually live along pristine rocky and gravelly streams, often have short flight seasons, and some are quite uncommon. Males are slightly but distinctly clubbed, females scarcely so; the legs are short. Like ringtails, these clubtails have a green thorax, but light markings on abdomen are not in the shape of distinct rings. The abdomen is black and yellow, not as strongly tinged with orange as in most ringtails. In almost all eastern species S1–2 are green with wide, somewhat irregular dorsolateral brown stripes, and the remaining segments are marked with yellow and/or white. Females of most species have one or two pairs of spinelike "horns" on or behind the occiput. Males perch on sandy or gravelly shores or streamside vegetation, usually fairly low, and alternate perching with steady flight up and down beats over shallow riffles and pools. Females are only at the water to breed but are often found nearby in clearings and open country. Probably females of all species produce egg masses while perched with abdomen elevated, often on rocks at breeding streams. There is substantial emergence at times, with immature individuals sometimes common in clearings near rivers. Bright green Eastern Pondhawks often perch on the ground and may generate snaketail fever until they are better seen. World 28, NA 19, East 14.

181 Boreal Snaketail *Ophiogomphus colubrinus* TL 41–48, HW 27–31

Description Bright green, heavily marked northern snaketail with dark facial stripes. *Male:* Eyes green, face green crossed by four narrow blackish lines. Thorax green with T1–2 fairly wide and partially fused, T4 prominent; lower end of T3 represented by dark point projecting upward. Femora mostly light tan, tibiae black. Abdomen black along sides; green on top of S1–2, duller and paler green  candles on top of next segments, turning to pale yellow spots by end of abdomen. Whitish on sides expanded to prominent spots on S8–10, each with variable brown smudges. *Female:* Colored as male but abdomen thicker, club less prominent, white more obvious on sides. Pair of blunt peglike horns on back of occiput adjacent to eyes, may be tiny pair behind them.

Identification Looks much like other northern snaketails with T3 incomplete and T4 complete, but more brown on abdomen than **Brook**, **Maine**, **Riffle**, and **St. Croix**, which have very black markings there. Dark lines across face also distinguish it from those species. Femora pale as in **Brook**, not black as in other species. Easily distinguished from **Rusty Snaketail** by more heavily striped thorax, more brightly marked abdomen. Probably no overlap with **Sioux Snaketail**, which also has brown-marked abdomen and pale femora but lacks dark lines on face.

181.1
Boreal Snaketail
male—Douglas
Co., WI, August
2008

181.2
Boreal Snaketail
female—Vilas
Co., WI, August
2008, posed

Natural History Males fly up and down low over water, sometimes hovering, and come to rest on rocks, logs, or shrubs up to head height or more. Most activity in morning and midafternoon, not at midday. Females oviposit in riffles or upstream of them by tapping water rather methodically, then perching, usually on an exposed rock in the stream, curving abdomen upward and extruding eggs for 5–15 sec, all the while wing-whirring. Then fly over water again to do the same, tapping 4–10 times for up to 30 sec, then fly up into trees.

Habitat Clear rapid streams and rivers with pools and riffles, gravelly or rocky beds.

Flight Season ON May–Sep, QC Jun–Sep, NS Jul–Sep, WI May–Sep, ME Jun–Jul.

Distribution West across southern Canada to British Columbia, north to Northwest Territories. The most northerly clubtail.

---

182 Riffle Snaketail *Ophiogomphus carolus* TL 40–45, HW 24–28

Description Small, vividly striped, rather dark snaketail of northeastern rivers with well-defined club. *Male*: Eyes green, face light green. Thorax bright green with dark brown stripes, T1 and T2 wide and mostly fused, T4 narrow and confined to suture; lower end of T3 represented by dark point projecting upward. Legs black. Abdomen black on sides, green on top of S1–2, yellow from there back, markings candle-shaped in midabdomen but smaller and smaller

182.1
Riffle Snaketail
male—
Penobscot Co.,
ME, June 2006

182.2
Riffle Snaketail
female—Bayfield
Co., WI, June
2008, Ryan Brady

to mere spots at end. Whitish markings low on sides turn into prominent spots on sides of S7–9 smudged with brown markings of variable size. *Female*: Colored as male but abdomen thicker, club scarcely evident. Some females have pair of minute horns on occiput.

Identification Differs from **Rusty** in black and yellow abdomen, from very similar **Boreal** in unmarked face (**Boreal** with fine cross-stripes) and black femora (mostly pale in **Boreal**). Also differs from **Brook Snaketail** by black femora and shorter dorsal abdominal markings with more indented edges. **Maine Snaketail** also with black femora but has even longer, thinner dorsal markings and usually lacks pale spot on S9 present in **Riffle**. Epiproct of **Maine** with two prominent teeth in side view, **Riffle** with only one. **St. Croix Snaketail** barely overlaps, quite similar but mostly pale S10.

Natural History Males perch on rocks out in current or on leaves of shrubs and low trees at shore, then fly short patrols up and down riffles just above surface. Difficult to follow because of low, swift flight over agitated water surface. Female oviposits in smooth flight over water, may rest beforehand extruding obvious mass of eggs. Both sexes in clearings near breeding habitat.

Habitat Clear rocky and sandy streams and rivers with pools and riffles bordered by riparian shrubs and trees.

Flight Season ON Jun–Aug, QC Jun–Jul, NS May–Aug, WI May–Aug, ME Jun–Aug, OH May–Jul, NJ May–Jul.

Description Rare, heavily striped snaketail of southeastern uplands. *Male*: Eyes somewhat blue to turquoise; face all green. Thorax with T1 incomplete above, just touching well-developed T2 at upper ends; T3 complete or interrupted at midlength, T4 well developed. Legs black, front and middle femora may be paler. Abdomen black with yellow spearpoints back to S7, changing to narrow streaks on S8–9. Sides of S7–9, S10, and appendages mostly yellow. *Female*: Color pattern as in male, yellow markings on top of abdomen less defined and blending with dark color; no yellow on top of S8–9.

Identification Several very similar snaketails occur in range of **Edmund's**. All have slightly less bold markings on thorax, T1–2 slightly narrower and only barely touching at upper end of T2, in some individuals not touching at all. T3 always absent (always with upper end clearly present in **Edmund's**). **Appalachian** has similar blue eyes, and a good look is necessary to distinguish them. **Edmund's** has S9 distinctly black above, same segment mostly yellow in **Appalachian**. Male **Edmund's** have cerci sharply pointed, **Appalachian** rounded at tip. Yellow dorsal marking on S3 narrower in **Edmund's** and femora black in male and mostly dark in female (mostly pale in **Appalachian**). **Brook** and **Maine** also differ by having green eyes. **Edmund's** typically at lower elevation than latter two species.

Natural History Males out on rocks, often at head of deeper runs, may be in swiftest current with slippery bottom to thwart photographer or collector. More rarely on shore.

Habitat Clean rocky rivers with good current.

Flight Season GA Apr–Jun.

183.1
Edmund's Snaketail
male—Oconee Co.,
SC, May 2008,
Marion M. Dobbs

183.2
Edmund's Snaketail
female—Rabun Co.,
GA, June 2008, Giff
Beaton, posed

Description A rare, heavily striped snaketail of southeastern uplands. *Male:* Eyes blue, face green. Thorax with T1–2 well developed, usually just separated at upper ends. T3 represented only at spiracle and below, T4 narrow but complete. Femora tan, black-tipped; tibiae black, pale on outside. Abdomen black with yellow spearpoints back to S7, changing to narrow streak on S8 and spot on S9. Sides of S7–8 and most of S10 and appendages yellow. *Female:* Colored as male but yellow markings on top of abdomen wider, almost touching white markings on sides; S9–10 with smaller dorsal spots. Pair of prominent spines on occiput.

Identification See **Edmund's** for differences between these two similar and co-occurring species. **Brook** and **Maine** with thoracic stripes like **Appalachian**, but both have green eyes and more black on femora. Approaches but does not overlap with higher-elevation **Riffle Snaketail** (which has heavier thoracic striping and black legs). **Rusty Snaketail** has reddish, obscurely patterned abdomen and virtually no stripes on thorax.

Natural History Males more easily found in early morning and late afternoon. Perch on grasses and shrub and tree leaves over streams or in nearby sunlit clearings, where females also found.

Habitat Small to medium spring-fed streams with mud and gravel bottoms.

184.1
Appalachian
Snaketail
male—
Oglethorpe Co.,
GA, May 2006,
Marion M. Dobbs

184.2
Appalachian
Snaketail
female—
Oglethorpe Co., GA,
May 2006

Flight Season GA Apr–Jun.

Comments Two moderately well-defined subspecies have been recognized, *O. i. incurvatus* from the east side of the Appalachians and *O. i. alleghaniensis* from the west. The latter is a bit larger, differing slightly in hamules and male appendages; female occipital horns are much larger and close together, and the occiput bulges behind. Specimens from Alabama are somewhat intermediate, and more study is needed.

185 Southern Snaketail *Ophiogomphus australis* TL 44–46, HW 24–28

Description A rare snaketail of southeastern lowlands. *Male*: Eyes blue, face yellow-green. Thorax with T1–2 well developed, T1 not in contact with antealar brown. T3–4 narrow but complete, although somewhat variable. Femora light brown, tibiae black. Abdomen black on S3–7 with white ventrolateral spots and yellow dorsal candle markings extending two-thirds of segment. S1–2 marked with yellow and white, not green as in most other snaketails. *Female*: Color pattern like male, yellow dorsal abdominal

185.1
Southern Snaketail
male—Pike Co., MS,
April 2006, Gayle and
Jeanell Strickland

185.2
Southern Snaketail
female—Early Co., GA,
March 2007, Giff Beaton

markings wider because abdomen wider. Some females have two small black occipital horns, tiny or lacking in Florida populations.

Identification No other snaketail in its limited range. No habitat overlap with rather similar-looking **Eastern Ringtail** of large rivers; latter species has brown at wing bases and middle segments of abdomen with whitish rings.

Natural History Both sexes found along streams and in nearby clearings. Rarity of appropriate habitat in known range contributes to scattered distribution and poorly known life history. Larvae can be common at known localities.

Habitat Small streams in woodland with at least some gravelly substrate.

Flight Season GA Mar–Apr, FL Mar–Apr.

Comments Some differences among populations and similarities to Appalachian Snaketail have led to ongoing confusion in knowledge of this species.

---

186 Brook Snaketail *Ophiogomphus aspersus*　　　TL 44–49, HW 24–32

Description Brightly marked snaketail of northeastern streams. *Male:* Eyes green, face unmarked green. Green thorax with T1–2 prominent but narrow, T1 incomplete above. T3 absent above spiracle, T4 very fine. Femora tan and black, tibiae black. Abdomen mostly black with yellow acute triangles (slightly indented at midlength) from S3 to S7, shorter marking on S8 and only spot on S9–10. S7–9 with large, irregular yellow lateral spots bordered by black.

186.1
Brook Snaketail
male—Sussex Co.,
NJ, June 2008

186.2
Brook Snaketail
female—Sussex Co.,
NJ, May 2007, Allen
Barlow

Female: Colored as male, eyes usually duller and broader abdomen emphasizes yellow dorsal markings. Pair of short but obvious hornlike spines on back of head just behind occiput.

Identification Extremely like **Maine** and **Riffle Snaketails** in having only lower end of T3 present, but that stripe often obscure even below the spiracle. Also base of femur pale in **Brook** (completely black in other two; close look necessary). Dorsal abdominal markings in both sexes more like broad-based triangles; those in **Maine** narrower, not much broader than lines, and those in **Riffle** broader, with "flame" distinct from "candle" and not as pointed. In hand, cerci of male **Brook** with bulge in middle, other two species more or less cylindrical. Look for postoccipital horns in female **Brook**. **Boreal** also similar but abdomen with brown markings, face with dark crosslines. Slight overlap if any with **Appalachian** and **Edmund's**, which have more yellow at abdomen tip, including all of S10.

Natural History Males perch on twigs or leaves, not far above water, and fly back and forth over stream. Disappear from water through middle of day.

Habitat Shallow, clear, sandy streams in woodland. Rocks also often present, but larvae in sand.

Flight Season QC Jun–Aug, NS Jun–Aug, ME Jun–Aug, NJ May–Jul.

---

187 Sioux Snaketail   *Ophiogomphus smithi*   TL 45–48, HW 26–29

Description Very restricted snaketail of sandy streams. *Male*: Eyes rather pale blue, face unmarked green. Green thorax with narrow T1–2, T1 incomplete above. T3 not evident above spiracle, T4 narrow but complete. Legs black and tan striped. Abdomen with typical dark brown dorsolateral stripes enclosing yellow dorsal markings, latter candles and then acute triangles extending most of length of segment S3–9, oval spot on S10. Large, irregular whitish spots on

187.1
Sioux Snaketail male—
Jackson Co., WI, June
2007

187.2
Sioux Snaketail
female—Jackson Co.,
WI, June 2007

sides of S7–9, only partially bordered on flange by brown. *Female:* Colored as male but eyes duller, blue-gray. Tiny black-tipped spine projects upward from either end of occiput.

Identification Differs from **Rusty Snaketail** in better-defined abdominal pattern, with yellow triangles above and more conspicuous thoracic stripes. Abdominal pattern less vivid (but with yellow dorsal markings almost continuous) and thoracic stripes less conspicuous than all other snaketails that might overlap with it (**Boreal, Extra-striped, Pygmy, Riffle, St. Croix**), most of them barely if at all. These other snaketails very likely lacking from sandy streams inhabited by this species.

Natural History Males perch on open sand and low vegetation along streams. Females and immatures mostly in sunny clearings nearby, in vegetation up to chest height.

Habitat Small to medium-sized sand-bottomed streams in largely wooded landscape.

Flight Season IA Jun–Jul, WI May–Jun.

Description Wide-ranging northeastern snaketail with sharply patterned thorax and abdomen. *Male:* Eyes and unmarked face green. Green thorax with well-developed T1–2, T1 incomplete above. T3 absent above spiracle, T4 narrow but complete. Legs black. Abdomen mostly black, finely pointed pale yellow dorsal stripes on S3–8 extending half length of each segment or slightly more; S9 with small basal spot. Pale yellow lateral spots on S7–9, covering most of sides of S8–9; S10 mostly pale. *Female:* Colored as male. Pair of close-set "horns" pointing straight up from center of occiput.

188.1
Maine Snaketail
male—Essex Co.,
VT, July 2008,
Bryan Pfeiffer/
Wings Photography

188.2
Maine Snaketail
female—Middlesex
Co., CT, June 2004,
Giff Beaton

Identification Very similar to **Boreal, Brook,** and **Riffle Snaketails**. See those species for differences. Yellow markings on S8–9 less in extent in **Maine** than in other three, so abdomen tip looks darker. Usually no spot on top of S8–9 (or at least S9; **Boreal** and others have spots on both). Also differs from **Boreal Snaketail** by unmarked face. Femora black in **Maine** and **Riffle**, mostly pale in **Boreal** and **Brook**. **Appalachian** and **Edmund's** might overlap but usually at lower elevation; both have pale S10.

Natural History Males perch on ground, logs, and shrubs in sunny clearings at breeding habitat. More likely on rocks than Brook Snaketail, which favors plants (Riffle Snaketail uses both commonly).

Habitat Small rocky streams and rivers in forest or open, typically smaller than many of those used by other snaketails.

Flight Season QC Jun–Jul, NS Jul, ME May–Jul, NJ May–Jul, KY May–Jul, GA Apr–Jun.

Comments Populations west of the Alleghany-Appalachian crest in Pennsylvania and West Virginia have been considered a distinct subspecies, *O. m. fastigiatus*, differing from *mainensis* in epiproct shape. The difference is sufficient that specific status has been suggested. Yet populations of typical *mainensis* occur farther south along the Appalachian chain.

---

189 Acuminate Snaketail *Ophiogomphus acuminatus* TL 49–53, HW 29–34

Description Rare and restricted snaketail with lightly marked thorax. *Male*: Eyes turquoise, face unmarked green. Lime-green thorax with T1–2 relatively narrow, T1 falling well short of upper end. T3 absent, T4 very fine, scarcely visible. Legs black and yellow striped. Base of abdomen looks largely pale above; dark brown to black markings relatively sparse on basal segments, increasing in size to rear until covering much of S7–9, leaving dorsal streak on S7–8 and  spot on S9; also large yellow-green spots on sides of S8–9. S10 and appendages yellow. *Female*: Colored like male.

Identification Overlaps only with **Rusty Snaketail** and like that species with very lightly marked thorax, including scarcely visible middorsal stripe; **Acuminate** easily distinguished by more conspicuous abdominal pattern. No other green-thoraxed clubtail in range except **Eastern Ringtail**, with much more prominent thoracic stripes and ringed abdomen.

Natural History Males rest on rocks and low vegetation near water. Activity seems to be greatest before midmorning.

Habitat Moderate-sized and typically spring-fed shallow streams with long pools and short riffles, gravel bottom overlain by small rocks, much shaded but some open shores.

Flight Season Entire range Apr–Jun.

189
Acuminate
Snaketail
male—Dickson
Co., TN, June 2006,
Richard Connors

Description Snaketail of large rivers with mostly brownish abdomen and very sparse thoracic striping. *Male*: Eyes green to turquoise, face green with tan labrum. Thorax lime green with T1–2 fairly narrow and partially fused, no other stripes. Legs mostly tan, black on inside of tibiae. Abdomen mostly brown, typical snaketail pattern present but quite obscure except for green markings on S1–2, hint of whitish spots on sides of S8–9. Club quite obvious from above. *Female*: Colored as male, again typical snaketail pattern present but obscured, overall impression light brown with white on lower sides and dark dorsal spots on posterior segments. Pair of prominent pointed horns on back of head adjacent to eyes, some females with second upward-pointing tiny pair just in front of occipital border.

Identification Only eastern snaketail with largely brownish rather than black and yellow abdomen in both sexes. Be aware that tenerals of other snaketails could look something like this species before fully colored, although even they should have more conspicuous mark-

190.1
Rusty Snaketail male—
Ashland Co., OH, July
2007

190.2
Rusty Snaketail female,
inset female—Ashland
Co., OH, July 2007

ings. Also distinguished by very narrow thoracic stripes, at a distance thorax looking entirely green.

Natural History Males perch on twigs over water or fly low and erratically over riffles. Present throughout day, although often reduced between around 10:30 a.m. and 4 p.m. Copulation away from water, once observed at dusk. Female oviposits in straight fast runs upcurrent, perches between brief bouts and extrudes orange-tan egg mass. Both sexes perch above ground in weedy fields near breeding sites.

Habitat Large streams and rivers with moderate current, typically larger and siltier and warmer than those used by other snaketails.

Flight Season ON May–Sep, QC Jun–Aug, NS Jun–Sep, IA May–Jul, WI May–Sep, ME Jun–Aug, OH May–Aug, NJ May–Aug, KY Jun–Jul.

Distribution Also records in southwestern Manitoba and central Saskatchewan.

191 Westfall's Snaketail *Ophiogomphus westfalli*   TL 49–50, HW 29–31

Description Only snaketail of the Ozark/Ouachita region. *Male*: Eyes light blue-green, face unmarked green. Green thorax with faint stripes, T1 incomplete above and sometimes not evident, T2 narrow but always present. T3 absent, T4 scarcely visible. Legs tan, ends of femora and inside of tibiae black. Abdomen with dark lateral stripes on S3–9, becoming paler toward rear; large yellow candle markings occupying all of upper surface of S3–6, shorter on S7 and

191.1
Westfall's Snaketail
male—Crawford Co.,
MO, June 2009

191.2
Westfall's Snaketail
female—Montgomery
Co., AR, May 2006,
Steve Krotzer

Clubtail Family **305**

basal spots on S8–9; S10 mostly pale. Irregular pale tan spots on sides of S7–9, flanges black. *Female*: Colored as male, eyes a bit duller. Pair of hornlike spines projecting up from middle of occiput.

Identification Only species of snaketail in its range, thorax virtually unmarked in comparison with **Eastern Ringtail**. Don't be fooled by female and immature **Eastern Pondhawks** with green head and thorax and black-marked abdomen perched on ground on paths along river.

Natural History Males on twigs or rocks in or at edge of rivers.

Habitat Fair-sized rivers with moderate current, at least partially gravel bottom, and emergent rocks and vegetation patches.

Flight Season Entire range May–Jul.

---

192 St. Croix Snaketail   *Ophiogomphus susbehcha*   TL 50–52, HW 27–29

Description Very local brightly marked snaketail of pristine rivers in upper Mississippi valley. *Male*: Eyes blue, faced unmarked green. Thorax green with T1–2 black and well defined, T1 almost reaching top of segment. T3 absent above spiracle, T4 narrow but well-defined. Legs black, femora pale at base. Abdomen mostly black with narrow yellow candles on S3–7 reaching about halfway down segments, shorter on S8, only spot on S9. Distinct pale yellow patches  on sides of S7–9 bordered by black; S10 pale, contrasts strongly with S9. Epiproct distinctly longer than cerci. *Female*: Colored as male, easily distinguished by thicker abdomen as in other clubtails. Pair of black horns on back of head at either end of occiput.

Identification Relatively long epiproct distinctive of male. Distinguished from similarly flashy snaketails by all-pale S10 (mostly black in **Extra-striped** and **Riffle**, some dark markings in **Boreal** and **Sioux**). **Boreal** also has dark markings on face, and it and **Sioux** have

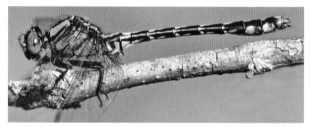

192.2
St. Croix Snaketail
male, female—
Burnett Co., WI,
June 1991, William
Smith

192.1
St. Croix Snaketail
male—Burnett Co., WI,
June 1991, William
Smith

pale femora. Usually not in same habitat as **Sioux**. **Rusty** with brown abdomen, **Extra-striped** with an extra lateral thoracic stripe, **Pygmy** much smaller with orange-tinted wing bases.

Natural History Little known. Adults difficult to find after emergence.

Habitat Large clear rivers with slow current and gravel and mud substrates.

Flight Season WI May–Jun.

Comments A population of snaketails in Maryland and Virginia, and probably elsewhere in that region, is close to this species but appears to be distinct in both color pattern and structure. It flies in April and May. Further studies are ongoing.

---

193 Extra-striped Snaketail *Ophiogomphus anomalus* TL 39–44, HW 24–27

Description Smallish snaketail with extra diagonal stripe on sides of thorax. *Male*: Eyes green, face green with narrow black crosslines. Green thorax with rather thick T1–2 connected at upper ends, T1 not quite complete. T3 complete or not, but diagonal stripe between it and complete T4. Legs black. Abdomen mostly black, yellow triangles or candles on S3–6 reaching about halfway down segments, becoming narrower and shorter on S7–8, basal spots on  S9–10; S10 otherwise black. Relatively small yellow spots on sides of S7–9. Epiproct distinctly shorter than cerci, sharply bent upward at midlength. *Female*: Colored as male. Pair of black spines project from middle of occiput.

Identification Short, bent epiproct characteristic of male. No other snaketail has diagonal stripe between T3 and T4; all others but **Boreal** lack black markings on face. **Extra-striped** has smallest lateral spots on club of any snaketail in its range. Thus, dorsal and lateral spots about same size in this species, lateral spots conspicuously larger in others. **Pygmy Snaketail** most similar in appearance of end of abdomen but smaller and with wider club and amber-tinged wing bases.

193.1
Extra-striped Snaketail
male—Piscataquis Co,,
ME, July 2006

193.2
Extra-striped Snaketail
female—Penobscot
Co., ME, June 2006

Natural History Both sexes perch on leaves and twigs in shrubs and trees and are seen more often away from than at water.

Habitat Wide variety of clean rivers, from small and swift to large and slow-flowing, more common in latter.

Flight Season ON Jun–Jul, QC Jun–Aug, WI May–Jun, ME May–Jul.

---

194 Pygmy Snaketail *Ophiogomphus howei* TL 31–34, HW 19–21

Description Tiny snaketail with orange wing bases. *Male:* Eyes green, darker than in some other snaketails; face unmarked green. T1–2 well-developed, barely contacting at upper ends; T1 incomplete above. T3 broken in middle, presence of upper part of stripe unusual in snaketails. T4 narrow but complete. Legs black. Abdomen black, short yellow triangles on S3–7 (shortest on S4–6); shorter lines or spots on S8–10, may be absent from S9–10 or S10.  Irregular yellow spots on sides of S7–9. Cerci more slender than in other snaketails, black. Yellow tinge at base of hindwings. *Female:* Colored as male, shows more pale markings on sides. Yellow on hindwings darker, more extensive. Short dark horns near each end of occipital ridge.

Identification Nothing else like this petite, tinted-winged species. **Extra-striped** is most similar snaketail, larger with relatively smaller club and no color in wings. All other very small clubtails lack prominent club present in both sexes of this species and, of course, lack green thorax.

Natural History Males fly rapidly over water, not looking different from numerous other species that do the same, but patrol time of any one individual usually brief, then back into forest. Mature individuals rarely seen otherwise. Both sexes when away from water are probably well up in trees, but mating pairs have been seen in forest clearings in morning not far above the ground, perched on large leaves. Females oviposit rapidly in large circles over areas of current, presence of males confirmed when female is suddenly grabbed and pair flies up into trees.

Habitat Moderate-sized pristine rocky rivers with shallow riffles and mud bottom, usually through woodland.

Flight Season WI May–Jul, ME May–Jul, KY May–Jun.

194.1
Pygmy Snaketail male—Northumberland Co., NB, June 2007, Denis Doucet

194.2
Pygmy Snaketail female—Rusk Co., WI, June 2007, posed

Snaketails - male appendages

Boreal Snaketail

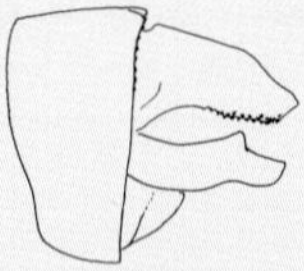

Riffle Snaketail

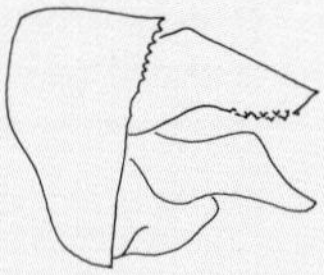

Edmund's Snaketail

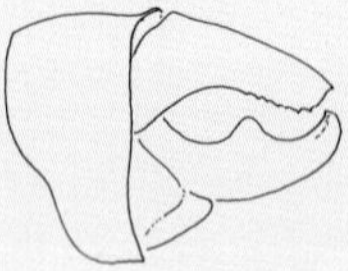

Appalachian Snaketail

Southern Snaketail

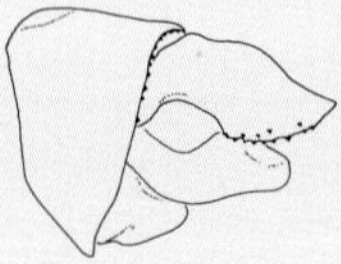

Brook Snaketail

Sioux Snaketail

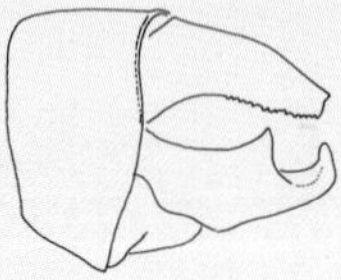

Maine Snaketail

Acuminate Snaketail

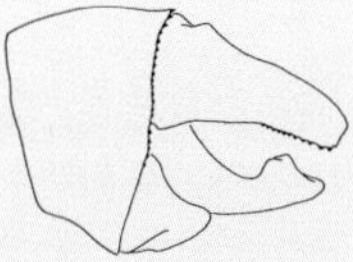

Rusty Snaketail

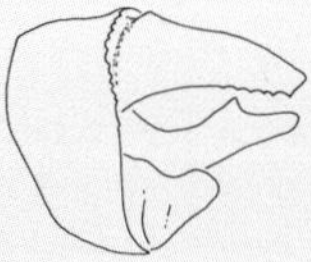

Westfall's Snaketail

St. Croix Snaketail

Extra-striped Snaketail

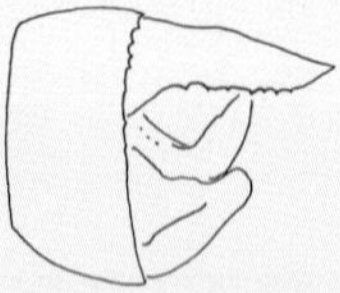

Pygmy Snaketail

These are the smallest of North American clubtails and among the smallest clubtails in the world. Might be mistaken for damselflies in flight. Related to pygmy clubtails by small size and similarities in larval shape and antennae. Both genera occur only in eastern Asia and eastern North America. World 11, NA 2, East 2.

195 Eastern Least Clubtail *Stylogomphus albistylus* TL 31–36, HW 20–23

Description Tiny clubtail of rocky streams with dark, yellow-ringed abdomen, scarcely any club, and white cerci. *Male*: Eyes turquoise to green, face pale yellow. Thorax yellow with dark stripes T1–4 well developed. Legs black. Abdomen black with yellow dorsal stripe on S1–3 , yellow rings on S3–7 almost broken on top, and yellow side spots at base of S8–9. Cerci white. *Female*: Colored as male with slightly larger areas of yellow on abdomen, especially on sides of basal segments. Yellow colors change to gray with old age.

195.1
Eastern Least Clubtail male—Murray Co., GA, June 2005, Marion M. Dobbs

195.2
Eastern Least Clubtail female—Renfrew Co., ON, July 2005, Bev Wigney

Identification Small size and slender body distinctive among clubtails in its range, as are white cerci in both sexes. Much smaller than black and yellow COMMON CLUBTAILS that occur with it. Same size as PYGMY CLUBTAILS, but less ringed abdomen, duller eye color in mature individuals, and dark cerci distinguish latter two species. Overlaps with **Interior Least Clubtail** in some areas (at least central Kentucky and Tennessee, possibly northern Alabama) and could not be distinguished in field. Male cerci in **Interior** slightly longer and more upcurved. Epiproct in **Interior** longer and more deeply forked. Females almost identical, subgenital plate of **Interior** more shallowly forked and with less pointed tips.

Natural History Males perch flat on rocks or in dense herbaceous vegetation, typically at riffles; less often on leaves of trees and shrubs above water. Patrol in circles in fast, bouncy flight low over rapids, when very difficult to follow. Probably come from surrounding trees, as they often fly back up into them. Emergence on flat rocks, tenerals sometimes rather common in trees above river. Females relatively rarely seen, probably up in trees, but when found usually perching on leaves above river. Females oviposit by tapping at intervals in circling path just above riffles, often at high speed.

Habitat Small, clear rivers with moderate current and sand to rock substrates, usually in woodland.

Flight Season ON Jun–Aug, QC Jun–Aug, NS Jul–Sep, ME May–Aug, OH May–Aug, NJ Jun–Sep, KY May–Aug, GA May–Aug.

Comments A few hybrids between the two least clubtail species have been found in central Kentucky and Tennessee, and more study may show additional areas of hybridization. Populations in northeast corner of Mississippi not identified to species.

---

196 Interior Least Clubtail *Stylogomphus sigmastylus* TL 34–37, HW 20–22

Description Just like previous species, ranges farther west. *Male*: Eyes turquoise, face pale yellow. Thorax yellow with stripes T1–4 well developed. Legs black. Abdomen black with yellow dorsal stripe on S1–3, yellow rings on S3–7 almost broken on top, and yellow side spots at base of S8–9. Cerci white. *Female*: Colored as male with slightly larger areas of yellow on abdomen, especially on sides of basal segments. Yellow colors change to gray with old age.

196.1
Interior Least Clubtail male—
Phelps Co., MO, June 2009

196.2
Interior Least Clubtail female—Washington
Co., MO, June 2009, Greg Lasley

Identification Small size and slender body distinctive among clubtails in its range, as are white cerci in both sexes. Much smaller than black and yellow COMMON CLUBTAILS that occur with it. See **Eastern Least Clubtail**.

Natural History Identical to that of Eastern Least Clubtail, as far as known.

Habitat Small, clear rivers with moderate current and sand to rock substrates, usually in woodland.

Flight Season WI Jun–Aug, KY Apr–Oct.

Comments The two least clubtails are known to hybridize, at least occasionally, where their ranges come together. Records of this species in Virginia and North Carolina seem anomalous.

Least Clubtails - male appendages

Eastern Least   Interior Least
Clubtail   Clubtail

Pygmy Clubtails   *Lanthus*

These are the smallest of North American clubtails other than the related least clubtails. With rather similar habits, they look darker overall, and their appendages are entirely black. They are restricted to pristine rocky streams in forested landscapes. The third species is in eastern Asia. World 3, NA 2, East 2.

197 Northern Pygmy Clubtail   *Lanthus parvulus*   TL 33–40, HW 21–26

Description *Male*: Eyes dull green, face cream-colored with black edges. Thorax with T1–2 fused, T3–4 close together and connected by crossbar in center. Legs black. Abdomen black, S1–2 extensively marked with yellow; S3–8 with tiny yellow basal spot low on each side, largest on S3. Appendages black. *Female*: Colored as male, yellow abdominal spots slightly larger and may be tiny spots on S9 as well.

Identification Smaller than all other clubtails in range except **Eastern Least Clubtail**, which has different thoracic pattern, more prominent markings on middle abdominal segments, a bit more of a club, and white cerci. Distinguished from **Southern Pygmy Clubtail** in their wide zone of overlap by different thoracic patterns, **Southern** with only one narrow stripe on sides.

Natural History Males perch on rocks in and at edge of streams, also leaves above them up to head height. Commonly obelisk at hot midday. Females spend much of their time in trees.

197.1
Northern Pygmy
Clubtail male—
Piscataquis Co., ME,
June 2006, Netta Smith

197.2
Northern Pygmy
Clubtail female—
Hampden Co., MA, May
2004, Glenn Corbiere

Habitat Clear, often spring-fed rocky streams with sand or silt deposits inhabited by the larvae. Streams can be tiny, usually within woodland but with light gaps to allow sunlight for adult perches. Only in mountains in southern part of range.

Flight Season QC Jun–Aug, NS Jun–Aug, ME Jun–Jul, OH Jun.

---

198 Southern Pygmy Clubtail *Lanthus vernalis* TL 29–40, HW 20–27

Description *Male:* Eyes dull green, face cream-colored with black edges. Thorax with T1–2 fused, T3 absent, T4 narrow and straight. Legs black. Abdomen black, S1–2 extensively marked with yellow; S3–8 with tiny yellow basal spot low on each side, largest on S3. Appendages black. *Female:* Colored as male, may be tiny yellow spots on S9 as well.

Identification See **Northern Pygmy Clubtail**.

Natural History More likely to perch in shade than Northern Pygmy Clubtail, also prefers to perch on leaves rather than rocks, from just above water to well above it. Immatures soon

198.1
Southern Pygmy
Clubtail male—White
Co., GA, May 2006

198.2
Southern Pygmy
Clubtail female—
Sussex Co., NJ, June
2007, Tom Murray

after emergence easier to find than mature adults, found foraging from leaves in sunny clearings. One female oviposited by tapping water every 3 feet or so while flying upstream not far above the surface. Oviposition flights usually fast and low.

Habitat Much like that of its close relative but also inhabits slightly larger streams.

Flight Season ME Jun–Jul, OH Jun–Jul, NJ May–Jul, KY May–Jun, GA Apr–May.

The four genera of this family are all very much alike in appearance and habits, large black or brown dragonflies with prominent yellow stripes on thorax and yellow-patterned abdomen. Most species occur in Eurasia, where they fly up and down small woodland streams and behave much as the North American species of our single genus do. World 51, NA 9, East 7.

Spiketails   *Cordulegaster*

Spiketails are large black or dark brown dragonflies with similar bright yellow thoracic stripes and species-specific abdominal markings. Relatively small, slightly separated or just touching eyes are either bright blue or bright green. They seem surprisingly unwary for such large dragonflies, easier to approach for photography or capture than most. They fly over sunny clearings, typically quite low, while foraging for small insects and then perch by hanging in herbaceous or shrubby vegetation right out in the open. They may be watching for flying prey from their perch. Wasps and bees seem to be common prey for these large dragonflies. Some individuals hang much like darners; others extend out from a branch at a 45° angle. Males are much more often seen in this situation than females, and they may be looking for females as well as prey. They do not wander as far from breeding habitats as do the similarly large darners that feed from the air. Males are also seen flying long beats up and down streams, from moderate-sized rushing rocky ones to shallow, mossy forest trickles, depending on the species. Cruising beats are often long, so expect to wait until a given individual returns. Mating pairs are rarely seen, but copulation is lengthy, lasting an hour or more, usually in trees near or away from water. Females tend to oviposit after midday, flying along and stopping suddenly to hover over a shallow spot and jab eggs into the substrate with pointed and spikelike (thus the group name) ovipositor, really a "pseudo-ovipositor" formed from the prolonged subgenital plate. Oviposition movements are characteristic of the genus and have been called "bouncing" or compared with a sewing-machine needle. Other black and yellow dragonflies are easily distinguished. Superficially similar river cruisers have much larger eyes and a single stripe on either side of the thorax; they tend to be on larger streams and hang straight down when perched. Dragonhunter has a different pattern on both thorax and abdomen. World 25, NA 9, East 7.

199 Tiger Spiketail   *Cordulegaster erronea*   TL 65–76, HW 42–51

Description   Rather rare large ringed spiketail of tiny forest streams. *Male*: Eyes bright green; face yellow, heavily patterned with black. Thorax blackish with bright yellow stripes, two in front and two on each side. Abdomen black, with yellow rings at base of S1–8. *Female*: Colored like male, with thicker abdomen and subgenital plate extended beyond tip.

Identification   No other spiketail is obviously ringed, except **Say's**, which is smaller, tinged with brown on thorax, has narrow yellow rings between the broad ones, and occurs on the coastal plain farther south. Few other brilliantly ringed dragonflies in range, but note **Zebra Clubtail** is black with yellow-ringed abdomen. Males of that species have a conspicuously clubbed abdomen, females yellow spots along sides of abdomen, and it often perches horizontally.

Natural History   Males patrol up and down streams through much of day, interrupting flights with frequent hovering and changing direction. Males that meet fight and fly off into forest. Oviposits in tiny streams for up to several minutes, tapping water almost twice a second, rising to one body length and dropping again. May lay 350 eggs or more at one

199.1
Tiger Spiketail
male—Floyd Co., GA,
July 2008, Marion M.
Dobbs, posed

199.2
Tiger Spiketail
female—Towns Co., GA,
July 2010, Marion M.
Dobbs

spot. The bouncing motion apparently attracts males, which will not attempt mating with a stationary female.

Habitat Small forest streams and seeps, often with skunk cabbage and interrupted fern.

Flight Season OH Jun–Sep, NJ Jun–Sep, KY May–Aug, GA Jun–Aug.

---

200 Twin-spotted Spiketail   *Cordulegaster maculata*   **TL 64–76, HW 38–49**

Description Large eastern spiketail with yellow-spotted abdomen. *Male*: Eyes green in North, pale blue to turquoise in South, duller and may be brownish below; face pale with dark bar across it, sometimes quite dark above. Thorax dark brown with two yellow stripes on front and pair of yellow stripes on each side. Abdomen blackish-brown with paired yellow spots or triangles on S2–9, two pairs each on S2–4, where each pair pointed toward the other. *Female*: Colored as male, but eyes duller, gray in some. Spots on abdomen distinctly smaller and only on S2–7 or 8. Recognized by long pointed ovipositor extending well beyond end of abdomen.

Identification One of four eastern spiketails with paired spots on abdomen (rings and unpaired central spots in others). **Brown, Delta-spotted,** and **Ouachita Spiketails** all slightly smaller, with smaller spots and yellow lateral stripe at abdomen

200.1
Twin-spotted Spiketail
male—Jackson Co., WI,
June 2007

200.2
Twin-spotted Spiketail
female—Franklin Co.,
NY, June 2008,
Steven Collins, posed

200.3
Twin-spotted Spiketail
female—Union Par., LA,
April 2010,
Kelby Ouchley

base. **Twin-spotted** shows no hint of stripe but usually has two pairs of spots per segment on these segments. Differs from **Arrowhead Spiketail** by paired rather than central markings on abdomen; also slightly smaller. Other large black and yellow dragonflies (**Dragonhunter**, RIVER CRUISERS) patterned differently.

Natural History Appears generally more common than other spiketails. Males fly rapidly up and down breeding streams a few inches above water. On wider streams they stay near one bank but often cross over on narrow streams. Not averse to wending their way through dense branches and flying through tunnels. Stand in water and they will fly around your legs. May become more common later in afternoon and often fly on cloudy and even rainy days. Both sexes feed low in clearings in woodland, where they can be found when away from water, and hang up not far above ground. Copulating pairs into treetops. Females oviposit by hovering a few inches above water with abdomen hanging down obliquely, then dropping quickly with it vertical to push eggs into mud, sand, or fine gravel, quickly ascending and doing it again, as many as 100 times a minute. May then move a few feet and repeat same actions. Typically oviposit in running water.

Habitat Small to midsized rocky streams with good current and muddy pools, typically in forest. Occasionally seen patrolling on larger rivers.

Flight Season ON May–Aug, QC May–Aug, NS May–Aug, WI May–Aug, ME May–Jul, OH May–Jul, NJ Apr–Jun, KY Mar–Jul, LA Mar–Apr, GA Mar–Jun, FL Feb–Apr.

201 Arrowhead Spiketail   *Cordulegaster obliqua*   TL 72–81, HW 41–50

Description Large eastern spiketail with arrowheads down abdomen. Southern individuals are larger. *Male*: Eyes pale green above, brownish below, more blue-green in South; face pale yellow with brown markings, an upper bar and lower spot. Thorax dark brown, almost black, with two broad vivid yellow stripes on each side and two narrower ones on front. Abdomen black with series of yellow arrowhead-shaped marks on S2–7, large blotch on S8, and smaller spot on S9. *Female*: Colored as male, usually lacks spot on S9. Recognized by long pointed ovipositor extending well beyond S10.

Identification Distinguished from other spotted spiketails by central rather than paired

201.1
Arrowhead Spiketail male—Chattooga Co., GA, May 2006; inset males—Early Co., GA, July 2007

201.2
Arrowhead Spiketail
female—Jasper Co., TX,
May 2005

markings on abdomen; also slightly larger. All other large black and yellow dragonflies (**Dragonhunter**, RIVER CRUISERS) patterned very differently.

Natural History Adults spend a week or more away from water until they mature sexually. Males perch in open on twigs or herbaceous stems or patrol up and down over breeding habitat, cruising slowly and steadily at knee to waist height and often having to thread way among tall herbaceous plants. May patrol entire length of small rivulets, stopping to hover occasionally. Males clash when they meet. Both sexes hang in shrubs at waist to chest height at or near water.

Habitat Small swift streams and soft-bottomed muddy seeps in forest, also streams reduced to series of small pools during drier weather. As in some other spiketails, skunk cabbage often present.

Flight Season ON May–Jul, QC Jun, WI May–Aug, ME Jun–Jul, OH May–Jul, NJ Jun–Jul, KY May–Jul, GA May–Aug, FL May–Jul.

Comments The southern populations of larger individuals with blue eyes have been considered subspecies *C. o. fasciata*, but the boundaries of the subspecies are not well defined.

---

202 Say's Spiketail   *Cordulegaster sayi*   TL 60–69, HW 37–42

Description Small ringed southeastern spiketail with brown on thorax, rather rare. *Male*: Eyes green, not especially bright, bordered behind by black; face whitish with single black crossband. Thorax with typical yellow stripes, one on front and two on sides, but also pale brown (magenta in some lights) markings between them. Abdomen black, S1–2 with yellow bands edged with brown; S3–8 with broad yellow ring in middle and narrow yellow ring at end, S9–10 with basal paired yellow spots. *Female*: Colored as male, eyes duller and abdomen thicker and with pointed subgenital plate projecting to extreme tip.

Identification Nothing else like this species within its range (brighter and larger **Tiger Spiketail** farther north).

Natural History Both sexes perch on grass stems and twigs near ground with abdomen from almost horizontal to depressed 45°, then fly around in open areas, presumably hunting. Females oviposit in mucky seepages, one dipping abdomen about 70 times at intervals of less than 1 sec. Often take bees and wasps as prey.

Habitat Small mucky seeps in woodland, either associated with bay swamps in sandhills or ravines in hardwood bluffs. Usually adjacent to open pinewoods used for foraging.

Flight Season GA Mar–Apr, FL Feb–Apr.

202.1
Say's Spiketail male—
Liberty Co., FL, April
2005

202.2
Say's Spiketail
female—Liberty Co.,
FL, April 2008

Description Black northern spiketail with paired yellow abdominal triangles. *Male*: Eyes fairly bright green, face white with black crossband. Thorax with usual yellow stripes, may be narrow stripe between lateral stripes. Abdomen blackish, with yellow lateral stripe running length of S1–3 and yellow backward-pointing triangles at base of S4–8. *Female*: As male but more yellow on abdomen, anterior markings on each segment extended to form an almost continuous stripe from S1 to S8 at most extreme. Also thicker abdomen, subgenital plate projecting to end of abdomen.

Identification Differs from **Twin-spotted Spiketail** by abdominal markings larger and more pointed but a bit smaller on mid abdo-

203.1
Delta-spotted Spiketail
male—Essex Co., VT, June
2007, Bryan Pfeiffer/Wings
Photography

203.2
Delta-spotted Spiketail
female—
Northumberland Co.,
NB, June 2007, Denis
Doucet

men, enough so that posterior markings look larger in flight or at rest. Basal yellow markings more extensive so that sides of S1–3 with a conspicuous stripe. All markings smaller and look about same size in **Twin-spotted**, and no stripe at base; in fact, looks crossbanded there. Abdominal stripe even more pronounced in female **Delta-spotted**, no trace of it in **Twin-spotted**. Female subgenital plate in **Twin-spotted** extends well past end of abdomen, only to end in **Delta-spotted**. **Delta-spotted** also overlaps with **Brown**; see that species.

Natural History Males perch on stems in sunny clearings at an angle of 45° and fly slowly up and down streams hunting for females. Stop often to hover and pivot. Females oviposit along pool edges by thrusting abdomen into shallow water with soft substrate. One female laid eggs into moss just above water in seep.

Habitat Spring-fed seeps and small streams, usually wooded but also in open glades and powerline corridors. Skunk cabbage commonly present.

Flight Season ON May–Aug, QC May–Aug, NS May–Aug, WI Jun–Jul, ME Jun–Jul, OH May–Jul, NJ Apr–Jul.

Description Brown southern spiketail with paired yellow abdominal triangles. *Male:* Eyes dull pale blue to turquoise; face whitish with black crossband. Thorax brown with usual yellow stripes. Abdomen brown, with yellow lateral stripe running length of S1–3 and yellow backward-pointing triangles at base of S4–8. *Female:* As male but thicker abdomen; pointed subgenital plate projects to end of abdomen.

Identification Differs from **Twin-spotted Spiketail** in same ways as **Delta-spotted** does. Differs from **Delta-spotted** only slightly, by usually being brown rather than black and usually with bluish eyes; dark stripe across face and leg color show this difference. **Delta-spotted** more likely to have additional fine pale stripe between lateral thoracic stripes. Minor structural difference in male appendages. Overlaps with **Delta-spotted** in narrow band through a number of states.

Natural History Both sexes forage and perch low in sunny clearings.

Habitat Small woodland streams.

Flight Season OH May–Jul, KY May–Jun, LA Mar–Apr, GA Apr–Jul.

Comments Where the range of this and Delta-spotted Spiketail approach one another, intermediate specimens have been found, and identification to species may not always be possible.

204.1
Brown Spiketail
male—Chattooga Co.,
GA, April 2006, Marion
M. Dobbs

204.2
Brown Spiketail
female—Murray Co.,
GA, May 2006

Description Arkansas spiketail with paired yellow abdominal triangles. *Male*: Eyes pale green; face whitish with black crossband. Thorax brownish-black with usual yellow stripes. Abdomen brown, with yellow lateral stripe running length of S1–3 and yellow backward-pointing triangles at base of S4–8. Abdominal spots wider toward rear. *Female*: As male but thicker abdomen; pointed subgenital plate projects to end of abdomen.

Identification Separated geographically from similar **Brown** and **Delta-spotted Spiketails**. Only other spiketails that occur in range are **Arrowhead** and **Twin-spotted**. **Arrowhead** has totally different abdominal pattern of central markings. **Twin-spotted** has paired abdominal spots but distinguished from **Ouachita** by smaller spots and no stripe at abdomen base. Female **Twin-spotted** has much longer subgenital plate than **Ouachita**, projecting well beyond abdomen tip. Also different breeding habitat.

Natural History Males fly low up and down streams; both sexes hang up low in herbaceous vegetation.

Habitat Tiny streams overhung by woodland vegetation.

Flight Season Entire range May.

205.1
Ouachita Spiketail
male—Montgomery
Co., AL, May 2006,
posed

205.2
Ouachita Spiketail
female—Montgomery
Co., AL, May 2006,
posed

Cruisers are easily recognizable large dragonflies with large eyes and long legs that fly up and down streams and rivers or along lake shores and then hang up vertically in trees and shrubs. They are brown to black with a single pale stripe on each side of the thorax and a spotted or ringed abdomen. The abdomen is often slightly clubbed in males, a good distinction from darners as they cruise overhead in feeding flight. Some species of cruisers have brilliant emerald green eyes, and some authors have considered this a subfamily of the emeralds, Corduliidae. Other authors combine both of those families with the skimmers, Libellulidae, but the long-legged sprawling larvae of cruisers are quite distinct from larvae of either emeralds or skimmers, and no other North American dragonflies are very similar to cruisers. Wing venation of the three groups is different, only emeralds and skimmers showing a distinct anal loop, and the triangles of cruisers are arranged more like those of clubtails and darners. Most species are in the Old World tropics, and the group probably reached North America relatively recently and extends only as far south as the Mexican Plateau in the New World. World 122, NA 9, East 7.

Brown Cruisers   *Didymops*

These are smaller, duller editions of the large and showy river cruisers, body color brown instead of black and pale markings cream rather than yellow. Eyes are greenish but much duller than those of river cruisers and meet over only a short distance. When perched, they often hold the abdomen more elevated than river cruisers do. The flight season is earlier, and the two genera probably seldom overlap in time. Brown cruisers are North American endemics, one species restricted to the extreme Southeast, where it is a lake-dweller. World 2, NA 2, East 2.

206 Stream Cruiser   *Didymops transversa*   TL 56–60, HW 34–38

Description Small brown cruiser of eastern streams. *Male*: Eyes brown with green highlight above. Thorax brown with narrow whitish to pale yellow stripe on each side. Abdomen brown with dull pale yellow to whitish spots on S3–8, becoming progressively shorter and wider toward rear; anterior ones split into pairs by narrow brown median line. Abdomen distinctly clubbed. Tiny brown spot at base of each wing. *Female*: Eyes brown. Colored as male but spots on basal abdominal segments may be larger, creating a more mottled effect. Abdomen thick, no hint of club.

Identification See **Florida Cruiser**, most similar species. Smaller and paler than RIVER CRUISERS, generally flies earlier in season. Cerci of **Stream Cruiser** whitish in both sexes, dark in RIVER CRUISERS. Abdominal spots often but not always conspicuous in flight. Might be mistaken for CLUBTAIL except for single pale stripe on each side of otherwise dark thorax, also large eyes and flying and perching behavior. **Springtime Darner** of similar size and flying in same season and habitat shows blue-spotted abdomen, two stripes on sides of thorax. No EMERALDS have dark abdomens with light spots.

Natural History Males fly rapidly and usually below waist height up and down streams in beats up to 100 yards long, also along lake shores; sometimes hover, unlike river cruisers. Otherwise hangs up from almost horizontal to almost vertical fairly low in trees and shrubs. Ovipositing female flies along shore or around tree trunks and taps water rapidly at varying intervals. Feeds on insects as large as other dragonflies, during short foraging beats in or out of woodland, from near ground to above head height; most foraging at lower levels than river cruisers.

Habitat Sandy forest streams and rivers, less commonly large lakes.

206.1
Stream Cruiser
male—Burnett Co., WI,
June 2007

206.2
Stream Cruiser
female—Aiken Co., SC,
May 2008

Flight Season ON May–Sep, QC May–Jul, NS May–Aug, WI May–Jul, ME May–Jul, OH May–
Aug, NJ Apr–Aug, KY Apr–Aug, LA Mar–Apr, GA Mar–Jun, FL Jan–May.
Distribution Extends slightly farther west in Oklahoma and Texas.

---

207 Florida Cruiser *Didymops floridensis*　　　　　**TL 65–68, HW 37–41**

Description A cream-ringed brown cruiser of Florida sand lakes.
Male: Eyes mostly dull green; face cream-colored, with broad black
markings. Thorax brown with single cream-colored lateral stripe
and blackish markings in sutures. Abdomen with S1–2 mostly
brown; S3–10 dark brown to blackish, with cream-colored basal
markings on S3–8, forming obvious rings on S3–6 and dorsal spots on S7–8. *Female*: Colored
much as male; abdominal spots may be larger and with pale areas between them. Abdomen cylindrical with scarcely hint of club.

207.1
Florida Cruiser male—
Leon Co., FL, April 2008,
posed

207.2
Florida Cruiser female—
Seminole Co., FL, March
2008, Paul Hueber

Identification Only similar species **Stream Cruiser**, which has smaller abdominal markings, looking like spots rather than rings and with many of them divided by brown midline. Facial markings brown in **Stream**, black in **Florida**. **Florida** also lacks brown markings present at wing bases in **Stream**. Typically in different habitats in range of **Florida**.

Natural History Males fly along shore on sexual patrol, usually quite low, or out over lake. Female oviposited in low flight at high speed with occasional tap. Rarely seen in feeding flight.

Habitat Sand-bottomed lakes, with or without fringing woodland. Often but not always belts of tall grasses around these lakes.

Flight Season FL Jan–May.

River Cruisers *Macromia*

These large to very large dragonflies with big green eyes and somewhat metallic bodies cruise long distances along river and stream banks. They are easily distinguished from other large fliers (darners, spiketails) by a single pale stripe on each side of thorax and slightly clubbed abdomen in males of most species. Most of the species are very similar to one another, but males have a low keel at the distal end of the mesotibiae (middle legs) that distinguishes some of them. This is almost impossible to see except in hand but may be visible in photos from some angles. And don't be fooled by prominent full-length keels on metatibiae (hind legs). Females can be very difficult to distinguish. The group is very diverse in tropical Asia, with only a few species extending into the temperate zone of Asia and one in Europe. In addition to the five eastern species with brilliant emerald-green eyes (brown when immature), there are two duller central and western species. Some eastern species apparently hybridize. World 78, NA 7, East 5.

Description Most common and widespread black and yellow club-tailed river cruiser. Description refers to southern subspecies *M. i. georgina*. *Male*: Eyes brilliant green, face black with yellow spots on top of frons and crossband on front. Thorax metallic green-black with upwardly pointed yellow stripe on front and wide yellow stripe on each side. Abdomen shiny black with yellow ring on S2; paired triangles on S3–6, smallest on 6; and median spots on S7–8. Also yellow lateral spots under S7–9. *Female*: Colored as male, but thorax browner, yellow abdominal markings averaging larger and

not much smaller on S6 than S7; abdomen not clubbed. Wings, especially tips, get increasingly orange-brown with age, not the case in males. The northern *M. i. illinoiensis* is much less marked with yellow in both sexes. Typically thorax with no anterior stripe in *illinoiensis*,

208.1
Swift River Cruiser
(*illinoiensis*) male—
Rusk Co., WI, June 2007

208.2
Swift River Cruiser
(*illinoiensis*) female—
Eau Claire Co., WI, June
2007

208.3
Swift River Cruiser (*georgina*)
male—Decatur Co., GA,
July 2007, posed

208.4
Swift River Cruiser
(*georgina*) female—
Travis Co., TX, June 2005

stripe usually prominent in *georgina*. In male of northern subspecies, abdomen with narrow, interrupted (or scarcely evident) ring on S2, very small spots on S3–4, and no yellow on S5–6. In northern females, abdominal spots vary from virtually absent to rather large, but yellow spot much larger on S7 than on S6. In southern females, spots all about same size.

Identification Most common river cruiser in most parts of range. Probably impossible to distinguish in flight from **Allegheny** or **Mountain River Cruisers**, must be captured and examined. See those species. See technical manuals for differences in male hamules in these three species. Females are extremely difficult. Female **Allegheny** and **Mountain** have slightly longer legs, hind tibiae usually 13 mm or longer (12 mm or shorter in this species), but enough size variation to prevent that difference from being definitive. Distinguished from larger **Royal River Cruiser** by abdominal club, complete stripe around S2 (broken at top in **Royal**), and pale spots on top of frons. Also, in both sexes, **Royal** usually with small paired spots or no markings on S8, **Swift** with single median triangle or crossbar. **Swift** differs from **Gilded** by much less pale color everywhere: small instead of large spots on top of frons, shorter and narrower stripes on front of thorax, and smaller abdominal markings. In any view, abdomen of **Swift** looks black with pale spots, that of **Gilded** banded or ringed black and yellow. Flight usually more rapid, higher, and farther out from shore than vaguely similar **Twin-spotted Spiketail**.

Natural History Both sexes cruise over clearings, from just above ground to well up in tree-tops, and hang up on bare limbs of shrubs and trees, even weeds, from knee height to high in canopy. Fly regular beats in small clearings, sometimes only at certain times, probably hanging up in intense heat. Males at water fly long beats not far above water, often sticking close to shore, often with abdomen slightly arched. Accelerate like rocket in lengthy chases of one another, especially when males after females. When ovipositing, females fly low and fast from near shore to midriver, much as males, tapping water at intervals of up to 30 feet in straight or curved path. Also seen flying slowly in smaller area, tapping water three to four times among branches of shrub fallen in water, then reversing direction and repeating. At least in northern areas, both sexes cruise over water from dawn until just about dark and may be active under cloudy skies.

Habitat Large streams and rivers, clear to muddy with slow to fast currents, rocks or not. At open lakes in northern part of range.

Flight Season ON Jun–Sep, QC Jun–Aug, NS May–Sep, IA Jul–Sep, WI May–Aug, ME May–Sep, OH May–Sep, NJ May–Sep, KY May–Sep, LA May–Aug, GA May–Oct, FL Mar–Nov.

Distribution Extends farther west in Oklahoma and Texas, also records from Montana and South Dakota.

Comments Populations on southern coastal plain, extending up Mississippi River valley, are subspecies *M. i. georgina*, often called Georgia River Cruiser. Northern populations, including those in Appalachian chain, are *M. i. illinoiensis*, often called Illinois River Cruiser (also former name for species).

---

209 Allegheny River Cruiser *Macromia alleghaniensis* TL 65–72, HW 45–50

Description Widespread long-legged river cruiser with short mesotibial keels and yellow ring around S7. *Male*: Eyes brilliant green; face black with yellow band across middle, pair of small yellow spots above. Thorax shiny black (brown in younger individuals) with single yellow lateral stripe. Abdomen mostly black, with yellow markings as follows: ring around S2 (interrupted at top), small paired spots on S3–6, ring surrounding S7, central spot on S8,

209.1
Allegheny River Cruiser male—
Cumberland Co., TN,
June 2006, posed

209.2
Allegheny River Cruiser female—
Rabun Co., GA, June 2008,
Giff Beaton, posed

and tiny spot low on each side of S8–9. *Female:* Colored much like male but yellow ring on S7 interrupted laterally. Wings usually clear, in some cases amber-tinged; perhaps amber, if acquired, appears later than in other river cruisers. Abdomen cylindrical, no hint of club.

Identification Occurs with and similar to **Mountain** and both subspecies of **Swift**. Male distinguished from all of these by complete yellow ring on S7. Further distinguished from male "Illinois" **Swift** by almost complete yellow ring on S2, continuous on sides and just broken at top. "Georgia" **Swift** seems always to have that ring broad and continuous at top, probably good distinction from **Allegheny** if it can be seen; **Mountain** also has it broken. For confirmation, tibial keel in male extends only about one-fifth length of mesotibia, around half or more in **Mountain** and **Swift**. Female indistinguishable from females of these other species in field, difficult enough in hand. Green eyes (maturity) and untinted wings in female might indicate **Allegheny**.

Natural History Males fly rapidly up and down streams, mostly but not always near shore, usually quite low but said also to fly higher and slower than Illinois. May prefer to fly late in afternoon. Cruise up and down roads through woodland, in sun and shade, or fly up higher into forest canopy. Female oviposited by flying fairly rapidly along vertical bank in shade, tapping water at 3- to 6-foot intervals.

Habitat Slow-flowing streams and rivers, rocky or not.

Flight Season OH Jun–Aug, NJ Jun–Sep, KY Jun–Aug.

---

210 Mountain River Cruiser *Macromia margarita*   TL 72–78, HW 46–52

Description A rather uncommon large, long-legged, brightly spotted river cruiser of the interior uplands. *Male:* Eyes brilliant green; face black with yellow band across middle, pair of small yellow spots above. Thorax shiny black (brown in younger individuals) with single yellow lateral stripe. Abdomen mostly black, with yellow markings as follows: ring around S2 (broken at top), small paired spots on S3–6, larger central spots on S7–8, and tiny spot low

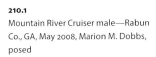

210.1
Mountain River Cruiser male—Rabun Co., GA, May 2008, Marion M. Dobbs, posed

210.2
Mountain River Cruiser male—
Franklin Co., NC, July 2008,
Marion M. Dobbs; arrow points to
tibial keel

210.3
Mountain River Cruiser
female—Macon Co., NC,
July 2008, Giff Beaton

on each side of S8–9. *Female*: Colored much like male but lower half of eyes duller, yellow ring on S2 interrupted laterally, abdominal spots usually larger than those of male. Abdomen cylindrical, no hint of club. Wings tinged with brown at maturity.

Identification River cruisers are among the biggest challenge of any eastern odonates to identify. **Mountain** averages very slightly larger than **Allegheny** and **Swift**, but size would not allow identification. **Mountain** has more prominent yellow stripe across face than **Alleghany** and northern ("Illinois") form of **Swift** (might be useful in field for both sexes), the two that most often might occur with it. Keel extends half length of male mesotibia in **Mountain**, slightly shorter in northern **Swift**, and even shorter in others. Yellow on sides of S2 continuous in **Mountain** and "Georgia" **Swift** (these two barely overlap), interrupted in "Illinois" **Swift** (present in most of range of **Mountain**). Spot on top of S7 distinguishes male from male **Allegheny**, which has ring around S7. Subgenital plate longer in **Mountain** than in **Allegheny**.

Natural History Habits apparently like other river cruisers. Little known because of difficulty of distinction from similar species in field.

Habitat Rocky mountain streams and rivers with good current.

Flight Season GA Jun.

Description Most brightly marked river cruiser, showing almost as much yellow as black. Smaller in southern part of range. *Male*: Eyes brilliant green, face white with wide black bar across front. Thorax metallic green-black with wide cream stripe on front and side. Abdomen shiny black with wide cream to yellow markings, ring on S2 (may be interrupted at top) and large basal spots on S3–8. Spots on S3–6 partially split by black middorsal line. Wings strongly amber-tinged throughout in some areas. *Female*: Colored as male, but pale spots on abdomen more separated, ring on S2 always interrupted at top; abdomen not clubbed.

Identification Largest expanse of yellow/cream of any river cruiser, with wide, complete stripes on front of thorax and large spots on abdomen, occupying almost half of each segment S3–8. Much yellow visible in flight, other species look black. Yellow at tip of vertex diagnostic for **Gilded** if it can be seen. **Swift River Cruiser** of *georgina* subspecies similar in size and shape, also with pale color on top of frons but black vertex. **Swift** usually has incomplete antehumeral stripe and smaller abdominal spots, encompassing much less than half of each segment and minuscule on S6, at least in males. Larger **Royal River Cruiser**

211.1
Gilded River Cruiser
male—Washington Co.,
MO, June 2009, Greg
Lasley, posed

211.2
Gilded River Cruiser
female—Clark Co., AR,
May 2006, Giff Beaton,
posed

differs in same way, also has no evident club at abdomen tip. **Royal** also has top of frons almost entirely black. **Gilded** is only river cruiser in which males, at least in Ozark/Ouachita area, have gold-tinted wings.

Natural History Males fly long beats over river, often near shore, even when this involves deviating around beds of water plants and overhanging shrubs. Females only occasionally encountered hanging in woods, both sexes in cruising flight over clearings.

Habitat Clear rivers with long pools and moderate current, in or out of woodland.

Flight Season OH Jun–Aug.

Distribution Extends south through central Texas.

Comments Perhaps hybridizes locally (best known from Ohio) with Royal River Cruiser to produce distinctive populations named *Macromia wabashensis*; this is considered a valid species by some workers, and the situation needs further research.

---

212 Royal River Cruiser *Macromia taeniolata* TL 75–91, HW 46–59

Description Largest river cruiser, with no abdominal club, yellow markings relatively restricted. *Male*: Eyes brilliant green, face mostly metallic green-black with yellow crossband. Thorax metallic green-black and brown with wide yellow side stripe and more restricted yellow antehumeral stripe pointed above. Abdomen shiny black with yellow markings: interrupted ring on S2, small paired spots on midsegment S3–8, those on S7 larger and fused into one. *Female*: Colored as male but abdominal spots slightly larger, usually double on S7 and may be lacking from S8. Wings largely suffused with amber.

Identification Overlaps with all other river cruisers. Distinguished from all by larger size (not always easy to determine in field), very little indication of abdominal club in male (quite

212.1
Royal River Cruiser
male—Travis Co., TX,
August 2007, Greg
Lasley

212.2
Royal River Cruiser
female—Hillsborough
Co., FL, August 2009,
Marion M. Dobbs

distinctive in males overhead), generally less yellow all over (much less than **Gilded**). Other three species (**Allegheny**, **Mountain**, and **Swift**) have large central pale spots on S7–8, **Royal** smaller and/or divided spots, easily visible on perched individuals and perhaps discernible on passing ones. Females also with smaller abdominal spots than other species; most like "Georgia" **Swift** because of partial anterior thoracic stripes. No yellow spots under abdomen tip as in other species, would be diagnostic in ventral view along with narrow abdomen.

Natural History Males cruise up and down rivers or over lakes at knee height or a bit above, often near shore but at times farther out, going long distances in one direction before returning on same path. Close enough to shore and steady enough in flight that capture is not difficult. Sexual patrol flights more common in morning but also seen in afternoon. Both sexes hang up in trees near breeding areas and feed well above ground in open areas or among treetops, sometimes in feeding swarms with other large dragonflies. Copulating pairs also hang up in trees. Oviposition may be leisurely at one spot or in rapid flight with tapping at long intervals.

Habitat Wooded streams and rivers, sometimes at large, sand-bottomed lakes. Tends to be at larger, slower rivers than other river cruisers.

Flight Season ON Jul–Aug, IA Jul–Oct, WI Jun–Jul, OH Jul–Sep, KY Jun–Sep, LA May–Aug, GA May–Sep, FL Apr–Nov.

Comments Probably hybridizes ("*Macromia wabashensis*") with Gilded River Cruiser, situation still poorly understood.

This family is named for the brilliant green eyes (red-brown when immature) characteristic of most species and metallic green bodies of some. The body is generally dark, with pale markings at abdomen base same color as pale areas on thorax and typically a pale ring at junction of S2 and S3, continued on other segments in some "ringed" species. No other North American odonates have such coloration, but not all emeralds exhibit it. Most of northern affinities, they seem well protected against low temperatures by hairiness (not of the same origin as mammal hairs) of thorax and, often, abdomen. Hairs usually golden, producing golden haze around otherwise very dark thorax. Few structural characters distinguish emeralds from skimmers, but note short anal loop in hindwings, not very foot-shaped, and soft keel variously developed on tibiae of at least third pair of legs. Male emeralds also have a small auricle on each side of S2 and slightly angulate hindwing bases, like other dragonfly families but unlike skimmers. Emeralds are all fliers except for the rather aberrant boghaunters that perch like skimmers. When they perch, the larger, long-bodied emeralds hang up like darners, but the smaller ones often perch flat on leaves. Many emeralds are restricted to characteristic northern habitats—bogs and fens. World 251, NA 50, East 47.

Boghaunters *Williamsonia*

The two species in this genus are rather different from the other emeralds, the smallest on the continent and the only ones that typically perch on the ground and tree trunks. The eyes are duller than in most other emeralds and the bodies dark and nonmetallic with white or yellow markings. Both species are restricted to acid bogs and thus quite local over much of their ranges. They are among the earliest odonates to emerge in spring. World 2, NA 2, East 2.

213 Ebony Boghaunter *Williamsonia fletcheri* TL 29–35, HW 21–23

Description Very small dark emerald that behaves like a skimmer. *Male*: Eyes pale greenish-gray, becoming bright green with age; face metallic greenish-black. Thorax brown with hints of metallic green and fine whitish transverse lines at upper edge of front. Abdomen glossy black with white rings at base of S3–4, rarely further. Extreme base of wings tinged with orange. *Female*: Eyes duller and darker than those of male, abdomen thicker.

Identification Distinguished from quite similar **Ringed Boghaunter** by mostly plain abdomen. Basal rings narrow and whitish rather than broad and yellow. Size, shape, color, and perching habits make it also likely to be mistaken for **Black Meadowhawk** or WHITEFACE. All WHITEFACES have white faces (dark in boghaunter), brown eyes (gray to greenish in

213.1
Ebony Boghaunter
male—Jackson Co., WI,
June 2007

213.2
Ebony Boghaunter
female—Worcester
Co., MA, May 2004,
Tom Murray

boghaunter), and red or yellow markings on thorax and/or red or yellow spots on abdomen. **Black Meadowhawk** has brown eyes, more slender abdomen, and, except for mature males, yellow spots on thorax and abdomen. Also almost no overlap in flight season. Among other emeralds, **Petite** and **Racket-tailed** small enough to be confusing, but note different abdomen shape and perching and flight habits.

Natural History Both sexes rest flat on ground, logs, or tree trunks. Although other emeralds from time to time land on flat surfaces, most hang from leaves or twigs. Male boghaunters perch on twigs and bog mat at small bog pools and make short flights over the pools, but copulating pairs often seen away from water. Oviposits in small pools with or without floating sphagnum. Early-season species.

Habitat Acid bogs, usually surrounded by woodland and full of sphagnum and other mosses but always with at least some open water, if only small pools.

Flight Season ON May–Jul, QC May–Jun, NS May–Jun, WI May–Jul, ME May–Jun.

214 Ringed Boghaunter *Williamsonia lintneri* TL 32–34, HW 20–22

Description Very small black bog-dwelling emerald with gray eyes and yellow-ringed abdomen. *Male*: Eyes gray, face yellow. Thorax black, somewhat metallic and with yellow band crossing front at wing bases. Abdomen with prominent terminal yellow rings on S2–8. Touch of yellow at all wing bases. *Female*: Colored as male, with thicker abdomen.

214.1
Ringed Boghaunter
male—Wood Co., WI,
May 2007, Ken
Tennessen

214.2
Ringed
Boghaunter
female—
Worcester Co., MA,
May 2007, Bryan
Pfeiffer/Wings
Photography

Identification Most similar to **Ebony Boghaunter**, easily distinguished by prominent golden rings entire length of abdomen. Much smaller, and with broader rings, than **Ringed Emerald** and other similar STRIPED EMERALDS. Note female **Petite Emerald** has yellow-spotted abdomen, not complete rings. No other emeralds perch flat on ground or logs like boghaunters. Early flight season also a good clue for these rare emeralds.

Natural History About the same as Ebony Boghaunter, perching on ground in sandy clearings or on roads or tree trunks. Similar behavior at water and similarly early flight season. Rather inactive, seldom seen breeding. Adult maturation time around 10–14 days away from water.

Habitat Acid bogs with scattered open pools in wooded landscape; submerged sphagnum usually present.

Flight Season WI May–Jun, ME Apr–Jun.

Common Emeralds   *Cordulia*

This genus is most closely related to the striped (*Somatochlora*) and little (*Dorocordulia*) emeralds, distinguished from them by forked epiproct of males and minor differences in venation. Single European and Asian species closely related to American one. World 3, NA 1, East 1.

215 American Emerald   *Cordulia shurtleffii*   TL 43–50, HW 29–32

Description Medium-sized, unmarked dark emerald with slight abdominal club. *Male*: Eyes brilliant green, face dull brownish, iridescent green-black above. Thorax brown with metallic green stripes in sutures between sections. Abdomen shiny black, S1–2 mostly orange-brown on sides. *Female*: Colored as male, abdomen obviously thicker. Wings become brownish with age.

Identification Petite Emerald rather similar but smaller and lacking narrow white ring around abdomen base characteristic of **American**. **Racket-tailed Emerald** also similar but smaller, with more pronounced club. **American** lacks yellow spots at base of S3 present in both of these species. Smaller and shorter-bodied than STRIPED EMERALDS with which it might occur, no trace of yellow markings on thorax, and appearing earlier in season. Superficially most like smallest species **Brush-tipped** and **Ocellated Emeralds**, but those with prominent thoracic markings. In hand, thorax bronzy brown, not metallic green-black of most STRIPED EMERALDS. Darker and with brighter

215.1
American Emerald male—
Penobscot Co., ME, July 2006

215.2
American Emerald female—150 Mile
House, BC, July 2006

green eyes than BASKETTAILS of similar size and flight habits. SUNDRAGONS are also similar but have yellow lateral spots on most abdominal segments and color at the wing bases; they breed in streams.

Natural History Males fly over open water or along shore vegetation beds, typically at waist to knee height, alternating rapid flight and brief hovering. Shoreline patrols 30–80 feet long but not territorial; males change patrolling areas frequently. Can be very common. Activity greater on cool mornings and afternoons than at warmer middays, when most leave water. Perch by hanging up from twigs or landing horizontally on leaves, sometimes ground vegetation. Copulation at least partly in flight, fairly lengthy. Females oviposit by flying rapidly in straight line, touching water every few feet, typically along shores overhung by vegetation. Oviposition continues late into afternoon in shade. Sometimes in mixed feeding swarms in open areas with other emeralds, especially baskettails in spring; flight from just above ground to head height. Crane flies preferred diet in some areas. Sometimes hovers among plants in an effort to flush prey, often successful.

Habitat Great variety of lakes and ponds, mostly but not always in forested country. Beaver ponds and bog lakes typical.

Flight Season ON Apr–Aug, QC May–Sep, NS May–Aug, WI May–Aug, ME May–Aug, OH May–Jun, NJ May–Jul.

Distribution West across northern North America to Alaska, south in mountains to California, Utah, and Colorado.

American Emerald - male appendages

American Emerald   American Emerald

Little Emeralds *Dorocordulia*

This small genus of northeastern North American species includes some of the smallest of our emeralds. With bright green eyes and dark, metallic body, they could be mistaken for the smallest striped emeralds (*Somatochlora*), and in fact they are closely related. They perch more often in plain sight (perhaps just lower) than other emeralds and commonly perch on top of leaves. World 2, NA 2, East 2.

216 Petite Emerald *Dorocordulia lepida*   TL 37–43, HW 26–29

Description Very small dark emerald with yellow at base of very slightly clubbed abdomen. *Male*: Eyes brilliant green, face dull yellowish-brown. Thorax metallic brown with metallic green markings on front and toward rear of each side. Abdomen black, some yellow-orange on S1–2 and large spots on each side of S3; those markings and tiny yellow basal side spots on S4–7 obscured with age. *Female*: Colored about as male but green on thorax less vivid. More yellow on abdomen, including entire sides of S1–3 and large basal lateral spots on S4–7, becoming smaller toward rear.

Identification Male distinctive by small size and narrow abdomen as well as typical emerald-green eyes and dark body. Abdomen of male much narrower than similar **Racket-tailed Emerald**, easily distinguished in flight or at rest. Females of the two species similarly shaped, but **Petite** with much more prominent yellow markings on midabdomen. Much smaller than similarly colored STRIPED EMERALDS, not so much smaller than **American Emerald** and shaped about the same. Fine whitish ring at end of S2 distinguishes either sex of **American**; that ring lacking in **Petite**, and female **Petite** has yellow markings along abdomen lacking in **American**. **Petite** much more limited in range. Female **Petite**, with yellow spots on abdomen, somewhat like **Uhler's Sundragon**, which is larger and has dark markings at wing bases.

Natural History Males fly low over water, often near shore, perhaps lower and closer than Racket-tailed with less hovering. Both sexes forage over small clearings in woodland, often lower than other emeralds.

216.1
Petite Emerald male—Ocean Co., NJ, June 2007, Steven Collins

216.2
Petite Emerald female—Hillsborough Co., NH, July 2006

Habitat Lakes, ponds, and small slow-flowing streams, most common at acid bog ponds.
Flight Season NS Jun–Aug, ME May–Aug, NJ May–Jul.

217 Racket-tailed Emerald *Dorocordulia libera* TL 37–43, HW 26–31

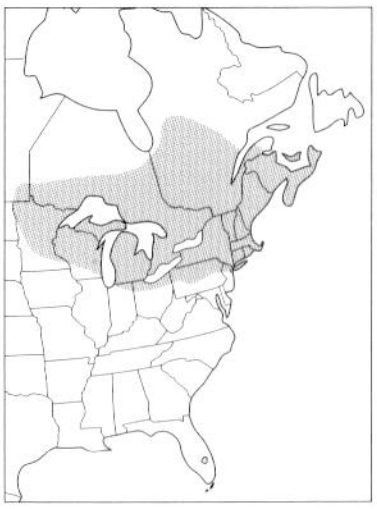

Description Small, dark emerald with conspicuous club. *Male*: Eyes brilliant green, face shiny black. Thorax metallic green or bronze, mixed with brown. Abdomen shiny black, yellow markings low on sides of S1–2 and small paired spots at base of S3. End of abdomen dramatically widened (like tennis racket). *Female*: Colored as male but pale spots on S3 larger, more obvious from above; "racket" not so wide.

Identification Smaller than most other green-eyed emeralds, with more prominently expanded abdomen. With metallic thorax and black abdomen, most similar to **American Emerald**, which is larger, with more pale color on face, less prominent club, white ring at abdomen base, and no pale spots on S3. Smallest STRIPED EMERALDS, **Brush-tipped** and **Ocellated**, with yellow markings on sides of thorax and expanded part of abdomen farther forward and not as wide. Female might be confused with **Uhler's Sundragon**, but that has yellow spots along abdomen and no hint of club.

Natural History Males fly back and forth somewhat irregularly over marsh vegetation or farther out over open water at knee to waist height, a bit higher than the larger American

217.1
Racket-tailed Emerald
male—Wood Co., WI,
June 2007

217.2
Racket-tailed Emerald
female—Penobscot
Co., ME, June 2006

Emeralds often found in the same spots. Females oviposit by tapping surface in open water or in vegetation beds. When feeding, both sexes cruise around over short beats in open areas, usually below tops of tall shrubs and very often in tiny forest clearings. Land more frequently than other emeralds, even occasionally on ground. Because of this, easiest emerald to photograph. Also, like other emeralds, cruise around people to take attendant black flies!

Habitat Lakes and large ponds, commonly associated with bogs.

Flight Season ON May–Aug, QC May–Aug, NS May–Aug, WI May–Aug, ME May–Aug, OH May–Jul, NJ May–Aug.

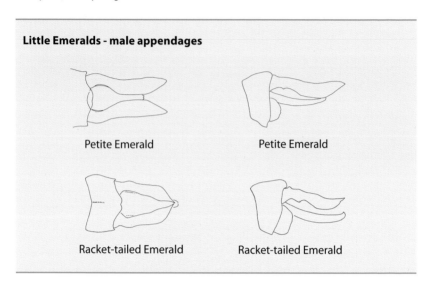

Little Emeralds - male appendages

Petite Emerald   Petite Emerald

Racket-tailed Emerald   Racket-tailed Emerald

Sundragons *Helocordulia*

These are small, dark, emeralds of eastern forests with green eyes but no conspicuous green on bodies. The male abdomen is more obviously expanded toward the tip than in other small emeralds. They have bright yellow spots on a black abdomen, some color at the wing bases, and often visible (especially at close range) dark spots to mark crossveins at front of all wings. They fly up and down streams or cruise lightly over sunny clearings, then hang up on a stem at an oblique angle. Perhaps closely related to baskettails, they differ in color and wing venation as well as details of the genitalia. World 2, NA 2, East 2.

218 Selys's Sundragon *Helocordulia selysii*   TL 38–41, HW 26–28

Description Small dark southeastern emerald with small but obvious wing spots. *Male*: Eyes blue or blue-green, face yellow-orange. Thorax brown with metallic green highlights. Abdomen black, S3 orange at base and tiny orange basal spots along sides of S4–8. *Female*: Colored as male, spots on S4–8 larger. Both sexes with series of dark brown markings at crossveins along front edge of wings, more prominent toward base; larger spots at base.

Identification Only **Uhler's Sundragon** very similar. **Uhler's** has orange marking mixed with black at hindwing base, **Selys's** not.

218.1
Selys's Sundragon
male—McCurtain
Co., OK, March 2008,
Berlin Heck

218.2
Selys's Sundragon
female—McCurtain
Co., OK, March 2008,
Berlin Heck

Yellow spots on abdomen average slightly larger in **Uhler's** than in **Selys's**, especially in females. Other small emeralds in range of sundragons include BASKETTAILS and SHADOW-DRAGONS, both with brown or mostly brown abdomen not expanded toward tip. SHADOWDRAGONS have brown eyes and a yellow spot on either side of the thorax. Female **Double-ringed Pennant** somewhat similar, with black, yellow-ringed abdomen, but that species has black and yellow thorax, reddish eyes, and different behavior.

Natural History Males fly up and down streams, not far above water. Pairs copulate in flight, then perched. Both sexes cruise for food in clearings and perch low in vegetation. Very early flight season.

Habitat Woodland streams.

Flight Season LA Mar–Apr, GA Mar–Apr, FL Mar–Apr.

---

219 Uhler's Sundragon *Helocordulia uhleri*   **TL 41–46, HW 25–29**

Description Small dark northeastern emerald with small but obvious wing spots, orange at wing bases. *Male*: Eyes green, face yellow-orange. Thorax brown with metallic green highlights, some obscure yellow markings in front of wings. Abdomen black, S3 orange at base and orange basal spots along sides of S4–8. *Female*: Colored as male, spots on S4–8 larger. Both sexes with series of

219.1
Uhler's Sundragon
male—Sussex Co.,
NJ, June 2008,
posed

219.2
Uhler's Sundragon
female—Berkshire
Co., MA, June 2004,
Glenn Corbiere

dark brown markings at crossveins along front edge of wings, more prominent toward base; larger spots at base with orange spots just behind them.

Identification See **Selys's Sundragon** for differences from that and other species. No other emeralds fly low and fast up and down streams during day. Looks small and dark, with abdomen expanded toward tip. Green eyes visible if light is right, perhaps not as bright as in some other emeralds. **American Emerald** and LITTLE EMERALDS somewhat similar, lack yellow spots along abdomen (except female **Petite Emerald**, see that species). SHADOW-DRAGONS often have spots at wing crossveins but are brown, with brown eyes and yellow lateral thoracic spots.

Natural History Males fly rapidly along streams below knee height, often just offshore, and may hover. Perch by hanging in trees and shrubs. Include pools and riffles in lengthy flights. May be quite difficult to see when flying in shade. Sexual patrol flight often lasts until dark. Oviposition by tapping water among floating debris. Both sexes feed in flight in sunny clearings, including over paths through woodland.

Habitat Wide habitat choice, from small rocky woodland streams to large open rivers, usually with good current.

Flight Season ON May–Jul, QC May–Jul, NS May–Jul, ME May–Jul, OH May–Jun, NJ Apr–Jul, KY Apr–Jun, GA Apr–May.

Sundragons - male appendages

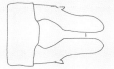

Selys's Sundragon

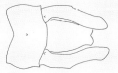

Uhler's Sundragon

Sundragons - female subgenital plate

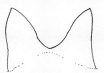

Selys's Sundragon

Uhler's Sundragon

Striped Emeralds   *Somatochlora*

This represents the most diverse group of emeralds and among the most sought by dragonfly enthusiasts, as many are limited to very specific habitats and thus are often rare and local. Appearing dark from a distance, they are surpassingly beautiful up close, almost all with brilliant green eyes (not included in species descriptions, reddish-brown in immatures) and dark metallic bodies, some of them conspicuously marked with yellow. Yellow thoracic markings are brightest in immatures and may become obscured in older individuals of some species. Largest species are about twice the size of smallest. Males of most species have S1–2 bulging, then S3 rapidly narrowed to a wasp waist and the abdomen widening out somewhat beyond that, in some cases spindle-shaped or almost clubbed. Female abdomens are more parallel-sided. Striped Emeralds are typical of bogs and fens and forest streams, with a few species at lakes and none at the marshy ponds favored by skimmers. Some forest-stream-based species occupy limited ranges in the South, other bog and fen species are common and widespread in the North.

Because the group is diverse, the species with very similar overall coloration, identification is a real challenge. Some species can be identified in the field, especially once the observer is familiar with the local fauna and the habitats in which each species is to be expected. Identification can often be by breeding habitat, but all species feed in flight and may be well away from their breeding habitat, even feeding in mixed-species swarms. As many are uncommon and local, familiarity with common species may not provide the knowledge to identify another one entering the picture, so with any doubt, they should be captured for identification. In hand, species are distinguished by thoracic markings and appendages, including cerci in males and subgenital plates in females, as well as size and abdomen shape. Female subgenital plates vary from short and skimmer-like to large and projecting, a "pseudo-ovipositor" for inserting eggs into substrates denser than water. The latter may be short or long, parallel or obliquely slanted, or dramatically perpendicular to the abdomen. Some field marks allow quick assignment to a small group, for example, brown spots at hindwing bases (Delicate, Muskeg, Whitehouse's), bright yellow stripes on the thorax (Calvert's, Hine's, Ozark, Plains, Ski-tipped, Texas, Treetop), or narrow but obvious white rings around the abdomen (Hudsonian, Lake, Ringed). In some others (Brush-tipped, Clamp-tipped, Whitehouse's), male appendages are immediately distinctive. World 42, NA 26, East 24.

220 Ringed Emerald   *Somatochlora albicincta*   TL 45–52, HW 28–33

Description Medium-sized, white-ringed northern emerald. *Male*: Face black, yellow on sides. Thorax metallic green-black with small vertically elongate pale yellow spot on each side of mesothorax. Abdomen black with faint brown markings at base, narrow but conspicuous white ring formed by joint at ends of S2–9. Cerci typical of ringed group, straight in top view and then sharply angled inward; in side view, thin upcurved tips. *Female*: Colored much like  male, thorax brown mixed with green. Subgenital plate projecting but short, not half length of S9, and notched or bilobed.

Identification One of small group of white-ringed species. Distinguished from **Lake Emerald** by smaller size, less than 2 inches in length (**Lake** more than 2 inches), as well as marked thorax. Distinguished from **Quebec Emerald** by more prominent rings on abdomen. Very similar to **Hudsonian Emerald**, only very slight color differences. Look for pale spots on each side of S10 at base of cerci, often in **Ringed** but not in **Hudsonian**. Males of **Hudsonian** with prominent basal tooth on edge of cerci that makes appendages look wider at base (narrow throughout in **Ringed**, without prominent tooth). Subgenital plate of female **Ringed** shorter than in **Hudsonian** and strongly notched.

220.1
Ringed Emerald
male—Kittitas Co., WA,
September 2007

220.2
Ringed Emerald female—
Baker Co., OR, August 2004

Natural History Males fly over open water and typically just off shorelines, usually quite low. Rapid flight over water, sometimes hover over vegetation. May be common in morning, then decrease when darners dominate flight lanes. Females oviposit in open water or near shore or floating objects; fly along slowly and tap once, then rise and move a few feet in any direction before dropping to tap again. May reverse direction to remain in one small favorable area.

Habitat Lakes of all sizes down to rather small bog ponds, in open or forest, also slowly flowing wide streams. Typically no aquatic vegetation except shore emergents. Up at elevation in southern parts of range.

Flight Season ON Jun–Aug, QC Jun–Sep, NS Jul, ME Jul–Aug.

Distribution Across Canada to Alaska, south in mountains to California and Montana, but virtually no records between Hudson Bay and Rockies.

221 Hudsonian Emerald *Somatochlora hudsonica*	**TL 50–54, HW 30–34**

Description White-ringed northern emerald, very similar to some others. *Male*: Face black, yellow on sides. Thorax metallic green with barely evident dull yellowish elongate spot on each side. From above, cerci well separated at base, straight and then sharply angled inward and then curved gently outward to almost meet at tip; extreme tip pointed and curled upward. From side, with a tooth on both exterior and interior surface, exterior one near base. Abdomen black with whitish rings at rear of S2–9. *Female*: Colored as male. Subgenital plate projecting, rounded, less than height of S9.

Identification Member of small group with prominently ringed abdomen, identical to **Ringed** in field and distinguished by appendages in hand. **Hudsonian** male cerci with

221
Hudsonian Emerald male—Old Crow, YT,
July 1983, Rob Cannings

prominent exterior tooth near base lacking in **Ringed**. Female subgenital plate distinctly longer than that of **Ringed** and not notched. Only other conspicuously ringed species is **Lake**, which is much larger. Rings of these species often not visible in flight, when **Hudsonian** looks like many others. Capture always advised for striped emeralds until local fauna well understood, and even then, additional species are always possible in this diverse group.

Natural History Males fly low over water along shore much like Ringed Emerald. Females oviposit by tapping open water.

Habitat Lakes, ponds, and slow streams, especially large muskeg pools with abundant sedge growth. Often with Ringed Emerald.

Flight Season ON Jun–Sep.

Distribution Across southern Canada to Alaska and British Columbia, south in Rockies to Colorado.

---

222 Quebec Emerald   *Somatochlora brevicincta*   TL 47–50, HW 29–31

Description Dark northern emerald of ringed group but with no conspicuous field marks. *Male:* Face black, yellow on sides. Thorax shiny green-black with vertically elongate faint yellow spot on each side of mesothorax. Abdomen shiny black with faint indication of whitish rings between terminal segments. Cerci with tiny lateral tooth at base, tips angled inward and then curved upward in long, slender point. *Female:* Colored much like male, thorax brown and green. Subgenital plate not projecting but almost as long as S9.

Identification Not easily distinguished from other similar-sized far northern species except in hand. No brown at wing base as is present in **Delicate, Muskeg,** and **Whitehouse's Emeralds** (first more slender) but looks much like them. Also like **Forcipate** but spots on thorax not as evident and never two of them. Pale abdominal rings recall **Hudsonian** and **Ringed Emeralds** but much less distinct, even when present interrupted in center. In group of species with cerci slightly angled in top view and curled up at tip in side view, most similar to those of similar-sized **Hudsonian** and **Ringed** (**Lake** is much larger), but show only one projecting tooth near base in side view (others show two, much more prominent in **Hudsonian**). Epiproct of **Quebec** long, over half length of cerci, as in **Hudsonian** (in **Ringed** less than half). Female subgenital plate as long as S9 and rounded in **Quebec**, half length of S9 and notched in **Ringed**, projecting ventrally in **Hudsonian**.

222.1
Quebec Emerald male—Lake Co., MN, July 2005, June Tveekrem

222.2
Quebec Emerald female—McBride, BC, August 2000, Sid Dunkle, posed

Natural History Males fly slowly at knee height over fens. Females oviposit among water-logged vegetation in small pools. Has been found in feeding swarms of several striped emerald species in East.

Habitat Shallow patterned fens with sedges and mosses, those also inhabited by Muskeg and Whitehouse's Emeralds.

Flight Season QC Jun–Sep, NS Jun–Sep, ME Jun–Jul.

Distribution Isolated population in Rockies of eastern British Columbia, presumably occurs elsewhere between there and Minnesota.

223 Lake Emerald *Somatochlora cingulata* TL 55–68, HW 33–41

Description Large, white-ringed northern emerald of large lakes. *Male*: Face black, yellow on sides. Thorax metallic green and brown, otherwise unmarked. Abdomen black, with whitish rings at ends of all segments 2–9. Cerci with prominent lateral tooth at base, tips sharply angled inward and then curved upward in slender point. Epiproct broad at tip, unusual for this genus. *Female*: Colored as male. Subgenital plate short, not projecting.

223.1
Lake Emerald male—St. Lawrence Co., NY, July 2007, Steven Collins, posed

223.2
Lake Emerald male—Bennington Co., VT, June 2007, Bryan Pfeiffer/ Wings Photography, posed

223.3
Lake Emerald immature female—St. Louis Co., MN, July 2008, Aaron Brees, posed

Identification Very large size for an emerald distinctive, combined with rather conspicuous white rings (more so than in smaller species). Both **Hudsonian** and **Ringed Emeralds** somewhat similar, and they also fly over open water, but **Lake** larger by 10–15 percent. In silhouette much like a darner, but green eyes and black body distinguish it from MOSAIC DARNERS, the other large dragonflies that fly over northern lakes.

Natural History Males fly low and swiftly over lakes with no hovering, usually 6–15 feet off-shore but sometimes approaching shore, easy to observe but difficult to capture. Males curve abdomen down at end, reminiscent of cruiser in flight rather than one of the smaller, slower-flying striped emeralds. Pairs form at water and immediately fly off into woods, but also seen far from water, perhaps also pairing away from it. Females oviposit by flying rapidly back and forth or in broad circles, tapping water every few feet.

Habitat Lakes, with or without much floating and/or emergent vegetation; also large, slow-flowing rivers.

Flight Season ON Jun–Sep, QC May–Sep, NS Jun–Aug, WI Jun–Aug, ME Jun–Sep.

Distribution Also in Rockies of British Columbia and Alberta, isolated records in Saskatchewan and Wyoming.

224 Whitehouse's Emerald *Somatochlora whitehousei* TL 46–48, HW 26–30

Description Small northern emerald with brown patch at base of hindwing. *Male:* Face black with yellow on sides. Thorax metallic green and brown; narrow, elongate dull yellow-orange spots below each wing that become obscure with age. Abdomen black with orange-brown dorsolateral spots on S2, white ring at base of S3. Dark brown triangle at base of each hindwing. Cerci in top view narrowing from base, then suddenly expanded and finally angled together; in side view curled up at tip. *Female:* Colored as male. Subgenital plate projecting at right angle and scoop-shaped but very short, half length of S9.

Identification Only two other striped emeralds have moderately visible brown spot at hind-wing base, **Delicate** and **Muskeg**. **Delicate** has longer and much more slender abdomen than **Whitehouse's**. **Muskeg** looks identical, must be distinguished in hand by differences

224.1
Whitehouse's Emerald male—Heckman Pass, BC, July 2006, posed

224.2
Whitehouse's Emerald female—Pend Oreille Co., WA, August 2008, Jim Johnson, posed

224.3
Whitehouse's Emerald
female—Pend Oreille Co.,
WA, August 2008, Jim
Johnson, posed

in male appendages and female subgenital plate (see that species). **Whitehouse's** usually more common than **Muskeg** at preferred habitats. If brown wing spots can not be seen, **Whitehouse's** could be mistaken for rarer **Quebec Emerald**, which has different appendages. Other striped emeralds have longer abdomen and/or brighter yellow spots on thorax.

Natural History Males fly back and forth at knee height and below in relatively short beats over water with open stands of low vegetation, then wander across ridge to next depression or into woods to perch before returning to water. They drop to water surface from time to time, presumably looking for females. Females oviposit by flying low and slowly through vegetation in shallow ponds, tapping water or wet moss once and moving short distance before doing it again; usually near shore or emergent plants where slow flight and leisurely tapping renders them quite inconspicuous.

Habitat Classical muskeg, small to moderate-sized open ponds with abundant sedges, buckbean, and algae, clean water but soft mud bottom and quaking substrate.

Flight Season ON Jun–Jul, QC Jul–Aug.

Distribution Also widespread in western Canada, from Yukon south in Rockies to western Montana, with isolated record in Saskatchewan.

---

225 Muskeg Emerald *Somatochlora septentrionalis*   **TL 39–48, HW 26–30**

Description Far-northern emerald with brown in wing bases. *Male*: Face blackish with yellow on sides. Thorax metallic green and brown, faintly indicated yellow spot under forewing. Abdomen glossy black with brown markings on S1–2, white ring and brown spots at base of S3. Dark brown triangle at base of hindwing. Cerci sharply angled inward in top view, strongly swept up at tip, with basal tooth visible in side view. *Female*: Colored as male, pale spots on S3 slightly larger. Subgenital plate short and not projecting, with two lobes.

Identification In size, abdomen shape, and brown at base of hindwing, both sexes look exactly like comparable sex of **Whitehouse's Emerald**. Check appendages to distinguish males (in top view, **Whitehouse's** cerci converge and cross, **Muskeg** cerci remain parallel than turn sharply inward), side view of subgenital plate (projecting downward in **Whitehouse's**, flat against abdomen and bilobed at tip in **Muskeg**) to distinguish females. Differs from all other species in same ways as **Whitehouse's**. Male appendages somewhat like those of ringed group, and could be confused with **Quebec Emerald**, which also lacks rings, but prominent downward-directed spine under base of cerci should distinguish **Muskeg**.

225.1
Muskeg Emerald male—
Heckman Pass, BC, July 2006

225.2
Muskeg Emerald male—Whitehorse,
YT, August 2009, Syd Cannings, posed

Natural History Males fly low over water in continued patrol flights, only hovering occasionally. Apparently roost near breeding sites, in shrubs and at edge of tiny pools with overhanging sedges that effectively hide them. Copulating pairs fly into woods, and one observer reported female returning in 15 min to lay eggs. Females oviposit in slow flight by
tapping steadily both in open water and on mat of decayed vegetation floating on it.

Habitat Open fens with shallow pools of open water, typical muskeg in boreal forest
habitats.

Flight Season ON Jun–Jul, QC Jul–Aug, NS Jun–Aug.

Distribution Also in western Canada, from Yukon and Northwest Territories to southern British Columbia.

---

226 Forcipate Emerald *Somatochlora forcipata* TL 43–51, HW 29–33

Description Slender northern emerald with spotted thorax and
faintly dotted abdomen. *Male:* Face black, some yellow on sides.
Thorax mostly metallic green except brown just behind prothorax
and with two oval pale yellow spots on each side. Abdomen black
with light brown markings on sides of S1–2, whitish ring at end of S2,
and obscure orange lateral dots at front end of S5–7. Abdomen narrowest on S3–4, widens on S5 and back. Cerci with long, slightly incurved and sharply pointed tips. *Female:* Colored as male. Subgenital plate broad, projecting downward obliquely, about as long as S9.

Identification Only other species with two well-defined round
spots on thorax is **Ocellated**, much smaller, with abdomen clubbed in middle and quite
different appendages. At a distance could be easily mistaken for other species of similar
size but without yellow thoracic spots, for example **Delicate**, **Incurvate**, and **Kennedy's**,
or the shorter-abdomened **Muskeg** and **Whitehouse's**.

Natural History Males fly up and down above small streams, from just above surface to
waist height. Females oviposit in open water, even tiny pockets, by tapping water leisurely;
also in mats of moss and stonewort. Foraging flight in clearings or over roads, usually at not
much more than head height, and ascending up to 20 feet in trees to perch.

226.1
Forcipate Emerald
male—Coos Co., NH, June
2006, Glenn Corbiere

226.2
Forcipate Emerald
female—Bayfield Co., WI,
July 2008, Ryan Brady

Habitat Small spring-fed boggy streams, in or out of woodland.
Flight Season ON May–Sep, QC May–Aug, NS Jun–Sep, WI Jun–Aug, ME May–Sep.
Distribution Scattered records west to Northwest Territories and British Columbia.

227 Incurvate Emerald *Somatochlora incurvata* TL 49–59, HW 31–37

Description Obscurely patterned slender emerald of northeastern bogs. *Male*: Face mostly black, yellow on clypeus and sides of frons. Thorax all brown with metallic green highlights in narrow stripes. Abdomen black, brownish on S1–2 and base of S3; poorly defined dull orange-brown lateral spots at base of S4–8. Abdomen very narrow on S3–4, from above conspicuously wider on S5–10. Cerci quite straight and pointed in side view, from above strongly curved inward at tips. *Female*: Color pattern identical to male, recognized by abdomen shape. Subgenital plate pale, large and scoop-shaped, rounded at rear and extending beyond base of S10.

Identification Very much like **Kennedy's Emerald** but slightly duller than that species, usually showing no pale spots at all (**Kennedy's** has dull yellowish spots on thorax and abdomen base). Cerci similar from side, but more forceps-like in **Incurvate**. Subgenital plate distinctly shorter in **Kennedy's**, not reaching end of S9. Also like **Forcipate Emerald** but a

227.1
Incurvate Emerald
male—Penobscot Co., ME,
September 2004, David
Reed

227.2
Incurvate Emerald
female—Iron Co., WI,
August 2008, Ryan Brady

bit larger and duller, the latter species with distinct and contrasty pale spots on thorax and abdomen. Cerci in **Forcipate** arched downward in side view. Female subgenital plates rather similar in these two, just overlapping in size (usually longer, surpassing base of S10, in **Incurvate**). Also rather similar to other slender-bodied emeralds with no more than obscure spots on thorax, although not as slender as **Delicate** and without its brown hindwing spots. **Mocha** and **Williamson's** have cerci that broaden toward tip in male and ventrally projecting subgenital plate in female. Further, **Mocha** has distinct yellow spot on abdomen base, notable in a species lacking thoracic spots.

Natural History Males fly over bogs and hover over small pools. Females oviposit in pools by tapping water, also commonly in animal paths through bogs.

Habitat Sphagnum bogs.

Flight Season ON Jul–Aug, QC Aug–Sep, NS Jul–Oct, WI May–Aug, ME Jun–Sep.

---

228 Delicate Emerald *Somatochlora franklini*   TL 44–54, HW 25–30

Description Very slender far-northern emerald with brown at wing bases. *Male*: Face black, yellow on sides. Thorax metallic green mixed with some brown, when young with dull yellowish spot evident under forewing base that disappears with maturity. Abdomen black with dull brown side spots on S1–2, dull yellow ring at end of S2. Dark brown triangle at each hindwing base. Abdomen narrow throughout. Cerci from above like forceps, from side a simple slightly droopy and pointed finger. *Female*: Colored as male but thorax brown mixed

228.1
Delicate Emerald male—
Penobscot Co., ME, June 2000,
Blair Nikula, posed

228.2
Delicate Emerald male—
Westmorland Co., NB, June
2008, Denis Doucet, posed

228.3
Delicate Emerald
female—Whitemouth
River, MB, July 2009,
Larry de March

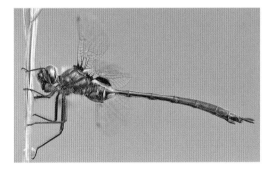

with green, abdomen with dull orange dorsolateral spots on S3. Eyes stay reddish for much of life, finally turn green. May be indistinct brown stripes extending out front of all wings. Subgenital plate length of S9, not projecting.

Identification Very slender abdomen good clue, even more slender than others similar enough for confusion, including **Forcipate, Incurvate, Kennedy's**, and **Quebec**. Comparison of appendages in hand may be necessary for certainty. One of few species with obvious brown at base of hindwing, not that easy to see in field. **Muskeg** and **Whitehouse's**, also with brown in wing and often in same habitat, have shorter abdomen and very different appendages and subgenital plates.

Natural History Males fly back and forth and hover frequently at waist height over beds of tall grasses and sedges and among shrubs. Females oviposit by tapping onto wet moss or in tiny pools, even within dense vegetation.

Habitat Sedge- and moss-filled fens, at foot of hillsides below seepage or in wide-open meadows; usually not at open water.

Flight Season ON May–Aug, QC Jun–Aug, NS Jun–Jul, WI May–Aug, ME Jun–Aug.

Distribution West across Canada to Alaska, south to northeastern Washington.

229 Kennedy's Emerald *Somatochlora kennedyi* TL 47–55, HW 29–34

Description Slender northern emerald with no distinctive markings. *Male*: Face brown with paler sides. Thorax metallic green and brown, in younger individuals with dull yellowish spot below forewing. Abdomen black with paler brownish areas low on sides of posterior segments. Cerci somewhat forcipate, long and fingerlike, narrowly pointed at tip. Epiproct relatively short, less than half length of cerci. *Female*: Colored as male but dull yellowish dorsolateral spots on S2–3. Subgenital plate projecting slightly, scooplike, as long as S9.

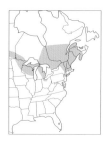

Identification If well seen, **Kennedy's** should be mistaken only for other slender-bodied species without strong thoracic markings,

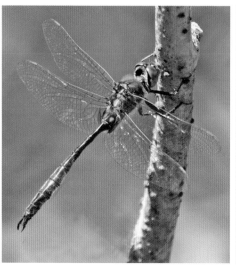

229.1
Kennedy's Emerald male—Bayfield Co., WI, June 2008, Ryan Brady

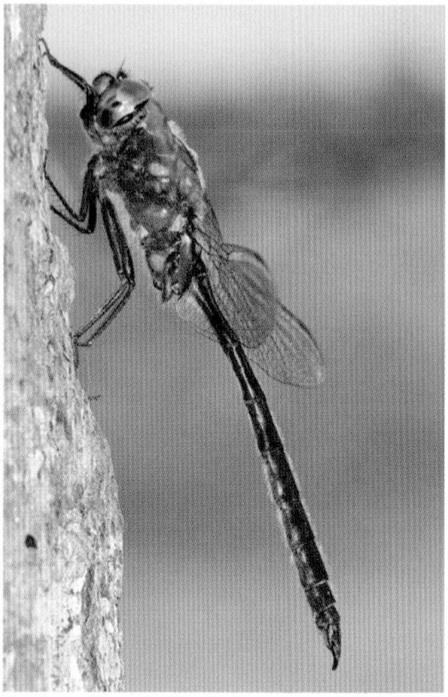

229.2
Kennedy's Emerald male—Westmorland Co., NB, June 2008, Denis Doucet

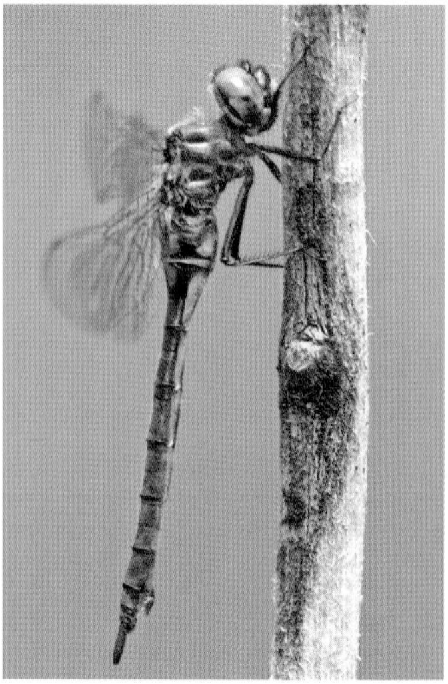

229.3
Kennedy's Emerald female—Sussex Co., NJ, June 2005, Allen Barlow

especially **Delicate**, **Mocha**, and **Williamson's**. Differs from **Delicate** in slightly larger size and in having abdomen slightly more expanded and lacking brown at hindwing base; from **Mocha** in relatively shorter abdomen; and from **Williamson's** in smaller size. But these differences are not at all obvious as one goes flying past. Male cerci slender and almost touching at tips in **Kennedy's**, well separated at tips in **Delicate**, upcurved and tipped with hairs in **Williamson's**, and distinctly shorter in **Mocha**, epiproct almost as long as cerci. Habitat and flight season, of course, separate some of these species, particularly **Kennedy's** from **Mocha**. Note also probability of confusion at a distance with other slender emeralds of high latitudes such as **Forcipate**, which has brightly spotted instead of plain thorax.

Natural History Males patrol over water at knee to waist height, hovering regularly and changing orientation ("pivoting") while doing so. Fly into nearby shrubbery and hang up in shade for short period, then resume patrolling. Females oviposit by flying leisurely among clustered plant stems or over floating moss, tapping surface frequently in one spot of open water for few seconds, then moving to another nearby to repeat. Both sexes in feeding swarms in morning and at dusk.

Habitat Open bogs or fens with sedge and mosses, often at small ponds.

Flight Season ON May–Aug, QC May–Aug, NS May–Jul, WI May–Aug, ME Jun–Jul, NJ May–Jun.

Distribution Also farther west in Manitoba, then wide gap to range in Yukon and Northwest Territories south to northern British Columbia and Alberta, with one Alaska record.

230 Ski-tipped Emerald *Somatochlora elongata* TL 52–62, HW 34–38

Description Brightly spotted emerald of eastern forests. *Male*: Face black above and below, yellow band across middle. Thorax metallic green and brown with pair of bright yellow elongate spots, anterior one longer. Abdomen black with bright yellow spot on S2. Cerci straight and pointed from above, from side with flattened and sharply upcurved (ski-shaped) tip. *Female*: Color pattern just like that of male, abdomen less slender at base with conspicuous pointed subgenital plate projecting down at right angle.

230.1
Ski-tipped Emerald male—Washington Co., VT, July 2005, Bryan Pfeiffer/Wings Photography, posed

230.2
Ski-tipped Emerald female—Grafton Co., NH, June 2006, posed

Identification Compare with other species with two yellow spots on thorax, the front one longer. **Forcipate** lacks bright yellow spot on S2 and "ski" tip of cerci. **Brush-tipped** smaller, with brush-tipped cerci in male. Yellow markings in **Ocellated** are same-sized spots. Slight range overlap with **Plains**, which is a bit smaller and has more yellow on face. Female subgenital plate points down at right angle in **Ski-tipped**, thus rather similar to females of two other species with yellow thoracic markings, **Clamp-tipped** (with duller spots) and **Plains**. Broad, almost equilateral triangle in side view in **Ski-tipped**, very narrow triangle in **Clamp-tipped** and **Plains**.

Natural History Males fly slow and regular patrols over water with frequent hovering. Females oviposit by flying along shore and tapping water at intervals.

Habitat Slow-moving streams in bogs and swamps.

Flight Season ON Jun–Aug, QC Jun–Aug, NS Jun–Sep, WI Jun–Aug, ME Jun–Sep, NJ Jun–Jul.

Comments Previously called Ski-tailed Emerald.

---

231 Williamson's Emerald *Somatochlora williamsoni*   TL 53–59, HW 35–40

Description Large northeastern emerald without pale thoracic markings and with male abdomen gradually wider to near end. *Male*: Face blackish with dull yellow-orange sides. Thorax metallic green and brown. Abdomen black, with faint pale ring at base of S3. Cerci straight in side view, curling up at tips and quite hairy above; exterior basal tooth visible from side or above. *Female*: Colored as male but orange-brown anterior ventrolateral spots on S4–8. Subgenital plate projecting at right angle, longer than height

231.1
Williamson's Emerald
male—Bayfield Co., WI, August
2008, Ryan Brady, posed

231.2
Williamson's Emerald
female—Eau Claire Co., WI,
June 2007

of S9 and very sharply pointed. Cerci longer than S9 + S10. Immature with pair of fine yellow lines on each side of thorax.

Identification Rather similar to other slender striped emeralds, distinguished from **Delicate**, **Forcipate**, and **Kennedy's** by larger size. **Kennedy's** also distinguished by usually evident dull yellow mesothoracic spot, straight rather than upcurled tips of male cerci, and short, rounded subgenital plate. **Forcipate** distinguished by two pale spots on each side of thorax, **Delicate** by brown spots at hindwing bases. Much larger than **Brush-tipped Emerald**, only other species with visibly hairy cerci, and tip of cercus long and pointed in side view rather than blunt. Long, pointed, perpendicular subgenital plate of female different from most other emeralds, but see more brightly marked **Clamp-tipped** and **Plains**, with similar plates.

Natural History Males patrol streams and lake shores, alternating rapid flight and brief hovering, typically at knee to waist height. Foraging flight high in air along woodland borders. Females usually oviposit on wet muddy banks above water, alternating series of thrusts into mud with tap in water, presumably to clear ovipositor. Both sexes in feeding swarms in morning or late afternoon.

Habitat Slow forest streams and clear sand- or rock-margined lakes with wave-washed shores.

Flight Season ON Jun–Sep, QC Jun–Sep, NS Jun–Aug, WI Jun–Sep, ME Jun–Sep, NJ May–Jul.

Distribution Also few records west to central Saskatchewan.

232 Ocellated Emerald *Somatochlora minor* TL 42–50, HW 30–34

Description Very small northern emerald with small but conspicuous thoracic spots. *Male*: Face metallic green, dull yellow-brown at sides. Thorax brown and metallic green with two pale yellow oval spots on each side. Abdomen black with conspicuous yellow spots on sides of S2 and base of S3. Cerci slender, straight but slightly angled inward in top view with two minute teeth along outside; meet at end where pointed and slightly upswept. *Female*: Colored as male. Subgenital plate projecting at right angle, pointed, not as long as height of S9.

Identification Brush-tipped only other striped emerald this small, and both sexes have quite different terminal appendages. Color patterns similar, but anterior spot on sides of

232.1
Ocellated Emerald
male—Bayfield Co., WI,
July 2008, Ryan Brady

232.2
Ocellated Emerald
female—Bayfield Co., WI,
July 2008, Ryan Brady

thorax of **Brush-tipped** elongate, whereas both spots oval and same size in **Ocellated**; also, **Brush-tipped** has tiny pale spots on sides at midabdomen. From above, **Ocellated** abdomen looks spindle-shaped (widest at middle), **Brush-tipped** closer to club-shaped (widest slightly behind middle) in both sexes. Also like **American Emerald**, latter in different habitat and with no yellow on thorax. Still smaller **Racket-tailed Emerald** has wide club nearer end of abdomen. Other species in range with fairly bright markings on thorax (**Clamp-tipped**, **Forcipate**, **Ski-tipped**) all larger.

Natural History Males fly back and forth along small stream or hover above it for lengthy periods, usually close to water, as close as a few inches above it; patrol length averages around 30 feet. Often perch on grasses, sedges, or pale rocks at stream after lengthy flying bout, also on tree trunks nearby. Foraging flight relatively low, usually below head height in woodland clearings, sometimes a bit higher with high-flying larger emeralds. Some females oviposit by alternating taps on water surface near shore and wet mossy bank above, then short move to new location to repeat process. Others just tap surface of shallow flowing water.

Habitat Small to medium, slow to moderately fast clear streams with pools, in both woodland and open. Good habitat is where stream drops out of forest onto meadow.

Flight Season ON Jun–Aug, QC Jun–Sep, NS Jun–Aug, ME Jun–Aug.

Distribution West to Yukon and British Columbia, south in uplands to Oregon, Wyoming, and South Dakota.

---

233 Brush-tipped Emerald *Somatochlora walshii*   TL 41–52, HW 25–34

Description Small northern emerald with prominently clubbed abdomen and distinctive brushy appendages. *Male*: Face black with yellowish-brown on sides. Thorax metallic green and brown with prominent yellow spots on sides, front one longer and narrower than rear one. Abdomen black with dull yellowish ventrolateral spots and pale yellow apical ring on S2. Pale basal spots or half-rings on sides of S5–7. Cerci curved slightly downward, broader toward tip, then abruptly swept up; "brush" of hairs at tip obscures shape. *Female*: Colored as male but orange dorsolateral spots at

233.1
Brush-tipped Emerald
male—Hampden Co., MA,
August 2009, Glenn
Corbiere

233.2
Brush-tipped Emerald
male—Piscataquis Co., ME,
June 2006, posed

233.3
Brush-tipped Emerald
female—Bayfield Co., WI,
July 2008, Ryan Brady

base of S3, larger pale spots or half-rings at bases of S5–7. Subgenital plate projecting obliquely, scoop-shaped with rounded tip, about as long as height of S9.

Identification Small size and pronounced wasp-waisted look distinguish it from most other striped emeralds in its range. **Ocellated Emerald** equally small but has two rounded spots on each side of thorax rather than two unequal-sized ones and lacks any markings on midabdomen. Appendages of both sexes quite different; note especially short epiproct of **Brush-tipped**, leaving gap in appendages not notable in **Ocellated**. Breeding habitats different but both may be feeding anywhere away from water. Otherwise could be mistaken for **American Emerald**, with no yellow on thorax, shorter appendages, and different habitat (lakes and ponds). **Racket-tailed Emerald** still smaller and with wider abdominal club. **Ski-tipped Emerald** has thoracic pattern quite similar to **Brush-tipped** but is perceptibly larger and has quite different appendages in both sexes.

Natural History Males fly slowly back and forth or hover over narrow stream or marsh, usually at knee to waist height. Fly with characteristically arched abdomen. May also cruise fairly rapidly over lengthy beat of 30 to 65 feet. Both sexes fly rapidly around at all heights over forest clearings while foraging. Females usually oviposit by slow flight over water surface, rhythmically tapping water while maneuvering around plant clumps; often in animal paths within dense vegetation.

Habitat Typically small, slow streams flowing through sedge fens and meadows, sometimes at woodland edge.

Flight Season ON Jun–Aug, QC Jun–Sep, NS Jun–Oct, WI Jun–Aug, ME Jun–Sep, OH Jun–Jul, NJ Jun–Aug.

Distribution Also throughout southern British Columbia south in mountains to Oregon and Montana; few scattered records across central Canada.

234 Plains Emerald *Somatochlora ensigera* TL 48–51, HW 33–35

Description Midsized emerald of prairie region with dramatic yellow spots on sides. *Male*: Face yellow, black on top of frons. Thorax dark brown with green highlights; pale yellow stripe on mesothorax, smaller but brighter yellow spot on metathorax. Abdomen black, with large yellow spot on sides of S2 and yellow markings on sides of S3. Cerci unique in side view, relatively short and curved downward with short tooth projecting upward near end and

234.1
Plains Emerald male—
Cherry Co., NE, July 1998,
Sid Dunkle, posed

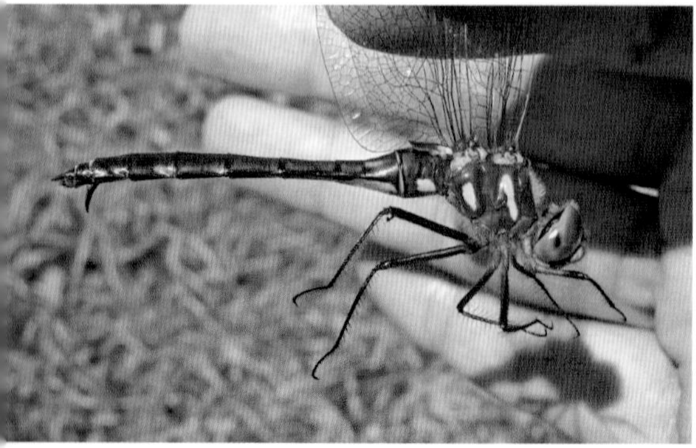

234.2
Plains Emerald female—
Pinewood, ON, July 2005,
Ilka Milne

epiproct only slightly shorter than cerci. *Female*: Colored as male, face duller. Subgenital plate projecting at right angle, longer than height of S9 and sharply pointed. Cerci relatively short, shorter than S9 + S10.

Identification Should be distinguished from other species with brightly marked thorax. **Ocellated Emerald** similarly patterned but smaller and with quite different abdomen tip in both sexes. Farther east, **Plains** barely overlaps with a few other species with prominent yellow stripes or spots on sides of thorax. Perhaps no overlap with **Ski-tipped**, very similarly colored but with very different male appendages and subgenital plate broader in side view. **Clamp-tipped** male has quite different appendages, although females are more similar, but in **Plains** subgenital plate longer than cerci, in **Clamp-tipped** shorter than cerci. In fact, short cerci are good mark for female **Plains**. **Brush-tipped** smaller, appendages of both sexes quite different. Mostly yellow face diagnostic of **Plains** when it can be seen.

Natural History Males fly beats up and down streams, usually low and with intermittent hovering; quite territorial. Females oviposit by hovering and tapping clay bank or gravel bed above water level or in water itself; may begin in early morning. Both sexes and pairs perch on streamside vegetation.

Habitat Slow-flowing streams and small rivers with pools and riffles, wooded in East but mostly in open areas in plains, where typically lined with band of riparian shrubs and trees.

Flight Season ON Jul–Aug, IA Jul–Sep, WI Jun, OH Jun–Aug.

Distribution Quite rare east of plains. Scattered records across northern plains to Saskatchewan, Wyoming, and Colorado.

---

235 Mocha Emerald *Somatochlora linearis* TL 58–68, HW 39–47

Description Long, slender southern emerald with unmarked thorax and yellow spot on abdomen base. *Male*: Face dark brown with paler sides. Thorax dark brown overlaid with metallic green. Abdomen black with dull but fairly conspicuous yellowish spot on sides of S1–2, slightly indicated pale basal dots on sides of S3–7. Cerci with long, pointed tooth projecting downward near tip in side view; in top view, widened and clublike in terminal half. *Female*: Colored as male, but thorax with less obvious metallic green. Abdominal

235.1
Mocha Emerald male—Floyd
Co., GA, September 2009,
Marion M. Dobbs

235.2
Mocha Emerald female—
Baltimore Co., MD, September
2008, Steven Collins

spots often larger. Subgenital plate projecting at right angle, narrowly pointed, about as long as height of S9. Wings become suffused with brown in older individuals, more so in females.

Identification Compare with other striped emeralds with unspotted dark thorax and no rings on abdomen (note very little range overlap with any of them). **Mocha** unique in having conspicuous yellow spot on each side of abdomen base. Others (**Kennedy's, Incurvate, Williamson's**) lack that spot or may have it very obscure. Very different appendages also differentiate **Mocha** from **Kennedy's** and **Incurvate** (both bog species), but **Williamson's** (a lake species) also has square-tipped male cerci and right-angle projecting female subgenital plate. As a southern species, **Mocha** overlaps mostly with other species with brightly marked thorax.

Natural History Males patrol a few feet above stream, hovering frequently in sunny spots and cruising over long beats of 60–100 feet. Beats may be longer when stream shrinks to isolated pools. Most active in morning and evening, more likely to be hanging from tree branches in forest during midday. May be found hanging vertically or obliquely from twigs over stream, even quite low. Females oviposit in muddy areas by thrusting eggs into mud or fine gravel at shore or above it, even quite early in morning. Often seen at small intermittent pools. Both sexes cruise over open areas to forage, all the way up to treetops.

Habitat Small streams with mud and leaf litter a few yards in width in forest, with rocky riffles or not. In late summer may decrease to series of pools.

Flight Season ON Jul–Sep, IA Jun–Aug, OH Jun–Oct, NJ Jun–Sep, KY May–Sep, LA Jun–Aug, GA Jun–Sep, FL May–Aug.

---

236 Coppery Emerald *Somatochlora georgiana*   TL 44–46, HW 29–32

Description Rare small eastern emerald with red eyes and reddish body. *Male*: Eyes dull red over gray; face golden-brown. Thorax medium brown with two dull creamy-whitish stripes on either side. Abdomen medium brown with cream markings on sides of S2, dark stripe on top of S8–9 when mature. Cerci long, slender, and straight, curled up at flattened tip. *Female*: Colored as male. Subgenital plate with rear edge at right angle to abdomen, sharply pointed and about as long as height of S9.

Identification Structurally a typical striped emerald, but differently colored and the smallest species. No other striped emerald, or emerald for that matter, has eyes red above and a brown body with two pale thoracic stripes. BASKETTAILS are duller

236.1
Coppery Emerald male—Middlesex Co., MA, August 1997, Blair Nikula, posed

236.2
Coppery Emerald female—Stone Co., MS, June 2008, Steve Krotzer, posed

brown and thicker-bodied with different appendages in both sexes and no trace of pale stripes on thorax. Perhaps more likely mistaken for some sort of elongate tropical skimmer, for example, female **Four-spotted Pennant**, but of course **Coppery Emerald** is a flier that hangs up rather than a percher. Emerald-type appendages in both sexes, with long terminal appendages in male and well-developed subgenital plate in female show it clearly to be an emerald, as does abbreviated anal loop in hindwing. Remember that all emeralds have brown or reddish-brown eyes when very young.

Natural History Males patrol streams at midday but more intensely later in evening. Rarely in mixed feeding groups over clearings with other striped emeralds. One of our rarest dragonflies, very seldom encountered in most of its range.

Habitat Small, sandy forest streams.

Flight Season NJ Jul, LA Aug, GA Jun, FL May–Aug.

---

237 Fine-lined Emerald *Somatochlora filosa*   TL 55–66, HW 36–45

Description Long, slender southeastern emerald with fine white stripes on sides of thorax. *Male:* Face dull brown, metallic green above. Thorax mixed brown and metallic green with two well-defined but narrow white stripes on each side. Abdomen black, white rings on S1–2 continuing thoracic patterning. Cerci long and slender with slightly outcurved and pointed tip. *Female:* Colored as male but thorax and base of abdomen with more brown. Wings orange-tipped in immature, entirely tinged brown with maturity. Subgenital plate projecting obliquely and upcurved at end, longer than S9 and rather like sled runner.

Identification No other striped emerald in its range has fine white vertical stripes on thorax and abdomen base. Other species in range with patterned thorax (**Calvert's, Clamp-tipped, Texas, Treetop**) all have wider, bright to dull yellow thoracic stripes. **Mocha Emerald**, often flying with **Fine-lined** when foraging, has very different appendages and subgenital plate as well as unmarked thorax. Orange-tipped wings might be clue to female **Fine-lined** overhead.

237.1
Fine-lined Emerald male—Leon Co., FL, October 2005, Giff Beaton

237.2
Fine-lined Emerald female—Brantley Co., GA, October 2005, Giff Beaton, posed

Natural History Usually encountered in feeding flight in open pine woods, often way up in treetops. Males patrol at waist height or lower at edges of swamps and over small, slow streams and seeps, pivoting often. One female seen pushing eggs into sandy bank overlain by silt.

Habitat Poorly known, probably small sandy forest streams and tiny, tannin-stained seeps.

Flight Season NJ Jun–Nov, KY Jun–Sep, LA Jul–Sep, GA Aug–Nov, FL Jun–Dec.

| 238 **Calvert's Emerald** *Somatochlora calverti* | TL 50–52, HW 36–37 |

Description Limited-range southeastern emerald with yellow thoracic stripes and finely ringed abdomen. *Male:* Face mostly brown, metallic green on top of frons. Thorax metallic green, much brown and short yellow stripes on front and two long yellow lateral stripes. Abdomen black with large irregular yellow spot on S2 and pair of yellow spots at base of S3, often faint pale ring at end of all segments. Cerci straight in dorsal view, greatly arched and meeting long epiproct in lateral view. *Female:* Color pattern as in male, but yellow markings on top of S3 longer stripes. Subgenital plate narrow, pointed, scoop-shaped, extending to end of S10. Wings with dark brown streak between costa and nodus.

Identification Brightly yellow-striped thorax unique in its range except for quite similar **Treetop Emerald**. Male **Treetop** differs by appendages, from above cerci angled inward, from side shorter epiproct not meeting cerci. Besides stripes, pale rings at tip of abdomen diagnostic of females of **Calvert's** and **Treetop**; **Treetop** extremely similar to **Calvert's** except for lacking brown stripes in wings and cerci usually shorter than S9 + S10 (about length of those segments in **Calvert's**); also, **Calvert's** usually shows rings along entire abdomen, **Treetop** only at tip. **Clamp-tipped** also flies with **Calvert's**, distinguished by spots on thorax, dramatically angled cerci in side view, and right-angled subgenital plate of female. **Coppery Emerald** also with striped thorax, but stripes obscure and on a smaller, brown dragonfly.

Natural History Individuals of both sexes, but especially males, fly rapidly up and down roads through sandy pinewoods with wavy (up and down) flight at head height. The flights

238.1
Calvert's Emerald
male—Gadsden Co., FL,
July 2009, posed

238.2
Calvert's Emerald
female—Gadsden Co., FL,
June 2005, Giff Beaton,
posed

seem to be unidirectional. Both sexes hang up in trees, not often within range of net or camera.

Habitat Probably small sandy streams; not definitely known but worthy of intense field work because of rarity.

Flight Season FL Jun–Aug.

239 Treetop Emerald *Somatochlora provocans* TL 53–56, HW 33–37

Description *Male*: Face dull brownish yellow, metallic black on top of frons. Thorax mixed metallic green and brown, with two long yellow stripes on each side. Abdomen black, S2 with elongate yellow spot, continuing striped look; also pair of small basal yellow spots on top of S3. Cerci slender, pointed, angled inward in dorsal view and slightly downcurved in lateral view *Female*: Color pattern as in male, but abdomen without basal constriction. Pair of pale stripes on S3 and prominent white rings at base of S9–10. Subgenital plate narrow, pointed, scoop-shaped, extending to end of S10.

Identification One of several species in range with pair of bright yellow stripes on each side of thorax. See **Calvert's** for distinction from that species. Male appendages and female subgenital plate very different from **Clamp-tipped**. No overlap in range presently known for rather similar **Ozark** and **Texas Emeralds**; check those species for differences in areas where their ranges approach. Emeralds hover enough that thoracic pattern sometimes obvious, but not necessarily. Then must be distinguished from additional species with plain or spotted thorax pattern. **Coppery**, **Fine-lined**, and **Mocha** also in range of **Treetop**; all easily distinguished if well seen.

Natural History Adults fly back and forth over roads through sandy pinewoods, from head height to well up in trees, move into shade at midday. Males patrol at knee height over seeps, often stopping to hover.

Habitat Sand-bottomed forest streams and seeps.

Flight Season NJ Jun–Sep, KY Jun–Jul, FL Jul–Aug.

239.1
Treetop Emerald male—
Gadsden Co., FL, June 2005, Giff
Beaton, posed

239.2
Treetop Emerald female—
Gadsden Co., FL, June 2005, Giff
Beaton, posed

240 Ozark Emerald *Somatochlora ozarkensis* TL 55–58, HW 34–39

Description Brightly marked emerald of Ozark region. *Male*: Face yellow, top of frons metallic green. Thorax metallic green and brown with two bright yellow stripes on each side, front one narrower. Abdomen black with bright yellow markings on sides of S1–2, small dull yellow dorsolateral spots at base of S3. Cerci straight to half length, then abruptly bent downward at 45° angle; tip widened in side view. *Female*: Colored as male. Subgenital plate very long, reaches end of abdomen; scoop-shaped, pointed.

240.1
Ozark Emerald male—McCurtain Co., OK,
June 2009, Berlin Heck

240.2
Ozark Emerald female—McCurtain Co., OK,
August 2007, David Arbour

Identification In limited range in Missouri and Arkansas, could be confused only with **Clamp-tipped** and **Hine's Emerald**, both a bit larger with more obscure thoracic markings. Abdominal appendages very different in both sexes. Probably no range overlap with very similar **Texas Emerald** of lowlands to the south. Male cerci in **Texas** straighter in lateral view, female subgenital plate narrower in ventral view. Also, stripes on thorax average slightly wider in **Texas**. RIVER CRUISERS larger, with single stripe on sides of thorax and patterned abdomen.

Natural History Has mostly been encountered feeding in open areas in wooded country, often over roads. Poorly known but may be locally common.

Habitat Small, clear, rocky forest streams in hills.

Flight Season Entire range Jun–Aug.

241 Texas Emerald *Somatochlora margarita* TL 51–59, HW 32–37

Description Slender southeastern emerald with vividly striped thorax and abdomen base. *Male*: Face black, faint yellow on sides. Thorax black with green iridescence, vivid yellow stripes running from top to bottom of meso- and metathorax. Abdomen black, S2 with contrasty pale yellow markings on lower sides and ring at end. Pale yellow markings at base of S3. Cerci long, slender, and finger-like, parallel in top view and arched downward in side view. *Female*: Colored as male. Subgenital plate very long, extending to end of abdomen, rounded at end and narrowly scoop-shaped.

Identification In limited range could be confused with no other species because of vivid thoracic markings, visible even on flybys. Range overlaps with **Clamp-tipped**, **Coppery**, **Fine-lined**, and **Mocha**, all different in color pattern and structure. See also **Ozark Emerald**, no known overlap. Green eyes and bright thoracic stripes might invite confusion with RIVER CRUISERS, but distinctly smaller and with unmarked abdomen.

241.1
Texas Emerald male—
Jasper Co., TX, June 2010,
Troy Hibbitts, posed

241.2
Texas Emerald female—
San Jacinto Co., TX, June 2010,
Troy Hibbitts, posed

Natural History Seemingly rare and very poorly known, mostly encountered in high feeding flight over roads in wooded country.
Habitat Breeding habitat unknown, probably small forest streams. Feeds in open pine forests, often well above ground. First specimens collected from roof of pickup truck with long-handled net! Foraging flights in early morning and late afternoon, not midday.
Flight Season LA Jun–Jul.

---

242 Hine's Emerald *Somatochlora hineana* TL 58–63, HW 40–42

Description Midwestern emerald of restricted range and habitat with striped thorax. *Male*: Face dull yellow-brown, top of frons black. Thorax metallic green and brown with two short yellow stripes on each side, anterior one longer. Abdomen black with round yellow spot on sides of S2. Cerci straight and blunt-ended in dorsal view, strongly arched down and ending beyond tip of epiproct. *Female*: Color pattern as male, abdomen not constricted. Subgenital plate long, scoop-shaped and pointed, projecting backwards at 45° angle.

Identification Although restricted in range, this species potentially occurs with numerous other striped emeralds. Most similar, and often occurring with it, is **Clamp-tipped**. Hine's differs from **Clamp-tipped** in having cerci straight (curved inward in **Clamp-tipped**) in top view and less angulate in side view. In **Clamp-tipped** anterior thoracic stripe usually more obscure than posterior one, often not evident, whereas both equally bright in **Hine's**. **Plains** not known to occur near any **Hine's** populations but very similarly marked, distinguished by brighter yellow-orange face and quite different appendages. **Brush-tipped** has somewhat similar thoracic markings but is smaller and with very different appendages. **Ocellated** is small, with round spots on thorax. **Ozark** has long rather than short stripes on thorax. **Forcipate** has smaller thoracic markings and yellow dots along abdomen. **Delicate**, **Incurvate**, **Kennedy's**, **Mocha**, and **Williamson's** lack conspicuous thoracic markings.

Natural History Prereproductive adults fly up to 2 miles from emergence site, become sexually mature in 7–10 days. Most activity at breeding sites is for 3–4 hr in late morning, before temperatures rise in early afternoon; perched individuals near breeding sites most likely to be found early in day. Feeding flights last 15–30 min, typically in clearings in woodland, and

242.1
Hine's Emerald male—Dent Co., MO, June 2009, Bryan Pfeiffer/Wings Photography
242.2
Hine's Emerald female—Will Co., IL, July 2007, David Jagodzinski

foraging individuals may be several miles from breeding habitats. Much feeding in morning but may feed as late as dusk. Breeding males fly slowly around their territories, frequently hovering, for many minutes. Fly at knee to head height over territories 6–30 feet in length. Trespassing males quickly chased away. Males capture females that visit their territory, fly off in tandem, and copulate in nearby shrubs. Oviposit by hovering, then dropping to substrate and dipping abdomen in water or soft mud, typically in small water-filled depressions surrounded by sedges. May tap water up to 200 times on one visit and lay >500 eggs during lifetime. Mature adults can live at least 2 weeks.

Habitat Grass and sedge fens (meadows) with no more than shallow sheet of water in depressions, often with at least slight current (flat or on a slight slope). Usually fed by ground water, underlain by dolomite, and in wooded/shrubby landscape. Larvae overwinter in crayfish burrows.

Flight Season Entire range Jun–Aug.

Distribution Not found in Ohio or Alabama in recent decades.

Comments Only North American odonate on U.S. Endangered Species List. Recent searching has shown it as much more widespread than was known when it was listed.

243 Clamp-tipped Emerald *Somatochlora tenebrosa* TL 48–54, HW 34–40

Description Slender eastern emerald with distinctive appendages. *Male*: Face black above, light brown below. Thorax mixed brown and metallic green, two elongate yellow spots on sides that become obscure with age. Abdomen black with yellow ventrolateral spot and pale yellow apical ring on S2. Cerci from side sharply bent downward in middle, overlap strongly curved epiproct like clamp; in top view tips angled inward, then parallel. *Female*: Colored as male but orange dorsolateral spot on S3. Subgenital plate sharply pointed, projecting almost at right angle, longer than height of S9.

243.1
Clamp-tipped Emerald male—Greene Co., OH, September 2009, William Hull

243.2
Clamp-tipped Emerald female—Northumberland Co., NB, July 2007, Denis Doucet, posed

Identification Good side view of clamplike appendages of male definitive. Same for long, perpendicular, pointed subgenital plate of female, although much like that of **Mocha** and **Williamson's Emeralds**, which have unmarked thorax. **Hine's, Ozark,** and **Texas Emeralds** also have yellow-spotted thorax but more vividly marked, quite different appendages. Often flies with **Calvert's** and **Treetop** on southeastern Coastal Plain; males distinguished easily by different appendages. Female **Calvert's** and **Treetop** show faint white rings at abdomen tip, yellow stripe down each side of S3, all missing from **Clamp-tipped**.

Natural History Males fly up and down streams at knee height or above, at both pools and riffles, with frequent hovering and pivoting, then may perch at knee height. Longer beats necessary on series of pools. Female oviposits by tapping water or pushing eggs into wet moss, decaying leaves, or mud; often in tiny depressions among dense herbaceous vegetation. Foraging flight throughout day at woodland edge, rapid and over wide range of altitudes, even persisting until after sunset.

Habitat Small forest streams with rapids and pools and much leaf litter, almost always in shade. May dry to series of pools in late summer. Also sedgy fens in western part of range.

Flight Season ON Jul–Sep, QC Jul–Aug, NS Jul–Sep, WI Jul–Aug, ME Jun–Sep, OH Jun–Sep, NJ Jun–Sep, KY Jun–Oct, GA May–Sep, FL Jun–Aug.

Striped Emeralds - male appendages

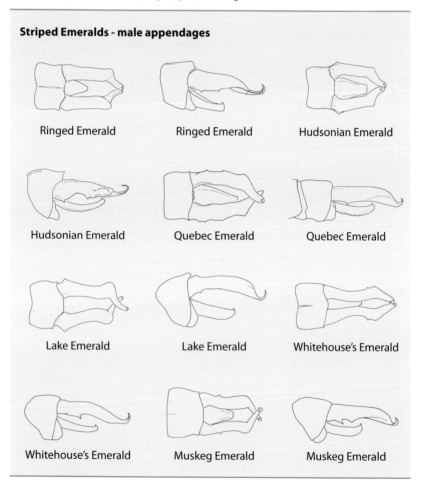

Ringed Emerald

Ringed Emerald

Hudsonian Emerald

Hudsonian Emerald

Quebec Emerald

Quebec Emerald

Lake Emerald

Lake Emerald

Whitehouse's Emerald

Whitehouse's Emerald

Muskeg Emerald

Muskeg Emerald

Striped Emeralds - male appendages *(continued)*

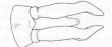

Forcipate Emerald

Forcipate Emerald

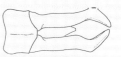

Incurvate Emerald

Incurvate Emerald

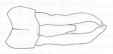

Delicate Emerald

Delicate Emerald

Kennedy's Emerald

Kennedy's Emerald

Ski-tipped Emerald

Ski-tipped Emerald

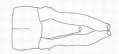

Williamson's Emerald

Williamson's Emerald

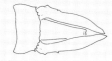

Ocellated Emerald

Ocellated Emerald

Brush-tipped Emerald

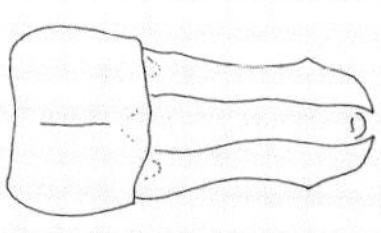

Brush-tipped Emerald

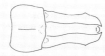

Plains Emerald

Plains Emerald

Striped Emeralds - male appendages *(continued)*

Mocha Emerald

Mocha Emerald

Coppery Emerald

Coppery Emerald

Fine-lined Emerald

Fine-lined Emerald

Calvert's Emerald

Calvert's Emerald

Treetop Emerald

Treetop Emerald

Ozark Emerald

Ozark Emerald

Texas Emerald

Texas Emerald

Hine's Emerald

Hine's Emerald

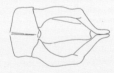

Clamp-tipped Emerald

Clamp-tipped Emerald

Striped Emeralds - female abdomen tip

Ringed Emerald

Hudsonian Emerald

Quebec Emerald

Lake Emerald

Whitehouse's Emeraldn

Muskeg Emerald

Forcipate Emerald

Incurvate Emerald

Delicate Emerald

Kennedy's Emerald

Ski-tipped Emerald

Williamson's Emerald

Ocellated Emerald

Brush-tipped Emerald

Plains Emerald

Mocha Emerald

Coppery Emerald

Fine-lined Emerald

Striped Emeralds - female abdomen tip *(continued)*

Calvert's Emerald

Treetop Emerald

Ozark Emerald

Texas Emerald

Hine's Emerald

Clamp-tipped Emerald

Shadowdragons *Neurocordulia*

Shadowdragons are characterized by dull brown coloration (including the large eyes), entirely pale face, yellow spot on each side of thorax in most species, and relatively broad wings with dense venation. Dark pigment forming dots at anterior crossveins is usually present, more prominent in some species. Note the pigment is between the subcostal and medial veins inward from the nodus, not at the front edge of the wing. A few species have dark basal hindwing patches. They roost during the day in woodland, and their flight time is restricted to dusk and into darkness. When warm enough, they also fly at dawn. The large eyes and broad wings are characteristic of crepuscular dragonflies. It is hard to imagine that their flight period is long enough to accomplish either feeding or breeding, but they manage. Because of their time of activity, they are generally very poorly known, but all species may have rather similar habits. Most live on streams and rivers, but a few also patrol along the shores of large lakes. They are fast and often erratic fliers, a challenge to the most skillful collector and probably impossible to identify without capture when flying at dusk. Roosting individuals may be distinguished at close range. World 7, NA 7, East 7.

244 Stygian Shadowdragon *Neurocordulia yamaskanensis* TL 45–55, HW 33–35

Description Large shadowdragon with basal wing spots. *Male:* Largely brown, including eyes. Thorax darker in front than on sides, with conspicuous white median line on front and small yellow spot at spiracle. Abdomen darker brown with dull yellow stripes along sides of S2–8. Wings with orange basal spots, veins therein outlined in brown. *Female:* Color pattern as in male, abdominal pattern a bit more pronounced, darker with more prominent yellow patches on sides. Basal wing spots may be entirely brown, and antenodal crossveins may be faintly marked with pigment.

Identification Only other shadowdragon in range with conspicuous brown basal wing patches is **Umber**, which averages about one centimeter shorter and has much more distinct dots at crossveins, a larger one at nodus of each wing. **Stygian** also occurs widely with

244.1
Stygian Shadowdragon
male—Sussex Co., NJ, June
2008, Allen Barlow

244.2
Stygian Shadowdragon
female—Sussex Co., NJ, June
2007, Tom Murray

Broad-tailed and **Smoky** and very narrowly overlaps **Cinnamon** and **Orange Shadowdragons**. Configuration of basal wing spots different from those of BASKETTAILS, and brown coloration eliminates SUNDRAGONS. SPOTTED DARNERS, also brown and flying over streams at dusk and roosting in forest by day, much larger and with two yellow spots on each side of thorax.

Natural History Come to river as early as half hour before sunset, both sexes apparently in equal numbers. Presumably for both sexual rendezvous and feeding, as small insects often abundant at that time and place. Pairs meet over water, hook up in wheel, then fly up into trees. Freshly emerged individuals found near breeding habitat in herbaceous and shrubby vegetation.

Habitat Large rivers and lakes with unvegetated shallows.

Flight Season ON Jun–Sep, QC Jun–Jul, IA Jun–Jul, WI Jun, ME Jun–Jul, OH Jun–Aug, NJ May–Jul, KY May–Aug.

---

245 Umber Shadowdragon   *Neurocordulia obsoleta*   TL 43–48, HW 30–33

Description Shadowdragon with basal wing spots and prominent spot at nodus. *Male*: Largely brown, including eyes. Thorax darker in front than on sides, with conspicuous white median line on front and small yellow spot at spiracle. Abdomen with narrow, faint yellow stripes along sides of S2–8. Wings with brown basal spots. *Female*: Color pattern as in male, abdominal pattern a bit more evident, with more prominent yellow patches on sides.

Identification Smaller than similar **Stygian Shadowdragon**, with much better developed dots at crossveins, largest one at nodus. Other co-occurring shadowdragons (**Alabama**, **Broad-tailed**, **Cinnamon**, **Smoky**) and other emeralds lack combination of basal wing spots and nodal spots.

Natural History Appears at rivers as it is getting dark, but before sunset, and flies into darkness. Flight fast and a bit erratic, low over water surface and poking into nooks and crannies along edge. More commonly over swift than quiet water. As in other shadowdragons, both sexes present, but very difficult to understand what they are doing. Mating pairs fly up into forest. Freshly emerged individuals found near breeding habitat in herbaceous vegetation.

Emerald Family   **377**

245.1
Umber Shadowdragon
male—Middlesex Co., CT,
June 2004, Giff Beaton,
posed

245.2
Umber Shadowdragon
female—Sussex Co., NJ, June
2007, Tom Murray, posed

Habitat Rocky rivers with fairly swift current in pools and riffles through woodland.
Flight Season ME May–Sep, OH Jun–Jul, NJ May–Sep, FL Apr.
Distribution Records very sparse over most of range away from Atlantic states.

246 Broad-tailed Shadowdragon *Neurocordulia michaeli* TL 40–43, HW 28–31

Description Northern shadowdragon with broad, boldly marked abdomen and dark legs. *Male*: Eyes dull greenish (to yellowish) over gray, face light brown. Thorax brown, darker in front and with pale carina and yellow spot around spiracles. Abdomen blackish with fairly bold yellow rectangles on sides of S3–8. Wings with variable amount of orange suffusion at base, inner crossveins with faint pigment spots. *Female*: Color pattern as male, eyes duller green or reddish-brown. Yellow spots on abdomen wider, more prominent. Gravid females with very swollen abdomen.

Identification Only shadowdragon with entirely dark legs and sometimes yellowish eyes. Abdominal pattern more contrasty than any other. Different from **Stygian** and **Umber** in lacking brown basal wing spots. Body color rather like a BASKETTAIL, but latter lack pale carina on thorax and have yellow on either side of spiracle, not over it; also no hint of pigmented crossveins.

Natural History Adults come to breeding habitat at sundown, initially flying high over water and then coming lower, staying less than 45 min. Pairs meet at water surface, form wheel, and then fly into understory of marginal forest. Females oviposit by tapping smooth stretches of water while flying at high speed up center of rapids.

Habitat Rapid streams and rivers with boulders and cobbles.

Flight Season ON Jun–Jul, ME Jun–Jul.

246.1
Broad-tailed
Shadowdragon
male—Charlotte Co., NB,
June 1996, Blair Nikula,
posed

246.2
Broad-tailed
Shadowdragon
female—Renfrew Co., ON,
July 2005, Greg Lasley,
posed

247 Alabama Shadowdragon   *Neurocordulia alabamensis*   TL 42–46, HW 29–33

Description Small, very plain shadowdragon of Southeast. *Male:* Entirely orange-brown to dull brown, including eyes; sides of thorax become yellowish with maturity. *Female:* Colored as male, recognized by thicker abdomen. Wings with anterior edges heavily dotted with brown in both sexes; entire wings of older individuals suffused with brown.

Identification Distributions poorly known but may overlap with **Cinnamon** and **Smoky Shadowdragons**, southern species also lacking large hindwing patch. In hand, look at dots along front edge of wing. In **Alabama**, dots evenly colored and extend out to nodus and often to stigma, the most heavily dotted wings of any of the species in this group. In **Cinnamon**, dots smaller and extend only halfway to nodus. In **Smoky**, dots may extend to nodus but are darker on edge than along crossvein. **Cinnamon** and **Smoky** also usually show bright yellow spot on each side of thorax lacking in **Alabama**. Slightly larger **Umber** has large basal wing spots. No other small, virtually unmarked brown dragonfly in range (until **Evening Skimmer** moves farther north).

247.1
Alabama Shadowdragon
male—Bibb Co., AL, Jul
2003, Giff Beaton, posed

247.2
Alabama Shadowdragon
female—Bibb Co., AL, June
2008, Steve Krotzer, posed

Natural History Only seen in dusk flight over breeding habitat; nothing known of behavior otherwise.

Habitat Small to medium-sized slowly flowing streams with sand and muck bottoms, usually in woodland.

Flight Season FL May–Jul.

---

248 Cinnamon Shadowdragon *Neurocordulia virginiensis* TL 42–49, HW 32–35

Description Southern shadowdragon with faint yellow thoracic spots and wing dots. *Male*: Entirely medium brown, including eyes. Thorax with median dark area in front, inconspicuous yellow spot low on sides. Abdomen with faint narrow yellow rings most obvious on basal segments, faint dark markings most obvious on middle segments. *Female*: Colored as male. Both sexes with faint dots on some antenodal crossveins.

Identification Least-marked wings of any shadowdragon, less than **Alabama** and **Smoky** with which it overlaps. Very similar **Smoky** has brown dots at crossveins margined with darker, not the case in **Cinnamon**. Yellow thoracic spot not bordered behind by black, as in **Smoky**. **Orange** and **Umber** have much more heavily marked wings.

Natural History Both sexes fly beats just above water's surface from about sundown until dark (or later?). Males may appear before dark at times. Patrol flights usually over riffles, may be short up and down or may cruise one riffle for short time, then move to a different one, both at shore and out over open water. Day and night roosting apparently in forest near breeding habitat.

Habitat Medium-sized to large rivers with some current in wooded country.

Flight Season GA May–Jun, FL Mar–Jun.

248.1
Cinnamon Shadowdragon male—Rabun Co., GA, June 2008, Giff Beaton, posed

248.2
Cinnamon Shadowdragon female—Buckingham Co., VA, May 2009, Allen Bryan

Description Shadowdragon with bold yellow thoracic spots and prominent wing dots. *Male*: Entirely light brown, including eyes. Thorax with dark area on front and prominent elongate yellow spot low on sides. Abdomen with yellow basal spot low on sides of S2, narrow yellow rings on about S3–8, and faint dark patterning along middle segments. *Female*: Colored as male. Both sexes with dots at all antenodal crossveins, larger dot at nodus.

Identification Differs from **Cinnamon Shadowdragon** in larger and more extensive wing dots, extending out to nodus and darkly outlined on edges. Dark area behind yellow lateral thoracic spot a bit more prominent in **Smoky** than **Cinnamon**, which often lacks it. **Alabama** has many wing dots but lacks obvious yellow spot on each side of thorax present in both **Cinnamon** and **Smoky**. Slightly larger and brighter **Orange Shadowdragon** has much more extensive wing markings. **Stygian** and **Umber** have prominent basal wing spots.

Natural History Both sexes appear at river as dusk is falling, usually last half-hour before darkness and as much as half-hour before sunset. Individuals can be seen coming from forest through clearings to river. Remain at water until scarcely visible and perhaps into full dark, flying up and down river very low and mostly over open water away from shore. Much interaction among individuals, details not obvious (just among males? males checking for females?). Females oviposit by flying rapidly, tapping water every few feet. Roosts in trees and shrubs in forest.

Habitat Large, swift-flowing rivers with sandy shores, wooded banks.

Flight Season IA May–Jul, WI Jun–Jul, OH Jun–Aug, GA Apr–Jun, FL Jun–Aug.

249.1
Smoky Shadowdragon
male—Long Co., GA, June 2005,
Giff Beaton, posed

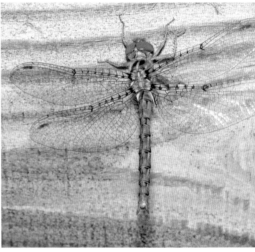

249.2
Smoky Shadowdragon
female—St. Charles Co., MO,
June 2008, Dale Hallett

Description Large orange-brown shadowdragon of southern plains with heavily marked wings. *Male*: Eyes light brown. Body entirely orange-brown. Thorax with faint yellow spot low on sides. Abdomen with faint yellow basal spots on sides of S4–8. *Female*: Colored as male. Both sexes with wings heavily marked with orange or brown, typically dark dots and blotches along anterior edges but may be heaviest across base; in older individuals, entire wing may become brownish.

Identification Larger and more orange-looking than other shadowdragons, often apparent even at dusk. Extensive wing markings also distinguish it from others of its group. Day-flying habits make it appear when various brown skimmers present, but none of them really looks like it.

Natural History Both sexes fly over rivers beginning at dusk or shortly before and continuing at least until completely dark. Also fly at dawn on warmer mornings and occasionally during cloudy periods at midday. Flight usually just above water but at times a bit higher, from just off shore to well out in open water; beats may be short or much lengthier. Mating seen in dawn flight, with copulating pair flying from water to perching site in tree. Oviposition seen after dawn flight, female scattering eggs in rapid flight. Many roost in forest, but

250.1
Orange Shadowdragon male—Gonzales Co., TX, July 2009, Troy Hibbitts

250.2
Orange Shadowdragon female—Montgomery Co., AR, May 2006

only shadowdragon that also regularly roosts in herbaceous and shrubby vegetation adjacent to breeding habitat, perhaps because often in open country. Thus more easily found in daytime than other shadowdragons, usually hanging below knee height in small shrubs and perhaps showing preference for small islands in rivers.

Habitat Rivers with slow to moderate current in open or wooded landscape.

Flight Season Entire range Apr–Aug.

Distribution Extends farther west in Oklahoma and Texas, one New Mexico record.

Baskettails *Epitheca*

Among the dullest emeralds, their eyes are less brilliant green and there is little or no metallic color on the light brown and black body with spindle-shaped abdomen. The eyes are reddish over gray in immatures of all species, then in most males turn emerald green with maturity (but there is individual variation, and eyes may be blue in at least several species). The flight season is typically early. Males cruise over water, apparently also over land, in sexual patrol flight, but females are not often seen, mostly in foraging flights over clearings that may be aggregated when prey is common. Baskettail feeding swarms are a daily occurrence wherever one of the small species is common, often the most conspicuous dragonflies over roads and clearings. They perch with abdomen held at around 45° below horizontal except for the long-bodied Prince Baskettail, which hangs vertically. Mating pairs are rarely seen, and mating may always occur away from water. After mating, the female accumulates a large egg cluster at the end of her abdomen, held in place by the very long, forked subgenital plate, very conspicuous as she flies low over water. Females spend much time in flight with abdomen elevated and a conspicuous egg mass at the tip, looking for optimal oviposition opportunities. When the right place is found, the abdomen is dragged along the water surface, draping a long string packed full of eggs over plant stems. These masses can be up to several feet long and an inch or more wide as the jelly expands. Numerous females may oviposit at the same spot. The American species of this genus are often separated in genera *Epicordulia* (Prince Baskettail) and *Tetragoneuria* (all other species). The two Eurasian *Epitheca*, intermediate in size between these two American groups, share the egg strings that appear to unite them all. Body patterns are also rather similar, and all species have at least small brown basal hindwing spots, some quite a bit larger patches. Some *Tetragoneuria* are frustratingly similar in structure and variable in wing patterns, which vary geographically as well as individually. Field identification is almost impossible for most species, as all are colored essentially the same, and they present difficulties even in hand. Drive slowly along roads that pass through their habitats and look for feeding swarms to capture and identify baskettails. Another way to see these and other flier dragonflies is to go out early and look in sunny clearings, where they may be perched in the open trying to warm up to start their feeding flight. Extralimital distribution records in this genus are especially suspect because of identification problems. World 12, NA 10, East 9.

251 Common Baskettail *Epitheca cynosura*   TL 38–43, HW 26–31

Description In most areas the most common baskettail. Size, darkness of body, and darkness and extent of wing markings increase toward northern part of range. *Male:* Eyes red over gray for much of life but eventually becoming bright emerald green or blue (perhaps geographic variation); face dull yellow-orange with black on top of frons varying from small black triangle at base to entire top of frons black. Thorax brown with darker markings and small yellow spots low on sides. Abdomen with S1–2 brown, black beyond that with elongate yellow spots on sides of S3–8. *Female:* Colored as male; abdomen thicker and cerci much shorter. Over much of region hindwing markings

251.1
Common Baskettail
male—Santa Rosa Co., FL,
April 2008

251.2
Common Baskettail
male—Jackson Co., WI,
June 2007, posed

251.3
Common Baskettail
female—Union Co., SC,
May 2008

vary from tiny brown basal spot to triangular brown spot that extends almost to nodus, but large-spotted individuals make up all or almost all of northern populations.

Identification Indeed the common baskettail over much of eastern North America, serving as a standard from which other species must be distinguished. Other species dominate numerically at northern and southern ends of its range, however. Male **Beaverpond** and **Spiny** with limited brown at base of hindwings, whereas **Common** often with prominent hindwing spot where it overlaps with them. Cerci of **Beaverpond** very different, those of **Spiny** similar but with spine that can be seen only in hand. In fact, most identification of small baskettails not possible except in hand. See **Mantled** and **Slender** for distinctions from those species in southern part of region. Female cerci distinctly shorter (shorter than S9) than those in **Slender** and **Spiny** (longer than S9). Note that wing pattern alone may distinguish it in some areas, as **Common** only species (outside range of **Mantled**) that has extensive black markings at hindwing bases. But not all **Common** have prominent wing markings. See also **Florida** and **Sepia Baskettails**, overlapping with **Common** in limited area.

Natural History Males fly at knee height over pools in streams as well as along shores of ponds and lakes, often with extended hovering; patrol length 12–30 feet. Males often patrol clearings near but not at water, perhaps also sexual patrol flights; these are usually higher, often head height. Copulation in flight, with movements over water at waist height up to hundreds of yards and as long as 5 min. Females at times fly very rapidly across water, stop suddenly to inspect potential oviposition site, apparently find it wanting, and zoom off again. Appropriate oviposition sites may attract numerous females simultaneously. Often survey an area in low flight before even starting to lay eggs. Feeding singly or in small swarms over open areas, from head height to well up in trees and each individual moving back and forth rapidly, then pursuing prey and changing height. Small insects such as flying fire ants are eaten in flight, their wings dropped.

Habitat Ponds and lakes with open or wooded margins, also pools in slow streams.

Flight Season ON May–Aug, QC May–Jul, NS Jun–Aug, IA May–Aug, WI May–Sep, ME May–Jul, OH Apr–Jul, NJ May–Jul, KY Apr–Jul, LA Feb–May, GA Mar–Jul, FL Jan–May, Oct–Nov.

Distribution Few records farther west in Nebraska. Western range limits may be inaccurate because of confusion with similar species.

---

252 Mantled Baskettail *Epitheca semiaquea* TL 32–37, HW 23–28

Description Small baskettail of Atlantic Coastal Plain with broad abdomen and largest dark spots in hindwings. *Male*: Eyes red over gray for much of life but eventually developing small green areas along front; face dull yellow-orange with black on top of frons varying from small black triangle at base to entire top of frons black. Thorax brown with darker markings and small yellow spots low on sides. Abdomen with S1–2 brown, black beyond that with elongate yellow spots on sides of S3–8. Hindwings with large dark markings, extending back to wing margin and out to nodus in Southeast. Wing markings smaller in New Jersey and farther north, not reaching nodus and rear of wing. *Female*: Colored as male, thicker abdomen and much shorter appendages evident.

252.1
Mantled Baskettail
male—Nassau Co., NY,
May 2009, Steve Walter

252.2
Mantled Baskettail
female—Cape May Co.,
NJ, May 1999, R. A.
Behrstock/Naturewide
Images

252.3
Mantled Baskettail
male—Evans Co., GA,
March 2005, Giff Beaton

252.4
Mantled Baskettail
female—Chesterfield Co.,
SC, May 2008

Identification Large hindwing spots, extending almost to nodus and rear edge of wing, should allow easy identification whether on territory or in feeding flight. Confusion most likely with some **Common Baskettails** with especially large hindwing spots, although most **Common** in range of **Mantled** have smaller markings. Markings a bit different, usually a clear area at base (midbasal space and just beyond) in **Mantled**, entirely or mostly dark in that space in **Common**, especially those that have larger markings. This mark especially useful in northern and western part of region, where **Mantled** have smaller wing spots. **Common** a bit larger with more slender abdomen, although difference in females not easily detected. S4–5 in both sexes of **Mantled** obviously wider than long, in **Common** square to longer than wide. Relatively broad abdomen makes yellow spots on sides of it more prominent than in other baskettails. **Robust Baskettail** also wide-bodied, but larger and with very limited wing markings. Quite different habits, flying around and then hanging up vertically, should distinguish any baskettail from small skimmers with dark hindwing patches, for example **Marl Pennant**. **Black Saddlebags** much larger.

Natural History Males fly over water on sexual patrol; back and forth beat may be as short as 15 feet. May also patrol beat over land in shady areas. Oviposition as in other baskettails, eggs dropped in floating algal mats. One female dragged abdomen tip through 10-inch algal mat quite slowly. Because of large wing spots, flight usually looks fluttery.

Habitat Sandy lakes and ponds with much vegetation. In northern part of range, much more a species of the low coastal plain than is the more upland Common Baskettail.

Flight Season ME May–Jul, NJ Apr–Jun, KY May–Jun, GA Mar–Apr.

253 Slender Baskettail *Epitheca costalis* TL 38–48, HW 25–32

Description Rather slender southeastern baskettail. *Male*: Eyes red over gray for much of life but eventually becoming emerald green or dark blue; face dull yellow-orange with small black triangle at base of top of frons. Thorax brown with darker markings and small yellow spots low on sides. Abdomen with S1–2 brown, black beyond that with elongate yellow spots on sides of S3–8. *Female*: Colored as male; abdomen slightly thicker, but very similar, as appendages of both sexes rather long. Some females with dark stripe along anterior edge of wings, apparently restricted to north Florida and nearby Georgia (one specimen from coastal South Carolina) and rare even there.

Identification Overlaps extensively with **Common Baskettail** in eastern part of region. Differs in having more slender abdomen, constricted to form distinct "wasp waist." Look at S3 from directly above if possible. In male **Slender**, width at narrowest point about one-half length; in male **Common**, distinctly more than that. In female, S4–5 are distinctly longer than wide in **Slender**, more or less square in **Common**. Yellow dorsolateral markings on S3 elongate, usually more than twice as long as wide and often tapering sharply to rear in **Slender**, as an indicator of segment shape. In **Common**, these markings more rectangular, no more than twice as long as wide. Difficult to quantify, but differences becomes apparent with experience. However, more difficult to distinguish in side view. Male appendages very

253.1
Slender Baskettail
male—Laurens Co., GA,
April 2005, Giff Beaton

253.2
Slender Baskettail
female—Tattnall Co., GA,
March 2005, Giff Beaton,
posed

253.3
Slender Baskettail
female—Bay Co., FL,
March 2008, May
Lattanzio

similar, but cerci of **Slender** slightly longer and with more obvious bump at ventral angle, of **Common** slightly shorter and with more of a narrow keel at that angle. Females differ by **Slender** having distinctly longer cerci, about three times length of S10, not quite two times in **Common**. Many **Common** have extensive dark markings at hindwing bases, not so in **Slender**. **Slender** overlaps slightly with **Florida** and **Sepia Baskettails**, distinguished by yellow dashes along abdomen sides rather than continuous or nearly continuous yellow stripe. Probably no overlap in range with quite similar-looking **Spiny Baskettail**.

Natural History Males fly patrol flights over water like other baskettails but seem slightly more common in wooded areas, often flying in shade and among trees and shrubs. Forage in open areas from just above ground to treetops, often in swarms and may be mixed with other baskettails.

Habitat Sandy ponds, lakes, and slow streams. More likely to be on streams than other small baskettails.

Flight Season IA May–Jul, NJ May–Jun, KY May–Jun, LA Mar–Apr, GA Mar–Jun, FL Jan–Apr.

Distribution Records of this species farther west may all refer to Dot-winged Baskettail.

Comments Called Stripe-winged Baskettail in some books. Perhaps the Dot-winged Baskettail, *Epitheca petechialis*, of farther west may occur in Louisiana and Arkansas. Western individuals of Dot-winged have dotted wings, but eastern ones do not, and they are difficult to impossible to distinguish from Slender; there is speculation that they are the same species. Finally, as difficult as baskettail identification seems, it gets worse. Some specimens from Ohio and other states are intermediate, possibly hybrids, between this and the Common Baskettail!

254 Florida Baskettail *Epitheca stella* TL 40–48, HW 27–32

Description Slender baskettail mostly restricted to Florida. *Male*: Eyes red-brown over gray, with faint greenish tinge in front; face dull yellow-orange with only faint dark marking above. Thorax brown with sparse darker markings in sutures and very faint yellow spots low on sides. Abdomen with S1–2 brown, black beyond that with sides of S3–8 yellow to orange-brown. Cerci long, slender, and cylindrical, divergent at ends. *Female*: Colored as male, distinguished by abdomen shape and appendages. Cerci shorter than S9.

Identification Overlaps in northern part of range with superficially very similar **Slender Baskettail**; the two could be distinguished in the hand by the male cerci (longer and with a distinct projecting angle visible in side view in **Slender**, shorter and with less projecting angle in **Florida**) and female cerci (usually longer than S9 in **Slender**, shorter in **Florida**).

254.1
Florida Baskettail male—
Palm Beach Co., FL, March
2008, Steve Walter

254.2
Florida Baskettail
female—Broward Co., FL,
March 2006, Steve Walter

The abdomen in **Slender** is also a bit more constricted, widening more after the very constricted S3; thus S4 distinctly wider at posterior than anterior end in **Slender**, less obvious difference in **Florida**. **Florida** also occurs with **Common Baskettail**, differs from that species in more slender abdomen (best seen in dorsal view) and lack of dark basal wing markings. Amount of yellow on sides of abdominal segments might be good field mark; extends almost entire length of segment in **Florida**, not so in **Common** and **Slender**, which thus show series of dashes rather than (almost) continuous yellow edges. **Sepia Baskettail** also has no or very limited markings at wing bases and full-length yellow abdominal markings but is darker than **Florida**, with shorter and broader abdomen, showing no abdominal constriction at all. Female **Sepia** also have shorter cerci. They are the only two baskettails in southern Florida, readily distinguished when together in feeding swarms if their shape can be noted. Their breeding habitat is different as well as the time of their sexual patrol flights.

Natural History Most often seen away from water, and large unidirectional flights away from breeding habitats have been seen in Everglades area. Often in feeding assemblages with Sepia Baskettails in peninsular Florida. Males fly short back-and-forth beats over streams and ponds and over land near marshes in broad daylight, from waist to head height. As no females are seen at these times, these are probably sexual patrol flights.

Habitat Extensive marshes and marsh-bordered lakes, habitats not used by other baskettails in the southeastern coastal plain. The Everglades is an important habitat, as are coastal marshes farther north in Florida.

Flight Season FL Jan–Apr.

Distribution Isolated records of this species, well away from the main range, may not represent breeding populations. The species should be sought in marsh habitats farther west along the Gulf Coast.

---

255 Sepia Baskettail *Epitheca sepia* TL 35–45, HW 26–32

Description Small, dark, somewhat stocky baskettail of Florida and nearby states. *Male*: Eyes red-brown over gray; face dull brownish. Thorax brown with black markings in sutures and pair of fairly conspicuous yellow spots at mesothoracic spiracle. Abdomen with S1–2 brown with black markings. S3–9 with broad black dorsal stripe, yellow-orange sides, pale markings becoming narrower and narrower as abdomen becomes narrower toward rear, and S10

255.1
Sepia Baskettail male—Leon Co., FL,
April 2005, posed

255.2
Sepia Baskettail female—
Orange Co., FL, April 2008,
Eric Haley, posed

black. *Female*: Colored as male, distinguished by abdomen shape and appendages. Cerci short, about twice length of S10.

Identification This is a small baskettail, only the **Mantled** as small, and that species has large black markings on the hindwings. **Sepia** usually lacks dark wing markings entirely and is smaller and stockier than other clear-winged baskettails, with which it often flies in feeding swarms. The abdomen is unconstricted, the middle segments almost as wide as long (much longer than wide in **Common**, **Florida**, and **Slender**). Sides of abdomen show continuous yellow-orange stripes, contrasting highly with dark thorax. Other baskettails (except **Florida**) have these stripes obviously broken. See **Florida Baskettail**, seen in feeding flights with this species.

Natural History Males engage in sexual patrol flights from midafternoon until dark. They fly fairly low in short beats along shorelines of both streams and ponds. Patrol beat around 20–30 feet long at knee to waist height, back and forth flight with no hovering and abdomen elevated slightly. Both sexes feed throughout the day, often in small assemblages and up to treetops, but apparently much more later in day. It would be interesting to know why this small species has such a long flight season in comparison with its close relatives.

Habitat Lakes, ponds, and streams with sand bottom, some vegetation.

Flight Season GA May–Jul, FL Jan–Nov.

256 Spiny Baskettail *Epitheca spinigera*   TL 43–47, HW 29–34

Description Slender northern baskettail with dark body and clear wings. *Male*: Eyes bright emerald green or blue-green at maturity; face dull yellow-orange with black on top of frons as broad-based T-spot. Thorax brown with darker markings and small yellow spots low on sides. Abdomen with S1–2 brown, black beyond that with elongate yellow spots on sides of S3–8. Cerci with small spine under base visible from side, rarely reduced or even lacking. *Female*: Colored as male, eyes duller, dark green and brown at maturity. Cerci rather long.

Identification Wide overlap with **Beaverpond Baskettail**, distinguished by differently shaped cerci in male, longer cerci in female. Also, in hand, T-spot on top of frons and black rear of head can be seen in **Spiny**, frons mostly dark and back of head pale in **Beaverpond**. Probably not distinguishable in flight, although appendages might be visible in binoculars in slow or hovering flight. Also overlaps with slightly smaller **Common Baskettail** in much

256.1
Spiny Baskettail male—
Bayfield Co., WI, June
2008, Ryan Brady

256.2
Spiny Baskettail
male—Rusk Co., WI, June
2007

256.3
Spiny Baskettail
female—Bayfield Co., WI,
June 2008, Ryan Brady

of eastern range. In hand, male **Spiny** distinguished from **Common** by small downward-pointing spine at base of cerci (very rarely lacking), very difficult to see in field. Pattern of top of frons different, prominent dark T-spot in **Spiny** and usually only stem of that marking in **Common**; again, most readily seen in hand. Females more easily distinguished by length of cerci, longer than S9 in **Spiny** and shorter than S9 in **Common**; this could be seen in perched individuals. Many **Common** have prominent dark markings at base of hindwings (lacking in **Spiny**).

Natural History Males fly low over water in sexual patrol flight, but also do so in open areas near water, often at woodland edge. Cruise back and forth at waist to above head height over beats 10–40 feet in length. Copulating pairs rarely seen; one was in tall grass near water. Females fly with raised abdomen, then tap water at intervals releasing short egg string, as late as dusk. Favored oviposition sites may be inundated with egg clusters, looking much like amphibian eggs. Both sexes feed over clearings, knee height to treetops, sometimes far from breeding localities.

Habitat Ponds and lakes of all sizes and kinds in wooded country, including beaver ponds and bog ponds, more rarely at slow streams.

Flight Season ON May–Aug, QC May–Jul, NS May–Aug, WI Apr–Aug, ME May–Jul, NJ May–Jun, KY Apr–Jun.

Distribution West across southern Canadian provinces to northern Alberta and British Columbia, then south in Pacific states to northern California.

---

257 Beaverpond Baskettail   *Epitheca canis*   TL 43–48, HW 30–31

Description Northern baskettail with distinctive male appendages, otherwise much like other species (but note brown-winged females). *Male*: Eyes bright emerald green or blue-green; face dull yellow-orange with black triangle on top of frons. Thorax brown with darker markings and small yellow spots low on sides. Abdomen with S1–2 brown, black beyond that with elongate yellow spots on sides of S3–8 or 9. Cerci strongly angled downward near

257.1
Beaverpond Baskettail
male—Columbia Co., WI,
May 1997, Dave Westover

257.2
Beaverpond Baskettail
female—Hampden Co.,
MA, June 2004, Glenn
Corbiere

tips. *Female*: Colored as male, eyes more likely to be red over gray. Mature females in eastern populations with entirely brown wings, very distinctive in flight.

Identification Beaverpond differs from both **Common** and **Spiny Baskettails** by pale rear of head (black in other species) and very different angulate male appendages. More slender abdomen than **Common**, about like **Spiny**. Brown wings allow easy distinction of mature female **Beaverpond**, although uncolored in younger individuals. **Beaverpond** has female cerci about twice length of S10, slightly more than that in **Spiny**, distinctly less than that in **Common**, but some variation and perhaps overlap. **Common** often has prominent dark hindwing patches, **Beaverpond** only tiny ones. In hand, ventral view of subgenital plate diagnostic, two lobes almost parallel in **Beaverpond**, diverging in **Common** and **Spiny**.

Natural History Alternate hovering and continuous flight along shore or over open water, knee to waist height. Territories may be as small as 12 × 6 feet or up to 100 feet long depending on water area. Fierce territorial aggression between males at boundaries. Males at times in what looks like sexual patrol over clearings near water. Ovipositing female may fly around with abdomen elevated for long time, even with 2- to 3-inch egg string hanging from abdomen, before finally dragging it through water to release eggs on substrates such as twigs. Numerous females often oviposit at same place, presumably attracted to optimal sites where eggs persist, thus "safe." Male once found tangled in female egg string. Both sexes hunt by cruising over clearings away from water, sometimes well up in trees.

Habitat Slow streams and sloughs as well as lakes and ponds, including bog ponds. Aquatic vegetation usually prominent.

Flight Season ON Apr–Aug, QC May–Jul, NS May–Jul, WI May–Oct, ME May–Jul, OH May–Jun, NJ May–Jun.

Distribution Scattered records across southern Canadian provinces to interior British Columbia, then west of Cascades from southern British Columbia to northern California.

Description Heavy-bodied baskettail, seemingly rare in most parts of range. Very small brown spots at base of hindwings. *Male*: Eyes bright emerald green at maturity; face dull yellow-orange with black basal triangle on top of frons. Thorax brown with darker markings and small yellow spots low on sides. Abdomen with S1–2 brown, black beyond that with elongate yellow spots on sides of S3–8. Cerci strongly angled downward near tips. *Female*: Colored as male, abdomen thicker at base and appendages slender. Cerci about length of S9.

Identification A "wide-body," distinctly bulkier than other baskettails, can be distinguished in flight by this. Both sexes have broader-looking abdomen than **Common Baskettail**, more like **Mantled**, but lack extensive dark markings in hindwings as **Mantled** and many **Common** have. As in **Mantled** (but with much smaller markings), midbasal space usually clear with dark markings before and after it. Other species rarely if ever have this exact condition, usually having some pigment in the midbasal space if the marking is more extensive or lacking it in the cell just behind that space if the marking is more limited. Relatively broad abdomen makes yellow spots on sides of it more prominent than in other baskettails. Capture or good photo would be necessary for certainty; uniquely shaped cerci in male diagnostic, with upward-pointing spine near tip.

Natural History Males fly along shore and over water as other baskettails, hovering frequently, perhaps a bit harder to approach. Often fly among trees in sunny clearings like other baskettails. Much less often seen than other species but occasionally common. Very early flight season.

258.1
Robust Baskettail
male—Cumberland Co.,
NJ, May 2005, Steve Walter

258.2
Robust Baskettail female—
Tuscaloosa Co., AL, April 2006,
Steve Krotzer

Habitat Swampy woodland ponds.
Flight Season NJ Apr–Jun, LA Apr, FL Mar.
Distribution The sparseness of records south and west of North Carolina is puzzling.

259 Prince Baskettail *Epitheca princeps* — TL 59–75, HW 36–49

Description More like darner than emerald, large and with long abdomen, but note green eyes and big dark spots on wings. *Male*:
Eyes bright emerald green at maturity; face light brown, darker on
top of frons. Thorax brown with darker markings and small yellow
spots low on sides. Abdomen with S1–3 mostly brown, thereafter
black above with elongate light brown spots on sides of S4–7 or 8
(may be larger and whitish on S3). Fine white ring borders each abdominal segment. Large irregular dark spots at base, middle, and
tip of each wing. Geographic and individual variation striking, individuals of populations on the southeastern Coastal Plain much larger and with larger wing
markings. Individuals in some northern populations all across region almost completely
lack wing markings (tip spots almost always present), yet fully marked individuals may
occur in same populations. *Female*: Colored as male, eyes more likely to be red over gray;
abdomen slightly thicker, cerci straight instead of diverging at ends.

Identification When wing spots can be seen, nothing else like it; easy when overhead,
sometimes difficult against dark water. Much larger than female **Common Whitetail** and
Twelve-spotted Skimmer, with somewhat similar wing patterns, and, as flier and hanger,
Prince Baskettail shows quite different behavior. If wing spots not evident, note it is

brown rather than green as in the large STRIPED EMERALDS with which it might be confused. Only common all-brown DARNER in its range and habitat is **Fawn Darner**, with bright yellow spots on thorax.

Natural History Wary and difficult to capture. Males fly long beats along lake shores or over pools in streams, typically from waist to head height, alternating fluttering and gliding and occasionally hovering. Also fly far out over water of large lakes. Much chasing of other dragonfly species while on sexual patrol. Land in shrubs or trees, even at treetop level, and hang straight down like darner, not with abdomen extended outward as do other baskettails. Both sexes may hold abdomen curved strongly upward when perched, especially exaggerated in females holding ball of eggs. Feeding in flight in open areas from near ground to treetop level, in swarms (occasionally very large) with its own species, darners, and/or river cruisers. Prey mostly quite small. Feeding seems to peak in early morning and evening and extends at least until dusk. Mating also peaks in morning and evening; pairs couple over water and then fly back and forth for considerable periods, perhaps all of copulation in flight. Females oviposit as smaller baskettails by forming egg mass, flying over water with abdomen strongly curled upward, then dropping to water to drag out egg string.

Habitat Moderate-sized streams to fair-sized rivers, usually slow-flowing, and large ponds and lakes. Most have sandy to muddy bottoms. Tendency to be more at lakes in northern part of range.

259.1
Prince Baskettail male—Liberty Co., FL, July 2009, posed

259.2
Prince Baskettail female—Polk Co., WI, June 2007

259.3
Prince Baskettail male—Ottawa, ON, June 2005, Chang-Won Seo

Flight Season ON Jun–Sep, QC May–Jul, NS May–Jul, IA Jun–Sep, WI Jun–Sep, ME Jun–Sep, OH May–Sep, NJ May–Sep, KY May–Nov, LA May–Aug, GA May–Sep, FL Mar–Dec.

Distribution Occurs farther west in plains states from Nebraska to Texas; one record from New Mexico.

Comments Populations of the larger southeastern individuals with more heavily marked wings have been considered a separate species *E. regina* or subspecies *E. p. regina*. However, size and wing markings vary widely, so this form is not currently recognized.

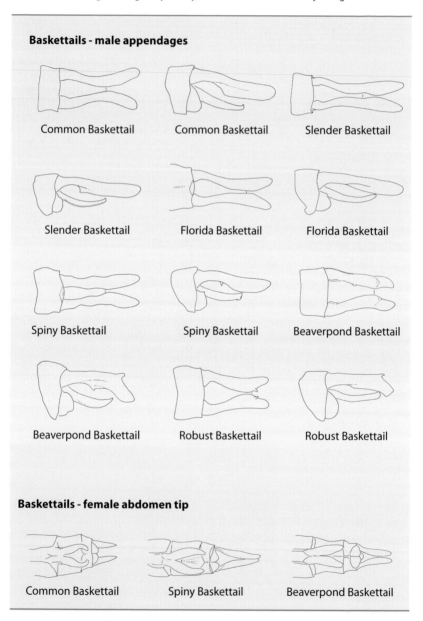

Baskettails - male appendages

Common Baskettail

Common Baskettail

Slender Baskettail

Slender Baskettail

Florida Baskettail

Florida Baskettail

Spiny Baskettail

Spiny Baskettail

Beaverpond Baskettail

Beaverpond Baskettail

Robust Baskettail

Robust Baskettail

Baskettails - female abdomen tip

Common Baskettail

Spiny Baskettail

Beaverpond Baskettail

Skimmers comprise the largest odonate family (although barely larger than the clubtail family) and include the species most likely to be seen by a casual dragonfly watcher. It is sensible for beginners to become familiar with common skimmers before attempting to learn more difficult species of other dragonfly families. The entire array of dragonfly colors is represented among skimmers, although few of ours have the metallic finish of cruisers and emeralds. Some species are strikingly patterned, recognizable as far as you can see them, and many have distinctive color patterns on their wings. On the other hand, some groups of skimmers consist of a set of similar-looking species and present real identification challenges. Large eyes touching in the center of the head and a foot-shaped anal loop in the hindwings are characteristic of this family. Hindwings are similar in males and females, unlike other dragonfly families, which in males have an angled base on each hindwing and auricles that project on either side of S2.

Most libellulids are perchers, but several genera of tropical origin are fliers. One group of fliers includes rainpool gliders, saddlebags, pasture gliders, hyacinth gliders, and evening skimmers; another group clubskimmers. Perchers often spend much time in flight when on sexual patrol, but they feed from a perch, like flycatchers rather than swallows. Most species are sexually dimorphic in coloration, sometimes dramatically so (for example, whitetails). In many cases, males become pruinose, females not; pruinosity much less common in other dragonfly families. In most species, immature males are colored like immature females, and usually immature females are a paler version of mature females. Thus, the sex of many individuals you see, especially away from water, will have to be determined by shape. Males typically have longer, more tapered and pointed abdomen than females, which have slightly thicker, blunt, or truncate abdomen. Keep in mind **tapered tails in dragon males.** Of course the characteristic bump of genitalia under the male's abdomen base is always diagnostic of that sex, and males usually have basal segments more swollen in side view than do females. World 982, NA 112, East 77.

Whitetails   *Plathemis*

Among the best known of our dragonflies, these are stocky skimmers of muddy ponds and streams that spend much of their time perching on the ground and other flat substrates. Males have spectacularly pruinose abdomens, both sexes striking wing markings. One species is common continent-wide, the other restricted to the Southwest. Corporals and king skimmers are close relatives, and *Plathemis* was formerly combined with *Libellula*. World 2, NA 2, East 1.

260 Common Whitetail   *Plathemis lydia*   TL 42–48, HW 30–35

Description One of our most common and widespread dragonflies. Unmistakable pied males always notable but different from spotted females. *Male*: Eyes and face dark brown. Thorax dark brown with two faintly indicated pale stripes on each side. Abdomen white (some see it as pale blue) with pruinosity when mature. Wide black crossband near tip and black streak at base of each wing, white behind basal streak at maturity. Immature with spotted abdomen as female but typical male wing pattern; becomes gradually bluish-white, then white. *Female*: Eyes and face brown. Thorax  brown with two white stripes on each side, turning yellow at lower ends. Abdomen brown with white to pale yellow spots along each side, forming lines on S2–3 and extending diagonally on S4–8. Pale spots outlined in black. Three dark spots on each wing, quite different from male. Just-emerged individuals show only very faint wing spots, but distinctive abdominal pattern apparent.

Identification Sexual differences in wing color pattern greater than in any other North American dragonfly. Male like nothing else in region. Vaguely like **Band-winged Dragon-**

260.1
Common Whitetail
male—Wayne Co., OH,
July 2007

260.2
Common Whitetail
female—Burnett Co., WI,
June 2007

260.3
Common Whitetail
immature male—Burnett
Co., WI, June 2007

let and **Four-spotted Pennant**, both of which have similar black bands on each wing but no white on wing bases and abdomen slender and black. Female wing pattern much like that of female **Twelve-spotted Skimmer**, differs in abdomen pattern. Skimmer has yellow squares at outer edge of each segment that make abdomen appear bordered along edges, **Whitetail** paler yellow-white slashes that make abdomen appear spotted along edges.

Whitetail commonly perches on ground and logs, skimmer usually on branches and leaves. See **Banded Pennant** and **Prince Baskettail**, with similar wing patterns but otherwise very different.

Natural History Most of perching away from water is on ground, rocks, or logs, usually very low and in more open areas than where most skimmers perch. Capture small insects that pass by in flight. Males perch at waterside and fly up and down shore, very aggressive to other male whitetails and other somewhat similar-looking species. Strongly territorial, defending an area 12 feet on either side of an oviposition site. Territorial males remain at a breeding site for several hours each day, not necessarily every day, at maximum for 18 days. Larger males defend larger territories and mate more times. Subordinate males may be allowed in dominant male territories, but dominants mate. Patrol flight typically very low, just above water. Broad white abdomen elevated in face-to-face display in flight; one turns and lowers abdomen (still displayed) or both may fly in parallel flight for up to a minute or more. Females visit breeding sites only every few days, peaking at midday but second peak in late afternoon, presumably fertilized females returning to water. Copulation brief (averaging 3 sec) and in flight, followed immediately by oviposition. Female usually guarded by male, often hovering about a foot above her. Where common, especially at small ponds, both guarding and territorial defense ineffective, female often snatched up by second male or leaves water. Some females drop to ground at waterside when harassed, then apparently invisible to males. Females oviposit by tapping water near floating vegetation or on clumps of mud or vegetation with glistening surfaces, with frequent position changes or not. May remain in same spot for up to several minutes with male in attendance. Often flick water drops forward with eggs, laying 25–50 eggs at each tap. Females lay around 1000 eggs total, at around 25/sec. Reproductive adults can live up to 36 days.

Habitat Lakes, ponds, and slow streams, including those constructed by humans. Larvae on mud bottom and tolerant of a wide range of conditions, so adults often seen at "yucky" sites, for example cattle-trodden stock ponds. Sometimes only species present.

Flight Season ON May–Sep, QC May–Sep, NS May–Sep, IA May–Oct, WI May–Sep, ME May–Sep, OH Apr–Sep, NJ May–Oct, KY Apr–Oct, LA Mar–Nov, GA Mar–Nov, FL Feb–Nov.

Distribution Across United States to Pacific coast, south to southern border, recorded from every state and southern British Columbia but large gaps in arid West; also south in eastern Mexico to Nuevo León.

Corporals *Ladona*

This small North American genus is closely related to king skimmers (*Libellula*) and has often been combined with them. The nearest relative may be the Scarce Chaser (*Libellula fulva*) of Europe, which some have considered *Ladona*. Two light stripes on the thorax of females and immature males, like those that indicate the military rank, give the group its name. Both forewings and hindwings have conspicuous basal markings. Corporals, like whitetails, perch on the ground and other flat surfaces, whereas king skimmers (*Libellula* and *Orthemis*) usually do not. World 3, NA 3, East 3.

261 Blue Corporal *Ladona deplanata* TL 34–38, HW 26–29

Description Small, wide-bodied, blue or brown southeastern skimmer of early spring with dark streaks at base of all wings. *Male*: Eyes dark brown; face black. Thorax dark brown, pruinose blue in front. Abdomen entirely pruinose blue above. *Female*: Eyes and face brown. Thorax brown with narrow pale stripe at each side of front, equal width darker stripe behind it. Abdomen brown with black stripe down middle becoming wider to rear, on each middle segment wider at rear than front of segment.

261.1
Blue Corporal male—Leon
Co., FL, April 2008

261.2
Blue Corporal female—
Richmond Co., GA, May
2006

261.3
Blue Corporal immature
female—Walton Co., FL,
April 2008

Identification Nothing much like male of this species, especially early in spring when it flies. Much smaller and duller than blue KING SKIMMERS such as **Spangled** and **Yellow-sided Skimmer**. Much duller than **Eastern Pondhawk** males that also perch on ground, wider abdomen than **Pondhawk** or **Blue Dasher**. Brown sides of thorax further distinguish it from all blue species. Male easily distinguished from **White Corporal** by abdomen color. Female much like female **White Corporal**; see that species. Dark basal marking in hindwings distinctly longer than wide in **Blue**, more or less rectangular, whereas same markings triangular in **Chalk-fronted**, about as wide as long. **Blue** also has clear to orange mid-basal space within wing markings (brown covers that space in most **Chalk-fronted**, but some show orange stripe). Distinctive stripes on thorax and down middle of broad abdomen distinguish female from other types of skimmers.

Natural History Males perch on logs and shore, much like associated clubtails, and are quite aggressive toward one another. Also fly low fluttery patrols over water, with some hovering. Both sexes commonly perch on ground in clearings, on roads and paths, and on sunny side of tree trunks and buildings; also on plant stems at times. Elevated individuals may droop wings slightly. Copulation brief and in flight. Females oviposit by flying low and slowly to rapidly, tapping water regularly or erratically; may be guarded by male. Can be very common at optimal habitats, dominating southeastern spring odonate fauna. One of earliest dragonflies to emerge in its range, flying in midwinter in southern Florida.

Habitat Lakes, ponds, slow streams, and ditches with wooded or open borders and at least some mud. Common at nutrient-poor glacial lakes and ponds.

Flight Season OH Apr–Jun, NJ Apr–Jul, KY Apr–Jun, LA Feb–May, GA Mar–Jun, FL Nov–May.

---

262 White Corporal *Ladona exusta* TL 37–46, HW 31–33

Description A white-tailed skimmer of the Atlantic coast with dark basal wing markings. *Male*: Eyes dark brown, face blackish. Thorax dark brown with narrow gray stripe on either side of front. Abdomen pruinose whitish except dark tip pointed forward to S8. Both forewings and hindwings with elongate dark basal spot. *Female*: Colored like male but abdomen brown with darker central stripe, all but central stripe becoming increasingly frosted with pruinosity with age (never as white as male).

Identification Occurs with both **Blue** and **Chalk-fronted Corporals** along Atlantic coast, males easily distinguished by color pattern. Note **Blue** has pruinosity on front of thorax as well as almost entire abdomen; **White** has entirely dark thorax and prominent black at abdomen tip, a much more conspicuous insect. **Chalk-fronted** has white only on front of thorax and abdomen base. Females of all three more similar, however. **Blue** and **White** look about the same, but thorax of **White** is darker, especially in front, and stripes narrower, so marked more conspicuously. Black stripe down abdomen expands toward rear of each seg-

262.1
White Corporal
male—Hillsborough
Co., NH, July 2006,
Netta Smith

262.2
White Corporal
female—Hillsborough
Co., NH, July 2006, Netta
Smith

ment in **Blue**, stays same width in **White**. **Blue** has clear dividing line (midbasal space) down center of dark basal wing spots, that area suffused with color in **Chalk-fronted** and **White**. These details difficult to see except from directly above. **Chalk-fronted** larger than **White**, with both front and sides of thorax paler, contrasting with dark stripe just behind pale stripe on each side. Also, pruinosity only at base of abdomen in female **Chalk-fronted**, as in male. Male **White Corporal** in flight looks much like small **Common Whitetail**.

Natural History Like other corporals, most perching on open ground, commonly on boardwalks through habitat. Also perches on plants, perhaps more than Blue Corporal. Males commonly chase and are chased by male Blue Corporals, but their flight season averages a bit later. One male snatched a teneral Elfin Skimmer as it rose from a bog.

Habitat Sandy lakes and ponds, especially common at acid bogs with abundant vegetation. Also common at nutrient-poor glacial lakes and ponds.

Flight Season NS May–Sep, ME May–Aug, OH May–Jun, NJ Apr–Aug.

---

263 Chalk-fronted Corporal *Ladona julia* TL 38–45, HW 28–34

Description Chunky dark northern skimmer with dark markings at base of all wings. Distinctly larger at western end of region. *Male*: Eyes dark brown; face black. Thorax dark brown, pruinose white on front. Abdomen black, S1–4 pruinose white. *Female*: Eyes brown; face tan. Thorax brown, paler front bordered by darker stripe. Abdomen brown with black lines on all keels, black stripe down middle narrow on basal segments, becoming wider to rear. Older individuals become darker, eventually become pruinose like males.

Identification No other skimmer colored like males and older females with front of thorax and base of abdomen strikingly pale. Combination of robust skimmer-shaped body, paler front of thorax, and clear wings with markings only at extreme base will suffice to identify younger females. Larger than other two corporals, distinguished by color pattern in mature individuals. Basal wing markings average shorter in **Chalk-fronted** than other species, can be either entirely dark or sometimes with pale stripe like **Blue Corporal**. Dull female sometimes mistaken for dull brown **Four-spotted Skimmer**, but wing patterns are different.

Natural History Adults at very high densities at times all across their range, in appropriate habitats outnumbering all other species put together. Often common far from water in early part of flight season. Males perch on shore or on vegetation over water at edge of lakes and ponds, alternating lengthy periods of both perching and flying back and forth

263.1
Chalk-fronted Corporal
male—Jackson Co., WI,
June 2007

263.2
Chalk-fronted Corporal
female—Penobscot Co.,
ME, July 2006

263.3
Chalk-fronted Corporal
immature female—
Worcester Co., MA, June
2006

over short distances. Quite aggressive toward one another and somewhat similar-looking Four-spotted Skimmers. Defended territories may be 30–80 feet of shoreline, but some males are nonterritorial, with long flights along shore. Both sexes perch flat on ground when away from water, often on light-colored surfaces and commonly on roads. Also perch on sides of trees facing sun, very likely to land on dragonfly net. Feeding occurs away from water, wide variety of prey up to size of whitefaces. Copulation brief (averaging about 5 sec) and in flight. One female seen to copulate with three males in quick succession. Females oviposit by tapping water and moving short distances between taps, in open and dense vegetation but usually near shore; even in puddles on roads. Males guard ovipositing females by hovering over them; females finished with oviposition fly rapidly into nearby forest. Male reproductive period averages 10 days, extreme 40 days.

Habitat Wooded and open lakes and ponds, especially associated with acid waters of bog lakes. Mud bottom favored habitat of larvae.

Flight Season ON May–Sep, QC May–Aug, NS May–Aug, WI May–Oct, ME May–Aug, OH May–Jun, NJ May–Jul.

Distribution West across southern Canadian provinces to coast, then south to northern California and central Idaho.

King Skimmers *Libellula*

Species in this group include some of the most familiar dragonflies to the general naturalist, as they are large and conspicuous, often with distinctive wing patterns. They range all across the North Temperate Zone and extend south into mainland American tropics, one species throughout much of South America. Typically, they perch with the front pair of legs folded behind the head. Males of some species undergo slow and gradual color change, becoming more and more pruinose with maturity. Copulation is brief and in flight in most species. Females of some species have an obvious flange on each side of S8 that facilitates splashing eggs on the bank during oviposition. On hot days in bright sunshine, members of this group and related genera droop their abdomen downward rather than raising it in obelisk position. Some North American species fall in distinct groups of species pairs or trios that are most similar to one another and can present identification problems. World 27, NA 19, East 12.

264 Four-spotted Skimmer *Libellula quadrimaculata* TL 42–46, HW 33–36

Description Yellow-marked brown northern skimmer with lightly spotted wings. *Male*: Eyes brown above, greenish below, becoming all brown with age; face tan. Thorax rich brown in front, sides similar but yellow below with black lines along sutures. Abdomen rich brown, even orange-brown, at base with bright yellow stripe down outer edge of segments back to S8 or S9; rear ends of S4–5 and all of S6–10 black above. Color becomes duller with age, matte brown, and very different-looking from brilliant orange-brown individuals. Air spaces in abdomen, probably important insulation for this northernmost of all king skimmers, show up clearly through thin cuticle. Moderate-sized black spot at hindwing base, tiny spot at nodus of each wing; anterior wing veins yellow to orange in some individuals. *Female*: Colored as male, with same variation. One of few king skimmers in which sexes indistinguishable except at close range.

Identification No other brown skimmer with small wing spots at base and nodus, although those not visible in flight. Not really much like anything else in its range and habitat, but very orange individuals with large wing markings could be mistaken for **Painted Skimmers**. Female sometimes mistaken for brown but differently patterned **Chalk-fronted**

264.1
Four-spotted Skimmer male—Jackson Co., WI, June 2007

264.2
Four-spotted Skimmer female—Kittitas Co., WA, September 2007

Corporal. Individuals flying cross country could be mistaken for RAINPOOL GLIDERS, which have either unmarked wings or round hindwing spot; very unlikely to be breeding in same habitat.

Natural History Males perch at waterside, usually well above water, much less conspicuous than most other king skimmers. May perch on ground, unlike other king skimmers. Abdomen held pointing downward in intense sunlight. Also fly incessantly at times. Highly territorial; some males adopt satellite behavior (subordinate to territorial male but chance of mating) at high densities. Pairs copulate briefly (but up to a minute or more) in flight; oviposition may begin immediately, or female flies away. Females oviposit by tapping several times in small area, then moving a foot or two to repeat, in open water or shallow seep. May contain up to 3000 or more eggs in a single clutch. Male guards in many cases. During maturation period, sometimes seen far from water. Prey taken up to size of meadowhawk. Cyclic migration events, with huge numbers of individuals, seen in Europe; no such flights recorded in North America.

Habitat Lakes and ponds with mud bottoms and from little to much emergent vegetation. Prefers acid waters, common at northern bog lakes and ponds.

Flight Season ON Apr–Aug, QC May–Aug, NS May–Sep, IA May–Jul, WI May–Aug, ME May–Aug, OH Jun–Jul, NJ May–Jul.

Distribution West across northern North America to Alaska, south through most of West in mountains. Also occurs all across northern Eurasia, from UK to Japan.

Description Brightly patterned rich brown skimmer with spotted wings. *Male:* Eyes reddish-brown; face orange, tan at sides. Thorax brown, sides with two conspicuous stripes varying from white to yellow. Abdomen brown with yellow sides, and these black markings: fine lines on sutures, triangles at rear of S6–7, and wide median stripe on S8–10. As Four-spotted Skimmer, thin cuticle shows air spaces beneath. Wings with basal pattern of brown streak surrounded by orange, brown nodal spot, and brown subapical band; stigma brown. Veins along front of wing bright yellow to orange.
Female: Patterned as male, usually duller, brownish instead of orangey-brown.

Identification Nothing else like it in range. Note, however, that extremely orange **Four-spotted Skimmers** could cause confusion. Looks quite golden-orange in flight, but wing pattern and smaller size immediately distinguish it from **Golden-winged** and **Needham's Skimmers**. **Calico Pennant**, with spotted wings, much smaller and with pale-spotted black abdomen and pale stigmas.

Natural History Males spend much time perching from waist to head height over water and chasing others of their species that approach. Females in woods nearby. Both sexes fly-catch from twig tips. Copulation in flight. Females oviposit in low flight by vigorous and well-spaced tapping and moving some distance between groups of a few taps, often guarded by male. Probably migratory in northern part of range, mature males appearing

265.1
Painted Skimmer male—
Wayne Co., GA, May 2006

265.2
Painted Skimmer
female—Aiken Co., SC,
May 2008

earlier than most other skimmers. Midsummer movements have been observed on New England coast.

Habitat Boggy ponds and ditches with much emergent vegetation, usually associated with woodland.

Flight Season ON May–Jul, WI Jun–Aug, ME Jun–Jul, OH Apr–Aug, NJ May–Oct, KY Apr–Jul, LA Mar–Aug, GA Mar–Jul, FL Feb–Sep.

Distribution Extends slightly farther west in Oklahoma and Texas.

266 Twelve-spotted Skimmer *Libellula pulchella* TL 52–57, HW 42–46

Description Large, striking skimmer with three big black spots on each wing. *Male*: Eyes dark brown; face brown, paler on sides. Thorax brown with two pale stripes on each side, gray above and bright yellow below. Abdomen pruinose gray, underlying female-like pattern often showing through. Wings with three large dark spots, at base, nodus, and tip; pruinose white spots almost fill in clear areas between dark spots. *Female*: Eyes dark brown; face brown, yellow on sides. Thorax brown with two slanted yellow stripes on each side. Abdomen broadly brown above, continuous

266.1
Twelve-spotted Skimmer male—Travis Co., TX, September 2008, Eric Isley

266.2
Twelve-spotted Skimmer female—Floyd Co., GA, May 2009, Marion M. Dobbs

yellow stripe down each side. A small percentage of females develop white wing spots like those of males.

Identification Distinguished from all other king skimmers by 12 dark wing spots (three in each wing). Although males quite different, female **Common Whitetail** poses identification problem, as she has same 12 wing spots. In addition to being distinctly smaller, female **Whitetail** has series of yellowish-whitish spots not contacting edge of each abdominal segment, whereas female **Twelve-spotted** has continuous parallel yellow stripes on either edge of abdomen. In side view of thorax, female **Whitetail** has additional yellow dot in front of anterior yellow stripe, lacking in **Twelve-spotted**. Note that much larger **Prince Baskettail** can have similarly twelve-spotted wings, much smaller **Banded Pennant** superficially similar wing spots.

Natural History Males fly short beats back and forth along shore and over water with regular hovering, also perch on twigs and other prominent perches at edge of open water and may return to preferred ones. Territories changed daily, may be up to 1000 square feet in area. Quite aggressive to other species as well as its own. Males display face to face while hovering, wing spots forming blurry pattern. Copulation fairly brief and in flight. Females oviposit, with peak visitation at midday, by splashing eggs into water with much aquatic vegetation; also at floating logs. Stay in place or move up to a few feet between series of taps, remaining at water for about 3 min. Guarded by males, guarding effective only at low population densities. Suspected migrants have been seen in some numbers in northeastern coastal locations in midsummer and fall. Possibly only a migrant in extreme South, where uncommon and usually seen in fall.

Habitat Lakes and ponds with emergent vegetation.

Flight Season ON May–Oct, QC Jun–Sep, NS Jun–Sep, IA May–Sep, WI May–Sep, ME Jun–Sep, OH May–Oct, NJ May–Oct, KY May–Sep, LA Mar–Nov, GA Apr–Oct, FL Sep–Oct.

Distribution Quite uncommon in southernmost part of range. West across the continent, north to the southern edge of Canada; sparsely distributed in drier regions and absent from parts of the Southwest, just entering Mexico in Sonora.

---

267 Widow Skimmer *Libellula luctuosa*   TL 42–50, HW 38–40

Description Big, showy skimmer with dark wing bases. *Male*: Eyes and face dark brown. Thorax dark brown, pruinose white on front. Abdomen entirely pruinose white above. Wings dark brown from base to nodus, paler at base, then pruinose white from nodus almost to stigma. *Female*: Eyes brown; face light brown. Thorax brown with large tan spots low on sides. Abdomen with black central stripe widening toward rear, bordered by wide yellow stripes on each side; brown low on sides at base. Wing bases become dark but not as dark as male and without pruinosity; extreme tips also  dark. Some females develop abdominal pruinosity. Rare female variant has only dark streaks at wing bases, something like pattern of corporal, but abdominal pattern typical Widow Skimmer.

Identification No other king skimmer patterned like this, with large dark basal wing patches. Most similar to **Black Saddlebags**, which has smaller patches only in hindwing and no white beyond them. Similarly showy and white-tailed **Common Whitetail** has black bands toward tips of wings, smaller black markings at bases. **Twelve-spotted Skimmer** also with showy black and white wings but very differently patterned. Female **Widow** just as distinctive as male because of wing pattern.

Natural History Both sexes may be common in meadows and on roadsides well away from water, where they perch on herbs and shrubs. Males at water most of day, perching at water's edge or flying conspicuously back and forth over short beats at ankle to head height, aggressive to males of their own and other species. May hover and flip abdomen up and

267.1
Widow Skimmer
male—Wayne Co., OH,
July 2007

267.2
Widow Skimmer
female—Green Co., KY,
June 2006

down during patrol flights. May maintain expansive territory or defend group territory in which dominant male most likely to mate. However, territories move and dominance relationships change regularly. Copulation brief (10–20 sec) and in flight, sometimes briefly at rest. Females oviposit, guarded by male or unattended, by tapping open water steadily or flicking eggs onto surface from just above it. Oviposition brief, no more than a few minutes. Longevity after maturation up to 43 days. Individuals with very heavy water-mite loads may have shortened and distorted abdomen.

Habitat Lakes, ponds, and pools in slow streams of all kinds with mud bottoms and usually much vegetation, in open and wooded habitats. Common at farm ponds and other created habitats.

Flight Season ON May–Sep, QC Jun–Aug, NS Jul, IA May–Oct, WI Jun–Sep, ME Jun–Sep, OH May–Oct, NJ Apr–Oct, KY May–Sep, LA May–Aug, GA Apr–Oct.

Distribution West across plains almost to Rockies, also across southwestern states to California, then north to western Washington. Also south in Mexico to Baja California and Durango.

268 Yellow-sided Skimmer *Libellula flavida*   TL 48–51, HW 38–40

Description Southeastern skimmer with bright yellow sides and blue male. *Male*: Eyes dark blue-green; face blackish. Thorax mostly pruinose blue, sides obviously yellow under pruinosity. Abdomen pruinose blue, bright yellow under base. Wings with amber stripe on front, stigma dark brown. *Female*: Eyes brown; face tan. Thorax dark brown in front, yellow on sides divided by narrow dark brown stripe. Abdomen yellow with fairly wide brown to black central stripe, also dark basal side stripe. Wings colored as male but with wide dark tips and paler, usually yellow, stigma.

268.1
Yellow-sided Skimmer
male—Santa Rosa Co., FL,
July 2009

268.2
Yellow-sided Skimmer
female—Richmond Co.,
GA, May 2006

Identification Both sexes distinguished from other similarly patterned king skimmers and all other skimmers by yellow sides of thorax (obscured in mature males) and amber or golden stripe along wing. Superficially like **Spangled Skimmer** but with dark stigmas and distinctly yellow sides of thorax. Females very similar, but brown costal vein contrasts with bright yellow longitudinal and crossveins right behind it in **Yellow-sided**, all these veins brown in **Spangled**. Females also somewhat like **Golden-winged** and **Needham's Skimmers**, which have much duller thoracic pattern and wingtips unmarked or with narrower dark markings. Female **Yellow-sided** have broadly dark wingtips. Anteriormost vein entirely dark in **Yellow-sided**, mostly pale in others. Dark abdominal stripe on **Yellow-sided** female wide throughout its length (similar in **Spangled**), in **Golden-winged** and **Needham's** narrow and then suddenly widening at abdomen tip. Male could be mistaken for **Eastern Pondhawk** but larger, with dark face, brownish wings, and different perching habits.

Natural History Weakly territorial males perch on stems and twigs at tops of low vegetation and fly back and forth over small area with frequent hovering for a few seconds; more flying than perching. Females in nearby open woodland, usually not far from breeding habitat. Copulation at rest for about 30 sec, then female perches for 10–15 sec before ovipositing by hovering 6 inches above the water, dropping to the water to tap once, then rising again, repeating process for up to several hundred times with brief perching at intervals. Male guards at first but not throughout process.

Habitat Boggy ponds, seeps, slow streams, and weedy ditches.

Flight Season OH Jul–Aug, NJ May–Sep, KY Apr–Aug, LA Apr–Sep, GA Apr–Oct, FL Apr–Sep.

Description Midsized eastern skimmer with mostly white stigmas. *Male:* Eyes dark, brown to blue-green; face metallic black. Thorax and abdomen entirely pruinose blue. Stigmas white proximal two thirds, black distal one-third. *Female:* Eyes brown; face tan. Thorax dark brown in front, cream on sides with brown stripe across middle. Abdomen yellow to orange-brown with dark brown central stripe widening toward rear. Dark stripe on lateral carina sometimes expanded upward. Wings suffused with amber, especially in front, and with broad dark tips.

Identification White stigmas glitter in sun. **Yellow-sided Skimmer** rather similar but has dark stigmas in male (paler in female), yellow veins just behind front edge of wings, and thorax with yellowish sides in male, bright yellow sides in female. Male **Spangled** unlikely to be confused with other all-blue species in range, including smaller **Eastern Pondhawk**

269.1
Spangled Skimmer
male—Washington Co.,
MO, June 2009

269.2
Spangled Skimmer
female—Clark Co., AR,
May 2006

and **Blue Dasher**. **Spangled** looks a bit darker, duller blue than these sky-blue species (including **Great Blue** and **Yellow-sided Skimmers**). Female patterned like several other king skimmers, but white stigma always diagnostic.

Natural History Males perch in shrubs and marsh vegetation over water or fly back and forth along shore at waist height or below. Copulation brief and in flight, may be followed by brief rest (total <1 min) before separation. Female oviposits on water or wet mud, sometimes in dense vegetation. Both sexes can be very common in roadside weeds and meadows well away from breeding habitat.

Habitat Lakes, ponds, and marshes, primarily those with silty/muddy bottoms, in open or woodland.

Flight Season IA Jun–Jul, WI May–Jul, ME Jun–Aug, OH May–Sep, NJ Apr–Sep, KY Apr–Sep, LA May–Jul, GA Apr–Sep.

Distribution Few records to west in Oklahoma and Texas.

---

270 Bar-winged Skimmer *Libellula axilena* TL 60–62, HW 43–49

Description Large southeastern skimmer with black bars along wings. *Male:* Eyes dark reddish brown; face metallic black. Overall blackish, front of thorax and base of abdomen pruinose bluish-white. In older individuals, sides of thorax and sides of abdomen become somewhat pruinose; top of abdomen remains black. Many males on territory retain some spots on abdomen from immature coloration. Wings typically with well-defined basal streak, dark spot at nodus, interrupted dark line along front edge between nodus and entirely dark stigma, and narrow dark tip. Sometimes nodal  spot and front-edge stripe connected. Extreme base of hindwing becomes pruinose white with age. Immature colored as female. *Female:* Eyes dark reddish brown above; face brown in center, white on edges. Thorax brown in front, mostly pale gray on sides, with dark stripe extending below hindwing conspicuous, wider toward lower end. Abdomen yellow to light brown on sides, paler at base, with black dorsal stripe becoming wider toward rear, covering much of top by S8–10. Wings as in male, dark tip slightly more extensive. Old females may become colored almost exactly like males but lack the white at the hindwing base.

Identification Mature males differ from rather similar **Great Blue** and **Slaty Skimmers** by blue-gray and black pattern (**Great Blue** all blue, **Slaty** all black), wing markings (usually

270.1
Bar-winged Skimmer
male—Liberty Co., FL,
June 2009, Troy Hibbitts

270.2
Bar-winged Skimmer
female—Wakulla Co., FL,
July 2009

270.3
Bar-winged Skimmer
immature male—Taylor
Co., FL, April 2005

best developed in **Bar-winged**), and face (white in **Great Blue**, black in **Bar-winged** and **Slaty**). Black stigma and duller color distinguish from **Spangled** and **Yellow-sided Skimmers**. Female and immature male very similar to female **Great Blue** and **Slaty**. Both differ from **Slaty** by dark face with sharply defined white edges and dark marking on sides of thorax below hindwing more conspicuous, wider near lower end. Also, black on lower side of thorax more likely to reach spiracle in **Bar-winged** than in **Slaty**. Differs from **Great Blue** in same ways and also by entirely black femora. Wing markings usually diagnostic, but **Slaty** can be as heavily marked.

Natural History Males typically perch over water on twigs but can be seen in wide variety of situations. Females oviposit by splashing water drops up as in related species; sometimes closely guarded by hovering male. Both sexes, along with other skimmers, have been found perched in numbers all along fence wires. Experiences periodic northward irruptions along Atlantic coast, when it may breed, but populations not established in northernmost part of range.

Habitat Wooded slow streams and sloughs, forest pools. Occurs with both Slaty and Great Blue Skimmers.

Flight Season NJ May–Sep, KY Jun–Aug, LA May–Sep, GA May–Aug, FL Mar–Oct.

Description Large black skimmer with dark legs, dark stigma, and dark face at maturity. *Male*: Eyes dark brown; face metallic blue-black. Thorax and abdomen black, overlaid with dark slaty-blue pruinosity. Wings usually clear but may have narrow dark tips and tiny spot at nodus; small number with stripe on anterior edge from nodus to stigma. *Female*: Eyes brown; face dull brown, paler below. Thorax brown in front, yellow to gray on sides. Dark marking below hindwing base elongate, varying from quite narrow to slightly more conspicuous; if expanded, widest toward base. Abdomen

271.1
Slaty Skimmer male—
Calhoun Co., FL, July 2009

271.2
Slaty Skimmer female—
Natchitoches Par., LA, May
2005

271.3
Slaty Skimmer immature
female—Penobscot Co.,
ME, July 2006

yellow to light brown with wide black central stripe becoming wider to rear. Dark side stripe on basal segments narrowing to rear. Old females can become entirely dark gray pruinose. Wings always with dark tips more extensive than in males, also often with dark basal streak, usually with small spot at nodus, often with dark streak along front edge between nodus and stigma. At most heavily patterned, broad dark stripe along front edge of wing from nodus to extensive dark tip.

Identification No other large, all black skimmer. Females and immature males very similar to female **Bar-winged** and **Great Blue Skimmers**. Differ from **Bar-winged** by face whitish to light tan, never black except in mature male; and dark marking on each side of thorax less conspicuous, not wider near lower end. Males distinguished from **Bar-winged** by less extensive wing markings, never with basal streak. Females much more difficult, some with identical wings and some female **Slaty** with even more heavily marked wings than **Bar-winged**. Thoracic pattern only clear distinction, with black streak below hindwing broader in **Bar-winged**. Differs from **Great Blue** by entirely black femora (pale at base in **Great Blue**) and somewhat darker face, especially during maturation. Also perceptibly smaller.

Natural History Males perch on shrubs and other vegetation, from knee height to well above water, and fly back and forth along shorelines. Sometimes flights long-lasting. Territorial aggression involves circling around one another, then rapid chase. Copulation for 30–60 sec, both perched and in flight. Females oviposit by splashing eggs into vegetation, alternating brief hovering a few inches up and dropping to water for several taps. Male may guard by flying back and forth above her.

Habitat Wide variety of lakes, ponds, and long pools in streams, mostly in wooded areas; regularly at bog ponds. Sometimes in swamps with Bar-winged and Great Blue Skimmers, but also at marshy lake edges where those species absent.

Flight Season ON Jun–Sep, QC Jun–Aug, NS Jun–Sep, WI May–Sep, ME Jun–Sep, OH May–Sep, NJ May–Oct, KY May–Sep, LA May–Sep, GA May–Nov, FL Mar–Nov.

Distribution Extends slightly farther west in Oklahoma and Texas.

---

272 Great Blue Skimmer   *Libellula vibrans*   TL 56–63, HW 48–51

Description Very large blue skimmer with white face. *Male*: Eyes bright blue or turquoise; face white. Thorax and abdomen entirely pruinose blue with maturity. Wings usually with dark streak at base, dark spot at nodus, and faint dark tip; small percentage lack one or more of these markings. Immature colored as female, thorax becoming pruinose first. *Female*: Eyes dark reddish-brown over dull greenish; face dirty white. Body pattern typical of skimmers. Only dark marking under wings on each side of thorax a faint line under hindwing, barely visible at any distance; if expanded at all, widest  toward upper end. Femora mostly pale, dark only at tips (pale color always extends beyond half length). Females become duller and darker with age, eyes may become blue. Wings as males but with dark tips slightly more extensive.

Identification Large size, bright blue eyes, and white face distinctive, other blue king skimmers (**Spangled**, **Yellow-sided**) somewhat smaller and with darker eyes and face. With strikingly marked dark-and-light thorax and abdomen, immatures and females very similar to **Bar-winged** and **Slaty Skimmers** but femora extensively pale-based. Differs further from **Bar-winged** in white face and much less conspicuous marking on sides of thorax below hindwing base, from **Slaty** in white face (but female **Slaty** may have very pale face) and slightly less conspicuous marking on each side of thorax. Only one of three with no black under forewing, lacking pale point (ear of "wolf's head") of other two (but this area obscured in older females of all). Typically **Great Blue** females with more color at wingtips than close relatives.

272.1
Great Blue Skimmer
male—Lewis Co., TN, June
2006

272.2
Great Blue Skimmer
female—Caldwell Co., TX,
June 2009, Eric Isley

Natural History Immatures and females may be common in sunny clearings or at forest edge, perching from low to high. Males defend small territories over woodland pools and in dense swamps, usually perching in sun from waist height to well above head height. Few other skimmers are such confirmed swamp dwellers, and males often seen at places lacking most other odonates. Copulation at rest for about 25 sec, then male hover-guards female. Female taps water vigorously, splashing water drops and eggs up to 8 inches away, sometimes on bank. Seen to oviposit in muddy tire tracks in sandy road.

Habitat Wooded swamps and slow streams with dark, mucky water. May breed in pools isolated from stream. Most restricted swamp-dweller of king skimmers.

Flight Season ON Jun–Aug, WI Jul–Aug, OH Jun–Sep, NJ May–Sep, KY May–Sep, LA Mar–Sep, GA Apr–Oct, FL Mar–Oct.

Distribution Extends slightly farther west in Oklahoma and Texas. Recent northerly range extensions (New England) may be from global warming, or perhaps wetter period in East has brought about more swampy conditions. However, some of these extensions are episodic, alternating with declines and disappearance from same areas.

---

273 Golden-winged Skimmer *Libellula auripennis* **TL 51–58, HW 39–43**

Description Yellow-orange southeastern skimmer with mostly golden-tinted wings. *Male:* Eyes orange over brown; face red-orange. Thorax brown, sides paler. Abdomen orange, paler at base and with narrow brown stripe down center, becoming darker to rear and widest on S9. Wings amber-tinted, brightest on front edge; almost all veins and stigma orange. *Female:* Eyes brown over pale greenish; face tan, paler at edges. Thorax brown in front, whitish on sides. Abdomen yellow with narrow black stripe down cen-

273.1
Golden-winged Skimmer
male—Charlton Co., GA,
July 2007

273.2
Golden-winged Skimmer
female—Jefferson Co., FL,
June 2004

ter, widening on S8–9. Wings less colored than male, but anteriormost (costal) veins yellow, faint dusky tips. Some females almost as bright as males.

Identification Few North American species as bright golden-orange as males of this one, with similarly bright wings. Males really look orange, not the red to scarlet of some other species in their range, and that together with colored wings makes identifying them easy. Look-alike **Needham's Skimmer** poses only difficulty (see that species). Female and immature **Needham's** have basal part of costal vein darker than other wing veins, pale on sides of thorax extends as "thumb" onto brown front. Female **Golden-winged** with thorax and abdomen patterned much as females of other king skimmers, for example **Slaty Skimmer** and its near relatives, but yellow anterior wing veins and orange stigma are sufficient distinction. Females of golden-winged pair of species do not typically show prominent dark wingtips as in clear-winged group, but occasional individuals show distinctly darkened tips and might be mistaken for **Yellow-sided Skimmer**, which has dark costal vein, bright yellow sides of thorax, and dark abdominal stripe wide throughout its length.

Natural History Males perch on twigs and leaves near and at shore or in tall grass over water, even quite high; also much cruising between perches. Appears to be more aggressive than Needham's Skimmer, with larger territories. Females and immature males feed in sunny clearings near breeding habitat, perching from ground level to well up in shrubs. Copulation in flight for around 30 sec; male often guards ovipositing female.

Habitat Open ponds and lakes with much shore vegetation; shallow ponds with tall grasses scattered throughout are preferred habitat in many areas. More commonly associated with fishless flatwood ponds than any other king skimmer but apparently not limited to them.

Flight Season NJ May–Oct, LA May–Sep, GA Apr–Oct, FL Feb–Nov.

Distribution Also record in northwestern Nebraska.

Description Vividly distinctive orange-winged purple species of Florida lakes. *Male:* Eyes purplish-red, face dark purple. Body pruinose blue-purple, with pattern much like that of Golden-winged showing through when pruinosity lighter; abdomen tip usually shows some orange. Wings bright orange, including stigmas, as in

274.1
Purple Skimmer male—
Bay Co., FL, July 2009,
Marion M. Dobbs

274.2
Purple Skimmer
female—Lake Co., FL,
July 2009

274.3
Purple Skimmer
female—Lake Co., FL,
July 2009

Golden-winged except extreme basal veins blue. *Female*: When fully mature, entirely covered with gray-purple pruinosity, pattern on thorax and abdomen (exactly like Golden-winged) evident in many individuals. Distinctly duller than males. Wings quite variable, from very slightly tinged with amber to entirely orange (most highly colored individuals just like males); tips dusky in some but not all individuals. Unlike males, stigmas may develop darkish tips and even become entirely purple.

Identification Nothing else like mature males. The slightly purplish-looking male **Slaty Skimmer** has uncolored wings. Mature purple females may look dull gray, most distinguished from **Slaty Skimmer** by gold tones in wings, or reddish veins in clear-winged individuals. Such individuals distinguished also by unpatterned sides of thorax (pattern usually evident on **Slaty**). Immature male **Purple** develop purplish on front of thorax first, recognizable from that time on. Immature females not distinguishable from female **Golden-winged Skimmer**, although dark-tipped stigmas may allow recognition of some.

Natural History Males hold territories on tall grasses at the edge of their chosen habitat. Both sexes in sunny clearings near breeding habitat, usually perching on twigs at head height and lower. Males have been seen mating with orange females, but there is no way to determine whether these were Purple or Golden-winged.

Habitat Often found at cleanest, least-vegetated small lakes on white sand soil, usually with a narrow band of tall grasses along the edge. Also at larger lakes with broad vegetation band and even ponds with much vegetation throughout, but always on white sand. May occur commonly with Golden-winged.

Flight Season Apr–Sep.

Comments This species is anomalous in the absolute minimum number of characters that differentiate it from its closest relative, Golden-winged Skimmer, the only difference the presence or absence of pruinosity. The restricted range and narrow habitat choice of the Purple Skimmer have led odonatologists to consider it a valid species, but the possibility exists that it is a localized pruinose color morph.

---

275 Needham's Skimmer *Libellula needhami* **TL 53–56, HW 39–44**

Description Red-orange skimmer with golden-tinted wings, mostly of coastal regions. *Male*: Eyes red over greenish-brown; face red-orange. Thorax orange-brown in front, tan on sides, with extension of tan forward just onto lower part of front. Abdomen red-orange to almost red with narrow brown stripe down center, becoming black at rear and widest on S8–9. Costa between base and nodus slightly duller than other veins. In brightest individuals, entire body bright red-orange, stigma and wing veins, especially anterior ones, bright orange; entire wings suffused with orange. *Female*: Eyes  brown over pale greenish; face tan, paler at edges. Thorax brown in front, whitish on sides. Abdomen yellow with narrow black stripe down center, widening on S8–9. Pattern on thorax much more evident than in mature male. Wings with veins fairly dark, stigma and anteriormost veins yellow except basal part of costa dark before nodus.

Identification Very much like **Golden-winged Skimmer**. Males look identical in field, with same degree of variation in brightness, but Needham's abdomen averages a bit redder. Difference in thoracic pattern so evident in females may be visible in mature males. Some **Needham's** have costal vein darker before nodus, contrasting slightly with bright orange veins behind it (same color as rest of wing in **Golden-winged**). Smaller wing veins behind prominent anterior veins tend to be orange in **Golden-winged**, browner in **Needham's**, so **Needham's** wings present a more bicolored effect. Females are easier, with difference in costal vein color more pronounced, difference in pattern on sides of thorax obvious. **Needham's** has thumblike extension of pale sides onto front; this shows in younger males and sometimes in mature ones. Hind tibiae black in **Golden-winged**, brown in **Needham's**, but

275.1
Needham's Skimmer
male—Fayette Co., TX,
July 2008, Eric Isley

275.2
Needham's Skimmer
male—Fayette Co., TX,
July 2008, Eric Isley

275.3
Needham's Skimmer
female—Franklin Co., FL,
July 2009

difference not easy to see. Learn which species occurs where; they seem to coexist rarely. **Needham's** most common on and near coast, both species widespread throughout peninsular Florida. Male TROPICAL KING SKIMMERS (**Antillean** and **Roseate**) much redder, with uncolored wings. No females other than **Golden-winged** very similar, although various king skimmers without yellow in wings have similar body patterns. Dark brown front and bright yellow sides of thorax, as well as wide dark abdominal stripe, distinguish female **Yellow-sided Skimmer**.

Natural History Males perch along shore and in tall marsh vegetation, typically at waist to head height on stems or tips of grass stalks and cattails. Both sexes forage in sunny clearings in woodland or in open areas. Can be very abundant locally, especially associated with extensive marshlands such as the Everglades and Louisiana coastal marshes. At times swarms disperse from breeding habitat, many individuals moving across open areas like rainpool gliders but landing more frequently.

Habitat Large ponds and lakes and open marshland, including coastal marshes. Typically larger water bodies than preferred by Golden-winged Skimmer and most common near coast. These two species rarely occur together.

Flight Season NJ May–Sep, LA Apr–Oct, GA Mar–Aug, FL Jan–Nov.

Distribution Extends slightly farther west in Texas and south in Mexico to Jalisco and Tamaulipas, but nowhere common in that country; also in Quintana Roo, Bahamas, and Cuba, but residency status unknown.

Tropical King Skimmers *Orthemis*

These large dragonflies are shaped and sized much like the king skimmers of temperate latitudes that they replace in the New World tropics (and much like *Orthetrum* skimmers in the Old World tropics). Wing venation is also similar in these genera, wings with many antenodals and wavy distal veins. Males of most but not all tropical king skimmers are red, females brown. Their presence at ponds at lower latitudes in the United States show the tropical affinities of those regions; their increase in recent years may present evidence of the effects of global warming. They typically perch with front legs folded up behind head, usually with wings and abdomen level, like king skimmers. Copulation is brief and in flight, so mating pairs seldom seen, but watch for males guarding ovipositing females. World 23, NA 3, East 2.

276 Roseate Skimmer *Orthemis ferruginea*   TL 48–53, HW 36–44

Description Large rosy-purple skimmer of southern states. *Male*: Eyes dark red; face metallic red-violet above, dull reddish below. Rare individuals have eyes and face brighter red. Thorax purplish, overlaid by matte pruinosity. Abdomen red, pruinosity gives it pinkish cast. Wings unmarked, veins reddish. *Female*: Eyes reddish-brown above, tan below; face dull brownish. Thorax brown with complex pattern on sides of pale yellowish stripes, black markings  (below as well as on lower sides). Contrasty whitish median stripe on thorax and abdomen base. Abdomen reddish-brown; conspicuous pale, dark-edged flaps on sides of S8. Old females can become dull and even somewhat purplish-pruinose.

Identification Nothing else like it in eastern North America except **Antillean Skimmer** of southern Florida, which see. Female superficially like other large skimmers but thoracic pattern distinctive. Entirely clear wings (rarely tiny brown area at bases) also distinguish it from some other large reddish skimmers. Other red, clear-winged species in its range include much smaller **Red-tailed Pennant**, without pruinosity.

Natural History Males perch at and actively patrol territories along water's edge, often with much interaction with adjacent males, also with male Antillean and other large skimmers. Copulation brief (usually less than 10 sec) and in flight, then egg-laying female guarded by male. Females oviposit by tapping water and releasing eggs, more commonly by splashing up water droplets that land either on water or on adjacent moist bank. Female may remain in small circumscribed area for surprisingly long periods. Both sexes perch on twigs in sunny clearings with abdomen usually below horizontal (obelisking very rarely seen), sometimes several in small area; may be well up in trees. Long flight season but often most common in fall.

276.1
Roseate Skimmer male—
Hidalgo Co., TX,
September 2008

276.2
Roseate Skimmer
female—Collier Co., FL,
December 2007

276.3
Roseate Skimmer
immature male—Bexar
Co., TX, July 2004

Habitat Very broad habitat tolerance, prefers mud bottoms for larval habitat. Ponds, ditches of all size, and open marshes with mud bottoms, also scummy stock tanks and slow-flowing streams. May be tall emergent vegetation or virtually none, but open water seems necessary. Completely open or wooded country. May breed in very small, including artificial, water bodies, and very successful in sewage lagoons.

Flight Season LA Apr–Dec, GA Mar–Nov, FL all year.

Distribution West to southern California and southern Utah, south to Costa Rica; also in Cuba.

Description Bright red, clear-winged skimmer of far southern Florida. *Male*: Eyes and face red. Body red, thorax pruinose and abdomen not. *Female*: Eyes dark reddish over gray, face reddish-tan.
Body light brown, thorax with fine pale median stripe and several
fine pale diagonal lateral stripes, also horizontal stripe at lower
edge of thorax. Stripes obscure in some individuals, perhaps with age. Abdomen with segments finely bordered by black; S8 with conspicuous brown, black-edged, flap. Immature
male colored like female.

277.1
Antillean Skimmer
male—Monroe Co., FL,
December 2007

277.2
Antillean Skimmer
female—Monroe Co., FL,
December 2007

277.3
Antillean Skimmer
immature male—Monroe
Co., FL, December 2007

Identification Both sexes superficially like **Roseate Skimmer**, but good differences. Male **Antillean** has red head and thorax, **Roseate** much more purplish. **Antillean** has bright red abdomen, pruinosity on **Roseate** abdomen makes it look pinkish rather than red. Female **Antillean** has set of fine parallel stripes on sides of thorax, **Roseate** has more complex pattern with prominent black spot above middle legs and anterior stripes coalescing in an H pattern. Immature males distinguished similarly. Thoracic markings may become obscured with age in female **Antillean**, those of **Roseate** remain prominent. Only other perching red dragonflies in range of **Antillean** are the smaller **Red-tailed Pennant** and **Scarlet Skimmer**, but note the presence of several species of similar-sized red SADDLEBAGS, all of which have basal wing markings and fly incessantly or perch at the tips of twigs.

Natural History Males hold territories around edges of open water. Both sexes feed in open areas and woodland clearings near breeding habitat, perching from ground level to well up in trees. Mating is brief, in flight, and females oviposit by hovering 6–8 inches from shore and flicking drops of water onto shore just above waterline. May be guarded by male.

Habitat Ponds and lake margins, both natural and artificial.

Flight Season FL all year.

Distribution Known to occur through Greater Antilles to Virgin Islands, perhaps on peripheral Caribbean islands and/or locally on Central or South American mainland.

Comments The species is as yet undescribed, although it had long been listed as *Orthemis ferruginea* in the literature. There is still some confusion about its taxonomic limits and distribution.

Amberwings   *Perithemis*

Amberwings are very small unmistakable skimmers, males with yellow to orange wings and females usually with complex and variable wing patterns. Their abdomen is spindle-shaped, narrower at front and back than in the middle. The legs are long and support the small body well above the substrate. Males are found low over the water, but both sexes perch from ground level to well up in trees when away from it, where they appear to be wasp mimics. Most species are tropical. World 13, NA 3, East 1.

278 Eastern Amberwing   *Perithemis tenera*   TL 20–25, HW 16–19

Description Tiny skimmer with orange wings and legs. *Male:* Eyes reddish-brown above, pale greenish below; face orange-brown. Thorax brown with faint yellowish anterior stripes, two prominent yellow lateral stripes. Abdomen orange with brown to black dorsolateral streaks slanted toward midline at rear. Series of yellow triangles down middle of abdomen in more brightly marked individuals. Cerci yellow. Wing veins orange, stigma usually darker orange, membrane about same darkness. Just-emerged males with faintly amber-tinged wings. *Female:* Wings clear but with irregular  black spot between base and nodus and another, larger one between nodus and stigma; typically both surrounded by orange. Also orange costal stripe; stigma orange-brown. Considerable variation in extent and darkness of markings. Populations from southeastern Coastal Plain have males with distinct dark spots at each triangle and females with rather more heavily marked wings. Very rare andromorph females may have entirely yellow-orange wings as males, with some dark smudging.

Identification Nothing else in region like either sex of this species, if small size, swollen abdomen, and colored wings seen. Some females so sparsely marked as to be almost clear-winged, but still identifiable by size and body shape and color.

Natural History Roosts in trees at night. Males stay at water through much of day, perching and patrolling small areas (10–15 feet in diameter) just above open water, and may remain

278.1
Eastern Amberwing male—
Callaway Co., MO, June 2009

278.2
Eastern Amberwing female—McCurtain
Co., OK, November 2009, Berlin Heck

278.3
Eastern Amberwing female—
Clay Co., FL, June 2004

278.4
Eastern Amberwing
andromorph female—Putnam
Co., TN, June 2006, posed

at one site for at least several days. Typically perch on flat or elevated water-lily leaves or projecting twigs. Quite aggressive toward other insects of their own size and color, probably mistaken identity. Males examine potential oviposition sites at great length and then defend a small territory that includes a good one. Territories may be as tight as one per 100 square feet. They choose lookout perches farther from shore than their oviposition sites, perhaps to avoid conflicts with neighboring males, but much conflict with wandering males. After quick copulation (averaging 17 sec) at rest, female led to oviposition site, typically something wet at water level to which eggs will adhere. Common sites are floating algal mats, wet logs or projecting twigs, or cups of water in water-lily leaves. Females may tap water or wet substrate 100 times or more in one spot, often just above waterline, changing direction at intervals. Males may take other males in tandem, perhaps to keep them from mating with nearby female. Both sexes feed away from water, especially females, which may be found widely in weedy fields or perched well up in shrubs or low tree branches. Often perch with wings, or hindwings only, elevated and may point abdomen toward or away from sun at midday. Both sexes, especially females, may be effective wasp mimics. Wing-waving when perched seems to enhance this similarity, and female in flight, with dark wing bases and spindle-shaped abdomen, is sufficiently wasplike to fool an odonate enthusiast and presumably an insect-eating bird.

Habitat Wide variety of ponds, slow streams, and lake shores, usually with mud bottom; in open areas but sometimes associated with woodland.

Flight Season ON Jun–Sep, IA May–Sep, WI Jun–Sep, ME Jun–Sep, OH Jun–Sep, NJ Jun–Sep, KY May–Oct, LA Feb–Nov, GA Mar–Nov, FL all year.

Distribution West across central tier of plains states from South Dakota south, also to southeastern Arizona; south in Mexico to Durango and Tamaulipas.

Comments Florida specimens were described as *Perithemis seminole*, which has also been considered a subspecies of *tenera*. This form is distinguished by heavier wing markings in both sexes, especially females, which usually have a dark border on the posterior edge of all wings, lacking in populations to the west and north. These females really do look different, but they also turn up outside Florida, and there is much variation. Observers in southern Florida should watch for the Slough Amberwing, *Perithemis domitia*, common on wooded streams and sloughs in the West Indies. Both sexes have mostly dark legs and distinctly striped patterns on both thorax and abdomen. Females have each wing entirely orange basally, bounded by a brown crossband at the nodus and brown around the tip.

Tropical Pennants *Brachymesia*

Two species of tropical pennants are often seen perching at tips of vertical twigs and reed stems, males over open water. With abdomens held horizontal, they look like little flags and may be whipped about by the wind. Often, they hold wings elevated, perhaps an adaptation to stabilize them in the breeze, and all species are likely to obelisk at midday. Only somewhat smaller metallic pennants, marl pennants, and small pennants normally perch over water in the same way. The Red-tailed Pennant is more varied in perching habits, more like other skimmers in perching on more solid perches and often nearer the water and in vegetation. All of them commonly perch on fence wires. Away from water, they may be found perching on twigs of shrubs and trees, even well above ground. Abdomen shape, with basal segments dramatically expanded in side view, is a good mark for all three species (except female Red-tailed). World 3, NA 3, East 3.

279 Red-tailed Pennant *Brachymesia furcata* TL 41–46, HW 32–36

Description Small tropical skimmer with unpatterned wings, red male and brown female. *Male*: Eyes red over blue-gray; face red, varying to paler reddish-tan. Thorax reddish-brown. Abdomen bright red, often with limited black markings on top of S8–9. *Female*: Eyes dark reddish-brown over blue-gray. Thorax tan, abdomen light reddish-brown, marked as male. Some individuals (oldest?) become about as red as males on abdomen.

Identification Much larger **Antillean** and **Roseate Skimmers** also common at tropical latitudes; males fly back and forth over water at same ponds and lakes but are larger and do not show contrast of browner thorax and redder abdomen. These larger species also slightly more pruinose purplish looking, especially on thorax. Male **Scarlet Skimmer** even brighter red, with thorax and abdomen equally bright, and larger hindwing patches. **Scarlet** has red legs, **Red-tailed** dark brown to black. **Scarlet** has fine black line down length of abdomen, **Red-tailed** black markings only near tip. Female and immature **Scarlet** have obviously striped abdomen, **Red-tailed** not. Male **Autumn Meadowhawk** scarcely overlaps with **Pennant**; smaller and more slender, thorax and abdomen same color, unlikely to be perched over open water. Female **Red-tailed** could be mistaken for **Tawny Pennant** but much more compact, with shorter abdomen. Much smaller than female **Antillean Skimmer**, which usually has striped thorax. Female **Band-winged Dragonlet** also rather plain but with more slender abdomen, usually dark rectangles visible along sides. Female **Autumn Meadowhawk** smaller and more delicate with scoop-shaped subgenital plate.

279.1
Red-tailed Pennant
male —Monroe Co., FL,
December 2007, Netta
Smith

279.2
Red-tailed Pennant brown
female—Hidalgo Co., TX,
September 2008

279.3
Red-tailed Pennant red
female—Monroe Co., FL,
December 2007

Natural History Males perch on exposed branches or stems over water or fly back and forth along shore and over water, sometimes far over open water and for lengthy periods, with or without some hovering. Wings held flat or slightly lowered, not raised as is common in two larger tropical pennants. Patrol beat up to 50 feet in length. Usually perch horizontally but may elevate abdomen in obelisk. Very aggressive to other species as well as its own. Females seldom seen, usually in clearings in wooded areas, may be high in trees. Copulation brief (about 10 sec, can be up to 1 min or more), in flight, then pair separates after landing. Ovipositing female dips to water every few feet in rapid flight, at times stopping to tap in one place on floating vegetation, usually with guarding male keeping up with her or flying round and round her.

Habitat Lakes and ponds, typically with open shores. Common at coast and may inhabit brackish waters.

Flight Season FL all year.

Distribution West along Mexican border to southern California, south to Argentina and Chile, also throughout West Indies.

---

280 Tawny Pennant *Brachymesia herbida* TL 43–46, HW 34–37

Description Long-bodied midsized skimmer with brown body and brownish-washed wings. *Male*: Eyes reddish-brown over blue-gray; face white with brown markings. Thorax brown. Abdomen light brown with black central line becoming wider toward rear of each segment and almost covering segment on S8-9. *Female*: Colored just as male, distinguished by structure.

Identification Only rather plain brown perching dragonfly with brownish wings. Immature **Four-spotted Pennant** looks very much like this species but always has white stigmas, **Tawny** brown stigmas. Also, **Tawny** lacks black lines on sutures of thorax present in **Four-spotted**, and **Tawny** usually has brown legs, **Four-spotted** black. Color in wings develops

280.1
Tawny Pennant male—
Dade Co., FL, September
2009, Sharon Weaver

280.2
Tawny Pennant
female—Laguna
Cartagena, Puerto Rico,
March 2009, Netta Smith

between base and nodus in **Tawny**, at and beyond nodus in **Four-spotted**. Female **Band-winged Dragonlet**, somewhat similar in size and shape, has different abdominal pattern. **Evening Skimmer**, similarly brown, hangs up to perch, lacks expanding black line down abdomen like **Tawny Pennant**.

Natural History Males perch on tips of plants over water, usually in smaller numbers and on smaller water bodies than Four-spotted. Alternate perching with patrolling along shore. Both sexes often perch with wings up. Habits probably generally similar to Four-spotted Pennant but less well known; may spend more time in flight. One female oviposited by tapping water surface at long intervals.

Habitat Lakes, ponds, and marshes, usually with more vegetation than typical of other tropical pennants.

Flight Season FL Apr–Oct.

Distribution Also from south Texas south to Argentina, including Galapagos and West Indies; vagrants north to Nebraska.

---

281 Four-spotted Pennant *Brachymesia gravida* TL 50–54, HW 35–42

Description Conspicuous slender spotted-winged skimmer of open wetlands. *Male*: Eyes dark brown; face metallic black. Thorax black, thinly overlaid with gray pruinosity. Abdomen dark brown, darker along top, may become black. Wings with large brown spots just beyond nodus, stigmas shining white. *Female*: Eyes brown over blue-green; face white, heavily marked with black. Thorax medium brown with dark lines in sutures. Abdomen light reddish brown with black lines along all sutures, black central line widening toward rear of segment on S7–9. Wing spots more dif-

fuse than in male, but old females may become almost black, with large wing spots, and look like male, only distinguished by shape and structure. Wing spots larger toward west.

281.1
Four-spotted Pennant male—Monroe Co., FL, April 2005

281.2
Four-spotted Pennant female—Wakulla Co., FL, June 2004

Identification Very slender abdomen distinguishes this species from most other skimmers, certainly from those that perch as it does. Only other dragonflies with large black mark on each wing are male **Common Whitetail** and male **Band-winged Dragonlet**, both of which have black mark larger and rectangular. **Common Whitetail** has abdomen short and broad, white in mature males, and perching habits entirely different. **Band-winged Dragonlet** perches and flies low in marshes, stigmas black instead of white. In south Florida, see **Tawny Pennant**, always with brown wings and dark stigmas. Much larger and longer-bodied than **Marl Pennant**, **Metallic Pennant** and SMALL PENNANTS that occupy same habitat and perches.

Natural History Males perch on tips of twigs, cattail leaves, and grass inflorescences, often waving in the breeze. May fly far out over water of large lakes and sometimes fly back and forth low over water very fast, with black wing spots conspicuous. Females perch similarly, more likely away from water but sometimes in mixed-sex groups and sometimes large numbers together. Relatively wary, perhaps because of wide-open perch sites. Both sexes may perch high in trees or on transmission lines. Both abdomen and wings usually much elevated with high temperatures and overhead sun. Copulation brief and in flight, then immediate oviposition with male in attendance (although more typically solo). Oviposition quite varied, flight from just above water to knee height, tapping water at very short to moderately long intervals, varying from regular and unidirectional to scattered with much course change. Perhaps the only regional perching skimmer that commonly feeds like flier, even in small to large swarms. Swarming is more common in early morning and late afternoon. Tiny flies most common prey in these circumstances, although larger prey occasionally taken. Reaches prodigious densities in large open lakes, especially near coast but even far inland.

Habitat Mostly lakes, often those with relatively low odonate diversity. Also at large coastal marshes in Texas and may be on large drainage canals and artificial lakes. Tolerates high alkalinity and perhaps some salinity.

Flight Season NJ Jul–Sep, LA Apr–Oct, GA May–Nov, FL all year.

Distribution West to southeastern Arizona; not yet recorded in Mexico.

Metallic Pennants *Idiataphe*

This small genus contains species somewhat like the small pennants *Celithemis* in shape and behavior. Their basically brown and black color, with no contrasty pale markings, includes patches of metallic overtones, quite unusual in the skimmer family. The venation is open, with fewer cells than most dragonflies of their size, and the legs are relatively long. They characteristically perch on the tips of stems along shorelines, the long hind legs probably an adaptation for keeping the abdomen horizontal while tip-perching, and fly well out over open water. When away from water, they may perch at the tops of trees. World 4, NA 1, East 1.

282 Metallic Pennant *Idiataphe cubensis* TL 36–41, HW 28–30

Description Slender dark dragonfly of southern Florida lakes. *Male:* Eyes dark metallic green with reddish areas. Face brown, metallic blue on top. Thorax brown, metallic dark green on front and in sutures along sides; some individuals become entirely metallic on thorax. Abdomen black, brown at extreme base and younger individuals with dull yellow-orange stripe along each side. Very small brown patch at base of hindwing. *Female:* Colored much like male, distinguished by slightly thicker abdomen and persistence of yellow lateral stripe.

Identification In its restricted range in southern Florida, both sexes could be mistaken for male **Marl Pennant**, especially when color of thorax (black in **Marl**, brown in **Metallic**) not evident. **Marl** has much larger hindwing spot. Female **Metallic** looks about like male, female **Marl** very different from both. All SMALL PENNANTS of similar size and behavior with

282.1
Metallic Pennant male—
Dade Co., FL, December
2007, Netta Smith

282.2
Metallic Pennant
female—Dade Co., FL,
October 2009, Janet
Roxburgh

which this species might overlap have more conspicuous basal hindwing markings and different body colors.

Natural History Males on tips of upright twigs and grass and sedge tips over water, usually in fringing bed. Usually perch with wings elevated, forming a right angle. Cruising flights well out over open water, sometimes with much hovering, then may return to same perch. Cruising beat out from shore and rarely as long as 100 feet. Females seldom seen, may usually perch in treetops near breeding habitat; males also often on bare twigs in treetops. One oviposited by flying around and around over water, then dipped to water and tapped once, repeated same behavior once, then landed at edge. Another tapped shallow water in small area at edge of lake repeatedly.

Habitat Prefers good-sized ponds and lakes with much open water and fringing beds of tall grasses and sedges; may tolerate brackish coastal waters. Readily colonizes borrow pits and lakes excavated as amenities, so likely to be very successful in Florida.

Flight Season FL all year.

Distribution Also in Bahamas and Greater Antilles and southern Texas south to Venezuela.

Small skimmers of marshy lakes and ponds, they are almost restricted to eastern North America north of Mexico and should be especially treasured as part of the rich odonate fauna of this region. With patterned thorax and central red or yellow spots on abdomen, they are somewhat similar to whitefaces but have colored faces, and most species have prominent wing markings. Like other pennants and very different from whitefaces, they perch at tips of vertical stalks, males over water and females away from it. This has been called "teed up," likening it to a golf ball on a tee. All species characteristically elevate wings, forewings higher than hindwings; at most extreme, forewings vertical, hindwings horizontal. They could be considered butterflies of the dragonfly world, and in flight, those species with most heavily marked wings are reminiscent of butterflies. They share that distinction with the distantly related tropical Old World genus *Rhyothemis* (flutterers), with amazing convergence in wing pattern between certain species in the two genera. Small pennants are among the relatively few skimmers that usually oviposit in tandem, but like meadowhawks and others, a pair may separate and the female continue on her own. World 8, NA 8, East 8.

283 Amanda's Pennant *Celithemis amanda* TL 27–31, HW 23–26

Description Small red or yellow pennant with large hindwing patches. *Male:* Eyes dark red over gray-brown; face dark red-brown. Thorax reddish-brown with black markings. Abdomen black with red-orange triangular or oval spots on S3–7, becoming smaller toward rear. Cerci red-orange (pale in immature). Hindwing patches dark brown, edged in orange; veins running through them bright red; stigmas orange. *Female:* Eyes reddish-brown over greenish;

283.1
Amanda's Pennant
male—Charlton Co., GA,
July 2007

283.2
Amanda's Pennant
female—Charlton Co., GA,
July 2007

face tan to yellow. Front of thorax with broad black stripe bordered by brown, sides yellow with very sparse brown to black markings. Abdomen black, S2–3 mostly yellow, S4–7 with large oval yellow spots. Cerci pale yellow. Wing patches orange with dark brown markings fore and aft; stigmas light brown.

Identification Only pennant with large, complex hindwing marking but otherwise clear wings. No other regional dragonfly exactly like this. Female **Marl Pennant** perhaps most similar but with much smaller markings, also larger and heavier-bodied. Body color rather like **Ornate Pennant**, but wing markings much larger, nearly reaching rear edge of hindwing, going back only about halfway in **Ornate**. For satisfying close-range confirmation, male **Amanda's** has red cerci (pale in immature), **Ornate** black. Female **Amanda's** has sides of thorax almost entirely yellow, female **Ornate** with conspicuous black markings.

Natural History Males in grass near breeding habitats or over open water like other pennants. Prefers more heavily vegetated areas than other small pennants. Pairs oviposit in tandem or female by herself. Tends to fly later in season than other small pennants.

Habitat Open shallow ponds with band of emergent vegetation at shore or ponds with dense grass, usually in open habitats.

Flight Season LA Apr–Sep, GA Jul–Oct, FL May–Nov.

284 Martha's Pennant   *Celithemis martha*   TL 25–33, HW 23–28

Description Black pennant of Atlantic coast with large wing spots. *Male*: Eyes dark brown, face metallic black. Entire body black, somewhat dusted with gray pruinosity. Base of hindwings with large black spot. *Female*: Eyes red-brown over gray or dull yellow, face dull tan. Thorax blackish in front, pale brown to yellowish-orange on sides. Abdomen black, with light orange-brown basal segments and large basal dorsal spots on S4–7, rounded toward rear.

284.1
Martha's Pennant
male—Ocean Co., NJ, July
2005, J. Lubchansky

284.2
Martha's Pennant female—
Burlington Co., NJ, July 2006, J.
Lubchansky

Becomes duller with age. Hindwing spot patterned dark brown and orange, basal antenodals in both wings with tiny brown spots.

Identification Males distinctive, easily distinguished from the other small black dragonflies in its range, **Double-ringed Pennant**, **Seaside Dragonlet**, and **Black Meadowhawk**, by large hindwing spots. Black male **Banded Pennant** has spots also farther out on wings. Might overlap with **Dot-tailed Whiteface**, distinguished as its name indicates. Female **Martha's** very like female **Amanda's**, although not known to overlap in range. **Martha's** has hindwing spots smaller, extending out to third antenodal (fourth antenodal in **Amanda's**). At close range, brown dots on basal antenodals can be seen in **Martha's**, lacking in **Amanda's**.

Natural History Typical of genus, but more often perches flat on ground, logs and rocks, especially during cool weather. Foraging in open fields from perches on tips of plants. Males patrol over vegetation, knee to waist height, and are most active in morning. Oviposition in tandem, most often in morning.

Habitat Sand-bottomed lakes and ponds with emergent vegetation along shore. Also nutrient-poor glacial lakes on New Jersey ridges.

Flight Season NS Jun–Sep, ME Jul–Sep, NJ Jul–Oct.

285 Ornate Pennant *Celithemis ornata* TL 33–35, HW 23–28

Description Orange-brown or yellow pennant with moderate-sized hindwing marking. *Male:* Eyes bright red over dull brown; face brown, top of frons metallic blue-black. Thorax orange-brown with wide black stripes on front and sides. Abdomen black with orange base and elongate orange triangles on S4–7. Cerci black. Hindwing patch of moderate size, extending back a bit more than halfway across wing and out to end of triangle; mostly dark brown with red veins. Stigma orange. *Female:* Eyes dark reddish-brown over pale greenish; face tan. Thorax brown in front, yellow mixed with brown  on sides, with black stripes as in male. Markings in abdomen as in male but dull yellow-orange. Immatures of both sexes strikingly black and yellow.

Identification Distinguished from other pennants by clear wings with midsized hindwing markings smaller than **Amanda's**. Thorax more heavily marked with black on sides than **Amanda's**, spots on abdomen narrower, cerci always black. Male can be quite reddish, but not as bright as **Red-veined** (which also has bright red face), basal wing veins not red, and hindwing markings larger. Female **Ornate** colored just like female **Red-veined**, latter only

285.1
Ornate Pennant
male—Taylor Co.,
GA, May 2006

285.2
Ornate Pennant
female—Lake Co., FL,
April 2008

distinguished by smaller wing markings (and some female **Red-veined** have dark wingtip spots). Other small dragonflies with red or yellow coloration and conspicuous basal wing markings include female **Marl Pennant**, heavier-bodied and with mostly pale abdomen; and **Checkered Setwing**, larger and with white markings on thorax and abdomen. Neither of these species usually where **Ornate Pennants** occur.

Natural History Both sexes, males mostly immature, can be common in weedy fields well away from water. Males perch on tips of grasses and sedges over water, often in fairly dense vegetation. Pairs oviposit in tandem flight among emergent and floating vegetation.

Habitat Grass and sedge beds at shores of sand-bottomed lakes and large ponds.

Flight Season NJ Jun–Jul, LA Mar–Sep, GA Mar–Nov, FL all year.

Comments Formerly called Faded Pennant.

286 Red-veined Pennant *Celithemis bertha* TL 28–36, HW 24–28

Description Bright red southeastern pennant with red veins but minimal wing markings. *Male*: Eyes and face bright red. Thorax mostly red with fine black median line and fine markings on sides. Abdomen black, red on basal segments and on narrow spots on S4–7. Anterior and basal veins red, filling small dark basal hindwing spot. *Female*: Eyes red-brown over gray, face yellowish. Thorax strongly patterned black and yellow, more brownish tinged in front. Abdomen black, mostly yellow at base and with narrow yellow dorsal spots on S4–7. Some females (polymorphism?) red instead of yellow. Wing veins dark. Many individuals in more northerly populations (outside peninsular Florida and southern Georgia) have small dark brown spots at wingtips, especially females.

Identification Bright red males not really like anything else. Female with strongly patterned thorax like female **Ornate Pennant** but virtually lacking hindwing spot. Female **Double-ringed Pennant** has markings only at abdomen base. No other pennant with dark markings only at wingtips like some **Red-veined**.

Natural History Males perch on tips of grass and sedge stems, often well out at edge of open water, too deep for anyone but the most intrepid photographer or collector. They cling to their precarious perches in all but the highest winds. Females and immatures less often found than is the case with other *Celithemis* pennants that forage commonly in weedy clearings. Pairs copulate briefly at rest in herbaceous vegetation, then fly rapidly in

Skimmer Family **437**

286.1
Red-veined Pennant
male—Laurens Co., GA,
July 2007

286.2
Red-veined Pennant
female—Liberty Co., FL,
April 2008

tandem and about 6–12 inches above the water, dipping to the surface at intervals of 2–5 feet. They oviposit in straight or circling flight and occasionally hover for a few seconds between dips. Eggs are laid in open water or dense vegetation with equal frequency.

Habitat Clean sand-bottomed lakes, usually with much open water and beds of grass around the shore.

Flight Season LA May–Sep, GA Apr–Oct, FL Apr–Dec.

| **287 Calico Pennant** *Celithemis elisa* | **TL 29–34, HW 27–28** |

Description Small red-brown or yellow pennant with prominently brown-spotted wings. *Male:* Eyes dark red; face red. Thorax red with black markings. Abdomen black with bright red dorsal triangles or heart-shaped spots on S3-7. Cerci red (pale in immature). Forewing reddish at extreme base, with brown spot just past nodus and dark brown tip. Hindwing with large patterned basal patch extending just past triangles, filled with red veins, and dark postnodal spot and tip as in forewing. Size of smaller spots vari-

287.1
Calico Pennant male—
Coffee Co., GA, July 2007

287.2
Calico Pennant female—
Carroll Co., NH, June 2006

287.3
Calico Pennant aberrant
male—Charlton Co., GA,
July 2007

able, tip spots may be absent. Stigma bright red, contrasting with dark wing spots. *Female*: Eyes red over pale greenish; face yellow-brown. Thorax brown on front, with black central stripe and bordered by black; yellow on sides, with two prominent black spots. Abdomen black with large yellow spots from base to S7. Veins in hindwing spot yellow, stigma orange.

Identification Wing pattern diagnostic; no other pennant with clear wings, large basal patch, and dots at midwing and tip. Basal patch much like those of other species, but markings beyond nodus distinctive. Rare individuals lack nodal and tip spots, rather similar to **Red-veined Pennant** but with much larger basal markings. **Banded Pennant** has larger spots, all of them dark. Abdominal spots, although not dramatically different from other pennants, more often heart-shaped and memorable because of that. Female **Eastern Amberwing** has heavily patterned wings but otherwise very different.

Natural History Often found in numbers feeding in weedy fields near water. Breeding males perch up on the tallest herbaceous or shrubby vegetation over water and fly actively back and forth along shore and over the water at knee height. Also perch on tips of herbaceous plants in nearby fields to watch for females; much pairing occurs away from water. Copulation for about 5 min, then pair flies to water to oviposit. Tandem oviposition for about 3 min, rarely followed by another few minutes of solo oviposition. About 700–800 eggs laid.

Habitat Ponds and lakes with vegetated margins, including bog ponds.

Flight Season ON May–Sep, QC Jun–Aug, NS Jun–Sep, IA May–Sep, WI May–Sep, ME May–Sep, OH May–Sep, NJ May–Oct, KY May–Sep, LA Mar–Oct, GA Mar–Nov, FL Apr–Oct.

Distribution Extends slightly farther west in Oklahoma and Texas, also in western Nebraska and adjacent states.

---

288 Banded Pennant *Celithemis fasciata*   TL 30–38, HW 25–32

Description Dark pennant with dark-banded wings. *Male*: Eyes dark brown; face brown, metallic blue-black above. Thorax black with faint paler markings. Abdomen black, may develop slight pruinosity at base. Black wing markings quite variable in size but typically include tip, incomplete band between nodus and stigma, and complex pattern across wing bases. Commonly yellow wash across wing base enclosed by black markings. Dark markings reduced in some individuals, especially farther north, but basic set always present. *Female*: Eyes reddish-brown over pale greenish; face cream, metallic blue-black above. Thorax bright black and yellow striped. Abdomen black with yellow spots, longer on S4–6 than on S3 or S7.

288.1
Banded Pennant
male—Laurens Co., GA,
July 2007

288.2
Banded Pennant
female—Laurens Co.,
GA, July 2007

288.3
Banded Pennant
male—Hampden Co.,
MA, September 2002,
Glenn Corbiere

Identification Easily distinguishable from **Halloween Pennant** by lack of color between dark wing markings except for wash at base. In very poor lighting could still be distinguished by greater extent of basal markings, continuous from base to nodus (interrupted in **Halloween**, basal spots separated from nodal spots). Mature male **Banded** all black, **Halloween** reddish. Female **Banded** with more black than yellow on abdomen, spots discontinuous (forming line in **Halloween**). Some KING SKIMMERS, WHITETAILS, and **Prince Baskettail** patterned somewhat like **Banded Pennant** but much larger and without complicated patterning of basal spots of pennant.

Natural History Both sexes roost and even feed well up in trees, also spend time in weedy fields near water. Males perch on leaf and branch tips at open-water shore or among marsh vegetation, often on grass stems. Abdomen and wings may be well elevated, forewings more than hindwings. Also spend much time flying low over water. Pairs oviposit in tandem, often flying around wildly covering large area. Then pair may separate and female continue by herself, more sedately in smaller area and with or without male guarding. Females oviposit by hovering, dropping to water and tapping once, then rising and moving to do it again.

Habitat Sandy lakes and ponds with emergent vegetation, also slow streams.

Flight Season OH Jun–Aug, NJ May–Sep, KY May–Aug, LA Apr–Oct, GA Apr–Nov, FL Apr–Oct.

Distribution Extends farther west in Oklahoma and Texas, also records from eastern New Mexico.

Description Medium-sized pennant with dark-spotted colored wings. *Male*: Eyes dull red over orange-brown; face red-orange. Thorax orange-brown with black stripes below each wing and third, incomplete, stripe between them. Abdomen orange at base, otherwise black with full-length orange spots forming stripe from base through S7. Cerci black, some orange at base. Wings entirely golden-tan to orange with black band just in from stigma and another on inner side of nodus, one black spot near base of forewing and two near base of hindwing. Most wing veins and stigma red-orange. *Female*: Eyes red over gray-green; face yellow-orange. Thorax brown in front, yellow on sides, stripes as in male. Abdomen black with pale yellow base and yellow stripe extending to S7. Wings as male, most veins and stigma yellow.

Identification Unmistakable because of wing color pattern. **Banded Pennant** most like it but has pale part of wings clear rather than orangey, abdomen all black in males. **Calico Pennant** similar but more restricted markings. KING SKIMMERS with spotted wings much larger and without overall tan color. Much smaller AMBERWINGS have unmarked or differently marked wings, as well as characteristic short, spindle-shaped abdomen.

Natural History Males perch on grass and sedge tips over water and fly at one another. Copulation while perched, lasting 3–6 min, oviposition immediately thereafter. Pairs and solo females oviposit in open water or among floating vegetation, more commonly in morning and even quite early, often over open water in windy weather. Where common, as in the Everglades, many tandem pairs seen in cross-country flight, up to 60 feet above ground. Both sexes perch similarly away from water, sometimes in large numbers, with wings elevated. Fluttery flight and colored wings recall butterfly, prompting speculation whether they look enough like Monarch to gain some protection from bird predators while away from water. Sometimes in great numbers away from water when blown out of extensive breeding habitat.

Habitat Open lakes and marshes of all kinds, with at least some emergent vegetation. Very common coastally, also in slightly brackish marshes.

289.1
Halloween Pennant
male—McCurtain Co., OK,
June 2008, David Arbour

289.2
Halloween Pennant female—
Charlton Co., GA, July 2007

Flight Season ON Jun–Sep, IA Jun–Sep, WI Jun–Sep, ME Jun–Sep, OH Jun–Oct, NJ Jun–Sep, KY May–Sep, LA Apr–Sep, GA Mar–Nov, FL all year.

Distribution West to eastern Wyoming and New Mexico, one record in southeastern Arizona; south in Mexico to Coahuila and Nuevo León. Also recorded, possibly not established, in Bahamas and Cuba.

Description Pennant with black or black and yellow body and tiny dark hindwing markings. *Male*: Eyes dark brown; face dark glossy brown. Thorax and abdomen black, overlaid with dark blue pruinosity. Small black spots at base of hindwing. *Female*: Eyes reddish over gray; face yellow, metallic blue above. Thorax yellow with wide median black stripe and lateral brown stripes on front, two black stripes on each side. Abdomen yellow at base with black on top of S1–2, yellow ring on base of S3–4, remainder black. Veins within black wing markings yellow. May become almost solid black with age, retaining hint of thoracic pattern.

Identification Male unlike other pennants in being entirely black, with very small wing markings. **Martha's Pennant** similarly black but with prominent hindwing markings.

290.1
Double-ringed Pennant male—Atlantic Co., NJ, June 2008

290.2
Double-ringed Pennant female—Chesterfield Co., SC, May 2008

Might be mistaken for other small black dragonflies with brown eyes that overlap in range although not in habitat. **Seaside Dragonlet** with pruinosity only between wings, lacks dark marking at wing base, at coast or alkaline lakes. **Marl Pennant** chunkier, with large hindwing spots, more common at coast. Mostly black abdomen of female **Double-ringed** with two pale rings distinguishes from other female pennants and any other dragonfly in range. Female with sides of thorax somewhat like other female pennants but with distinctive pattern of one stripe with lightning-bolt effect followed by narrow straight stripe. Females of both this species and **Seaside Dragonlet** can become virtually entirely black; note hint of pattern at base of **Pennant** wing versus projecting subgenital plate in **Dragonlet**.

Natural History Males perch on overhanging herbaceous vegetation at knee height and below and fly short beats along shore over open water. Often perch on sides of stems rather than tips. Pairs oviposit in tandem. Flies mostly in spring.

Habitat Open ponds and small lakes with band of emergent vegetation along shore.

Flight Season NJ May–Jul, KY May–Jul, LA Apr–Jun, GA Apr–Jun, FL Apr.

Whitefaces *Leucorrhinia*

Whitefaces constitute a north-temperate genus of small black dragonflies of lakes, ponds, and marshes with conspicuous white face and yellow and/or red markings. Females of most species have a dull morph and a bright, male-like morph. Usually there is a small brown triangular spot at hindwing base. The veins and stigmas are black, but the yellow costal vein just beyond the stigma is characteristic of the genus. They perch with wings flat or sometimes drooped forward. Male whitefaces seem more likely than other dragonflies to attempt tandem with males of pairs already in tandem. Well adapted to northern latitudes, they are almost always seen perched flat on light-colored rocks, logs, and tree trunks in the morning, where their dark coloration allows quick warming in the sun. Later in the day, they may be on leaves and twigs. Old females become quite pruinose on the underside of the abdomen. They are sometimes very abundant, with pairs commonly seen. Identification is often tricky, especially females and immatures. Examination of male hamules and female subgenital plates may be necessary for the last word. World 16, NA 7, East 7.

291 Frosted Whiteface *Leucorrhinia frigida* TL 28–32, HW 21–24

Description Small white-faced skimmer with pale-based black abdomen. *Male*: Eyes dark brown; face white. Entirely dark brown to black, mature males with abdomen base (typically S2–5) heavily white pruinose; also tiny spot of pruinosity on sclerite at each wing base. *Female*: Eyes brown; face white. Thorax ochre, black in front and scattered spots on sides. Abdomen black, yellow at base and with elongate spots on S4–7 becoming narrower to rear, that on S7  always a fine streak. Subgenital plate with two large, pointed lobes. Immature thorax almost entirely unpatterned golden with square black patch on front.

Identification Mature male most like **Belted Whiteface** but slightly smaller and with less vividly marked thorax, no trace of red between wing bases. Female **Frosted** much like other female whitefaces but thorax with reduced black markings in comparison with most other species, sides almost entirely pale. Immature **Dot-tailed** may have pale thorax but pale carina makes fine streak down front of thorax (all black in immature **Frosted**) and usually more broadly spotted abdomen.

Natural History Males perch low in emergent vegetation or on lilypads at water, sometimes defending small territories but not aggressive at other times. Females usually on ground or in herbaceous vegetation away from water. Copulation for 10–20 min on ground or vegetation, may fly briefly over water. Female then perches for few minutes, then oviposits with

291.1
Frosted Whiteface
male—Price Co., WI, June
2007

291.2
Frosted Whiteface
female—Wood Co., WI,
June 2007

male guarding. One female oviposited by tapping water twice, hovering briefly, and double-tapping again six times, then perching again.

Habitat Mud-bottomed lakes and ponds with abundant emergent vegetation, especially pools in fens and bogs.

Flight Season ON May–Aug, QC Jun–Aug, NS May–Sep, WI May–Sep, ME May–Aug, OH May–Jul, NJ May–Jul.

Distribution Also record in northern North Dakota.

292 Belted Whiteface *Leucorrhinia proxima* TL 33–36, HW 24–27

Description Small white-faced skimmer with pale-based black abdomen. *Male*: Eyes dark brown; face white. Thorax brightly marked red and black (yellow and black in immature), becoming darker and duller with age but red persisting between wings. Abdomen black with red-orange base (S1–3), with maturity pruinosity spreading and covering entire base back to S5 or S6; also tiny spot of white pruinosity at base of each wing. Pruinosity reduced at western end of region (Minnesota), some individuals remaining bright red and black. *Female*: Polymorphic, andromorph colored like male but heteromorph with light areas yellow. Tiny pale spots at base on sides of S4. Oldest females develop pruinosity between wings and at abdomen base. Subgenital plate with two short, rounded lobes.

Identification Mature pruinose males most like **Frosted Whiteface**, differs in having red be-

292.1
Belted Whiteface male—
Grafton Co., NH, June
2006

292.2
Belted Whiteface
heteromorph female—
Carroll Co., NH, June 2006

292.3
Belted Whiteface
immature male—Wood
Co., WI, June 2007

tween wings and often trace on thorax. Also slightly larger, and typically more abdominal segments pruinose. Western males with red thorax and abdomen base look just like **Canada** and **Crimson-ringed**, latter most similar species. **Crimson-ringed** differs in wing venation (usually two or more cells in radial planate on each wing doubled in **Crimson-ringed**, not so in **Belted**) and hamule shape (inner branch straight and then hooked at tip in **Crimson-ringed**, smoothly curved in **Belted**). Female **Belted** looks like females of most other whitefaces, almost exactly like female **Crimson-ringed** (see that species for slight differences); capture and scrutiny may be essential for identification. Lobes of subgenital plate barely evident in **Crimson-ringed**, short but quite obvious in **Belted**, still longer in other species. Wing venation also good separation from female **Crimson-ringed**, sometimes visible in field. **Canada** smaller and more slender and lacks pale spot on S7.

Natural History Males perch on leaves and twigs over and near water, defending small territories. Away from water, perches from ground to well up into trees. Pairs couple at water, immediately fly in wheel away from water into shrubs and trees, where copulation quite lengthy. Mating pairs often in numbers, seen throughout day.

Habitat Lake shores and ponds with much aquatic vegetation, often boggy margins; usually in forested landscapes.

Flight Season ON May–Aug, QC May–Aug, WI May–Aug, ME May–Aug.

Distribution West across southern Canada to Alaska, south sparsely in mountains to northern California, Utah, and Colorado.

Comments Called Red-waisted Whiteface in earlier publications.

293 Dot-tailed Whiteface *Leucorrhinia intacta* TL 29–33, HW 23–25

Description Small all-black dragonfly with white face, yellow dot on abdomen. *Male:* Eyes dark brown; face white. Thorax and abdomen black, abdomen with paired contiguous yellow dots on S7. Immatures brown with spotted abdomen as female, males at water may retain some pale markings. *Female:* Eyes brown, face white. Thorax brown with dark spots below base of forewings and scattered smaller spots. Abdomen yellow at base, yellow extending down sides of S3–5, shorter on S5. Large yellow dorsal spots on S3–7, shortest on S7. Thorax and abdominal spots become darker with age, and oldest females have dark brown thorax and black abdomen except for pale streaks on sides of S3–5 and pale dots on S7, looking just like mature male except for abdomen shape. Subgenital plate with pair of peg-

293.1
Dot-tailed Whiteface
male—Kittitas Co., WA,
June 2009, Netta Smith

293.2
Dot-tailed Whiteface
female—Carroll Co., NH,
June 2006

293.3
Dot-tailed Whiteface
immature female—
Waushara Co., WI, July
2009, Ken Tennessen

like projections. Small percentage of females have amber-based wings. Immatures of both
sexes with mostly pale thorax, dark in front split by conspicuously pale carina.

Identification Nothing looks exactly like mature male with yellow abdominal dots. **Black
Meadowhawk** lacks dots on abdomen, has dark face. Females, especially younger ones,
much like other female whitefaces, but yellow spot on S7 usually wider than long and
squared off (longer than wide and pointed in others), also often partially divided in two,
but a few **Dot-tailed**, especially younger ones, have long, pointed spots. Other whitefaces
(**Belted, Crimson-ringed, Hudsonian**) usually with more vivid pattern on thorax, although **Frosted** has less pattern. Pale carina on front of thorax excellent mark for younger
individuals, although **Hudsonian** may show same character; look for pale veins in dark
basal wing spots and (usually) narrowly pointed spot on S7 characteristic of **Hudsonian**. To
be sure, check subgenital plate in captured females (difficult to get below one to see this).
Pale immature females with amber-based wings could be mistaken for **Band-winged
Meadowhawk** but color diffuse, not cleanly cut off as in **Meadowhawk**, and abdominal
spots usually obvious.

Natural History Both sexes commonly seen at some distance from breeding sites, especially
immatures. Males at water often perch on water-lily leaves, also in emergent vegetation,

including tall grasses; obelisk at midday on hot days. Males remain in one spot for as little as 15 min or as much as 6 hr, then move somewhere else or wander through other males' domains. Fixed territories not defended, but the closer another male comes, the more likely it is to be chased. Copulating pairs may fly for lengthy periods looking for landing site in low vegetation or up in trees, then copulate for 5–25 min. Females oviposit by flying rapidly over open water tapping irregularly, tend to localize in one spot when over submergent aquatics or floating algal mats. Usually guarded by male.

Habitat Wide variety of lakes and ponds with emergent vegetation, typically in open. More widespread and common than other whitefaces, less tied to "northern" habitats such as bog lakes and ponds.

Flight Season ON May–Aug, QC May–Aug, NS May–Aug, IA May–Aug, WI May–Oct, ME May–Aug, OH Apr–Jul, NJ Apr–Jul, KY Jun–Jul.

Distribution West to Pacific coast, from British Columbia south in mountains to northern California and New Mexico.

294 Canada Whiteface *Leucorrhinia patricia* TL 24–29, HW 18–25

Description Delicate, small, far northern cream-faced whiteface with pale-based black abdomen. *Male*: Eyes dark brown; face cream-colored. Thorax red with black triangle on front and extensive black markings on sides. Abdomen black, S2 and base of S3 red; may be fine red streaks down middle abdominal segments. *Female*: Polymorphic, either colored just like male or red replaced by

294.1
Canada Whiteface
male—Grayling Lake,
AK, June 2008, Bob
Armstrong, posed

294.2
Canada Whiteface
andromorph female—
Heckman Pass, BC, July 2006,
Netta Smith

yellow; S4–6 may or may not have narrow yellow spots on basal half of segment. Subgenital plate with two short, rounded lobes.

Identification Smallest whiteface in range, more slender than others and perhaps recognizable by this alone. Both sexes like small, slender-bodied **Crimson-ringed Whiteface**, abdominal spots smaller than in **Boreal** and **Hudsonian**. At close range, both sexes distinguished from other whitefaces by creamy-yellow tint on face; all others have chalk-white faces. Because it is small, only two cell rows in trigonal interspace, obvious lengthy field of cells distal to triangle in forewing. Similar-looking species have three rows there.

Natural History Males perch low in breeding habitat, often right on moss; otherwise seen on ground, rocks, and logs as in other whitefaces.

Habitat Bog ponds and fens with much low emergent vegetation and especially mats of floating mosses, more restricted to this habitat than any other whiteface; not in dense sedges with Hudsonian Whiteface.

Flight Season ON Jun–Jul, QC Jun–Aug, NS Jul, ME Jun.

Distribution Also from Alaska and Northwest Territories south to British Columbia.

---

295 Hudsonian Whiteface *Leucorrhinia hudsonica* TL 27–32, HW 21–27

Description Small marsh-dwelling whiteface with prominently spotted abdomen. *Male*: Eyes dark brown; face white. Thorax red with black triangle on front and extensive black markings on sides. Abdomen black, most of S1–2 and base of S3 red and rather narrow red spots extending about halfway down top of S4–7. Spots very rarely lacking. *Female*: Polymorphic, andromorph colored about like male and heteromorph with light areas ochre on thorax and brighter yellow on abdomen; spots on abdomen longer, extending much of length of segments. Small pale basal spot on sides of S4, rarely another on S5. Subgenital plate with two prominent lobes, their inner edges touching.

Identification Red spots along most of abdomen distinguish male from other whitefaces except **Boreal**; smaller than **Boreal** and with no spot on S8. Superficially like **Belted**, **Canada**, and **Crimson-ringed**, but all of them have little or no red on middle abdominal segments, and only **Canada** as small as **Hudsonian**. Rare individuals without abdominal spots would have to be distinguished structurally. Female similar to female **Belted** and **Crimson-ringed** but smaller and spots on abdomen usually wider and longer, reaching two-thirds

295.1
Hudsonian Whiteface
male—Heckman Pass,
BC, July 2006, Netta
Smith

295.2
Hudsonian Whiteface
heteromorph female—
Kittitas Co., WA, August
2006, Netta Smith

295.3
Hudsonian Whiteface
andromorph female—
Heckman Pass, BC, July
2006

length or more of each middle segment (usually halfway in other species); also like **Canada** but somewhat more robust. See **Crimson-ringed** for spots on side of abdomen. **Hudsonian** only species among these with pale veins within dark basal hindwing spot. Look at subgenital plate for definitive identification; large in **Hudsonian**, with two prominent lobes or projections touching one another; in other species projections well separated (**Boreal, Canada, Dot-tailed, Frosted**) or not much more than bumps (**Belted, Crimsonringed**).

Natural History Males perch on sedge and grass stems and defend small territories. Females away from water, often perch on ground or light-colored logs in woodland clearings. Pairs leave water for lengthy copulation at rest. Females oviposit in open water in sedge beds, often guarded by male hovering nearby.

Habitat Marshes, sedge meadows, coldwater fens, and bog ponds with sphagnum, occupying denser vegetation than most whitefaces.

Flight Season ON Apr–Aug, QC May–Sep, NS May–Aug, WI May–Aug, ME May–Aug, NJ May–Jul.

Distribution West across much of Canada to Alaska, south in mountains to California, Utah, and Colorado.

Description Small white-faced skimmer with pale-based black abdomen. *Male:* Eyes dark brown; face white. Thorax brightly marked red and black, becoming darker and duller with age. Abdomen black, red at base (S1–2) and sometimes with fine red streaks down center of middle segments. *Female:* Polymorphic, andromorph colored as male; heteromorph thorax varies from brown and dull yellowish to rather contrasty black and yellow. Subgenital plate barely visible.

Identification Male easily distinguished from all other whitefaces in most of East except **Canada** by bright red thorax and abdomen base and almost entirely black abdomen. Obviously larger than **Canada**, otherwise looks the same; check wing venation and other structural differences. Nonpruinose male **Belted Whiteface** at western edge of region and immature males anywhere also similar to **Crimson-ringed**, and capture would be necessary for identification unless wing venation could be clearly seen or photographed. Presence of doubled cell rows in radial planate on all wings (rarely not doubled on one or two wings) in **Crimson-ringed** often visible with close-range binoculars. **Canada** has single row, and most **Belted** have single cell row, rarely one or more doubled rows in one or two wings, but a few just like **Crimson-ringed,** and identification only by venation would be flawed on rare occasions. Slight difference in male appendages (epiproct extending beyond half of rather slender cerci in **Belted**, about half of slightly thicker cerci in **Crimson-ringed**) might also be visible in binoculars, but distinct difference in hamules impossible to see except in hand.

296.1
Crimson-ringed Whiteface
male—Grafton Co., NH,
June 2006

296.2
Crimson-ringed Whiteface
pair with heteromorph
female—Hillsborough
Co., NH, June 2006

Female virtually identical in coloration to female **Belted**, although dark area on front of thorax more likely to narrow smoothly to point above; same dark area usually remains wider and angled before end in **Belted**, but with overlap. Good close-range character on abdomen for females is tiny pale spot at base of each side of S4 in **Belted**, almost always lacking in **Crimson-ringed**. **Frosted** and **Hudsonian** have spot (**Hudsonian** also has even tinier spot at base of S5), **Canada** lacks it. **Dot-tailed** has hint of pale stripe along sides of S4–5. Wing venation in both sexes, hamule shape in male, and/or subgenital plate in female furnish definitive identification. Female distinctly larger than similar-looking female **Hudsonian Whiteface**, usually has smaller spots along abdomen and lacks spot on sides of S4 (spot prominent in **Hudsonian**).

Natural History Males often flat on water-lily leaves but also commonly on stems of emergent vegetation as well as waterside trees and shrubs. Perch flat on ground away from water but also very often in trees. Females rarely seen except in pairs in wheel, seen as they approach lake from surrounding woodland. Lengthy copulation at rest, as long as 30 min or more.

Habitat Lakes and ponds in forested regions, often with boggy margins; vary from very little to abundant aquatic vegetation.

Flight Season ON May–Aug, QC May–Sep, NS May–Aug, WI May–Aug, ME May–Oct, NJ Jun–Aug.

Distribution Also southern Alaska and Northwest Territories south in mountains to California and Wyoming, very few records in middle Canada.

297 Boreal Whiteface *Leucorrhinia borealis*   TL 44–46, HW 29–32

Description Largest whiteface, with heavily red-spotted abdomen. *Male*: Eyes dark brown; face white. Thorax with red-brown and black pattern. Abdomen black, S1–2 mostly red, S3–8 with large red spots almost covering top of each segment; less often, little or no red on S8. *Female*: Polymorphic; colored just like male or pale color yellow to ochre; S8 usually all black but may show pale basal marking. Subgenital plate with two large, rounded lobes.

297.1
Boreal Whiteface male—Yarger Lake, AK, June 2003, Bob Armstrong, posed

297.2
Boreal Whiteface female—Riding Mountain National Park, MB, June 2011, Netta Smith

Identification Only whiteface distinctly larger than others of group. Similarly colored male **Hudsonian Whiteface** conspicuously smaller and lacks obvious spot on S8 (rarely also absent in **Boreal**). Larger size and full-length pale spot on S7 will distinguish female from females of other whitefaces such as **Belted** and **Crimson-ringed** that occur with it; subgenital plate shape also distinctive for each species in hand.

Natural History Males perch on grasses and sedges over water, also flat on algal mats and ground. May be abundant near optimal open-marsh habitats. As many as 10 per square foot seen perching on sunny sides of aspen trees and other pale surfaces in early morning. Only whiteface restricted to short, early flight season.

Habitat Marshy ponds and lake margins, bogs and fens, typically with much upright emergent vegetation, even tall grasses. Most common in open country.

Flight Season Entire range Jun–Jul.

Distribution West to Alaska, south to Washington and in mountains to northern New Mexico.

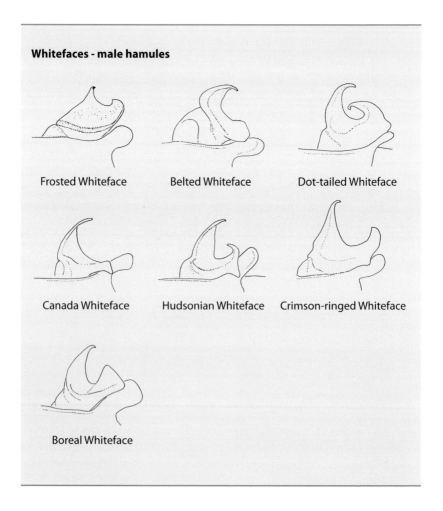

Whitefaces - male hamules

Frosted Whiteface

Belted Whiteface

Dot-tailed Whiteface

Canada Whiteface

Hudsonian Whiteface

Crimson-ringed Whiteface

Boreal Whiteface

Whitefaces - female subgenital plate

Frosted Whiteface

Belted Whiteface

Dot-tailed Whiteface

Canada Whiteface

Hudsonian Whiteface

Crimson-ringed Whiteface

Boreal Whiteface

Elfin Skimmer *Nannothemis*

This monotypic genus may be related to the Old World *Nannophya*, a group of equally tiny dragonflies. The wings are so small that there is no space for the development of an anal loop, and it wouldn't take long to count all the cells in each one. The forewing triangle is four-sided as in some primitive skimmers of Old World rain forests, although not necessarily indicating a relationship. The specialized habitat preference makes for a localized, if widespread, distribution. World 1, NA 1, East 1.

298 Elfin Skimmer   *Nannothemis bella*   TL 18–20, HW 10–15

Description Barely big enough to be called "dragon," this tiny, distinctively colored skimmer occurs widely at bogs and sandy lakes. *Male*: Eyes blue-gray, stripe of reddish-brown around posterior edges. Face mostly white, body entirely pruinose blue-gray, black often showing through. Immature males shiny black. *Female*: Very differently colored at all stages. Thorax black and yellow striped; abdomen black with yellow bands, bands become narrower toward tip. Wings with dark streaks at base, also much orange suffusion. Note white tips of pterostigmas, much like some spreadwings. Very young tenerals of both sexes are lime green!

298.1
Elfin Skimmer male—
Richmond Co., GA, May
2006

298.2
Elfin Skimmer female—
Hillsborough Co., NH, July
2006

298.3
Elfin Skimmer immature
male—Richmond Co., GA,
May 2006

Identification Nothing else in range is so small. Male obviously smaller than male **Little Blue Dragonlet**, not as blue, and with mostly gray eyes and white face. **Dragonlet** has dark face and eyes and black abdomen tip. Males are so tiny and pruinose that a quick look could suggest mature female **Eastern Forktail**. Female looks like nothing else, might be mistaken for bee or wasp. Perhaps could be confused with female **Eastern Amberwing**, which has more patterned wings, less patterned abdomen.

Natural History Remains in breeding habitat, where it may be found during cloudy weather. Invariably droops wings when perching. Males spend much time perching on low shrubs and sedges around water, little time over open water, but quite territorial in very small territories. Females in vegetation at fringe of uplands, often both sexes present together at edges. Mating rarely seen. To oviposit, female taps water a few times, then perches for short while, then repeats. May be guarded by male. Males seen to be aggressive to male Frosted Whitefaces. Female coloration, both body and wings, makes them probable mimics of wasps and bees.

Habitat Sphagnum bogs and sedgy seepage areas at lake edges.

Flight Season ON May–Aug, QC Jun–Jul, NS May–Aug, WI May–Aug, ME May–Aug, OH Jun–Sep, NJ May–Sep, GA Apr–May, FL May–Aug.

Scarlet Skimmers *Crocothemis*

This Old World genus, occurring from southern Europe throughout Africa and southern Asia to northern Australia, is similar to and probably related to the New World pondhawks and dragonlets. Both wing venation, general form, and the expanded subgenital plate point to this relationship. Most species are red or brown, but one has black and blue males. A single species was introduced to the New World from Asia. They are called "scarlets" in Africa. World 10, NA 1, East 1.

299 Scarlet Skimmer *Crocothemis servilia*   TL 37–43, HW 31–33

Description The brightest of a small number of red species in peninsular Florida, with blue-edged eyes, this is our only nonnative odonate. *Male*: Eyes red, sides with blue edge. Face and body entirely bright scarlet-red. Hindwings with prominent reddish patch at base. *Female*: Eyes reddish-brown over gray, hint of bluish rear  edge. Thorax dull yellowish, brown on front with narrow yellow stripe on either side. Abdomen yellow with narrow stripes, a black median one and brown lateral ones. Hindwing patch paler than in male.

Identification Only one other very similar species (same size, rather bright red) in peninsular Florida. Male **Red-tailed Pennant** differs by having thorax darker brown than bright red abdomen; eyes duller reddish, blue-gray below rather than at rear edge; swollen abdomen base; and smaller hindwing patch. Male **Antillean Skimmer** distinctly larger and clear-winged, no blue in eyes. Female and immature **Scarlet Skimmer** rather nondescript but distinguished from others by overall yellowish color, pale stripes bordering front of thorax, and three dark stripes on abdomen (median one darkest). Female **Red-tailed Pennant** has no abdominal pattern. Female **Band-winged Dragonlet** has different abdominal markings, including black tip, and darker front of thorax.

Natural History Males perch on twigs, rocks, and ground near water; tend to perch low when over water. Very active at midday, with much aggression among males. Sometimes very wary, appropriate for such a brightly colored animal. Yellow immatures can be very common near breeding sites.

Habitat Ponds, lakes, canals, and ditches with aquatic vegetation. Very tolerant and widespread in its native range in southern Asia.

299.1
Scarlet Skimmer male—
Collier Co., FL, December
2007

299.2
Scarlet Skimmer
female—Collier Co., FL,
June 2004

Flight Season FL all year.

Distribution Also known from throughout the Greater Antilles, it may be slowly spreading northward in Florida. Native to Asia, from the Middle East, China, and Japan through the Greater Sunda Islands and Philippines.

Comments Introduced into the New World, the only such species. First found in Florida in mid 1970s and subsequently recorded in Cuba, Jamaica, Hispaniola, and Puerto Rico, it may have been originally introduced to one of the islands and spread from there. Called Oriental Scarlet or Crimson Darter or Ruddy Marsh Skimmer in parts of its Old World range.

Pondhawks *Erythemis*

Appropriately named, these medium to large skimmers are voracious predators of other insects, including dragonflies, up to their own size. They capture them by flycatching. Walking along the waterside, you may flush teneral odonates, and if there are pondhawks in the vicinity, you may see a swift attack and can watch the process of a meal being consumed. The genus is characterized by some extra-large spines on the hind femur, surely an adaptation to take large prey. Most species perch and fly low, often on the ground or broad leaves or logs. Perhaps low perching facilitates capture of larger prey, as this behavior is common in skimmers of Old World genus *Orthetrum*, similar in numerous ways, and also in many clubtails. Wings usually are held flat but may be drooped when on an elevated perch. Raising wings or pointing abdomen upward has not been noted in this group. The species fall into two categories, with either excessively slender and elongate or normally shaped abdomen. Pin-tailed and Great are the slender species of our fauna; the others belong to the "normal" group. World 10, NA 7, East 4.

300 Black Pondhawk *Erythemis attala* TL 42–44, HW 32–38

Description Medium-sized black or black and yellow skimmer, abdomen slender but not excessively so; vagrant in region. *Male:* Eyes dark brown; face black. Thorax and abdomen entirely black; appendages white. Some mature males retain pale bands of immaturity on abdomen. Basal dark hindwing markings extend out to triangle. *Female:* Eyes dark brown; face tan. Thorax brown. Abdomen black, yellow at base and with basal yellow bands on S4–7, bands

increasingly restricted with age to paired yellow blotches as abdomen darkens, then may

300.1
Black Pondhawk male—
Kleberg Co., TX, October
2004, Greg Lasley

300.2
Black Petaltail female—
Hidalgo Co., TX, June
2008, Martin Reid

302.1
Great Pondhawk
male—Laguna
Cartagena, Puerto
Rico, March 2009,
Netta Smith

302.2
Great Pondhawk
female—Cameron
Co., TX, November
2008, R. A.
Behrstock/
Naturewide Images

302.3
Great Pondhawk
immature
male—Monroe Co.,
FL, December 2007

to male, even in shape, and goes through same color changes with maturity. Cerci cream-colored, shorter than those of male.

Identification Much larger and longer-bodied than female and young male **Eastern Pondhawk** of same color. Abdomen of **Great** a bit longer than hindwing, very slender, and dramatically swollen at base; obviously shorter than hindwing and not such swollen base in **Eastern**. Dark markings on abdomen transverse in **Great**, pointed in front in **Eastern**. S1–3 entirely green in **Great**, all carinas marked with heavy black lines in **Eastern**. Abdominal markings always green, never white as they sometimes are in **Eastern**. Femora pale in

Great, entire leg black in **Eastern**. Female subgenital plate projects in **Eastern**, not in **Great**. In flight, easily mistaken for DARNER, in particular species with green thorax such as **Amazon, Blue-faced, Common Green**, or **Mangrove**, but green bands across abdomen distinctive, as well as perching habits.

Natural History As other pondhawks, perches on ground, but much more likely to perch higher, to head height and above. In dry season/winter, can be common within forest, perching in shade. Males usually perch below waist height at waterside or fly back and forth over open water, hovering from time to time with abdomen elevated and looking a bit like a darner. Mating rarely observed, copulation at rest. Oviposition by regular taps in one spot, then moving on to another area to repeat. Regularly takes large prey, including dragonflies and butterflies. Usually more common in fall and early winter than earlier in season.

Habitat Marshy ponds, including temporary ones; also fly over pools in streams, may not breed there.

Flight Season FL all year.

Distribution Also throughout West Indies and from Oklahoma south to Argentina, including Galapagos. Scattered records across Southwest, north to northern Arizona and southern Colorado, presumably vagrants.

---

303 Eastern Pondhawk *Erythemis simplicicollis* TL 38–44, HW 30–33

Description Medium blue or green skimmer with medium-length slender abdomen. *Male*: Eyes blue-green, with conspicuous dark pseudopupils; face green. Thorax and abdomen entirely pruinose blue; appendages white. Immature colored as female, becomes pruinose first on abdomen and then thorax. Color change begins at about a week of age and takes about 2–3 weeks, fastest at higher temperatures. *Female*: Eyes olive-brown to yellowish-green to fairly bright green; face green. Thorax and abdomen base bright green, rest of abdomen banded black and white or black and pale green, tip black; appendages white. Subgenital plate projects downward from abdomen at right angle. Notable geographic variation, females from northwestern part of area (Minnesota, Iowa) with slightly shorter, broader abdomens with black markings reduced. Tenerals bright lime green all over, even wings.

Identification Green females and immatures unmistakable; only thing similar are both sexes of **Great Pondhawk**, obviously larger and with much thinner abdomen (see that species). Blue males most likely mistaken for **Blue Dasher,** but that species has white face, bright green eyes, and a bit of color at hindwing base. Perching habits distinguish them, **Pondhawk** near and often on ground, **Dasher** up in vegetation, and males on territory above waist height. **Dashers** typically droop their wings, **Pondhawks** do not. Two of the most common species within their wide ranges, these two can be compared again and again. Green individuals may be mistaken for CLUBTAILS, especially as they fly swiftly and land on ground. Note very different abdominal pattern.

Natural History Often superabundant, clearly favored in wetlands of today, although sufficiently tied to still water that absent from many areas in hilly, wooded interior. Perches low, usually below waist height and with four legs; on ground and other flat surfaces, also leaves and branches. One of few skimmers that habitually chooses ground perching, although this makes it vulnerable to larval tiger beetles, known to grab the dragonfly and pull enough of it down into their burrow for a meal. Voracious predator, especially females, eating odonates of all kinds their own size and smaller, up to Blue Dasher and other pondhawks, and, rarely, even larger species such as Wandering Glider and immature king skimmers. May forage until almost dark. Males return to water at about 2 weeks of age, perch along shores and in marsh vegetation, and spend relatively little time in patrol flights. May

303.1
Eastern Pondhawk
male—Early Co.,
GA, July 2007

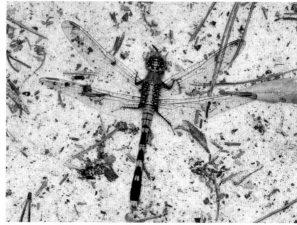

303.2
Eastern Pondhawk
female—Lake Co.,
FL, April 2008

303.3
Eastern Pondhawk
immature
male—
Hillsborough Co.,
NH, July 2006

remain on territory for up to 5 hr in a day. Interacting males fly in parallel flight and then have mutual display, "vertical circling," seeming to leapfrog but in fact rear one moving *under* the other, and pair usually repeating action at least several times. Copulation brief (averages 20 sec) and aerial, may be followed by resting period. Female usually continues to perch after separation, quite inconspicuous to males. Her mate, remaining on territory, may guard her once she starts laying eggs. Most oviposition without male in attendance,

303.4
Eastern Pondhawk
female—Bremer Co.,
IA, July 2004

usually in beds of vegetation and fairly brief, often under a minute spent at water (but returning repeatedly). Quite variable in distance moved and taps made per site, but up to several hundred when undisturbed. Often abdomen conspicuously raised above horizontal before hitting water. Clutch size averages 900 eggs, released at 8–10/sec.

Habitat Almost any body of water—lakes, ponds, slow streams, ditches, canals—with emergent vegetation. Seems especially to prefer carpets of floating plants such as water hyacinth and water lettuce. Shuns unvegetated wetlands.

Flight Season ON May–Sep, QC Jun–Aug, IA May–Oct, WI May–Sep, ME Jun–Sep, OH May–Oct, NJ May–Oct, KY Apr–Oct, LA Feb–Nov, GA Mar–Nov, FL all year.

Distribution West to eastern Colorado and New Mexico (also recorded from southern Arizona) and south in eastern Mexican lowlands, then to Costa Rica, although very scarce south of Mexico. Also in Bahamas and Greater Antilles.

Dragonlets *Erythrodiplax*

This large genus of small to medium skimmers of New World tropics has few species reaching North America and one found only there. Most live in marshes with dense vegetation. In our area, we see a large black species with black wing markings, a much smaller pruinose blue species, and a slender black coastal species. Immature males are colored just like females, and immatures are often common. At rest, the wings are held level or drooped forward, the perching position usually parallel to the branch; they are likely to obelisk in midday sun. World 58, NA 6, East 3.

304 Little Blue Dragonlet *Erythrodiplax minuscula*   TL 25–27, HW 17–21

Description Very small clear-winged skimmer with blue male. *Male:* Eyes dark brown, blue-tinged in oldest individuals; face metallic blue. Thorax pruinose blue or blackish, abdomen pruinose blue with S8–10 black, appendages pale. *Female:* Eyes reddish over blue-gray, blue in oldest individuals; face yellowish-tan. Thorax brown in front, yellowish to tan on sides; abdomen yellowish with rectangles on sides, stripe down middle, and tip black. Immature similarly patterned but pale colors yellow.

Identification No other skimmer in its range is tiny and blue (male **Elfin Skimmer**, even smaller, is blue-gray and lacks conspicuous black at abdomen tip). Dark face and reddish-brown/gray eyes readily distinguish mature male from male **Eastern**

304.1
Little Blue Dragonlet
male—Early Co., GA,
July 2007

304.2
Little Blue Dragonlet female—Collier Co., FL,
December 2007, Netta Smith

304.3
Little Blue Dragonlet immature
male—Telfair Co., GA, May 2006

Pondhawk (green face, dark blue-green eyes), male **Blue Dasher** (white face, brilliant green eyes), and male **Blue Corporal** (dark brown eyes, face, and thorax and conspicuous basal wing spots). All of these mostly blue dragonflies are obviously larger. Females and immature males drab but recognized by small size. Dark stripe down center of abdomen and black tip distinguish female **Little Blue** from female MEADOWHAWKS.

Natural History Males not very conspicuous as they perch below knee height in marsh vegetation, but they fiercely chase others from their small territory. Often perch with wings depressed and abdomen elevated, like miniature Blue Dasher. Copulation brief and in flight, followed immediately by oviposition, male often hovering in attendance. Females oviposit in dense vegetation or in open water at edge of vegetation, either moving rapidly over open water and tapping at irregular intervals or remaining in restricted area and tapping slowly and methodically.

Habitat Shallow marshy ponds and lake margins.

Flight Season KY Jun–Sep, LA Apr–Dec, GA Mar–Dec, FL all year.

Distribution Extends slightly farther west in Oklahoma and Texas.

Comments The Antillean Dragonlet (*Erythrodiplax justiniana*) of the Greater Antilles might occur in Florida. It looks much like this, but both sexes have big brown basal spots in the hindwings.

Description Small slender skimmer of coastal habitats, including full salt water. *Male*: Eyes dark red-brown over pale greenish; face metallic blue-black. Entirely glossy black at maturity, eventually overlaid by dusky pruinosity in some. *Female*: Seemingly quite variable. Eyes red-brown over greenish-gray; face cream colored, metallic blue-black on top of frons. Thorax yellow to orange, with many narrow black stripes. Abdomen black on S1–3 and S8–10; S4–7 orange above, black on lower sides. Many individuals with black thorax and bright orange abdomen, some becoming entirely black

as male. Other individuals have striped thorax, entirely black abdomen. Many individuals, especially in more northerly populations, show brown wing spots beyond nodus. Subgenital plate conspicuous—long, pointed, and extending downward from abdomen.

Identification Unique habitat and range make identification relatively easy; no other similar species occurs with it. **Double-ringed Pennant**, also small and black, becomes more bluish pruinose and has small brown spot at hindwing base. Overlap in habitat unlikely. Quite similar-looking **Black Meadowhawk is** a northern species of fresh water, with limited overlap in range. Males probably not distinguishable if one strayed into the habitat of the other, perhaps by remnant markings of immature coloration or length of stigma (shorter than width of face in **Meadowhawk**, longer than that in **Dragonlet**). Female **Seaside Dragonlet** distinctive because of bright orange and black or yellow and black in various combinations. Brightly marked female **Black Meadowhawk** also similar, has chainlike pattern on sides of thorax instead of stripes. Some female SMALL PENNANTS closest in appearance,

305.1
Seaside Dragonlet
male—Brevard Co., FL,
April 2008

305.2
Seaside Dragonlet
female—Brevard Co., FL,
April 2008

305.3
Seaside Dragonlet
female—Sagadahoc
Co., ME, July 2002,
Glenn Corbiere

305.4
Seaside Dragonlet
female—Wakulla Co.,
FL, July 2005, Marion M.
Dobbs

305.5
Seaside Dragonlet
female (*naeva*
type)—Monroe Co., FL,
December 2007

but most have colored patch at hindwing base and black abdomen with pale spots down middle, whereas **Dragonlet** has orange on both sides or covering entire segments. When changing from orange to black, thorax in **Seaside Dragonlet** becomes black when only top of abdomen orange, a unique combination. Female **Double-ringed Pennant** has light color only at abdomen base.

Natural History Both sexes often in large numbers in breeding areas, seem less territorial than other dragonlets, but males aggressive to other males at close range. Often at freshwater locations near coast and occasionally disperse well inland, perhaps with prevailing winds. Perch in marsh vegetation, also on shrub and tree branches when in wooded habitats. Tandem oviposition unique in genus, and pairs may fly long distances in tandem. Oviposition slow and methodical, often with repeated dips to water at same spot (up to 50 on one occasion), especially on algal mats, then moving a few inches to repeat the procedure.

Habitat Only American dragonfly that breeds in salt water. Salt marshes in much of range, mangrove swamps in tropics. Favored habitats at least in some areas are brackish sites somewhat inland from outer coast, but larvae also develop in fresh water in similar situations. Breed at upper fringe of mangroves and salt marshes in fresh water.

Flight Season NS Aug, ME Jun–Aug, NJ May–Sep, LA Apr–Nov, GA Apr–Oct, FL all year.

Distribution Surprisingly many scattered records away from coast, but probably all wandering individuals. Ranges south around Gulf and Caribbean, including throughout West Indies, to Venezuela. Also on Pacific coast of Mexico from Baja California and Sonora to Oaxaca and in interior of west Texas and New Mexico.

Comments Tropical representatives of this species have been considered a distinct subspecies, *E. b. naeva*, differing in smaller size and very slight average differences in hamules and penis. There is substantial overlap. Populations in the Florida Keys have been considered *naeva*, as they are small, and females lack the brown wing spots that are common in populations farther north. Also, females seem more likely to become pruinose, as in populations in the West Indies.

306 Band-winged Dragonlet *Erythrodiplax umbrata* TL 38–45, HW 25–33

Description Midsized slender skimmer, male with black bands across wings. *Male*: Eyes dark brown; face black. Thorax and abdomen black, each wing with rectangular black band past midwing. Immature males fairly quickly develop light brown hint of definitive wing pattern. *Female*: Eyes brown over gray; face brown. Tan to brown with dark markings on front of thorax, dark markings like pointed rectangles along abdomen, and clear wings. Polymorphic, small percentage of mature females with black body and banded wings as males.

Identification Nothing else like mature male except **Four-spotted Pennant**, especially those that have larger wing spots. **Pennant** differs by having edges of spots rounded rather than straight across and white stigmas, also very different habit of perching high on tips of vegetation. Note that male **Common Whitetail** also has black band on each wing, but very different otherwise, with wide abdomen and different body colors. Female **Band-winged** rather drab but can be recognized by dark, pointed in front, spots along sides of abdomen. Female **Little Blue Dragonlet** much smaller; abdomen looks relatively shorter.

Natural History Males perch low in or at edge of tall grasses and fly low over water, often chasing one another. Flight looks fluttery, perhaps a consequence of patterned wings. Females and immatures perch on branches and herbaceous stems, even at some height in shrubs and trees, sometimes aggregated in one small area in what seems extensive similar habitat. Mating pairs rarely seen, copulation brief and in flight. Ovipositing female guarded by male or not, taps slowly and methodically without rising far from water. Ovipositing andromorph females, with black wing bands, may display to males as if they were also males and thus avoid harassment. Huge numbers of this species seen on Texas coast in July 2004, estimated to be millions. This magnitude of occurrence remains unexplained, although species probably in part migratory and seen in great numbers in fall in eastern Mexico. Has bred in Ohio, but perhaps immigrant rather than resident there. Immatures often retire to woodland until ready to breed, may spend entire dry season there in tropics. Abundant and widespread in tropics.

306.1
Band-winged Dragonlet
male—Monroe Co., FL,
December 2007

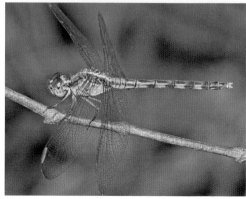

306.2
Band-winged Dragonlet
heteromorph female—
Dade Co., FL, December
2007, Netta Smith

306.3
Band-winged Dragonlet
andromorph female—
Charlotte Co., FL,
September 2008, Marion
M. Dobbs

Habitat Shallow, marshy ponds, often temporary, with scattered to dense, low to high sedges and grasses.

Flight Season OH Jun–Oct, LA Sep–Oct, FL all year.

Distribution Extends farther west in Oklahoma and Texas and south to Argentina, also throughout West Indies.

Meadowhawks are the only small red dragonflies seen over most of North America and all across Eurasia. The only other small, clear-winged red dragonflies in the East are the Red-tailed Pennant and Scarlet Skimmer, of limited distribution in our region, and few meadowhawks occur in the same range and habitat. Other red dragonflies in region are larger or have much more black patterning mixed with the red. Black Meadowhawk is an exception to the red coloration prevalent in this genus, and it could be mistaken for several species of whitefaces except for its dark face. Female meadowhawks are more problematical, as most are brown, and there are other small, brown dragonflies, for example dragonlets. Note the dark markings on the abdomens of female dragonlets are usually rectangular, not so for meadowhawks. Also, dragonlets are of tropical origin, meadowhawks of temperate, so there is relatively little overlap in range. Immature meadowhawks may be everywhere in meadows at high density, often more than one species. Immature males are colored just like females but are easily distinguished by their more slender abdomen. Some female meadowhawks, perhaps oldest individuals, turn entirely red as in males. Both sexes may be seen away from water, sometimes far away, especially in the migratory Variegated Meadowhawk. Perching with wings drooped forward is common, even when on tips of grass inflorescences where pennants perch with wings level or raised. All meadowhawks oviposit in tandem, and some of them fly long distances in tandem between mating and egg laying. Other red dragonflies that oviposit in tandem, including saddlebags and small pennants, look quite different. Some species oviposit in water, but others lay eggs on dry ground, with hatching after winter rains fill temporary ponds. Larvae develop quickly during summer, and the cycle begins again. These species lay relatively large eggs, up to 3 mm in diameter. This breeding cycle is characteristic of species that fly in late summer, and most meadowhawks are seen in late summer and well into fall. Variegated is an exception, also appearing early in spring. World 61, NA 13, East 10.

Description Robust migratory meadowhawk with fancy abdominal pattern and pair of wide white stripes or yellow spots on either side of thorax. *Male*: Eyes red above, pinkish to gray below; face red in front, brownish on sides. Thorax brown with pair of small bright yellow spots on either side. Abdomen overall reddish but complexly patterned brown and red at close range. Legs black with brown stripe on outside of femur and tibia. Anterior wing veins red. Younger males (common away from breeding habitats) patterned as females, with white lateral spots persisting, but with much red on abdomen. *Female*: Eyes and face brownish-tan. Thorax brown with yellow spots as in male. Abdomen brown with whitish lateral spots on S3–8. Sutures between segments richer orange-brown. Anterior wing veins yellow. Immature of both sexes more vividly marked, with wide white stripes on sides of thorax leading down to yellow spots; bright white spots low on sides of S2–8, bordered by black above and below; and black dorsal markings on S8–9, all producing variegated look that gives species its name. Stigma at all stages darker in center than at ends. Legs prominently black and yellow striped.

Identification Yellow spots low on sides of thorax diagnostic in combination with complexly patterned abdomen in immatures; no other dragonfly so patterned. **Red-veined Meadowhawk** (very restricted in region) also has pale stripes on thorax but has abdomen plain except for dark ventrolateral markings. Most mature male **Variegated** retain variegated abdominal pattern, but those that become entirely red might be confused with other meadowhawks or other red skimmers. Reddish anterior wing veins and (usually) yellow dots on thorax are distinctive. **Saffron-winged** has similarly brighter anterior wing veins

307.1
Variegated Meadowhawk
male—Hidalgo Co., TX,
November 2005

307.2
Variegated Meadowhawk
male—Brewster Co., TX,
November 2007,
Netta Smith

307.3
Variegated Meadowhawk
female—Harney Co., OR,
July 2006

but has stigma uniformly colored, **Variegated** darker in center; **Saffron-winged** body also scarcely patterned.

Natural History May feed in flight in swarms with other fliers but more typically a flycatcher like most skimmers. Males alternate perching on twigs, sedges, and grasses and frequent flights low over water. Pairs oviposit in tandem, staying fairly low between descents and often tapping repeatedly before moving a short distance to do it again. Pairs at times very common, even at small pools or flooded parking lots. Away from water, commonly perches on ground; during migration, seen well up in trees. More likely to droop abdomen downward during midday heat than elevate it, as other meadowhawks do. Presumably mostly a migrant in the East, with mature males appearing in early spring in northwestern part of region (Minnesota, Iowa) before any sign of emergence. Large numbers, including tandem pairs, seen in late fall at western edge of region, for example, southwestern Arkansas. Individuals seen over much of East in fall may be migrants/vagrants displaced from farther West, where abundant. Migrating individuals seen all the way to southern Florida along

Gulf Coast, but most disappear before spring. In core of range in West, many individuals present through winter, even with subfreezing nights. Winter breeding not definitely established in Southeast but possible. Recently emerged immatures in spring in eastern Tennessee. Farther west along Gulf coast, present in both spring and fall but rarely in winter and never in summer.

Habitat Breeding habitat shallow open or marshy lakes and ponds, often alkaline. Also pools with shore vegetation in streams and rivers. Oviposition seen in temporary ponds in many areas, even rain puddles on roads; not known if larvae develop to emergence.

Flight Season ON Apr–Nov, IA Mar–Oct, WI Apr–Oct, ME Jul–Aug, OH Apr–Nov, NJ Jun–Oct, LA Oct–Apr, GA Oct–Apr, FL all year.

Distribution Records sparse east of Mississippi River, especially in South; for example, no record from very well surveyed North Carolina. Also occurs throughout West, north to southern Canada. Recorded south to Belize and Honduras, perhaps only as vagrant. Regular south onto Mexican Plateau, southern limits of breeding not known.

| **308 Red-veined Meadowhawk** *Sympetrum madidum* | **TL 42–45, HW 28–31** |

Description Fairly large meadowhawk with conspicuous thoracic stripes, red-veined wings, barely entering region. *Male*: Eyes and face red. Thorax red, faint indication of black lines on sutures and trace of two pale spots low on each side. Abdomen red, in some with black specks on posterior segments corresponding to areas where other species have more black. Legs black. Veins on front and base of wings reddish, may be orange suffusion in basal wing

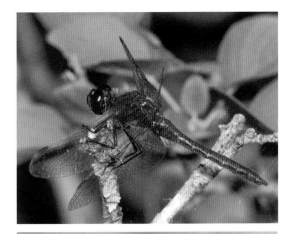

308.1
Red-veined Meadowhawk
male—70 Mile House, BC,
July 2006

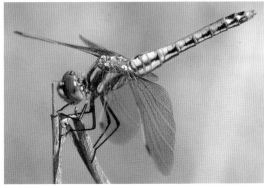

308.2
Red-veined Meadowhawk
female—West Shoal Lake,
MB, June 2008, Deanna
Dodgson

membranes. *Female*: Eyes red-brown over pale greenish; face tan. Thorax brown with two broad white stripes on either side, in some individuals fainter whitish stripes on front. Abdomen tan with narrow black lateral stripe on S4–9, whitish areas below that; narrow black median line on S8–9. Some females become red like males, retaining much of pattern.

Identification Male **Cherry-faced Meadowhawk** also bright red like **Red-veined** but has prominent black markings along sides of abdomen and cerci with long point and prominent ventral tooth (blunt-ended, no tooth in **Red-veined**); also a bit smaller. No other eastern meadowhawk has the bright pale thoracic stripes of this one, although see also **Variegated Meadowhawk**.

Natural History Males perch low in herbaceous vegetation or on ground around marshy areas. Females may be nearby, often perched on rocks or ground when temperature low in morning. Oviposits in tandem or alone, typically with male hovering nearby to guard female. Eggs laid in shallow water about to dry up or in dry pond basins, presumably overwintering and hatching in spring after ponds fill in winter.

Habitat Shallow, open, often somewhat saline ponds with abundant emergent vegetation, usually or perhaps always drying up by mid or late summer. Also marshy pools in small slow-flowing streams, not much associated with open water.

Flight Season Probably all summer.

Distribution Widespread in West from southern Canada to southern California and Colorado, scattered records north to Northwest Territories.

---

309 Blue-faced Meadowhawk   *Sympetrum ambiguum*   TL 36–38, HW 26–28

Description Brightly marked southeastern meadowhawk with blue face in male. *Male*: Eyes pale blue, brownish-tinged above; face white overlaid by blue to turquoise, sometimes looks greenish or just whitish (old individuals?). Thorax mostly creamy gray with rather faint brown stripes. Abdomen red, black apical rings on S4–9, widening to rear to cover most of S9. Appendages pale. *Female*: Eyes brown over gray; face tan. Thorax as male. Abdomen tan, black apical dorsolateral spots on S3–9 becoming larger to rear and covering most of S8–9. Abdomen red in small proportion of individuals.

Identification Male only red dragonfly with bright blue to green face and bluish eyes. Even in those with whitish face, eyes have some blue. Gray, brown-striped thorax of both sexes

309.1
Blue-faced Meadowhawk
male—Cape May Co., NJ,
October 2008, Steven
Collins

309.2
Blue-faced Meadowhawk
female—Travis Co., TX,
November 2007, Eric Isley

309.3
Blue-faced Meadowhawk
immature male—Floyd
Co., GA, May 2006

not like thorax of any other meadowhawk or, actually, any other species in its size range. Abdomen also has more ringed look than in other meadowhawks. **Autumn Meadowhawk** is a brown-legged species that lacks black rings. **Cherry-faced, Ruby, Saffron-winged,** and **White-faced Meadowhawks** all differ by having black markings low on sides of most abdominal segments rather than rings or partial rings. Those species also have dark legs, **Blue-faced** tan.

Natural History Both sexes perch in trees at woodland edge or within forest when away from water. Males perch low around edge of shallow pools or dried-up ponds, often inconspicuous. Copulation at rest. Females oviposit by dropping eggs in grass or on mud, guarded by male hovering or perched.

Habitat Ponds, including temporary ones, in or out of woodland; also on some wooded streams. More characteristic of wooded habitats than any other North American meadowhawk but also common at edge of large Atlantic-coast marshes.

Flight Season IA Jun–Oct, OH Jul–Oct, NJ Aug–Oct, KY May–Oct, LA Jun–Nov, GA Apr–Nov, FL May–Nov.

Distribution Extends farther west from Kansas to Texas, one Nebraska record.

Description Meadowhawk with white face, black abdominal markings, and black legs. *Male:* Eyes red-brown over pale greenish to grayish; face white. Thorax brown, may look paler on sides than front with faint indication of ventrolateral pale spots. Abdomen bright red, black ventrolateral triangles on S4–8, most of lower surface of S9 black. Appendages reddish. *Female:* Eyes reddish-brown over pale greenish; face pale yellowish. Thorax brown in front, lighter brown on sides with pale yellowish areas below. Abdomen tan with wide black ventrolateral stripe from S4–9, covering larger parts of segments toward rear. Wings may have some orange suffusion at base. Some females may become red as in other meadowhawks but rarely seen in this species.

Identification Mature male only one of three species with vivid black triangles on red abdomen (producing jagged line where they meet) that has white face. **Cherry-faced** has red to tan face (redder in western part of region), **Ruby** light brown face. Female like **Cherry-faced** but usually paler face, darker wing veins, and more contrasty thoracic pattern. Even more like **Ruby**, probably these three species not distinguishable except by examining subgenital plates in hand. Even some males will be puzzling without a look at the hamules. See **Cherry-faced** for structural details.

310.1
White-faced
Meadowhawk male—
Kittitas Co., WA,
September 2007

310.2
White-faced
Meadowhawk female—
Kittitas Co., WA,
September 2007

Natural History Males can be superabundant in extensive sedge meadows, as many as one per 10 square feet. Copulation presumably lengthy, as pairs in wheel can also be abundant at times when scarcely one in tandem is seen. Oviposits in tandem or alone, usually with male hovering nearby to guard female. Male may release female and both land, then he guards her when she flies up to lay eggs again, or she may lay eggs even while perched. Eggs dropped from above in shallow water about to dry up or in dry pond basins, presumably overwintering and hatching in spring after ponds fill in winter.

Habitat Shallow marshes, bogs, and fens that may or may not dry up each summer; also similar habitats at edge of lakes. Often most common meadowhawk in cold, boggy wetlands, and associated with forest over most of its range.

Flight Season ON Jun–Oct, QC Jun–Oct, NS Jun–Oct, IA Jun–Oct, WI Jun–Oct, ME May–Oct, OH Jun–Oct, NJ Jun–Oct, KY Jul–Nov.

Distribution West across southern Canada to Northwest Territories and British Columbia, south in mountains to northern California and northern New Mexico.

Comments Thought to hybridize with Cherry-faced and Ruby Meadowhawks, at least at eastern end of range.

---

311 Ruby Meadowhawk *Sympetrum rubicundulum*　　　TL 33–34, HW 24–30

Description Red meadowhawk with sharply defined black triangles along abdomen and tan face. *Male*: Eyes red over grayish-green; face tan, slightly more reddish above. Thorax red. Abdomen bright red with elongate black ventrolateral triangles on S4–9. Populations at west end of region (Minnesota, Iowa) with orange wing bases. *Female*: Eyes reddish-brown over pale greenish; face yellowish to chartreuse. Thorax brown, paling to yellowish on sides. Abdomen tan with black markings similar to those of male but more like rectangles than triangles. Some females bright red like males.

Identification This species easily confused with very similar **Cherry-faced** and **White-faced Meadowhawks**. **Ruby** averages slightly larger than the other two, so size alone might be clue. Tan face color distinguishes male from mature male **White-faced**, but easternmost **Cherry-faced** populations quite similar. Hamules distinctive but must be seen in hand or extreme close-up photograph. Females of these three not distinguishable in field. In this

311.1
Ruby Meadowhawk male—Walker Co., GA, August 2007, Marion M. Dobbs

311.2
Ruby Meadowhawk red female—Wayne Co., OH, July 2007

species, lobes of subgenital plate much expanded, bulging downward and pointing straight to rear. See more details under **Cherry-faced**. Orange wing bases, where found, good field mark in both sexes to distinguish **Ruby** from **Cherry-faced** and **White-faced**, but some female **Cherry-faced** similar, in which case capture and examination of subgenital plate necessary for identification. Orange wing bases in those populations superficially like those of **Band-winged Meadowhawk**, which has brown crossband at midwing where it occurs with **Ruby**, also black markings on thorax.

Natural History Males perch in tall grasses and shrubs at breeding locations. Tandem pairs and lone females oviposit by dropping eggs into grass near water; also lay in water, unlike near relatives Cherry-faced and White-faced.

Habitat Edges of extensive marshes and marshy ponds and lake shores.

Flight Season ON Jun–Oct, QC Jun–Aug, NS May–Oct, IA Jun–Oct, WI Jul–Sep, ME Jun–Oct, OH Jun–Oct, KY Jun–Oct.

Distribution West to western South Dakota and Nebraska, possibly farther. Because of much confusion in literature among similar species, western edge of range may need revision. Isolated records in Ontario need to be confirmed.

Comments Thought to hybridize with Cherry-faced and White-faced Meadowhawks, at least at eastern end of range.

312 Cherry-faced Meadowhawk   *Sympetrum internum*   TL 31–36, HW 23–27

Description Small meadowhawk with reddish face, colored basal wing veins, prominent black markings on sides of abdomen, black legs. *Male*: Eyes red, shading to dull pale greenish below; face reddish in most of range, tan in New England region. Thorax and abdomen bright red. Abdomen with elongate black ventrolateral triangles on S4–9, widening to rectangles to rear; may be fine median black line on S7–8. Veins of wing base, or most of wing, may be yellow-orange in western areas, and sometimes yellowish suffusion in this area. Farther east, populations with relatively dark veins, only costa yellowish. *Female*: Eyes red-brown over tan; face tan. Thorax and abdomen tan; latter with continuous black ventro-

lateral stripe on S4–9, continuous with narrower stripe higher up on S2–3. Wings as in male, more likely to have extensive orange suffusion on hindwing base. Small percentage of females get quite red on upper surface of eyes, front of thorax, and all of abdomen.

312.1
Cherry-faced
Meadowhawk
male—
Westmorland Co.,
NB, August 2006,
Denis Doucet

312.2
Cherry-faced
Meadowhawk
brown female—70
Mile House, BC, July
2006, Netta Smith

312.3
Cherry-faced
Meadowhawk
red female—
Gatineau Park,
QC, August 2008,
Chang-Won Seo

Identification One of three small species with plain thorax, black legs, vivid black triangles low on each side of abdomen. Male distinguished from otherwise very similar **White-faced Meadowhawk** by reddish or tan face; more readily in westernmost part of region by reddish wing-vein color. In that region (Minnesota, Iowa, Missouri) differs from **Ruby Meadowhawk** in same ways, also usual lack of orange color at wing bases. Immature males and all females impossible to distinguish from **Ruby** and **White-faced** in field; must examine hamules or subgenital plates in hand for certainty. **White-faced** has small notch in hamule, **Cherry-faced** and **Ruby** large notch; this difference easily visible with hand lens. Other two more difficult to distinguish, **Ruby** with slightly larger notch than **Cherry-faced**, with more prominent shelf extending inward visible in view from below. Mature female **Cherry-faced** like **White-faced** but face somewhat redder, wings with yellow costa in western part of region. Subgenital plates similar, all narrowing toward tip and then notched, with groove between two halves. Paired tips point outward in **Cherry-faced**, parallel in other two. In side view, each half bulges dramatically in **Ruby**, flatter and more parallel with abdomen in **White-faced**. Much more black on abdomen than in other clear-winged red eastern meadowhawks with reddish or brown faces (**Autumn**, **Red-veined**, **Saffron-winged**).

Natural History Males set up small territories, often close to one another, over dry grassy, weedy basins. Copulation presumably lengthy, as pairs in wheel common. Male holds wings backward to touch female to signal tandem flight, which may be lengthy. Oviposits in tandem or solo, dropping eggs from below knee height on dry ground of pond basin, often persistent at one spot and usually collecting in clusters. May lay eggs unproductively in grass on wet lawns.

Habitat Shallow marshy ponds and lake edges that dry up during summer.

Flight Season ON Jun–Oct, QC Jun–Oct, NS May–Oct, IA Jun–Oct, WI Jun–Sep, ME Jun–Oct, OH Jun–Oct, NJ Jun–Oct, KY Jul–Oct.

Distribution West across southern Canada to Alaska and Northwest Territories, south to northern California and northern New Mexico.

Comments Populations of this species in New England have been named as Jane's Meadow-hawk, *Sympetrum janeae*, differing in structure in minor ways and with tan face and dark wing veins. There is still debate over the validity of that species, and many authors call them all Cherry-faced, although many eastern populations do not have a red face. Typical red-faced, red-veined individuals occur east to the Great Lakes and farther, with red faces seen as far east as New Brunswick, but any area of intermediacy is poorly defined. In addition, hybridization is thought to take place, perhaps only in some areas, among Cherry-faced, Ruby, and White-faced Meadowhawks.

---

313 Saffron-winged Meadowhawk *Sympetrum costiferum* TL 31–37, HW 25–28

Description Meadowhawk with brightly colored line down front edge of wings and long, black-bordered stigma; male all dark red. *Male:* Eyes dark red, paler below; face reddish-tan. Thorax red-brown with fine black lines in sutures. Abdomen red, duller at base and with black ventrolateral lines from S3 to S9, not always present, and narrow black median stripe on S8–9. Legs light brown to mostly black. Anterior wing veins reddish; stigma red, strong black border fore and aft. *Female:* Eyes dull reddish over tan; face tan. Thorax and abdomen tan to reddish, black abdominal markings as male but much reduced. Legs brown on outer surfaces. Anterior wing veins yellowish to orange; stigma clear yellow, bordered fore and aft by black. Small percentage become almost as red as male.

Identification Mature male dark red all over with dull brown face; no other meadowhawk exactly like this, and most a bit brighter red. However, brightest **Saffron-winged** much like **Autumn** because of entirely red body and (in some populations) brown legs; distinguished most readily by wing coloration, **Autumn** lacking saffron stripe along front. For differences in details of abdomen pattern, see **Autumn**. **Cherry-faced**, **Ruby**, and **White-faced Mead-**

313.1
Saffron-winged
Meadowhawk
male—Ashland Co.,
WI, August 2008

313.2
Saffron-winged
Meadowhawk
female—Benton Co.,
WA, August 2007, Netta
Smith

313.3
Saffron-winged
Meadowhawk
immature female—
Grant Co., WA, August
2007

owhawks with black legs, much more prominent black abdominal markings. Female **Saffron-winged** colored much like female **Autumn,** but legs usually darker, less color at wing bases, and easily distinguished by end of abdomen (**Autumn** with expanded scoop-shaped subgenital plate). Female **Saffron-winged** wing color also distinctive, with dark-bordered yellow stigmas and saffron stripe along front edge. Female **Variegated Meadowhawk** with somewhat similar wings but yellow stripes on thorax and patterned abdomen.

Natural History Males on territory at and near shore, perched low over open water on twigs or hovering at knee to waist height offshore, more hovering over water than is typical of meadowhawks (except Variegated). Breeding habitat more open than in most other meadowhawks. Oviposits in tandem, usually in open water but also on wet shore. Some pairs tap water half-dozen times, then move slowly to next nearby spot, very methodical.

Habitat Permanent marshes, ponds, and lakes with much emergent vegetation.

Flight Season ON Jun–Oct, QC Jul–Oct, NS Jul–Oct, IA Jun–Oct, WI Jul–Oct, ME Jul–Nov, OH Jul–Oct.

Distribution West across southern Canada to Pacific coast, north to Northwest Territories and south to upland California, Utah, and Colorado; one record from southeastern New Mexico.

Description Meadowhawk with extensive orange-brown patches at wing bases. *Male:* Eyes red-brown over greenish-tan; face reddish-brown. Thorax brownish-red. Abdomen bright red with conspicuous black ventrolateral stripe on S2–10, expanding toward rear, and black median line on S8–9. *Female:* Eyes reddish over paler reddish or greenish. Duller than male, usually brown on front of thorax and yellow on sides. More darkly marked individuals with dark lateral stripe on S1–4 or 5, continuous black low on sides of entire abdomen. Wing patches usually paler than those of males. Some older females with red on top of abdomen. Westernmost populations (Minnesota, Iowa) with distinct darker margin on outer edge of basal wing

314.1
Band-winged
Meadowhawk male—
Dade Co., GA, June 2006,
Giff Beaton

314.2
Band-winged
Meadowhawk female—
Ottawa, ON, August 2004,
Chang-Won Seo

314.3
Band-winged
Meadowhawk western
male—Chaves Co., NM,
September 2008, Jerry
Hatfield

markings, well-developed black lines on sides of thorax extending from legs up toward wing bases.

Identification Only meadowhawk with extensive orange-brown patches at bases of all wings. Female **Black Meadowhawk** sometimes has orange wing bases but has heavy black markings on thorax, even heavier than western populations of **Band-winged**, and lacks upper dark stripe on basal abdominal segments. Western populations of **Ruby Meadowhawk** and some female **Cherry-faced Meadowhawks** also with orange wing bases but less extensive than **Band-winged** and without dark outer marking of co-occurring *fasciatum* subspecies of **Band-winged**, nor dark thoracic lines.

Natural History Individuals of both sexes at times fly back and forth over clearings up to 30 feet above ground, like little saddlebags and with much hovering. Are these individuals feeding or on display? Both sexes tend to perch higher than other meadowhawks, males high on twigs and leaves at breeding sites. Pairs often seen away from water, flying cross-country in tandem. Perhaps conspicuous wing markings, as in saddlebags, facilitate sexes finding one another away from breeding sites, and pairs probably come together away from water. Oviposits in tandem in shallow open water, often among plants.

Habitat Open ponds and marshes, usually permanent but sometimes small seepage areas; in open or wooded country. Also spend much time in grassy meadows.

Flight Season ON Jun–Sep, QC Jun–Sep, NS Jun–Oct, IA Jun–Sep, WI Jun–Sep, ME Jul–Oct, OH May–Sep, NJ Jun–Oct, KY Jun–Aug.

Distribution West across southern Canada to Vancouver Island, south to central California and southern Arizona and New Mexico.

Comments Western populations of this species were long considered a separate species, Western Meadowhawk, *Sympetrum occidentale*. Subsequently intermediate specimens have been found in midcontinent, but no one has conducted a thorough study to document the extent of intermediacy. Those in most of the East are *S. s. semicinctum*, but populations in Minnesota and Iowa are at the eastern end of the range of the plains subspecies *S. s. fasciatum*.

---

315 Black Meadowhawk *Sympetrum danae* TL 30–33, HW 22–23

Description Small black or black and yellow meadowhawk of northern regions. *Male*: Entirely dark brown to black from face to appendages. Face becomes metallic. Younger individuals colored as females, become increasingly dark with age but retain showy pattern for some time. *Female*: Eyes reddish-brown over pale green; face tan. Thorax rich brown in front, pale yellow on sides with complex black pattern of anastomosing stripes. Abdomen yellow at base, otherwise tan with continuous black lateral stripe from S2 to S9 or S10, black median stripe on S8–9. Legs black as in male. Costa yellow.

Identification Male unmistakable by all-black coloration, easily distinguished from whitefaces if face can be seen. Also more slender-bodied than typical of whitefaces. Female distinguished by striking pattern on thorax. Pale sides of thorax of **Black** contrast strongly with brown front, differing from most other meadowhawks. **Seaside Dragonlet** is another small species with black males and black and yellow to orange females, but restricted to coastal areas. With close look, longer stigmas might distinguish male, differently patterned thorax and projecting subgenital plate female **Dragonlet**. See also **Ebony Boghaunter**, a small, mostly black dragonfly that does not overlap seasonally with **Black Meadowhawk**.

Natural History Males scattered through marshy wetlands, very conspicuous against bright green sedges but not particularly territorial. Immatures and females often common nearby, perching in herbaceous and shrubby vegetation or sometimes on ground; females more likely higher up in shrubs. Much mating takes place away from water, then pairs in tandem come to water by midday. Copulation averages about 20 min. Lone females also become

315.1
Black Meadowhawk
male—Kittitas Co.,
WA, September 2007

315.2
Black Meadowhawk
female—Kittitas Co.,
WA, September 2007

315.3
Black Meadowhawk
immature
male—Kittitas Co.,
WA, September 2007

more common at water after midday. Oviposits in tandem or solo in open water or on moss, less often mud, even dropping eggs from air; usually attracted to one another. Pairs dip toward surface about 1.6 times/sec. Eggs scattered widely in open or among dense vegetation, but most pairs use single site while present. Perches in obelisk position in sun at midday.

Habitat Typically shallow lake borders, marshes, and fens with abundant emergent vegetation, especially sedges; also quaking bogs.

Flight Season ON Jul–Oct, QC Jun–Oct, NS Jun–Oct, WI Jul–Oct, ME Jun–Oct.

Distribution West across southern Canada to Alaska, south to northern California and northern New Mexico; one record in central Arizona. Also occurs all across northern Eurasia.

316 Autumn Meadowhawk *Sympetrum vicinum*	TL 31–35, HW 21–23

Description All red or yellow late-season meadowhawk. *Male*: Entirely red, only black narrow median spot on S9; however, some older individuals with additional dark markings toward end of abdomen. Legs reddish-brown. *Female*: Eyes reddish over tan; thorax and abdomen tan or red, same black on S9 as male but also may be on S8. Legs light brown to yellowish. Subgenital plate prolonged into large scoop-shaped structure.

Identification Pale legs usually distinctive, as is entirely red color, including face, with little or no black. Lacks dark markings on thorax, abdomen, wings, or legs that characterize most other meadowhawks, but isolated dark spot on S9 distinctive. Some **Saffron-winged** almost lacking in black markings but a bit larger, distinctly darker red in male, than **Autumn**, with characteristic wing coloration. Black dorsal markings in male **Saffron-winged** always on S8–9, not just S9 as in **Autumn**. Scoop at end of abdomen of female **Autumn** easily visible from side.

Natural History Adults common in clearings and at forest edge near breeding sites, males not defending territory at water. Usually perch well up in shrubs, also on tree trunks, wood piles, and ground in sun on cool days. Arrive at water already paired by late morning or midday and accumulate in certain spots, in or at edge of dense vegetation, but often fly far and wide around area before laying eggs. Dipping movements at water may in fact precede and stimulate copulation, which lasts about 6 min. Pairs oviposit in tandem and seem attracted to one another, show no aggression at all to others within inches. Pair usually oriented toward and close to shore while laying eggs, either in shallow water, on wet vegetation, including moss-covered logs, or on wet mud. Female forms ball of eggs within subgenital plate, pair drops to substrate from 3–6 inches up, rises and hovers, then drops again, often moving a few inches each time. Often alternate tapping shore and water. Emergence may be in midsummer with long interval before returning to water. Latest species to fly in northern parts of range, usually until first heavy frosts. Able to maintain activity by constant basking in sun.

316.1
Autumn Meadowhawk
male—Grays Harbor Co.,
WA, October 2007

316.2
Autumn Meadowhawk
female—Grays Harbor
Co., WA, October 2007

316.3
Autumn Meadowhawk
immature male—
Washburn Co., WI, August
2008

Habitat Well-vegetated ponds and lakes, usually permanent and usually associated with woodland and forest.

Flight Season ON Jun–Dec, QC Jul–Nov, NS Jun–Nov, IA Jul–Nov, WI Jun–Nov, ME Jul–Nov, OH May–Nov, NJ Jun–Dec, KY Jun–Nov, GA May–Nov, FL May–Aug.

Distribution Eastern populations west to western Nebraska, south to eastern New Mexico, then large gap with few records and western populations from southern British Columbia to northern California.

Comments Called Yellow-legged Meadowhawk in some recent publications.

Meadowhawks - male hamules

Red-veined
Meadowhawk

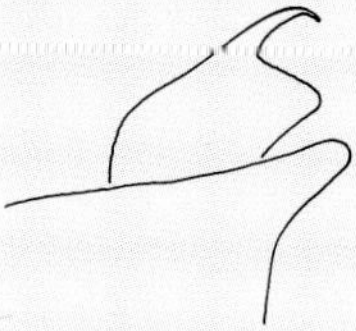

Blue-faced
Meadowhawk

White-faced
Meadowhawk

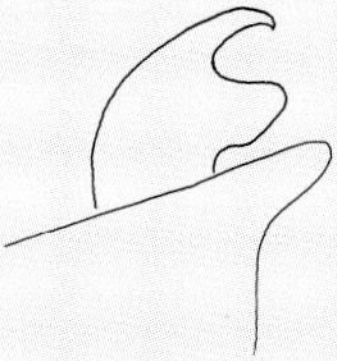

Ruby Meadowhawk

Cherry-faced
Meadowhawk

Saffron-winged
Meadowhawk

Meadowhawks - female subgenital plate

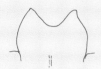

Red-veined
Meadowhawk

Blue-faced
Meadowhawk

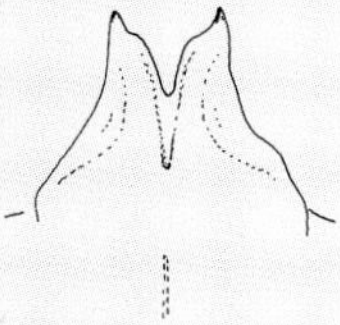

White-faced
Meadowhawk

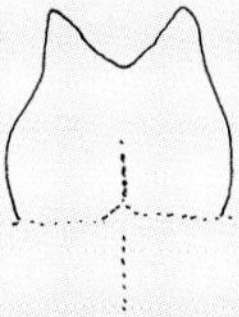

Ruby
Meadowhawk

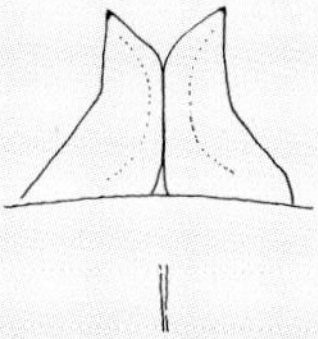

Cherry-faced
Meadowhawk

Saffron-winged
Meadowhawk

These neotropical skimmers have glowing green eyes and white faces, metallic above, just like related Blue Dasher. Species vary from tiny to midsized, all with clear wings but variably patterned bodies, typically including a strongly striped thorax. Almost all have pale spots on S7, a common marking in dragonflies the function of which badly needs explanation. Two bridge crossveins in each wing are diagnostic of the genus, one such vein in all similar North American genera. They perch at the edge of ponds and swamps, drooping wings and elevating abdomen in midday sun. Females have very varied egg-laying behavior, including doing so while perched. This is a large genus, extending barely north into North America. World 46, NA 4, East 3.

317 Spot-tailed Dasher   *Micrathyria aequalis*   TL 28–33, HW 21–25

Description Small south Florida dasher with triangular spots on abdomen. *Male*: Eyes brilliant green; face white, top of frons metallic purple. Thorax and abdomen base pruinose blue, posterior abdomen black with conspicuous triangular yellow spots on S7. *Female*: Eyes dull green over blue-gray, face white. Thorax brown in front

with narrow pale green stripe on either side not reaching top; sides more or less evenly striped brown and pale green, IYI-pattern usually clearly indicated with half-height dark

317.1
Spot-tailed Dasher
male—Sonora, Mexico,
August 2006, Netta Smith

317.2
Spot-tailed Dasher
female—Sonora, Mexico,
August 2006, Netta Smith

stripe after that, behind hindwing. Abdomen dark brown to blackish with dorsolateral pale green stripe on S2–4, interrupted to form narrow triangles on S5–7, triangle often wider on S7. Pale green ventrolateral areas as well on S2–3. Old females can become very dull, grayish pruinose all over.

Identification No other similar smallish skimmer in range like mature male, with pruinose blue thorax and black abdomen with pale spots on S7. Abdomen like that of male **Dot-tailed Whiteface** but ranges far separated and **Whiteface** all black. Still larger male **Three-striped Dasher** with striped thorax, larger square spot on S7. Male **Blue Dasher** also larger, with thorax striped and abdomen pruinose blue. Female and immature much like female **Blue Dasher** but smaller and with more complex lateral thoracic stripes; abdomen with only one row of pale markings on each side rather than two.

Natural History Males perch low in herbaceous vegetation at shore or in grasses and sedges in open marshes, some individuals staying at water all day. Droops wings and raises abdomen when perching in midday sun. Females usually away from water, surprisingly hard to find (but sometimes in numbers where species especially common); often roost up in shrubs and low trees. Females oviposit by hovering over low aquatic vegetation, then landing on it and applying eggs to substrate, both on surface and curling abdomen beneath leaves and algal mats. Male stays nearby in flight and perched.

Habitat Ponds, ditches, and marshes, often those formed during rainy season and usually with much aquatic vegetation. Tolerant of habitat degradation, breeding at sites with sewage runoff.

Flight Season FL all year.

Distribution Also throughout West Indies and southern Arizona and southern Texas south to Ecuador and Guianas.

---

318 Thornbush Dasher *Micrathyria hagenii*   TL 33–35, HW 25–29

Description Medium-small tropical dasher with multispotted abdomen. *Male*: Eyes brilliant green; face white, top of frons metallic purple. Thorax complexly striped dark brown and pale greenish, with dark stripe pattern looking like letters YI, with no dark stripe under hindwing. Abdomen black with pale elongate bluish spots on basal segments and square whitish spots on S7, black beyond that. At maturity, pruinose blue between wings. *Female*: Colored much like male, but no pruinosity between wings, and abdominal spots larger and those

318.1
Thornbush Dasher male—Hidalgo Co., TX, September 2008

318.2
Thornbush Dasher
female—Travis Co., TX,
July 2004

318.3
Thornbush Dasher
female—Hidalgo Co., TX,
September 2008

on S1–6 yellow; wings may be extensively orange at base. Old females develop some pruinosity on abdomen.

Identification Not known to overlap with other two tropical dashers in this region. Lack of blue on thorax and abdomen easily distinguishes from male **Blue Dasher**, but immatures more similar. Female and immature male **Thornbush** with large spots on abdomen back through S7, just as in **Blue Dasher**, but in one row rather than two on each side. **Blue** has straight and separated stripes on thorax, **Thornbush** with at least one Y-shaped stripe that joins other stripes at top. **Thornbush** has vivid flattened X at top of front of thorax, formed from yellow line across top and yellow sclerites before wing bases; with pale median line looks like tiny dragonfly in flight! In **Blue Dasher** only lower yellow line evident (sometimes faint upper line evident, but never such an obvious "pair of wings"). **Thornbush Dasher** also smaller than **Swift Setwing** and from below shows unique dark marking on underside of thorax with pointed rear corners.

Natural History Males on twigs and other prominent perches at water's edge, up to head height. Both sexes common in shrubs away from water. Wings of males at water typically drooped but away from water may obelisk with raised wings. Copulation brief and in flight, oviposition immediately thereafter. Females drop clusters of eggs from above water or land on floating submergent vegetation and walk along it, extruding eggs.

Habitat Ponds and open marshes, frequent at rain pools.

Flight Season Entire range probably all summer.

Distribution Also Greater Antilles and southern Arizona and southern Texas south to Panama.

---

319 Three-striped Dasher *Micrathyria didyma* TL 35–41, HW 25–33

Description Slender south Florida dasher with square-spotted abdomen. *Male:* Eyes brilliant green; face white, top of frons metallic purple. Thorax somewhat evenly striped brown and pale yellowish-green, abdomen black with fine yellow streaks on base and large squareish white spots on S7. Well-developed blue pruinosity between wings at maturity. *Female:* Essentially as male in color and pattern but abdomen slightly thicker with more color at base and no pruinosity between wings; may have wide dark wingtips.

Identification Distinctly larger than **Spot-tailed Dasher**, with large, square to rectangular spots on S7 that fill segment rather than narrower, triangular spots of **Spot-tailed**; also no

319.1
Three-striped Dasher
male—Sonora, Mexico,
August 2006, Netta Smith

319.2
Three-striped Dasher
female—Boqueron,
Puerto Rico, March 2009

pruinosity on sides of thorax or abdomen. Much more slender and elongate than **Blue Dasher**; thoracic pattern somewhat similar to that species, but abdomen very different. Immature **Three-striped**, before green eyes acquired, distinguished from superficially quite similar female and immature **Swift Setwing** (might overlap in south Florida) by lack of crossbars between thoracic stripes. When mature, eye color differentiates them. Pruinosity only between wings also distinguishes **Three-striped** from **Swift**. Finally, male **Three-striped** has distinctive large, forward-extending hamules that are easily seen in side view.

Natural History Both sexes perch in shade at waist height or higher, often with greatly drooped wings. Males at edge of or over water, females just away from it. Copulating pairs typically in trees away from water, but breeding biology poorly known.

Habitat Wooded swamps and borders of wooded ponds and sloughs, typically in shaded areas.

Flight Season FL all year.

Distribution Also throughout West Indies and southern Texas south to Ecuador and Guianas.

Blue Dasher *Pachydiplax*

This monotypic North American genus may be most closely related to the tropical dashers *Micrathyria*. Superabundant at times and places. The large space with no crossveins behind the stigma is diagnostic for genus and species. World 1, NA 1, East 1.

320 Blue Dasher *Pachydiplax longipennis*   TL 28–45, HW 30–42

Description Small skimmer with striped thorax and abdomen, becoming blue. Size more variable than in many other species, tends to be large in spring and small in autumn. *Male*: Eyes green; face mostly white, metallic blue on top. Thorax dark brown in front with narrow yellow stripes not reaching top; sides evenly striped dark brown and yellow. Abdomen pruinose blue when mature. Wings with dark streaks at extreme base in most individuals, tinted brown between and around streaks. In older individuals brown suffusion covering wing distal to nodus. *Female*: Eyes red  over gray, becoming green in older individuals; face white, metallic blue at extreme top. Thorax striped as in male, abdomen longitudinally striped in two rows, lower markings

320.1
Blue Dasher male—
Lake Co., FL, April
2008

320.2
Blue Dasher
female—Dade Co., FL,
December 2007

320.3
Blue Dasher old
female—Dade Co., FL,
December 2007, Netta
Smith

triangular; yellow to green on brown to black. Abdomen and between wings of older females may become largely pruinose blue. Immatures and some females may lack wing markings entirely. Female with notably short abdomen (named *longipennis*, or "long-winged," because of this).

Identification Male most like male **Eastern Pondhawk**, which has no color at wing base and no indication of stripes on body. PONDHAWKS very often perch flat on ground or other flat substrates, dashers usually well above ground. Females of two smaller TROPICAL DASHERS (**Spot-tailed** and **Thornbush**) very similar to **Blue**; differ most in thoracic pattern (see those species) and wing venation. **Blue Corporal**, with heavier body, brown eyes, and larger basal wing patches, also perches on ground. **Little Blue Dragonlet** has pruinose blue abdomen but is smaller and with brown eyes and plain brown or blue thorax. Pruinose blue **Spangled Skimmer** has similar stigmas but dark face; **Yellow-sided Skimmer** has gray to white eyes and white on the sides of the thorax; **Great Blue Skimmer** much larger, with blue eyes and all blue thorax. Female **Blue Dasher** unique in overall striped pattern, as well as relatively short abdomen. Similar-sized skimmers with mostly clear wings and patterned bodies typically have yellow central or paired spots on top of abdomen (see DRAGONLETS, WHITEFACES). Note that dark postnodal areas can look quite conspicuous in flight, making wings look patterned.

Natural History Abundant in many regions, favored in low, vegetated wetlands typical of so much of coastal plain. Much less common in wooded uplands, where streams predominant habitat. Perching at all levels, commonly up in trees, and often with wings drooped forward like setwing. Abdomen held in obelisk position on sunny midday, wings may also be elevated at that time. Common in wooded areas near breeding habitat but usually at sunny edges. Small feeding territories away from water defended by both sexes, capture prey on three-fourths of foraging flights. Prey all seems tiny, unlike co-occurring pondhawks. Males spend most of their time perching but defend breeding territories aggressively, displaying at each other head to head in flight with raised abdomens. Also fiercely aggressive to other skimmers with blue pruinosity. At times display to perched females, swinging back and forth in front of one with raised abdomen. Mating pairs infrequently seen considering abundance. Copulation in flight, less often at rest, relatively brief (10–40 sec). Female, often at first guarded by male perched or hovering, oviposits among vegetation, hovering in one spot and tapping numerous times before moving to another; slow and sedate, often around once a second. Very productive, 300–700 eggs laid in about 35 sec. Females often peak at breeding habitats in late afternoon after male numbers decline. Apparent migratory movements have been observed in midsummer on the Atlantic coast.

Habitat Any body of standing water with some aquatic (floating or emergent) vegetation might be appropriate, including lake shores, ponds, ditches, and even wooded wetlands where some sunlight penetrates. Also at slow streams with abundant vegetation. Although they commonly perch in trees and shrubs, these are not necessarily present. Adults are more likely to be in tall (for example, cattails) than in short emergent vegetation, but larvae abundant in floating carpets of water lettuce and water hyacinth. Shuns unvegetated wetlands.

Flight Season ON May–Oct, IA May–Sep, WI May–Sep, ME Jun–Oct, OH May–Oct, NJ May–Oct, KY Apr–Sep, LA Mar–Nov, GA Mar–Nov, FL all year.

Distribution West to western edge of Nebraska, then south through eastern Colorado and across Southwest to Pacific coast and north to southern British Columbia. South into upland Mexico, less common in tropical lowlands but rarely to Belize, and in Bahamas and Cuba.

Setwings *Dythemis*

This small neotropical genus is related to sylphs (*Macrothemis*), clubskimmers, and rock skimmers (*Paltothemis*). As do its near relatives, the female has underside of S9 characteristically elevated, curved, and keeled, plainly visible from the side and different from the flat segment in other skimmers. They are named for their characteristic perching with wings depressed and abdomen up, like the "ready, set, go" of a runner at a track meet. However, all species also perch like small pennants, with abdomen and forewings raised substantially, hindwings level or a bit raised. and they may assume full vertical obelisk position at midday. Most species have a slender abdomen. Most females have prominent dark wingtips. World 7, NA 4, East 2.

321 Checkered Setwing *Dythemis fugax*   TL 44–50, HW 36–38

Description Setwing with red-brown, black, and white pattern and dark brown wing patches. *Male:* Eyes red over red and gray; face red. Thorax mostly reddish-brown with indistinct black markings, pale gray on lower sides. Abdomen black with cream streaks at base and pair of long spots on S7. All wings with large brown patches at bases, darker veins running through them. *Female:* Eyes red over blue-gray, face tan. Thorax heavily striped brown and  white. Abdomen black with each of S2–7 irregularly marked white at base, black at tip. Wings like male but narrowly dark-tipped.

321.1
Checkered Setwing
male—Graham Co.,
AZ, September 2006,
Doug Danforth

321.2
Checkered Setwing
female—Howard Co.,
AR, June 2009,
Charles Mills

Identification Nothing else in range like male, with reddish head and thorax, black and white abdomen, and prominent brown wing patches. Except for basal wing patches, female rather like female **Swift Setwing** with which it occurs. Female **Marl Pennant** also with brown hindwing patches, but forewings with only tiny patches and abdomen shorter and thicker, mostly pale rather than strongly patterned as in **Checkered Setwing**. Patterned abdomen and different wing pattern distinguish from vaguely similar SMALL PENNANTS that often perch similarly. No other eastern skimmer has abdomen so vividly patterned black and white.

Natural History Males perch on twigs along shore. Much more active than other setwings, floating over water in flash of color much like appearance of small pennants. Fly back and forth slowly over pools, and two males may engage in very rapid and lengthy parallel flights. Copulation brief and in flight, female often leaving water to return later.

Habitat Slow streams and rivers and open lakes, sometimes ponds, usually in open country with a shore belt of low trees or shrubs.

Flight Season Probably throughout summer.

Distribution West to southern Arizona and south in Mexico to Tamaulipas.

Description Brightly marked slender setwing with conspicuously spotted abdomen and usually obviously dark wingtips. *Male*: Eyes red-brown over blue-gray; face brown, paler on outer edges. Thorax heavily marked with brown and cream in complex stripes. Abdomen mostly black, white basal markings on S1–3 and small spots on S4–7, largest on S7 where they form an oval half length of segment. Very small brown spot at base of hindwing, indication of

dark border at wingtips. *Female*: Colored as male but pale abdominal markings larger, spots on S7 cover much of segment. Usually prominent dark wingtips.

Identification Nothing exactly like this species, slender with complex thoracic pattern and big spot on S7. Female **Checkered** has big basal wing patches. Female, with thicker abdomen, also has dark wingtips to distinguish it from **Blue Dasher** and TROPICAL DASHERS. Female actually something like **Three-striped Dasher** (only in south Florida), but **Swift Setwing** with YIY instead of III thoracic pattern.

Natural History Males perch on twigs over water and defend small territories against other males. Spend most time perching, relatively seldom in flight, but males sometimes fly rapidly back and forth in restricted space, then land on tip of branch, or two males fly together in parallel flight. Females in open on elevated perches nearby. Commonly in shade on sunny days.

322.1
Swift Setwing male—
Travis Co., TX, August
2009, Eric Isley

322.2
Swift Setwing female—
Travis Co., TX, September
2004, Eric Isley

Habitat Streams and rivers with slow to moderate current, less often pond and lake shores. Usually wooded or shrubby banks.

Flight Season LA Aug–Sep, GA May–Oct, FL May–Sep.

Distribution West locally to southeastern Arizona and south in Mexico to Durango and Nuevo León; one record from Colorado.

Clubskimmers *Brechmorhoga*

This group includes rather large skimmers with expanded abdomens reminiscent of some tropical clubtails, especially tropical species of sanddragons and leaftails. Like those clubtails, they have a black abdomen with big pale markings on S7 that show conspicuously as they fly past. Unlike clubtails, they are fliers rather than perchers and hang vertically or diagonally when they perch, although some species also perch on rocks. In the tropics, they are often found in feeding swarms. World 16, NA 3, East 1.

323 Pale-faced Clubskimmer *Brechmorhoga mendax*   TL 53–62, HW 34–43

Description Large southwestern skimmer zipping up and down streams with long, slightly clubbed abdomen with conspicuous spots near tip. *Male*: Eyes light blue-gray; face light brown. Thorax striped dark brown and light gray-green. Abdomen black with whitish markings around S1–3 and whitish streaks on S4–5. Large whitish pair of spots almost touching and almost filling up S7. Often small pale spots at base of either side of S7. *Female*: Eyes light  brown over blue-gray. Colored as male, abdominal club less evident because abdomen base somewhat thicker. Wing color polymorphic, some individuals with both tips or only forewing tips amber or brown. Wings may become entirely brown with age.

323.1
Pale-faced Clubskimmer
male—Graham Co., AZ,
August 2007

323.2
Pale-faced Clubskimmer
female—Travis Co., TX,
June 2006, Eric Isley

Identification Nothing else like this species in the East. No other dragonfly that flies up and down streams and hangs in trees has a dark abdomen with bright pale spot on S7. RIVER CRUISERS hang similarly but larger and with green eyes when mature, one thoracic stripe on each side, and more spots on abdomen.

Natural History Males fly low and either slowly or rapidly up and down riffles, less often over pools between them. May land on rock. Beats often 15–30 feet long, probably dependent on length of riffle. Difficult to see under those conditions, sometimes only spots on abdomen apparent. Copulation brief, in flight over water while hovering or flying slowly. Females oviposit by flying along rapidly, striking water at fairly lengthy intervals. Both sexes perch by hanging vertically or with abdomen projecting well outward, usually below chest height in shade in woods. Feeds in flight in open areas from just above ground to well up in trees, sometimes with other swarm feeders such as gliders.

Habitat Shallow rocky streams with riffles and pools, some current. Banks wooded or open but must have sun.

Flight Season Entire range Apr–Nov.

Distribution West across Southwest to central California and south in Mexico to Baja California Sur, Nayarit, and San Luis Potosí; isolated population in Black Hills.

Evening Skimmers *Tholymis*

This small tropical genus of dusk-flying skimmers is thought to be related to gliders and saddlebags, although the wings are less broad and flight activity is mostly at dusk and dawn. The unusual anal loop is narrow and extends to the edge of the wing. Males of the Old World species, *T. tillarga*, are red but have the same habits as our species. The egg-laying apparatus, unique to this genus, consists of not only the standard subgenital plate but behind it an inverted trough with hairs that hold egg clusters within it. World 2, NA 1, East 1.

324 Evening Skimmer *Tholymis citrina* TL 48–53, HW 36–39

Description Slender brown tropical skimmer that flies actively at dusk and dawn. *Male*: Eyes dark gray; face dark gray, metallic blue on top. Entirely brown with front of thorax becoming dark gray. Golden-brown spot at middle of each hindwing, sometimes hint of same in forewing. *Female*: Similar but face, eyes, and thorax paler, light brown or yellowish (eyes may have bluish tinge). From above, easily seen that female cerci diverge, males are parallel. Also, cerci of females long and curved downward. Wings become brownish in older individuals of both sexes.

Identification Tawny-winged Pennant most similar species in overall brown coloration and slender abdomen, but typical skimmer, perching horizontally in open during day and not performing evening flights. SHADOWDRAGONS, also brown and with similar evening flight, not known to occur within **Evening Skimmer's** tropical range, although latter might overlap with **Alabama Shadowdragon** in Florida. **Shadowdragon** has dots at wing bases, **Evening Skimmer** larger spot at each hindwing nodus. **Pale-green, Phantom**, and **Twilight Darners**, brown to greenish dusk-fliers, are much larger.

Natural History Roosts at forest edge, hanging like small darner; flies erratically when flushed and then suddenly lands again, sometimes in plain sight (but brown coloration renders it very cryptic). Feeding tends to be in short period before and at dusk, along with dusk-flying tropical darners and, if early enough, with gliders and saddlebags. Also probably flies at dawn as other species of genus. Feeding flight rapid and erratic. Breeding also takes place at those times, males flying back and forth over shallow water bodies with occasional hovering. Pairs of Old World *Tholymis tillarga* copulate briefly in flight, then male guards female as she oviposits. Females sometimes hit water to oviposit, then twist around

324.1
Evening Skimmer
male—Cameron Co., TX,
November 2008, Terry
Fuller

324.2
Evening Skimmer
female—Zapata Co., TX,
November 2004, Martin
Reid

180° to repeat. Also lay eggs on leaves at water surface. Our species probably with similar reproductive behavior, but no observations.

Habitat Shallow ponds and marshes, often but not always associated with forest.

Flight Season FL Oct–Jan.

Distribution Also from southern Texas south to Argentina and Chile and widely in West Indies. Vagrants in Oklahoma and southern Arizona.

Pasture Gliders   *Tauriphila*

Species of this small New World tropical genus exhibit the same incessant flight and hanging style of perching as rainpool gliders but are somewhat smaller and more slender. Closely tied to floating plants, they are probably most closely related to hyacinth gliders. Some species have brown spots at wing bases. Pasture gliders may be only vagrants to eastern North America, without breeding populations. World 5, NA 3, East 1.

325 Garnet Glider   *Tauriphila australis*   TL 42–47, HW 36–38

Description Rare Florida gliding skimmer with dark head and thorax, red abdomen, and dark hindwing spots. *Male*: Eyes and face dark reddish-brown, face metallic purple above. Thorax dark brown in front, paling to dull reddish on sides. Abdomen brown on S1–2, then red, segments outlined finely in black. Narrow black me-

325.1
Garnet Glider male—
Sonora, Mexico, August
2006, Doug Danforth

325.2
Garnet Glider male—
Guanacaste, Costa Rica,
August 2010, Netta Smith

dian stripe on S8–9. Hindwings with dark basal spot, anterior and basal wing veins reddish. *Female*: Duller than male, face all brown, and thorax and abdomen brownish; abdomen with narrow black median stripe. Hindwing spot smaller, may be virtually absent. Wings often tinged with golden, especially toward tips.

Identification No other gliding dragonfly just like this one. **Hyacinth Glider** smaller, with orange rather than red abdomen; also hindwing markings narrower and extend width of wing, wings more strongly suffused with orange. Red abdomen as in various SADDLEBAGS, but all those have red thorax and hindwing spot either narrow but longer or much wider. **Spot-winged Glider** bulkier, hindwing spot smaller and less obvious in flight. **Red-tailed Pennant** colored somewhat like **Garnet Glider**, but behavior quite different.

Natural History Males patrol all morning and until midafternoon, often flying over beds of water hyacinths with no open water. In foraging flight, faster and more erratic than larger rainpool gliders.

Habitat Lakes and ponds, usually associated with floating vegetation such as water hyacinth and water lettuce.

Flight Season FL Jun–Oct.

Distribution Encountered so rarely that it probably is only a vagrant from farther south; no known occurrence after 1963. Also Greater Antilles and from northern Mexico south to Bolivia and Paraguay.

Hyacinth gliders are small skimmers related to pasture gliders, saddlebags, and rainpool gliders, and, with similarly broad hindwings, they fly for long periods and then hang up more or less vertically. They are among the few dragonflies closely tied to particular plant species, primarily water hyacinth but also water lettuce. The other species in the genus, the Dwarf Glider (*Miathyria simplex*), is smaller and red, with a round hindwing spot, and occurs throughout much of the New World tropics. World 2, NA 1, East 1.

326 Hyacinth Glider   *Miathyria marcella*   TL 37–40, HW 29–33

Description Small gliding skimmer of Southeast with dark hindwing saddles and orange abdomen, addicted to water hyacinths. *Male*: Eyes reddish-brown; face brown, blue-purple above. Thorax pruinose violet (plum-colored), including between wings, when fully mature. Abdomen yellow-orange with narrow black median line widening on S7–8; S9–10 black. Wing veins reddish, hindwing with dark brown base. *Female*: Eyes reddish above, gray below. Thorax  brown with whitish diagonal stripe running from front to below forewing, parallel whitish ventrolateral stripe, and broader blackish stripe between them. Abdomen orange-brown with black markings as male. Wing veins dark.

Identification No other small North American skimmer flies back and forth over aquatic vegetation beds or feeds with larger RAINPOOL GLIDERS and SADDLEBAGS in swarms in open country. Much smaller than feeding associates, although superficially like narrow-saddled SADDLEBAGS. Purple and yellow-orange males uniquely colored. Could be mistaken for **Garnet Glider**, slightly larger and very rare in Florida. See that species.

326.1
Hyacinth Glider male—
Starr Co., TX, October
2005, Marion M. Dobbs

326.2
Hyacinth Glider female—Fort Bend
Co., TX, November 2007, R. A.
Behrstock/Naturewide Images

Natural History Males fly back and forth, usually low, over beds of aquatic vegetation and search closely for females; then hang up in herbs, shrubs, or low trees, where females also perch. Perch like rainpool gliders, hanging on vertical stem with abdomen projecting outward. Pairs in tandem and single females oviposit by dropping into tiny gaps in floating vegetation where water visible. Few skimmer species as closely tied to a few plant species as this one. Both sexes feed in groups at head height and above, often in tighter swarms than other fliers with which they associate such as pasture gliders, rainpool gliders, and saddlebags. Swarms may be at some distance from water; also involved in migratory movements with other gliders and saddlebags.

Habitat Ponds and lakes with abundant water hyacinths or water lettuce, less commonly over other floating vegetation.

Flight Season LA Apr–Nov, GA Apr–Nov, FL all year.

Distribution From Sonora and central Texas south to Argentina, also Greater Antilles.

Comments Increased North American range with spread of water hyacinths. Has dramatically declined wherever that plant largely eliminated in Southeast and could disappear from large parts of range with hyacinth-control programs.

Saddlebags *Tramea*

These are gliding dragonflies with broad hindwings with conspicuous dark markings at their bases ("saddles"), more conspicuous than the spots on the rather similar Spot-winged Glider. They fly incessantly over open areas, even up to the treetops, then most commonly perch at tips of twigs like pennants (often with front legs tucked behind eyes). When in full resting mode, they hang from branches like rainpool gliders. Even when perching horizontally, they may droop their abdomen almost straight down (the reverse of obelisking behavior) to avoid overheating at midday, and they often fly with abdomen drooping, a behavior unique to these and rainpool gliders, when it is hot. For breeding habitat, they do best in fishless ponds. Pairs join in flight, then fly to nearby vegetation and perch for 10 min or so, then head for water in tandem flight, with unique oviposition behavior. The pair flies rapidly at knee height or lower and pauses at intervals for female to be released, tap water, and be reclaimed by male, almost too quick to see the details. The long, slender male cerci surely facilitate this action. A pair may fly all over a pond before stopping again. The distance between taps may be as little as a few feet but is often longer. The eggs are held by the female with a large, divided subgenital plate. Saddlebags are easily divided into two groups from the width of their hindwing markings, "broadsaddle" with the spot on each side wider than the abdomen and "narrowsaddle" about as wide as the abdomen. Any sighting should first determine which type is involved. Most individuals seen in the United States are broadsaddle, but three species of narrowsaddle occur along the southern border and are often seen in southern Florida, and another has been found only once. Distinctions can be difficult within each group. The genus is distributed worldwide but primarily in the tropics. World 21, NA 7, East 7.

327 Vermilion Saddlebags *Tramea abdominalis* TL 44–50, HW 38–42

Description Red-faced narrowsaddle saddlebags of extreme southern Florida. *Male:* Eyes above and face bright red. Thorax dull red, abdomen bright red with small black spots on top of S8–9. Cerci long and black, red at extreme base. Basal wing veins red. *Female:* Eyes red over gray, face reddish-tan. Thorax tan. Abdomen red with black spots as male. Appendages long, black. Wing veins black except red within dark hindwing saddles.

Identification Males of **Antillean** and **Striped Saddlebags** also entirely red with narrow saddles. **Vermilion** differs from **Antillean** in entirely red face (no trace of purple), but this can be very difficult to see in field. Shorter ap-

327.1
Vermilion
Saddlebags
male—Broward Co.,
FL, November 2009,
J. Lubchansky

327.2
Vermilion
Saddlebags
female—Curaçao,
March 2009, Mars
Muusse

pendages of **Vermilion** might also be seen on perched male; not much longer than S9–10, distinctly longer in **Antillean**. With even better look, longer hamules of **Vermilion** might be evident, longer than genital lobe (shorter in **Antillean**). Female **Antillean** and **Vermilion** impossible to distinguish in field unless really good look shows purple on top of frons of **Antillean**. In hand, subgenital plate extends to end of S9 in **Vermilion**, not that far in **Antillean**. Differs from **Striped** in untinted wings (but wash of color in **Striped** not obvious against sky), unstriped thorax, and black spots at tip of red abdomen (**Striped** has most of abdomen tip black). See that species for additional differences.

Natural History Males fly at waist height or above along edge and over middle of breeding ponds. Both sexes feed, often in swarms and often mixed with other saddlebags species, in open areas away from water. Occasionally seen perched over or near water.

Habitat Vegetated ponds, including small and temporary ones. Also ditches and drainage canals, apparently able to coexist with fish.

Flight Season FL all year.

Distribution Also throughout West Indies and from southern Texas south to Argentina.

Description Purple-faced narrowsaddle saddlebags of southern Florida. *Male*: Eyes dark reddish-purple; face brown, top of frons metallic purple. Thorax dull reddish-brown, abdomen bright red with small black spots on top of S8–9. Cerci very long and black, red at extreme base. Basal wing veins red. *Female*: Eyes dull reddish over gray, face tan with hint of purple on top of frons. Thorax tan, abdomen reddish with black spots as male. Appendages long and black. Wing veins black except reddish within dark hindwing saddles.

Identification One of narrowsaddle group, very similar to **Vermilion Saddlebags** but distinguished by darker head and eyes, with purple on face. Less like **Striped Saddlebags**, which usually shows stripes on thorax and has much more black at abdomen tip. Male appendages in **Antillean** longer (obviously longer than S9–10) than those of **Striped** and **Vermilion** (barely if at all longer than S9–10). Female **Antillean** and **Vermilion** extremely similar, distinguished in hand by entirely red frons of **Vermilion**, touch of purple on upper surface in **Antillean**. Subgenital plate of female **Antillean** shorter than S9, longer in **Vermilion**. See also **Sooty Saddlebags**, vagrant to East.

Natural History Males fly over breeding habitat at waist to chest height or perch near shore, often on dead tree branches. Males of this and other species with narrow saddles perhaps more likely to perch over water than the broadsaddle species. Oviposits in pair as is typical

328.1
Antillean Saddlebags
male—Frio Co., TX, June
2005, Martin Reid

328.2
Antillean Saddlebags
female—Frio Co., TX,
August 2005, Martin Reid

of saddlebags or alone; solo females fly rapidly and tap water much more frequently than pairs, without hovering. Both sexes feed away from water, often in small swarms of their own and other species.

Habitat Ponds and lakes with open water, relationship with fish not established. Seems well adapted to life in small artificial water bodies.

Flight Season FL all year.

Distribution Ranges south throughout West Indies and west to eastern edge of Mexico, also disjunct populations in south Texas and southeastern Arizona to Sonora.

Comments Called *Tramea binotata* in earlier literature.

Description All black narrowsaddle saddlebags, vagrant in North America. *Male*: Eyes very dark brown. Entirely black, all but last three segments of abdomen dusted with gray pruinosity; face metallic purple above. Cerci very long. *Female*: Face purple above, eyes red over dark gray. Rest of body reddish-brown, S8–10 almost  entirely black. Become darker brown with maturity. Immature male similar, reddish at first, then maroon when darker and finally black or pruinose gray.

329.1
Sooty Saddlebags
male—Guadeloupe,
March 2006, Claudine and
Pierre Guezennec

329.2
Sooty Saddlebags
immature male—
Guadeloupe, March 2006,
Claudine and Pierre
Guezennec

Identification Mature male easily distinguished from any other saddlebags by black color and very small hindwing spots. **Black Saddlebags** are a bit larger, with much larger saddles. Female and immature male much like same stages of **Antillean Saddlebags** but with more black on abdomen tip (only on top of S8–10 in **Antillean**).

Natural History Habits seem identical to other saddlebags, males flying rapidly or hovering over water when on territory, feeding widely away from water. Perches high on plant tips at water.

Habitat Lakes and ponds for breeding, foraging over open country anywhere.

Flight Season All year in tropics.

Distribution A single record from the region, in northwest Florida in September. Also throughout Greater Antilles and widespread from northern Mexico to Argentina. Recently recorded in southeast Arizona.

Comments Called *Tramea walkeri* in earlier West Indian literature.

Description Brown to reddish tropical narrowsaddle saddlebags with pale stripes on sides of thorax. *Male*: Eyes red over brown; face red with small metallic purple area at top of frons. Thorax brown, darker on sides with pair of dull yellowish stripes on each side. Abdomen bright red with most of S8, all of S9–10, and appendages black. Wing veins light brown, wings tinted with amber. *Female*: Eyes red over gray; face tan with purple area smaller than in male. Thorax and abdomen light brown, thoracic stripes whitish. Wing veins darker than in male. Individuals wandering north from Mexico would have amber-tinted wings; this color lacking in West Indian and Florida populations.

Identification Distinguished from other narrowsaddle saddlebags by pale stripes on sides of thorax. These stripes may be obscure in mature males, obliterated by overall reddish color of thorax. Such individuals distinguished from both **Antillean** and **Vermilion** by largely black S8–10, producing black-tipped abdomen (other species have black spots on top of S8–10, abdomen looking entirely red), and slightly lighter, more orange-red color of

330.1
Striped Saddlebags
male—Laguna
Cartagena, Puerto Rico,
March 2009, Netta
Smith

330.2
Striped Saddlebags
female—Laguna
Cartagena, Puerto Rico,
March 2009, Netta Smith

abdomen. Face of **Striped** also a bit duller than the bright red face of **Vermilion**. Pronounced amber tinge to wings (not visible in some lights) also distinctive of Mexican populations of **Striped**. Male appendages distinctly shorter than those of **Antillean**, same length as **Vermilion**. Note **Hyacinth Glider** has similar behavior and striped thorax, but differently colored otherwise and much smaller.

Natural History Males fly over water at waist height or lower, seem more likely to perch on branches at water than other saddlebags. Feeding flight mostly head height and above, often mixed with other saddlebags and gliders.

Habitat Shallow ponds with much open water and beds of vegetation.

Flight Season NJ May–Oct, FL Jan–Oct.

Distribution Perhaps resident in southern Florida; records farther north probably represent vagrants, perhaps associated with frontal passages. Records spotty in both space and time, present some years and not others but increasingly detected. Record numbers came north in 2010 (not mapped). Also resident in south Texas, with sporadic records farther north and in New Mexico, Arizona, and southeastern California, and ranges south in lowlands to Argentina and throughout West Indies.

331 Red Saddlebags *Tramea onusta* — TL 41–49, HW 38–43

Description Red broadsaddle saddlebags locally common in South. *Male*: Top of eyes bright red; face bright red, extreme top of frons with slight purple tinge. Thorax reddish-brown, sometimes with scattered black markings. Abdomen bright red with black spots on top of S8–9; cerci long, reddish at base. Basal wing veins red. *Female*: Duller all over, with same black markings as male but slightly more reduced, in some scarcely evident. Cerci long and black. Immatures with all pale areas tan.

Identification One of two red saddlebags with broad saddles. Distinguished from **Carolina Saddlebags** by entirely red face (**Carolina** purple), slightly smaller size. Best field mark if it can be seen: black spots only on top of S8–9 in **Red**, black on S8 extends to bottom of segment in most **Carolina**. More difficult in females, in which black less extensive. Check thorax for purple highlights characteristic of **Carolina** and lacking in **Red**. Also check wing pattern, similar except clear "window" (not always easy to see) on inside of wing patch in **Red Saddlebags** oval or circular, larger than width of abdomen

331.1
Red Saddlebags
male—Hidalgo Co.,
TX, September 2008

331.2
Red Saddlebags
female—Travis Co.,
TX, August 2005, Eric
Isley

331.3
Red Saddlebags
pair—Denton Co.,
TX, June 2009, Troy
Hibbitts

and usually smaller than that in **Carolina** (typically a small, acutely pointed triangle). Two subtle differences in hindwing markings might be seen in photos. First, red stripe between subcosta and median often completely isolated from rest of spot in **Red**, usually continuous with it beyond basal space in **Carolina** (overlap, however). Second, **Carolina** has almost entire anal loop colored, if not then outer row of cells partially colored; **Red** usually has that row and sometimes even more of "foot" clear. See **Carolina Saddlebags** for discussion of male abdomen base. From below, different-sized subgenital plates might be evident in females.

Natural History Often seen far from water, feeding in swarms with Black Saddlebags and rainpool gliders. Both sexes roost on dead twigs high in treetops. Males fly incessantly along shore and over open water, defending territories as large as 100 by 30 feet. Pairs oviposit in tandem as typical of saddlebags, often on algal mats; where common, constantly interact with one another, circling round and round. Ovipositing pairs only harassed by lone males when female released to oviposit. Female may also oviposit solo in very different way, moving slowly and tapping constantly in vegetation bed, scarcely rising between taps; perhaps true of all saddlebags.

Habitat Lakes and ponds, also ditches and canals and large pools of slow rivers. Probably breeds most successfully in fish-free waters such as rainy-season ponds.

Flight Season ON May–Oct, IA May–Sep, WI Jun–Jul, OH May–Oct, NJ Jul–Sep, KY May–Sep, LA Mar–Oct, FL Mar–Jan.

Distribution Sparse through most of Southeast except peninsular Florida; for example, no North Carolina records. West to eastern Colorado and throughout Southwest, north to central California and southern Utah; few records farther north. Ranges south to Venezuela and throughout West Indies.

---

332 Carolina Saddlebags *Tramea carolina* TL 48–53, HW 44–45

Description Purple-faced red broadsaddle saddlebags of the Southeast. *Male*: Eyes dark reddish-brown; face reddish with top of frons dark purple. Thorax dull reddish to brown, sometimes with scattered black markings. Abdomen bright red with much of S8–9 black; cerci long, reddish at base. Basal wing veins red. *Female*: Eyes red over brown, face tan with metallic purple just at base of top of frons. Duller all over, with same black markings as male except a bit more reduced, typically covering much of S8 and upper half of S9, in some individuals covering only upper half of S8. Cerci long and black. Immatures with all pale areas tan.

Identification One of two large broadsaddle saddlebags with red coloration. See **Red Saddlebags** for differences. Easily distinguished from all black **Black Saddlebags**, as red usually evident even when backlighted. Male broadsaddles can be distinguished with good look in side view. In **Red**, hamule long and narrow, extending past genital lobe; in **Carolina**, hamule and genital lobe same length, hard to distinguish; in **Black**, hamule shorter than genital lobe, forming two bumps.

Natural History Males fly along shorelines at waist to head height, circling out over open water and back along shore. Also perch on dead twigs near water, often above flight height. Copulation at rest in herbaceous or woody vegetation for 8–10 min. Most oviposition among emergent vegetation. Both sexes feed in open areas from low over ground to treetops, singly or in small to moderate swarms and often with other species. Feeds at all times of day, including until dusk, for example when feeding with Regal Darners. May be at least partially migratory, mature individuals appearing suddenly in northern areas in spring.

Habitat Ponds, both marshy and open, and lakes with much submergent vegetation. May breed in wetlands with fish populations.

332.1
Carolina Saddlebags
male—Aiken Co., SC,
May 2008

332.2
Carolina Saddlebags
female—Lake Co., FL,
April 2005

Flight Season ON May–Sep, IA May–Aug, WI May–Jul, ME Aug–Sep, OH May–Sep, NJ May–Sep, KY Apr–Oct, LA Feb–Nov, GA Mar–Dec, FL all year.

Distribution Few records farther west in Oklahoma and Texas. As in all saddlebags, northerly records may be vagrants outside breeding range.

---

333 Black Saddlebags *Tramea lacerata* | **TL 51–55, HW 45–47**

Description Widespread black broadsaddle saddlebags. *Male*: Eyes dark brown, face dark purple. Thorax dark brown to blackish, sometimes with scattered metallic black markings. Abdomen black, often showing yellow squares on S7 indicative of immaturity. Cerci very long (more than twice as long as epiproct) and black. *Female*: Duller all over, usually showing pale markings on S7; cerci long, black. Immatures dark brown, with yellow markings along most abdominal segments to S7. Some individuals of both sexes have dark markings at forewing bases.

333.1
Black Saddlebags male—Travis Co., TX,
July 2007, Eric Isley

333.2
Black Saddlebags female—Richmond
Co., GA, September 2005, Lois Stacey

333.3
Black Saddlebags pair—Hamilton Co., OH, July 2007, William Hull

Identification Other broadsaddle saddlebags are red; only other black saddlebags is **Sooty Saddlebags**, narrowsaddle species unlikely to be encountered. Big yellow spots on dark abdomen of female and immature **Black** are distinctive. "Windows" on inside of hindwing markings of **Black Saddlebags** variable, overlap with both **Carolina** and **Red**. **Black** is only species among these three that sometimes has black markings at forewing bases, useful overhead. Immature **Widow Skimmer**, lacking white bands on wings, might be confusing but perches and flies like skimmer, not saddlebags, and has patterned abdomen. Male **Marl Pennant** also black with hindwing spots but much smaller, with smaller spots.

Natural History Males cruise just out from shorelines and over open water, typically at waist height and often rather erratically; length of territory may exceed 100 feet. One male stayed at same pond for 30 min. Copulation brief and in flight or somewhat lengthier on perch, followed by rapid tandem flight low over water, hovering briefly and then moving again, until some stimulus for oviposition causes them to drop to the water, male releasing female for one tap, then rejoining and moving on to do it again. Very tentative at this time, not surprising as fish such as bass follow them underwater and strike when they drop to surface. Both sexes roost on dead twigs high in treetops. Highly migratory, migrants appearing in northern part of range in summer and breeding, their offspring apparently migrating back to South. Large-scale movements in fall on Atlantic coast.

Habitat Shallow open lakes and ponds with much aquatic vegetation; wanders far and wide away from water.

Flight Season ON May–Oct, NS Jul–Aug, IA May–Oct, WI Jun–Oct, ME Jun–Sep, OH May–Oct, NJ Apr–Nov, KY May–Oct, LA Apr–Nov, GA Mar–Nov, FL Mar–Jan.

Distribution West to Pacific coast, north to Washington, absent from much of Rockies. Ranges south in Mexico to Baja California Sur and Veracruz, also Yucatan Peninsula, Bahamas, and Cuba.

Saddlebags - male hamules

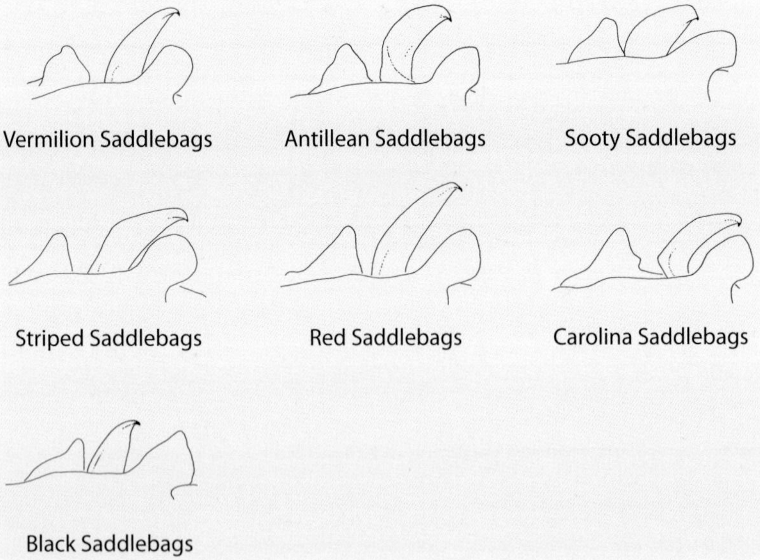

Vermilion Saddlebags   Antillean Saddlebags   Sooty Saddlebags

Striped Saddlebags   Red Saddlebags   Carolina Saddlebags

Black Saddlebags

These broad-winged skimmers are the champion gliders of the odonate world, on the wing for hours and even days at a time as they wander even across oceans. Because of this, one species is the only dragonfly with worldwide tropical distribution. Perching is always by hanging up, unlike most skimmers, and perches are usually the underside of slender branches about 20–40° from the vertical, the long hind legs propping the dragonfly well out from the branch. The very broad hindwings represent an important adaptation for gliding, as does the ability to deposit fat and then use it for energy during a long flight just as a migratory bird does. The abdomen is drooped in flight at midday to reduce heat load from sun. Saddlebags are similar in many ways and are presumably close relatives. World 2, NA 2, East 2.

334 Wandering Glider *Pantala flavescens* TL 47–50, HW 36–42

Description Gliding skimmer that looks yellow to yellow-orange in flight. *Male*: Eyes reddish; face orange. Thorax and abdomen yellow, upper part of abdomen orange. Darker orange median line on abdomen, expanded on each segment and forming black spots toward rear, on S8–10. Cerci black, obviously pale at base. *Female*: Much as male, but lacks reddish-orange colors of that sex. Sexes shaped very similarly but female cerci slightly longer and more slender than in male, less pale color at base.

Identification Nothing else gives quite the impression of this species in flight. **Spot-winged Glider** similar in size and habits but darker, looks more brownish in flight, and spot at base of hindwing visible with good look; may have to pass overhead to see spots. Perching behavior distinguishes both gliders from most other skimmers and from all others that are yellowish (especially **Golden-winged** and **Needham's Skimmer** and immatures of other KING SKIMMERS). A bright orange-brown **Four-spotted Skimmer** could cause confusion, but the two species overlap little in distribution and none in habits and breeding habitat.

Natural History Feeding and territorial patrol in rapid and sweeping flight, at or away from water. Hangs up at a slant or almost vertically when not active. Typically perches low in

334.1
Wandering Glider male—
Hidalgo Co., TX,
September 2008

334.2
Wandering Glider
female—Monroe Co.,
FL, December 2007

grass or weeds, sometimes up in trees. Males patrol over or near water, rapidly back and forth over large water bodies. Patrol area 30–150 feet in length, at head height, with some hovering. Sexes meet there or nearby for brief copulation (30 sec to 5 min) and then go into tandem and fly rapidly in a fairly straight course, tapping water at intervals of a few feet. Female can lay up to 800 eggs during one mating. Oviposition often early in morning before sun hits water, especially by lone females. Females often tap surface of shiny automobiles as perceived tiny ponds, eggs apparently harming paint job! Perhaps much egg laying in inappropriate habitat, including swimming pools and brackish lagoons. Tandem pairs as well as singles seen far from water. Feed singly or in small to large swarms, sometimes clearly aggregated with no individuals for some distance from swarm. Individuals have been seen to chase large darners flying near a feeding group. Alternates short feeding flights with hanging in shade on hot days. Stops feeding well before dusk, unlike some other swarm-feeders. Prey presumably small swarming insects. Highly migratory and with great dispersal powers, including far out over ocean, where they fly at night as well as during day. Presumably breeding individuals at high latitudes have migrated up there from lower latitudes, often associated with warm fronts, and recently emerged immatures may be seen in late summer before they head south. In tropics apparently fly toward areas of lower pressure, where rain likely. Flight season tends to be better correlated with rainy season than with "summer." Usually becomes more common in north later in summer.

Habitat Seen anywhere in feeding flight over open country, attracted for breeding to ephemeral habitats such as temporary wetlands in newly filled basins, including drainage ditches. Often breeds in artificial ponds, even swimming pools or small garden ponds, and may appear at new wetlands immediately. Fishlessness probably prerequisite for breeding habitat, as larvae conspicuous in waters without vegetation. Also oviposits in canals and large shallow pools of rivers in rainy season. Because of shiny cars, parking lots often frequented.

Flight Season ON Jun–Oct, QC Jun–Sep, NS Jun–Sep, IA Jun–Sep, WI Jun–Sep, ME Jun–Sep, OH Jun–Oct, NJ Jun–Nov, KY May–Sep, LA Apr–Dec, GA Apr–Dec, FL all year.

Distribution Basically a tropical species, sparse at north end of summer range, perhaps many records north of breeding distribution. West to Pacific coast, north to northern California, Nevada, and Nebraska; scattered records north of that, northernmost in Washington and Alberta. Ranges south throughout tropics of both hemispheres. Very widespread, even on most oceanic islands in tropical latitudes, but absent from Europe.

Description Robust gliding skimmer, overall brown to brownish-red with prominent dark spot at base of each hindwing. *Male*: Eyes mostly gray with reddish cap; face dull red. Thorax brown with two pale gray stripes on each side. Abdomen brown with complex but not conspicuous pattern of fine lines on sutures, also black median line slightly expanded on each segment, expanded into spots on S8–10. Dark brown basal spot on hindwing blends with abdomen in flight. *Female*: Colored and shaped as male but face lighter reddish. Slightly longer and more slender cerci, if visible, good criterion for sexing. Color pattern on abdomen in immature may be more contrasty, actually quite striking.

Identification Distinguished from rather similar **Wandering Glider** by darker color and hindwing spots when they can be seen, but not always easy distinction, as spots not always very obvious. **Wandering** typically looks yellow, **Spot-winged** more reddish or brown, but bright male **Wandering** also quite orange in front. Could be mistaken for **Striped Saddle-**

335.1
Spot-winged Glider
male—Sonora, Mexico,
August 2006, Netta Smith

335.2
Spot-winged Glider
female—McCurtain
Co., OK, August 2008,
Berlin Heck

bags, both with restricted markings at hindwing base and stripes on sides of thorax. Close scrutiny or capture may be necessary. One difference is that saddlebags often perch horizontally at twig tips, rainpool gliders always hang down. Even more dissimilar, nevertheless **Four-spotted Skimmer** in rapid flight over open area could be mistaken for this species.

Natural History Feeding and territorial patrol in flight, hangs up at a slant or almost vertically when not active. Typically perches in trees, higher than Wandering Glider, but sometimes hanging from same branch. Often flushed from edge of woodland trails. Flight rapid and erratic, more so than Wandering, difficult to follow visually, and a real challenge to catch or photograph. Individuals may make distinctive undulating flight while foraging, tops of arcs no more than a foot above bottoms. Swarms of dozens of individuals often seen, flying back and forth from knee to head height but often higher. Individuals may be well spaced while moving all over landscape. Discrete swarms may move uphill during day. Oviposition usually by female alone, unlike Wandering Glider, but pairs seen flying cross-country in tandem and also ovipositing that way. Pairs make rapid approach to water, hit it once, then off again to swoop around and come back for another try; solo females more leisurely, often guarded by male. Also oviposits in large shallow pools of rivers in rainy season. Migratory, sometimes spectacular southbound flights encountered from midsummer to fall along Atlantic coast, more rarely elsewhere; may dominate such flights or be thoroughly mixed with other species. Massive northbound flights in spring also seen, often associated with low-pressure fronts with much rain.

Habitat Seen anywhere in feeding flight over open country, attracted for breeding to temporary wetlands in newly filled, usually shallow and open basins. Often breeds in constructed wetlands, even garden ponds or swimming pools, as long as they lack fish.

Flight Season ON Jun–Oct, QC Jul–Sep, NS Jun–Aug, IA Jun–Sep, WI Jun–Sep, ME May–Aug, OH Apr–Sep, NJ May–Oct, KY May–Sep, LA May–Oct, GA Apr–Oct, FL all year.

Distribution Also across much of western United States (absent from northern plains and Rockies), isolated records north to Alaska. South to Argentina, also Bahamas and Greater Antilles.

Coastal Pennants *Macrodiplax*

This small genus is at times placed in a family or subfamily separate from the other skimmers, along with several other Old World genera that share its very open venation. Most workers consider it a skimmer, and in habits it is much like other pennants, all of which are bona fide skimmers. A red species, *Macrodiplax cora*, replaces this one in the Old World tropics. It too is common in coastal habitats and disperses widely among islands. World 2, NA 1, East 1.

336 Marl Pennant *Macrodiplax balteata* TL 37–42, HW 32–35

Description Medium-sized black or brown pennant, mostly of coastal areas, with prominent hindwing spot. *Male:* Eyes dark brown; face shiny black. Thorax and abdomen black. Prominent basal black spot in hindwing. *Female:* Eyes red-brown over blue-gray; face cream. Thorax brown in front, whitish on sides with prominent W-shaped black marking. Abdomen light brown, blackish on sutures and low on sides; tip of S8 and S9–10 black. Hindwing spot dark brown.

Identification Should be no confusion with other species, especially in typical open, often coastal, habitat of **Marl Pennant**. Males of other black species in its range, **Double-ringed Pennant** and **Seaside Dragonlet**, have scarcely evident hindwing spots. No female SMALL PENNANT or other similar-sized skimmer duplicates wing pattern of female **Marl**. Thoracic pattern of brown front and pale sides with black W also distinctive. **Checkered Setwing** somewhat like female but has black and white banded abdomen and large color patch at

336.1
Marl Pennant
male—Palm Beach Co.,
FL, September 2008, J.
Lubchansky

336.2
Marl Pennant
female—Lee Co., FL,
July 2007, Marion M.
Dobbs

base of forewings as well as hindwings. Female could be mistaken for **Hyacinth Glider**, **Spot-winged Glider**, or SADDLEBAGS at first glance when in feeding flight.

Natural History Characteristically perches at tips of twigs, grass inflorescences, and tall leaves such as cattails and bulrushes with abdomen horizontal or up in obelisk position. Wings at times raised like other pennants. Often perched among larger numbers of Four-spotted Pennants at coastal lakes, and like them sometimes in dragonfly feeding swarms. Males may spend long periods flying over open water. Also common, especially females and immatures, in open areas near breeding habitats. Pairs oviposit in tandem in open water, dipping to surface in straight and rapid approach for one tap, then slowing and pre-paring for another run.

Habitat Lakes and large ponds in open areas, from fresh to brackish. Marl substrates charac-teristic but perhaps not essential. Stonewort often an indicator of potential breeding site. Can be quite common in restricted habitat. Individuals (wandering?) of both sexes often seen at more typical odonate habitats or away from water.

Flight Season LA May–Nov, GA Jun–Oct, FL all year.

Distribution Across Southwest to southern California, in western Mexico south to Sinaloa and along Gulf and Caribbean to Belize and Venezuela; also Greater Antilles.

Species Added to the Western Fauna in 2009 and 2010

Four species recently found in far southern Texas are not covered in *Dragonflies and Damselflies of the West*.

Red-tipped Swampdamsel   *Leptobasis vacillans*

This small, slender damselfly, the size of our Lucifer Swampdamsel, is easily recognized by the greenish thorax and black, red-tipped and red-based abdomen in mature individuals of both sexes. Immatures are entirely orange, then develop black on the abdomen and finally a green-striped thorax. Some numbers found in tall grass in woodland near pond. Large population found in Santa Ana National Wildlife Refuge in summer 2009, but no sign of them in 2010. Could also occur in southern Florida.

Marsh Firetail   *Telebasis digiticollis*

A bit larger than Desert and Duckweed Firetails, males look similar, but the thorax is mostly blackish in front. Females are entirely brown, again with thorax all dark in front rather than patterned as in the other two. Large populations found in dense water hyacinth in 2010 at San Benito.

Red-mantled Skimmer   *Libellula gaigei*

All-red skimmer with red at wing bases extending out to nodus. More color in wings and with narrower abdomen (more like Needham's) than Flame or Neon Skimmers, neither of which recorded from Lower Rio Grande Valley. Also darker red than Flame Skimmer. Female similarly marked, body reddish-brown. One male photographed at pond in Santa Ana National Wildlife Refuge in August 2009, far from known range in Mexico.

Caribbean Dasher   *Micrathyria dissocians*

This species looks much like Three-striped Dasher but has some of the thoracic stripes joined rather than all parallel. Males lack the projecting hamules of Three-striped, and the pale spots on S7 are a bit longer, occupying four-fifths of the segment or more (about two-thirds in Three-striped). It usually occurs in open marsh habitats. An immature was photographed at Laguna Atascosa National Wildlife Refuge in April 2009, and a few individuals were found at Santa Ana National Wildlife Refuge in June 2010. Should be watched for in southern Florida as well.

Appendix: Dragonfly Publications and Resources

Books on Dragonfly Biology and Natural History

Brooks, S. *Dragonflies*. 2003. Washington, DC: Smithsonian Books.

Corbet, P. S. *Dragonflies: Behavior and Ecology of Odonata*. 1999. Ithaca, NY: Cornell University Press.

Corbet, P., and S. Brooks. *Dragonflies*. 2008. London: Collins.

Miller, P. L. *Dragonflies*. 1995. Slough: The Richmond Publishing Co.

Silsby, J. *Dragonflies of the World*. 2001. Washington, DC: Smithsonian Institution Press.

North American Guides (Some Technical)

Dunkle, S. W. *Dragonflies through Binoculars*. 2000. New York: Oxford University Press.

Garrison, R. W., N. von Ellenrieder, and J. Louton. *Dragonfly Genera of the New World*. 2006. Baltimore: Johns Hopkins University Press.

Garrison, R. W., N. von Ellenrieder, and J. A. Louton. *Damselfly Genera of the New World*. 2010. Baltimore: Johns Hopkins University Press.

Needham, J. G., M. J. Westfall, Jr., and M. L. May. *Dragonflies of North America*. 2000. Gainesville, FL: Scientific Publishers.

Nikula, B., J. Sones, D. Stokes, and L. Stokes. *Stokes Beginner's Guide to Dragonflies and Damselflies*. 2002. Boston: Little, Brown, and Company.

Walker, E. M., and P. S. Corbet. *The Odonata of Canada and Alaska*, 3 volumes. 1953–1975. Toronto: University of Toronto Press.

Westfall, M. J., Jr., and M. L. May. *Damselflies of North America*. 2006. Gainesville, FL: Scientific Publishers. With color guide.

Eastern Regional Books

Abbott, J. C. *Dragonflies and Damselflies of Texas and the South-Central United States*. 2005. Princeton: Princeton University Press.

Barlow, A. E., D. M. Golden, and J. Bangma. *Field Guide to Dragonflies and Damselflies of New Jersey*. 2009. Flemington, NJ: New Jersey Division of Fish and Wildlife: Endangered and Nongame Species Program.

Beaton, G. *Dragonflies and Damselflies of Georgia and the Southeast*. 2007. Athens, GA: University of Georgia Press.

Carpenter, V. *Dragonflies and Damselflies of Cape Cod*. 1991. Brewster, MA: The Cape Cod Museum of Natural History.

Curry, J. R. *Dragonflies of Indiana*. 2001. Indianapolis, IN: Indiana Academy of Science.

DuBois, B. *Damselflies of the North Woods*. 2005. Duluth, MN: Kollath+Stensaas Publishing.

Dunkle, S. W. *Dragonflies of the Florida Peninsula, Bermuda and the Bahamas*. 1989. Gainesville, FL: Scientific Publishers.

Dunkle, S. W. *Damselflies of Florida, Bermuda and the Bahamas*. 1990. Gainesville, FL: Scientific Publishers.

Glotzhober, R. C., and D. McShaffrey, eds. *The Dragonflies and Damselflies of Ohio*. 2002. Columbus, OH: Ohio Biological Survey.

Jones, C. D., A. Kingsley, P. Burke, and M. Holder. *Field Guide to the Dragonflies and Damselflies of Algonquin Provincial Park and the Surrounding Area*. 2008. Whitney, ON: The Friends of Algonquin Park.

Lam, E. *Damselflies of the Northeast*. 2004. Forest Hills, NY: Biodiversity Books.

Legler, K., D. Legler, and D. Westover. *Color Guide to Common Dragonflies of Wisconsin*. 1998. Sauk City, WI: Karl Legler.

Mead, K. *Dragonflies of the North Woods*. 2009. Duluth, MN: Kollath+Stensaas Publishing.

Nikula, B., J. L. Loose, and M. R. Burne. *A Field Guide to the Dragonflies and Damselflies of Massachusetts*. 2003. Westborough, MA: Massachusetts Division of Fisheries & Wildlife.

Pilon, J.-G., and D. Lagacé. *Les Odonates du Québec*. 1998. Chicoutimi, QC: Entomofaune du Québec (EQ) Inc.

Rosche, L., J. Semroc, and L. Gilbert. *Dragonflies and Damselflies of Northeast Ohio*. 2008. Cleveland, OH: Cleveland Museum of Natural History.

Dragonfly Societies

Dragonfly Society of the Americas (http://www.odonatacentral.org/index.php/PageAction.get/name/DSAHomePage)

Foundation Societas Internationalis Odonato-
logica (http://bellsouthpwp.net/b/i/
billmauffray/siointro.html)
Worldwide Dragonfly Association (http://
ecoevo.uvigo.es/WDA/)

Dragonfly Listserves

Odonata-l (https://mailweb.ups.edu/mailman/
listinfo/odonata-l)
Northeast Odonata (http://tech.groups.yahoo.
com/group/NEodes/)
Great Lakes Odonata (http://tech.groups.
yahoo.com/group/gl_odonata/)
Southeast Odonata (http://tech.groups.yahoo.
com/group/se-odonata/)

General Dragonfly Websites

These sites are as varied as their names, and
they should be browsed to see what they have
to offer. Many of them will link to the abundant
sites that contain photos and still more
information on eastern odonates. Or just enter
"dragonflies" in a search engine and stand
back.
Odonata Central (http://www.odonatacentral.
org/)
International Odonata Research Institute
(http://www.iodonata.net/)
Dragonfly Biodiversity, Slater Museum of
Natural History (http://www.pugetsound.
edu/dragonflies)
Ode News (http://www.odenews.org/)
Odonata—Dragonflies & Damselflies (http://
www.windsofkansas.com/Bodonata/
odonata.html)
Digital Dragonflies (http://www.dragonflies.
org/)
Ed Lam (http://homepage.mac.com/edlam/)

Regional Dragonfly Websites

These are all excellent resources, and it is worth
conducting searches for other states and

provinces, as they may be added. There are
also innumerable photo sites showcasing
odonate photography by many individuals,
and searching for images of individual species
will take you to many of them.
Arkansas (http://www.hr-rna.com/RNA/
Dfly%20pages/Dragon%20list%20AR.htm)
Connecticut (http://ghostmoth.eeb.uconn.
edu/dragons/)
Georgia (http://www.mamomi.net/index.htm)
Georgia (http://www.giffbeaton.com/
dragonflies.htm)
Illinois (http://www.museum.state.il.us/
research/entomology/od_db.html)
Iowa (http://www.iowaodes.com/)
Maine (http://mdds.umf.maine.edu/)
Michigan (http://insects.ummz.lsa.umich.edu/
MICHODO/MOS.html)
Minnesota (http://www.mndragonfly.org/)
Missouri (http://members.sockets.
net/~tkulowiec/)
New Brunswick (http://www.odonatanb
.com/)
New Jersey (http://www.njodes.com/default.
htm)
North Carolina (http://149.168.1.196/odes/a/
accounts.php)
Ohio (http://www.marietta.edu/~odonata/)
Ontario (http://nhic.mnr.gov.on.ca/MNR/nhic/
odonates/about.html)
Vermont (http://campus.greenmtn.edu/dept/
NS/Dragonfly/)
West Virginia (http://www.insectsofwestvir-
ginia.net/d/nt/odonata.html)
Wisconsin (http://inventory.wiatri.net/
Odonata/)

Dragonfly Collecting Gear

BioQuip Products (http://www.bioquip.com/
default.asp)
Rose Entomology (http://www.roseentomol-
ogy.com/)

Glossary

abdomen: last section of body, the long and slender one, with 10 segments; often thought of as the "tail"

anal loop: foot-shaped cluster of cells in hind wing of skimmers and emeralds

anastomosing: branching and coming back together, like a braided river

andromorph: bright (usually male-like) morph in female odonates with two color morphs

angulate: edge of structure forming angle

Anisoptera: suborder to which "true" dragonflies belong

anteclypeus: narrow part of face between labrum and clypeus

antehumeral stripe: one of paired pale stripes extending along front of thorax

antenodal: crossveins proximal to the nodus

anterior: toward the front

apical: at the tip of a structure

appendages: structures at end of abdomen: two in females, three (two superior, one inferior) in male dragonflies, four (two superior, two inferior) in male damselflies; distinctive of species

arculus: prominent crossvein near base of wing where several longitudinal veins originate

auricle: projection from either side of abdominal segment 2 in males of most dragonflies (not skimmers), may be used to guide female abdomen during copulation

band: marking crosswise to axis of structure (body, wing, leg)

bar: as band

basal: at or near the base of a structure

carina: narrow keel running along or across a structure; prominent on front of thorax and along top and sides of abdominal segments in skimmers, across segments in all families

cercus (pl. cerci): paired appendage at end of abdomen, upper pair ("superior append-ages") in males, only appendages in females

clypeus: middle segment of "face"

congener, congeneric: species in the same genus

conspecific: in the same species

convergent: coming together

costa: anteriormost wing vein, forming front edge of wing

costal stripe: narrow colored area running along front margin of wing

crepuscular: active at dusk and, often, at dawn

cryptic: camouflaged, not easily detected

cuticle: outermost covering of insect

dimorphic: of two different shapes or colors, as in sexual dimorphism

distal: more toward tip of structure

divergent: going apart

dorsal: above, on top

dorsolateral: where top and sides meet

elongate: lengthened in one direction

emerge: to leave water and undergo metamorphosis into an adult; emergence is thus both from water and from exuvia

emergent vegetation: plants growing on bottom in shallow water that extend above water surface

endemic: occurring nowhere else

endophytic oviposition: laying eggs into plant tissue

ephemeral: not permanent; refers to ponds that fill up in wet season, go dry in dry season

epiproct: unpaired inferior abdominal appendage in male Anisoptera

exophytic oviposition: laying eggs onto water or land

exoskeleton: outer hard part of insect, including legs and wings

exuvia (pl. exuviae): cast skin from any larval molt (including transformation into adult)

femur (pl. femora): first long segment of leg, starting from base

flight season: period during which adults occur

frons: uppermost part of "face"

frontoclypeal suture: prominent line between frons and clypeus on face

genital lobe: projection from abdomen at posterior end of genital pocket on segment 2

genital valve: valves on either side of blade of ovipositor

gravid: full of eggs

Greater Antilles: large islands of West Indies—Cuba, Jamaica, Hispaniola, and Puerto Rico

hamules: paired structures that project from genital pocket under second segment and hold female abdomen in place during copulation

herbaceous: small plants with no woody tissue

heteromorph: dull morph in female odonates with two color morphs

heterospecific: of different species

humeral stripe: one of pair of dark longitudinal stripes extending along junction of front and sides of thorax

immature: adult past teneral stage but still not with mature coloration; usually not at water

instar: a larval stage; most larvae go through 10–13 of them

labium: jointed mouthpart below mandibles, visible from bottom of head, sort of a lower lip; also "lip" of larva that is extended during prey capture

labrum: lowermost part of "face," just above mandibles, sort of an upper lip

larva (pl. larvae): immature stage of Odonata (and other insects)

lateral: on the side(s)

lateral carina: keel that runs across middle of abdominal segments

lentic: term used for standing water, such as ponds and lakes

linear: like a line; usually lengthwise, from front to back or along a structure

lotic: term used for running water, such as streams and rivers

maiden flight: first flight of teneral away from water

mandibles: toothed structures with which a dragonfly bites and chews

mature: of reproductive age, fully colored

mediodorsal: at or near middle of top of region or structure

mesostigmal laminae (sing. lamina): paired plates in females, one on either side of front end of pterothorax, that engage cerci of male damselfly during copulation and tandem; males have same plates

mesostigmal plate: another term for mesostigmal lamina

mesothorax: middle segment of thorax, bears second pair of legs and first pair of wings

metamorphosis: process of changing from larva to adult; happens within larval exoskeleton

metathorax: rear segment of thorax, bears third pair of legs and second pair of wings

midbasal space: long clear space at wing base, behind subcosta and proximal to arculus in all wings

middorsal carina: keel that runs down middle of front of thorax and top of abdominal segments

molt: each time exuvia is shed; larval growth can take place only when larva is briefly soft at this time

monotypic: only one member in group

naiad: another term for larva, commonly used for aquatic insects with incomplete metamorphosis

neotropical: occurring in New World tropics

nodus: slight but noticeable notch in anterior margin of wing where some major veins originate

nymph: another term for larva, commonly used for insects with incomplete metamorphosis (no pupa)

obelisk: to hold abdomen pointing straight up, or the position of that abdomen

occipital bar: narrow bar between postocular spots in many pond damsels

occiput: posteriormost area on top of head, behind vertex and ocelli

ocellus (pl. ocelli): one of three simple eyes between the large compound eyes; on the vertex

odonate: another term for dragonfly/damselfly

ommatidium (pl. ommatidia): one division of a compound eye

oviposition: act of laying eggs

ovipositor: complex structure at posterior end of female damselflies, darners, and petaltails that functions in endophytic oviposition; also "spike" of spiketail; loosely applied to enlarged subgenital plate in emeralds and skimmers that holds clump of eggs

paraproct: paired inferior abdominal appendage in male Zygoptera

petiole: narrowed base of wing in damselflies

polymorphic: occurring in more than one form or color within one sex and age class of a species

posterior: toward the rear

postnodal: crossveins between nodus and stigma

prothorax: first segment of thorax, often considered the "neck" although true neck is membranous area between head and prothorax; bears first pair of legs

proximal: more toward base of structure

pruinescent: becoming pruinose

pruinose: exhibiting pruinosity

pruinosity: powdery (actually waxy) bloom on odonates that exudes from cuticle and turns it light blue, gray, or white, deposited on mature individuals (more commonly males) of many species of odonates

pterostigma: technically correct word for stigma

pterothorax: major part of thorax, fused meso- and metathorax

radiation: can be used to describe the evolution of numerous similar species from a single common ancestor

relict: formerly more widespread and common, now much restricted

rendezvous: where the two sexes normally meet to mate

riparian: narrow band of moist woodland or shrubland along rivers and streams

satellite: male allowed in other male's territory because of nonaggressive behavior and usual failure to mate

sclerite: small segment of exoskeleton, quite evident around wing bases

seminal receptacle: sperm-storage organ in female reproductive tract

seminal vesicle: sperm-storage organ in second abdominal segment of male

sexual patrol flight: characteristic flight of male odonates at water; either actively searching for females or defending a territory that females may enter

sinuous: a curved line, like a snake's body

sperm transfer: when male transfers sperm from tip of abdomen to accessory genitalia on second abdominal segment

spiracle: small opening to respiratory system on each side of thorax

stigma: thickened, colored cell at front of each wingtip in most Odonata

stripe: marking running along axis of structure (body, wing, leg), also used for markings on thorax that run between wings and legs, thus up and down

subapical: just before tip

subcosta: longitudinal vein just behind costa, runs only to nodus

subgenital plate: plate below S8 that holds bunches of eggs when enlarged; variable enough in shape to be of value in identification

submergent vegetation: plants growing below water surface

sympatric: occurring in same geographic area

synthorax: same as pterothorax

tandem, tandem linkage: position taken when male has grasped female by head or thorax

tarsus (pl. tarsi): third part of leg, with many segments and paired tarsal claws

teneral: freshly emerged adult, usually soft, minimally pigmented, and with shiny wings

tibia (pl. tibiae): second long segment of leg

transverse: crosswise, from side to side

trigonal interspace: row(s) of cells distal to triangle in forewing

truncate: cut off squarely

tubercle: a bump

ventral: below, underneath

ventrolateral: where sides and underside meet

ventromedial carina: keel that runs along lower edge of abdominal segments

vernal: during spring

vertex: conical tubercle or flat area on top of head between eyes or just in front of eye seam in groups with eyes in contact; bears the ocelli

vulvar lamina: subgenital plate

vulvar plate: another term for vulvar lamina

vulvar spine: spine projecting from rear edge of underside of S8 in some female pond damsels

wheel: the copulatory position in odonates

Zygoptera: damselfly suborder

Index